T0311801

Marx at 200

The book provides new vistas on Karl Marx's political economy, philosophy and politics on the occasion of his 200th birthday.

Often using hitherto unknown material from the recently published Marx-Engels Gesamtausgabe (the MEGA^2 edition), the contributions throw new light on Marx's works and activities, the sources he used and the discussions he had, correcting received opinions on his doctrines. The themes dealt with include Marx's concepts of alienation and commodity fetishism, the labour theory of value and the theory of exploitation, Marx's studies of capital accumulation and economic growth and his analysis of economic crises and of the labour contract. Novel developments in the reception of his works in France and the UK conclude the volume.

This book was originally published as a special issue of *The European Journal of the History of Economic Thought*.

Gilbert Faccarello is Professor at the University of Paris II Panthéon-Assas, France, a founding editor of *The European Journal of the History of Economic Thought* and co-Editor of the Routledge Historical Resources site devoted to the history of economic thought.

Heinz D. Kurz is Professor Emeritus at the Graz Schumpeter Centre, Austria, a founding editor of *The European Journal of the History of Economic Thought* and, together with Gilbert Faccarello, co-Editor of the Routledge Historical Resources site on the history of economic thought.

Marx at 200

New Developments on Karl Marx's
Thought and Writings

Edited by
Gilbert Faccarello and Heinz D. Kurz

Routledge
Taylor & Francis Group

LONDON AND NEW YORK

First published 2020
by Routledge
2 Park Square, Milton Park, Abingdon, Oxon, OX14 4RN

and by Routledge
52 Vanderbilt Avenue, New York, NY 10017

Routledge is an imprint of the Taylor & Francis Group, an informa business

© 2020 Taylor & Francis
Chapter 6 © 2018 Heinz D. Kurz. Originally published as Open Access.
Chapter 9 © 2018 Christian Gehrke. Originally published as Open Access.

British Library Cataloguing in Publication Data
A catalogue record for this book is available from the British Library

ISBN13: 978-0-367-43751-0
ISBN13: 978-0-367-49961-7 (pbk)

Typeset in Minion Pro
by Newgen Publishing UK

Publisher's Note
The publisher accepts responsibility for any inconsistencies that may have arisen during the conversion of this book from journal articles to book chapters, namely the inclusion of journal terminology.

Disclaimer
Every effort has been made to contact copyright holders for their permission to reprint material in this book. The publishers would be grateful to hear from any copyright holder who is not here acknowledged and will undertake to rectify any errors or omissions in future editions of this book.

Contents

Citation Information   viii

Notes on Contributors   xii

1 'Marx at 200': introductory remarks   1
Gilbert Faccarello and Heinz D. Kurz

The formative years

2 Not a man of solid principles. The relevance of Edgar Bauer's polemical portrait of Karl Marx in his 1843 novella *Es leben feste Grundsätze!*   15
Herbert De Vriese

3 "Alienation" and critique in Marx's manuscripts of 1857–58 ("*Grundrisse*")   46
Zacharias Zoubir

4 Error or absurdity? A non-cognitive approach to commodity fetishism   74
David Andrews

Around the new MEGA

5 Concepts in examining the legacy of Karl Marx   92
Regina Roth

6 Will the MEGA² edition be a watershed in interpreting Marx?   119
Heinz D. Kurz

7 Re-examining the authorship of the Feuerbach chapter in
    The German Ideology on the basis of a hypothesis of dictation   144
    Izumi Omura

8 Marx, primitive accumulation, and the impact of Sismondi   169
   Nicolas Eyguesier

9 Marx's reproduction schemes and multi-sector growth models   195
   Christian Gehrke

10 New aspects of Marx's economic theory in MEGA: Marx's
    original six-sector model   229
    Kenji Mori

11 The *Books of Crisis* and Tooke–Newmarch excerpts: a new
    aspect of Marx's crisis theory in MEGA   248
    Kenji Mori

12 Marx on rent: new insights from the new MEGA   262
    Susumu Takenaga

Analytical developments

13 Is Marx's absolute rent due to a monopoly price?   297
    Saverio M. Fratini

14 Use values and exchange values in Marx's extended
    reproduction schemes   322
    *Carlo Benetti, Alain Béraud, Edith Klimovsky and
    Antoine Rebeyrol*

15 James Steuart and the making of Karl Marx's
    monetary thought   358
    Rebeca Gomez Betancourt and Matari Pierre Manigat

16 Labour values and energy values: some developments on the
    common substance of value since 1867   388
    Wilfried Parys

17 The employment contract with externalised costs: the avatars
of Marxian exploitation 417
Rodolphe Dos Santos Ferreira and Ragip Ege

18 Marx and Kalecki on aggregate instability and class struggle 430
Michaël Assous and Antonin Pottier

Reception

19 Searching for New Jerusalems: P.H. Wicksteed's "Jevonian"
critique of Marx's *Capital* 449
Michael V. White

20 The reception of Marx in France: *La Revue Socialiste*
(1885–1914) 490
Michel Bellet

Index 536

Citation Information

The chapters in this book were originally published in *The European Journal of the History of Economic Thought*, volume 25, issue 5 (October 2018). When citing this material, please use the original page numbering for each article, as follows:

Chapter 1
'Marx at 200': introductory remarks
Gilbert Faccarello and Heinz D. Kurz
The European Journal of the History of Economic Thought, volume 25, issue 5 (October 2018), pp. 665–678

Chapter 2
Not a man of solid principles. The relevance of Edgar Bauer's polemical portrait of Karl Marx in his 1843 novella Es leben feste Grundsätze!
Herbert De Vriese
The European Journal of the History of Economic Thought, volume 25, issue 5 (October 2018), pp. 679–709

Chapter 3
"Alienation" and critique in Marx's manuscripts of 1857–58 ("Grundrisse")
Zacharias Zoubir
The European Journal of the History of Economic Thought, volume 25, issue 5 (October 2018), pp. 710–737

Chapter 4
Error or absurdity? A non-cognitive approach to commodity fetishism
David Andrews
The European Journal of the History of Economic Thought, volume 25, issue 5 (October 2018), pp. 738–755

Chapter 5

Concepts in examining the legacy of Karl Marx
Regina Roth
The European Journal of the History of Economic Thought, volume 25,
issue 5 (October 2018), pp. 756–782

Chapter 6

Will the MEGA² edition be a watershed in interpreting Marx?
Heinz D. Kurz
The European Journal of the History of Economic Thought, volume 25,
issue 5 (October 2018), pp. 783–807

Chapter 7

Re-examining the authorship of the Feuerbach chapter in The German
Ideology *on the basis of a hypothesis of dictation*
Izumi Omura
The European Journal of the History of Economic Thought, volume 25,
issue 5 (October 2018), pp. 808–832

Chapter 8

Marx, primitive accumulation, and the impact of Sismondi
Nicolas Eyguesier
The European Journal of the History of Economic Thought, volume 25,
issue 5 (October 2018), pp. 833–858

Chapter 9

Marx's reproduction schemes and multi-sector growth models
Christian Gehrke
The European Journal of the History of Economic Thought, volume 25,
issue 5 (October 2018), pp. 859–892

Chapter 10

*New aspects of Marx's economic theory in MEGA: Marx's original
six-sector model*
Kenji Mori
The European Journal of the History of Economic Thought, volume 25,
issue 5 (October 2018), pp. 893–911

Chapter 11

The Books of Crisis *and Tooke–Newmarch excerpts: a new aspect of Marx's crisis theory in MEGA*
Kenji Mori
The European Journal of the History of Economic Thought, volume 25, issue 5 (October 2018), pp. 912–925

Chapter 12

Marx on rent: new insights from the new MEGA
Susumu Takenaga
The European Journal of the History of Economic Thought, volume 25, issue 5 (October 2018), pp. 926–960

Chapter 13

Is Marx's absolute rent due to a monopoly price?
Saverio M. Fratini
The European Journal of the History of Economic Thought, volume 25, issue 5 (October 2018), pp. 961–985

Chapter 14

Use values and exchange values in Marx's extended reproduction schemes
Carlo Benetti, Alain Béraud, Edith Klimovsky and Antoine Rebeyrol
The European Journal of the History of Economic Thought, volume 25, issue 5 (October 2018), pp. 986–1021

Chapter 15

James Steuart and the making of Karl Marx's monetary thought
Rebeca Gomez Betancourt and Matari Pierre Manigat
The European Journal of the History of Economic Thought, volume 25, issue 5 (October 2018), pp. 1022–1051

Chapter 16

Labour values and energy values: some developments on the common substance of value since 1867
Wilfried Parys
The European Journal of the History of Economic Thought, volume 25, issue 5 (October 2018), pp. 1052–1080

Chapter 17

The employment contract with externalized costs: the avatars of Marxian exploitation
Rodolphe Dos Santos Ferreira and Ragip Ege
The European Journal of the History of Economic Thought, volume 25, issue 5 (October 2018), pp. 1081–1093

Chapter 18

Marx and Kalecki on aggregate instability and class struggle
Michaël Assous and Antonin Pottier
The European Journal of the History of Economic Thought, volume 25, issue 5 (October 2018) pp. 1094–1112

Chapter 19

Searching for New Jerusalems: P.H. Wicksteed's "Jevonian" critique of Marx's Capital
Michael V. White
The European Journal of the History of Economic Thought, volume 25, issue 5 (October 2018), pp. 1113–1153

Chapter 20

The reception of Marx in France: La Revue Socialiste *(1885–1914)*
Michel Bellet
The European Journal of the History of Economic Thought, volume 25, issue 5 (October 2018), pp. 1154–1199

For any permission-related enquiries please visit:
www.tandfonline.com/page/help/permissions

Notes on Contributors

David Andrews is Professor and Chair of the Economics Department at the State University of New York at Oswego, USA. He serves as an Associate Editor for the journal *History of Economic Ideas*. His research has been focused on the writings of J.M. Keynes, Piero Sraffa, Adam Smith and classical political economy. His publications include *Keynes and the British Humanist Tradition: The Moral Purpose of the Market* (2010) and papers in the *Cambridge Journal of Economics*, *Economic Thought, History of Political Economy* and *The European Journal of the History of Economic Thought*.

Michaël Assous is Professor of Economics at Lumière University Lyon 2, France. His research focuses on the history of macroeconomics and, more specifically, on the modelling of (in)stability in the works of Fisher, Harrod, Kalecki, Lange, Marx, Meade, Samuelson and Solow. In 2012, he was awarded the ESHET (European Society of the History of Economic Thought) Young Researcher Award.

Michel Bellet is Professor at the University of Saint-Etienne, France. He is the coordinator of a multi-disciplinary research programme on Saint-Simonism. He has published several works on utopia in economics and on socialist ideas in France before Marx. His studies have particularly focused on the main French socialist journal at a time when Marx and a special kind of Marxism gained influence. He is also interested in the intersection between the republican idea and economics during the nineteenth century and in Sismondi in particular.

Carlo Benetti is Emeritus Professor of Economics at Paris Nanterre University, France. His publications include books and articles on the history of economic thought, the theory of prices and the theory of money, primarily in Marx and in a classical approach with emphasis on disequilibrium economics.

Alain Béraud is Emeritus Professor at the University of Cergy-Pontoise, France, and a member of the Economic Theory, Modelling and Application research team. His recent research focuses on the history of economic thought in France.

Herbert De Vriese is Professor at the Centre for European Philosophy of the University of Antwerp, Belgium. He obtained his PhD in Philosophy with a dissertation on the concept of critique in the Hegelian school. His research focuses on nineteenth-century German philosophy, with special attention to the 'revolutionary rupture' between Hegel and Nietzsche and its place and role in larger societal processes such as secularisation and disenchantment.

Rodolphe Dos Santos Ferreira is Emeritus Professor of Economics at the University of Strasbourg, France, where he is a member of the Bureau d'Économie Théorique et Appliquée and an honorary senior member of the Institut Universitaire de France. His research activities are in the field of economic theory (industrial organisation, general equilibrium, macro-dynamics) and the history of economic thought. His contributions to the latter deal with Cournot, Keynes, Marx and their major predecessors.

Ragip Ege is Emeritus Professor of Economics at the University of Strasbourg, France, and a member of the Bureau d'Économie Théorique et Appliquée. His recent research activities focus on the history of economic thought (especially on eighteenth- and nineteenth-century authors) and the relations between economics and ethics. He is particularly interested in Marx's economic and political thought and in his criticism of Hegelian philosophy.

Nicolas Eyguesier is a member of the Groupe d'Analyse et Théorie Economique at the University of Saint-Etienne, France, and a member of the board of the publishing house La Lenteur in Paris. He obtained a PhD at the University of Lausanne, Switzerland. He is also co-Editor of Sismondi's *Œuvres Économiques Complètes* (2012–2017). His areas of research include republicanism and history of capitalism.

Gilbert Faccarello is Professor at the University of Paris II Panthéon-Assas, France, a founding editor of *The European Journal of the History of Economic Thought* and co-Editor of the Routledge Historical Resources site devoted to the history of economic thought. He also chaired the Council of the European Society for the History of Economic Thought.

His most recent publications include the three-volume *Handbook on the History of Economic Analysis* (co-edited with Heinz D. Kurz), *Political Economy and Religion* (ed.) and *Malthus Across Nations: The Reception of Thomas Robert Malthus in Europe, America and Japan* (co-edited with Masashi Izumo and Hiromi Morishita).

Saverio M. Fratini is Professor of Economics and coordinator of the three-year bachelor's degree in Economics at Roma Tre University, Italy. He holds a PhD in Economics from the Sapienza University of Rome, Italy. He is Managing Editor of the *Centro Sraffa Working Papers* series. His research interests concern economic theory and the history of economic thought, with particular reference to the contribution of Piero Sraffa.

Christian Gehrke is Associate Professor at the Department of Economics of the University of Graz, Austria, and co-Director of the Graz Schumpeter Centre. He has published several papers, mostly on classical economics, in various journals, and has edited and co-edited some books. He is co-Editor of the *Centro Sraffa Working Papers* series and serves on the editorial boards of *Metroeconomica*, *Bulletin of Political Economy*, and *The European Journal of the History of Economic Thought*. He is currently also a member of the Executive Committee of the European Society for the History of Economic Thought.

Rebeca Gomez Betancourt is Professor of Economics at Lumière University Lyon 2, France, where she is also a researcher at the Triangle Research Centre. She is the Vice-President of the Association Charles Gide pour l'Étude de la Pensée Économique and Director of the masters in History of Economics at Lumière University Lyon 2. Her work focuses on the history of monetary thought, but also on women and economics, Latin America, US monetary history and classical political economy. She has published on the history of the US Federal Reserve System, the quantity theory of money and monetary regimes in Latin America and India.

Edith Klimovsky is Professor at the Economics Department of the Universidad Autónoma Metropolitana, Mexico. Her research has focused on the contemporary classical theory of prices and distribution and its reconstruction in monetary terms. Her publications include several books and numerous articles in Spanish, English, French and Russian.

Heinz D. Kurz is Professor Emeritus at the Graz Schumpeter Centre, Austria, a founding editor of *The European Journal of the History of Economic Thought* and, together with Gilbert Faccarello, co-Editor of the Routledge Historical Resources site on the history of economic thought. His most recent publications include the three-volume *Handbook on the History of Economic Analysis* (co-edited with Gilbert Faccarello) and *Economic Thought: A Brief History* (2016).

Kenji Mori is Professor of Political Economy at the Graduate School of Economics and Management of Tohoku University, Japan. He is a member of the editorial board of the International Marx/Engels Foundation in the Netherlands. He co-edited Marx's and Engels's manuscripts of *Capital: Volume II* for MEGA^2, volumes II/12 and II/13, and Marx's *Books of Crisis* for MEGA^2, volume IV/14.

Izumi Omura is Emeritus Professor at Tohoku University, Japan. He is a member of the editorial board of the International Marx/Engels Foundation in the Netherlands. He edited three volumes of MEGA^2 and led the editorial team as Chief Editor of MEGA^2, volumes II/12 (2005) and II/13 (2008). He is also well-known as a critic of some of the MEGA^2 editing.

Wilfried Parys is Emeritus Professor at the University of Antwerp, Belgium. His research concentrates on the history of economic thought, especially on Sraffa, Leontief, Remak, Potron, Charasoff and other pioneers of linear economic models. His publications include papers in the *Quarterly Journal of Economics*, *American Economic Review*, and *The European Journal of the History of Economic Thought*.

Matari Pierre Manigat was trained both in economics and political science. He is a researcher at the Institute of Social Research, and Professor at the Faculty of Political and Social Sciences of the Universidad Nacional Autónoma de México. His work focuses on the history of economic thought, state theory and Latin American economic history. He has published on public debt, Marxist theories of finance capital and state and monetary regimes and crisis in Latin America.

Antonin Pottier is Associate Professor at the École des Hautes Études en Sciences Sociales, France. His research interests cover the history of economic thought and the relations between economics and the environment. His publications include *Comment les économistes réchauffent la planète* (2016).

Antoine Rebeyrol is Professor of Economics at Paris Nanterre University, France. He has been a member of the editorial board of *Cahiers d'Economie Politique* since 1978. He is a specialist in the history of economic thought. His recent research focuses on models of capital accumulation using a classical approach.

Regina Roth is an historian and co-Editor of MEGA^2 at the Berlin-Brandenburg Academy of Sciences, Germany. She co-edited *Capital II*, *Capital III* and *Capital*-manuscripts in the MEGA^2 (1871–1894). She is currently coordinating the digital edition of MEGA^2, containing the correspondence of Marx, Engels and their correspondents from 1866 onwards, and many excerpts from Marx (megadigital.bbaw.de).

Susumu Takenaga is Professor at Daito Bunka University, Japan, where he teaches the history of economic thought. He obtained a PhD in Economics at Paris Nanterre University, France. His research interests include the economic analyses of Marx and of classical political economy, particularly Ricardo. His recent publications include *Ricardo on Money and Finance: A Bicentenary Reappraisal* (2013; co-edited with Yuji Sato) and *Ricardo and the History of Japanese Economic Thought: A Selection of Ricardo Studies in Japan during the Interwar Period* (2016; ed.).

Michael V. White is an independent scholar. He has published extensively on the history of political economy, with a particular focus on the works of William Stanley Jevons.

Zacharias Zoubir is a PhD student in Philosophy at the Sophiapol Laboratory of Paris Nanterre University, France. His research explores the connections between political philosophy, social theory and the critique of political economy, especially with regard to racial issues. His publications include a chapter in the *Routledge International Handbook of Contemporary Racisms* (2020).

'Marx at 200': introductory remarks

Gilbert Faccarello and Heinz D. Kurz

The recurrence of debates concerning the work of an author, the lively controversies it raises among opponents and followers and the redirection of its interpretations as time goes by is a sign of its continuing fascination and complexity. These debates do not follow a steady path, but have their own ups and downs, change their topics and shift the emphasis, are carried out in academic circles or in the media and are often linked to some socio-economic or political event. However, the most intense periods of ferment, in terms of intellectual achievements and additions to our knowledge, are often closely linked to the publication of new, more comprehensive editions of the works under consideration, which allow novel and more accurate readings and perspectives. This was obviously the case with regard to David Ricardo and the Sraffa edition of his *Works and Correspondence* (1951–1973), Adam Smith and the 1976 edition of his writings published on the occasion of the bi-centenary of the *Wealth of Nations*, or John Maynard Keynes and the publication of his *Collected Writings* from 1971 to 1989.[1]

1. A return to Marx's texts

The work of Karl Marx is no exception to the rule, all the more so as Marx wrote a lot during his lifetime, only parts of which have been published every once in a while during more than one century after his death in 1883. With regard to political economy, for example, some manuscripts were brought out rather quickly: Volumes II and III of *Capital* contain a selection of manuscripts made by Friedrich Engels and published, respectively in 1885 and 1894; and the three volumes of *Theorien über den Mehrwert* (*Theories of Surplus Value*) contain another selection edited and published by Karl Kautsky in

---

[1] This is also the case, but to a lesser extent, with regard to the publication, from 1987 to 2005, of *Œuvres économiques complètes de Auguste et Léon Walras*, and the ongoing edition of Jean-Baptiste Say's *Œuvres complètes*.

1905–10, presented as Volume IV of *Capital*. However, some other important works had to wait much longer: the so-called 1857–58 *Grundrisse der Kritik der politischen Ökonomie* were first published in a not widely circulated edition in 1939–41, then in a more accessible one in 1953, and were only translated two decades later into different languages; the fragment of a draft ("Urtext") of the 1859 *Zur Kritik der politischen Ökonomie* (*A Contribution to the Critique of Political Economy*) had to wait until 1939–41 to come out, together with the *Grundrisse*; and some important material for Volume I of *Capital* was only available, for a small part, from 1933 — this is the case, for example, of the so-called "unpublished Chapter 6".

With regard to philosophy, things are still more striking.[2] For a long time, only Marx's introduction to the critique of Hegel's *Philosophy of Right*, "Zur Kritik der Hegelschen Rechtsphilosophie. Einleitung", and his article on the "Jewish question", "Zur Judenfrage" (both published in 1844 in the *Deutsch-Französische Jahrbücher*), were known. The pieces of Marx's 1841 doctoral thesis that have come down to us — *Differenz der Demokritischen und Epikureischen Naturphilosophie* (*The Difference Between the Democritean and Epicurean Philosophy of Nature*) — were only published in 1902; the 1843 essay *Zur Kritik der Hegelschen Rechtsphilosophie* (*Critique of Hegel's Philosophy of Right*) in 1927; and the celebrated *Ökonomisch-philosophische Manuskripte von 1844* (*Economic and Philosophic Manuscripts of 1844*) and the 1845 *Die deutsche Ideologie* (*German Ideology*), in 1932.

These facts ought to be recalled when trying to understand the history of the debates over Marx's thought, as well as the present state of the Marx studies. Without going into detail, five main points deserve to be stressed.

(1) First of all, it is clear that the availability, or lack thereof, of manuscripts, some of them of fundamental importance, had an impact on the various interpretations of Marx. During several decades after Marx's death, numerous writings that are now considered as essential to a correct understanding of his views were simply not available to the general public, and very often it was not even known that such writings existed. Yet, the first interpretations, sometimes very sketchy and *ad hoc*, adopted and frequently promoted by political organisations, dominated the debates for a long time. This is true, for

---

[2] Marx's more openly political writings were much better known and circulated, during and after his life, as pamphlets and newspaper articles.

example, with regard to the general understanding of the content and "method" of *Capital*, especially in the theory of value and price, the falling rate of profit or the approach to economic crises. This is also the case with regard to the philosophical aspects of Marxism. Engels' writings, sometimes tinged with Darwinism, coined a vocabulary and an orthodoxy, and were highly influential — whether on Ludwig Feuerbach and the Young Hegelians, the alleged "Utopian" and "scientific" socialisms, "historical materialism" (a phrase coined by Engels) or dialectics (that is, "materialist dialectic" or "dialectics of nature" based on a simplistic interpretation of Hegel's philosophy). It is basically Engels' line of thought, stated mainly in the 1880s after the death of Marx, and not Marx's, that was developed by Marxists in several countries, for example, in works popularising the "materialist conception of history", or in a book by Kautsky on "the three sources of Marxism"[3] (German philosophy, French socialism, and English political economy),[4] which involved a sketchy and questionable interpretation of Marx. Engels' views were also influential in Russia, with the development of the alleged "dialectical materialism", especially by Georgi Plekhanov and Lenin. In all this history, independent intellectuals such as Rudolf Hilferding, Isaak Illich Rubin, György Löwinger (alias Lukács), or Karl Korsch, were rare. Over the decades, the use and abuse of some words like "dialectics" by authors whose knowledge of Hegel apparently was poor or nonexistent, led the discussions astray into blind alleys. Even some very usual vocabulary like the German word "Praxis", used by Marx (and by Kant) to mean the ordinary practice of an activity, was misunderstood and, at best, confused with the Aristotelian distinction between "praxis" and "poiesis", thus obscuring Marx's intellectual developments. Needless to say, all this was a serious impediment to a better understanding of Marx's texts and thoughts.

(2) Second, this overall chaotic state of things showed the need of a comprehensive edition of Marx's works. Three attempts were made in this direction.

---

[3] The phrase was coined by Kautsky in 1908 and was taken up by Vladimir Ilyich Ulyanov, alias Lenin, in 1913.

[4] It is sometimes stated that a source of inspiration for this view is to be found in a celebrated book anonymously published by Moses Hess in 1841, *Die europäische Triarchie*, where a fundamental role in contemporary history is given to Germany, France, and above all the United Kingdom. But Hess' discourse was different.

In 1927, such a systematic and complete edition started to be published by the Marx–Engels Institute in Moscow, under the directorship of David Borisovich Goldendakh (alias David Rjazanov). However, in 1931, Stalin ordered Rjazanov's detention (Rjazanov was executed in 1938) and Vladimir Viktorovich Adoratsky replaced him in the project. The result was the first MEGA — that is, *Karl Marx. Friedrich Engels. Historisch-kritische Gesamtausgabe. Werke. Schriften. Briefe* (MEGA being the abbreviation of *Marx-Engels Gesamtausgabe*). This project was stopped in 1935 after 12 volumes[5] had been published.

After World War II, almost all work had to start again. A new publication project was launched: the *Marx–Engels Werke* (MEW). From 1956 to 1990, the Institutes for Marxism–Leninism in Moscow and in East Berlin published jointly 44 volumes.[6] While containing some of the most important writings and correspondence — but still deprived of many significant manuscripts — the edition is far from complete and lacks the characteristic features of a critical edition.

Hence, finally, a third attempt to bring out a complete critical edition. The *Marx-Engels Gesamtausgabe*, that is, the second MEGA or MEGA[2], was put on track by the same Institutes in 1970, but came to an end as a consequence of the breakdown of the German Democratic Republic and the Soviet Union. In 1990, the Internationale Marx Engels Stiftung (IMES) decided to resume the project in an academic context. However, the number of the originally planned 164 volumes was reduced to 114. This is still work in progress, but a large part of the project has by now been accomplished: the third attempt can be expected to be successful.

(3) Third, it is also clear that Marx's thought is much more complex and wide-ranging than the various Marxist vulgates claimed it to be as time went by and this raises significant questions: What is the link between all these writings? Is there a continuity, or a break, or a more complex relationship, between Marx's youthful philosophical ideas developed in the 1840s and his more mature work on political economy and politics — a question that includes an assessment of his relationship with Hegel's philosophy and the writings of the Young Hegelians? What is the meaning of his constant intention to write a "critique of political economy"? Is it possible to identify beyond reasonable doubt Marx's intellectual evolution and the elements of his thought that became permanent and stable? All these questions were,

---

[5] Volume I has been published in two parts.
[6] This edition is based on the second Russian edition published from 1954 onwards.

inter alia, discussed again since the 1960s, along with the republication of the *Grundrisse*, the progressive issuing of the volumes of MEW and MEGA[2], and the various translations of parts of them into English, French and Italian in particular.[7]

In this context, Marx's most important concepts and approaches have been questioned and studied anew, as for example, the definitions and role of "alienation" and "fetishism" in Marx's youthful writings and in *Capital*, the meaning of "abstract labour" in the theory of value and its links with "value-form" analysis and money, the precise description and role of some Hegelian dialectical devices used by Marx in his political economy, the meaning of his notion of "critique", etc. For this general work of reinterpretation — which swept aside much of the conventional discourses of the past — some critical reappraisals of central themes (dialectics, abstract labour, value and money, the deduction of concepts in *Capital*) played an important role: see, in particular, Lucio Colletti (1969, 1975) in Italy, Hans-Georg Backhaus (1967) and Helmut Reichelt (1970) in Germany, and the rediscovery of Rubin's work in the early 1970s. Many innovative developments were inspired by these analyses.

Another characteristic of the research during these last decades is a strong revival of the studies of the young Marx and his formative years. Warren Breckman (1999) and David Leopold (2007) cast new light on his relationships with the Young Hegelians, thus supplementing some classic studies like McLellan (1969) and Rosen (1977); see also the studies edited by Emmanuel Renault (2008), which focus on the *1844 Manuscripts* and insist, in particular, on the crucial role of Moses Hess in the development of Marx's thought. For his part, Rojahn (1983) showed how the *1844 Manuscripts*, traditionally presented as a coherent book, consist, in fact, of a simple juxtaposition of various texts written at different points of Marx's intellectual evolution and thus does not have the philosophical status attributed to them in the past. Other more or less youthful works have also been examined, for example, the *Grundrisse* (see, e.g., the contributions in Musto 2008), and reappraisals of Marx's overall philosophical development and its importance for his approach have been published (see, for example, Renault 2009, 2014; and Fischbach 2015).

---

[7] Attempts to assess the importance of MEGA[2] for the Marx studies and the interpretation of *Capital* have been made (see, e.g., the papers in Bellofiore and Fineschi 2009; Roth 2010; or Heinrich 2016).

(4) Of course, a great many of the new texts in the MEGA^2 have been made available in specific contexts, which had an impact on their reception and the ensuing post World War II controversies. With regard to political economy, one major event was the publication of Piero Sraffa's *Production of Commodities by Means of Commodities* (1960), which quickly became a focal point in the discussion of Marx's approach to the theory of value and distribution. Marx's "law of the falling tendency of the rate of profit" was also scrutinised with the help of Sraffa's theory and found to be wanting. In the course of the multiple controversies that Sraffa's work raised, many diverging attempts have been made to rescue or restate certain parts of Marx's analysis. The above-mentioned developments on abstract labour, value and money are cases in point, and so are the new readings of the concept of alienation, which replaces, in some authors' views, that of exploitation, which is considered to be too much tied to an ill-founded labour theory of value. Some other approaches were put forward, either in favour of a more traditional understanding of Marx's labour value-based reasoning, at least on an aggregative level (see e.g., Foley 1982, 2000), or in a radically diverging way. A celebrated example of the latter is the so-called "analytical Marxism", launched by Gerald Cohen (1978), John Roemer (1981, 1982, 1986) and Jon Elster (1985), trying to reformulate certain ideas of Marx within a marginalist or neoclassical framework, using rational choice and game theory. In a still different perspective, some developments were inspired by the "critical theory" of the Frankfurt School (see, e.g., Postone 1993, and the "critique of value" approach by Larsen et al. 2014).

(5) Finally, some useful additions to Marx studies have been made in synthetic or historiographical perspectives. Some collective syntheses of Marx and Marxism, in general, or Marxian economics in particular, have been published (Carver 1991, Bidet and Kouvelakis 2008, or Fine, Saad-Filho and Boffo 2012), together with reading guides of *Capital* (inter alia Heinrich 2004 and Harvey 2010–13). Then there is the highly ambitious and necessarily only partial attempt by Jan Hoff (2009) to review the Marx debates across the entire world since the mid 1960s. Last but not least, the classic biographies of Marx, sometimes politically tinted, by Franz Mehring (1918), Boris Nikolaevskij and Mänchen-Helfen (1937), or David McLellan (1973), were complemented by several new, more academic accounts of the life and works

of Marx by Jonathan Sperber (2013), Gareth Stedman Jones (2016), and the first of a projected three-volume work by Michael Heinrich (2018).

2. Some new developments

The articles included in this special issue deal first with Marx's formative years. The main part then turns to some developments in Marx's political economy — among which those dealing with the new MEGA are grouped under a specific heading. Some new research on the immediate reception of Marx's work in the United Kingdom and France concludes the issue.

2.1. The formative years

As was noted above, the recent Marx studies have been characterised by a significant revival in research of Marx's formative years and his (sometimes quick) philosophical developments, all themes which prove now to be of importance for the understanding of the "mature" Marx. The three chapters included in this part exemplify this.

The first chapter, by Herbert De Vriese, deals with the controversies between Marx and the Young Hegelians at the beginning of the 1840s. Focusing on an hitherto neglected novel published in 1843 by a former close friend of Marx, Edgar Bauer, it shows how the young Marx was negatively depicted by his former friends, and uncovers the element of truth in this portrait but also the theoretical reason lying behind the attitudes of the protagonists: a different conception of the role of critique.

Zacharias Zoubir then examines the concept of alienation in the 1857–58 *Grundrisse*, a concept which is not confined to Marx's more youthful writings but reappears strategically in his mature work. Zoubir shows that this reflects an evolution in Marx's thought during this period, the terminology of alienation acquiring a philosophical and economic content different from that of his earlier work — the 1844 *Manuscripts* for example — and leading to a different conception of an emancipated society.

The following chapter, by David Andrews, focuses on the related concept of fetishism. Rather neglected in the course of the history of the interpretations of *Capital*, the importance and centrality of "commodity fetishism" for an understanding of Marx's main opus was nevertheless stressed in the past by authors like Rubin or Colletti (who directly linked it with the concept of alienation). Andrews re-examines the "mysterious" or "occult" quality attributed to the products of labour and shows how in terms of Marx's use of "natural" in the Aristotelian sense it pervades the entire "absurd" functioning of a capitalist economy.

2.2. Around the new MEGA

The altogether eight articles in this part deal with a number of themes spurred by the MEGA^2 edition and the new material it contains, which has not been publicly available in the past and which is bound to change some of the received views on Marx. It also sheds light on Friedrich Engels' work as an editor of volumes II and III of *Capital*.

The first chapter is by Regina Roth who is involved in the MEGA project as an editor and researcher and informs about the status of the editorial work and also about the novel concept of *MEGAdigital*. The latter puts Marx's manuscripts and the published version of *Capital* in the context of Marx's overall writing and then relates it to Marx and Engels' correspondence and to excerpts and notes in Marx's notebooks. Examining Marx's manuscripts and studies on rent, reproduction and the rate of profit, the article illuminates the way Marx worked and why he failed to accomplish his huge economic project.

The second chapter, by Heinz D. Kurz, asks whether and in what sense the MEGA^2 edition will turn out to be a watershed in interpreting Marx. The edition is said to be a watershed, because it documents that Marx apparently got doubts as regards the correctness of his "law of motion" of modern society, centred on the falling tendency of the rate of profits. It will not be a watershed, since Marx unswervingly stuck to his "law of value", which, however, is difficult to sustain.

In his chapter, Izumi Omura, who is a part of the Japanese MEGA^2 team on economics, turns again to the question of who was the author of the chapter on Feuerbach in the *German Ideology*, Marx or Engels? Omura elaborates an argument that has all the characteristic features of a forensic, evidence-based account. He argues that Rjazanov's contention that the chapter was written by Engels alone and not dictated by Marx is difficult to sustain. Omura also rejects Mayer's view that the two co-authored the piece for a lack of evidence in support of it: according to him, the Feuerbach chapter was indeed dictated by Marx to Engels.

Nicolas Eyguesier, in the fourth chapter, re-examines the concept of "primitive accumulation" against the background of Marx's explanation of the birth of "capitalism". He compares Marx's concept with that of the development of Sismondi and argues that while the latter was essentially "romantic" and cyclical, the former was based on the idea of progress and assumed an eschatological aim of the history of mankind. While Marx took notice of Sismondi's doctrine, he rejected its core message.

The following two chapters are dedicated to an assessment of Marx's extensive work on multi-sector models of expanded reproduction. Christian Gehrke in his chapter shows that balanced growth, which plays a prominent role in Engels' edition of the second volume of *Capital*, is not to be found in Marx's original manuscripts. The reader is rather confronted with Marx's investigation of the problem of the traverse between systems of production, which he analysed in terms of an intricate model with six sectors. Marx also pointed out the "elasticity" of industrial production, which is due to the possibility of varying the intensity of labour and the rate of capacity utilization.

In the following chapter Kenji Mori, who is a part of the Japanese $MEGA^2$ team on economics, also deals with Marx's six-sector model of extended reproduction and the traverse problem. His attention focuses on Marx's attempt to understand the dynamics of prices in a world characterised by the diffusion of new methods of production. It is shown that Marx was well aware of some fundamental problems in dynamic analysis, which were tackled only a century later by economists such as Adolph Lowe.

The next chapter is also by Kenji Mori. It is devoted to Marx's empirical research in his notebooks known as *Krisenhefte* (*Books of Crisis*) dealing with the 1857 crisis, arguably the first economic crisis in history that affected the world economy. Marx's studies continued the work of Thomas Tooke and William Newmarch on *A History of Prices*, published in the same year. His meticulous work has recently been published for the first time in the MEGA edition (Part IV, Vol. 14).

In his chapter, Susumu Takenaga, who is a part of the Japanese $MEGA^2$ team on economics, sheds new light on Marx's various attempts to come to grips with the problem of rent and draws the attention to notes and manuscripts not contained in volume III of *Capital*, edited by Engels on the basis of a manuscript Marx wrote in

1865. The author shows how much Marx struggled with Ricardo's rent theory, the concept of "absolute rent" he elaborated and his absorption of Justus von Liebig's path-breaking work on agro-chemistry.

2.3. Analytical developments

This part consists of altogether six articles, which elaborate analytically on some of the problems Marx tackled in his works.

In the first chapter, Saverio Maria Fratini investigates whether Marx's concept of "absolute rent" reflects the existence of a monopoly in agriculture. Marx had argued that this kind of rent has an upper limit given by the difference between the (labour) value and the production price of agricultural products. Critics disputed the existence of such an upper limit. The author argues that while the criticism is correct, it still makes sense to distinguish absolute rent from rent reflecting a monopoly.

The second chapter is by Carlo Benetti, Alain Béraud, Edith Klimovsky and Antoine Rebeyrol and analyses the numerical illustrations of the two-sector model of extended reproduction in volume II of *Capital*. The attention focuses on the problem of whether or not the economy converges to a balanced growth path and which role is played in this context by the way prices are determined. While Marx assumed prices to be given in terms of labour values, they introduce an endogenous price model that allows for an adjustment of prices according to the state of the accumulation process.

Rebeca Gomez Betancourt and Matari Pierre Manigat, in the following chapter, turn to James Steuart's influence on Marx's monetary economic thought. Steuart was critical of the quantity theory of money and provided arguments in support of breaches of the link between the quantity of money and prices, which Marx took up and elaborated in various directions. The focus is inter alia on the functions money performs and the difference between advances of capital and the spending of income.

The chapter by Wilfried Parys scrutinizes critically Marx's view of the "common third" in the exchange of any two commodities. Marx identified "abstract labour" to be the sought substance. His idea was soon challenged not only by marginalist authors who insisted that "use value in general" is the *tertium comparationis*, but also by various scholars who pointed out that commodities entering directly or indirectly in the production of all commodities could serve the purpose. Energy is such a thing.

Rodolphe Dos Santos Ferreira and Ragip Ege in their chapter have a closer look at Marx's concept of the labour contract, which was supposed to substantiate exploitation and confront it with the neoclassical concept. While the latter refers to a particular service, the former refers to the labour power the worker sells to the employer. The employer is entitled to make the best use of labour power with the wage covering its cost of reproduction. Externalisation of part of this cost, via the social security system or higher flexibility of the labour contract, allows the employer to increase exploitation.

The final chapter in this part is by Michaël Assous and Antonin Pottier, who compare the analyses of Marx and Michal Kalecki on the macroeconomic (in)stability of capitalism and the role of the class struggle between workers and capitalists in it.

2.4. The reception of Marx's works

The reception of Marx's works in different countries has long been neglected, first because, like for other authors, this field of study was not really topical or fashionable, but also more probably because of the role played, until recently, by the official discourses of political organisations. Both obstacles being now absent, the two chapters included in this part offer analyses of two important moments in the reception of Marx in the United Kingdom and in France prior to World War I.

Michael White focuses on one author, Philip Henry Wicksteed, and deals with his developments in what was called the Jevonsian critique of Marx: how Wicksteed was led to criticise Marx while defending Henry George's views, and why this was done in a questionable way, based on some misreading of Jevons's analysis.

Michel Bellet, in turn, studies a large group of authors who wrote in *La Revue socialiste*, the main French socialist journal prior to the First World War. He shows that Marx's writings, while judged important, were nevertheless received critically within an intellectual context deeply shaped by the ideas of the main French socialist writers of the nineteenth century (Constantin Pecqueur in particular), and how the role of Benoît Malon was central in this reception.

All these studies bring new material and fresh results. No doubt, thanks to the MEGA^2 edition, they are part of a novel start in Marx studies.

Acknowledgements

The present issue of *The European Journal of the History of Economic Thought* offers a selection of papers presented at the conference "Marx 1818/2018. New Developments on Marx's Thought and Writings", Lyon, France, 27–29 September 2017. This conference was organised with the financial help of *The European Journal of the History of Economic Thought*, the research centre Triangle (UMR CNRS 5206), the École Normale Supérieure de Lyon, the Labex COMOD, the University of Lyon 2 and the ANR "Saint-Simonisme 18–21".

Disclosure statement

No potential conflict of interest was reported by the authors.

Funding

The financial support of the publication by Labex Comod (ANR-11-LABX-0041) of the University of Lyon — as a part of the program "Investissements d'Avenir" (ANR-11-IDEX-0007) managed by the Agence Nationale de la Recherche (ANR) — is gratefully acknowledged.

References

Backhaus, Hans-Georg. 1967. "Zur Dialektik der Wertform". In Alfred Schmidt (ed.), *Beiträge zur marxistischen Erkenntnistheorie*, second edition, 1970, Frankfurt am Main: Suhrkamp, 128–152. As in H.G. Backhaus, *Dialektik der Wertform. Untersuchungen zur Marxschen Ökonomiekritik*, Freiburg: Ca Ira Verlag, 1997, 41–64.
Bellofiore, Riccardo, and Roberto Fineschi, eds. 2009. *Re-reading Marx. New Perspectives after the Critical Edition*. London: Palgrave Macmillan.
Breckman, Warren. 1999. *Marx, the Young Hegelians, and the Origins of Radical Social Theory: Dethroning the Self*. Cambridge: Cambridge University Press.
Bidet, Jacques, and Stathis Kouvelakis, eds. 2008. *Critical Companion to Contemporary Marxism*. Leiden: Brill.
Carver, Terrell, ed. 1991. *The Cambridge Companion to Marx*. Cambridge: Cambridge University Press.
Cohen, Gerald A. 1978. *Karl Marx's Theory of History: A defence*. Princeton: Princeton University Press.

Colletti, Lucio. 1969. *Il Marxismo e Hegel*. Bari: Laterza. English translation of Part II by Lawrence Garner, *Marxism and Hegel*, London: New Left Books (NLB), 1973.

Colletti, Lucio. 1975. "Introduction" to Karl Marx, *Early Writings*. Harmondsworth: Penguin Books, 7–56.

Elster, Jon. 1985. *Making Sense of Marx*. Cambridge: Cambridge University Press and Paris: Maison des Sciences de l'Homme.

Fine, Ben, Alfredo Saad-Filho, and Marco Boffo, eds. 2012. *The Elgar Companion to Marxist Economics*. Cheltenham: Edward Elgar.

Fischbach, Franck. 2015. *Philosophies de Marx*. Paris: Vrin.

Foley, Duncan. 1982. "The Value of Money, the Value of Labor Power und the Marxian Transformation Problem." *Review of Radical Political Economics* 14: 37–47.

Foley, Duncan. 2000. "Recent Developments in the Labor Theory of Value." *Review of Radical Political Economics* 32: 1–39.

Harvey, David. 2010-13. *A Companion to Marx's Capital*. London and New York: Verso.

Heinrich, Michael. 2004. *Kritik der politischen Ökonomie: Eine Einführung in Das Kapital von Karl Marx*. Stuttgart: Schmetterling Verlag. English translation by Alexander Locascio, *An introduction to the three volumes of Karl Marx's Capital*, New York: Monthly Review Press, 2012.

Heinrich, Michael. 2016. "Capital After MEGA: Discontinuities, Interruptions, and New Beginnings". *Crisis and Critique* 3 (3): 92–138.

Heinrich, Michael. 2018. *Karl Marx und die Geburt der modernen Gesellschaft. Band I: 1818–1843: Biographie und Werkentwicklung*. Stuttgart: Schmetterling Verlag. English translation by Alexander Locascio, *Karl Marx and the Birth of Modern Society. The life of Marx and the Development of his Work*. Volume I: 1818–1843, New York: Monthly Review Press, 2019 (forthcoming).

Hoff, Jan. 2009. *Marx global. Zur Entwicklung des internationalen Marx-Diskurses seit 1965*, Berlin: Akademie Verlag. English translation by Nicholas Gray, *Marx Worldwide. On the Development of the International Discourse on Marx since 1965*, Chicago: Haymarket Books, 2017.

Larsen, Neil, Mathias Nilges, Josh Robinson, and Nicholas Brown. 2014. *Marxism and the Critique of Value*. Chicago: MCM' Publishing.

Leopold, David. 2007. *The Young Karl Marx. German Philosophy, Modern Politics and Human Flourishing*. Cambridge: Cambridge University Press.

McLellan, David. 1969. *The Young Hegelians and Karl Marx*. London: Macmillan.

McLellan, David. 1973. *Karl Marx. His Life and Thought*. London: Macmillan. Third edition as *Karl Marx. A Biography*, London: Papermac, 1995.

Mehring, Franz. 1918. *Karl Marx. Geschichte seines Lebens*. Berlin: Leipziger Buchdruckerei.

Musto, Marcello, ed. 2008. *Karl Marx's Grundrisse. Foundations of the Critique of Political Economy 150 Years Later*. London: Routledge.

Nikolaevskij, Boris and Otto Mänchen-Helfen. [1937] 1963. *Karl Marx. Eine Biographie*. Hanover: J.H.W. Dietz.

Postone, Moishe. 1993. *Time, Labor, and Social Domination. A Reinterpretation of Marx's Critical Theory*. Cambridge: Cambridge University Press.

Reichelt, Helmut. 1970. *Zur logischen Struktur des Kapitalbegriffs bei Karl Marx*. Frankfurt am Main: Europäische Verlagsanstalt.

Renault, Emmanuel, ed. 2008. *Lire les manuscrits de 1844*. Paris: Presses Universitaires de France.

Renault, Emmanuel. 2009. "Philosophie". In *Lire Marx*, edited by Gérard Duménil, Michael Löwy, and Emmanuel Renault. Paris: Presses Universitaires de France, 93–192.

Renault, Emmanuel. 2014. *Marx et la Philosophie*. Paris: Presses Universitaires de France.

Roemer, John E. 1981. *Analytical Foundations of Marxian Economic Theory*. Cambridge: Cambridge University Press.

Roemer, John E. 1982. *A General Theory of Exploitation and Class*. Cambridge, Mass: Harvard University Press.

Roemer, John E., ed. 1986. *Analytical Marxism*. Cambridge: Cambridge University Press and Paris: Maison des Sciences de l'Homme.

Rojahn, Jürgen. 1983. "Marxismus. Marx. Geschichtswissenschaft. Der Fall der sog. Ökonomisch-Philosophischen Manuskripte aus dem Jahre 1844'". *International Review of Social History* 28 (1): 2–49.

Rosen, Zvi. 1977. *Bruno Bauer and Karl Marx. The Influence of Bruno Bauer on Marx's Thought*. The Hague: Martinus Nijhoff.

Roth, Regina. 2010. "Marx on Technical Change in the Critical Edition." *The European Journal of the History of Economic Thought*, 17 (5): 1223–1251.

Sperber, Jonathan. 2013. *Karl Marx. A Nineteenth-Century Life*. New York: Liveright.

Sraffa, Piero. 1960. *Production of Commodities by Means of Commodities. Prelude to a Critique of Economic Theory*. Cambridge: Cambridge University Press.

Stedman Jones, Gareth. 2016. *Karl Marx. Greatness and Illusion*. London: Penguin Books.

Not a man of solid principles. The relevance of Edgar Bauer's polemical portrait of Karl Marx in his 1843 novella *Es leben feste Grundsätze!*

Herbert De Vriese

ABSTRACT

The protagonist of Edgar Bauer's 1843 novella *Es leben feste Grundsätze!* is a young intellectual named "Karl". It can hardly be doubted that Bauer's novella is a polemical character study of Karl Marx: the rather demeaning picture of "Herr Karl" belongs to the heat of controversy between Marx and *die Freien*, the Berlin Young Hegelians, after the end of their participation in the *Rheinische Zeitung* in late autumn 1842. So far, Bauer's novella has never been used as a potential source to shed light on the deeper causes of animosity between Marx and *die Freien*.

Das Skandal, die Polissonerie müssen laut und entschlossen in einer Zeit desavouirt werden, die ernste, männliche und gehaltene Charaktere für die Erkämpfung ihrer erhabenen Zwecke verlangt.

Karl Marx, *Rheinische Zeitung*, 29. November 1842

Karl war aber im Grunde kein sehr starker Geist. Er war reizbar; er konnte daher wohl so lange fest bleiben, als es ihm äußerlich nicht zu schlecht ging.

Edgar Bauer, *Es Leben feste Grundsätze!*, 1843

This article is an inquiry into the theoretical relevance of Edgar Bauer's polemical portrait of Karl Marx in his 1843 novella *Es leben feste Grundsätze!* [*Long Live Solid Principles!*]. It is divided into two main parts. The first part focuses on the life, thought and personality of the young Marx. It examines whether the novella provides new knowledge that may be relevant to the intellectual-biographical study of the young Marx. The second part concentrates on the philosophical

issue of "principledness", both in the sense of intellectual integrity
and in the sense of steadfast allegiance to the good cause. Taking into
account how the issue divided Marx and the Berlin Young Hegelians
from late autumn 1842 onwards, it is argued that the central theme of
Edgar Bauer's novella helps underline the importance of this issue.
Taken together, these elements justify a call for more scholarly attention to Bauer's novella in the context of the study of Karl Marx and
the Young Hegelians.

1. A portrait of Karl as a young man

The two parts of this article each have a different tone and distinctive
approach to Edgar Bauer's novella *Es leben feste Grundsätze!* Whereas
the second part aims to bring new and reliable findings to an already
well-documented interpretation of the 1842 conflict and eventual schism
in the Young Hegelian movement, the first part is of a more speculative
nature, because it will attempt to get a grip on the "real Marx" through
a medium as seemingly untrustworthy as a polemical novella. However,
in order not to repel the reader in this first part, I will set out from a
concrete and down-to-earth observation, which may be of special interest to the historian of Marxism and the Marx biographer. My article is
built on the basis of a sufficiently solid and intriguing discovery: the
protagonist of the 1843 novella by Edgar Bauer entitled *Es leben feste
Grundsätze!* – one of two novels in a compilation under the title
Berliner Novellen, which is now a rather rare and hard to find book[1] –
is a portrayal of Karl Marx. As I will argue in this article, it can hardly
be doubted that the novella's protagonist, a young intellectual who bears
the name "Karl", is consciously intended by the author to be understood
(and even to be recognized by the intellectual in-crowd) as a lively representation of Karl Marx.

The difficulties arise, however, as soon as we try to gain fruitful
insights from this discovery and to cast them into an original and
useful contribution to Marx scholarship. The major dilemma in the
interpretation of the 175-page novella may be put as follows. On the
one hand, the book appears to be a new and reliable biographical

---

[1] This was particularly the case until just a few years ago, when I discovered and studied the
book at the *Staatsbibliothek zu Berlin* during a research stay in Berlin. In the meantime, a
digital copy has become available through Google Books. As for the published editions,
according to an extensive worldwide search with Karlsruhe Virtual Catalog, today only five
public libraries, all located in Germany, appear to own a copy.

source since Edgar Bauer (1820–1886) had been a contemporary and one of Marx's close friends during his student years in Berlin.[2] It can easily be proven by passages from the book that the author was well aware of the personal situation in which Marx found himself at that time. By extension, it is evident to assume that Edgar Bauer, as a philosophical companion and good friend, must have had first-hand knowledge of the young Marx's most precious ideas, thoughts, worries and ambitions, and must have been well acquainted with his distinctive character traits.[3] On the other hand, we must take into account that the novella was meant as a strategic vehicle (but apparently, for reasons which I have not been able to detect, never came to adopt such a function) in the bitter conflict in 1842–43 between Marx and the Berlin Young Hegelians (also known as "*die Freien*" or "the free ones"), of whom Bruno Bauer, Edgar Bauer, Ludwig Buhl, Eduard Meyen, Karl Friedrich Köppen and Max Stirner may be mentioned here as the most prominent figures. Hence, Edgar Bauer's book is anything but an attempt at an authentic representation of Karl Marx, but rather a piece of defamatory writing boiling down to a "literary revenge" on his former friend. So, the question arises: how can a purposely distorted and degrading picture of a young German intellectual of the 1840s named Karl ever lend itself to revealing new insights into the life and personality of the young Marx?

Here is where the speculative undertaking sets in. In the interpretation of the novel, I have adopted the heuristic principle that a polemical character study, in order to hit its mark and be effective, must to a large extent be truthful, since it attempts to gain the attention of the well-informed reader by playing on the effect of recognition. Only a largely authentic approach can produce the critical impact of *unmasking* a person – as a powerful strategy of destructive criticism that should be distinguished from less refined and more innocent procedures such as mere travesty or caricature – and we can imagine that it is precisely this kind of

---

[2] During Bruno Bauer's two and a half year stay at the University of Bonn, Marx's regular visits to the house of the Bauer family in Charlottenburg attest to an enduring friendship with Bruno's younger brother Edgar Bauer (Bruno Bauer and Edgar Bauer 1844, 55–56; Bruno Bauer to Karl Marx, April 1841, in *MEGA III/1*, 356).

[3] The energetic portrait of Karl Marx, 'ein schwarzer Kerl aus Trier', in the mock epic *Der Triumph des Glaubens* (Edgar Bauer and Friedrich Engels 1842, 28; Blumenberg 2000, 36) is by Edgar Bauer, because Engels had not yet met Marx in person: "Who comes last, wild and free? / A black lad from Trier now we see. / (…) / His fist is clenched, he rages without compare, / As if then thousand devils had him by the hair."

destructive impact which Bauer sought to generate. To support this general consideration, three specific arguments must be taken into account. First, the similarities between the protagonist's trials and tribulations in the book and those of the young Marx in his real life are considerable, even to the extent that one may assume that most of the significant character traits of "Herr Karl" are truthful or at least not entirely fictionalized. Second, when situated in the larger context of Young Hegelian hypercritical discourse, excelling in the art of writing controversial and satirical pamphlets (such as Bruno Bauer's *Die Posaune des jüngsten Gerichts über Hegel den Atheisten und Antichristen. Ein Ultimatum* (1841b), Ludwig Buhl's *Die Noth der Kirche und die christliche Sonntagsfeier. Ein Wort des Ernstes an die Frivolität der Zeit* (1842) and indeed the notorious mock epic *Die frech bedräute, jedoch wunderbar befreite Bibel. Oder: Der Triumph des Glaubens* (1842) written by Friedrich Engels and Edgar Bauer himself), it would have been a surprisingly weak and unconvincing gesture if the novella's protagonist had only received the first name of Karl Marx and not some of his most remarkable and easily recognizable characteristics.[4] Third, it must be underlined that the novella's polemical force is not so much produced by the description of the protagonist, but rather by the imaginary future course of his life, which is projected in the then near future of the years 1843–1845 (Bauer 1843a, 179 and 261). So, it could work perfectly with a more or less reliable character sketch of Marx.

Drawing these threads together, I will defend the hypothesis that Edgar Bauer's novella *Es leben feste Grundsätze!* is a valuable source of information to obtain a richer understanding of the life and personality of the young Marx. More fundamentally, when it comes to the question of examining the possible motives behind Marx's theoretical and ideological development in the early 1840s, I will pursue the idea that there may be a significant core of truth in the way Edgar Bauer pictures the existential choices and attitudes of "Karl". I realize that this is a somewhat daring approach to interpret the book,

---

[4] The strategy of making a 'Charakteristik', originally developed by Arnold Ruge in *The Hallische Jahrbücher* as a new form of critical journalism, must also be taken into account here as a potentially illuminating source of influence. 'Charakteristik' was based on the (orthodox Hegelian) conviction that genuine criticism is not an active interference with the object of criticism, but simply a detached representation allowing the object 'to criticize itself' (viz. to expose and even eliminate itself). This idea was central to the method of 'pure critique' employed by many of the Berlin Young Hegelians, and was the hallmark of Edgar Bauer's conception of 'die Ruhe des Erkennens' (see De Vriese 2011, 575–77, 583).

founded on a heuristic principle that is far from self-evident. Nevertheless, I think it makes sense to confine myself in the first part of this article to developing a clear hypothesis and to elaborating its most obvious consequences. Insofar as my findings are new and unconventional, they may serve as an invitation to other scholars to take Bauer's novella and read it, in the light of their own expertise. And even if one retains a healthy measure of skepticism about the potential authenticity of Edgar Bauer's portrait of "Karl" as a young man, there still may be value in the less controversial claim that this is how Karl Marx was viewed by some of his former friends and associates at that time.

1.1. Autumn 1842: the split in the young Hegelian movement

The period in which Edgar Bauer's *Es leben feste Grundsätze!* was written can quite accurately be determined: during the two and a half months between 31 January and 16 April 1843.[5] This interval of time is important for a correct interpretation of the polemical function of the book. It coincides with the last months of Marx's occupation as executive editor of the *Rheinische Zeitung*: he resigned on 17 March because of the rigorous and double censorship regime that had been imposed on the newspaper, and presumably in a final attempt to save the newspaper by making this sacrifice.[6] Yet, the suppression of the journal had been officially decreed by the King of Prussia on 19 January 1843, leaving a "period of grace before execution" (Marx to Ruge, 25 January 1843, in *MEGA III/1*, 40) until the end of March 1843, and the decision was not reversed. The guidelines of stricter censorship were officially articulated in the new Prussian censorship instruction of 31 January 1843, which prohibited the discussion of

---

[5] There is only one exact time reference in the novella, and it is written in the conditional mood: "If our story took place in the year 1843, then you would consider the latest censorship instruction for the beginning of how the curse of the father was fulfilled on Karl." (Bauer 1843a, 179) The fact that Edgar Bauer mentions in his book the latest censorship instruction – the Prussian censorship instruction of 31. Januar 1843 (on which Edgar Bauer wrote a 60-page pamphlet, by the way) – and gives it a crucial role to develop the plot of the novella may be taken as a fairly certain starting date for the conception and writing of the book. The time of publication can be determined between 16 April and 1 May 1843, because the book is mentioned in *Allgemeines Verzeichniß der Bücher, welche von Ostern 1843 bis Michaelis 1843 neu gedruckt oder aufgelegt worden sind*, 197 (Easter Sunday 1843 was on 16 April), and because Carl Biedermann's *Deutsche Monatsschrift für Litteratur und öffentliches Leben* of May 1843 has a review of the book.

[6] Attempts to save the newspaper continued until the end of March (Klutentreter 1966, 128–133).

ideas and theories that were critical for the Christian religion and the
Prussian state – a stipulation so stringent that the censor complained
that he would have to strike two-thirds of the articles (Klutentreter
1966, 137; Ruge 1886, 325). The date of this censorship instruction is
a key date in Edgar Bauer's novella: it is described as the beginning of
the fulfilment of the curse that had been laid upon the protagonist
Karl (Bauer 1843a, 179).

What had happened before that time belongs to the
established knowledge on the Young Hegelian movement[7] and
has often been described in secondary literature. In late autumn
1842, it came to a clean break between Marx and the Berlin
Young Hegelians, who up till then had been regular contributors to
the *Rheinische Zeitung*. The tension had built up since 15 October
1842 when Marx became the executive editor of the newspaper.
Marx was annoyed by the radical ideas and provocative style of many
of the Berlin contributions because he felt they might endanger the
continued existence of the newspaper, while at the same time
being hardly beneficial to the good cause. He demanded a more
profound and more serious investigation of new political
ideas. Moreover, he did not believe that an ongoing critique of
religion, let alone the aggressive display of the label of atheism,
was a viable strategy to stimulate social and political change
in Germany.

However, the event leading to a definitive break was not situated
in the Rhineland, in the editorial office of the *Rheinische
Zeitung* in Cologne, but in the capital of Prussia. In November 1842,
Arnold Ruge brought a visit to *die Freien,* the Berlin
Young Hegelians, in one of their favorite bars. His ambition was to
bring the progressive movement of philosophical-political
journalism in Germany into line again, and more specifically, to

---

[7] For the sake of convenience, I will capture the 'left', 'progressive' or 'young' wing of the
Hegelian school here by the term of a Young Hegelian *movement*. With this general term, I
refer to the journalistic activity and outspoken political activism undertaken in the period
between 24 December 1841 (date of the Prussian censorship instruction that opened a period
of relative freedom of the press) and 31 January 1843 (date of the Prussian censorship
instruction that reversed the liberal measures) and supported by a large group of Hegelians
participating in Arnold Ruge's *Deutsche Jahrbücher*, the *Leipziger Allgemeine Zeitung* and the
Rheinische Zeitung (these three organs of publicity were all suppressed at the end of 1842 and
the beginning of 1843). However, the sociological dynamic of the Young Hegelians is much
more complicated, as is convincingly shown by Wolfgang Eßbach's useful distinction between
philosophical school, political party, literary bohemia and atheist sect. In view of that, the
category of 'movement', which favors the connotation of a political party, is misleading. See
Eßbach 1988.

bring a "thorough ethical principle" to the Young Hegelians in Berlin.[8] This attempt ended in a complete failure. The Berlin philosophers stuck to their uncompromising intellectual radicalism. Ruge was openly ridiculed as a reactionary. As a result, the former unity of the Young Hegelian movement was broken beyond repair. Still, Ruge did not intend to give publicity to what had happened, but the rumor of the conflict spread and was brought out into the open by two German newspapers, albeit in a severely distorted account. It was incorrectly reported that it was Ruge's travel companion in Berlin, the poet Georg Herwegh, who had visited *die Freien*, and who had passed the scathing judgment that they were beneath the dignity of criticism. In order to rectify the situation, Herwegh sent a letter to Marx in which he confirmed his contemptuous judgment of *die Freien*, while clarifying, though, that he had not visited the group in Berlin. Herwegh suggested that Marx could publish those parts of his letter which he thought appropriate for a contribution on this issue in the *Rheinische Zeitung*. Marx did not hesitate to publish an abridged version of Herwegh's letter and even added a self-written paragraph to it. When it appeared on 29 November, the Berlin Young Hegelians were shocked and felt deeply betrayed by Marx, who in their eyes was now openly taking sides with Herwegh, against the group of *die Freien*. This was nothing less than a clear decision to expel *die Freien* from Germany's most progressive philosophical-political movement of that time. The conflict aggravated when it became clear that Marx had not only *published* Herwegh's letter but edited and altered it, which quickly grew into the gossip that Marx had written the entire Herwegh letter himself (see Ruge to Marx, 10 December 1842, in *MEGA III/1*, 385). One specific sentence, which today can be verified as Marx's proper statement, may indeed be regarded as Marx's personal and decisive farewell from *die Freien*:

> Rowdiness and roguery must be loudly and resolutely repudiated in a period which demands serious, manly and self-restrained characters for the achievement of its lofty aims (*MEGA I/1*, 372).

---

[8] M.L. 1844, 28–29: "I still remember with joy the summer of the year 1842. What a united life we had among us 'radicals', in spite of all debates over atheism and popularity and Jacoby and Königsberg. We were connected by the *Rheinische Zeitung* – in short, we almost felt like a party. But then, in autumn, the Anhalt railway brought us those two 'men of freedom' [*Freiheitsmänner*], who appeared to have come to Berlin, which seemed too free and too frivolous in their eyes, with the exclusive aim of bringing a thorough ethical principle and the anchor of the religion of freedom." See also Ruge, Letter to Prutz, 18 November 1842, Letter to Marx, 4 December 1842, Letter to Prutz, 7 December 1842, Letter to Fleischer, 12 December 1842, in Ruge 1886.

What followed was a fury of letters from Berlin to Cologne, of which only a few explicit references (the letters from Eduard Meyen) and only one letter, from Bruno Bauer to Karl Marx, have survived. Marx replied to Meyen with a sharp and violent letter, which has neither survived, but must have had the effect of making the breach irreparable. Bruno Bauer adopted a calm and measured tone in his letter but reproached Marx bitterly that he had taken sides against the Berlin philosophers without good reason.

Ruge, for his part, was not directly involved in this dispute, but almost immediately joined in with Marx's resolute behaviour and encouraged him to make the break with *die Freien* definitive. Furthermore, he openly attacked the "blasé theoreticians" of the Prussian capital in his famous essay "Eine Selbstkritik des Liberalismus", published in January 1843 – a publication which, for other reasons than those addressed here, provoked the official ban of the *Deutsche Jahrbücher*. In a curious way, the explicit articulation of the schism in the Young Hegelian movement coincided with the suppression of its principal organs.

In Marx's editorial office in Cologne, too, the definitive break with *die Freien* was easily detectable. From December 1842 onwards until the suppression of the *Rheinische Zeitung* in April 1843, one would no longer read Berlin contributions in the newspaper.[9] In Berlin, the former allies of the Young Hegelian movement were outraged. They began to affirm their radical philosophical profile against the "accommodating" political liberalism of Marx and Ruge. It is in this context that Edgar Bauer decided to write a novella with a protagonist named Karl.

1.2. Herr Karl = Karl Marx

So, let us turn our attention to the book itself. Two possible misunderstandings must be clarified here. Bauer's novella is much more than just a demeaning picture of Karl Marx. It is a *philosophical* novella full of interesting thoughts, especially on the

---

[9] A significant observation is that Friedrich Engels, who started writing correspondence from England to the *Rheinische Zeitung* from the beginning of December 1842 onwards, abruptly stopped his cooperation after four weeks. Klutentreter believes this to be an obvious consequence of Engels' awareness, probably through letters from Berlin that have been lost, of Marx's break with *die Freien*. According to this hypothesis, one should include Engels within the group of the 'Berlin' Young Hegelians (Klutentreter 1966, 107).

themes of censorship and love and marriage. It is a *social* novel making a sharp accusation against the hardship and crying abuses of the time.[10] The polemic with Karl Marx is interwoven in other literary registers, and even remains hidden in the first three-quarters of the book: there, the protagonist Karl is a principled and even admirable character. But, the blow in the last quarter of the book strikes hard. Karl is manoeuvred into a compromising and degrading situation, in which he renounces all of his earlier principles, and shows his true colours: not so much does he appear to be a weak and fainthearted person, but rather a sly character merely searching for his own benefit and (social) improvement. Yet, before describing and interpreting the plot, let me first ascertain that the Karl of Bauer's novella is Karl Marx.

What does the book teach about Karl that conforms remarkably well to the life of Marx? I will present three obvious similarities. I believe that these similarities, when combined with each other and placed in the above-sketched context of bitter disagreement between Marx and the Berlin Young Hegelians, establish a sufficiently strong argument to read the fictional Karl as an allusion to the real Karl.

First, there is the story of a severe conflict between Karl and his father. The son Karl openly confesses that he is not willing to aspire to the kind of job his father has in mind for him (Bauer 1843a, 162–63). On top of that, he has to acknowledge that he is engaged to a woman of the upper class. According to his father, this is an offense against the "sanctity of class society":

> My son, my son, what nonsense are you talking! For sure, when I was in France, every once in a while I heard such insane rubbish against the sanctity of the classes and against common decency. But you don't want to poison my house with the immoral principles of the frivolous French people, do you? (164)

The father speaks harsh words to his son, and tragically enough, before they can be reconciled to each other, Karl's father dies – which is interpreted in the novella as a major burden of guilt on the

---

[10] To the best of my knowledge, research on the genesis of the social novel in German literature is the only scholarly context in which Edgar Bauer's novella has been discussed so far. See Edler 1977, 118, 169.

protagonist's conscience.[11] It is generally agreed in Marx scholarship that the conflict with his father, broken off by his untimely death on 10 May 1838, thus destroying any hope of reconciliation, was the central personal experience for Marx as a young man.[12]

Second, Karl follows the only profession "with which one can content oneself in all honesty under the given circumstances" (178): he is a writer, a journalist, and a talented one at that (303, 305). A personal letter by Karl, which constitutes the fifth chapter of the book, expresses his ambition to spread new thoughts among the people and to make it conscious of its rights (192).[13] On behalf of his progressive and liberal ideas, another character in the novella sizes him up in a second as a journalist of the *Rheinische Zeitung* (176). In this light, the fact that the latest censorship instruction of 31 January 1843 is interpreted as the beginning of how the curse of Karl's father comes to fulfilment (179), points manifestly in the direction of Marx, because by that time all Berlin Young Hegelians had already stopped their cooperation with the journal and hence could not suffer personal misfortune by a stricter censorship regime and the eventual suppression of the journal. If there was one "journalist" of the *Rheinische Zeitung* for whom this was a personal disaster, it was Marx, because he was the only one who was to lose a, by the standards of that time, secure, honourable and very well-paid position.[14]

Third, the aristocratic father with whose daughter Karl is engaged – in Bauer's novella, that daughter's name is Marie and she is pictured as a bright and self-conscious woman – is Privy Councilor [*Geheimrat*] to the Prussian government. This may be taken as an

---

[11] The psychological analysis of Edgar Bauer distinguishes between Karl's conscious rejection of the influence of his father's admonishment and its disastrous effects on an unconscious and existential level: "And this Karl! He doesn't *seem* affected by the curse, that he has taken upon him." (Bauer 1843a, 168, my italics)

[12] See for instance Blumenberg 2000, chapter "Life at the University – Conflict with his Father", 16–32.

[13] Karl's ideas in the novella on censorhip and marriage can easily be traced back to some of Karl Marx's articles in the *Rheinische Zeitung*. Especially striking is the analogy between Marx's main argument in "Der Ehescheidungsgesetzentwurf" and the lengthy and well-elaborated critique of marriage in the novella (Bauer 1843a, 251–255). See also Marie's correspondence to Karl (213): "Again, you will come to me and say: marriage is not a free relationship, because it rests on the belief in the sanctity of its institution." Whether the novella contains substantial and sufficiently reliable material to extend our knowledge on the thought of the young Marx, should be investigated more deeply. In my reading, the philosophical reflections in the book are in part allusions to ideas of Karl Marx that were well-known in the intellectual in-crowd of that time, and in part those of Edgar Bauer himself.

[14] Mehring (2003, 44) underlines that Marx was 'heart and soul' in his work for the *Rheinische Zeitung* and succeeded in steadily increasing the number of subscribers under his editorship. According to Mehring, the goal of turning the *Rheinische Zeitung* into a successful journal appeared important enough to Marx "to risk a breach with his old companions in Berlin".

almost explicit reference to Jenny's father Ludwig von Westphalen, who was Privy Councilor to the Prussian Provincial Government of the Rhine Province. The specific details of his Prussian honorary decoration – Fourth Class Order of the Red Eagle [*roter Adlerorden vierter Klasse*] – are historically correct (Schöncke 1993, 876).

> At that moment the Privy Councilor came in. (...) If it strikes you as something characteristic, then I want to tell you that he had the Fourth Class Order of the Red Eagle (...). (Bauer 1843a, 183)

The fact that the relationship between Karl and Marie is a central theme in the novella is yet another sign that Edgar Bauer is turning his book into an adaptation of the real life of Karl Marx.

Without a doubt, the third motive is the strongest and most decisive one to confirm the identity between Herr Karl and Karl Marx. For the novella is placed in a time when Marx and Jenny von Westphalen were betrothed but not yet married. The time of writing is February, March, April 1843. At that time, no one could imagine how the engagement between Karl Marx and Jenny von Westphalen would develop, especially with the prospect of Marx's loss of his job. Was this not the death-blow to Marx's final hopes that his marriage with Jenny, "the queen of the ball" and one of the most eligible young ladies of his home town Trier, would ever be established?

We can safely assume that feelings among the Berlin Young Hegelians were not excelling in compassion and sympathy. In Bauer's novella, published at least one and a half months before Marx's and Jenny's marriage on 19 June 1843, the marriage does not take place: when Karl takes the decision to leave temporarily for another German city, where he has his "main professional connections" (191),[15] his fiancée is seduced by a cynical and opportunistic nobleman. It is to this man that Marie will consent yes.

1.3. Dramatic development and plot

In what follows, I will sketch the dramatic development of *Es leben feste Grundsätze!* in order to illuminate the sudden twist of fate that makes up the plot of Edgar Bauer's story. In the beginning, Bauer's protagonist is depicted as a courageous and strong-minded character, whose longing

---

[15] An allusion to the distance between Marx's romantic life in Trier and his professional life in Cologne?

for authentic human freedom is more precious than any desire for material prosperity and social recognition (Bauer 1843a, 165). Karl refuses to accept the position his father has arranged for him because holding an appointment in a society dominated by privilege and tyrannical patronizing is irreconcilable with his principles (166). In addition, he comes to the fore as a sensitive and self-sacrificing character. After the death of his father, Karl decides to take care of his younger sister. They face hardship and poverty, but Karl is not the man to waver in his conviction or lose his sense of self-worth. When he bumps into his aristocratic rival, the idle creature that has won the heart of his former fiancée, he does not shrink at lecturing this person, his superior in social rank, for his behaviour (176).[16]

As one might expect, the aristocratic man, named Arthur, who will soon afterwards succeed in marrying the Privy Councilor's daughter Marie, is not willing to accept the humiliation. Instead of meditating on revenge, however, he simply plans to find out more about the arrogant fellow. More particularly, Arthur wishes to discover the weaknesses hidden behind this display of self-absorbed rectitude and firmness of character. And even more importantly, he resolves to see the very moment that Karl is no longer able to stick to his lofty principles and is forced to renounce his convictions.

The years pass by. Through an intermediary, Arthur is kept informed of how Karl and his sister are doing. The misery of their condition has slowly begun to erode the proud and energetic spirit of Karl. He has lost his temper and inspiration: no longer as a journalist or a writer does he work, but as a low-wage copyist (285). Only a person with an exceptionally strong self-consciousness, the novelist explains, is capable of resisting the humiliating treatment of harsh conditions. And Karl is not such a strong spirit. "He was an excitable person; therefore, he could only keep his strength as long as external things were not too bad for him." (286) Karl is no longer the independent and unyielding man he used to be.

Yet, for Arthur, the awareness that Karl has succumbed to the external pressures of life and is no longer able to live up to his former ideals and ambitions, does not suffice. He wants to see the renouncement of his former principles as an expression of free will. Hence, he sends his intermediary to the place where Karl and his sister live and creates the conditions for "an offer that cannot be refused".

---

[16] I make abstraction from a much more complicated narrative thread (see 239–47).

Well, this Karl was always a thorn in my flesh: it annoyed me that he wanted to be better than other people. Sometimes I would get downright furious when I realized that this Karl wanted to keep himself proud and pure. But now, who knows where he will adapt himself to! (...) As soon as we have bound him in the shackles of an appointment and daily bread, we will be able to have a reasonable conversation with him. He will finally become ordinary and conform to our regulations. (306)[17]

Karl accepts a well-paid position at the government and justifies his decision with the argument that he needs to take care of his sister (311). His sister, by contrast, leaves him in anger and swears never to return. Shocked by his complete reversal of ideals, she reproaches him of merely following his own selfish impulses, and advises him to stay in that part of society that is best suited for this sort of "eternal preoccupation with oneself" (315).[18]

Karl, however, has chosen a new direction in life and does not look back. He works as a censor specialized in the radical press. His former expertise now helps him to see through and uncover the radical ideas, however cleverly they may be hidden in veiled terms. And the final stage of his progressive insight is highly appreciated in the upper-class circles:

Karl. Yes, I admit, our thoughts were stupid fancies, empty chimeras, in which we considered ourselves great beyond compare. Using general ideas of the state, of freedom, of justice, of equality – ideas which are present in the heart of each man – nothing seemed more credible to us than our capacity to call into existence a national consciousness [Volksbewußtsein], a nation, on the basis of these ideas. (321–22)

---

[17] Without a doubt, this plan to 'buy' Karl out of his situation – and out of his solid principles – is the most curious passage of the entire novella. For it is a historical fact that Karl Marx had effectively received an offer to enter the state service in Berlin. This occurred in the period between the banning of the Rheinische Zeitung and his marriage to Jenny von Westphalen – the period in which Edgar Bauer wrote his novella. Is it credible that Bauer knew about this offer, which was most probably arranged thanks to the efforts of Jenny's half-brother Ferdinand (who would later become the Prussian interior minister) in order to turn her improper liaison into a decent and respectable marriage? If so, it can hardly be doubted that the entire novella Es leben feste Grundsätze! has sprung from this specific knowledge, because in Bauer's eyes this unexpected move from the Prussian government could be nothing else than unambiguous proof of Karl Marx's secret connections and intriguing with the powers that be, and thus as the real cause of his sudden break with the too radical Berlin Young Hegelians in autumn 1842. I will leave it an open question. At any rate, if it should be answered affirmatively, it is sure that Bauer had not (yet) been informed that Marx had rejected the offer. Probably – but I am building speculation upon speculation here – this may also explain why Bauer's book completely missed its mark at that time. The Cologne censor of the Rheinische Zeitung, who wrote a final evaluation of Karl Marx to the Prussian government, acknowledged that Marx might be accused of "anything, but not a lack of principles [Gesinnungslosigkeit]" (Peters 1984, 42–48; Hosfeld 2009, 32).

[18] Bauer 1843a, 304, for the deeper reasons of her repugnance, and 313.

Karl has liberated himself from his youthful idealism and now speaks the words of a real adult. And more importantly, he has arrived where he had always wanted to come: in the upper-class circles, where he is finally recognized as a man of talent and a man of sufficient wealth. Long live solid principles!

1.4. Edgar Bauer's polemical character study

The hidden agenda behind the novella's plot speaks for itself. The embarrassing situation at the end of the book could not be in sharper contrast to the position Karl Marx actually held until March 1843 as a successful and widely admired editor of a liberal newspaper. Still, the way in which the unexpected turn of the story is carried out by Edgar Bauer, as a vitriolic attack and merciless mockery in the last 20 pages of the book after a generous and predominantly sympathetic picture of Karl, catches the reader by surprise. Indeed, the abrupt exposure of Karl's true nature creates the effect of having been completely wrong about this character. All of a sudden, this laudable person is unmasked as one who is fundamentally unreliable and has until then had the dexterity to conceal his true motives and inclinations. I am convinced that the abruptness of change in the protagonist's character, this sudden twist from loyalty to disloyalty, reflects how the Berlin Young Hegelians felt in autumn 1842 when Marx was no longer prepared to publish their articles in the *Rheinische Zeitung*. Hence, it can be interpreted as Bauer's literary revenge on the objectionable behaviour of his former friend.

Still, this purely imaginary attempt to square the account with Marx might be seen as a rather cheap travesty and totally impotent gesture. I even dare to assume that Bauer would not engage in such literary strategy if the sudden twist at the end of his book was not such as to make it (at least partly) recognizable for the intellectual in-crowd as one in line with the real motives and distinctive mindset of Marx. What we have read then, according to this hypothesis, is not just bitter situation humour, but a sharp and relentless character study of Marx, resulting in a personal indictment. For the sake of the argument, I have singled out three conspicuous character traits that grasp the essence of Bauer's demeaning portrait: weakness, untrustworthiness and selfishness.

Karl's weakness is defined in a dialectical fashion. Weakness is the state of being of a person who is determined and molded by the external circumstances in which he finds himself

(Bauer 1843a, 310).[19] It stands in contrast to the condition of a person who has the strength of spirit to transcend the established order and to shape or reshape it according to his own will (286). More specifically, weakness is related to "irritability" [*Reizbarkeit*], which may refer both to a nervous state of mind that is easily affected by influences and stimuli from the outer world, and to a thin-skinned and hot-tempered personality. The novella often highlights this irritable state of mind, in Karl's contact with his father (164), in his insolent conduct towards others, especially his superiors in social rank and power (176, 245–48, 286–87), and in his private life too (285, 315). Karl's weakness, which is contrasted with the strength of character of his sister,[20] openly comes to the fore in a personal confession at the end of the novella (310): "it is solely my own weakness," Karl writes, "that inspires me this doubt: but a weak and doubtful human being is no longer worthy to be a fighter for reason."

The main point of Karl's untrustworthiness is the sudden renouncement of the lofty ideals and adamant principles he held as a journalist of the radical press. But the most striking illustration of his untrustworthiness occurs at the end of Bauer's novella, in relation to his younger sister. Karl has always been there to take care of her, after the death of their father, as if such attitude of sisterly love could not be shaken by any misfortune. Yet, the final chapter of the book reveals that Karl has only pretended to be such a laudable and reliable person. All of a sudden, he does not care about his sister anymore, and this happens as soon as he has taken the step to accommodate to upper-class life. When he is questioned about her fate, and about whether she has recovered from her misery, he simply answers: "Do not speak me about that vile creature." (325) In view of that, his untrustworthiness is of the specific kind that he is able to devote himself intensively to someone during a particular time, but then suddenly and without remorse cuts such person out of his life completely: he is able to break off an affectionate relation by the same kind of evidence as that by which he formerly showed himself fully dedicated and reliable.

---

[19] The dialectical relationship between individual and society is an important philosophical theme in the book (see 155, 178, 182, 191, 194–95, 209, 214, 218, 259–60, 283, 292).

[20] The following passage (289) depicts Karl's sister as a strong, and therefore exceptional, human being: "The uncomplicated dignity, the serene elevation, with which she resigned herself to her misery, reconciled him [August, another character in the novella] with his own misery. It was the first time that he had seen a strong human being."

The suspicion of Karl's selfishness is only revealed at the end of the novella but may be reconstructed as a continuous thread all through the book. It constitutes the core of his sister's condemnation: she reproaches him of being eternally preoccupied with himself (315). Most concretely, this is illustrated in her criticism that Karl, when he makes his decision to accept the government position that will drag him and his sister out of their miserable condition, has not even thought a second about what his sister might think of such a change of life and the motives behind it, let alone considered to ask her about her personal opinion. Hence, Karl's selfishness extends to the need to dominate and exercise his powers over others, so as to direct the course their lives (or thoughts) must take (313–14; 287).

Now, what does this all imply for gaining a better understanding of the life and personality of the young Marx? In order to soften the impression of a purely speculative undertaking, resulting in a completely new image of Marx, it must be underlined that this is not a new perspective. Rather, it is one that may yield extra support to already existing discussions on intriguing choices and behaviors in Marx's life, especially those concerning his intellectual and ideological orientation, and those related with bitter and rather unexpected personal conflicts in his life as the ones with Arnold Ruge (1844), Bruno Bauer (1845), Wilhelm Weitling (1846) and Proudhon (1847), all of which testify to an abrupt shift from deep sympathy to outright hostility.

In the context of the 1842 split in the Young Hegelian movement, with Marx and Ruge taking sides against *die Freien*, the Berlin Young Hegelians, it is significant that the pattern of a totally unexpected break and personal betrayal repeats itself in the relation between Marx and Ruge during their stay in Paris. Untrustworthiness, lack of character and selfishness are at the heart of Ruge's judgment of Marx's personality, which should not pass unnoticed here:

> Marx is merely the afforced Bauerian orientation: the unscrupulous, groundless critique, with lack of character, disloyalty and fierceness as its fundamental principle. (…) Marx professes communism, but he is a fanatic of egoism, and with a conscience even more concealed than Bauer's. (Ruge to Fröbel, 6 December 1844, in Ruge 1886, 381)[21]

---

[21] The reference to Bauer is to Bruno Bauer, Edgar's brother. With respect to Marx's 'egoism', see also Ruge 1886, 350: "Marx (…) has attracted the German laborers for no other reason than to have a party and to have people as servants." Cf. Hosfeld 2009, 28–29. With respect to Marx's 'excessive irritability', see Ruge 1886, 344. For a broader analysis, see Weigel 1976.

In a long flood of letters, Ruge described how deeply he felt betrayed by Marx and how much this betrayal had caught him by surprise.[22] Ruge realized that Marx's behaviour could not be explained by an argument they had had over a mutual friend, but simply resulted from his refusal to put all his personal wealth in a publication project that was bound to fail – the *Deutsch-französische Jahrbücher* or a similar book project – and which until then had provided Marx with a medium of intellectual influence and a steady job and income.[23]

In sum, the hypothesis that Edgar Bauer's character sketch of Marx is more or less authentic, sides with a specific position in a range of existing scholarly disputes. With respect to Marx's attitude vis-à-vis the philosophical radicalism of *die Freien*, it supports the argument that his rejection of *die Freien* was not a question of principle but sprouted from strategic considerations on professional success and perhaps even personal gain and ambition. With respect to Marx's intellectual and ideological reorientation during the early 1840s in the direction of economic and socialist thought, it supports the argument that this reorientation was not a steady and logical development but a sudden turnabout after the failure of "Rhineland liberalism". With respect to the deeper sources of Marx's communism, it supports the argument that his choice for communism was not merely the expression of genuine dedication to the cause, nor the outcome of an inner theoretical development, but also the result of a somewhat coincidental series of conflicts with people who had been incapable of securing his social position, and from whose authority he sought to emancipate himself as soon as it could suit the quest for social recognition and intellectual influence. These are extreme positions, to be sure. Even if Bauer's novella might succeed in reviving some of these disputes, it certainly lacks the potential to settle any of them definitively.

2. The issue of principledness

It the next part of this article, I will try to clarify my own position on these matters. Even though I am convinced that Edgar Bauer has hit

---

[22] Ruge to Fröbel, 6 December 1844, in Ruge 1886, 380: "In his eyes, I am the cause of the failed project." Ibid., 343–45, 351, 367.

[23] An analogous argument can be developed for the conflict between Marx and Bruno Bauer: it was mainly due to the latter's radicalism in his theological writings, which in March 1842 led to Bauer's removal from his academic post at the University of Bonn, that Marx himself lost a viable prospect on a future academic career (Rosen 1977, 128).

the mark of the young Marx's irritable temperament and has persua-
sively exposed some of the deeper motives behind his actions and
decisions in the early 1840s, I do not believe that such psychological
account suffices to explain Marx's behaviour and position in his conflict with the Berlin Young Hegelians. I will attempt to show this in a
less speculative, and more conventional and fact-based approach to
the question of the hidden agenda of Edgar Bauer's polemical portrait
of Karl Marx. More specifically, I will argue that Bauer's novella helps
underline the importance of the issue of "principledness" within the
Young Hegelian movement, both in the sense of intellectual integrity
and in the sense of steadfast allegiance to the good cause. I will show
that the novella provides significant clues to understand how Marx
and the Berlin Young Hegelians were taking completely different positions on this issue in late autumn 1842, and why Marx's position on
this issue, even though it could be perceived in the circles of Berlin
Young Hegelianism as a sudden and strategic change of perspective,
boiling down to nothing less than defection and perfidy, must be seen
as springing from deeper motives than sheer opportunism and want
of social recognition.

2.1. The riddle in the title

In light of the dramatic development and plot of *Es leben feste
Grundsätze!*, it does not take much reflection to realize that the title
of the novella must be read ironically. Karl pretends to have solid
principles but in due course renounces all and each of them. When at
the end of the novella the catchphrase "Long live solid principles!"
resounds, this occurs at a festivity in the upper-class circles.
Apparently, it is a well-known toast, proposed to the guests as an
invitation to repeat it. It comes as no surprise that the solid principles
which are thus celebrated are in complete opposition to those which
Karl previously held as a journalist: the necessity of censorship, the
authority of the state, the sanctity of marriage, the consolation of religion and the pride of serving one's government (Bauer 1843a, resp.
320, 321, 324, 327, 328).

> In sum, Mr Karl, my brother in faith, for you as well I can wish nothing
> better than this: get married, return to God and then exclaim with me:
> long live solid principles! (327)

In so doing, the novelist sketches a scenario where his protagonist makes a complete turn from liberal principles to utterly conservative ones.

But there is more to solving the riddle in the title than that. Quite apart from the specific principles in question, the central theme of the novella is about a personal virtue or character trait, namely the capacity or strength of character to stick to specific principles. Time and again, Karl is pictured as a person who adheres to his principles, even in the face of great practical obstacles and dire personal and social consequences, and who attempts to arrange his entire life according to solid principles.[24] As the story progresses, the ideal of "principledness" is submitted to a critical analysis, in part by some of the characters, in part by the novelist himself. It turns out that the virtue or talent to remain faithful to one's principles is not so much a praiseworthy, self-sacrificing attitude, but rather a source of self-pride, a shield to protect one's selfish desires, and even – when used as a subtle instrument of subordination – a strategy to gain power and influence over others (resp. 262, 208; 313; 305–306). Step by step the ideal of "principledness" loses its lustre. In view of that, the main question of the novella is not so much whether the protagonist is able to stick to his lofty principles, but whether such achievement would be really a virtue at all. In pursuing this question, the novella turns into a philosophical investigation of what it means to be a man of solid principles.

These observations help explain why precisely the issue of "solid principles" was chosen as the central feature of a polemic with Marx. When put in the broader context of the Young Hegelian movement, it must be emphasized that the issue of "principledness" was a shared concern among many members of the Young Hegelian movement and had a specific philosophical relevance and connotation. The "feste Gesinnung" (steadfast conviction) and the capacity to hold on to "feste Grundsätze" (solid principles) were key concepts to denote the unity of the Young Hegelians' philosophical-political radicalism during the year 1842. One of the clearest instances of the importance of this issue is given in the following account of Albert Fränkel, one of

---

[24] The following passage (Bauer 1843a, 242) clearly expresses a world view in which everything is arranged and determined according to a formula: "Deep down, he is a good guy – Arthur thought – but it is his misfortune, that he sees all things too sharply and that he wants to act according to principles everywhere. (...) With this Karl, everthing must go according to a formula." See also 176 ("the principles of a radical"), 246–47, 249, 262.

the minor figures and lesser-known members of *die Freien*, when he explains in 1844 how much intellectual life in Berlin has changed when compared to the year 1842:

> What you still expected to find here, was the standpoint of 'steadfast conviction' and 'principle' [*den Standpunkt der 'festen Gesinnung' und des 'Princips'*], the standpoint of the *Deutsche Jahrbücher* and the *Rheinische Zeitung*. But in two years' time, critique has made a consistent development beyond the major and decisive works that were then completed. Critique started to criticize its former essence, with all of its words and phrases. As a logical consequence, it had to break with all those who held on to these words and phrases as eternal, unassailable truths, as dogmas and idols (...). Critique, however, should not be the cause of a party (...). For critique no longer possesses a firmly established, dogmatic 'conviction' [*feststehende, dogmatische 'Gesinnung'*] or 'principle' [*'Princip'*]. Its work has liberated itself from this presupposition, as from each and every presupposition as such. (Fränkel 1844, 23–25)

In Edgar Bauer's article "1842", too, written in 1844, the Young Hegelian philosophical-political radicalism of the year 1842 is epitomized by the "so-called thorough conviction [*gediegene Gesinnung*]". This concept is further elaborated as the belief in the superior powers of the free state – and the determination to "seriously hold on to" such belief (Bauer 1844, 2).

Still, these characterizations remain highly abstract. And that is precisely the point: even though "principledness" (*feste Gesinnung*) appears to have been a catchphrase to describe the unity of the Young Hegelian movement, there was little consensus as to what the concept meant or implied. Here was a potential source of dispute and animosity, hidden behind the formal cohesion of the Young Hegelians' concerted efforts in their main organs of publicity: the *Deutsche Jahrbücher* and the *Rheinische Zeitung*. Frequently comparing themselves with the French encyclopaedists, the Young Hegelians felt united by their shared discontent with the existing order and their common purpose to transform it through a new period of Enlightenment. Yet, they never reached a shared agreement on a particular political program or party program (McLellan 1978, 24, 28–31). Even more problematically, the ways in which to achieve social and political change in Germany by the medium of philosophical theory and critique were on sharply diverging paths. Ruge, who pleaded for a serious, manly and morally exemplary dedication to the good cause, found himself in increasing opposition to the mischievous and frivolous radicalism of *die Freien*, which in his eyes was detrimental to the objective of realizing profound and long-lasting historical change in Germany. "Without moral earnestness, even the best cause in Germany is a lost cause" (Ruge to Marx, 4 December 1842, in *MEGA III/1*, 383).

When Ruge visited *die Freien* in autumn 1842 in Berlin, in an attempt to bring the Young Hegelian movement into line again, his mission was captured in the statement that he had resolved to bring "a thorough ethical principle" to Berlin (M.L. 1844, 29). Ruge made clear that the tendency among Young Hegelians in the capital was too free and too frivolous in his eyes. In my opinion, there is no doubt that the term "principle" [*Grundsatz*] was at the heart of his disagreement with *die Freien*. I even dare to assume that Ruge had literally blamed the Berlin Young Hegelians for having "no solid principles" when he broke with them in autumn 1842 because the kernel of his argument was that the "unprincipled" freedom of "the free ones" [*die Freien*] thwarted the attempt to bring freedom to man and people.[25] Unmistakably, there were completely different orientations when it came to a more accurate understanding of the "feste Gesinnung" of the Young Hegelian movement. So, let us delve a bit deeper into this subject.

2.2. Pure critique

In the early 1840s, Bruno Bauer had emerged as one of the intellectual leaders of the Young Hegelian movement. His influence was most pronounced in Berlin. From May 1842 onwards, after his dismissal from his academic post at the University of Bonn and his return to the capital of Prussia, Bruno Bauer increased his theoretical influence by his personal presence as a source of lively inspiration and agitation. In the circles of young intellectuals in the city, where he was heralded as the "Messiah of critique" (Schwegler 1843, 278), he soon took a leading position in the philosophical-political struggle against the reactionary forces of religion, political authority and the institution of the Christian state. The notorious mock epic *Der Triumph des*

---

[25] According to an eyewitness account, this is how one of Ruge's reproaches rang: "You want to be free and do not notice, that you are up to your ears in the mud! One cannot liberate people and populations by means of dirty tricks [*Schweinereien*]!" (Ruge 1886, 286 footnote). Ruge defined political freedom as "serious passion for a *particular* formation and transformation, not for revolution as such" (291, my italics).

Glaubens [*The Triumph of Faith*] testifies to the wide support Bruno Bauer enjoyed among the Berlin Young Hegelians:

> Praise to Bauer, Our Hero! He must lead us to battle! (Edgar Bauer and Friedrich Engels 1842, 419)

To a considerable extent, Bruno Bauer's return to Berlin had the effect of reviving the "Doctor Club" of the late 1830s, replacing the fairly innocent internal-theoretical debates on Hegel's philosophy of that time with a much more subversive agenda of philosophical radicalism and historical change.

The major influence of Bruno Bauer was not so much related to a specific set of ideas but to a new method of critique. Bauer had elaborated his method of "pure critique" [*reine Kritik*] in his theological magnum opus, the four-volume *Kritik der evangelischen Geschichte* [*Critique of the Gospel History*], written in 1840–42. More specifically, his new critical method was designed to solve an intrinsic problem of philosophical criticism: being a negative approach to the object of criticism, any philosophical criticism was bound to be determined by the object it had criticized. This discovery of the inner dialectical relationship between philosophical criticism and its object was nothing but sound reasoning within the confines of Hegelian logic. A lucid example in this context is Feuerbach's critique of Christianity, which in spite of (or more exactly, following Bauer's analysis, by virtue of) its destructive impact was deemed to undergo the implicit determination by the object of criticism: consequently, Feuerbach's human being was turned into a new God and his humanism into a new religion (Bauer 1845, 86–146; see also Stirner 1845, 43–45). Bauer's solution to the dialectical impurity of critique was as simple as original: do not criticize the object, but its most radical critic.[26] In Bauer's case, this critic was David Friedrich Strauss.

Bruno Bauer's controversy with Strauss had started after Strauss's publication of *Das Leben Jesu* [*The Life of Jesus*] in 1835–36. Bauer wrote a lengthy review in which he attacked the subjective standpoint of Strauss's approach. The controversy intensified after Strauss's reaction in the *Streitschriften* (1837) in defense of his work. Determined

---

[26] Bruno Bauer' method can be seen as a theoretical application of the theorem of the 'second *Aufhebung*', which had been proposed by August von Cieszkowki (1838) as a historical tool of analysis to compare the world-historical significance of the French Revolutions of 1789 and 1830: definitive emancipation is in need of a second negation, after the result of the first negation has been neutralized. The influence can also be traced in Marx's famous contention that great historical events always occur twice: once as tragedy, then as comedy.

to provide a definitive refutation of his opponent, Bruno Bauer wrote his own theological analysis of the Gospel history. When read in consecutive order, however, the four volumes of the *Kritik der evangelischen Geschichte* testify to a remarkable transformation of Bauer's theories and views on the historical veracity of the Gospel accounts. In addition, and more intriguingly, they show the religious crisis and dramatic apostasy of the author himself: from a staunch defender of the Christian faith to a serious and blasphemous critic of some of the principal facts and doctrines of Christianity. As Bauer's theoretical and ideological radicalization took place during a long-term process of research and writing, in which each of the four volumes of his work was separately published as soon as it was completed (respectively in 1840, 1841, 1841 and 1842), it was as if Hegel's dialectical progression through self-negation was literally applied to research results and preliminary conclusions which only a short time before had been communicated to the public.

Indeed, as the analysis of the Gospel narratives progressed, the initial objectives and ambitions of Bauer's Hegelian-inspired theological approach to Scripture, such as his guarantee to the reader that his "most destructive criticism" would eventually lead to an entirely new view of Jesus' personality and the creative power of Christianity (Bauer 1841a, xxiii, footnote), turned out to be completely unrealistic and unattainable. The basic presuppositions that had been presented in the first volume were gradually questioned in the course of further research, and finally reversed or abandoned as untenable. One of these basic presuppositions was the assumption that Jesus had lived in the first decades of the first century and had preached a message of love and repentance in order to renew the Jewish religion of his day. Bauer even assumed at the start of his study that this message had been preserved in the Synoptic Gospels. At the end of his work, Bauer arrived at the conclusion that there never was a historical person named Jesus and that the earliest and authentic Gospel narrative was a work of fiction created by one and only one original author (Bauer 1840, 38, 218; 1842a, 308, 314–15).

Slowly but surely, the negative potential of Strauss's critical approach to the Gospel history had gained influence over Bauer's original conception of the problem. In a sincere and candid manner, Bauer gradually came to accept the cogency of Strauss's approach, and eventually radicalized it. But instead of taking the emerging contradictions within his own work as imperfections or substantial damages to its scientific status, he underlined them as proof of its theoretical quality: "it would be a bad work, if it did not move itself through vivid, inner contradictions" (Bauer 1842b, 21).[27] According to Bauer, this procedure constituted a new method of critical inquiry, to which any conscientious thinker should commit himself: his famous model of "pure critique". It involved the gradual discarding of uncritically accepted assumptions in the exposition of one's theoretical outlook. More specifically, it shifted the focus from developing criticism of a specific object to developing criticism of the prevailing (and preferably most radical) critique of the object. In so doing, Bauer maintained, the critical process is gradually purified from the contaminations inherent in the object of criticism and will succeed in liberating itself from the dialectical determination by the object.

What is important here with respect to our question of the "feste Gesinnung" in the Young Hegelian movement, is the insight that the entire process of radicalization is not carried out in a preconceived manner, but reflects the author's sincere attitude to go along with the logical movement of destructive criticism, also when it undermines hard-earned results of earlier steps of research, and also when it runs counter to views and convictions that are precious to the author himself. Hence, Bauer's critical procedure inaugurates a new ideal of intellectual integrity (De Vriese 2017, 288–90). It sets the permanent and uncompromising task of critical self-purification, and even of "consistent inconsistency", for it implies calling into question again and again those steps of critical inquiry that have already been attained. In this process, the critic cannot stop at any sense of loyalty or attachment to personal beliefs, values or concerns – he must dedicate himself unconditionally to the higher demands of Critique. In Bauer's personal case, these higher demands ran counter to the practical concern of finding and keeping a steady job, or of advancing his career and social status, because the publication of his increasingly radical ideas led to the dismissal from his teaching post at the university.

---

[27] In the opinion of his brother Edgar Bauer (1843c, 41), the presence of apparent contradictions in Bruno Bauer's work is a proof of the *purity* of his critique: "This inner and necessary development of the critique of Bruno Bauer explains why apparent contradictions can be found in it – contradictions, however, that eventually resolve themselves. They, in specific, are proof of the purity of Bauer's critique. Only those who do not understand a thing about the organic growth of a scientific work, can use them to refute Bauer."

2.3. Uncompromising struggle

It can be shown that Bruno Bauer's model of pure critique and the new critical mindset it requested, was extremely influential in the circles of *die Freien* and even in the entire Young Hegelian movement.[28] It demanded the organization of sharp oppositions and the negation of half-hearted compromises. It inspired the concerted effort of destructive criticism and hypercritical self-reflection, generating a relentless logic of surpassing the existing critical achievements along the lines of the "critique of critique". Furthermore, it not only supported the belief that such "terrorism of true theory" (Bauer to Marx, 28 March 1841, in *MEGA III/1*, 353) would result in a major world-historical crisis, but that history itself was able to create the positive organization of a better society after the theoreticians' purely negative work. To be sure, although this was proof of orthodox Hegelian faith in the blessings of dialectical progression, this was a rather naïve and "uncritical" idea.

In sum, there was method in the flotilla of destructive criticism launched by the Berlin Young Hegelians in the early 1840s. Moreover, the method of pure critique explains why they were engaging in the expression (and discovery) of extreme and particularly confrontational positions. As the major goal was the organization of theoretical conflict, their style and tone were often destined to provocation and agitation. Mockery rather that a serious and moderate exposition of ideas, uncompromising struggle instead of strategic considerations. In *Die gute Sache der Freiheit und meine eigene Angelegenheit* [*The Good Cause of Freedom and My Own Affair*], the book written during the summer of 1842 to defend himself after his dismissal from the university, Bruno Bauer explicitly argued in favour of a philosophical strategy of ridicule. His argument reflects the essential aim of pure critique, namely the philosophical ambition of getting beyond the "dialectical sphere of influence" of the object of criticism:

> In a particular phase of the battle, ridicule is a necessary weapon. It is the proof that theory has so far finished with the object, that its dominion has completely come to an end and that spirit has attained its freedom also in a practical manner. Ridicule sets in at that moment – and only at that precise moment – when theory completes itself and has to deny the former practical validity of the object also in a practical manner. Ridicule (...) is

---

[28] For an extensive analysis, see De Vriese 2011, the chapter "Reine Kritik", 547–602.

the prophecy of a world condition, in which the power that has been theoretically overthrown, will be conquered practically as well. (1842b, 195)[29]

Joined to a disposition to provoke conflict and to carry matters to extremes, such kind of philosophical struggle for freedom was not likely to gain wide support among the German population, let alone to forge a strong political movement in Germany. For some members of the Young Hegelian movement, in particular, for a determined democrat like Ruge, this became a growing concern.

In the *Rheinische Zeitung*, the confrontational method of pure critique was most consistently pursued by none less than Edgar Bauer, in his critique of liberalism and of any moderate critique of the Prussian state. And again it was Edgar Bauer, with the publication of *Der Streit der Kritik mit Kirche und Staat* [*The Struggle of Critique with Church and State*] in August 1843, who gave the most striking example of philosophical radicalism at the cost of one's personal freedom and well-being. After *Der Streit der Kritik* had been banned and confiscated by the Prussian government, Edgar Bauer was convicted of insurrection, lese majesty and defamation of religious groups. He was sentenced to four years in prison (Gamby 1985, 21).[30] Indeed, provocative ridicule was not just for fun. It was pursued in earnest as an intrinsic dimension of what was considered to be the only appropriate vehicle for social and political change in Germany.

---

[29] The historical example Bruno Bauer has in mind, is the French Enlightenment. I am reminded here of a striking characterization of the French *philosophes* by Will and Ariel Durant (1965, 324): "Never in literature had there been such subtle wit, such delicate pleasantry, such coarse buffoonery, such lethal ridicule. Every orthodoxy of Church or state trembled under the assault of these sharply pointed, sometimes poisoned, usually nameless, pens."

[30] Gamby's study of Edgar Bauer's stay in London during the 1850s and his regular contact with Karl Marx at that time throws an entirely new light on the issue of 'principledness'. Under the cover of friendship and devotion to the communist cause, Bauer actually spied on the activities of Marx and other revolutionaries in London. Working as a secret agent for the Danish government, he sent more than hundred reports with information on revolutionary movements and organizations, including reports on Marx and Engels (Gamby 1985, 30–37). The irony of history? Because my focus in this paper is on the split in the Young Hegelian movement of the early 1840s, I have decided to leave out this dubious episode of Edgar Bauer's later life. I feel obliged to mention it here succinctly, in order to remove the false impression that it is Edgar Bauer who, in contrast to 'Karl', is the more laudable and 'principled' character: strong, reliable and self-sacrificing. Moreover, my main concern in this paper is about better understanding the personal and philosophical motives behind the split in the Young Hegelian movement, not about passing a moral judgement. If one were to embark on such a precarious investigation, one would certainly have to pay attention to personal and philosophical developments of the later 1840s, and in particular to the impact of the failed 1848 revolution in Germany.

2.4. Serious, manly and self-restrained characters

What about Marx? The early writings of Marx, at least until autumn 1842, demonstrate how much he was under the spell of Bruno Bauer's method of pure critique (Brudney 1998, 109–142; De Vriese 2011, 587–92; Leopold 2007, 9, 129–131; McLellan 1978, 69–75; Rosen 1977, 127–161). Among the Young Hegelians, Marx was widely regarded as one of the promising representatives of Bruno Bauer's philosophical radicalism. On 25 December 1841, Ruge wrote to Feuerbach:

> Bruno Bauer works together with a young man named Marx, whom he credits with extraordinary talent and erudition. They aim to produce a definitive critique of everything positive, in its full extent [einer definitiven Kritik des Positivismus nach seiner ganzen Ausbreitung]. (Pepperle 1985, 837)

This view accords with much of Marx's life and work in the early 1840s. It was no coincidence that Marx had consented to contribute to the follow-up of Bruno Bauer's satirical Die Posaune des jüngsten Gerichts über Hegel den Atheisten und Antichristen [The Trumpet of the Last Judgement Against Hegel the Atheist and Antichrist], eventually published without Marx's cooperation in 1842.[31] It was no coincidence that Marx had enthusiastically responded to Bruno Bauer's idea to launch a scientific journal with the provocative label "atheism" in the title (Rosen 1977, 128, 205). In autumn 1841, when Marx was living in Bonn and entertained a close friendship with Bruno Bauer, the two "critics" had amused themselves to gallop like madmen on donkeys in order to shock decent Bonn society out of its petty bourgeois conventions (Bruno Bauer and Edgar Bauer 1844, 192). More fundamentally, when it comes to Marx's journalistic activity in the Rheinische Zeitung, both the decision to publish the "Ehescheidungsgesetzentwurf" and the substance of the critical footnote "by the redaction" (written by Marx), breathe the confrontational and uncompromising attitude of pure critique. And this was one of the first contributions to the journal that threatened its continued existence.

In Edgar Bauer's novella, too, "Karl" is pictured as a radical and uncompromising theorist. The dispute with his former fiancée, Marie, centers around the word "critique". Karl's favorite expression, she writes, is "criticize" (Bauer 1843a, 214). Marie reproaches him,

---

[31] That book was entitled Hegel's Lehre von der Religion und Kunst von dem Standpuncte des Glaubens aus beurtheilt. See also Rosen 1977, 159.

however, that his eternal criticism prevents people from finding rest and satisfaction, and she expressly forbids him to criticize the way she is leading her life.

> Therefore, I urge you, don't come to me with your critique. Criticize as many books as you want. But the empire of your goddess should not extend further. (215; see also 225–32)

Gradually, the pieces of my analysis of "principledness" fall into place. The main source of disappointment and anger towards Karl Marx among the Berlin Young Hegelians, after the split of the Young Hegelian movement in autumn 1842, was that Marx had made an unexpected shift from uncompromising idealism to strategic pragmatism, and from the "frivolity" of *die Freien* to the "seriousness" of Ruge's conception of theoretical influence.[32] In other words, I believe it is plausible that *die Freien* were not so much insulted by the fact that they were openly portrayed as anything but serious, manly and self-restrained characters, but rather by the fact that Marx had implicitly presented himself as such a laudable character.[33] And more importantly, the deeper grounds of animosity were not about moral excellence but about the philosophical principles of profound and effective critique of the existing order. At this juncture, we must realize, however, that Marx, probably under the influence of Arnold Ruge,[34] may have had sound theoretical reasons for rethinking his conception of critique and hence for making a clean break with his former friends and allies.

Against this backdrop, the self-written statement by Karl Marx that was added to the publication of Herwegh's letter on 29 November

---

[32] Unlike Strauss and Feuerbach, Ruge had for a long time been sympathetic to, and even in support of the Bauerian method of 'extreme liquidation' (Ruge to Prutz, 8 January 1842, in Ruge 1886, 258–60). In his introduction to the 1842 volume of the *Deutsche Jahrbücher*, he had even developed similar views: "Can one reproach theory with being extreme? Isn't extremity its mode of existence?" (1842, 3–4). One year later, in his introduction to the 1843 volume of the *Deutsche Jahrbücher*, Ruge offered a sharp philosophical refutation of the 'blasé consciousness' of the Berlin Young Hegelians, unmasking their 'frivolity' as sheer vanity and their 'self-satisfied theory' as a 'vain movement inside one's own subjectivity'. Instead of promoting dedication to the philosophical cause, Ruge now realized, the frivolous radicalism of *die Freien* would only engender 'lack of character' and 'cowardice' (1843, 9–12).

[33] An alternative view is that this was essentially a dispute over the *correct interpretation* of 'earnestness and manliness'. See Bauer to Marx, 12 April 1841, in *MEGA III/1*, 357: "They cannot bear earnestness and acuteness and manliness."

[34] In light of Ruge's visit to the Young Hegelians in Berlin, it seems obvious to conclude that Ruge was the principal instigator of a philosophical campaign against the 'frivolity' of *die Freien*, eventually succeeding in winning Marx's support for his view. Nonetheless, the opposite interpretation can be developed, with Marx being (partly) responsible for the change in Ruge's opinion. See Marx to Ruge, 9 July 1842, in *MEGA III/1*, 28–30.

1842 in the *Rheinische Zeitung*, the event that had the effect of banishing the Berlin Young Hegelians from one of the main organs of the *Young Hegelian movement*, appears in a new light:

> Rowdiness and roguery must be loudly and resolutely repudiated in a period which demands serious, manly and self-restrained characters for the achievement of its lofty aims.

The peculiar sharpness of Marx's statement does not arise from a prescription of ethical standards but from his definition of the exigencies of the time: the heart of the matter is not what moral decency demands, but what a historical period of critical transition demands. As I have argued in this article, I believe here is the key to find the deeper sources of the ironic title *Long live solid principles!* of Edgar Bauer's 1843 novella and of its polemical function in the broader conflict between Karl Marx and the Berlin Young Hegelians.

Acknowledgements

The seminal ideas of this article were presented at the conference "Marx 1818/ 2018. New developments on Karl Marx's thought and writings", Lyon, 27–29 September 2017. I owe special thanks to Gilbert Faccarello who encouraged me to broaden my initial approach of a predominantly intellectual-biographical study of Edgar Bauer's novella and to deeper investigate the theoretical relevance of the book. Furthermore, I would like to thank the anonymous peer reviewers of *EJHET* for their careful reading of the manuscript and their valuable suggestions to improve it. I am particularly grateful for their insistence to better explain the connection between both parts of this article and to clarify my own position on Edgar Bauer's polemical portrait of Karl Marx.

References

Allgemeines Verzeichniß der Bücher, welche von Ostern 1843 bis Michaelis 1843 neu gedruckt oder aufgelegt worden sind, mit Angabe der Verleger, Bogenzahl und Preise. 1843. Leipzig: Weidmann'schen Buchhandlung.

"Berliner Novellen" [Anon.]. 1843. Buchbesprechung von A. Weil und Edgar Bauer, *Berliner Novellen*. In "Litterarischer Monatsbericht für Mai 1843", *Deutsche Monatsschrift für Litteratur und öffentliches Leben*, herausgegeben von Carl Biedermann, 80.

Bauer, Bruno. 1840. *Kritik der evangelischen Geschichte des Johannes*. Bremen: Carl Schünemann.

Bauer, Bruno. 1841a. *Kritik der evangelischen Geschichte der Synoptiker. Erster Band*. Leipzig: Otto Wigand.

Bauer, Bruno [Anon.]. 1841b. *Die Posaune des jüngsten Gerichts über Hegel den Atheisten und Antichristen. Ein Ultimatum,* Leipzig: Otto Wigand.

Bauer, Bruno. 1842a. *Kritik der evangelischen Geschichte der Synoptiker und des Johannes.* Leipzig: Otto Wigand.

Bauer, Bruno. 1842b. *Die gute Sache der Freiheit und meine eigene Angelegenheit.* Zürich: Verlag des literarischen Comptoirs.

Bauer, Bruno [Anon.]. 1842c. *Hegel's Lehre von der Religion und Kunst von dem Standpuncte des Glaubens aus beurtheilt.* Leipzig: Otto Wigand.

Bauer, Bruno [Anon.]. 1845. "Charakteristik Ludwig Feuerbachs." *Wigand's Vierteljahrsschrift* 3, 86–146.

Bauer, Bruno and Edgar Bauer. 1844. *Briefwechsel zwischen Bruno Bauer und Edgar Bauer während der Jahre 1839–1842 aus Bonn und Berlin.* Charlottenburg: Egbert Bauer.

Bauer, Edgar and Friedrich Engels [Anon.]. 1842. *Die frech bedräute, jedoch wunderbar befreite Bibel. Oder: Der Triumph des Glaubens. Das ist: Schreckliche, jedoch wahrhafte und erkleckliche Historia von dem weiland Licentiaten Bruno Bauer: wie selbiger vom Teufel verführet, vom reinen Glauben abgefallen, Oberteufel geworden und endlich kräftiglich entsetzet ist. Christliches Heldengedicht in vier Gesängen.* Neumünster bei Zürich: Heß.

Bauer, Edgar. 1843a. "*Es leben feste Grundsätze!*" In *Berliner Novellen,* A. Weil and Edgar Bauer, 153–328. Berlin: Berliner Verlags-Buchhandlung.

Bauer, Edgar. 1843b. *Die Censur-Instruktion vom 31. Januar 1843.* Leipzig: Otto Wigand.

Bauer, Edgar. 1843c. *Der Streit der Kritik mit Kirche und Staat.* Charlottenburg: Egbert Bauer.

Bauer, Edgar [Anon.]. 1844. "1842," *Allgemeine Literatur-Zeitung,* no. 8: 1–8.

Blumenberg, Werner. 2000. *Karl Marx: An Illustrated History.* London: Verso.

Brudney, Daniel. 1998. *Marx's Attempt to Leave Philosophy.* Cambridge, MA: Harvard University Press.

Buhl, Ludwig. 1842. *Die Noth der Kirche und die christliche Sonntagsfeier: Ein Wort des Ernstes an die Frivolität der Zeit.* Berlin: Hermes.

Cieszkowski, August von. 1838. *Prolegomena zur Historiosophie.* Berlin: Veit.

De Vriese, Herbert. 2011. *De Roes van de Kritiek: Bruno Bauer en 'die Freien'.* Brussel: ASP.

De Vriese, Herbert. 2017. "Intellectual Integrity in the Philosophy of Bruno Bauer and Max Stirner." *SGEM Conference Proceedings,* Vol. I, 285–292.

Durant, Will and Ariel. 1965. *The Age of Voltaire. A History of Civilization in Western Europe from 1715 to 1756, with Special Emphasis on the Conflict between Religion and Philosophy.* New York: Simon and Schuster.

Edler, Erich. 1977. *Die Anfänge des sozialen Romans und der sozialen Novelle in Deutschland.* Frankfurt a.M.: Klostermann.

Eßbach, Wolfgang. 1988. *Die Junghegelianer: Soziologie einer Intellektuellengruppe.* München: Wilhelm Fink Verlag, 1988.

Fränkel, Albert [Anon.]. 1844. "Briefe aus Berlin." *Norddeutsche Blätter, für Kritik, Literatur und Unterhaltung,* no. 2: 20–27.

Gamby, Erik. 1985. *Edgar Bauer: Junghegelianer, Publizist und Polizeiagent. Mit Bibliographie der E. Bauer-Texte und Dokumentenanhang.* Trier: Schriften aus dem Karl-Marx-Haus.

Hosfeld, Rolf. 2009. *Die Geister, die er rief: Eine neue Karl-Marx-Biografie.* München: Piper Verlag.

Klutentreter, Wilhelm. 1966. *Die Rheinische Zeitung von 1842/43 in der politischen und geistigen Bewegung des Vormärz.* Dortmund: Fr. Wilh. Ruhfus.

Leopold, David. 2007. *The Young Karl Marx: German Philosophy, Modern Politics, and Human Flourishing.* Cambridge: Cambridge University Press.

Marx, Karl and Friedrich Engels. 1975a. *Karl Marx Friedrich Engels Gesamtausgabe. Erste Abteilung: Werke Artikel Entwürfe. Band 1 (MEGA I/1).* Berlin: Dietz Verlag.

Marx, Karl and Friedrich Engels. 1975b. *Karl Marx Friedrich Engels Gesamtausgabe. Dritte Abteilung: Briefwechsel. Band 1 (MEGA III/1).* Berlin: Dietz Verlag.

M.L. [Anon.]. 1844. "Correspondenz aus der Provinz. 6." *Allgemeine Literatur-Zeitung*, no. 6: 28–30.

McLellan, David. 1978. *The Young Hegelians and Karl Marx.* London: Macmillan.

Mehring, Franz. 2003. *Karl Marx. The Story of his Life.* London: Routledge.

Pepperle, Heinz und Ingrid, ed. 1985. *Die Hegelsche Linke: Dokumente zu Philosophie und Politik im deutschen Vormärz.* Leipzig: Philipp Reclam.

Peters, Heinz F. 1984. *Die rote Jenny. Ein Leben mit Karl Marx.* München: Droemersche Verlagsanstalt Knaur.

Rosen, Zvi. 1977. *Bruno Bauer and Karl Marx: The Influence of Bruno Bauer on Marx's Thought.* The Hague: Martinus Nijhoff.

Ruge, Arnold. 1842. "Die Zeit und die Zeitschrift. Zur Einleitung." *Deutsche Jahrbücher für Wissenschaft und Kunst* 5 (1): 1–4.

Ruge, Arnold. 1843. "Vorwort. Eine Selbstkritik des Liberalismus." *Deutsche Jahrbücher für Wissenschaft und Kunst* 6 (1): 1–12.

Ruge, Arnold. 1886. *Briefwechsel und Tagebuchblätter aus den Jahren 1825–1880.* Erster Band: 1825–1847, herausgegeben von Paul Nerrlich. Berlin: Weidmannsche Buchhandlung.

Schöncke, Manfred. 1993. *Karl und Heinrich Marx und ihre Geschwister: Lebenszeugnisse, Briefe, Dokumente.* Köln: Pahl-Rugenstein.

Schwegler, Albert. 1843. "Die Hypothese vom schöpferischen Urevangelisten in ihrem Verhältniss zur Traditionshypothese." *Theologische Jahrbücher* 2 (2): 203–278.

Stirner, Max. 1845. *Der Einzige und sein Eigenthum.* Leipzig: Verlag von Otto Wigand.

Strauss, David Friedrich. 1835–36. *Das Leben Jesu, kritisch bearbeitet.* Tübingen: Osiander.

Strauss, David Friedrich. 1837. *Streitschriften zur Vertheidigung meiner Schrift über das Leben Jesu und zur Charakteristik der gegenwärtigen Theologie.* Tübingen: Osiander.

Weigel, Siegfried. 1976. *Der negative Marx: Marx im Urteil seiner Zeitgenossen. Eine Dokumentation.* Stuttgart: Hohe Warte – v. Bebenburg

"Alienation" and critique in Marx's manuscripts of 1857–58 ("*Grundrisse*")

Zacharias Zoubir

ABSTRACT

The debate on alienation in Marx has either tended to neglect Marx's manuscripts of 1857-58 ("*Grundrisse*") or has failed to provide a detailed account of that terminology in this text. This article is a philological contribution to this debate, i.e. an immanent reading of alienation in the *Grundrisse* with a systematic textual basis. By providing a general overview of how Marx uses terms like "alienation" (*Entfremdung*), "to alienate" (*entfremden*), "alien" (*fremd*), "alien character" (*Fremdartigkeit*) and the close yet distinct "externalisation" (*Entäußerung*) in the *Grundrisse*, we set out to show precisely how the meanings and functions of this terminology can be distinguished from alienation in the so-called "*Economic and Philosophical Manuscripts of 1844*" (EPM). Indeed, in the EPM, the concept of alienation refers to the inhibition of Man's generic forces by private property. There, it is thus a philosophical standpoint external to economic phenomena. In the *Grundrisse*, by contrast, the concept delineates three dimensions of the social and historical determination of these phenomena. First, the subordination of workers or independent producers to capital or money; second, the constitution of capital or money into independent social relations; third, the transcending character of the social reality hence produced. Nevertheless, a certain aspect of the system of alienation outlined in the EPM is taken up again in the Grundrisse: the idea that alienation calls for the integration of that which has been alienated (the productive forces) into the alienated subject (the producers).

Historically, the debate on the concept of alienation in the works of Marx has been more of a political than a philological one. The French conditions were long dominated by the Althusserian dismissal of alienation in the "young Marx", seen as the ideological basis for the humanist turn within the French Communist Party (Althusser 1965). The problem with this approach is its reconstruction of the Marxian oeuvre from the point of view of *Capital*, which makes it impossible to consider the "young Marx" in and for himself and, more specifically, to understand why references to alienation are still present in the later formulations of the critique of political economy. For other prominent thinkers of those decades, like Herbert Marcuse and Guy Debord, the system of alienation in late published works like the so-called *Economic and Philosophical Manuscripts of 1844* (hereafter EPM) were seen instead as a new resource for the critique of both an ever more integrated capitalist society and the Stalinist betrayal of the revolution (Marcuse 1941; Debord 1967). Both Marcuse and Debord made major contributions to Marxian theory, but their point was not so much to distinguish between the different meanings of alienation in the stages of development of Marx's critique. In this regard, Stéphane Haber's *L'aliénation. Vie sociale et expérience de la dépossession* has provided a more systematic overview of the different models of alienation in Marx (Haber 2007).[1]

More specifically, to our knowledge, readings of Marx's conception of alienation in the *Grundrisse* are rare. Friedrich Tomberg was probably the first to propose a somewhat systematic overview of the notion of alienation in the 1857–58 manuscripts. However, following Wygodski, he presupposes that all of Marx's works can be seen as one long preparation of what was to become *Capital*. On this view, Marx progressively moved from an analysis of the superstructure – bourgeois thought, religion, politics, etc. – in his early writings to an analysis of the economic base in his works of maturity, before providing a kind of synthesis of these studies in *Capital* (Tomberg 1969, 187–189). In this structural mode of reading, the *Grundrisse* are seen as a part of a greater system, and therefore terms like *Entfremdung* and *entfremden* in those manuscripts tend to be treated not in and for themselves but as examples of more general themes of the Marxian oeuvre. David McLellan's reading of alienation in the *Grundrisse* is similar to Friedrich Tomberg's insofar that he insists upon the continuity of the Marxian project of a critique of political economy. What is at stake for David McLellan is to show that the 1857–58 manuscripts are the keystone of Marx's

---

[1] Nevertheless, as we hope will become clear in our reading of the *Grundrisse*, it is not so certain that alienation in the later works focuses primarily on what Stéphane Haber calls "autonomised systems of action". Indeed, the other models defined by Stéphane Haber, namely "mediums of coordination [...] that imply the disclosure of the different aspects" of individuals' actions and the "functional differentiation" of individuals and activities do also apply to the 1857-58 manuscripts (2007, 337, our translation).

work, against Erich Fromm who considered that the EPM had to be given that position. For McLellan, passages on alienation in the *Grundrisse* are to be understood as more mature and accomplished variations of themes already covered in the EPM (McLellan 1972, 12–15). Also, McLellan reads such passages as digressions from Marx's economic considerations. What both Friedrich Tomberg and David McLellan fail to address is thus the way in which the terminology of alienation is used precisely in the *Grundrisse* since they both assume that there is a continuity in the theme of alienation and its critical function in the works of Marx. This assumption is problematic because the particularity of this terminology in the *Grundrisse* is that it is inextricably linked to Marx's critique of economic categories and not a phenomenon distinct from the economic base or from economic considerations.

An analysis of Marx's use of terms like "alienation" (*Entfremdung*), "to alienate" (*entfremden*), "alien" (*fremd*), "alien character" (*Fremdartigkeit*) and the close yet distinct "externalisation" (*Entäußerung*) in the manuscripts from 1857 to 1858 referred to as "*Grundrisse*" leads us to challenge Friedrich Tomberg's and David McLellan's perspectives. In so doing, we hope to endorse Terrell Carver's insight according to which the terminology of alienation in the 1857–58 manuscripts has a precise philosophical *and* economic content that can be distinguished from the earlier works (Carver 2008, 61–64). Drawing upon the idea that Marx's critique can be seen as a discontinuous project which went through numerous reformulations (Rancière 1965; McLellan 1972; Elliott 1979; Renault 1995), this article sets out to show that the terminology of alienation in the *Grundrisse* is neither a philosophical intruder, nor a simple repetition of Marx's former critiques, but a locus where the critique of economic categories is informed by Marx's (Young) Hegelian philosophical training. Our contribution aims to be a primarily philological one to the more general debate on alienation in Marx which has often either neglected the *Grundrisse* or not engaged with that precise terminology. What is at stake is thus to provide an analysis of alienation in the *Grundrisse* with a systematic textual basis, and to refer to the other works only insofar that it informs an immanent reading of alienation in 1857–58.

We will begin by distinguishing the different meanings and functions of the terminology of alienation in the EPM and the *Grundrisse*.

Second, we would like to describe the diverse contexts in which the terminology of alienation appears in the *Grundrisse*. Finally, one may wonder what new light this sheds on the model of alienation of 1857–58 and its political implications.

1. Alienation and the "critique of economic categories"

It was precisely in 1843–44, when Marx was in the process of breaking with the Hegelian conception of the political and with the Young Hegelian critique of religion, that the concept of alienation came to play an important role for the first time. Both in his *Critique of Hegel's Philosophy of Right* and in his *Contribution to the Critique of Hegel's Philosophy of Right*, the use of the concepts *Entäußerung* and *Entfremdung* indicates an evolution towards the idea of a critique of the "profane" (*unheilige*) aspects of life. However, we choose the EPM as a point of comparison with the terminology of alienation in the *Grundrisse* for two reasons. First, it is only in the EPM that the concept is developed in a systematic fashion. Second, as opposed to the *Jewish Question*, a text in which Marx merges Feuerbach's, Bruno Bauer's and Moses Hess' conceptions of alienation into his critique of liberal rights, the EPM offer an original concept of alienation (Renault 2008; Wittmann 2008).

1.1. The closely related yet distinct terms Entfremdung and Entäußerung. Some remarks on terminology and translation

Before beginning our study, some remarks on terminology and translation are needed. David Wittmann's contribution to the volume *Lire les* Manuscrits de 1844 ("*Reading the* 1844 Manuscripts") shows that what we call alienation has its roots in the term *Entäußerung* in Hegel's *Elements of the Philosophy of Right* (Wittmann 2008, 89–93). Here, *Entäußerung* was to be understood as the process through which a person's will is objectivated in an external thing, in the sense that personal freedom takes the concrete form of property. In Marx's texts – both in the *EPM* and in the *Grundrisse*, as we will see – *Entäußerung* retains something of this juridical meaning. Indeed, in its various formulations, the term is used by Marx to describe the process through which a subject evolves into something different. The far more speculative meaning of alienation is to be found in Hegel's *Phenomenology of Spirit*, a work widely discussed in the EPM. In the *Phenomenology*, Hegel uses the verb *sich entäußern* to show how self-consciousness departs from itself so as to become one with an objective spiritual reality. Then, *Entäußerung* can be defined both as self-detachment and self-alteration (Wittmann 2008, 93–94).

The term *Entfremdung* is closely related to *Entäußerung* although its source is Young–Hegelian rather than directly Hegelian. As Jean–Christophe Angaut has shown in another contribution to *Lire les Manuscrits de 1844*, the notion of *Entfremdung* was used by Marx in his EPM in part as an internal critique of Hegel, insofar that the different figures of consciousness exposed in the *Phenomenology of Spirit* were to be seen as theoretical symptoms of a practical pathology (Angaut 2008, 53–54). What is at stake in the EPM is thus the relation between material and ideal *Entfremdung*. Hegelian consciousness is an expression of the system of private property in which subjectivity is purely theoretical, i.e., separated from the practical means of its realisation (Angaut 2008, 54–55). The Young–Hegelian sources in this regard are Feuerbach on the one hand and Moses Hess on the other. Feuerbach provided Marx with the notion of humans as objective beings, as beings that can only live by consuming and producing objects. Humans are thus primarily sensuous beings, both dependent of, and limited by, nature. This Feuerbachian influence was in turn mediated by Marx's reading of Moses Hess' "*Über das Geldwesen*" (Hess 1921), a text in which *Entfremdung* is to be understood not as the projection of human beings' essence upon God, but as the projection of human relations upon money, a separate and abstract entity. This is what gives the concept of *Entfremdung* its critical function as the description of a negative situation (Fischbach 2008). Generally speaking, as we hope to show in our overview of alienation in the EPM, *Entfremdung* can then be defined as the historical process through which human beings create their reality in an entity which is alien to them in the sense that it transcends, inhibits and mutilates their activities.

Since the German language bears this distinction between *Entäußerung* and *Entfremdung*, the present article will translate the former with the etymologically close "externalisation" and the latter with "alienation". Despite the difference between the terms, we should also bear in mind Lukács' suggestion that *Entäußerung* and *Entfremdung* are so closely related that they can, given the way in which they were granted philosophical meaning by the likes of Hegel, Feuerbach and Moses Hess, be considered simply "as German translations of the English word 'alienation'" widely used in the more profane, juridical sense by Anglophone economists like Adam Smith (as quoted in Arthur 1986, 132).

1.2. From alienated labour to the form of alienation

Central to Marx's system of alienation in the EPM is the notion of a "contradiction" (*Widerspruch*) of alienated labour with itself. This means that human labour is inhibited by the system of property:

> Political economy starts from labour as the real soul of production; yet to labour it gives nothing, and to private property everything. [...] We understand, however, that this apparent contradiction is the contradiction of alienated labour [*entfremdeten Arbeit*] with itself, and that political economy has merely formulated the laws of alienated labour. (Marx 1982, 373; Marx and Engels 1975, 280, translation modified)

Here, Marx focuses on human nature, which requires a form of objectivation, a realisation of its abilities through the production of objects that satisfy its physical and spiritual needs. What political economy does not see and therefore tends to naturalise is the fact that the institution of private property separates human beings from their products and the very activity of production. More than 13 years later, when Marx uses the term "alienation" in the *Grundrisse*, he refers not to this inhibition of human productive activity but to the capitalist process of production, in which the products of labour are incorporated into capital, thus constituting an objectivity that dominates the labourer. Marx states that this process acquires the "form of alienation":

> The bourgeois economists are so much cooped up within the notions belonging to a specific historic stage of social development that the necessity of the *objectification* [Vergegenständlichung] of the powers of social labour appears to them as inseparable from the necessity of their *alienation vis-à-vis* [*der* Entfremdung *derselben gegenüber*] living labour. But with the suspension of the *immediate* character of living labour, as merely *individual*, or as general merely internally or merely externally, with the positing of the activity of individuals as immediately general or *social* activity, the objective moments of production are stripped of this form of alienation [*Form der Entfremdung*] [...]. (Marx 1976b, 698; Marx 1973, 832)

In other words, the historical determination of production as production for the market creates a situation in which social productive activities serve the individuals taking part in this process only indirectly, as commodities on the market, and not directly, as objects satisfying their needs. In this situation, the "*objectification*" of all workers' labouring capacities, i.e., their constitution as a collective power over which they do not have control individually, is also at the same time a process of "*alienation*" insofar that it serves a purpose that transcends their individual needs and activities. Here, then, the term "alienation" characterises a social relation in which production is an end in itself, whereas the individuals engaged as wage labourers only exist as executors of the latter. For Marx, however, this is true only for bourgeois society, where the activity of the individual labourer is social only to the extent that its products become commodities. Again, what the bourgeois economists do not see is that this historical "form of alienation", this specific configuration of social relations, can give rise to radically different conditions under which individual activities are immediately social, that is, not separate from the collective interactions they are producing for. Interestingly, this leads Marx to criticise John Stuart Mill's distinction between production as a physical phenomenon and distribution as the result of human institutions, as developed in the latter's *Principles of Political Economy* (Mill 2008):

> It is therefore highly absurd when e.g. J. St. Mill says [...]: 'The laws and conditions of the production of wealth partake of the character of physical truths ... It is not so with the distribution of wealth. That is a matter of human institutions solely.' [...] The 'laws and conditions' of the production of wealth and the laws of the 'distribution of wealth' are the same laws under different forms, and both change, undergo the same historic process; are as such only moments of a historic process. (Marx 1976b, 699; Marx 1973, 832)

For Marx, the fact that the workers are deprived of the products of their labour is not due to some institutional mode of distribution separate from the conditions of wage labour. Rather, it is an outcome of the "form" of these conditions as the conditions of production of surplus value. The notion of a "form of alienation" reveals that to which Mill was blind: that economic relations consist not so much in things as in the type of social conditions that they presuppose and produce.

1.3. From an internal to an external critique of alienation

This is only one example of how, in the *Grundrisse*, the function of the philosophical concept of alienation is to characterise the social-historical determination of the objects of political economy. In Marx's earlier formulation of the project of a critique of political economy in the EPM, alienation plays a different role. There, the philosophical notion of an objective being allowed for a detachment from the field of political economy – in Marx's own words, this implies that one "rise[s] above the level of political economy":

> Let us now rise above the level of political economy and try to answer two questions on the basis of the above exposition, which has been presented almost in the words of the political economists: (1) What in the evolution of mankind is the meaning of this reduction of the greater part of mankind to abstract labour [*abstrakte Arbeit*]? (2) What are the mistakes committed by the piecemeal reformers, who either want to *raise* wages and in this way to improve the situation of the working class, or regard *equality* of wages (as Proudhon does) as the goal of social revolution? (Marx 1982, 333; Marx and Engels 1975, 241)

To "rise above the level of political economy" has a two-fold meaning according to Marx in the EPM. On the one hand, that "mankind" is subject to a "reduction […] to abstract labour" cannot be treated as a mere fact of political economy but must be granted a "meaning" within the framework of "the evolution of mankind". Put differently, the fact of "abstract labour", of labourers being separated from all aspects of their own labour – its conditions, its means, its interactions, its products – has to be granted a historical signifi-cance which can only be formulated in terms of alienation. Indeed, abstract labour corresponds to the historical stage of bourgeois soci-ety in which humans posit their own objective being in a reality alien to them: that of private property. But this is only a temporary stage, of which the necessary outcome lies in the return of that which has been alienated to the human species. In other words, the alienation of our generic forces only proves the necessity of the overcoming of this alienation through a re-appropriation of that which has been alienated. On this view, inherited from Feuerbach's critique of Hegel, in order to accomplish itself, mankind first has to confront and recognise its own alienation. On the other hand, this act of "rising above political economy" calls for a critique of all par-tial opponents to the system of private property and wage labour.

To put forwards demands to either "raise" or "equalise" wages is to focus only on the quantitative side of labour, i.e., its remuneration in the form of a wage, and not on its qualitative dimension, that is, the kind of social relations and the kind of relation to objects it gives rise to.

This passage makes clear that in the EPM, Marx seeks to develop an external critique of political economy. In the EPM, the function of the terminology of alienation is then to reveal the immanent relations between certain economic objects and alienated labour (Monferrand 2016, 188–189). The "economic fact" of private property, for example (Marx 1982, 364; Marx and Engels 1975, 271, translation modified), is immediately redefined as the contradiction of alienated labour, in which the product of labour "confronts [the worker] as an alien being":

> If the product of labour does not belong to the worker, if it confronts him as an alien power [*eine fremde Macht ihm gegenüber ist*], then this can only be because it belongs to some other man than the worker. If the worker's activity is a torment to him, to another it must give satisfaction and pleasure. Not the gods, not nature, but only man himself can be this alien power over man. (Marx 1982, 243; Marx and Engels 1975, 278, translation modified)

This passages alludes to the fact that the effect of the economic fact of private property is that the products of the workers' own labour become a means of the exploitation of said labour since the profit gained through the capitalists' selling of those products is reinvested in the same process of exploitation of labour. Here, then, considered from the standpoint of alienation, private property can only be explained with reference to another supposedly more fundamental level, namely that of the relations between humans and between humans and nature. Private property is thus presented as a consequence of an underlying "alien power".

Then, we may conclude that even if both the EPM and the *Grundrisse* contain some similar formulations when it comes to the terminology of alienation, the different status of alienation in these two texts indicates two distinct ways in which the critique relates to its object, political economy. Of course, there are striking similarities between the two different manuscripts, especially if we consider that in both cases, Marx refers to the historical determinacy of alienation as that which bourgeois economists have failed to apprehend other than as a fact of nature. Nevertheless, in the EPM, economic facts are analysed as expressions of the alienation of human beings. In Feuerbach's and Moses Hess' footsteps, the task of the critique is then to bring back economic facts to their historical significance (Renault 2008, 16). Alienation implies that Man's generic forces cannot be activated and accomplished through free human cooperation. In the *Grundrisse*, by contrast, the philosophical dimension of alienation does not offer a standpoint external to economic phenomena, because Marx uses the terminology of alienation to characterise the social-historical determination of these phenomena. The critique sets out not to "rise above" political economy but to reveal, through the lens of the concept of alienation, the specific bourgeois conditions of production to which economists like John Stuart Mill are blind.

However, how are we to explain that Marx, after having rejected the notion of alienation at least twice in 1845 and 1846, as the symbol either of a misguided focus on religion (Marx 1969, 5) or of a misconception of history as a development of consciousness (Marx and Engels 1970, 24), took up that same terminology in his manuscripts written in 1857–58? In the *Theses on Feuerbach*, alienation is indeed associated with Feuerbach's focalisation on the projection of mankind's essence upon God, whereas the *German Ideology* associates the term "alienation" with the ideological conception of history as a development of the human mind. Despite these former rejections of the term, and even if we were to follow Althusser's assumption according to which *Capital* is the ultimate endpoint of the Marxian oeuvre, we must admit that the terminology of alienation is used extensively in the *Grundrisse*, a text which can be considered as a laboratory for *Capital*. Therefore, Terell Carver's suggestion that once Marx's polemic with the Young Hegelians was over, the terminology of alienation ceased to be a foil, seems accurate (2008, 57–58).[2] In 1857–58, the point is no longer to break with a certain philosophical strategy but to create the framework for a "critique of economic categories"[3] with all available conceptual resources – including those of German idealism and the Young Hegelians.

---

[2] Given the often highly *ad hominem* character of said polemic, it is interesting to note that Marx renewed contact with the Bauer brothers during his years in London (Gamby 1985, 32-33).

[3] That is how Marx qualified his own research in his letter to Lassalle from the 2nd of February 1858.

Under the conditions of an intellectual confrontation such as the one that led Marx and Engels to attack the likes of Feuerbach and Stirner in the *German Ideology*, the enemy had to be clearly identified, and it is not surprising that the terminology of alienation then came to be connected with the interlocutors in question. Indeed, what was at stake was to break with the primacy that the Young Hegelians granted to philosophy, and what could be more Young Hegelian than Feuerbach's and Hess' re-elaborations of Hegel's conception of alienation? The *Grundrisse*, by contrast, are not intended as an intervention against the primacy given to philosophy, but as a direct engagement with political economy. So, in this context, "alienation" does not come with the symbolic weight it had in 1845–46 and can even be used as a conceptual resource to frame the historical specificity of bourgeois society. As we will see, after all, this allows for a relative continuity between the EPM and the *Grundrisse*. Although alienation in the EPM refers to something external to economic phenomena, whereas in the 1857–58 manuscripts alienation immanently characterises the configuration of those phenomena, traces of the former model of alienation can be found in the *Grundrisse*.

2. Alienation in exchange and alienation in production

That the terminology of alienation is endorsed in the *Grundrisse*'s project of a foundation of this critique of economic categories calls for a close study of the way this vocabulary is used in the various notebooks of these manuscripts. Since it appears both in the so-called "Chapter on Money" and in the "Chapter on Capital", its referential ambivalence is obvious.

2.1. Money and alienated social relations

In the "Chapter on Money", the terms related to alienation are particularly important in Marx's analysis of the historical advent of money. In this context, what is at stake is to grasp how money emerged not only as the result of a supposed subjective convention concluded by the exchanging partners but also as a form of the social act of exchange. Put differently, Marx suggests a distinction between the general acceptance of money as an instrument of exchange on the one hand and money as a social form, on the other hand, i.e., value as something inherent to all commodities which is to be expressed in money (Reichelt 2005, 53–58). It is precisely in the terminology of alienation that these two levels are articulated. Marx writes that if, as Aristotle suggested in his *Nicomachian Ethics* (Aristotle 2002, bk V, ch. 5, para. 14), money can be seen as the "dead pledge of society", it is only because the members of that society have "alienated this relation as an object", as the pieces of metal and paper that we call money, thus investing the latter with the "social (symbolical) property" of pledge:

> But why do they have faith in the thing? Obviously only because that thing is an *objectified relation* between persons [*offenbar nur als* versachlichtem Verhältniß *der Personen unter einander*]; because it is objectified exchange value [*als versachlichtem Tauschwerth*], and exchange value is nothing more than a mutual relation between people's productive activities. Every other collateral may serve the holder directly in that function: money serves him only as the "dead pledge of society', but it serves as such only because of its social (symbolical) property; and it can have a social property only because individuals have alienated this relation as an object [*ihre eigne gesellschaftliche Beziehung als Gegenstand sich entfremdet haben*]. (Marx 1976a, 93; Marx 1973, 160, translation modified)

From the point of view of the critique of economic categories, the fact that money bears the signification of a promise of a certain kind of remuneration is not due to some intrinsic character of money itself. It is due to the mediating function that money plays in the relations between producers. Money is the vehicle of the relation of exchange, in which a given exchange-value is quantified as a number of units. However, for the individuals taking part in production for the market, money can be characterised as "an *objectified relation*" because its mediating function is not understood as such by these individuals, but rather as a characteristic of money itself. They thus attribute that which is, in fact, a matter of their own active social relations to an inert object. In this regard, this object, money, has acquired an existence of its own, because it is not invested with its "social (symbolical) property" in a practical process of signification. Instead, this "social (symbolical) property" is perceived as a fact of nature, i.e., as something out-of-reach and unchangeable. Therefore, money is also characterised as something that has become "different from and alien to" the immediate existence of commodities (*etwas von ihr Verschiednes, ihr Fremdes…*):

By existing outside the commodity as money, the exchangeability of the commodity has become something different from and alien to [*etwas von ihr Verschiednes, ihr Fremdes*] the commodity, with which it first has to be brought into equation, to which it is therefore at the beginning unequal; while the equation itself becomes dependent on external conditions, hence a matter of chance. (Marx 1976a, 82; Marx 1973, 148)

The mediating function of money is that of representing exchange-value *as such*. Money is that in which the exchange-value of a commodity, i.e., its relation to all other commodities on the market, is represented. The commodity is not exchanged against another commodity, against another of its own kind, but against what could be called the element of exchange itself, namely money. In this regard, money is "different from" the commodity. But it is also "alien to" the commodity in the sense that it incarnates the element of exchange itself, as opposed to the commodity which, in its immediate existence, is also a use-value, a thing with material properties and a specific function. So, in this context, alienation is understood as the individuals' exteriorisation of their own social relations into a specific object which then, in a kind of inversion, becomes the bearer of those social relations. In another passage of the "Chapter on Money", the adjective "alien" (*fremde*) is used to describe the relation between the members of society and the process they take part in through exchange. Here, Marx seeks to understand the unity of society and individual interests without presupposing that unity:[4]

Circulation is the movement in which the general externalization [*allgemeine Entäusserung*] appears as general appropriation [*allgemeine Aneignung*] and general appropriation as general externalization. As much, then, as the whole of this movement appears as a social process, and as much as the individual moments of this movement arise from the conscious will and particular purposes of individuals, so much does the totality of the process appear as an objective interrelation [*als ein objectiver Zusammenhang*], which arises spontaneously from nature; arising, it is true, from the mutual influence of conscious individuals on one another, but neither located in their consciousness, nor subsumed under them as a whole. Their own collisions with one another produce an *alien* social power standing above them [*eine über ihnen stehende, fremde gesellschaftliche Macht*], produce their mutual interaction [*Wechselwirkung*] as a process and power independent of them. (Marx 1976a, 126; Marx 1973, 197, translation modified)

---

[4] On this theme, see Lukàcs 1976 and Hippolyte 1955.

In the process of circulation, individuals are continuously completing particular acts of exchange. That is the moment of "appropriation", of acquiring property by means of property. This is only possible if one part of the exchange relation is transferring the ownership of its property in return for money. Here, "externalisation" (*Entäusserung*) is used in the economic, juridical sense. One should speak of "general" appropriation and externalisation because all those particular acts of exchange are what compose circulation as such. On this view, circulation appears as a "social process", in the sense of intersubjective activity. Nevertheless, the "totality" of this "process", in other words the kind of conditions this intersubjective activity of exchange gives rise to, "appear[s] as an objective interrelation" insofar that said conditions are those of private production for the market – production of exchange values – set to be mediated by the incarnation of exchangeability, namely money. We have here "an objective interrelation" since all individual interactions are determined primarily by the production and exchange of commodities. It also seems as if this interrelation "arises spontaneously from nature" because each particular act of exchange is a disappearingly small part of a general movement on which no one can have bearing individually. It is this act of taking part in a process of which the general conditions are out of one's control that makes circulation appear as an inevitable and self-acting phenomenon. Therefore, the continuous acts of exchange are qualified as a supra-individual "*alien* social power" ("fremde *gesellschaftliche Macht*"). So, the actors of exchange are only unconsciously interacting with the social process, and the market forces the individuals to subject themselves to its laws. Then, "alien" is that which unifies individuals *in their separation* as independent producers and which makes that separation a condition of their social interaction.

2.2. Money, exchange and socialisation

The second context in which the terminology of alienation plays a significant role in the "Chapter on Money" is that of the description of the specific kind of socialisation created by exchange. This socialisation is characterised as a "development" of "alienation" (*Entwicklung dieser Entfremdung*):

> Since, 'if you please', the autonomization [*Verselbstständigung*] of the world market (in which the activity of each individual is included), increases with

the development of monetary relations (exchange value) and vice versa, since the general bond and all-round interdependence in production and consumption increase together with the independence and indifference of the consumers and producers to one another; since this contradiction leads to crises, etc., hence, together with the development of this alienation [*mit der Entwicklung dieser Entfremdung*], and on the same basis, efforts are made to overcome it: institutions emerge whereby each individual can acquire information about the activity of all others and attempt to adjust his own accordingly, e.g. lists of current prices, rates of exchange, interconnections between those active in commerce through the mails, telegraphs, etc. (Marx 1976a, 93; Marx 1973, 160-161)

The development of a greater mutual interconnection of production and consumption through the world market does also, at the same time, lead to a greater "independence and indifference" of consumers and producers. Put differently, in this society, individuals are objectively dependent of one another. Each one of them is increasingly specialised in the production of a specific commodity for the market, so individual A needs individuals B, C, D, etc. only insofar that individuals B, C, D, etc. are producing other commodities than individual A, and that individual A needs those specific commodities for its own (productive) consumption. Hence, those individuals are objectively dependent since they are interconnected only by their products and needs for other products. So, at the same time, this increased "interdependence" implies a greater "independence" because it only reinforces the specialisation of each individual producer. It also implies a greater "indifference" since it does not actually matter *who* produces *what* as long as the product in question is being produced. The bonds created by the market can be said to be impersonal. In this passage, the term "alienation" describes the process through which those who take part in the market do so as independent producers, as separated individuals that only meet in the subsequent act of exchange. Later in this same passage, Marx goes on to characterise the conditions under which all particular acts of production must conform themselves to a social norm which is forced upon them:

The alien and independent character [*Die Fremdartigkeit und Selbstständigkeit*] in which [the bond created by the market] presently exists *vis-à-vis* individuals proves only that the latter are still engaged in the creation of the conditions of their social life, and that they have not yet begun, on the basis of these conditions, to live it. It is the bond natural to individuals within specific and limited relations of production. [...] The degree and the universality of the development of wealth where *this* individuality becomes possible supposes production on the basis of exchange values as a prior condition, whose universality produces not only the alienation of the individual from himself and from others [*der Entfremdung des Individuums von sich und von andren*], but also the universality and the comprehensiveness of his relations and capacities. In earlier stages of development the single individual seems to be developed more fully, because he has not yet worked out his relationships in their fullness, or erected them as independent social powers and relations opposite himself. (Marx 1976a, 94–95; Marx 1973, 162, translation modified)

Marx seems to consider that the "alien and independent character" of the bond created by the market corresponds to a necessary historical stage. The fact that individual producers are taking part in the process of circulation without having any bearing on this process as a whole is supposed to prove that they are still in a moment of "creation of the conditions of their social life", i.e., merely gathering the social stuff – relations, powers and wealth – of which an emancipated society would "live", that is repurpose for the sake of individual and collective autonomy. Under these conditions, not only are the individuals relating to themselves strictly as producers-for-the-market ("alienation of the individual from himself"); they are also relating to others merely as bearers of commodities of which they are in need ("alienation of the individual [...] from others"). "Alienation" here resides in this substitution of interconnected objects to relations between individuals. It characterises a situation in which specific products are the bearers of individuals rather than the opposite since those products are what determine the form (exchange) and content (the bonds created by the market) of individual interactions. As opposed to the feudal community, in which each individual had its function according to its gender or age and was thus directly a part of a whole, bourgeois society is that in which individuals play multilateral roles interconnected only by the "alien relation" (*fremden Verhältnis*) of exchange (Marx 1976a, 80–81; Marx 1973, 146, translation modified). In the rear-view mirror of history, this assessment may create the illusion that in past communities, individuals were taking part in their social life more actively. However, what Marx seems to be arguing here against this romantic position is that the development of a social process of an "alien and independent character" brings us closer to the conditions of social autonomy by confronting us with the necessity of taking over the powers of which we are now

continuously being deprived. Therefore, the kind of socialisation realised in exchange, which the terminology of alienation serves to
describe, is a kind of trans-socialisation, insofar as it only makes the
individuals part of a social process that stands beyond their control
and that they are yet to subsume under their own powers.

2.3. Capital as an "alien power"

In the "Chapter on capital", the terminology of alienation is first of all
used in a distinct but related context: that of the process of production. As we hope to have made clear in our comparison with the
EPM above, the fact that workers are subject to alienation is not to be
understood as their deprivation of their "generic forces". In the
Grundrisse, Marx formulates this differently. Workers are deprived of
everything but a certain quantity of commodities, namely those commodities that their wage allows them to buy for the sake of their own
reproduction:

> Just as labour, as a *presupposed* exchange value, is exchanged for an
> equivalent in money, so the latter is again exchanged for an equivalent in
> *commodities*, which are consumed. In this process of exchange, labour is
> not productive; it becomes so only for capital; it can take out of circulation
> only what it has thrown into it, a *predetermined* amount of commodities,
> which is as little its own product as it is its own value. (Marx 1976a, 227;
> Marx 1973, 307)

Again, the situation of the worker is characterised in terms of its
exchange relation with the capitalist and not, as in the EPM, in terms
of man's "alien power over man". In the context of the analysis of the
process of production, the terminology of alienation has a meaning
which seems very close to that of the "Chapter of Money" in the analysis of the relation between the independent producers and the social
process of exchange. Indeed, just like the social act of exchange or the
social character of the commodity were said to be "alien" to these
producers or to the immediate existence of their products, both the
property of the capitalists and the aim of production are defined,
respectively, as "*alien objectivity*" and "*alien subjectivity*":

> Labour itself, like its product, is *negated as the labour of the particular,
> isolated worker*. This isolated labour, negated, is now indeed communal or
> combined labour, posited. The *communal or combined labour* posited in
> this way – as activity and in the passive, objective form – is however at the
> same time posited as an other towards the really existing individual labour

– as an *alien objectivity* [fremde Objektivität] (alien property) as well as an *alien subjectivity* [fremde Subjektivität] (of capital). (Marx 1976b, 378; Marx 1973, 470)

This is because capital brings together the different activities of individual labourers in the process of production with the sole purpose of its own self-perpetuation as capital. The productive activity of the individual is directly part of a wider process of production for the market over which it has no bearing. It is thus put in relation with the productive activities of other individuals, each with their particular task, but both the origin and the result of this combination of productive activities belong to the capitalist and to the investment of capital. For this reason, in this same passage, Marx grasps science as part of the productive forces of capital, and qualifies the scientific knowledge that is invested in the different technological components used in the process of production as an "alien intelligence" since the workers and their activities are mere objects of the capitalists' rationalisation of the process of production:

The combination of this labour appears just as subservient to and led by an alien will and an alien intelligence [*einem fremden Willen und einer fremden Intelligenz dienend, und von ihr geleitet*] – having its *animating unity* elsewhere – as its material unity appears subordinate to the *objective unity* of the *machinery*, of fixed capital, which, as *animated monster*, objectifies the scientific idea, and is in fact the coordinator, does not in any way relate to the individual worker as his instrument; but rather he himself exists as an animated individual punctuation mark, as its living isolated accessory. (Marx 1976b, 377; Marx 1973, 470)

It is the private property of the capitalist and the project linked to the latter's investment of capital that grants the process of production with its determining "will" and "intelligence". "Alien" is then that which, from the outside, imposes a motivation and a rationale upon the combined activities of individual labourers. The "machinery", the commodities that are progressively consumed in this same process of production, are imposed upon the individual labourers in the same way. The latter are there as mere executors of the predetermined functions of those commodities, functions that are in turn determined by the sole purpose of valorisation and capitalisation. Therefore, capital can be said to be a separate and autonomous social process – an "alien power" – that unifies the labourers just like the market unifies the independent producers, namely *in their separation*, as executors of a particular task in a greater project over which they have no control (Marx 1976b, 572; Marx 1973, 693).

2.4. Capital as alienation

Closely linked to his account of the process of production is Marx's analysis of the specific subject–object relation that this process gives rise to. Here, labour is characterised as dominated by capital, not in the sense of a certain individual depriving another of its freedom, but in the sense of living labour being "alien" to the bearer of the "labour capacity" (*Arbeitsvermögen*). Because of its separation from the means of production, this labour capacity can only be actualised, i.e., realised as a productive activity, when it is sold as a commodity to the capitalist:

> The objective conditions of labour attain a subjective existence *vis-à-vis* living labour capacity – capital turns into capitalist; on the other side, the merely subjective presence of the labour capacity confronted by its own conditions gives it a merely indifferent, objective form as against them – it is merely a *value* of a particular use value *alongside* the conditions of its own valorization [*Verwertung*] as *values* of another use value. Instead of their being realized [*realisiert*] in the production process as the conditions of its realization [*Verwirklichung*], what happens is quite the opposite: it comes out of the process as mere condition for *their* valorization [*Verwertung*] and preservation as values for-themselves opposite living labour capacity. The material on which it works is *alien* material [*fremdes Material*]; the instrument is likewise an *alien* instrument [*fremdes Instrument*]; its labour appears as a mere accessory to their substance and hence objectifies itself in things not *belonging to it*. Indeed, living labour itself appears as *alien vis-à-vis* [*als* fremd *gegenüber*] living labour capacity, whose labour it is, whose own life's expression [*Lebensäusserung*] it is, for it has been surrendered to capital in exchange for objectified labour, for the product of labour itself. (Marx 1976b, 370; Marx 1973, 462, translation modified)

Since the conditions and the modalities of the workers' own productive activities belong to capital, only capital exists as a "subject" in the sense of a being that actualises its own purpose through different moments. The "labour capacity" in itself is then no more, no less than one commodity among others combined for the purpose of productive consumption. As such, it has no subjective or idiosyncratic specificity. It can be the labour capacity of anyone ("indifferent") and it has the status of a use-value among others ("objective"). Hence,

rather than producing for their own material and moral needs –
rather than "realising" themselves in production – labourers are only
there to add an increment of value to the commodities produced. Just
like the commodities exchanged are in fact the bearers of their individual producers, the individual labourers are really the appendage of
the commodities with which they are producing other commodities.
So, both the material and the instrument of labour are "alien" to the
labourer insofar that they are directly a part of this productive consumption controlled by the capitalist. Marx goes as far as to say that
"living labour itself appears as *alien vis-à-vis* living labour capacity"
because the worker's own productive activity is not motivated, determined or directed by its own will or needs but only according to the
will and needs of the production of commodities itself. Indeed, it
would not be completely accurate to say that the worker's activity
belongs to the individual capitalist because under the conditions
described by Marx, the individual capitalist is in fact no more than
"an alien commanding personification", the particular expression of
the domination of living labour by objectivated labour:

> … in the new act of production itself – which merely confirmed the
> exchange between capital and living labour which preceded it – surplus
> labour, and hence the surplus product, the total product of labour in
> general (of surplus labour as well as necessary labour), has now been
> posited as capital, as independent and indifferent towards living labour
> capacity, or as exchange value which confronts its mere use value. Labour
> capacity has appropriated for itself only the subjective conditions of
> necessary labour – the means of subsistence for actively producing labour
> capacity, i.e. for its reproduction as mere labour capacity separated from
> the conditions of its realization – and it has posited these conditions
> themselves as *things, values,* which confront it in an alien, commanding
> personification [*fremder gebietender Personifikation*]. (Marx 1976b, 362;
> Marx 1973, 452–453)

Once the labour capacity has been productively consumed in the
process of production, it appears that the individual labourer contributes actively to its own separation from the objective conditions of
production. The "total product" of both labour necessary for the
reproduction of the worker and non-remunerated labour is "capital",
i.e., money that is to be invested for the sake of accumulation. The
labourer contributes actively to this total product by not only preserving exchange value but also adding an increment of value through the
consumption of its labour capacity beyond that which is necessary for

its own reproduction. Capital is "independent and indifferent towards living labour capacity" because its purpose is its own self-perpetuation, a purpose over which the labour capacity has no control. Also, it does not matter for money invested for the sake of accumulation who's labour capacity is being used as long as the increment of value can be added. So, in its productive consumption, through which it adds an increment of value to the product, the labour capacity is contributing to a process which lies beyond itself, namely that of the valorisation of capital. The *"things, values"*, i.e., commodities "confront" the labour capacity not only in the sense that they belong to something else but also because they are the result of a process to which he only contributed as an individual appendage without any bearing on it as a whole. The capitalist is the "alien, commanding personification" of these commodities insofar that this individual executes production for the sake of production – it is merely a "personification" of this social compulsion – and it does so by having the labour capacity at its disposal ("commanding"). If "alien" it is to the labour capacity, it is precisely because it directs the process of which this capacity is just a particular executor among others. At such moments, it is tempting to draw parallels between Marx's approach and Feuerbach's and to conclude that, just like human beings give rise to God through a projection of their own qualities onto a supposedly divine reality, workers give rise to the subject of capital through the alienation of their productive activity (e.g., Feuerbach 1960, 14–40). If we get back to Marx's analysis of the process of production, however, Marx seems to reject any notion of a *real* – and not just analytical – separation between the essential attributes of labour and the alien reality of capital:

> Labour, such as it exists *for itself* in the worker in opposition to capital, that is, labour in its *immediate being*, separated from capital, is *not productive*. Nor does it ever become *productive* as an activity of the worker so long as it merely enters the simple, only formally transforming process of circulation. Therefore, those who demonstrate that the productive force ascribed to capital is a *displacement*, a *transposition of the productive force* of labour, forget precisely that capital itself is essentially this *displacement* [*Verrückung*], this *transposition* [*Transposition*], and that wage labour as such presupposes capital, so that, from its standpoint as well, capital is this *transubstantiation* [*Transsubstantiation*]; the necessary process of positing its own powers as *alien* to the worker [*ihre eignen Kräfte als dem Arbeiter fremde zu setzen*]. (Marx 1976a, 227–228; Marx 1973, 308)

Against Proudhon's theses in *Gratuité du crédit. Discussion entre M. Fr. Bastiat et M. Proudhon*, Marx claims that the "*displacement*" or "*transposition*" of the productive force of labour into a private property of the capitalist is not some aberration, but a normal characteristic of the process of production. Capital *is* the process through which labour poses "its own powers as *alien*" to the worker by contributing actively to the worker's own separation from and opposition to the product of its labour. Indeed, in the bourgeois mode of production, the actualisation of productive activities is subordinated to the production and capitalisation of surplus value. This "*displacement*" or "*transposition of the productive force* of labour" consists in the active contribution of the labour capacity to a process which lies beyond itself. From the moment it is consumed in the process of production, the physical and mental power of the labourers is actualised in something separate from and opposed to themselves. One could even speak of a "*transubstantiation*" insofar that this power is incorporated into capital by becoming an element of this reality separate from and opposed to itself. The alienation of labour is inscribed in its existence as a pure capacity of labouring separated from the means of production.

2.5. The meanings and functions of the terminology of alienation in the Grundrisse. An attempt at a unified presentation

After this overview, we may now attempt a unified presentation of the terminology of alienation in both "The Chapter on Money" and "The Chapter on Capital". This terminology serves to describe:

1. how the activities of workers or independent producers become subordinated to capital or money. Although capital or money only have an effect through the activities of the former, they acquire the status of autonomous beings. Indeed, the actors of exchange are acting as if money was really creating the exchangeability of their products, while the workers are actively contributing to the fact that their powers become a determinate quantity of commodities. Social relations are thus experienced and produced as things that live their own life.
2. how capital or money constitute independent social relations that stand beyond the control of workers or independent

producers. The result of the combination of labour faces the worker as something separate, while exchangeability appears in money as something opposed to the product. The social dimension of both labour and its products is thus, in fact, an external reality founded in a strictly economic compulsion. The different labourers and products are socialised only insofar that they remain separate from each other and from this social dimension as such.

3. how capital or money take part in constituting a social reality that transcends the workers or independent producers. The social dimension which is, in fact, an external reality supposes that the workers or independent producers exist as the mere appendage of the realisation of capital or money. Their individual activities contribute to exchange becoming an autonomous process and to the objective conditions of labour becoming something separate from and opposed to the workers. These activities produce a reality that is alien to the individuals conducting them.

Now, is there something that unifies these different moments described by the terminology of alienation in the *Grundrisse*? When reflecting upon the link between the process of production and the process of valorisation, in preparation of the critique of Proudhon mentioned above, Marx suggests an analogy between, on the one hand, the productivity of labour in relation to capital; on the other hand, exchange values in relation to money:

> The *transformation of labour* (as living purposive activity) into *capital* is, *in itself*, the result of the exchange between capital and labour, in so far as it gives the capitalist the title of ownership to the product of labour (and command over the same). *This transformation* is *posited* only in the *production process* itself. Thus, the question whether capital is productive or not is absurd. Labour itself is *productive only* if absorbed into capital, where capital forms the basis of production, and where the capitalist is therefore in command of production. The productivity of labour becomes the productive force of capital just as the general exchange value of commodities fixes itself in money. (Marx 1976a, 227; Marx 1973, 308)

Because the material basis of production is actually the product of past labour, the "productivity of labour" appears as the "productive force of capital". Indeed, the social relations that constitute this productivity "become" such a productive force insofar that they are functions within the alien reality of capital. An analogy can thus be made with the relation between exchange values and money since the basis of the process of circulation is this production of commodities for the market of which money represents the social character, i.e., the exchangeability. Just like the productivity of labour "becomes" the productive force of capital because it corresponds to functions within the alien reality of capital, this exchangeability "fixes itself" in money in the sense that all exchange relations must be mediated by the representation of this exchangeability. So, in both cases, social relations are concentrated upon an object (capital or money). In most cases, the terminology of alienation in the *Grundrisse* serves to analyse the movement of this concentration, the character of this object and the relation between the latter and the individual activities of workers and independent producers.

Conclusion. The political implications of the *Grundrisse's* model of alienation and their link to subsequent works

To conclude, one could say that the *Grundrisse* offers a specific model of alienation which is not that of a human being inhibited in its objectivation. Indeed, in the *Grundrisse*, alienation is conceived of not as the state of a certain being, but as the form of social relations that are separated from, opposed to and that transcend the individuals taking part in production and exchange. Nevertheless, it seems clear that certain aspects of the system of alienation from the EPM are embraced again in the *Grundrisse*, as when Marx writes that living labour "repulses" its own "realization" from itself (*ihre Verwirklichung* [...] *als fremde Realität von sich abstösst*) insofar as the conditions, the modalities and the purpose of its own activity are all part of the "alienated [...] reality" of capital (*entfremdeten* [...] *Realität*):

> Living labour therefore now appears from its own standpoint as acting within the production process in such a way that, as it realizes itself in the objective conditions, it simultaneously repulses this realization from itself as an alien reality, and hence posits itself as insubstantial, as mere penurious labour capacity in face of this reality alienated [*entfremdet*] from it, belonging not to it but to others; that it posits its own reality not as a being for it, but merely as a being for others, and hence also as mere other-being [*Anderssein*], or being of another opposite itself. (Marx 1976b, 363; Marx 1973, 454)

As described above, the labourer contributes actively to its own separation from the conditions and means of production as well as to the opposition of the latter to itself. Hence one witnesses a tension throughout these manuscripts between two conceptions of an emancipated society. One is close to the conception of alienation that Marx developed in the EPM with reference to Feuerbach and Hess, namely the idea that alienation calls for a resorption of the subject's alienated attribute (the productive forces) in the subject itself (the producers). Alienation is then understood as a necessary historical negative stage which unmistakeably leads the subject to bring back its essential attribute to itself. Antonio Negri's notion of an emerging "social worker" could be seen as an application of this idea (Negri 1979). Nevertheless, in other passages of the *Grundrisse*, small hints are given of how an emancipated society would not only bring back the productive forces to the producers but also qualitatively change the relations between individuals, their activities and their products.[5] For example, in his analysis of the process of circulation, Marx refers negatively to that which is *not* the "point of departure" of bourgeois conditions, namely the "free social individual" engaged in a collective development of her own forces with no other purpose than her self-fulfilment:

> Circulation, because a totality of the social process, is also the first form in which the social relation appears as something independent of the individuals, but not only as, say, in a coin or in exchange value, but extending to the whole of the social movement itself. The social relation of individuals to one another as a power over the individuals which has become autonomous, whether conceived as a natural force, as chance or in whatever other form, is a necessary result of the fact that the point of departure is not the free social individual. (Marx 1976a, 126; Marx 1973, 197)

If "the point of departure" was "the free social individual", the socialisation of individuals would not occur unconsciously and without them having any control over the process, as is the case when we consider the process of circulation in bourgeois society. The opposite would be true. The purpose of production would be the satisfaction of moral and material needs, and the socialisation of individuals would

---

[5] For interesting developments on French and German readings that have emphasised the subject-object relation in the *Grundrisse* since the 1960s, see Endnotes 2010.

be the result of their own conscious interactions rather than of a force operating behind their backs through the bonds between products.

Later, in *Capital*, it is the former conception of alienation that prevails, namely that of a negative stage that must lead to emancipation. In volume 3, for instance, Marx states that the "alienated, autonomised social power" (*entfremdete, verselbständigte gesellschaftliche Macht*) of capital will be overcome through a collective re-appropriation of that power (Marx 2004, 260, our translation). In other words, the social relations that are concentrated upon capital's self-perpetuation are to be repurposed for the development of free social individuals.

Acknowledgements

We are indebted to both Jean-Christophe Angaut and Pauline Clochec for their careful and considered comments on the Master's thesis upon which this paper is based. We also thank Camilla Brenni, Frédéric Monferrand, Herbert De Vriese as well as the two anonymous referees for their helpful remarks on earlier versions of the text.

Disclosure statement

No potential conflict of interest was reported by the authors.

References

Althusser, Louis. 1965. *Pour Marx*. Paris: Maspero.
Angaut, Jean-Christophe. 2008. "Un Marx feuerbachien?" In *Lire les Manuscrits de 1844*, edited by Emmanuel Renault, 51–70. Paris: PUF.
Aristotle. 2002. *Nicomachean Ethics*. Translated by Joe Sachs. Newburyport, MA: Focus.
Arthur, Chris J. 1986. *Dialectics of Labour: Marx and His Relation to Hegel*. Oxford: Basil Blackwell.
Carver, Terrell 2008. "Marx's Conception of Alienation." In *Karl Marx's Grundrisse. Foundations of the Critique of Political Economy 150 Years Later*, edited by Marcello Musto, 48–67. London: Routledge.
Debord, Guy. 1967. *La Société du spectacle*. Paris: Buchet/Chastel.
Elliott, John E. 1979. "Continuity and Change in the Evolution of Marx's Theory of Alienation: From the *Manuscripts* through the *Grundrisse* to *Capital*." *History of Political Economy* 11 (3): 317–362. doi:10.1215/00182702-11-3-317.
Endnotes. 2010. "Communisation and Value-Form Theory." *Endnotes* 2. https://endnotes.org.uk/issues/2/en/endnotes-communisation-and-value-form-theory

Feuerbach, Ludwig. 1960. *Das Wesen des Christenthums. Vol. 6, Sämtliche Werke*, edited by Wilhelm Bolin. Stuttgart-Bad Cannstatt: Frommann Verlag Günther Holzboog.

Fischbach, Franck. 2008. "Transformations du concept d'aliénation. Hegel, Feuerbach, Marx." *Revue germanique internationale* 8 (2008): 93–112. doi: 10.4000/rgi.377

Gamby, Erik. 1985. *Edgar Bauer – Junghegelianer, Publizist und Polizeiagent. Vol. 32, Schriften aus dem Karl-Marx-Haus*. Trier: Karl-Marx-Haus.

Haber, Stéphane. 2007. *L'aliénation. Vie sociale et expérience de la dépossession*. Paris: PUF.

Hess, Moses. 1921. "Über das Geldwesen." In *Sozialistische Aufsätze (1841–1847)*, 158–188. Berlin: Welt Verlag.

Hyppolite, Jean. 1955. "Aliénation et objectivation: À propos du livre de Lukács sur la jeunesse de Hegel." *Chap. 4 in Études sur Marx et Hegel*. Paris: Librairie Marcel Rivière et Cie.

Lukács, Georg. 1976. "'Entäusserung' ('externalization') as the central philosophical concept of The Phenomenology of Mind." Chap. 4 of part IV in *The Young Hegel. Studies in the Relations between Dialectics and Economics*. Translated by Rodney Livingstone. Cambridge, MA: MIT Press.

Marcuse, Herbert. 1941. *Reason and Revolution*. Oxford: Oxford University Press.

Marx, Karl. 1969. *Thesen über Feuerbach. Vol. 3, Karl Marx. Friedrich Engels. Werke*. Berlin: Dietz Verlag.

Marx, Karl. 1973. *Grundrisse*. Translated by Martin Nicolaus. London: Penguin Books.

Marx, Karl. 1976a. *Ökonomische Manuskripte 1857-58, Teil 1. II.1.1, MEGA*. Berlin: Dietz Verlag.

Marx, Karl. 1976b. *Ökonomische Manuskripte 1857-58, Teil 2. II.1.2, MEGA*. Berlin: Dietz Verlag.

Marx, Karl. 1982. *Ökonomisch-philosophische Manuskripte (Zweite Wiedergabe). I.2., MEGA*. Berlin: Dietz Verlag.

Marx, Karl. 2004. *Das Kapital. Kritik der politischen Ökonomie. Dritter Band. Hamburg 1894. II.15, MEGA*. Berlin: Akademie Verlag.

Marx, Karl and Friedrich Engels. 1970. *Die Deutsche Ideologie. I.5, MEGA*. Glashütten im Taunus: Detlev Auvermann KG.

Marx, Karl and Friedrich Engels. 1975. *Economic and Philosophic Manuscripts of 1844. Vol. 3, Karl Marx and Frederick Engels: Collected Works*. Translated by Richard Nixon et al. London: Lawrence and Wishart.

McLellan, David. 1972. "Introduction." In K. Marx, *The Grundrisse*, translated and edited by David McLellan, 1–16. New York: Harper Torchbooks.

Mill, John Stuart. 2008. *Principles of Political Economy and Chapters on Socialism*, edited by Jonathan Riley. Oxford: Oxford University Press.

Monferrand, Frédéric. 2016. "Marx: ontologie sociale et critique du capitalisme. Une lecture des Manuscrits économico-philosophiques de 1844." PhD diss., Université Paris Nanterre.

Negri, Antonio. 1979. *Marx au-delà de Marx*. Paris: Christian Bourgois.

Rancière, Jacques. 1965. "Le concept de critique et la critique de l'économie polit-ique des *Manuscrits de 1844* au *Capital*". In *Lire le Capital*, vol. 1, edited by Louis Althusser, 93–210. Paris: Maspero.

Reichelt, Helmut. 2005. "Social Reality as Appearance: Some Notes on Marx's Conception of Reality." In *Human Dignity: Social Autonomy and the Critique of Capitalism*, edited by Werner Bonefeld and Kosmas Psychopedis, 31–68. Aldershot, Burlington: Ashgate.

Renault, Emmanuel. 1995. *Marx et l'idée de critique*. Paris: PUF.

Renault, Emmanuel. 2008. "Comment lire les *Manuscrits de 1844?*" In *Lire les* Manuscrits de 1844, edited by Emmanuel Renault, 7-32. Paris: PUF.

Tomberg, Friedrich. 1969. "Der Begriff der Entfremdung in den „Grundrissen" von Karl Marx." *Das Argument* 11 (3): 187–223.

Wittmann, David. 2008. "Les sources du concept d'aliénation." In *Lire les Manuscrits de 1844*, edited by Emmanuel Renault, 89–110. Paris: PUF.

Error or absurdity? A non-cognitive approach to commodity fetishism

David Andrews

ABSTRACT
Karl Marx presented his theory of commodity fetishism as an explanation of the mysterious appearance of social relations in a system of commodity production as natural phenomena. The standard interpretation of this as a failure to perceive capitalist social relations correctly depends on a particular modern sense of 'natural'. If classical political economy and Marx used 'natural' in the Aristotelian sense, commodity fetishism appears quite differently: not as a cognitive error but rather as a manner of living under commodity production, one that is not wrong but absurd, the word fetishism tying commodity production to pre-Enlightenment, preliterate peoples.

1. Introduction

Karl Marx's theory of commodity fetishism has often been described as an important component of his thought, but it typically plays only a small role in actual discussions of his economic theory. For example, in the two volume "*A History of Marxian Economics*" by M.C. Howard and J.E. King (1989, 1992), commodity fetishism is only mentioned occasionally, never as the focus of a sustained analysis.[1] The limited interest in commodity fetishism today may be due to the way it has commonly been interpreted, as a failure to correctly perceive or understand capitalist social relations, a cognitive failure resulting from the experience of alienated life under a system of capitalist commodity production. Insofar as it is a question of how people understand or perceive the world, commodity fetishism can be remedied by learning Marx's theory and has little significance for economic theory.

---

[1] Almost the only writer to make it a focus, Isaak I. Rubin, argued that commodity fetishism is central to Marx's theory of value and to his critique of political economy, but his interpretation has not been assimilated in the literature.

In this essay, I present an alternative interpretation in which commodity fetishism appears not as a cognitive error but rather as a fact of life under a system of capitalist commodity production. In such a system, value necessarily plays a dominating role as individuals participate in markets to acquire the means to their continued survival. To fetishize commodities is to believe that they have value and to act on the basis of that belief. This is not an error, because commodities do have value in such a system. In this sense, commodity fetishism cannot be remedied merely by viewing the world as Marx did, but can only be resolved through a change in social organization.

If commodity fetishism is not an error, however, the question arises as to the sense in which it may play a role in Marx's critique of political economy. Marx indicates his position on this question with his use of the term fetishism, a practice that is not a simple mistake, but one that does not adhere to scientific norms of rationality. Marx suggests that capitalist commodity production is a practice carried on in a most bizarre fashion, based on the attribution of an occult property to certain inanimate but useful things produced by humans. Production and consumption decisions are made on the basis of the supposed existence of an invisible quality, believed to be present in differing quantities in the useful things of ordinary life, although not discernible through any human senses. Moreover, this occult property entails a capacity for self-movement that it exercises through human beings organized in support of its on-going reproduction and expansion. Political economy, on this reading, is the theory that purports to explain this bizarre practice as a natural and rational process.

2. A standard interpretation

Marx's mature and most famous characterization of commodity fetishism is in the third edition of the first volume of *Capital*: "a definite social relation between men, that assumes, in their eyes, the fantastic form of a relation between things ... This I call the Fetishism which attaches itself to the products of labour, so soon as they are produced as commodities" (MECW 35: 83).[2] Widely taken as a case of people making a mistake, the logic of this interpretation is not difficult to discern. Marx seems to say that what is in fact a social relation

---

[2] References to Marx's writings are to the *Marx Engels Collected Works* (MECW) unless otherwise noted.

between people "assumes, in their eyes" a form that is "fantastic" or
unbelievable. The world looks as if it were some way that in fact it is
not, that it could not be. The problem is in "their eyes," with how the
world looks. People are deceived by appearances. On this view,
commodity fetishism can be overcome by learning the theory of commodity fetishism, enabling people to recognise that the social relations
are relations among people rather than things, remedying a confusion
of the material and the human.

   This interpretation of commodity fetishism can be seen, for
example, in the recent sixth edition of Ben Fine's and Alfredo Saad-
Filho's *Marx's 'Capital'* (2016), a standard Marxian source, in which
commodity fetishism is described as a misperception contrasting with
Marx's correct perception:

> Marx perceives that the exchange of produced use values reflects the social
> organization of labour that has produced these commodities. But to many
> of his contemporary economists and to nearly all subsequent ones,
> the relationship between workers and the products of their labour
> remains merely a relationship between things, of the type × loaves of
> bread = 1 shirt, or one worker week is worth so much of a standard of
> living (the wage bundle). Thus, while capitalism organises production in
> definite social relationships between capitalists and workers, these
> relationships are expressed and appear, in part, as relationships between
> things. These relationships are further mystified when money enters into
> consideration and everything is analysed in terms of price. Marx calls such
> a perspective on the capitalist world the fetishism of commodities
> (2016: 23).

Commodity fetishism here is understood to be an error, a cognitive
failure, a "perspective" that is mistaken in that it fails to properly recognize the social character of production, with the result that people
make the mistake of viewing other human beings as things. In order
to overcome commodity fetishism, it is necessary to perceive society
as Marx perceived it.

   Another standard work on Marx's major work, Duncan Foley's
Understanding Capital (1986), expresses the same point, that
commodity fetishism is a cognitive failure, a misinterpretation of the
nature of social production, leading to instrumental human
relationships:

> The commodity form of production imposes a paradoxical consciousness
> on the human beings who live through it. One the one hand, the
> commodity form of production is a social form of production because in

practice the exchange of products establishes an extensive social division of labour and makes every person highly dependent on a multitude of other people for means of subsistence and means of production. The commodity form creates a vast web of cooperation and interdependence of people. On the other hand, the exchange process creates an illusion of privacy and individual self-reliance; it allows and forces people to construe their existence subjectively as a matter of relations between themselves and things rather than as a matter of relations between themselves and other people. The result is that things are treated as people and people as things. Commodity relations tend to make people view each other instrumentally rather than intersubjectively and to induce people to enter into personal and emotional relations with things. This curious and pervasive distortion is what Marx means by the fetishism of commodities (Foley 1986: 29).

This passage expresses an idea very close to Fine's and Saad-Filho's definition, identifying commodity fetishism as a "curious and pervasive distortion" or "paradoxical consciousness," a problem in the mind, resulting from the experience of life under capitalism that leads people to believe something that is not true, an "illusion" about social relations with the result that they treat others as objects. Again, it can be overcome by helping the afflicted to see social relations as "a matter of relations between themselves and other people."

I.I. Rubin described "the generally accepted view" of commodity fetishism among Marxists in the mid-1920s (which he did not share) in similar terms:

It consists of Marx's having seen human relations underneath relations between things, revealing the illusion in human consciousness which originated in the commodity economy and which assigned to things characteristics which have their source in the social relations among people in the process of production ... The theory of fetishism dispels from men's minds the illusion, the grandiose delusion brought about by the appearance of phenomena in the commodity economy, and by the acceptance of the appearance ... as the essence of economic phenomena (1972: 5).

As in the passages cited above, commodity fetishism here is a belief in something that is not true, a distorted perspective that can be overcome by learning the theory of commodity fetishism, which explains that what appears to be the case is actually not true, correcting the misperception.[3]

---

[3] Cf. Ehrbar 2010, Meikle 1985, Harvey 2010.

There are at least two powerful objections against this standard interpretation. First, it is not at all clear that political economists have fetishized commodities in the manner in which it has been described. Eduard Bernstein claimed that they have not: "He denied that Marx's theory of fetishism marked any significant advance over the Classical theory of value, whose advocates were well aware that individual workers were part of a wider division of labour" (Howard and King 1989: 74). Based on this interpretation, not even Adam Smith could be said to have fetishized commodities. His *An Inquiry into the Nature and Causes of the Wealth of Nations* (1976 [1776]), begins with the division of labour, presupposing that labour is originally a social unity in need of division rather than a set of individual labours in need of aggregation. Smith set his discussion of the division of labour in the context of the overwhelming mutual dependence people share, due to their inability to provide for themselves individually:

> In civilized society he stands at all times in need of the co-operation and assistance of great multitudes, while his whole life is scarce sufficient to gain the friendship of a few persons. In almost every other race of animals each individual, when it is grown up to maturity, is intirely independent, and in its natural state has occasion for the assistance of no other living creature. But man has almost constant occasion for the help of his brethren. (WN I.ii.2)[4]

It cannot be said that in Smith "the relationship between workers and the products of their labour remains merely a relationship between things".

A second objection to the standard interpretation is that it does not involve fetishism in its conventional sense. The word 'fetishism,' since its earliest usage, has involved attributing some sort of divine or magical power to physical materials. The term was coined in 1760 by Charles de Brosses in his book "On the worship of fetish gods; or, a parallel of the ancient religion of Egypt with the present religion of Nigritia": "Though in its proper signification it refers in particular to the beliefs of African Negroes, I signal in advance that I plan to use it equally in speaking of any other nation whatsoever, where the objects of worship are animals or inanimate objects that are divinized" (de Brosses 2017: 45). One might expect that when Marx chose to use

---

[4] References to Adam Smith's writings are to the Glasgow edition of his collected works.

the term 'fetishism of commodities,' it would refer to the attribution of some sort of divine or magical power to commodities.

3. An alternative interpretation

These objections to the standard interpretation, if not decisive, at least invite an alternative. If we return to the passage with which the previous section begins, we find that it can be interpreted differently: "[A] definite social relation between men, that assumes, in their eyes, the fantastic form of a relation between things" (MECW 35: 83) might also plausibly be taken to mean that a social relation assumes the form of a relation between things in people's eyes in that it does actually take that form in the world. In this case, people are correct to see a particular social relation as a relation between things, even though this may be a bizarre form for a social relation to take. The problem in this case is not in the eyes of people, but rather in the constitution of the society.

This is consistent with the idea of fetishism in its conventional sense of attributing power or divinity to material objects. In the case of commodity fetishism, the material objects are commodities. The social relation to which Marx refers is value. Value is a social relation in that it is the result of a particular way of organizing social production, but it is stamped on commodities practically in market relations as exchange values, putting all commodities in relation with each other, a relation of the form: there exists Y such that X units of commodity A is worth, or equal in value, to Y units of commodity B, for any A or B. This relation obtains across the entire world of commodities, allowing any commodity's value to be expressed in terms of money or in terms of any other commodity. Value is thus a social relation between things. To fetishize commodities, then, is to hold that commodities have value, a property they do possess in a system of commodity production.[5]

This involves a reinterpretation of the word "appears" in Marx's claim that "the social character of men's labour appears to them as an objective character stamped upon the product of that labour."[6] To say that

---

[5] Cf. I.I. Rubin: "The labour theory of value discovered the fetish, the reified expression of social labour in the value of things" (1972: 72); "Value is not the product of labour but is a material, fetish expression of the working activity of people" (1972: 147); "Thus value is 'reified,' 'materialized' labour and simultaneously it is an expression of production relations among people" (Rubin 1972: 153).

[6] Cf. Bellofiore 2014, Ehrbar 2010 on the distinction between scheinen and erscheinen.

something appears in a certain way may be understood in at least two different senses. It might be taken to refer to a situation of 'seeming' in which what appears to be the case on the surface is not really the case: "He appears to be hard working" suggests at least uncertainty, perhaps scepticism, doubt that he is actually hard working. In this case, to accept appearances is a mistake, or at least may be. This contrasts with appearance in the sense of becoming visible, in which the appearance is actually also the reality of the situation: "He appears every day at supper time." In this case, to accept appearances is not to make a mistake.

The standard interpretation has assumed that Marx's use here of the word "appears" should be understood in the first sense, but the relevant passages support the second sense: "the relations connecting the labour of one individual with that of the rest appear, not as direct social relations between individuals at work, but *as what they really are, material relations between persons and social relations between things*" (MECW 35: 84; emphasis added). In a system of commodity production, things do have value in an important sense, with what Marx described as "social validity": "The categories of bourgeois economy consist of such like forms. They are forms of thought expressing with social validity the conditions and relations of a definite, historically determined mode of production, namely, the production of commodities" (MECW 35: 87). If people believe that things have value, and act as if they have value, then in some sense they do have value. To cite an example Marx employs in a different context, commodities have value in a sense similar to that in which the Delphic Oracle had power, because it influenced the activities of living human beings (MECW 1: 104).

In this sense, commodity fetishism is not a not a mistake: not a cognitive error, not a distorted perception, not a false consciousness. The social relation "value" does appear to people as the property of things. Value is treated as an objective property of things both in the language of economists and in ordinary language, in the assertion that commodities have value. In ordinary life, value is treated as an objective property when people engage in market behaviour, in buying and selling. There is something strange or mysterious about commodity fetishism, but it is strange or mysterious behaviour, not misperception. Commodity fetishism is an aspect of a social practice, a way of acting and being in the world, a way of life, namely, the way of life based on the production of commodities by means of commodities.[7] As Rubin writes: "Fetishism is not only a phenomenon of social consciousness, but of social being" (Rubin 1972: 59). To perceive social relations as a property of things is to perceive accurately a contorted world.

Commodity fetishism according to this account cannot be overcome by perceiving the world as Marx did. Someone in Marx's household purchased food and supplies with money and thereby participated in commodity fetishism. All people who live under a system of capitalist commodity production participate in fetishism insofar as they base their behaviour to some extent on the idea that commodities have value.

According to several writers, including Lewis and Jacob (1977), Cohen (1978), Elster (1986) and Arthur (2002), commodity fetishism is the attribution of value to commodities, but only when it is attributed to them in a particular way, as something inherent or intrinsic to the commodity rather than as something relative. There are several reasons to reject this view. First, Marx addresses this point specifically in *Theories of Surplus*, explicitly rejecting the "inherent property" view of fetishism: "Bailey is a fetishist in that he conceives value, though not as a property of the individual object (considered in isolation), but as a relation of objects to one another, while it is only a representation in objects, an objective expression, of a relation between men, a social relation, the relationship of men to their reciprocal productive activity" (MECW 32: 334). Second, it is not clear that anyone believes that value is intrinsic to a commodity. The widely held marginal theory of value and distribution, for example, teaches that rather than being intrinsic to a commodity, value depends on scarcity. Most importantly, however, value as it exists in practice does belong to commodities individually, even as the values of commodities may be related to each other. Commodity fetishism only requires that we attribute value to commodities in the sense in which they do actually have value.[8]

---

[7] Cf. Andrews 2002.

[8] That commodity fetishism has been understood as a mistake may also be due to a common construal of the supposed misunderstanding or misperception as the reification of social relations. Reification has been used as the translation of Marx's *Verdinglichung*, a noun meaning the act or process of making what is not a thing into a thing. The etymological logic of using reification to translate *Verdinglichung* is easy to understand. *Res* is a Latin word for thing. Reification would seem to mean to make something that is not a thing into a thing, similar to purification or sanctification, to make something impure pure or to make something profane holy. Reification, however, is typically used in a different sense, to refer to the action of treating something abstract, for example, an idea or a concept, as if it were concrete, of treating something as if it were something that it is not. Reification in latter typical sense involves making an error; in the abnormal former sense it does not.

4. The absurdity of capitalist commodity production

If commodity fetishism is not an error based on the alienating character of capitalist production, questions arise as to the sense in which it
might contribute to the critique of political economy promised in the
subtitle of *Capital*. Assuming that we take critique in a broad sense to
refer to a reasoned evaluation of political economy, Marx's answer
appears to be that commodity fetishism points to the bizarre character
of capitalist commodity production, in a sense that purports, at least,
to be objective, the same sense in which fetishism may be recognized
as a clinical disorder. This implies that political economy is the theory
of a certain type of non-rational behaviour, but fails to recognise and
therefore participates in its non-rationality.

The word 'fetishism' suggests the contemptuous attitude taken by
eighteenth and nineteenth century European intellectuals toward the
religious practices of Africans, attributing magical or divine powers to
material objects. As noted above, the word 'fetishism,' since its earliest
usage, has involved attributing some sort of divine or magical power to
material objects. The Enlightenment, according to its champions such
as Condorcet, represented a shift of enormous world historical significance, in which human beings had for the first-time abandoned beliefs
grounded on superstition, authority and tradition in favour of free and
fearless pursuit of scientific truth with methods that had only recently
become clear. Fetishism belongs to the class of ideas abandoned. From
the rational Enlightenment perspective, fetishism was not a cognitive
error in the sense that modern science could demonstrate its falsity. It
was bizarre. A person believing in such absurd things had not made a
mistake, but displayed mental deficiency or derangement that could
not be corrected with a rational explanation. Fetishism was considered
to be pre-scientific, excluded by the scientific approach, unsuitable for
scientific investigation, to be dismissed rather than refuted.

In *Capital* Marx repeatedly suggests that there is something problematic about commodities, emphasizing their strangeness and mys-
teriousness. A commodity is "a very queer thing abounding in
metaphysical subtleties and theological niceties" (MECW 35: 81), as
well as an indication of "magic and necromancy" (MECW 35: 87). As
a use-value there is nothing strange about it, but as a commodity it
"transcends sensuousness": "It not only stands with its feet on the
ground, but, in relation to all other commodities, it stands on its head
and evolves out its wooden brain grotesque ideas" (MECW 35: 82).

What turns out to be mysterious and strange, even absurd, is the value relation among commodities:

> When I state that coats or boots stand in a relation to linen, because it is the universal incarnation of abstract human labour, the absurdity of the statement is self-evident. Nevertheless, when the producers of coats and boots compare those articles with linen, or, what is the same thing, with gold or silver, as the universal equivalent, they express the relation between their own private labour and the collective labour of society in the same absurd form. (MECW 35: 86–87)

Marx claims that it is absurd to say that a certain quantity of coats and boots are worth a certain quantity of linen. To claim that particular quantities of diverse commodities are equal in terms of an invisible or occult quality is absurd.

As absurd as commodity production might be, Marx understood that things being perceived as having value might not seem strange to many people: "the conventions of our everyday life make it appear commonplace and ordinary that social relations of production should assume the shape of things, so that the relations into which people enter in the course of their work appear as the relation of things to one another and of things to people" (MECW 29: 276). If strange and mysterious are contrasted with familiar then social things are not strange or mysterious at all.

What is it, then, that makes the practice of commodity fetishism absurd? Marx's answer is that the absurdity lies in the fact that value appears as a "socio-natural" property of commodities: "The mysterious character of the commodity-form consists therefore simply in the fact that the commodity reflects the social characteristics of men's own labour as objective characteristics of the products of labour themselves, as the socio-natural properties of these things." (Marx 1976: 164–165).[9]

I suggest again that in this context 'appears' should be read to mean that value does in fact take the form of a socio-natural property of commodities rather than seeming to take that form without really doing so. However, what is a socio-natural property? That things have social properties is not strange. In some sense, many things have social properties. The corner office, a badge, a coffee shop. Marx

---

[9] Here I use the Fowkes translation rather than the *MECW* because it translates "gesellschaftliche Natureigenschaften" as "socio-natural properties" rather than as simply "objective properties."

points out that value is not a physical or chemical property of things. However, beauty is not a physical or chemical property either. Beauty is a social concept we assign as a property to things, paintings and sculptures, for example, but we do not find it mysterious that we do so.[10] That value is social is not controversial. The answer to the question of the absurd, mysterious, bizarre character of commodities appears to depend on the sense in which value is natural in classical political economy, especially the writings of Smith, whose notion of "natural price" was adopted by David Ricardo.

5. The absurdity of things with self-motion

Nature is a notoriously complicated idea, but it is ubiquitous in Smith's writings. A common interpretation has been to understand 'natural' as opposed to 'artificial,' as what occurs in the absence of human interference. If value and market behaviour it organizes were natural in this sense, it could be taken to imply that market behaviour is universal and inevitable. Marx and others certainly held that this is not true, but it is an error, not an absurdity.

But Smith's use of nature is very different, rooted in Aristotle, for whom the nature of an animal was its internal principle of the activity that provides for its survival and reproduction, allowing it to persist and to be what it is over time: "the internal activity that makes anything what it is" (Sachs 1995: 250).[11] In order to exist over time, that is, a natural being's more or less diverse organs work together in an ongoing process of self-maintenance, primarily through assimilation of nourishment. In order for the species to continue to exist, reproduction must take place. In this sense, nature

---

[10] Cf. "In the first part of my book, I mentioned that it is characteristic of labour based on private exchange that the social character of labour "manifests itself" in a perverted form—as the "property" of things; that a social relation appears as a relation between things (between products, values in use, commodities). This appearance is accepted as something real by our fetish-worshipper, and he actually believes that the exchange-value of things is determined by their properties as things, and is altogether a natural property of things" (MECW 32: 317)

[11] "Nature is not just a sum of bodies but is an activity, seen in the birth, growth and self-maintenance of independent things and in the equilibrium of the cosmos. The cluster of central ideas in Aristotle's thinking is built on a few word roots that overlap in meaning: the phu of phusis, meaning birth and growth; the erg of energeia, meaning work, the ech of entelecheia (enteles echein) meaning holding-on in some condition (in this case completeness); and the en of to tie en einai, meaning being in the progressive aspect of that verb. This active dynamic character is present in the very material (hule) of each thing, as a potency (dunamis) spilling over into the activity that gives the thing its form (oidos or morphe)." (Sachs 1995: 31)

was teleological for Aristotle, with activity serving a purpose or a goal, of self-preservation of individuals and the reproduction of species.[12]

Smith embraced final causes in Aristotle's sense, and the final causes Smith embraced were precisely those of Aristotle. Smith repeated that the purposes of nature are the self-preservation of individuals and the propagation of species:

> Thus, self-preservation, and the propagation of the species, are the great ends which Nature seems to have proposed in the formation of all animals" (*TMS* II.i.5.9: 77); "In every part of the universe we observe means adjusted with the nicest artifice to the ends which they are intended to produce; and in the mechanism of a plant, or animal body, admire how every thing is contrived for advancing the two great purposes of nature, the support of the individual, and the propagation of the species. (*TMS* II.ii.3.5: 87)

This idea of nature is at the foundation of both Smith's *Theory of Moral Sentiments* and *Wealth of Nations*. In the *Theory of Moral Sentiments*, Smith described how the moral sentiments, inner feelings that regulate social activity, such as sympathy, gratitude, resentment, a sense of justice and beneficence, etc., function so as to allow coexistence and cooperation among human beings. These moral sentiments serve as internal sources of motion guiding human beings to behave in a manner that promotes the purposes of nature, their continuing survival and the reproduction of the human species.

In the *Wealth of Nations* Smith identifies two other instincts, belonging to humans by nature that dominate economic life and support the purposes of nature, namely, the "propensity" to exchange and the instinct to improve one's condition. Of the two, the former plays a much more prominent role, giving rise to the division of labour, a characteristic distinguishing humanity from other species:

> This division of labour, from which so many advantages are derived, is not originally the effect of any human wisdom, which foresees and intends that general opulence to which it gives occasion. It is the necessary, though very slow and gradual consequence of a certain propensity in human nature which has in view no such extensive utility; the propensity to truck, barter, and exchange one thing for another." (WN I.ii.2)

---

[12] See Andrews 2014, 2015.

Smith also considered the other internal principle of activity at the heart of the *Wealth of Nations*, the instinct to improve one's condition, to be very important:

> The uniform, constant, and uninterrupted effort of every man to better his condition, the principle from which publick and national, as well as private opulence is originally derived, is frequently powerful enough to maintain the natural progress of things toward improvement, in spite both of the extravagance of government, and of the greatest errors of administration. Like the unknown principle of animal life, it frequently restores health and vigour to the constitution, in spite, not only of the disease, but of the absurd prescriptions of the doctor. (WN I.ii.31)

Marx, whose close connection with Aristotle has been studied extensively,[13] argues to the contrary: Instead of being driven by human beings possessing inner principles of motion, capitalist commodity production is driven by commodities and money possessing an inner principle of motion—value—which makes them capital, which Marx defines as self-moving value. The change in agency is a constant theme in Marx's writing leading up to and including *Capital*. His language with respect to value and capital parallels Aristotle's (and Smith's) on individual survival and propagation: "the return of the capital, which includes the maintenance of its value and posits it as a self-maintaining and self-perpetuating value" (MECW 32: 454–455). Or again:

> Since, in the capitalist production process, the value of capital is perpetuated and reproduced in addition to its surplus-value, it is therefore quite in order that, when money or commodities are sold as capital, they return to the seller after a period of time and he does not alienate it [money] in the same way as he would a commodity but retains ownership of it. In this way, money or commodities are not sold as money or commodities, but in their second power, as capital, as self-increasing money or commodity value. Money is not only increased, but is preserved in the total process of production. It therefore remains capital for the seller and comes back to him. (MECW 32: 452)

---

[13] The literature on Marx and Aristotle is now extensive. As a student, Marx was immersed in Aristotle. The importance of Hegel for the young Marx is well known, but Marx viewed Hegel specifically in the context of Aristotle, as analogous to Aristotle with respect to his synthesis of early competing philosophies: Marx's doctoral dissertation juxtaposed pre- and post-Aristotelian philosophies of nature, giving Aristotle a pivotal role, preparing the way for an academic career in which ancient philosophies of nature and Aristotle would be a central focus. See, for example, McCarthy 1990, 1992, 1999; Depew 1982, 1992.

Here value is perpetuated and reproduced through the movement, especially the returning, of money and commodities. People are no longer the agents. Commodities, as values, are able to move themselves. This is obviously absurd.

Human labour plays a role, but only as a subordinated part of the activity of capital, which Marx describes with the word "entelechy," the derivation of a word coined by Aristotle, *entelecheia*, which Sachs translates as "being-at-work-staying-itself," (Sachs: 1995: 245), a principle of activity, of doing what must be done in order for something to continue as it is:

> We have seen that money is transformed into capital, i.e. a given exchange-value is converted into self-valorising exchange-value … However, it is not this … exchange between money and labour capacity, or the mere purchase of the latter, which converts money into capital. This purchase incorporates into capital the use of the labour capacity for a certain time, or, in other words, it makes a definite quantity of living labour one of the modes of existence of capital itself, its entelechy, so to speak. (MECW 34: 129–130)

In his discussion of the general formula of capital, Marx emphasizes that value is the "active factor," expanding as it continuously changes form, linking it to commodity fetishism as an "occult quality":

> both the money and the commodity represent only different modes of existence of value itself, the money its general mode, and the commodity its particular, or, so to say, disguised mode. It is constantly changing from one form to the other without thereby becoming lost, and thus assumes an automatically active character. If now we take in turn each of the two different forms which self-expanding value successively assumes in the course of its life, we then arrive at these two propositions: Capital is money: Capital is commodities. In truth, however, value is here the active factor in a process, in which, while constantly assuming the form in turn of money and commodities, it at the same time changes in magnitude, differentiates itself by throwing off surplus value from itself; the original value, in other words, expands spontaneously. For the movement, in the course of which it adds surplus value, is its own movement, its expansion, therefore, is automatic expansion. Because it is value, it has acquired the occult quality of being able to add value to itself. It brings forth living offspring, or, at the least, lays golden eggs. (MECW 35: 164–165)[14]

---

[14] Cf. "If production be capitalistic in form, so, too, will be reproduction. Just as in the former the labour process figures but as a means towards the self-expansion of capital, so in the latter it figures but as a means of reproducing as capital – *i.e.*, as self-expanding value – the value advanced" (MECW 35: 566).

The word 'automatic' here must be taken to mean self-moving, again emphasizing the dynamic element.

Marx's description of value's quality of being able to expand itself as "occult" points to its absurdity, the same absurdity, self-moving value, expressed in his use of the term "fetishism." Marx ties self-movement as automatic self-expansion even more strongly to fetishism in his description of interest bearing capital, value preserving itself and generating additional value without the mediation of production and circulation, as the "perfect fetish" and "the consummate automatic fetish" (MECW 32: 451); "the automatic fetish, self-expanding value, money generating money ... consummated in the relation of a thing, of money, to itself" (MECW 37: 389). In this case, the production process has been shoved into the background and finance appears as simply self-expanding, money generating more money.

Capital mimics the activity of a natural being, generating the conditions for its own production and reproduction. The idea of value as the active, moving element of the economic system is part of classical political economy. We find it in the *Wealth of Nations* when Smith writes of the return of wages advanced: "Though the manufacturer has his wages advanced to him by his master, he, in reality, costs him no expence, the value of those wages being generally restored, together with a profit, in the improved value of the subject upon which his labour is bestowed" (WN II.iii.1). Invested value is "restored" or returned with profit, but not by anyone in particular, evidently moving by itself.

However, the idea that commodities are self-moving is bizarre. Inanimate material objects cannot have inner principles of motion, but in a system of capitalist commodity production, they do.

6. Conclusion

Considerations of value have enormous power to shape human decision-making, because reflection on the value of things is essential for survival in a system of commodity production in which virtually everyone must sell something with value in order to purchase their subsistence, actions guided by judgements of value with respect to those things sold and purchased. In this way, value serves as the central organizing principle of a society based on commodity production, dominating the lives of those who live in such societies.

This attribution of value to things is what Marx described as commodity fetishism. Marx's use of the word *fetishism* mocks the Enlightenment pretensions of European society, asserting an equivalence between the behaviour of preliterate peoples and the behaviour of individuals living under capitalist conditions. The behaviour is not mistaken, not in the sense that has been or could be shown to be scientifically false. It is behaviour that is considered to be anterior to scientific consideration, excluded not through observation and evidence but by assumptions of rationality.

Marx gives an account of capitalist commodity production that is in some ways very similar to Smith's. Both describe a system of independent but social beings with inner principles of activity, leading them to maintain and reproduce themselves and their species. In Marx's account, however, the independent beings are not human beings but commodities and their inner principle, value, is oriented toward the survival and reproduction of capital, not the wellbeing of people. The survival and reproduction of human beings, insofar as it occurs, becomes an incidental by-product of the self-sustaining movement of capital.

But capital, or self-moving value, is commodities and money, that is, inanimate things. The idea that commodities, inanimate products of human labour, have an inner principle of self-moving activity, is self-evidently absurd. As artificial intelligence and robotics advance the idea of self-moving things becomes more plausible, but this was not relevant for Marx's analysis of capitalism or classical political economy. Commodities, insofar as they are material objects, neither plant nor animal, do not have internal principles of motion. A society that organizes production around the idea that things can move themselves engages in the same kind of non-rational behaviour that fetishists engage in.

As severe as this may be as a criticism of capitalist reality, it is no less significant as a criticism of classical political economy. If people organizing their lives around value is absurd, political economists participate in this as much as anyone else, but they are also responsible for formulating the social practice in abstract theoretical terms as if it were not absurd, equivalent to the intellectuals of preliterate societies, the guardians of irrationality, those whom Condorcet called the "quacks and sorcerers" of "the least civilized tribes of savages" (1796: 30).

Acknowledgments

The author is grateful for comments from participants in the Marx 1818–2018 conference in Lyon in September 2017, especially Riccardo Bellofiore, Jacob Abolafia, Gilbert Faccarello and Denis Melnik, and for the comments of two anonymous referees.

Disclosure statement

No potential conflict of interest was reported by the author.

References

Andrews, David. 2002. "Commodity Fetishism as a Form of Life." In *Wittgenstein and Marxism*, edited by G. Kitching and N. Pleasants, 78–94. London: Routledge.

Andrews, David. 2014. "Adam Smith's Natural Prices, the Gravitation Metaphor, and the Purposes of Nature." *Economic Thought* 3(1): 42–55.

Andrews, David. 2015. "Natural Price and the Long Run: Alfred Marshall's Misreading of Adam Smith." *Cambridge Journal of Economics* 39(1): 265–79.

Arthur, Christopher J. 2002. *The New Dialectic and Marx's Capital*. Leiden: Brill.

Bellofiore, Riccardo. 2014. "Lost in Translation: Once again on the Marx-Hegel Connection." In *Marx's Capital and Hegel's Logic: A Reexamination*, edited by Fred Moseley and Tony Smith, 164–188. Chicago: Haymarket Books.

de Brosses, Charles. [1760] 2017. "On the Worship of Fetish Gods; or, a Parallel of the Ancient Religion of Egypt with the Present Religion of Nigritia." In *The Returns of Fetishism: Charles de Brosses and the Afterlives of an Idea*, edited by Rosalind C. Morris and Daniel H. Leonard, 44–132. Chicago: University of Chicago Press, 2017.

Cohen, Gerald A. 1978. *Karl Marx's Theory of History: A Defence*. Princeton: Princeton University Press.

Condorcet, Jean-Antoine-Nicolas de Caritat, marquis de. 1796. "Outlines of an Historical View of the Progress of the Human Mind, being a Posthumous Work of the late M. de Condorcet." Philadelphia: M. Carey. Accessed June 20 2018. http://oll.libertyfund.org/titles/condorcet-outlines-of-an-historical-view-of-the-progress-of-the-human-mind.

Depew, David J. 1992. "The Polis Transfigured: Aristotle's Politics and Marx's Critique of Hegel's Philosophy of Right." In *Marx and Aristotle: Nineteenth-Century German Social Theory and Classical Antiquity*, edited by George E. McCarthy, 37–73. Savage, Md.: Rowman & Littlefield.

Depew, David J. 1982. "Aristotle's De Anima and Marx's Theory of Man." *The Graduate Faculty Philosophy Journal*. 8(1–2): 133–187.

Elster, Jon. 1986. *An Introduction to Karl Marx*. New York: Cambridge University Press.

Ehrbar, Hans. 2010. "Glossary to Marx's Capital and other Economic Writings." Accessed June 20 2018. http://content.csbs.utah.edu/~ehrbar/glossary.pdf

Fine. Ben and Alfredo Saad-Filho. 2016. *Marx's Capital*. Sixth ed. London: Pluto.

Foley, Duncan. 1986. *Understanding Capital*. Cambridge: Harvard University Press.

Harvey, David. 2010. *A Companion to Marx's Capital*. London: Verso.

Howard, Michael C. and John E. King. 1989 *A History of Marxian Economics*, Volume I, 1883–1929. Princeton: Princeton University Press.

Howard, Michael C. and John E. King. 1992 *A History of Marxian Economics*, Volume II, 1929–1990. Princeton: Princeton University Press.

Lewis, Haskel and Jacob Morris. 1977. "Marx's Concept of Fetishism." *Science and Society* XLI (2): 172–190.

Marx, Karl and Friedrich Engels. 1975. *Marx Engels Collected Works*. London: Lawrence and Wishart.

Marx, Karl. 1976. *Capital: A Critique of Political Economy*. Translated by Ben Fowkes, Harmondsworth, Eng.: Penguin.

McCarthy, George E. 1999. "Karl Marx and Classical Antiquity: A Bibliographic Introduction." *Helios* 26 (2): 165.

McCarthy, George E. 1992. *Marx and Aristotle: Nineteenth-Century German Social Theory and Classical Antiquity*. Savage, Md.: Rowman & Littlefield.

McCarthy, George E. 1990. *Marx and the Ancients: Classical Ethics, Social Justice, and Nineteenth-Century Political Economy*. Savage, Md.: Rowman & Littlefield.

Meikle, Scott. 1985. *Essentialism in the Thought of Karl Marx*. La Salle, Ill: Open Court.

Rubin, Isaak I. 1972. *Essays on Marx's Theory of Value*. Translated by Miloš Samardžija's and Fredy Perlman. Detroit: Black and Red.

Sachs, Joe. 1995. "A Note on Aristotle's Central Vocabulary" and "Glossary." In *Aristotle's Physics: A Guided Study*. New Brunswick: Rutgers University Press.

Smith, Adam. [1776] 1976. *An Inquiry into the Nature and Causes of the Wealth of Nations*. Oxford, Oxford UP. (WN)

Smith, Adam. [1759] 1976. *The Theory of Moral Sentiments*. Oxford: Oxford UP. (TMS).

Smith, Adam. 1978. "Early Draft of the Wealth of Nations (ED)." In *Lectures on Jurisprudence*, edited by Ronald L. Meek, David D. Raphael and Peter Stein, 562–581. Oxford: Oxford UP.

Concepts in examining the legacy of Karl Marx

Regina Roth

ABSTRACT

The editorial work on the Marx-Engels-Gesamtausgabe (MEGA) indicates that there is no finished masterpiece of *Capital*, and it reveals that the earlier economic manuscripts are far from being only "preparatory studies" culminating in *Capital*. To learn more about Marx' process of research, it is useful to consult all his manuscripts, letters and notebooks. The critical edition focusses on the connections between different passages in all of them; modern technologies offer new possibilities to visualize these connections. This article will present a survey on material presented by MEGA in print and online, and highlight some features and results of MEGAdigital.

1. Introduction

In portraying Karl Marx in his *Economic Theory in Retrospect,* Mark Blaug (1997, 215) affirms that "Marx the economist is alive and relevant today". Blaug identifies two handicaps for a thorough examination of this author: firstly, separating him from neo-Marxian or Leninised reformulations, and secondly, doing him justice, as Marx "created a system that embraced all the social sciences", from economics to philosophy, sociology, and history. Nevertheless, Blaug appears to feel "inspired by Marx's heroic attempt to project a systematic general account of the 'laws of motion' of capitalism". A solid basis for an examination of Marx' manifold thought is offered by the comprehensive edition of his works and writings, the Marx-Engels-Gesamtausgabe, or MEGA.

MEGA presents the complete legacy of Marx and Engels in four sections, dedicated to different sorts of texts: works, articles and drafts in Sections I and II with Section II focussing on Marx' magnum opus

Capital –, the letters Marx and Engels wrote and received from their many correspondents all over Europe and America in Section III, and Marx' and Engels' excerpts, notes and marginalia in Section IV. Important in terms of economics are Marx' manuscripts devoted to *Capital* and its preparatory studies, all of which are now available in the second section of MEGA, completed in 2012. One of the main results of our editorial labour shows that Marx left an unfinished work in progress and a variety of research methods. There are different approaches as well as new beginnings for his drafts of *Capital* which are unfinished, at least in Book 2 and 3, and there are also extensive studies on all sorts of topics, mostly documented in the fourth section of MEGA. All in all, Marx' work resulted in a massive interdisciplinary project that is rarely found elsewhere.[1] One reason for the unfinished and diversified state of Marx' research is his way of balancing arguments, identifying new material and approaches, and the manner in which he critically examines his own concepts to find the adequate model for them. By looking closer at MEGA, we can better understand this aspect of Marx' working process.

This paper will address the status of the editorial work and the new concept of *MEGAdigital,* firstly regarding manuscripts and printed versions of *Capital* in the context of Marx' writing, then turning to the correspondence of Marx and Engels with their many correspondents, followed by information on the excerpts and notes of Marx which have survived in many notebooks. The main section will offer some examples, highlighting results of the editing process in MEGA, and exposing a variety of connections between these different parts of Marx' legacy to shed light on the way Marx worked and illuminate the extent to which he did not complete his economic project. Some of them are already realised in the digital edition and some are presented in printed form but clearly demonstrate their potential for a – future – digitised presentation. Letters from the year 1866, Marx' discussion of rent and agricultural production in excerpts and manuscripts in the 1850s and 1860s, as well as Marx' last manuscripts for *Capital* from the 1870s in the edition of Engels (Marx's ms dates from the 1870s, not Engels' edition), will be presented in greater detail, followed by some concluding remarks.

---

[1] According to one handbook on Marx, his works and writings have had effects not only on economics, sociology, politics and history, but also on 10 other disciplines (Quante and Schweikard 2016, 367–423).

2. MEGA in print and online: status of our editorial work

Every printed MEGA-volume consists of two books: the first present-ing all texts from Marx and/or Engels, the second offering extensive commentaries on these texts. Every volume has an introduction (*"Einführung"*) which gives a survey on the structure and contents of the volume,[2] and an essay on *"Entstehung und Überlieferung"* for each of our authors' texts which provides basic information on the circum-stances accompanying the emergence of those texts, including proof of authorship and authentification of data to elucidate the contexts of their origin.[3]

With regards to Marx work on economics, his balancing of argu-ments can best be observed in the 12 volumes in the second section of MEGA (Marx [1863–1894] MEGA^2 II/4 to II/15), which since 2012, has provided all manuscript materials that Marx left behind for his economic project on *Capital*, complemented by all printed versions of this work (Hubmann and Roth [2014] for a survey on these texts). *Firstly*, there are Marx' drafts for *Capital*; most of them published for the first time in MEGA, written down between 1863 and 1881. The most important drafts scribed by Marx for Book 2 of *Capital* (on the circulation process) are to be found in MEGA-volumes II/4.3 and II/11; those for Book 3 (on the capitalist produc-tion process as a whole) in MEGA-volumes II/4.2, II/4.3, and II/14.[4] *Secondly*, we offer Marx' editions of *Capital*; he provided several versions of Volume and Book 1 (in 1867 and 1872, in French in 1872–1875) in addition to lists for a third edition and an American edition.[5] *Thirdly*, we present Engels' editions of *Capital*, which he pre-pared from 1883 up to 1894; comprising the third and fourth edition

---

[2] The introductions of the MEGA-volumes, which have appeared since 1998 are available at http://mega.bbaw.de/, Accessed 31 May 2018. The page on "Struktur" leads to the four sections of MEGA; in every section the corresponding volumes are listed with their bibliographical data and a link to their introductions; for instance, you may look at the introduction of MEGA-volumes II/4.3, II/11, II/12, II/13, II/14, and II/15.

[3] Only recently, in the fourth section, both texts and commentary are presented in one volume (MEGA^2 IV/5, IV/14). Yet, the ordering – first all texts, followed by all commentaries, starting with the introduction – is retained.

[4] The few manuscripts for Book 1 and 2, edited in Marx [1864] MEGA^2 II/4.1 (on "The Results of the Immediate Production Process", a text intended as a transition from Book 1 to Book 2; a first draft for Book 2), had been published in earlier versions. All other drafts are new texts, presented in MEGA for the first time. Meanwhile, Marx' manuscript for Book 3 (MEGA^2 II/ 4.2) has been translated into English (Marx [1864/65] 2016); an English translation of the general commentary on Marx' Manuscript of 1864/65 has been published in Roth and Moseley (2004).

[5] They are to be found in: MEGA^2 II/5 (German edition), II/6 (2nd rev. German edition), II/7 (French edition), II/8, 5–36 (Modifications for the 3rd German and an American edition).

as well as an English edition of Volume and Book 1, and an arranged edition of Book 2 and 3, compiled from Marx' legacy.[6]

These volumes make up the heart of the second section of the comprehensive edition of MEGA. To judge Marx' work on economic issues as a whole, however, one must also take into account numerous additional materials: namely, the voluminous 1861–1863 Manuscript,[7] and his first economic manuscript summarised as "Political Economy. Criticism of", known under its editorial title, *Grundrisse* (1857/58).[8] (For a survey on MEGA-texts available in English in MECW see Appendix.) But also his first plans and writings in the 1840s – his first contract with a publisher dates from February 1845 – have to be taken into account. Most important are his so-called *Economic-Philosophical Manuscripts*, written from the end of May/June to August 1844 (MEGA^2 I/2), together with many excerpts (MEGA^2 IV/2) that are interwoven with the manuscripts.[9] The same applies to his intensive studies and several newspaper articles from the 1850s, as well as his work and studies after 1867, in conjunction but separate from *Capital*.[10]

From his later writings, the intense studies on the history of economics in the seventeenth and eighteenth century and some responses on the works of Eugen Dühring in spring 1877 (MEGA^2 I/27, 131–216), as well as his correspondence with the Russian revolutionary, Vera Zasulich, in March 1881 (Marx [1875–1883] MEGA^2 I/25, 217–242) might be worth mentioning here. In general, for a study of Marx' economic views, it might be useful to look at all sorts of texts which have been written in the same period as his economic treaties in volumes of other sections of MEGA.[11]

---

[6] They are to be found in: MEGA^2 II/8 (3rd German edition), II/9 (English edition), II/10 (4th German edition), II/12 and II/13 (Book 2), II/15 (Book 3).

[7] Marx [1861–1863] MEGA^2 II/3; also to be found in English in MECW, vol. 30–34.

[8] MEGA^2 II/1. After writing *Grundrisse*, Marx published his first text in 1859 (*Contribution to a Critique of Political Economy. Issue 1*; MEGA^2 II/2).

[9] See Rojahn, "Die Marxschen Manuskripte aus dem Jahre 1844 in der neuen Marx-Engels-Gesamtausgabe (MEGA)". For Marx's contract with Carl Wilhelm Leske, see MEGA^2 III/1, 851–852. Marx's polemic against Joseph Proudhon's much discussed views on political economy, *La Misère de la Philosophie*, written in 1847, is currently prepared for publication in MEGA^2 I/6.

[10] For a survey on these texts, see Heinrich (2016). For the articles, especially in the 1850s, see also Hecker, Sperl, and Vollgraf (2006). Up to now, MEGA^2 I/10 to I/14 have been published, which contain several articles on economic and social developments; MEGA^2 I/16, including several articles on economic crises and the Bank of France, is scheduled to be published this year.

[11] For instance, the discussion 1867/68 in the International Working Men's Association on "Effects of Machinery" (Marx [1867–1871] MEGA^2 I/21, 535, 538–539, 577, 581, 585, 1835) or the record of a discussion Marx had with the trade unionist J.H.W. Hamann in Hannover in 1869 (906–907, 2141–2144).

Perhaps, a note on the structure of MEGA is appropriate here. The overall criterion for the ordering of texts in MEGA is chronology, as far as the dates when texts were written can be identified. The aim is to carve out and document the formulation of ideas and thought as a process, presenting the influences of the respective contexts of this formulation. However, there are some exceptions to this rule, and one of them is the existence of the second section of MEGA. It may be of interest to have a closer look at its origin which is traceable back to the first edition of texts from Marx and Engels in Moscow in the late 1920s and early 1930s.

David Rjazanov and his team at the Marx-Engels-Institute decided to separate the materials belonging to Marx' economic main work, *Capital*, in a special section, to prevent them from disappearing in the abundance of Marx' texts (Roth [2013, 58, 60] for evidence). Apart from several editions of the three volumes, having appeared from 1867 to 1894, all manuscripts for them should be included in this section, but also Marx' earlier economic texts from 1857/58 onwards, considered as preparatory studies. The order was chronological up to the publication of the first book and volume of *Capital* in 1867 (that is MEGA-volume II/1 up to II/5)[12], implying all materials were written before September 1867; next, the materials should be presented according to their contents and according to sequence of the three books – suggesting they were all written after 1867 – starting with all texts considering Book 1 of *Capital* (the different editions in Marx [1872 up to 1890] MEGA[2] II/6 up to II/10), then Book 2 of *Capital* (Marx' manuscripts in II/11, Engels' manuscripts while editing Book 2 in II/12, and the printed version of Book 2, edited by Engels, in II/13),[13] and lastly, Marx' and Engels' manuscripts belonging to Book 3 (in II/14), followed by the printed version of Book 3 (in II/15).

---

[12] The strict chronological order was also disrupted in MEGA-volume II/4 in favour of a presentation of material according to the sequence of the three books: the manuscript for Book 3, edited in MEGA[2] II/4.2, was started, as Marx himself noted, before writing the one for Book 2, edited in MEGA[2] II/4.1 (Marx [1864/65] MEGA[2] II/4.2, 225, 919–920). The texts collected in two folders and presented in MEGA[2] II/4.3 also proved to be written only after the publication of Book and Volume 1 of *Capital* (Marx [1863–1868] MEGA[2] II/4.3, 429–437).

[13] For Book 2, two of Engels' versions have emerged: firstly, the editorial manuscript (II/12) where you can trace the composition of the text out of several different Marx' manuscripts, secondly, the printed version which appeared in 1885 (II/13). In the commentary to the editorial manuscript in II/12 you will find a list documenting the provenance of every passage in the corresponding manuscripts. In *MEGAdigital*, a cumulated subject index correlates many passages in Marx' manuscripts to the corresponding ones in the Engels' editorial

Although it is a commonly used method to collect several versions of an author's comprehensive work, in the case of MEGA, difficult presuppositions were identified, proving to be false, through work on the historical-critical edition itself. Firstly, Marx' *Capital* was not a finished work, but a long-lasting project, revealing a research process that highlighted discontinuities and open questions in addition to improvements; secondly, it is no longer adequate to classify the manuscripts written before 1863 as preliminary studies for *Capital*.[14]

In 2008, we started our digital project, *MEGAdigital*, presenting central texts from the second section of the MEGA (http://megadigital.bbaw.de/, button *Kapital*). Unlike any previous edition of *Capital*, this section, as already mentioned, includes all versions and drafts for the three Books or Volumes of *Capital* written by Marx and partly published by Engels. In their editorial commentary, the volumes of Section II provide detailed documentation of the relations and connections between these various versions; it is an essential instrument for understanding the development of Marx' ideas and thoughts in the last two decades of his life. The purpose of *MEGAdigital* is to create a visual platform so that these relations and connections can be followed up by the reader. Thus, all present versions of texts, manuscript or printed, can be easily compared with each other (the reader can open a separate window for every text and move it on the screen just as he or she needs it – using the screen as a virtual desktop). Moreover, the intertextual linkage between individual manuscripts and print versions is made available for research either through accumulated registers or through full-text retrieval. Line and page enumeration of the edited texts are presented identically with the printed MEGA² volumes, which facilitates citation.

At present, the following texts are available on our *MEGAdigital* platform:

- *Capital* Vol. 1, first edition from 1867 and fourth edition (by Engels) from 1890;

---

manuscript and in his printed version, and vice versa (http://telota.bbaw.de/mega/ Accessed 31 May 2018).

[14] When MEGA was transferred to the Berlin-Brandenburg Academy of Sciences at the beginning of the 1990s, the editorial work on the second section was already completed to a large extent so that there was little scope left to change this editorial decision.

- *Capital* Vol. 2, manuscripts from 1864 to 1885, together with Engels' printed version from 1885;
- *Capital* Vol. 3, edited by Engels in 1894;
- *Grundrisse* from 1857/58.

We are planning to add the one existing comprehensive draft for Book 3, written by Marx in 1864/65, so that the essential manuscripts Marx had written for *Capital* will be available as an alternative to the printed versions prepared by Engels.

Since the beginning of 2016, we have largely restructured and extended MEGA online presence (http://megadigital.bbaw.de/), and have moved beyond just displaying printed books in digital form. Initially, we are going to include the third section of MEGA: the *correspondence* between Marx, Engels, and their many correspondents. Thirteen MEGA-volumes covering the correspondence from 1837 up to 1865 have already been published in printed volumes.

You can now find online the correspondence between Marx, Engels, and third persons from January 1 to December 31, 1866, comprising firstly, the letters they have written and received, and secondly, the commentary to these letters, developed using all the instruments of historical-critical editing. There are notes explaining the necessary context for understanding the contents of the letters and notes indicating connections to other letters, writings, excerpts, and so on, as well as information regarding the witnesses of the letters, the correspondents, dates, previous editions, etc. If you are interested, you can also view the variety of revisions which Engels, and more often, Marx, used by consulting the so-called "historical-critical text" (*KritischerText*) of the letter. Otherwise, a "reading text" (*Lesetext*) is presented.

The main advantages of the digital edition of the correspondence are: free access via the Internet all over the world and different gateways to the letters which means they may be ordered chronologically, or assorted by individual correspondents, or presented via central topics present in the letters. A full-text retrieval for passages in texts and commentary is also at your disposal as well as indexing which aids the user in searching for persons, firms, works and writings. We will soon offer indexes for periodicals as well as locations.

The same benefits can be gained for the digital edition of the *excerpts and notes*, which make up the fourth section of MEGA.

Fourteen volumes, mostly from the early years up to the beginning of the 1850s, have already been published as books, together with one volume on the library of Marx and Engels.[15] However, many of the approximately 220 notebooks still have to be edited. Thus, for our next step, we will include excerpts and notes in our digital presentation. Many notebooks were filled in chronologically, often in a short period of time, with different excerpts for special subjects, for instance, the notebooks dedicated to "*Physiology*", or the so-called "*Beihefte*" A to H. In many other cases, Marx and Engels used their notebooks in different periods of time to jot down information on a range of subjects.

The digital edition offers an opportunity unavailable in the printed edition: the reader can decide if he or she wants to see the excerpts in a variety of modes such as the order in which they appear in the notebook, chronological or subject order, or order of source from which the excerpts were drawn.

As soon as we have integrated these different sections into our digital MEGA, we will start to digitize MEGA-volumes, presenting works, drafts and articles from the first section of MEGA. They will give us particular challenges because these volumes will also be offered in a printed version. The first result of digital work on the first section may already be mentioned here. The "*Neue Rheinische Zeitung*", founded and edited by Marx and Engels as an "Organ of democracy" during the Revolution 1848/49, has been digitized during the editorial work on the MEGA-volumes I/7, I/8 and I/9. At present, the articles from this newspaper may be read and searched, using full-text retrieval, at http://www.deutschestextarchiv.de/nrhz/.[16]

3. New concept of *MEGAdigital*: connections realised as hyperlinks

One of the major tasks of the critical edition is to provide the connections between any work, writing, or draft collected from our authors and, on the one hand, the sources they used, directly or indirectly, and, on the other hand, the corresponding passages in other parts of their legacy. These connections to corresponding passages will play a

---

[15] MEGA² IV/1-9, IV/12, IV/14. Moreover, one volume covers Marx' chemical studies, another his geological studies (MEGA² IV/31 and IV/26). The library of Marx and Engels is documented in Bibliotheken 1999 MEGA² IV/32.

[16] Except the articles from Marx or Engels, due to the copyright of our publisher. Their articles from February to October 1848 have already appeared in MEGA² I/7 in 2016.

special role in *MEGAdigital* because the supply of hyperlinks will offer
an essential addendum for the readers of the digital edition. This will
allow immediate identification of all the connections between different
texts as soon as they are available in the digital presentation, thus giving the reader the opportunity to actively study Marx' "work in progress". This feature was already offered in *MEGAdigital* (we could call
it 1.0) with the cumulative index for the manuscripts and the printed
version of Book 2 of *Capital*. For the many terms collected in this
index, all corresponding passages in Marx' manuscripts and Engels'
printed versions, and vice versa are displayed. In the actual digital
presentation, *MEGAdigital* (we could call it 2.0), additional possibilities will be implemented. Some examples may illustrate the utility of
these new possibilities, at the same time shedding light on the way
Marx worked, or, in some cases, highlighting the extent to which he
did not realise his economic project.

3.1 Letters and works

In 1866, Marx was active in different fields, as is documented in the
index of topics already available in the letters from this year. He was
deeply involved in the politics of the *International Working Men's
Association*, discussing its statutes at its first conference in Geneva,
September 1866, after its initiation in London in 1864. The correspondence of Marx, Engels, and third persons is an important source
for studying the politics of the *International*.[17] Moreover, the letters
reflect the political situation in Europe, especially since the German
War in 1866 (June to August) and the Constitutional Conflict in
Prussia (since 1862) as well as Marx' growing interest in the natural
sciences. Furthermore, he wrote the final version of Book 1 of *Capital*
that eventually appeared in autumn 1867. This work may be illustrated by the following example.

Opening the site of *MEGAdigital* (http://megadigital.bbaw.de), you
can choose *"Register"* and select the topics (*"Themen"*); there, when
opting for *"'Das Kapital' (Arbeit an Manuskripten, Veröffentlichung)"*,
you will find passages in the letters from 1866, where Marx comments
on the manuscript for Book 1 of *Capital*. For example, in his letter of
February 10, 1866, Marx tells Engels, that he had to stop working on

---

[17] Einführung. In: MEGA² I/21. S. 1139–1219. (https://edoc.bbaw.de/files/13/i21_einfuehrung.pdf
Accessed 31 May 2018).

theoretical parts of his book, because: "My brain was not up to that". He expanded the chapter on the "Working Day", which he considered to be a complement to Engels' *Condition of the Working Class in England* from 1845. In our note to this passage, you find a link connecting to the beginning of the chapter Marx refers to. Later in this letter, Marx asks Engels to write to John Watts because he needs Watts' latest book dealing with machinery. In our note you find a link taking you to the passage in Book 1, where Marx quotes Watts.

In the future, every year of correspondence will be presented in *MEGAdigital* in this way, so that anyone can discover these connections between different parts and texts of MEGA in the form of hyperlinks. In particular, this will give background information on the texts that Marx and Engels wrote, the excerpts they created and the books they read.

3.2 Excerpts and manuscripts

MEGA is a unique provider of existing connections between manuscripts and excerpts, documenting Marx' method of operation and influences of other works and authors on his research. We thereby use a method which Marx himself preferred, as he reflected in his encounter with Eugen Dühring in 1877. Marx ([1876–1877] MEGA^2 I/27, 155) stated that he "took the liberty" of looking for the sources of political economists when analysing their ideas and thoughts, whereas, according to Marx, Eugen Dühring asserted that an author would be offended by such a step, because this would shed doubt on his singularity. It is widely known that Marx filled in many notebooks with excerpts from numerous works and authors, from the beginning of his work in the 1840s up to his last years in the 1880s. The MEGA edition of the manuscripts and excerpts has shown a strong connection between both parts of Marx' legacy; in many cases, we might even call it an interaction between both these parts. In the digital edition, which is now prepared for the first excerpts, we shall offer all connections, identified during the process of editing the texts, via hyperlinks to the texts available online.[18] Two examples will demonstrate the direction of this method.

---

[18] It will possibly take some time to realise these features in the digital edition because the technical instruments we need are still being developed.

The *first example* refers to the excerpts from August 1865 to February 1866 (IISH, Marx-Engels-Collection, B 106) regarding debates on productivity in agriculture and their potential limits and the manuscript dedicated to Book 3 of *Capital* hitherto dated 1864/65 (MEGA² II/4.2), anticipated to be published this year in MEGA² IV/18.[19] In his thesis, Kōhei Saitō (2016), one of the editors of MEGA² IV/18, scrutinised the many connections between excerpts and manuscript with regard to these debates on productivity in agriculture.[20] In the manuscript for Book 3, written in the mid-1860s, Marx adopted the idea of diminishing returns in his considerations and examined them in great detail in his chapter on "Differential Rent", although without excluding "increasing productive power of successive capital investments" (Marx [1864/65] MEGA² II/4.2, 830; for diminishing returns see f.i. 789, 790–791, 818, and 832). At the end of his chapter on ground rent, he explicitly stated that on declining productivity of the soil "Liebig should be consulted" (833; Saitō 2016, 172).

In the 7th edition of his *Agricultural Chemistry*, Justus von Liebig (1862, vol. 1) contends that an increase in the productivity of the soil, even when using chemical fertiliser, could only provide a short-term increase of crop yields; because, in the long run, the fertilisers were not able to replace all the mineral substances necessary for the optimal nourishment of the plants; therefore a regular cultivation of the fields would eventually exhaust them. Liebig coined the term "*Raubbau*" (exhaustive cultivation or robbery economy) to mark this method. Thus, the spectre of Malthusian over-population rose, now with a scientific argument in the background (106, 154–155; Saitō 2016, 172, 224). Marx read this version of Liebig's theory in 1865/66, making meticulous excerpts of passages, explaining the reasons for diminishing returns (IISH, Marx-Engels-Collection, B 106, 30–36, 58–59; Saitō 2016, 225–226). Henceforth, Marx defends the existence of a law of diminishing agricultural returns and warns his readers about the destructive potentials of capitalist agriculture, identifying

---

[19] MEGA-volume IV/18 will appear first in print, then we shall prepare it for the digital edition. As the manuscript from 1864/65 for Book 3 (Marx [1864/65] MEGA² II/4.2) will soon be available online (the printed version edited by Engels (Marx [1894] MEGA² II/15) is already available), it will then be possible to realise the many connections between both parts of Marx' legacy as hyperlinks.

[20] Moreover, work on the edition of the excerpts has gathered evidence to suggest that Marx did not finish the work on his manuscript for Book 3 in December 1865 (as he reported to Engels on February 13, 1866), but that he was still working on it in January, and possibly February 1866.

large landed property as a leading factor in this process (Marx [1864/65] MEGA² II/4.2, 752–753). Moreover, Marx warns about the same threat caused by the use of technology in manufacture. Later, in Vol. 1 of *Capital*, he writes: "Capitalist production, therefore, develops technology, and the combining together of various processes into a social whole, only by sapping the original sources of all wealth — the soil and the labourer" (Marx [1867] MEGA² II/5, 410, 413).[21]

This argument contrasts with earlier views of Marx. From the 1840s onwards, he was concerned with the question regarding the potential of improvements in agriculture. In *Manifesto of the Communist Party*, he and Engels praised the achievements of science and technology, in agriculture as well as in industry, mentioning explicitly the application of chemistry to agriculture; they were clearly optimistic about future developments and potentials of science and technology (MECW, vol. 6, 489).[22] Already in 1844, in his *Outlines of a Critique of Political Economy*, Engels reckoned, that the "productivity of the soil can be increased *ad infinitum* by the application of capital, labour and science". As an example, he mentioned the remarkable increase of population and the corresponding agricultural product in Great Britain since the beginning of the nineteenth century, referring to Chapters 1 and 2 from Archibald Alison's *The Principles of Population* from 1840 (MECW, vol. 3, 436). In 1845, Marx took notes particularly from these two chapters during his and Engels' studies in Manchester (Marx [1845–1850] MEGA² IV/5, 272–275, 365).[23]

In the 1850s, after having emigrated to London, Marx argued against the concept of diminishing returns in agricultural production by suggesting the improvement of soil, in particular, by chemical fertiliser. Marx' argument was based on his reading of Justus von Liebig, James Johnston, and others, documented in his *"Londoner Hefte"* from 1851. Up to the late 1850s, Liebig always argued against diminishing returns and advocated the use of chemical fertilisers to assure proportional or even increasing returns (Marx [1851a and b] MEGA²

---

[21] See Vollgraf (2016, 110–111), indicating further passages in *Capital* where Marx talks of dangers threatening the vitality of whole nations (Marx [1867] MEGA² II/5, 184–185, 208, 211, 335).

[22] See also Saitō (2016, 294–295), and, for an extensive examination of excerpts and manuscripts regarding rent, Takenaga. "Marx on rent: new insights from the New MEGA" (in this issue).

[23] At latest in Summer 1844, Engels had also taken notes from Alison's work but only a fragment has survived which does not cover these passages (MEGA² IV/2, 583–891, 813–814).

IV/8 and IV/9). It might be noteworthy that in his letter to Engels on 7 January 1851, Marx argued against the proposition of diminishing returns and of an expansion to ever less fertile land, because this proposition was "everywhere refuted by history". His evidence was based on an article in *The Economist* from 14 December 1850, which he had read shortly before (Marx [1849–1851] MEGA² IV/7, 358–360).[24] Besides, it should be taken into account that in this early discussion it had already become apparent that Marx and Ricardo were developing differing concepts as to the origin of rent (Gehrke 2011; Saitō 2016, 216). At the beginning of the 1860s, in his 1861–1863 Manuscript, Marx still favoured proportional, if not, increasing returns, based on findings in chemistry and the application of the capitalistic mode of production to agriculture (Marx [1861–1863] MEGA² II/3, 912a, 749, 762; Saitō 2016, 169–170).

In fact, we do not know how Marx would have arranged his section on ground rent in Book 3 of *Capital* after his reading of Liebig. We do know, after editing the excerpts from 1865/66, that Marx made more extensive use of them in this manuscript for Book 3, without noting all references in detail.[25] After the publication of Vol. 1 of *Capital*, he still worked on this subject, without producing another comprehensive draft on it. What has emerged is a collection of passages on "Differential Rent". It was written possibly in the first half of 1868, definitely after the publication of Vol. 1 of *Capital*, and dealt with the forms, causes, and effects of differential rent in agriculture as treated by various authors. Most of the references were drawn from the excerpts of 1865/66, but Marx also turned to the 1861–1863 Manuscript and to his excerpts from the 1840s.[26]

Looking at his excerpts, we find that Marx continued his studies on the exhaustion of the soil, or *Raubbau*, its causes and effects. In new excerpts written in 1868, he took particular notice of the debates on Liebig's position. He read several books defending or challenging Liebig's arguments. Perhaps the destructiveness of agriculture was

---

[24] Some weeks later, probably in May 1851, Marx began an intense study of Ricardo's *Principles*, including the chapter "On Rent" (Marx [1851a] MEGA² IV/8, 350–361). In July 1851, he turned to Edward West, in particular to his propositions on the effects of agricultural improvements (Marx [1851b] MEGA² IV/9, 147–152).

[25] See Vollgraf (2011, 87, Fn. 32) denoting numerous references between the manuscript and the excerpts from 1865/66.

[26] Marx [1863–1868] MEGA² II/4.3, 399–400, 903–927. (See also the introduction pp. 843–905 at http://mega.bbaw.de/struktur/abteilung_ii/dateien/mega_ii-43_inhalt-einf.pdf Accessed 31 May 2018.)

based on different assumptions from the ones that Liebig had alleged to; other writers argued against the claim that the exhaustion of the soil was a natural law, valid always and everywhere.[27] Marx referred to a book by Carl Fraas on *Climate and Plant Life* (1847), and to its main thesis that civilization resulted in the devastation of the land cultivated by civilized people — a thesis Fraas illustrated with several historical cases. Marx mentioned his new findings in a letter to Engels (March 25, 1868), and his excerpts highlight interest in the examples Fraas presents for his hypothesis. In particular, Fraas' statements on deforestation appear to have caught Marx' attention.[28]

However, it is difficult to trace the effects of these studies in the manuscripts that Marx dedicated to *Capital* after 1868/69. Saitō (2016, 292–293) suggests drawing a line from these excerpts to a passage in Manuscript II for Book 2, written between 1868 and 1870, where Marx discusses the length of the time it takes for timber to grow as a factor in influencing the turnover of capital.[29] Marx' last short comments on differential rent were recorded in February 1876 in a notebook where he had collected materials on the first *International Working Mens' Association* (around 1871) and studies on Russia, as well as on early history (after May 1876); these commentaries were published by Engels in his edition of Book 3 in 1894 as a supplement to Marx' chapter on differential rent in his main manuscript on Book 3 from 1864/65 (RGASPI, f. 1, op. 1, d. 2940; Marx Engels [1871–1895] MEGA² II/14, 151, 689; Marx [1894] MEGA² II/15, 722–725). In spite of a detailed study of Carl Fraas, there appears to be no more than a faint reverberation of Fraas' theory of alluvion, when Marx states that one meadow was naturally irrigated or covered with layers of silt, the other had to be made so by labour. What we can deduce is that after publishing the first volume of *Capital*, Marx still showed a great deal of interest in the relations between nature,

---

[27] IISH, Marx-Engels-Collection, B 111, 112; Saitō 2016, 294ff.; Vollgraf 2016, 112ff. Vollgraf presents Marx' field of reading, comprising authors such as Carl Fraas, Friedrich A. Lange, Julius Au, Friedrich Kirchhof et al.

[28] IISH, Marx-Engels-Collection, B 112; Marx wrote down his excerpts up to p. 53 of Fraas' work (about 10 pages in Marx' notebook), then he continued to place marginalia into the book itself, which he had acquired (123; Bibliotheken 1999 MEGA² IV/32. Nr. 436; Saitō 2015).

[29] Marx did not mention Fraas but another author, Friedrich Kirchhof (Marx [1868–1881] MEGA² II/11, 203; see also Vollgraf 2016, 114–115). In general, Marx appears to have neglected the distinction between renewable and exhaustible resources, apart from some casual references, f.i. to the exhaustion of forests, coal or other mines as influencing the productivity of labour (Marx [1864/65] MEGA² II/4.2, 334).

science and economics, though the substance of these later studies needs to be investigated in greater depth.[30]

The *second example* turns to the so-called *"Beihefte"*, written most likely between May and June 1863, and to its connection to the 1861–1863 Manuscript, devoted to Marx' critique of political economy. Probably in May 1863, while still working on his manuscript, Marx began to collect new information in separate notebooks which he later called "Beihefte", and still later labelled with letters "A" to "H".[31] To Engels, in a letter from May 29, 1863, he referred to these notebooks as results of reading and making "excerpts from all kinds of earlier literature relating to the part of the political economy I had elaborated". Marx thus produced notes from around 150 works on about 700 pages (Marx [1863–1868] MEGA² II/4.3, 462–463, 902). In addition, two pages have come to our attention which may have been an index allocating Marx' quotes to specific subjects, at least for the first pages of "Beiheft A". They were, as the editor has discovered, interconnected with some additional passages in his voluminous 1861–1863 Manuscript.[32] Eventually, it was disclosed that several of these quotes were already included in the main text, in fact within the pages of the last Notebooks XXI to XXIII of this manuscript. Marx himself either noted a quote in his text or referred to a quote in one of his "Beihefte". Thus, we are now able to observe Marx in his repeated discussions with the views of the authors he read.[33]

An illustration on this point is Marx' engagement with François Quesnay and his *Tableau économique*. Having referred to this

---

[30] See e.g., Marx' chemical and geological studies (MEGA² IV/31 and IV/26), as well as the library of Marx and Engels, documented in Bibliotheken 1999 MEGA² IV/32; Krader 1974 for his ethnological studies; Vollgraf (2016, 112ff.) with additional evidence for the activities of Marx in these fields in the 1870s.

[31] The first of these notebooks. "Beiheft A" also offers about 30 pages containing references to the history of Poland, Russia and Prussia, which was another subject Marx was very interested in throughout this period (RGASPI, f. 1, op. 1, d. 1691). Moreover, Marx had collected several more excerpts on the remaining 200 pages of a notebook he had used for the last entries of his first comprehensive economic manuscript from 1857/58, known today as *Grundrisse* (IISH, Marx-Engels-Collection, B 91a).

[32] Marx [1863–1868] MEGA² II/4.3, 399/400, 902–927. The index and the additions in the manuscript dealt with reasonings for property and interest, especially by John Locke, David Hume and Joseph Massie, identifying them as belonging to a "Pettysche line" (Marx [1861–1863] MEGA² II/3, 2318).

[33] Marx [1861–1863] MEGA² II/3, 2320ff.; for example "S. 13 Beiheft C" (2320.18). For Marx, an intense engagement with other authors, alive or dead, was an essential way to develop his own ideas and concepts, while criticising their thoughts. This may be observed from his very early studies onwards (see f.i. the recently published MEGA-volume I/5, in particular the extensive manuscript on a critique of Max Stirner, dedicated to a project, which has become known under the post festum title *German Ideology*). For Marx' notion of critique see also Heinrich (2016, 71).

economist in the 1840s,[34] Marx turned his full attention to him in his 1861–1863 Manuscript on economics and in the "Beiheft C and D", at least three times: May and June 1862, May 1863, and July 1863. In 1862, he started a separate notebook with a "digression" *("Abschweifung")* on Quesnay, while dealing with Theodor Schmalz and Adam Smith's distinction of productive and unproductive labour. Shortly afterward, Marx decided to include these considerations on Quesnay as Notebook X into his chapter on the "Theories of Surplus Value" (Marx [1861–1863] MEGA^2 II/3. S. 624ff., 2909). In 1863, Marx began another examination on Quesnay's *Tableau* and other writings in *"Beiheft C" and "D"*. He then utilised his studies in Notebook XXII and XXIII of his manuscript, adding many references to his *"Beihefte"*. On 6 July 1863, Marx reported to Engels on his new findings about the reproduction process and asked for Engels' opinion.[35] Attached to this letter, Marx sent the second version of the later so-called reproduction schemes, after having established the first version in Notebook XXII. In both, he distinguished two sections: one to produce food and another to produce constant capital or machinery and raw materials (Marx [1861–1863] MEGA^2 II/3, 2271ff.; Gehrke and Kurz 1995, 63ff., 80ff.).[36] Explicitly, Marx appreciated the physiocrats' important insights into the reproduction process.

3.3 Different manuscripts and printed versions

Presenting connections between manuscripts and printed versions for *Capital* is already established in *MEGAdigital*. At the moment, any two or more versions may be compared directly by opening them in

---

[34] The first excerpt from Quesnay which has emerged, was probably written at the end of 1846 or beginning of 1847. It dealt, firstly, with what Quesnay termed "droit naturel" and is contained in the theoretical basics of the physiocratic views on the economy, and, secondly, with Quesnay's *Analyse du Tableau Économique*, both in the edition of Eugène Daire's two-volumes on "Physiocrates" from 1846. The excerpt has recently been edited in MEGA^2 IV/5, 281–288. The collection from Daire was early (probably in autumn 1844) on in Marx' reading list as is documented in his notebook from 1844–1847 (MEGA^2 IV/3, 8, 10, 13). There are also several respectful references to the physiocrats having systematized economics in the manuscript dedicated to Max Stirner which has been produced by Marx and Engels for an envisaged quarterly since November 1845; it was written as part of the collection for a *German Ideology* (Marx Engels [1845–1847] MEGA^2 I/5, 466, 469, 1046ff.).

[35] See MEGA^2 III/12, Br. 256 (398–404, 1149–1150) for the connections between the letter and the Manuscript 1861–1863.

[36] Before and afterwards, Marx literally reproduced Quesnay's *Tableau*, as presented in the *Collection Des Principaux Economistes: Physiocrates* by Eugène Daire in 1846 (Beiheft C, RGASPI, f. 1, op. 1, d. 1691, 10; Marx [1861–1863] MEGA^2 II/3, 2337–2338 [XXIII-1433–1434]).

different windows in *MEGAdigital*.[37] Via the button *"Inhalt"* you may get tables of contents for the respective MEGA-volume and the text or texts therein. Moreover, there is a cumulative index of subjects *("Kumuliertes Sachregister")* for all texts belonging to Book 2 of *Capital*. This index offers, for every term, the corresponding passages in a manuscript of Marx, the editorial manuscript of Engels, and the printed version prepared by Engels; all parallel references are listed in one line. This allows one to follow the genesis of terms, phrases or passages.[38] Thus, Marx' very last manuscript for *Capital* written between 1877 and 1881 (*Manuscript VIII*, MEGA^2 II/11) may be compared with Engels' versions (MEGA^2 II/12 and II/13) in *MEGAdigital*. In the printed MEGA-volumes, a list of provenance in Engels' editorial manuscript (II/12, 896–934, *"Provenienzverzeichnis"*) is added to denote the matching passages in Marx's manuscripts (in II/11, and II/4.3). A similar list is provided for Book 3 in II/15 (946–974), referring to Marx' manuscripts (in II/4.2, II/4.3, and II/14). Furthermore, the edition has disclosed connections to other texts in the legacy of Marx. Up to now, they are offered and discussed in the printed commentary to the text. In future, it is intended to set up such connections as hyperlinks in *MEGAdigital*.[39]

The very last manuscript for *Capital* dealt with subjects of Book 2: the circulation process of capital, among them a critique of Smith's dogma, the role of money in circulation, and the analysis of expanded reproduction.[40] In his preface to the printed version, Engels presumed Marx was not satisfied with his presentation of the reproduction process in the third section of his book, and he, therefore, set out to elaborate another draft for it. The findings of the editors, however, cast

---

[37] Our Web-Application is organized like a large virtual desk on which many windows may be placed independently from each other, e.g. to compare two versions of one text you can place them parallel to each other; or several hits from a list of results by full text retrieval may be displayed parallel to each other, each one in the context of its page.

[38] Additionally, for every page of these texts, the subjects being dealt with on this page and their corresponding parts in other versions, may be displayed via buttons *"Apparat"*, then *"Kumuliertes Sachregister"*.

[39] This will be a multistage process, first presenting texts online, one by one, then by and by implementing the identified connections. We shall start with texts in MEGA-volumes from the first section which are going to be edited in future years. Moreover, for the volumes of the second section of *Capital*, the lists of provenance shall be used to realise more connections between manuscripts and printed versions than are presently identified via the cumulative index. In the long term, according to the resources the MEGA project disposes of, selected texts already published in printed volumes should be digitized.

[40] Marx [1868–1881] MEGA^2 II/11, 865ff. (The whole introduction pp. 843–905 is to be found at: http://mega.bbaw.de/struktur/abteilung_ii/dateien/mega_II-11_inhalt-einf.pdf Accessed 31 May 2018.)

doubts on this view. Rather, this manuscript emerged from a collection of material and ideas, which Marx began when he prepared some responses to the works of Eugen Dühring in spring 1877. These were intended to aid Engels in his polemic against the German economist whose ideas on capitalist production fuelled considerable debate among Social Democrats in Germany (Welskopp 2000, 712–722).

Marx directed his attention to the origins of political economy to prove the fallaciousness of Dühring's analysis and, at the same time, to reject Dühring's critique of Marx' own analysis in *Capital*. Marx declared Quesnay and his *Tableau* to be part of this controversy. Apart from many polemic statements, Marx offered a detailed analysis of the *Tableau* to present to readers, indicating that, in his view, the *Tableau* was "one of the most brilliant generalisations of political economy" (Marx Engels [1876–1877] MEGA^2 I/27, 137ff., 210ff.).[41]

The publication of Engels' *Herrn Eugen Dührings Umwälzung der Wissenschaft*, 1877/78, included for the first time some of Marx' considerations on Quesnay and his *Tableau*, however, as Marx explained to Engels in a letter from March 7, 1877, he did not want to present "his own peculiar way to deal with the physiocrats" without having the possibility of arguing about it in greater detail (Marx Engels [1876–1877] MEGA^2 I/27, 847). Instead, more of his ideas were to be found in a separate note that was to become the starting point of his last manuscript. There, Marx interpreted the *Tableau* using his own categories (Marx [1868–1881] MEGA^2 II/11, 701).

It was in this way that Marx started to work on his last draft for *Capital*, and it explains the fragmentary character of this last text. It also sheds light on the outward appearance of this manuscript: in contrast to other drafts for his books, Marx did not leave any space for footnotes on any page of this last manuscript; there were rarely any headings to be found, and he often used square brackets and horizontal lines to separate thoughts or passages on different topics.

Yet it is not only formalities that allude to the character of a collection of material, but also its contents. At least the first 23 pages show obvious connections to his notes on Dühring, sent to Engels in August 1877. The title was only added later, and it was in a rather

---

[41] Marx added a reproduction of the *Tableau* with some explications for Engels' private use. It is similar to the one in "Beiheft C", complemented by some symbols to identify the different flows of money and products.

cryptic form: "Ch. III, b. II.)".[42] Every now and then Marx noted thoughts that had no connection to the reproduction process or to *Capital* at all. For instance, one can find an annotated excerpt from the reports of the Secretary of Embassy and Legation, Victor Drummond, reporting on the cotton industry in Massachusetts and his ideas of workers as "rational consumers",[43] or one can find a short note referring to a book by James Geikie on *Prehistoric Europe*.[44]

If we compare Marx' last manuscript with Engels' edition of it in the printed version of Book 2, we find that Marx tentatively discussed several "difficulties", especially when he recorded what was to become his first – and only – elaboration on expanded reproduction.[45] Marx chose various numerical examples to prove his ideas, often without capturing the premises or clarifying the propositions of his argument. To give an example: he wanted to calculate the process of accumulation and, as a result, gained decreasing numbers for the organic composition of capital. That, as he noted, "contradicts the course of capitalist production" (Marx [1868–1881] MEGA² II/11, 814). He dropped this calculation and started new ones: one deleted at once, another soon marked as finished in a separate line. In his presentation, Engels did not mention any of the difficulties Marx encountered. Instead, he offered a numerical example reflecting a process of accumulation that functioned well. He could do so because he avoided Marx' mistake of distributing the additional capital in a lower composition than the original parts of the constant and variable capital.[46] In general, the questions Marx articulated in his manuscript appear, if at all, in Engels' presentation as mere rhetorical questions. And to questions that Marx had left open or insufficiently answered, Engels, looked for answers in other parts of the

---

[42] Its meaning was "Chapter III, book II" (Marx [1868–1881] MEGA² II/11, 698.1, 1609).

[43] Marx [1868–1881] MEGA² II/11, 818–819; Engels adopted this passage on the spot, but he left out the square brackets Marx had used to mark them as a special part (Marx [1885] MEGA² II/13, 479–480).

[44] Marx [1868–1881] MEGA² II/11, 826. These, together with the passages on the following pages, Engels, of course, did not adopt into his printed version as Marx had left some empty pages after his last notes on expanded reproduction.

[45] Marx [1868–1881] MEGA² II/11, 873ff. (Introduction also at http://mega.bbaw.de/struktur/abteilung_ii/dateien/mega_II-11_inhalt-einf.pdf Accessed 31 May 2018.)

[46] MEGA² II/13, 475–477, 543ff. (The whole introduction pp. 497–548 is to be found at http://mega.bbaw.de/struktur/abteilung_ii/dateien/mega_II-13_inhalt-einf.pdf Accessed 31 May 2018.) For a concise summary of the argument presented by Marx see also Marx [1868–1881] MEGA² II/11, 873ff.

manuscripts and presented them without further information as to their origins.[47]

Furthermore, the role of money proved to be one of the questions that would need further reflection, particularly, as in some of his examples, Marx still explicitly excluded it from his considerations.[48] As interpreters of Marx since the twentieth century have noted, among other questions overlooked was a detailed discussion of factors influencing the process of expanded reproduction like the development of technology and its impacts on the surplus rate, the profit rate and the composition of capital, let alone the effects of irregularities in circulation and crises.[49] Moreover, Marx had only alluded briefly to the potentials of credit in the process of reproduction (Marx [1868–1881] MEGA^2 II/11, 794, 799). Thus, the "real conditions of reproduction, that is of a continued production", as Marx stated at least up to 1872, were still required to be studied in greater detail.[50]

Similar results are unveiled when we have a closer look at Marx' last manuscript on the rate of profit and its precursors. This category and its relationship to the surplus value and the rate of surplus value, or, in a broader context, the transformation from values to production prices had already caused many problems in his main draft for Book 3 which Marx wrote in 1864/65 (MEGA^2 II/4.2). The investigation of the laws which were governing the rate of profit proved to be difficult,

---

[47] One example: when Marx spoke of two sources providing the money necessary to realise accumulation, he only mentioned one of them. Engels offered a second one, in an additional sentence, and he referred to a – not very clear – passage, which he presented in his last point "Supplementary remarks" (Marx [1868–1881] MEGA^2 II/11, 809–810; MEGA II/13, 474–475, 485–486). Moreover, this first possibility presented by Marx is that capitalists may betray one another, but this is hardly a systematic solution, inherent to the capitalist system. See also Marx' refutation of cutting wages as a valuable explanation for the accumulation of money, several pages before (808–809).

[48] Marx discussed five examples for his reproduction schemes with different settings, whereas Engels presented only one. The exclusion is to be found in Marx' second example (Marx [1868–1881] MEGA^2 II/11, S. 812). To the state of elaboration of these last considerations on expanded reproduction, see also Einführung: In Marx [1885] MEGA^2 II/13, 543–545.

[49] It might be interesting to refer to a passage in the earlier manuscript of Marx from 1868 to 1870, where he discussed simple reproduction in a more detailed way by introducing six departments into his reproduction schemes. Marx started a digression on the development of his examples given that the rate of profit was generalised, but he deferred it quickly to a later examination which did not take place in the manuscripts that have emerged (Marx [1868–1881] MEGA^2 II/11, 495; Einführung: In Marx [1885] MEGA^2 II/13, 542–543).

[50] Marx [1872] MEGA^2 II/6, 522. In the changed wording of the introductory paragraphs to "the process of accumulation" in the French edition, which Engels adopted for the fourth edition, the "real conditions" were no longer mentioned (Marx [1872–1875] MEGA^2 II/7, 487–488; Marx [1890] MEGA^2 II/10, 504–505).

although their importance was often stressed.[51] We may identify at least three attempts to come to grips with this subject.

The first attempt covers the first 70 pages from the draft for Book 3 in 1864/65. On p. 4, Marx began to write a note on the difference between the rate of surplus value and the rate of profit, which he continued up to p. 31. This was followed by new considerations on the topic, including a remark on p. 51: "In the final version of this story, therefore, we only need to concentrate on what is rational here"; all these details, Marx continued, "should definitely not be inflicted on the reader".[52] Marx returned to this topic in 1867/68, after the publication of his first Book. Apart from writing four beginnings of Book 3, he discussed in several texts, on almost 130 pages, the laws of the rate of profit, the surplus rate, cost price and turnover of capital, using new concepts, for example a profit rate on cost-price, denominated "π" (Marx [1863–1868] MEGA^2 II/4.3, 451–453, 599ff., 610ff., 735ff.). Eventually, in 1875, he began a new effort in a separate notebook to fix the relationship of profit rate and surplus rate (Marx Engels [1871–1895] MEGA^2 II/14, 19–150). He noted several reflections to derive "laws of the rate of profit", for example on p. 8 and 21 (27–28, 38ff.). Many horizontal lines mark new attempts, in addition to Roman numerals (I to V) up to p. 125 (19–141) and new titles shortly before the end of the manuscript (141, 142).

The result of all these attempts was no clarity. Rather, a note in the last manuscript from 1875 appears to be symptomatic: "No further confusion necessary, bred by a bad night" (Marx Engels [1871–1895] MEGA^2 II/14, 72). There were, first, several points left undetermined and vague, which, second, Marx should have 'fixed' by investigating them from a new angle, as he had remarked in the manuscript for Book 3 in 1864 (Marx [1864/65] MEGA^2 II/4.2, 77). In his printed version from 1894, Engels condensed all these pages and considerations of Marx into less than 20 pages. There are some passages, where Engels kept Marx' original words without any modification. On the other hand, he introduced a systematic discussion about the factors affecting the rate of profit, standardised the notation, and produced

---

[51] For instance, Marx to Engels, 30 April 1868; also in Book 1 Marx more than once emphasised the relevance of this question and confirmed his plan to deal with it in Book 3 (Marx [1872] MEGA^2 II/6, 488, 522, 541 or 557).

[52] Up to p. 8, there were some additional remarks, before Marx only wrote on the lower part of the page, reserved for footnotes. On p. 31 he resumed the thought of the main text and marked the "close of the footnote" (Marx [1864/65] MEGA^2 II/4.2, 13, 50, 83).

introductory paragraphs as well as a summarising sentence which stated clear dependencies. Furthermore, there are some topics that Marx had only hinted at, which Engels analysed in greater detail (Roth 2002, 67–68). With regards to Marx' discussion concerning the falling rate of profit, a final decision was never reached so that Engels inserted the familiar sentence: "But in reality [...] the rate of profit will fall in the long run".[53]

4. Concluding remarks

In summarising the few aspects on economic questions presented in this paper, it remains doubtful if, as Engels assumed in his preface to Book 2 in 1885, "what Marx intended to say is said there, in one way or another" (MEGA^2 II/13, 8). This does not only apply to the circulation of capital but also applies to other subjects, still incomplete when Marx died in 1883. First, none of his several drafts and treaties offers the clarity on the laws governing the rate of profit, promised in Book 1. Secondly, the exposition of the mechanisms of expanded reproduction remained in an unfinished state. Thirdly, a concise comment on rent reflecting his later studies was missing. Moreover, looking at other parts of Marx's *Capital* we find that a chapter on credit and its influences on the economic processes were still to be written, and Marx left his analysis of the "economic law of motion of modern society" without detailed reflection on classes.[54]

We are left to soberly observe Marx confronting the limits of new methods and thereby failing to come to grips with some of his ideas. On the other hand, recent research has uncovered a Marx, who, by integrating scientific findings into his economic analysis, was considering results of economic processes, not only for society but also for the ecological system, in the short and long term. In general, Marx scrupulously tracked discussions in the many fields and disciplines connected with his project and checked developments in the economy of his time to see if they were consistent with his analysis. MEGA, in printed volumes, and, increasingly, in digital form, offers rich material to study his encounter with numerous subjects and his repetition in

---

[53] Marx [1894] MEGA^2 II/15, 227 and Marx [1864/65] MEGA^2 II/4.2, 319. See also Heinrich 2011, 194.

[54] His draft from 1864/65 only offered one page on this subject (Marx [1864/65] MEGA^2 II/4.2, 901–902), and no other considerations on this important topic have been disclosed up to now.

looking at them from different perspectives. Although the explanations he offers may not always prove satisfactory, many of the phenomena and problems that he identified in the nineteenth century still resonate today.

Acknowledgements

I would like to thank the conference participants in Lyon for their valuable discussion, and the two anonymous referees for their helpful comments. I also thank Jacob Blumenfeld and Catriona Brown who checked my English. Responsibility for the final text is, of course, my own.

Disclosure statement

No potential conflict of interest was reported by the author.

References

Writings from Karl Marx not yet published are to be found in the International Institute for Social History in Amsterdam (IISH, Marx–Engels Collection) or at the Russian State Archive of Social and Political History in Moscow (RGASPI, fonds 1, opis 1). Letters or content of letters from Marx and Engels are quoted from either the MEGA or MECW and are identified only by date without reference to special editions and volumes. For details on the publications of the MEGA and the introductions available online see their website: http://mega. bbaw.de.

Bibliotheken, Die, von Karl Marx und Friedrich Engels. 1999. "MEGA^2 IV/32. Annotiertes Verzeichnis des ermittelten Bestandes." In   Karl Marx and Friedrich Engels, *Gesamtausgabe, Fourth Section*, Berlin: Akademie.

Blaug, Mark. 1997. *Economic Theory in Retrospect*. 5th ed. Cambridge: Cambridge University Press.

Gehrke, Christian. 2011. "Marx's Critique of Ricardo's Theory of Rent, A Re-Assessment". In *Classical Political Economy and Modern Theory: Essays in Honour of Heinz Kurz*, edited by Christian Gehrke, Neri Salvadori, Ian Steedman, and Richard Sturn, 51–84. London: Routledge.

Gehrke, Christian, and Heinz D. Kurz. 1995. "Karl Marx on Physiocracy". *The European Journal of the History of Economic Thought* 2 (Spring): 53–90. doi: 10.1080/10427719500000095

Hecker, Rolf, Richard Sperl, and Carl-Erich Vollgraf, Eds. 2006. *Die Journalisten Marx und Engels. Beiträge zur Marx-Engels-Forschung, N.F. 2005*. Hamburg: Argument Verlag.

Heinrich, Michael. 2011. "Entstehungs- und Auflösungsgeschichte des Marxschen ,Kapital". In *Kapital and Kritik. Nach der "neuen" Marx-Lektüre*, edited by Werner Bonefeld and Michael Heinrich, 155–193. Hamburg: VSA-Verlag.

Heinrich, Michael. 2016. "Das Programm der Kritik der politischen Ökonomie; Grundbegriffe der Kritik der politischen Ökonomie". In *Marx-Handbuch: Leben – Werk – Wirkung*, edited by Michael Quante and David P. Schweikard, 71–118; 173–193. Stuttgart: J. B. Metzler.

Hubmann, Gerald, and Regina Roth. 2014. "Die Kapital-Abteilung der MEGA. Einleitung und Überblick". *Marx-Engels-Jahrbuch* 2012/13: 60–69.

Krader, Lawrence. Ed. 1974. *The Ethnological Notebooks of Karl Marx (Studies of Morgan, Phear, Maine, Lubbock)*. 2nd ed. Assen: Van Gorcum.

Liebig, Justus von. 1862. *Die Chemie in ihrer Anwendung auf Agricultur and Physiologie*. 7th ed. Braunschweig: Vieweg.

Marx, Karl. 2016. *Marx's Economic Manuscript of 1864–1865*. Ed. by Fred Moseley. Translated by Ben Fowkes. Historical Materialism Book Series 100. Leiden: Brill.

Marx, Karl, and Frederick Engels. 1983–2003. *Collected Works*. New York: International Publishers. (MECW).

Marx, Engels. [1845–1847]. "MEGA² I/5: Marx, Karl, and Engels, Friedrich. Werke. Artikel. Entwürfe. Deutsche Ideologie. Manuskripte und Drucke." In Karl Marx and Friedrich Engels, *Gesamtausgabe*, First Section, Vol. 5. Berlin: DeGruyter. Akademie Forschung, 2017.

Marx, Engels. [1848]. "MEGA² I/7: Marx, Karl, and Engels, Friedrich. Werke. Artikel. Entwürfe. Februar bis Oktober 1848." In Karl Marx and Friedrich Engels, *Gesamtausgabe*, First Section, Vol. 7. Berlin: DeGruyter. Akademie Forschung, 2016.

Marx, Engels [1867–1871] "MEGA² I/21: Marx, Karl, and Engels, Friedrich. Werke. Artikel. Entwürfe. September 1867 bis März 1871." In Karl Marx and Friedrich Engels, *Gesamtausgabe*, First Section, Berlin: Akademie, 2009.

Marx. [1875–1883]. "MEGA² I/25: Marx, Karl, and Engels, Friedrich. Werke. Artikel. Entwürfe. Mai 1875 bis Mai 1883." In Karl Marx and Friedrich Engels, *Gesamtausgabe*, First Section Berlin: Dietz, 1985.

Marx, Engels. [1867–1877]. "MEGA² I/27: Engels, Friedrich. Herrn Eugen Dührings Umwälzung der Wissenschaft. In Karl Marx and Friedrich Engels, *Gesamtausgabe*, First Section Berlin: Dietz, 1988.

Marx [1857–1858]. "MEGA² II/1: Marx, Karl. Ökonomische Manuskripte 1857/1858." 2nd ed. In Karl Marx and Friedrich Engels, *Gesamtausgabe*, Second Section Vol. 1. Berlin: Akademie, 2006. (1. ed. 1976/81.)

Marx. [1861–1863]. "MEGA² II/3: Marx, Karl. Zur Kritik der politischen Ökonomie (Manuskript 1861–1863)." 2. ed. In Karl Marx and Friedrich Engels, *Gesamtausgabe*, Second Section, Berlin: Akademie, 2013. (1. ed. 1976–82.)

Marx. [1864]. "MEGA² II/4.1: Marx, Karl. Ökonomische Manuskripte 1863–1867. Part 1." In Karl Marx and Friedrich Engels, *Gesamtausgabe*, Second Section, Berlin: Dietz, 1988.

Marx. [1864–1865]. "MEGA² II/4.2: Marx, Karl. Ökonomische Manuskripte 1863–1867. Part 2." In Karl Marx and Friedrich Engels, *Gesamtausgabe*, Second Section, Berlin: Akademie, 2012 (1. ed. 1992.)

Marx. [1863–1868]. "MEGA² II/4.3: Marx, Karl. Ökonomische Manuskripte 1863–1868. Part 2." In Karl Marx and Friedrich Engels, *Gesamtausgabe*, Second Section, Berlin: Akademie, 2012.

Marx. [1867], [1872], [1883], [1890]. "MEGA² II/5, II/6, II/8, II/10: Marx, Karl. Das Kapital. Kritik der politischen Ökonomie. 1. Band. Hamburg 1867, 2. ed. 1872, 3. and 4. ed. 1883 and 1890 ed. by Friedrich Engels." In Karl Marx and Friedrich Engels, *Gesamtausgabe*, Second Section, Berlin: Dietz, 1983, 1987, 1989, 1991.

Marx. [1872–1875]. "MEGA² II/7: Marx, Karl. Le Capital. Paris 1872–75." In Karl Marx and Friedrich Engels, *Gesamtausgabe*, Second Section, Berlin: Dietz, 1989.

Marx. [1887]. "MEGA² II/9: Marx, Karl. Capital. London 1887." In Karl Marx and Friedrich Engels, *Gesamtausgabe*, Second Section, Berlin: Dietz, 1990.

Marx. [1868–1881]. "MEGA² II/11: Marx, Karl. Manuskripte zum zweiten Buch des Kapitals 1868 bis 1881." In Karl Marx and Friedrich Engels, *Gesamtausgabe*, Second Section, Berlin: Akademie, 2008.

Marx. [1884–1885]. "MEGA² II/12: Marx, Karl. Das Kapital. Kritik der Politischen Ökonomie. 2. Band. Redaktionsmanuskript von Friedrich Engels 1884/1885." In Karl Marx and Friedrich Engels, *Gesamtausgabe*, Second Section, Berlin: Akademie, 2005.

Marx. [1885]. "MEGA² II/13: Marx, Karl. Das Kapital. Kritik der politischen Ökonomie. 2. Band. Hamburg 1885. Ed. by Friedrich Engels." In Karl Marx and Friedrich Engels, *Gesamtausgabe*, Second Section, Berlin: Akademie, 2008.

Marx, Engels. [1871–1895]. "MEGA² II/14: Marx, Karl, and Engels, Friedrich. Manuskripte und redaktionelle Texte zum dritten Buch des Kapitals 1871 bis 1895." In Karl Marx and Friedrich Engels, *Gesamtausgabe*, Second Section, Berlin: Akademie, 2003.

Marx. [1894]. "MEGA² II/15: Marx, Karl. Das Kapital. Kritik der politischen Ökonomie. 3. Band. Hamburg 1894. Ed. by Friedrich Engels." In Karl Marx and Friedrich Engels, *Gesamtausgabe*, Second Section, Berlin: Akademie, 2004.

Marx. [1844–1847]. "MEGA² IV/3: Marx, Karl. Exzerpte und Notizen. Sommer 1844 bis Anfang 1847." In Karl Marx and Friedrich Engels, *Gesamtausgabe*, Fourth Section, Berlin: Akademie, 1998.

Marx. [1845–1850]. "MEGA² IV/5: Marx, Karl. Exzerpte und Notizen. Juli 1845 bis Dezember 1850." In Karl Marx and Friedrich Engels, *Gesamtausgabe*, Fourth Section, Vol. 5. Berlin: Akademie, 2015.

Marx. [1849–1851]. "MEGA² IV/7: Marx, Karl. Exzerpte und Notizen. September 1849 bis Februar 1851." In Karl Marx and Friedrich Engels, *Gesamtausgabe*, Fourth Section, Berlin: Dietz, 1983.

Marx. [1851a]. "MEGA² IV/8: Marx, Karl. Exzerpte und Notizen. März bis Juni 1851." In Karl Marx and Friedrich Engels, *Gesamtausgabe*, Fourth Section, Berlin: Dietz, 1986.

Marx. [1851b]. "MEGA² IV/9: Marx, Karl. Exzerpte und Notizen. Juli bis September 1851." In Karl Marx and Friedrich Engels, *Gesamtausgabe*, Fourth Section, Berlin: Dietz, 1991.

Marx, Engels. [1877–1883]. "MEGA² IV/31: Marx, Karl, and Engels, Friedrich. Naturwissenschaftliche Exzerpte und Notizen. Mitte 1877 bis Anfang 1883." In Karl Marx and Friedrich Engels, *Gesamtausgabe*, Fourth Section, Berlin: Akademie, 1999.

Marx. [1878]. "MEGA² IV/26: Marx, Karl. Exzerpte und Notizen zur Geologie, Mineralogie und Agrikulturchemie. März bis September 1878." In *Gesamtausgabe, Fourth Section*, edited by Karl Marx and Friedrich Engels. Vol. 26. Berlin: Akademie, 2011.

Quante, Michael, and David P. Schweikard, Eds. 2016. *Marx-Handbuch: Leben – Werk – Wirkung*. Stuttgart: J. B. Metzler.

Rojahn, Jürgen. 1985. "Die Marxschen Manuskripte aus dem Jahre 1844 in der neuen Marx-Engels-Gesamtausgabe (MEGA)". *Archiv für Sozialgeschichte* 25, 647–663.

Roth, Regina, and Fred Moseley, Eds. 2004. "Marx, Engels, and the Text of Book 3 of Capital. No. 1, Spring 2002." In *International Journal of Political Economy*. Vol.32. Armonk, N.Y.: M.E. Sharpe.

Roth, Regina. 2002. "The Author Marx and His Editor Engels. Different Views on Volume 3 of *Capital*". *Rethinking Marxism* 14, 59–72. doi:10.1080/00935690212331340951

Roth, Regina. 2013. "'Ich muß jetzt die Sache wieder ganz umarbeiten.' Zur Editionsgeschichte des *Kapital*". In *Prüfstein Marx*, edited by Matthias Steinbach and Michael Ploenus, 46–64. Berlin: Metropol.

Saitō, Kōhei. 2015. "Marx' Fraas-Exzerpt und der neue Horizont des Stoffwechsels." *Marx-Engels-Jahrbuch 2014*, 117–140.

Saitō, Kōhei. 2016. *Natur gegen Kapital: Marx' Ökologie in seiner unvollendeten Kritik des Kapitalismus*. Frankfurt, New York: Campus Verlag.

Takenaga, Susumu. 2018. "Marx on Rent: New Insights from the New MEGA" (in this issue). doi:10.1080/09672567.2018.1523936.

Vollgraf, Carl-Erich. 2011. "Marx' erstmals veröffentlichte Manuskripte zum 2. und 3. Buch des Kapitals von 1867/68 im MEGA²-Band II/4.3. Zu neuralgischen Punkten in der Ausarbeitung des Kapitals." *Beiträge zur Marx-Engels-Forschung. N.F. 2010, Das Kapital und Vorarbeiten. Entwürfe und Exzerpte*, 77–116.

Vollgraf, Carl-Erich. 2016. "Marx über die sukzessive Untergrabung des Stoffwechsels der Gesellschaft bei entfalteter kapitalistischer Massenproduktion." *Beiträge zur Marx-Engels-Forschung. N.F. 2014/15, Zu den Studienmaterialien von Marx und Engels*, 106–132.

Welskopp, Thomas. 2000. *Das Banner der Brüderlichkeit. Die deutsche Sozialdemokratie vom Vormärz bis zum Sozialistengesetz*. Berlin: Dietz.

Appendix

Economic Manuscripts and Printed Versions in the Second Section of the MEGA and in MECW			
Manuscripts on the "Economics" by Marx			
Grundrisse	1857/58	MEGA² II/1	MECW 28–29
Economic Manuscript 1861–1863	1861–1863	MEGA² II/3	MECW 30–34
Printed parts from the "Economics" by Marx			
A Contribution to the Critique of Political Economy	1859	MEGA² II/2	MECW 29
"Capital", Book 1			
Manuscript-Material, by Marx	1863/64	MEGA² II/4.1	MECW 34
	1871/72	MEGA² II/6	
	1877	MEGA² II/8, p. 5-36	
Printed versions, by Marx	1867, 1872, 1872–1875	MEGA² II/5–7	
Printed versions, by Engels	1883	MEGA² II/8	
	1890	MEGA² II/10	
	1887	MEGA² II/9	MECW 35
"Capital", Book 2			
Manuscript-Material, by Marx	1865	MEGA² II/4.1	
	1867/68	MEGA² II/4.3	
	1868–1881	MEGA² II/11	
Manuscript-Material, by Engels	1884/85	MEGA² II/12	
Printed versions, by Engels	1885, 1893	MEGA² II/13	MECW 36
"Capital", Book 3			
Manuscript-Material, by Marx	1864/65	MEGA² II/4.2	
	1867/68	MEGA² II/4.3	
	1871–1881	MEGA² II/14	
Manuscript-Material, by Engels	1883–1894	MEGA² II/14	
Printed version, by Engels	1894	MEGA² II/15	MECW 37

Will the MEGA² edition be a watershed in interpreting Marx?

Heinz D. Kurz

ABSTRACT

The MEGA² edition is a watershed in interpreting important aspects of Marx's oeuvre, but not all of them. It provides hints as to why Marx failed to complete his magnum opus, *Capital*, and informs about his doubts regarding the "law of motion" of capitalism centred on the "law of the falling tendency of the rate of profit" he was keen to establish.

> I pre-suppose, of course, a reader who is willing to learn something new and therefore to think for himself.

(Marx 1954, 19)

1. Introduction

In a letter to Friedrich Engels of 31 July 1865, Karl Marx wrote:

> As regards my work, I want to tell you the plain truth. … I cannot decide to send anything before the whole is in front of me. Whatever shortcomings they may have, it is the merit of my writings that they constitute an artistic whole, and this can only be achieved in my way by not allowing them to be printed, unless they are *fully* in front of me. (MEGA² II/5: 668–669; Marx's emphasis)[1]

The keywords in this letter are "artistic whole" and "fully in front of me". *The Marx-Engels Gesamtausgabe* carried out on behalf of the Internationale Marx Engels Stiftung (IMES), known as MEGA², is to be

---

credited with laying out almost "fully in front" of us the "artistic whole" of Marx' (and Engels') oeuvre. It does so almost because the original plans to publish basically each and every slip of paper showing the handwriting of the two has been abandoned and instead of the originally planned 164 volumes, now only 114 volumes are supposed to come out. This is still a gigantic enterprise and the probability is very high that we will eventually, once the entire edition is available, be able to see whatever is at least modestly important for an understanding of Marx's intellectual journeys. There is every reason to presume that no big fish will slip through the mesh of the net the editors of MEGA^2 have cast. Looking at what has already been published, I am inclined to say that some of the material available in print now could easily have been left out, because it does not really add to our apprehension of Marxs achievements and failures, as things may be.

To have easy access to (the main body of) Marx's works is, of course, to be welcomed and a boon. However, the sheer amount of material waiting for the reader is forbidding and ploughing through it in places very hard if not excruciating. The editors deserve our sincere thanks for their effort and meticulous work. In my view, they would deserve even greater praise had they been more selective or more outspoken in their editorial comments what merits to be read and what perhaps not. This would still leave the decision to the reader, but it would serve as a useful orientation for those who do not expect to be possessed of an infinite life.

The question now is: Will the MEGA^2 edition turn out to be a watershed in interpreting Marx? Asking this question is almost obviously rhetorical. I say almost because the answer given here is that it will and it will not. What I mean by this should become clear in the sequel.

The composition of the article is the following. Section 2 provides arguments in favour of the first half of the answer, that is, in important respects, the MEGA^2 edition will be a watershed or turning point, in interpreting central elements of Marx's oeuvre, especially his conceptualisation of the "law of motion" of modern society. It will at the same time provide some hints as to why Marx failed to complete his magnum opus, *Das Kapital*. Section 3 contains some observations on a central element of Marx's analysis in regard to which the edition will not serve as a watershed: his "law of value". This is so because it contains the nucleus of what he considered to be his main achievement in social theory and his advance beyond the state in which especially Aristotle had left it. Section 4 contains a critical discussion of the core piece of Marx's vivisection of capitalism and its demise, the "law of the falling tendency of the rate of profit", contained in Engels' edition of volume III of *Das Kapital*. It is argued that the material now available shows that Marx vacillated with regard to some of his propositions and assumptions and that Engels, the editor of the volume, actually assumed the role of a tough taskmaster. Section 5 concludes.

2. Several cases indicating a watershed

The most important reasons why in my view the MEGA^2 will be a watershed in interpreting Marx are the following.

First, for the first time we can assess the whole corpus of Marx's writings, his intellectual curiosities and wide-ranging interests, the richness of his thoughts, his multifarious talents and capabilities and the numerous influences he was exposed to coming from all kinds of directions. Marx, one can say without much of an exaggeration, was one of the last polymaths, a scholar seeking to absorb the essential parts of knowledge of mankind available at the time and furthering it, a *Renaissance man* and *homo universalis* in the best sense of the words. His erudition and immense knowledge spanning numerous disciplines, his command of several languages, his engagement in literary pursuits, his historical and political concerns are truly remarkable, impressive and admirable. At the same time, they indicate why he was bound to fail with his huge project, which amounted to nothing more nor less than revealing the law that governs the history of mankind, its "law of motion". Marx eventually had to admit that he could not master this formidable task, that he would have had to know a great deal more about many things and that every answer he came up with respect to a given question would result in a myriad of new questions cropping up – like in the story of Hydra in Greek mythology, with which he was so familiar. The obsession with which he buried himself at an advanced age in mathematics, the sciences and many other things were not an expression of someone seeking a pastime, as has been contended. As I see it, it was rather a sign of a final rebelling of a rebellious spirit, desperately trying to establish man's control over himself and the world and shaking off the yoke of religion and superstition, the forces that hid the exploitative nature of modern society. Alas, Marx had to admit self-critically that he had failed in this regard and could not escape the apocalypse, or ἀποκάλυψις, which literally means here the "revelation" of the fact that there is knowledge far superior to the one he had been able to accumulate over the years in the British Library and elsewhere. While Marx was an eminently political person, he was primarily a scrupulous and perfectionist scholar forced to acknowledge that his work was not yet and presumably never would be sufficiently mature. Aware of the fact that he had shouldered much too big a task, how could he possibly have accomplished writing *Das Kapital*?

Second, we have now for the first time general access to a number of manuscripts of great importance. These cannot but change several of the received views of Marx, which were formulated by scholars not knowing that such manuscripts existed. Therefore, not all misleading interpretations to be found in the secondary literature can be blamed on their authors, some simply reflect the limited access to Marx's papers. What is now displayed for the first time concerns a great many of Marx's philosophical articles, especially his *Economic-Philosophical Manuscripts* composed in late spring and summer of 1844 (MEGA² II/2), drafts of essays, preparatory notes, comments and newspaper articles, his 1857–1858 manuscript on political economy, known as the *Grundrisse* (MEGA² II/1), drafts and early versions of *Zur Kritik der Politischen Oekonomie*, published in 1859 (MEGA² II/2), and, last but not the least, a host of material documenting the work on his magnum opus, *Das Kapital*, which his literary executor and intellectual sparring partner, Engels, could have published, but did not.

In a short review of the MEGA² edition, I speculated about what would have happened had the MEGA project been completed shortly after Marx had passed away (see Kurz 2013b). The world would probably have seen less of the sterile debates about the true meaning of Marx's doctrines, the role of the labour theory of value in it and the law of the falling tendency of the rate of profits, not least because one would have been exposed to Marx's own doubts and self-criticisms and his vacillations with regard to some of his analytical propositions. Much more important, his statements could not have been treated as set in stone, as the words of a prophet who never errs, but rather as the propositions of a fallible scientist. Show trials in which intellectuals were accused of sinning against the eternal truths enunciated by the holy trinity, Marx, Engels and Lenin, would be more difficult to imagine, not to talk of scholars who were sent to the gulag for essentially the same reason.[2] In short, I am inclined to believe that an early publication of the MEGA[2] would have spared the world a lot of nonsense, confusion, capture of the mind, abuse of people and bloodshed.

The MEGA[2] edition contributes to the demystification of Marx. It also corroborates and further substantiates the picture of Marx, the dedicated scholar and scientist, ruthlessly trying to uncover the truth and unwilling to give in to what in the preface to the first volume of *Das Kapital* he had called the "furies of private interest". The widespread attitude to blame Marx for what happened in so-called "real existing socialism" finds little if any compelling support in the edition. The broad lines of his political agenda were closely tied to his scientific work and were only legitimate to the extent to which they reflected his analytical findings. His fierce confrontation with Wilhelm Weitling, for example, witnesses the clash between "scientific socialism" and political voluntarism. Marx was uncompromising in this regard and insisted on the scientific foundation of the working class movement. He saw himself as having discovered historical trends regarding the destiny of mankind that could be speeded up somewhat, but not fundamentally changed. Accordingly, his role was that of an obstetrician of the new society. By revealing the law of motion of modern society he saw himself in the role of an enlightener, who provided all people with the opportunity to understand what he felt was an irresistible historical trend. Whoever grasped it, he was convinced, could no longer oppose it: even the "bourgeois", he stressed variously, is offered the chance of humbly accepting his fate without resistance and therefore allowing for a non-violent social revolution. This hope reflects well Marx's humanist attitude and also his occasional naivety.

Third, the MEGA[2] edition allows us to see in great detail how Marx's ideas on particular themes developed – his sources of inspiration, the literature he studied, the obstacles confronting him and whether he managed to overcome them, irritations and doubts he developed in the course of time, the reasons why he abandoned some

---

[2] I only recently learned that as late as 1980, two scholars in the former German Democratic Republic were expelled from the university and banned from publishing because they had used Piero Sraffa's (1960) analysis in discussing environmental problems and thus had left the holy ground of the labour theory of value.

of the ideas and tried out new ones, and his analytical construction compared with the constructions of other political economists, especially Adam Smith and David Ricardo. Last but not least, the material contains some obvious and also some not so obvious indications why Marx did not manage to finish major parts of his enormous project, which he kept redefining time and again and cutting down in size and contents as time went by. The material displayed in this regard is essentially two-fold, historical and analytical. First, there are statements by Marx, which show that certain historical events had a deep impact upon him and made him rethink what he had advocated up until then. A most important case is the following one. In the preface to the first German edition of volume I of *Das Kapital* Marx had explained:

> In this work I have to examine the capitalist mode of production, and the conditions of production and exchange corresponding to that mode. Up to the present time, their classic ground is England. That is the reason why England is used as the chief illustration in the development of my theoretical ideas. (Marx 1954, 19)

Contributing numerous lead articles to the *New York Tribune* and other American newspapers, Marx (and Engels) kept a close eye on what was going on in the United States.[3] They were impressed by the rapid industrialisation of the United States, which took place within a few decades in the mid-nineteenth century, and its rise to a world economic, political, and military power. The United States was an impressive example of what unfettered capitalism could bring about in a short span of time. At the same time, the American form of capitalism differed markedly from the English one. Most importantly, it developed in parallel with political freedom extending to ever-larger segments of society and exhibited a comparatively high degree of social mobility. Unlike Britain, Prussia and Russia, the United States did not suffer from the remnants of a feudalist past. Therefore, the characteristic features of capitalism could be more clearly seen, since they were not contaminated by feudal elements. Marx felt he had erred in taking England as the "classic ground" – he should instead have taken the United States. The USA was able to make a fresh start, whereas Europe suffered from the yoke of history and tradition. Moreover, the USA did not show any signs of the retardation of

---

[3] For a summary account of Marx and Engels' respective activities, see Kurz (2014).

economic expansion or even decline. Was perpetual progress and growth possible? The developments in the United States and the way they differed from those in Europe are likely one of the reasons why the completion of his magnum opus eluded Marx.

The second reason is analytical, but connected to the historical one. Marx felt that in several regards, his previous convictions were perhaps not as well founded as he had thought and his criticism of some of the received economic doctrines could perhaps not be sustained. His conviction regarding the inescapable demise of capitalism stood or fell with the correctness of the "law of the falling tendency of the rate of profit", which hinged crucially on the type of technical progress Marx saw as being congenial to the capitalist mode of production. This type was characterised by rising levels of labour productivity and a rising "organic composition of capital", that is, the ratio of "dead" labour incorporated in the means of production ("constant capital") and living labour ("variable capital" and "surplus value").[4] Marx had to face the following challenges: First, was his reasoning regarding the trend of profitability vis-à-vis a rising organic composition correct? Secondly, Ricardo in discussing the type of technical progress under consideration had not concluded that the rate of profits was bound to fall. Who was right, Ricardo or he, Marx? Third, could the assumption of a rising organic composition without limit be sustained? Interestingly, Marx discussed several other types of technical progress that he considered less detrimental to profitability, including capital saving types. Why should these types be dominated by a form of technical progress that leads to a rise in the organic composition of the system as a whole without upper limit? What evidence, if any, spoke in its favour? What did the case of the United States of America tell us in this regard? Did it confirm or contradict Marx's view? Finally, what is the role of scarce natural resources in all this? Was Ricardo perhaps right in maintaining that for a given real wage rate, the rate of profits would fall, if and only if less and less fertile land (or natural resources in general) had to be employed or given qualities used more intensively and there was a lack of technical progress? Had Marx erred with regard to the core piece of his economic

---

[4] Interestingly, this is the kind of technical progress Ricardo in the chapter 'On Machinery' published in the third edition of his *Principles* in 1821 (Ricardo 1951: chap. 31) had identified as detrimental to the class of workers, because it implied a displacement of workers that would not swiftly be compensated by additional jobs (later called "technological unemployment"); see Kurz (2010).

analysis? He had put the stakes extremely (and as will be seen in Section 4: excessively) high: while Ricardo had argued that technical progress may counteract the "niggardliness of nature", which is ultimately responsible for any fall in the rate of profits, Marx put Ricardo's doctrine upside down and contended that the prevalent type of technical progress in capitalism caused a fall in profitability. In Ricardo, technical progress was the saviour, in Marx it was the villain. Who was right?

Fourth, given Marx's doubts about the correctness of certain propositions he had entertained, which are reflected in the MEGA^2 edition, and the unfinished state of his work on *Das Kapital*, the question is close at hand, how did Friedrich Engels interpret his role when putting together volumes II and III of it. Engels' editing of the two volumes from Marx's manuscripts was a Herculean challenge. He devoted 10 years of his life to the work of "creating as authentic a text as possible" (MEGA^2 II/14: 323). The two volumes confronted him with vastly different, and differently difficult, tasks. In the preface to volume II Engels wrote, among other things:

> I have contented myself with reproducing these manuscripts as literally as possible, changing the style only in places where Marx would have changed it himself [how could he possibly know?] and interpolating explanatory sentences or connecting statements only where this was absolutely necessary [why?], and, where, besides, the meaning was clear beyond any doubt. (Marx 1956, 1)

Engels added:

> The mere enumeration of the manuscript material left by Marx for Book II proves the unparalleled conscientiousness and strict self-criticism with which he endeavoured to elaborate his great economic discoveries to the point of utmost completion before he published them. This self-criticism rarely permitted him to adapt his presentation of the subject, in content as well as in form, to his ever widening horizon, the result of incessant study. (Marx 1956, 2)

In the preface to volume III we read instead:

> As the reader will observe from the following, the work of editing the third volume was essentially different from that of editing the second. *In the case of the third volume there was nothing to go by outside a first extremely incomplete draft.* The beginnings of the various parts were, as a rule, pretty carefully done and even stylistically polished. But the farther one went, the more sketchy and incomplete was the manuscript, the more excursions it contained into arising side-issues whose proper place in the argument was left for later decision, and the longer and more complex the sentences, in

which thoughts were recorded in *statu nascendi*. In some places handwriting and presentation betrayed all too clearly the outbreak and gradual progress of the attacks of ill health ... Between 1863 and 1867, Marx ... completed the first draft of the two last volumes of *Capital* and prepared the first volume for the printer. [However, deteriorating health] prevented Marx from personally putting the finishing touches to the second and third volumes. (Marx 1959, 2–3; first emphasis added)

The MEGA² largely confirms these observations. Marx's work had not reached a stage of maturity that warranted its publication. Worse, there were strong indications that it could perhaps never reach such a stage – too numerous and heavy-calibered were the problems he was struggling with. This must have come as a surprise to Engels, whom Marx for quite some time tried to leave in the belief that his work was advancing more or less smoothly and that at any rate its completion was in sight. Nothing of the sort! After Marx had passed away, Engels, his literary executioner, was confronted with a host of manuscripts, notes, excerpts, comments, observations, digressions and so on – a gigantic *pasticcio* – and had to make the best of it. He informed the reader about his editorial work. This, he wrote, he limited

to the essential. I tried my best to preserve the character of the first draft wherever it was sufficiently clear. I did not even eliminate repetitions, wherever they, as was Marx's custom, viewed the subject from another standpoint or at least expressed the same thought in different words.

He went on:

Wherever my alterations or additions exceeded the bounds of editing, or where I had to apply Marx's factual material to independent conclusions of my own, even if as faithful as possible to the spirit of Marx, I have enclosed the entire passage in brackets and affixed my initials. Some of my footnotes are not enclosed in brackets; but wherever I have initialed them I am responsible for the entire note. (Marx 1959, 3)

Seen against the background of the MEGA² edition, in my view, this is on the whole a correct account of the enormous task Engels had shouldered, which had all ingredients of a mission impossible. It also provides a fair description of what he did as an editor, or rather felt obliged to do. What he did, I am convinced, he did in good faith. And yet his above formulations already imply that not all 'alterations or additions' were indicated. As Regina Roth (2010) has pointed out, in some places in which Marx vacillated with regard to what Engels thought was the correct view, Engels added a short remark or changed a word to put Marx's reasoning back on track. He was not, at least not throughout, the innocent editor as which he portrayed himself, although there is reason to presume that he felt he was. While in my view accusing him of having manipulated the papers, Marx had left to posterity would be going too far, he was clearly intent on hiding Marx's doubts before the reader's eyes. This is highly unfortunate because it signalled firmness of conviction where there was none and supported people inclined to treat Marx's work as the enunciation of the truth about the matter under consideration and nothing but the truth. Up until recently, many readers of volumes II and III of *Das Kapital* appear to have wrongly started from the assumption that they were given the final versions of Marx's views on the issues at hand. Alas, there is no such thing as a final version and there is strong reason to presume that Marx was lost in despair given the analytical difficulties he got entangled in.

Let me now turn briefly to the question in which regard the MEGA² edition will not put upside down received interpretations of Marx.

3. No watershed: the 'law of value'

The MEGA² edition reproduces basically all relevant material from Marx's literary remains, only parts of which were already known. These parts cannot possibly change existing views about Marx's doctrines except for the information provided about Engels's interventions and the like. New perspectives on Marx are prompted essentially by material that is now published for the first time, and as has already been pointed out in the above, it concerns basically all fields he tried to till during his life – philosophy, political economy, politics, the sciences, agriculture, mathematics, ethnology and many more. We now have a much clearer idea of how much effort and energy he devoted to the different fields in terms of reading and writing and we learn, for example, that philosophy, physics, chemistry, geology and mathematics absorbed much more of his time than we had thought. His work in each of these fields will have to be assessed and an opinion formed whether or not received interpretations can be sustained and in which regard they have to be corrected.[5] This is a task far beyond

---

[5] There are altogether around 250 notebooks filled with excerpts, notes and comments on various subjects, dating from the 1840s up until Marx's final years in the early 1880s. Only

what I can do in this short article. I will rather focus on a single, but important theme only: Marx's concept of the "law of value" and its location in his overall social theory.

Marx was convinced that this law holds not only in the "state of nature", as John Locke had maintained, nor only in the "early and rude" state of society, as Adam Smith had been convinced, but also in capitalist society, which reflected the highest state of civilisation attained up until then. By establishing this law against the background of his distinction between "labour" and "labour power", Marx sought to show that capitalism, no less than former modes of production, was based on the exploitation of one class of society, workers, by another class, capitalists. He identified labour as the *source*, *substance* and *measure* of all value. Labour generated value, but was no part of the exploitative mechanism at work: it is the capital-labour relationship that is the source of social domination, control and exploitation.

The "law of value" is the cornerstone of Marx's analysis of capitalism. As far as I can see, he unswervingly stuck to it till the very end of his life. He did so not because he considered it the single most important achievement of his entire corpus of scientific work in which he managed to go beyond Aristotle, the "great thinker" and to Marx the "greatest thinker of antiquity" (Marx 1954, 64 and 384).

There is no need here to recapitulate Marx's respective argument. It suffices to say that his view with regard to the core concepts of his analysis – "abstract labour" and "value" – did not really change. In particular, I could not discern a serious attempt to overcome the different definitions of them that are incompatible with one another. These multiple meanings and incompatibilities of the concepts have been pointed out already a long time ago by authors such as Isaak Rubin. As Gilbert Faccarello (1997; see also Faccarello, Gehrke, and Kurz 2016) has argued, the different conceptualizations reflect different phases of Marx's work and the different influences he was exposed to (Hegel, the classical economists, the French utopian socialists and so on). Faccarello distinguishes between a physiological ("human brains, nerves, muscles and hands"), a historical (reflecting the trend

---

some of them have been edited by now. For example, as regards Marx's studies of the sciences, especially chemistry, in the period between 1877 and the beginning of 1883, see MEGA^2 IV/31; and as regards his geological and mineralogical studies carried out in 1878, see MEGA^2 IV/26. Remarks on agricultural chemistry, commenting inter alia on the works of Justus von Liebig, are to be found in MEGA^2 II/3 and again in MEGA^2 IV/26.

of de-qualification of workers), a sociological (value as a "social hier-oglyph") and a purely conceptual definition of abstract labour. To work with different definitions or specifications of abstract labour, emphasising different aspects of labour, does not necessarily cause harm, provided the spheres to which they belong are clearly separated. This would then be just another case of "horses for courses", and to some extent it is so also in Marx. Yet, he was also concerned with providing a quantitative determination of central magnitudes of the capitalist economy, first and foremost the general rate of profits and the corresponding prices of production, which were meant to demon-strate the superiority of his analysis compared to that of previous economists, especially Ricardo. For this purpose, it had to be abso-lutely clear, which concept of labour was to be employed and how its quantity was to be ascertained. In the absence of such clarity, how could one possibly enter into a serious discussion of Marx's theory of value and distribution?

The quantitative concept of abstract labour presupposes some con-version rate amongst different kinds of concrete labour. In Marx, we encounter essentially two such rates: first, the rate 1:1; and, secondly, the rate $w_i{:}w_j$. According to the first one, all kinds of labour, irrespect-ive of their skill level, their remuneration, the risk involved and so on, are possessed of the same capacity to generate value: "The labour ... that forms the substance of value, is homogeneous human labour, expenditure of one uniform labour-power" and thus "a productive expenditure of human brains, nerves, and muscles." (Marx 1954, 46 and 51) In this conceptualisation one hour of labour of type i produ-ces the same value as one hour of labour of type j. According to the second proposal, which Marx encountered in the classical economists Adam Smith and David Ricardo, the capacity of labour of kind i to produce value is proportional to the wage rate it fetches, w_i, relative to the wage rate of that kind of labour, w_j, that represents abstract labour, that is, in our example, labour of kind j. Marx stressed in vol-ume III of *Capital*: "If the wage of a goldsmith is paid at a higher rate than that of a day labourer, ... the former's surplus labour also pro-duces a correspondingly greater surplus-value than does that of the latter" (Marx 1959, 264). This mirrors Marx's assumption that the rate of surplus value is uniform across all spheres of production, which implies that differences in wage rates necessarily imply differen-ces in value creation. In order for this to be satisfied, the classical conversion of different kinds of labour via the structure of wages is required (see also Kurz and Salvadori 1995, chap. 11, 2010).[6]

Obviously, the two conversion rates yield different results with regard to important economic magnitudes, such as the sum total of value-added, surplus value, variable capital and, most importantly, the general rate of profits. Whereas a change in the composition of the total labour performed in the economy during a year would not affect the value magnitudes in case all kinds of labour were treated alike, it would affect some of them in case the structure of wages would be used to 'reduce' one kind of labour to some other kind. However, in his attempts to clarify the relationship between economic aggregates and the forces affecting the general rate of profits (see, especially, MEGA[2] II/4.3: 57 et seq., II/6: 224-5 and II/14: 491 et seq.), in rather tedious calculations he typically kept one variable constant in order to identify the impact of changes of some other variable on the rate of profits.[7] Marx was aware of the fact that this *ceteris paribus* reasoning is highly problematic and that the magnitude he treated as a constant should have been treated as a variable. More importantly in the present context, to the best of my knowledge he nowhere laid bare, or questioned, his scheme of social accounting and the concept of abstract labour assumed. He appears to have been convinced that some kind of law of conservation of mass (= value) applied, but refrained from telling the reader in terms of which unit this mass was defined and measured.

While Marx allowed for the fact that the ratio of prices of production of any two commodities would normally deviate from the corresponding ratio of (labour) values, he did not see that this insight carries over to the general rate of profits, which corresponds materially to a ratio of two vectors of commodities – the social surplus product on the one hand and the capital on the other. It thus is a

---

[6] One of the referees insisted that there is no tension or even contradiction between the two concepts on the ground that "Marx never held a version of abstract labour that ignored qualitative heterogeneity of labour." I do not dispute this but draw the attention to the fact that Marx used different and mutually incompatible schemes to reduce heterogeneous to homogeneous labour. To the best of my knowledge, in the relevant passages referred to in volume I of *Capital* there is at any rate no clear indication that a reduction scheme is to be applied different from the one treating all kinds of labour alike as simply "productive expenditures of human brains, nerves, and muscles".

[7] In his calculations, Marx blundered repeatedly. This would not deserve to be mentioned, had he not occasionally been inclined to infer from his (mistaken) results that they expressed something of importance about the capitalist economy. The perhaps crassest case in this regard are his numerical illustrations of extended reproduction; see the articles by Christian Gehrke and Kenji Mori in this volume.

relative price. Hence there is no presumption that in general the rate of profits ascertained in labour value terms equals the rate in price terms. Marx also glimpsed the fact that (relative) prices of production are bound to change when income distribution changes, but he failed to elaborate a consistent explanation of the dependence of relative prices on income distribution, given the system of production in use. In this regard he did not get beyond Ricardo's analysis and in some respects (regarding the treatment of fixed capital, for example) fell short of it.

Before we move on to the next section, the attention ought to be drawn to two important aspects that are relevant in the present context, but cannot be dealt with in any depth. The first one refers to a difference between the concept of labour in the classical economists, on the one hand, and Marx, on the other, which up until now has hardly ever been noticed, let alone emphasised, an exception being Piero Sraffa in his papers at Trinity College, Cambridge (see Kurz 2018). The second one refers to the relationship between abstract and concrete labour, on the one hand, and the different, but related, distinction between simple and complex or unskilled and skilled labour, on the other.[8]

With regard to the first aspect, it deserves to be emphasised that the classical economists did *not* reserve the concept of labour exclusively to *human* labour, but subsumed under it also the labour performed by horses or oxen and by machines. (Adam Smith even reckoned certain activities of nature amongst the total amount of labour performed in the economy.) Here, it suffices to mention that to the classical economists what mattered was that the different kinds of labour are, as Ricardo stressed, in "constant competition" with one another and that in conditions of free competition cost-minimising behaviour decides their employment.[9] The choice of technique of profit-seeking producers determines the physical real costs of production – the means of subsistence, the fodder of horses, the fuel of machines and the complementary inputs used. In this way it has an

---

[8] One of the referees rightly asked for a clarifying remark in this direction.

[9] It suffices to point out a single passage in Ricardo's *Principles* that provides evidence in support of this claim. In the machinery chapter, Ricardo discussed also the case in which "the *labour of horses* is substituted for that of man." He explained: "If I employed 100 men on my farm and if I found that the food bestowed on 50 of those men could be diverted to the support of horses and afford me a greater return of raw produce, after allowing for the interest of the capital which the purchase of the horses would absorb, it would be advantageous to me to substitute the horses for the men and I should accordingly do so; but this would not be for the interest of the men ... " (Ricardo *Works* I: 394; emphasis added).

impact on the productive metabolism of the economic system and necessarily affects its properties, which is reflected in the level of the general rate of profits and competitive normal prices. A proper analysis of value and distribution presupposes a correct analysis of the choice of technique problem.[10]

Marx did not share what we may call a *real cost*-approach to the different kinds of labour and therefore to the theory of value and distribution. In fact, he was strictly opposed to it and saw only human labour as the origin and substance of value. This indicates a fundamental divide between the analyses of Smith and Ricardo, on the one hand, and that of Marx, on the other. While the three authors shared several views, in this important respect they parted company with one another. "Labour" in different authors means different things. Readers ought be on the alert, when confronted with the concept.

With regard to the second aspect, abstract labour might indeed be seen, as one of the referees observed, as that kind of labour that is "transferable across producing activities". The referee added: "If there is transferability, perfect substitutability we might say, the conversion rate can only be 1:1." This case may be said to correspond to Marx's idea, mentioned in passing in the above, that technical progress leads to the de-qualification of labour. In the limit, all workers perform labour that can indiscriminately be employed in all lines of production. Marx did not go that far, and therefore, the problem of the conversion rate remains. The purely physiological definition of abstract labour he gives ("expenditure of human brains ... ") does not reflect, I surmise, the transferability or interchangeability of all kinds of labour, but rather the fact, as Marx perceived it, that in modern society, as opposed to the Greek polis, "all kinds of labour are equal and equivalent." This is said to be so, because "the notion of human equality has already acquired the fixity of popular prejudice." (Marx 1954, 65) Once commodity production and exchange are well established and have acquired "the stability of natural, self-understood forms of social life", "the labour-time socially necessary for [the production of various commodities] forcibly asserts itself like an *over-riding law of Nature*" (Marx 1954, 80; emphasis added).

---

[10] The classical authors did not stick consistently to this approach, but in an attempt to overcome the problem of the heterogeneity of commodities in terms of a search for an "ultimate measure of value" eventually adopted the labour embodiment rule as a makeshift solution and thus blurred the issues under consideration.

Now what about the distinction between simple and complex or unskilled and skilled labour? In the case of perfect substitutability discussed in the above, there is only simple labour. Complex labour is generated within the socio-economic system either as the result of special education processes in which simple labour is gradually transformed into complex labour or as a by-product of the production process (learning on the job, learning by doing). Adam Smith (1976a), for example, saw a strict analogy between an item of durable capital and skilled labour power and famously stressed that an educated man "may be compared to one of those expensive machines." He added: "The work which he learns to perform, it must be expected, over and above the usual wages of common labour, will replace to him the whole expense of his education, with at least the ordinary profits of an equally durable capital" (WN I.x.b.6). Hence according to Smith, the wages of skilled or complex labour cover interest or profit on the human capital involved (plus a depreciation share).[11] This compounds the difficulties of the labour value-based reasoning, which can only be regarded as a makeshift approach to the problem of value and distribution, but not a thorough and logically consistent basis from which a definitive solution can be elaborated, as Marx was inclined to think.

We now turn briefly to Marx's "law" of the falling tendency of the rate of profits. It constitutes the centrepiece of his conviction that capitalism is necessarily a transient mode of production.[12]

4. A hidden watershed: the "law" of the falling tendency of the rate of profits

The MEGA[2] edition bears impressive testimony to the fact that Marx in the course of his analytical work experienced the sobering feeling that he knew too little and that some of his earlier convictions did perhaps not stand up to critical scrutiny. This appears to apply especially with regard to the declared crowning of his entire economic analysis: the law of the falling rate of profits. Engels' edition of volume III of *Capital* did contain hints to Marx's growing doubts about the tenability of some of his propositions. But the selection of manuscripts from Marx's literary remains and Engels' passages interpolated

---

[11] For a summary account of the classical position and how its various aspects can be dealt with analytically, see Kurz and Salvadori (1995: chap. 11).

[12] For the following, see also Kurz (2013a).

in the text of the edition, some of which without informing the reader, hid the full extent of Marx's difficulties. The MEGA^2 edition allows us to see with much greater clarity which problems, in particular, stopped the accomplishment of Marx's *magnum opus*. In this section, we deal with elements of what may be called a hidden watershed, hidden by Engels' editorial efforts.

Marx's political economy represents a particular variant of the doctrine of the unintended consequences of self-interested behaviour that representatives of the Scottish Enlightenment had most forcefully advocated. Marx's version of it reads: capitalists do not want to fall victim to their "inimical brothers", as he called them, in the competitive struggle (MEGA^2 II/15: 249-50). The "coercive law of competition" (MEGA^2 II/15: 257) makes them restlessly pursue lower costs and higher profits through technical and organisational change. However, "behind their backs" (MEGA^2 II/15: 169; see also MEGA^2 II/1: 149), unknown to them, their nemesis was taking shape: the general rate of profits, the key variable of the entire system, was falling. The cunning of history was taken to ensure that the self-seeking behaviour of capitalists as a class spells their doom, and opens the way to socialism.

This is an "invisible hand" argument. Adam Smith (1976a, 1976b) had repeatedly made use of it by emphasising that socio-economic transformations of great significance are frequently brought about by people who promoted "an end which was no part of [their] intention" (WN IV.ii.9; also TMS IV.i.I.10). A most important case in point was the gradual demise of the feudal and the rise of the capitalist class. Smith explained:

> the silent and insensible operation of foreign commerce and manufactures … gradually furnished the great proprietors with something for which they could exchange the whole surplus produce of their lands, and which they could consume themselves without sharing it either with tenants or retainers. All for themselves, and nothing for other people, seems, in every age of the world, to have been the vile maxim of the masters of mankind. … For a pair of diamond buckles perhaps, or for something as frivolous and useless, they exchanged the maintenance … of a thousand men for a year, and with it the whole weight and authority which it could give them. (WN III.iv.10)

The implication was "decisive" and consisted in a dramatic loss of power of the landed gentry: "for the gratification of the most childish, the meanest and the most sordid of all vanities, they [the landlords] gradually bartered their whole power and authority." (WN III.iv.10) The Scotsman concluded:

> A revolution of the greatest importance to the public happiness, was in this manner brought about by two different orders of people, who had not the least intention to serve the public. To gratify the most childish vanity was the sole motive of the great proprietors. The merchants and artificers, much less ridiculous, acted merely from a view to their own interest, and in pursuit of their own pedlar principle of turning a penny wherever a penny was to be got. *Neither of them had either knowledge or foresight of that great revolution which the folly of the one, and the industry of the other, was gradually bringing about.* (WN III.iv.17; emphasis added)

Marx had begun to read Smith carefully in 1844 and formed a radical variant of this basic idea: with the self-transformation of capitalism eventually a classless society will come into being, ending the exploitation of man by man. In this final act, the invisible hand would itself become redundant, because man took control of his own destiny. Marx, the atheist, anticipated the salvation of mankind not in the hereafter, but on earth.

Marx considered the law of the falling rate of profits the "most important law from the historical standpoint" (MEGA^2 II/15: 255) because it captures the transient nature of the capitalist mode of production and the necessity of socialism. He rejected Ricardo's explanation that the fall of the rate of profits was due to diminishing returns in agriculture and mockingly said that Ricardo "flees from economics to seek refuge in organic chemistry." The rate of profit does not fall, he insisted, "because labour becomes less productive, but because it becomes more productive" (MEGA^2, part II, vol. 15: 236).[13] He contended that it falls in spite of technological progress, whereas for Ricardo technological progress works against its fall or is at worst neutral with regard to it.

The question is close at hand: should one then assume, conversely, that the rate of profits will rise with a falling productivity? Putting it in this way shows the difficulty into which Marx had manoeuvred himself. He had set the bar insurmountably high. He argued as follows. In order to survive in the competitive struggle, each capitalist has to accumulate capital and introduce new methods of production

---

[13] Ricardo explained the falling rate of profits by deliberately putting on one side technical progress, that is, by invoking a counterfactual argument. He stressed that with sufficient technical progress the rate of profits need not fall; see Kurz (2015).

that allow him to furnish new products or reduce the production costs of known products. Due to an increase in labour productivity the values of the different commodities will fall, and along with them their prices of production: less and less labour is needed to produce the various commodities. Marx based his respective argument on what he considered to be the dominant form of technological progress in capitalism. It is supposedly characterised by an increase in the 'organic composition of capital': more and more physical plant and equipment (tools, machines, etc.) is employed per worker – the production process gets ever more mechanised. As workers are replaced by machines, there emerges an "industrial reserve army of the unemployed". This reserve army holds the demands of workers in check and is a main reason why the workday is longer than necessary to just reproduce the worker's means of subsistence; correspondingly the real wage rate is lower than net labour productivity. Only for this reason is there surplus value and profit. But technological progress of this variety means that relatively less and less surplus value is created as variable capital and thus "living" labour is increasingly replaced by constant capital and thus "dead" labour. Since the organic composition – the ratio of dead to living labour – is the inverse of the *maximum* rate of profits, which obtains in the hypothetical case in which variable capital vanishes, a rising organic composition means a falling maximum rate of profits. However, a falling maximum rate of profits, Marx was convinced, increasingly narrows the leeway for the actual rate of profits, until it finally forces this to fall as well.

Is this reasoning convincing? Apparently Marx himself was not so sure. From summer 1865 to February 1866 he studied works on productivity-enhancing improvements in agriculture, which counteracted diminishing returns and undermined, or so he thought, Ricardo"s doctrine (MEGA^2 II/4.2).[14] But they would at the same time question the alleged falling tendency of the rate of profits. Constant or even increasing returns to scale in agriculture due to the scientific application of chemistry were difficult to reconcile with the tendency under consideration. However, shortly afterwards, Marx changed his view again. Under the influence especially of Justus von Liebig's views on the excessive cultivation of land, Marx took land to be an *exhaustible*

---

[14] It could not, of course, accomplish this task for the simple reason that Ricardo saw technical progress as a force countervailing the "niggardliness of nature" with the potential of preventing the rate of profits from falling.

resource (comparable to mineral deposits) that was actually getting exhausted. It was no longer the *renewable* resource possessed of "indestructible powers" that Ricardo had assumed in his theory of rent and profits. Marx went so far as to opine that capitalist production did not only exploit the original factors of production and sources of wealth – land and labour – but actually "exhausted" them (see MEGA² II/5: 410 and 413; see also MEGA² II/9: 442-3). By destroying the foundations of its own success, one may wonder, of course, how socialism could possibly prosper, inheriting a pauperised population and exhausted soil. To the best of my knowledge, Marx did not provide a clear-cut answer to the conundrum he had proposed.

Saito (2016) investigated Marx's respective studies and observations also after 1868 in some detail, but there are no compelling signs that Marx's respective thoughts on the role of nature in the course of socio-economic development became stable and permanent as time went by. Ricardo's legacy looms large even when the British economist does not get mentioned in person, but the problems he dealt with and the way he tackled them analytically are discussed.

Uncertainties and a lack of definiteness of certain views of Marx characterise also other parts of the MEGA² edition relating to preparatory notes, jottings, excerpts and manuscripts for volumes II and III of *Das Kapital*. When Engels selected from the host of material he had inherited what was to go into the edition, he was bound to decide what were in all probability Marx's most mature views on the various problems under consideration. This was anything but easy, and Engels had to find means and ways to go about Marx's vacillations, contradictions between different manuscripts and so on. In a couple of cases there is evidence that Engels patched over the editorial problems he was confronted with. A particularly significant case is the 'law' of the falling tendency of the rate of profits. Keen to keep things on track, Engels famously ended Marx's vacillations by insisting: "but in reality the rate of profit, as already seen, falls in the longer run" (MEGA² II/15: 227 and 977). For Engels, Marx was a "scientific socialist" on account of his identification of the "law of motion" of capitalism, and with that, of the inevitability of socialism. A falling rate of profits would decelerate capital accumulation and was a clear sign that capitalism was losing its vital force (MEGA² II/15: 255-6, 211).

However, as the MEGA² edition shows, Marx saw very clearly that there are forms of technical progress, which do not lead to a fall in the rate of profits, given the real wage rate. He anticipated, for example, what later became known as Harrod-neutral technical change and several other forms, some of which would even imply an increase, and not a decrease, in the general rate of profits! These forms would not lead to a rising trend in the organic composition of capital, the pivot of Marx's argument. How then could one establish beyond any reasonable doubt that the organic composition had to rise throughout, reflecting an inner necessity of the capitalist mode of production, relegating these other forms of technical progress to the realm of purely abstract possibilities?

Yet things were worse still. Even if the answer to this question would have been in the affirmative, it was far from clear that the rate of profits would have to fall. According to Marx's labour value-reasoning, the rate of profits is equal to the ratio of the total amount of "surplus value" and the total amount of capital, variable and constant. The surplus value is created by living labour (L) and is thus proportional to variable capital. The labour embodied in constant capital (C) is transferred in the course of its use and gradual wear and tear to the commodities produced. A rising organic composition implies an increase in C/L, which in turn is accompanied by an increase in labour productivity. Marx in fact insisted that in capitalism labour productivity grows "as in a greenhouse" (MEGA^2 II/5: 505), increasing "geometrically". Few writers have expressed such admiration for the productivity-enhancing properties of capitalism. But if labour productivity rises without limit, the quantity of labour needed in the production of the various commodities falls continually. This cheapens both the subsistence goods for the worker (variable capital) and the produced means of production employed (constant capital). The first implies that, for a given real wage, variable capital will shrink, and, for a given working day, the amount of surplus labour created daily per worker will increase. The latter means that as the elements of constant capital become cheaper, its value (C) increases more slowly than its "quantity", if at all.[15] The numerator in the expression of the rate of profits, the rate of surplus value, therefore increases,

---

[15] Marx spoke of the "technical composition of capital", which was meant to reflect some physical measure of constant capital relative to living labour as opposed to the organic composition, which is expressed in labour-value terms. However, he refrained from saying how changing technical inventories of heterogeneous capital goods are to be measured and compared with one another other than in labour value-terms, which, however, begs the question.

while it seems that nothing definite can be concluded about the denominator, which is an expression including as the only variable the organic composition. At any rate, there can be no talk of Marx's definitive "proof" of the "law" of the falling rate of profits.

Marx apparently became aware of the fact that his argument was not conclusive. For some time he tried hard to overcome its deficiencies. He buried himself in mathematics and differential calculus in particular, in order to deal with economic dynamics. He delved into the natural sciences, reading works on geology, biology, physiology and chemistry. Had Ricardo really been wrong with his reference to diminishing returns in agriculture? And would not Marx's claim that the capitalists' concern with short-term profit maximisation would necessarily lead to the desertification of land and nature more generally amount to an argument that is the dynamic equivalent of Ricardo's static reasoning? It should therefore come as no surprise that Marx would study the works of the eminent German pioneer in agricultural and biological chemistry, Justus von Liebig, and especially his theory of the exhaustion of soil. In addition, he read up on atomic theory and other fundamental issues, as is now evident from the published manuscripts. He also returned to the writings of Ricardo and other economists. While he had once seen Britain as the paramount example of capitalism, reflecting in a representative way the law of motion of capitalism, his attention was now increasingly drawn towards the USA, for which the statistical material was a great deal better, and which demonstrated no tendency of stagnation or decline. How did the development of limited liability, the separation of ownership and control and the stock exchange alter the picture? Capitalist economic development was cyclical, it evolved in leaps and bounds, but was the trend necessarily downward sloping? And could trend and cycles be predicted? The MEGA^2 edition shows impressively that Marx was scrupulous and a perfectionist. Given the number of unresolved questions, how could he possibly complete his work?

Interestingly, the organic composition of capital actually rose during the nineteenth century in several capitalist economies, rendering some support to Marx's intuition. Since there was no reason to presume that this trend would continue forever and even if it did, but was bounded from above and approached the boundary asymptotically, the maximum rate of profits would not fall to zero and in its wake the actual rate did not have to follow suit.

5. Concluding remarks

While Marx for a long time was convinced that socialism could be scientifically shown to be inescapable and once and for all do away with exploitative modes of production and establish a just and equitable society, in his later life he struggled with doubts regarding the correctness of his reasoning. He had not managed to accomplish his huge task, there were still many lose ends, and he got doubts about certain parts of the argument he had been able to develop up until then. He must have suffered greatly, confronted with the calibre of the problems he saw before him, on the one hand, and his waning mental and physical powers, on the other. If his view of the destructive impact of the capitalist mode of production on the environment happened to be correct: what kind of globe would capitalism leave behind? Could socialism prosper on a poisoned and despoiled planet? In his geological notebooks (see MEGA^2 IV/26), Marx treats the earth and humanity as two living and interacting organisms. The question he asked himself was: will they survive together in the long run or will the earth rid itself of humanity? Marx was exceptionally far-sighted, and although his analyses were not always cogent, but beset by difficulties, logical and others, he deserves to be credited with having posed the right questions and for having provided us with indications in which direction a correct answer may be sought.

Acknowledgments

An earlier version of this article was given at the conference 'Marx 1818/2018. New Developments on Karl Marx's Thought and Writings', 27–29 September 2017, Centre Jean Bosco, Lyon (France). I am grateful to the commentator of my article, Christian Gehrke, for his valuable observations, to the participants of the conference for interesting discussions and to Jurriaan Bendien, Gilbert Faccarello, Fabio Petri, and two anonymous referees for their comments and suggestions on aspects of the article. All remaining errors and misconceptions are, of course, entirely my responsibility.

Disclosure statement

No potential conflict of interest was reported by the author.

References

Faccarello, G. 1997. "Some Reflections on Marx's Theory of Value." In *Marxian Economics: A Reappraisal. Essays on Volume III of Capital. Volume I: Method, Value and Money*, edited by R. Bellofiore, 29–47. London: Macmillan.

Faccarello, G., C. Gehrke, and H. D. Kurz. 2016. "Karl Heinrich Marx (1818–1883)." Vol. II. In *Handbook on the History of Economic Analysis*, edited by G. Faccarello und H. D. Kurz, 211–233, Cheltenham und Northampton: Edward Elgar.

Kurz, H. D. 2010. "Technical Progress, Capital Accumulation and Income Distribution in Classical Economics: Adam Smith, David Ricardo and Karl Marx." *European Journal of the History of Economic Thought* 17 (5): 1183–1222. http://dx.doi.org/10.1080/09672567.2010.522242

Kurz, H. D. 2013a. "Das Problem der nichtintendierten Konsequenzen. Zur Politischen Ökonomie von Karl Marx, Marx-Engels Jahrbuch 2012/13", 75–112. Berlin: Akademie Verlag.

Kurz, H. D. 2013b. "Unintended Consequences: On the Political Economy of Karl Marx." *European Journal of the History of Economic Thought* 20 (5): 845–849. http://dx.doi.org/10.1080/09672567.2013.833673

Kurz, H. D. 2014. "Transatlantic Conversations: Observations on Marx and Engels' Journalism and Beyond." *Social Research* 81 (3): 637–655. http://dx. doi.org/10.1353/sor.2014.0035

Kurz, H. D. 2015. "David Ricardo: On the Art of 'Elucidating Economic Principles' in the Face of a 'Labyrinth of Difficulties'." *European Journal of the History of Economic Thought* 22 (5): 818–851. http://dx.doi.org/10.1080/ 09672567.2015.1074713

Kurz, H. D. 2018. "Marx and the 'Law of Value'. A Critical Appraisal on the Occasion of his 200th Birthday. Honorary Invited Lecture Given at the XIXth International Conference on Economic and Social Development." National Research University – Higher School of Economics, Moscow, April 10–13, 2018. To be published in Russian in the journal *Voprosny Economiki*.

Kurz, H. D., and N. Salvadori. 1995. *Theory of Production. A Long-Period Analysis*. Cambridge: Cambridge University Press.

Kurz, H. D., and N. Salvadori. 2010. "Sraffa and the Labour Theory of Value. A few Observations." In *Economic Theory and Economic Thought. Essays in Honour of Ian Steedman*, edited by J. Vint, J. S. Metcalfe, H. D. Kurz, N. Salvadori, and P. A. Samuelson, 189–215. London: Routledge.

Marx, K. 1954. *Capital*. Vol. I. London: Lawrence and Wishart.

Marx, K. 1956. *Capital*. Vol. II. London: Lawrence and Wishart.

Marx, K. 1959. *Capital*. Vol. III. London: Lawrence and Wishart.

Marx, K., and F. Engels. 1976–2012. *Gesamtausgabe* (MEGA), International Marx-Engels Foundation (IMES) (ed.). Zweite Abteilung: "Das Kapital" und Vorarbeiten, 15 vols in 23 separate parts, 1976–2012, several editors, Berlin: Akademie Verlag. http://www.oldenbourg-verlag.de/akademie-verlag/marx-engels-gesamtausgabe.

Ricardo, D. 1951. *On the Principles of Political Economy, and Taxation,* first published in 1817, third edn 1821. Vol. 1. In *The Works and Correspondence of David Ricardo,* edited by Piero Sraffa with collaboration of Maurice H. Dobb. Cambridge: Cambridge University Press.

Roth, R. 2010. "Marx on Technical Change in the Critical Edition." *European Journal of the History of Economic Thought* 17 (5): 1223–1251. http://dx.doi. org/10.1080/09672567.2010.522239

Saito, K. 2016. *Natur Gegen Kapital. Marx' Ökologie in Seiner Unvollendeten Kritik des Kapitalismus.* Frankfurt and New York: Campus Verlag.

Smith, A. 1976a. *The Theory of Moral Sentiments,* first published in 1759. In *The Glasgow Edition of the Works and Correspondence of Adam Smith,* edited by D. D. Raphael and A. L. Macfie. Oxford: Oxford University Press.

Smith, A. 1976b. *An Inquiry into the Nature and Causes of the Wealth of Nations,* first published in 1776. Two vols. In *The Glasgow Edition of the Works and Correspondence of Adam Smith,* edited by R. H. Campbell and A. S. Skinner. Oxford: Oxford University Press. In the text referred to as WN, book number, chapter number, section number, paragraph number.

Sraffa, P. 1960. *Production of Commodities by Means of Commodities.* Cambridge: Cambridge University Press.

Re-examining the authorship of the Feuerbach chapter in *The German Ideology* on the basis of a hypothesis of dictation

Izumi Omura

ABSTRACT

In the *Feuerbach* manuscripts, the core theses of the materialist conception of history were documented for the first time. Most of the handwriting of the manuscripts belongs to Engels. But later Engels repeatedly stated that the first discoverer of this conception is Marx, not him. This is a contradiction. This contradiction had been discussed for nearly a century, but it has not led scholars to a common result. Why? In my opinion, it was because no one, including the former and new MEGA editors, ever attempted to examine a very important problem, namely, the possibility that the *Feuerbach* manuscripts could have been dictated by Marx and written by Engels. If this possibility existed really, no contradiction will remain.

Preface

As is well known, Marx and Engels shared a common view of history, known as "the materialistic conception of history" or "historical materialism," the core theses of which were documented for the first time in the so-called Feuerbach manuscripts, which became the first chapter in *The German Ideology* (1845–1846). It is unclear, however, which writer should be regarded as the primary author of the Feuerbach chapter and thus as the founder of the materialistic conception of history. This is the well-known problem regarding the authorship of the Feuerbach chapter. Why has it remained controversial among scholars for such a long time?

Since most sections of the Feuerbach manuscripts were physically written by Engels, Marx's handwriting accounts for only a small percentage of the manuscripts. When identifying an author of an anonymous work, the handwriting is regarded as important. Thus, given the source of the physical handwriting seen on the manuscripts, it would be fair to say that Engels rather than Marx was the primary author of the Feuerbach chapter and was, therefore, the founder of the materialistic conception of history. Nevertheless, it was Engels himself who explicitly stated during Marx's life in 1877 that the founder of the materialistic conception of history was Marx[1]. This position of Engels remained unchanged even after Marx's death (1883[2]). Moreover, in 1885[3] and 1888[4], Engels clearly stated in the spring of 1845, immediately prior to beginning their collaborative project related to *The German Ideology* that he was not yet convinced by Marx's idea that the material conditions were the decisive force influencing history.

This apparent contradiction has been discussed for nearly a century, and scholars have been seemingly incapable of coming to a consensus. However, as the publication of *Marx-Engels-Gesamtausgabe* (1975–, hereafter referred to as *MEGA*②) and studies on excerpt notes proceeded, some began to argue that Marx took initiative in creating the Feuerbach manuscripts. At the same time, there is also another question to be answered: why is Engels the writer and Marx is not? Everyone, including the editors of *MEGA*② I/5, which contains *The German Ideology* and was published in November 2017, has been unable to answer this question. Why? In my opinion, this is because no one has ever attempted to examine a very important problem, namely, the possibility that the Feuerbach manuscripts could have been dictated. It is important to remember that the person who physically writes a text is not always its original author. Assuming this is the case, there would be no contradiction between Engels' statement in 1877 and the idea that he is the physical writer of the Feuerbach manuscripts. Furthermore, it would be problematic to establish Engels as the real author because his physical writing alone is no longer valid as persuasive evidence.

If this is the case, how can we investigate the possibility of dictation without any additional documents; for example, Marx and Engels' correspondence regarding the writing of the Feuerbach chapter? It is

---

[1] "These two great discoveries, the materialistic conception of history and the revelation of the secret of capitalistic production through surplus-value, we owe to Marx." (Engels 1988, 237)
[2] See, Engels 1989, 467–468.
[3] See, Engels 2011, 96–97.
[4] See, Engels 2002, 119–120.

very important to establish a scientifically valid criterion to establish convincingly whether the Feuerbach manuscripts were dictated. Since one's handwriting is not necessarily linked with his or her philosophy, a criterion for the extensive analysis of handwriting should be focused on its form and characteristic, to distinguish it from the theoretical analysis of the contents of manuscripts, which often results in a difference in interpretation.

In the case of analyzing the Feuerbach manuscripts, the best criterion is to focus on the peculiarities of composition[5] of Marx and Engels, including the number of corrections and the features of their modifications in the manuscripts. It is, therefore, essential to compare their peculiarities of composition with great care and accuracy, examples of which are evinced in the Feuerbach manuscripts and in their other manuscripts written just before the Feuerbach manuscripts.

I would like to turn my attention to two issues with the following arguments. The first is that the peculiarities of composition of the real author are reflected most powerfully in immediate variants (the so-called *Sofortvarianten* in *MEGA*②) because they were produced as part of process of composing a sentence; in other words, they were produced when the author delivered his own thoughts onto paper for the first time and created his base text (e.g. grammatically earliest completed text, so-called "rough draft", hereinafter base text.) The second issue is that, in the case of dictation, the peculiarities of composition on paper are identical to the style of the original author, and not to the "physical" writer, since the original author's judgment is given priority over that of the physical writer. Assuming that Engels was not only the physical writer but also the original author of the Feuerbach manuscripts, the peculiarities of composition in the manuscripts would correlate with those observed in Engels' other pieces written around the same period. If Engels is not the original author, we can assume that the peculiarities contained within the composition of the Feuerbach manuscripts would be similar to those of Marx. This would more effectively explain why Engels made very unusual mistakes in German grammar, such as the revision of homophones, "das" and "daß."

There are two main types of peculiarities of composition that are of interest here: the first occurs when one writes after deep consideration, composing the structure of one's sentences over and over in

---

[5] Peculiarities of composition refer to how sentences are formed, word choices, length and structure of sentences, how often items are crossed out and so on.

one's mind before writing them down. In this case, the number of immediate variants decreases. The other kinds of peculiarities of composition are those that arise when thinking and writing at the same time, which entail the repetition of the processes of writing and deletion. In this case, the process of writing is interrupted in the middle of producing the base text as the writer changes his mind, eventually increasing the number of immediate variants. As I will later demonstrate with concrete examples, while Engels' manuscripts belong to the first category, Marx's manuscripts belong to the second. Engels' manuscripts are often described as elegant, not only because each word is written in a refined way, but also because his peculiarities of composition belong to the first category. However, in the case of Marx, his peculiarities of composition are a classic example of the second category – scattered with corrections – and the illegible handwriting makes his manuscripts even less readable. To which category do the peculiarities of composition found in the Feuerbach manuscripts actually belong? This is the first question we must address.[6]

Because of space restrictions, I would like to limit my scope to the third portion of the manuscript, ranging from M36 to M72, as numbered by Marx himself (M36 to M39 is missing), that is, the so-called H^{5c} manuscript in $MEGA^{②}$ I/5. Ultimately, I would like to present my view on whether the first portion (M1 to M29: the H^{5a} manuscript in $MEGA^{②}$ I/5) and the second portion (M30 to M35: the H^{5b} manuscript in $MEGA^{②}$ I/5) were dictated.[7]

Indeed, the handwriting of Marx can be found in every page of H^{5c}, but these sections were inserted following the completion of the base text. The base text of H^{5c} is written by Engels alone, including its corrections and the additions known as the immediate variants. With respect to Marx, his handwriting remains in only 15 locations in the *Marx-Engels-Jahrbuch 2003*[8] and $MEGA^{②}$ I/5, excluding the page numbers. Moreover, they all belong to late variants (so-called *Spätvarianten* in $MEGA^{②}$), which were produced following the completion of a sentence in the base text. If we judge the authorship of

---

[6] This research method of this paper is based on the creation of its author himself and in the history of research about the authorship problem of *The German Ideology* it is a method that MEGA editors, including other Marx-Engels researchers, have never adopted.

[7] In the following, we refer the first portion of the Feuerbach manuscripts, M1 to M29, as H^{5a}, the second portion, M30 to M35, as H^{5b}, and the third portion as H^{5c}.

[8] This *Jahrbuch* was published as the pre-publication edition of $MEGA^{②}$ I/5 in 2004. Hereafter, it is referred to as the *MEJ 2003*.

H^{5c} purely on the basis of the differences between the handwriting and the sequential order of writing, we can more readily understand why Rjazanov argued – upon the presentation of the original Feuerbach manuscripts in 1926 – that Engels "seemed to have written these pages[9] alone, not based on dictation."(Rjazanov 1926, 217) It is also important to note that G. Mayer contended in 1921 that "Engels wrote more readably, he was quicker and steadier, and therefore constantly ready to commit to paper sections he had conceptualized with Marx jointly."(Mayer 1921, 776) This idea from Mayer is referred to as the hypothesis of the "co-authorship" of *The German Ideology* and the most influential view in the history of research. The editors of the *MEJ 2003* and also *MEGA*^{②} *I/5* take this position.[10] If, however, you look into my investigation of the Feuerbach manuscripts, I am quite confident that you will be convinced that neither Rjazanov's nor Mayer's assumptions are correct, and that the base text of H^{5c} was dictated by Marx and written down by Engels. In other words, there should be nothing like the Marx-Engels-Problem in the study of the Feuerbach chapter, which some scholars, such as Wataru Hiromatsu and Terrell Carver, insist on.[11] These scholars have tended to place significant weight on the fact that the Feuerbach manuscripts was physically written by Engels, which has rendered them incapable of exploring the more compelling possibility that the manuscripts were dictated by Marx. This seems to me a significant oversight.[12]

---

[9] These pages are M40 to M72, that is, the H^{5c} manuscript.

[10] As a member of the editorial board of the International Marx-Engels-Foundation (IMSF), I had been requesting that the editors of *MEGA*^{②} *I/5* to review the hypothesis of dictation from time to time since 2015. So, I was expecting it to be mentioned in the preface of *MEGA*^{②} *I/5*, but obviously they did not accept my suggestion. On the other hand, the preface not only states that *The German Ideology* was a collaborative elaboration of Marx and Engels, but also emphasizes that Marx had been far more ahead of Engels in terms of criticism of Stirner, Bauer and those called "Young Hegelian". It also mentions Marx's terrible handwriting. Therefore, it seems to me that they could have developed their argument related to the possibility of dictation. It is also possible that they abandoned such an effort since my argument was published after the completion of *MEGA*^{②} *I/5*'s editorial work (April 2017).

[11] See, *Hiromatsu edition* and *Carver edition*.

[12] *MEGA*^{②}(1975-) and *MEGA*^{①}(1927–1935) consist of both the text and critical apparatus of it, including the final text of the manuscript in the former, and the text variants separately in the latter. However, *Hiromatsu edition* (1974) and *Carver edition* (2014) do not distinguish between these texts, as they incorporate text variants into the final text of the manuscript. The text variants in *Hiromatsu edition* are based on *MEGA*^{①}*I/5*, in which there is no distinction made between the immediate and late variants. The text variants in *Carver edition* are based on the *MEJ 2003*. However, while immediate variants are clearly distinguished from late variants in the *MEJ 2003*, this distinction disappears in *Carver edition*. Thus, it is impossible to verify my hypothesis using either *Hiromatsu edition* or *Carver edition*. In other words, the possibility of dictation is excluded from the beginning by *Hiromatsu edition* and *Carver edition*, in which handwritings of Marx and Engels are printed with different fonts, giving readers an impression that the font represents its author. It is also important to note

Many immediate variants inconsistent with other manuscripts by Engels

Here, I would like to say that there are a significant number of immediate variants in manuscript H^{5c}. Table 1 (see, middle of this section) shows 433 immediate variants in H^{5c},[13] however, there is an issue regarding the number of immediate variants found in H^{5c}. To facilitate a comparative analysis using other manuscripts written by Engels and Marx around the same period, I have created reference charts and counted the number of immediate and late variants appearing in the text of H^{5c}. Table 1 and Table 2 (see, middle of this section) were created in consideration of the following three points:

(1) The first chapter of *The German Ideology* manuscripts was written in 1845 and 1846. To verify the peculiarities of composition of both Marx and Engels, it would be most convincing to examine their writing styles in other manuscripts written around the same period, particularly those written right before *The German Ideology*. While *The German Ideology* is contained in *MEGA*® *I/5*, other earlier manuscripts are going to be included in *MEGA*® *I/4*, which is not published. For these reasons, I selected the earlier works of Engels from *MEGA*® *I/3*, and Marx's work from *MEGA*® *I/2*. *MEGA*® *I/3* contains the early works of Engels up to August 1844, including facsimiles attached to some manuscripts (there are few posthumous manuscripts of Engels extant today). There are also 11 variant lists in *MEGA*® *I/3*; seven are related to the manuscripts, five of these seven record immediate variants, and only three of these five exceed ten pages when counted using the original manuscripts' page numbers. There are no manuscripts other than the three in *MEGA*® *I/3* that permit statistical processing, such as mean-value analysis. In Tables 1 and 2, the following three manuscripts are set as comparative objects:

"Eine Seeräubergeschichte" (1836–1837)

---

the issue of translation (*Carver edition*), because it is quite challenging to discuss subtle variances of complicated German grammar in English, such as a difference between German definite and indefinite articles.

[13] According to my study, the number of immediate variants in H^{5c} is 433, however, it is counted as 245 in the *MEJ 2003*. By comparing a text with the original clear image of H^{5c}, I supplemented the number of immediate variants written in the *MEJ 2003* with more reliable data. On the other hands, it is worthwhile to mention that the number of immediate variants in H^{5c} from *MEGA*® *I/5* has reached 407. I am currently editing the online edition of the first chapter of "Feuerbach" in the *German Ideology* (see, "Conclusion" of this paper). In the footnotes of the online version, I specifically report on the difference between my calculations and those from *MEGA*® *I/5*.

Table 1. Immediate variants in Marx and Engels Manuscripts compared to the Manuscript H^{5c}.

Immediate Variants / Manuscripts	(A) the manuscript H^{5c} (M40-72)	(B) Eine Seeräubergeschichte (1836-1837)	(C) Cola di Rienzi (1840-1841)	(D) Zur Kritik der preußischen Predgesetze (1842)	(E) Ökonomische-philoso-phische Manuskripte (Heft I: XXII-XXVI) (1845)	(F) Ökonomische-philoso-phische Manuskripte (Heft II: XL-XLIII)(1845)
(1) Number of immediate variants in the original manuscript's pages	433	32	37	9	118	57
(2) Number of the original manuscript's pages	33	16	26	10	5	4
(3) Frequency of immediate variants per one original manuscript page: (1)÷(2)	13.1	2	1.4	0.9	23.6	14.3
(4) Actual print number of the original manuscripts on basis of the format of MEGA²	25 (MEJ 2003, MEGA²I/5: 52Seiten)	12	12 (MEGA²I/3: 24Seiten)	7	13	6
(5) Frequency of immediate variants per MEGA² page: (1)÷(4)	17.3	2.7	3	1.3	9.1	9.5

(G) (32+37+9)÷(12+12+7)=2.5

Average frequency of immediate variants per MEGA² page

(H) (118+57)÷(13+6)=9.2

Table 2. Late variants in Marx and Engels Manuscripts compared to the Manuscript H^{5c}.

Late Variants \ Manuscripts	(A) the manuscript H^{5c} (M40-72)	(B) Eine Seeräubergeschichte (1836-1837)	(C) Cola di Rienzi (1840-1841)	(D) Zur Kritik der preußischen Preßgesetze (1842)	(E) Ökonomische-philosophische Manuskripte (Heftl: XXII-XXVI) (1845)	(F) Ökonomische-philoso-phische Manuskripte (Heftll: XL-XLIII)(1845)
(1) Number of late variants in the original manuscript's pages	210	47	125	81	73	61
(2) Number of the original manuscript's pages	33	16	26	10	5	4
(3) Frequency of late variants per one original manuscript page: (1)÷(2)	6.7	2.9	4.8	8.1	14.6	15.3
(4) Actual print number of the original manuscripts on basis of the format of MEGA²	25 (MEJ 2003, MEGA² I/5: 52Seiten)	12	12 (MEGA² I/3:24Seiten)	7	13	6
(5) Frequency of late variants per MEGA² page: (1)÷(4)	8.6	3.8	9.6	11.6	5.6	10.1
Average frequency of late variants per MEGA² page		(G) (47+125+81)÷(12+12+7)=8.2			(H) (73+61)÷(13+6)=7.1	

"Cola di Rienzi" (1840–1841)

"Zur Kritik der preußischen Preßgesetze" (1842)

(2) With regard to Marx's manuscripts, I selected two parts of *Economic and Philosophic Manuscripts of 1844* (*Ökonomisch-philosophische Manuskripte*) from *MEGA*[2] *I/2*, namely, pp. XXII–XXVI of manuscript I (Heft I) and pp. XL–XLIII of manuscript II (Heft II). The editors of MEW, Bd. 40 named the former as "Estranged Labor" [die entfremdete Arbeit] and the latter "On Private Property" [Das Verhältnis des Privateigenthuns].

(3) It would be meaningless to conduct a direct comparative analysis on the basis of the number of immediate variants because these manuscripts are written in a different format of verso leaves. Therefore, I decided to examine the average appearance number of immediate variants per page on the basis of the format of *MEGA*[2] (hereafter, frequency of immediate variants per *MEGA*[2] page). There is still a problem of composition originating from the nature of the texts, however. Although *MEGA*[2] *I/5* format is identical with the *MEJ 2003*, the Feuerbach chapter is set in a horizontal two-column format. Moreover, with regard to the *MEJ 2003* and *MEGA*[2] *I/5*, some insertions (mostly of late variants) in the right column of the manuscripts are reproduced in the left column, and it required only ten lines to reproduce the base text written by Engels in the left column of the manuscripts in M72. On the other hand, there is a large margin in the printed text of Engels' "Cola di Rienzi" because it was written for the drama. Therefore, in preparing the reference charts, I performed corrections when counting the actual print number or the frequency of immediate/late variants per page in each manuscript of *MEGA*[2]. H[5c] accounts for 52 pages in the *MEJ 2003* and the *MEGA*[2] *I/5*, but it can be also considered as 25 pages, based on the actual number of printed pages of the base text, taking up only the half space as the *MEJ 2003* and *MEGA*[2] *I/5*. "Cola di Rienzi" uses 24 pages in *MEGA*[2] for the reproduction, but is equivalent to only 12 pages using the printed number of the base text. My calculation of the frequency of immediate variants per *MEGA*[2] page in each manuscript is based on the actual printed numbers of the base text.

Thus, we can say the following, based on Tables 1 and 2. First, when one counts the number of late variants in the same way as immediate variants, in the case of Engels, it turns out that the average frequency of late variants is more than three times that of immediate variants in total (compare cells (5)-(G) in Table 1 and in Table 2, namely $8.2 \div 2.5 = 3.15$). In the case of Marx, the average frequency of late variants is 0.8 times ($7.1 \div 9.2 = 0.77$) that of the immediate variants. It is said that one who writes and thinks at the same time tends to produce a greater number of immediate variants whereas someone who writes following deep consideration does not produce so many immediate variants, recording his thoughts onto paper in a more orderly fashion. As mentioned in the preface of this paper, Marx represents the former approach, and Engels the latter. Their peculiarities of composition were not only used by Mayer when he proposed the "co-authorship" hypothesis but were also well known during the lifetimes of Marx and Engels. Thus, it seems reasonable to relate their peculiarities of composition to the number of immediate variants in their manuscripts, which are listed in Table 1.

Second, comparing the frequency of immediate variants per one original manuscript page (see also line (3) - (A) $\sim$ (F) in Table 1), Marx's manuscripts have the most, followed by H^{5c} and then Engels' three manuscripts. However, when counting the (average) frequency of immediate variants per $MEGA^{②}$ page (see also line (5)-(A),(G) and (H) in Table 1), the order becomes H^{5c}, Marx's manuscripts, and then the three manuscripts of Engels. Based on the usual print page number of the $MEGA^{②}$ format, it took approximately 25 pages to reproduce H^{5c}, and the frequency of immediate variants per $MEGA^{②}$ page is 17.3. For the three manuscripts of Engels, they took about 31 pages in total to reproduce, and the average frequency of immediate variants per $MEGA^{②}$ page is 2.5. It took 19 pages in total to reproduce fragments of Marx's manuscripts, and the average frequency of immediate variants per $MEGA^{②}$ page is 9.2.

As a consequence of the above, we should not dismiss the fact that there is a great divergence among these manuscripts in terms of the (average) frequency of immediate variants per $MEGA^{②}$ page. It is fair to say that, in comparison with other manuscripts written by Engels, the frequency of immediate variants per $MEGA^{②}$ page in H^{5c} is extremely significant. It would be rational to conclude that this portion was produced using dictation. In H^{5c}, there are many lines of strike-through written in Engels' hand, indicating corrections or deletions. However, the revisions are not messy in appearance. In fact, each word is written carefully, just like other manuscripts written by Engels. Moreover, Marx often wrote his commonly used nouns and definite articles in abbreviated form and there are few abbreviated forms here. Regardless, the frequency of immediate variants per $MEGA^{®}$ page in H^{5c} is almost seven $(17.3 \div 2.5 = 6.92)$ times that found in other manuscripts written by Engels, even exceeding that in other manuscripts penned by Marx. We cannot attribute these facts to mere coincidence. I believe that in order to explain rationally the reasons for such a great number of immediate variants in H^{5c}, there is no alternative but to conclude that despite the fact that the base texts of H^{5c} were written by Engels, they were nevertheless written on the basis of Marx's dictation and his thought. In the case of dictation, the peculiarities of composition reflected in the manuscripts belong to the original author, not to the physical writer. In addition, it is worth remembering that Marx's peculiarities of composition tended to produce many immediate variants. More importantly, in the case of dictation, it is inevitable that the number of immediate variants becomes higher than in a situation in which the original author himself takes the pen, not only because it is quite common for the writer to misunderstand dictation, but also because it requires the exchange of opinion between the original author and the writer in the case of long corrections. In other words, the greater frequency of immediate variants in H^{5c} compared to Marx's manuscripts (twice as much: 17.3/ 9.2) also reinforces the dictation hypothesis, because Marx alone would perhaps have done less immediate variants.

The miswriting of homophones

Most important of all, my argument may be supported by the fact that there are multiple examples of written homophone errors in H^{5c}. Immediate variants are created by two elements: (I) an interruption caused by one's thoughts and (II) a change in one's thought. In the case of an interruption, incomplete sentences remain within the texts as "unfinished." In circumstances in which one changes one's mind, words are developed in the text that follows after being amended in the process of writing; in light of amended sentences, pre-amended parts remain within texts as "miswriting." Many of the immediate variants from H^{5c} can be categorized in these two ways.

There is, however, a special case to be considered: the revision of homophones. How should we view the unusual revision of immediate variants made by the same author who happens to be a native

des Kapitals, na eines Eigenthums
dessen daß das bloß in der Arbeit &
im Austausch seine Basis hat.

M42:   Example 1   daß > das

& die durch die Nothwendigkeit der Beschäftigung
führ für die wachsende städtische Bet Bevöl-
kerung nöthig gewordene meist vom Auslande importirte
Industrie konnte der Privilegien nicht entbehren, die...

M48:   Example 2   führ > für

wie beiden bei den Nomaden das separate
Zelt jeder Familie. Diese getrennte

M53:   Example 3   beiden > bei den

Figure 1.   The miswriting of Homophones.

German? Based on my research, there are six cases in total related to revisions of homophones in H^{5c}(See, Figure 1). However, five cases (Examples 2–6 in Figure 1) are not mentioned at all in the previous editions of *The German Ideology*, including the *MEJ 2003*. In order to prove that my argument is valid, I am going to show the decipherable texts and the images of the corresponding parts of the original manuscripts in Examples 1 to 6[14] (see, Figure 1). Here, the text in hatching indicates the deleted text of the immediate variants; box designates word replaced the deleted text of immediate variants; and in M48

---

[14] These images of the manuscripts are now available on the website of IISH, free to download at the following link: https://search.socialhistory.org/Record/ARCH00860/ArchiveContentList# A595dad2f30

Figure 1. (Continued)

(Example 2 in Figure 1), <u>underline</u> is used to indicate insertion of immediate variants.

*MEGA*② *I/5* addressed immediate variants of homophones differently from *MEJ 2003*. As mentioned above, I found six cases of immediate variants related to homophones in H⁵ᶜ. While *MEJ 2003* included only one of the six cases, an immediate variant in M42, *MEGA*② *I/5* situated five of the six cases within the list of variants, excluding a case of "beiden → bei den" in M53 (Example 3 in Figure 1). However, this does not automatically mean that *MEGA*② *I/5* recognized the significance of these immediate variants, because it does not indicate any interest in the possibility that these immediate variants could have been misheard (no explanatory note in it). Needless to say, it does not explore the possibility of dictation through the examination of immediate variants related to homophones.

Table 3 Replacement and deletion of Definite/Indefinite articles in the manuscript H⁵ᶜ.

Manuscript	Examples	Page and Line of the MEJ 2003/Remarks
M40	... unter die ein Produkt der Arbeit.	47.22-23l
M42	...Modifikationen der des Zunftwesens, ...	51.13-14l/not listed
M44	...& le der die geringe Verbindung der einzelnen Städte...	53.33-34l/not listed
M47	... Auflösung des der Feudalität zusammenhängt.	58.27-28l/not listed
M49	...geschätzt. Das im Die Bearbeitung des im Lande...	62.20-21l/not listed
M52	... durch das die Bedürfnisse ...	67.36-37l/not listed
M53	...Einrichtung eines einer gemeinsamen Hauswirthschaft	70.6-7l/not listed
M55	... sie ein einen gemeinsamen Kampf	72.8l/not listed
M57	... gegen den das feudale Grundeigenthum	75.27-28l/not listed
M60	... waren. Das Der Unterschied zwischen persönliche persönlichem Individuum & zufälligem Individuum	79.34-36l
M61	... damit der eine Geschichte	82.3-4l/not listed
M62	... außer die den Individuen	83.11-12l
M63	...wurde) der die freie Bevölkerung fast verschwunden,	85.2-85.3/not listed
M66	...Während in der den früheren Perioden	89.19-20l
M70	...diese Entwicklung nicht von einer Entwicklung durch eine Ausdehnung	96.4l(see, MEJ 2003, 268)

Replacement and deletion of definite/indefinite articles

In addition to the miswriting of homophones, the exhaustive examination of immediate variants in H⁵ᶜ shows that there are two more cases related to dictation. The first case includes the replacement and deletion of definite/indefinite articles, pronouns, and relative pronouns; the swapping of verbs from singular to plural and vice versa; and the replacement of noun inflections. The second case is a situation in which deleted elements of immediate variants are restored within the main text. Cases of the first are listed in Table 3 and cases of the second are in Table 5. With regard to unreported cases in the apparatus of the *MEJ 2003*, I put notes "not listed" in the remarks column of reference Tables 3 and 5[15].

On the basis of Table 3, we can say the following. First, H⁵ᶜ includes a number of pages which contain multiple cases of the replacement and deletion of definite/indefinite articles as immediate

---

[15] These omissions do not exist in *MEGA*② I/5.

Table 4. Replacement and deletion of Definite/Indefinite qrticles in the Engels' three Manuscripts.

Page and line of the *MEGA*② I/3	Examples
Eine Seeräubergeschichte	
8.15	...noch eine die Freiheit
12.40	...; dies mein der Dolch....
19.5	..., der sein Schuß ...
19.22	ein ägyptisches eine ägyptische Galeere ...
19.37	... Unter den Hieben des seines tapern Gastes Gegners
Cola di Rienzi	
174.23	.. mei[nem] dem Wort
181.26	des Verräthers, der von dem den Schweiß des Volks
Zur Kritik der preußischen Preßgesetze	
nothing	

variants. We can find one on almost every page, excluding the two pages (M68 and M72). In Tables 3 and 4, definite/indefinite articles that were deleted are highlighted in hatching, and definite/indefinite articles replaced after deletion are highlighted in box. In Table 3, I cited 15 cases as representative examples of such immediate variants from H^{5c}. In practice, however, we can find about 60 such cases in H^{5c}.

Second, with regard to such immediate variants in the three manuscripts written by Engels by himself, there are five cases from "Eine Seeräubergeschichte," two cases from "Cola di Rienzi," and none from "Zur Kritik der preußischen Preßgesetze." These seven cases are all listed in Table 4. It takes 31 pages in total in the usual format of *MEGA*② to reproduce the three manuscripts, and it takes approximately 25 pages in the same format to reproduce H^{5c}. In 31 pages, these three manuscripts produced only seven cases of such immediate variants. By contrast, in 25 pages, H^{5c} produced about 60 cases of such immediate variants.

It is thus rational to believe that Marx dictated H^{5c} because this would explain why there is such a significant discrepancy – more than 10 times the difference – between H^{5c} and the other three manuscripts. In the case of dictation, the content of writing does not belong to the writer, but to the original author, as mentioned in the preface of this paper. Besides, there could be further instances in which the original author pauses in the middle, leading to a revision of written content. In light of these factors, I believe that it is reasonable to

Table 5. Immediate restoration of immediate variants after deletion in the Manuscript H^{5c}.

Manuscript	Examples	Jahrbuch 2003
M41	...der Konzentration der Produ[ktionsinstrumente] Bevölkerung, der Produktionsinstrumente,	49.24-261
M43	Die Arbe[eit] Theilung der Arbeit war...	53.231
M47	Die ... Manufaktur erhielt einen enormen Aufschwung durch die Entde[ckung] Ausdehnung des Verkehrs, welche mit der Entdeckung Amerikas & des Seeweges nach Ostindien eintrat.	59.18-231
M48	die Akkumulation des Kapitals mobilen Kapitals,	60.4-51
M51	die Anwendung von Elementarkräften, die M[aschinerie] zu industriellen Zwecken, die Maschinerie	65.1-31
M52	in jeder Lokalitäten Lokalität eines Landes	67.11-121 not listed
M53	entwickelter Industrie einen Wider[spruch] ähnlichen Widerspruch zu erzeugen	68.35-361
M54	Aus den vielen lokalen Bürgerschaften jeder der St[adt] einzelnen Städte entstand allmählig erst seh allmählig die Bürger*klasse*. (2 places)	71.8-111
M55	möglich. In der Gemeinschaft ist erst Erst in der Gemeinschaft existiren für jedes Individuum	73.28-291
M57	Der Unterschied tritt vom Stand tritt namentlich heraus im Gegensatz der Bourge.oisie gegen das Proletariat	75.17-201 not listed
M58	Während also die Leibei[gnen] entlaufenden Leibeignen	77.11-121
M61	& die verschiedenen Stufen werden Stufen & Interessen werden nie vollständig überwunden,	82.16-181 not listed
M62	England nach der Erob[erung] & Neapel nach der normännischen Eroberung	83.39-411
M65	Persönliche Energie der Nationen Individuen einzelner Nationen	88.9-101
M67	die Macht der bisherigen gesellschaftlichen Gliederung, Produktions & Verkehrsweise & gesellschaftlichen Gliederung	91.21-231

reach such a conclusion, and that my hypothesis can be proven by the examination of immediate variants in H^{5c}.

Immediate restoration of immediate variants after deletion

Now, I would like to discuss the second case, in which components of immediate variants are restored within the base text immediately after deletion. In Tables 5 and 6, deleted word and sentence are in hatching, with restored text in arial. There are 15 representative cases

Table 6. Immediate restoration of immediate variants after deletion in the Engels'
three Manuscripts.

Page and line of the *MEGA*[②] *I/3*	Examples
Eine Seeräubergeschichte	
8.24	..., zu thun dies zu thun,...
11.1	..., enge Matrosenjacken, weite Kaftans die enge Matorosenjacke, die weite Kaftan,...
Cola di Rienzi	
nothing	
Zur Kritik der preußischen Preßgesetze	
380.28-30	Bei Censurfällen mag es der Einsicht des Censors, als Polizeibeamten, und solange die Censur Polizeimaßregel ist, überlassen bleiben, ob er etwas für „unehrerbietig" hält; in Criminalkodex oder für „wohlmeinend" hält; die Censur ist eine Ausnahme,

here, selected from H[5c]. In practice, however, we can find over 60 cases of this kind of immediate variant in H[5c].

In the case of the three manuscripts by Engels included in *MEGA*[②] *I/3*, as listed in Table 6, there are two similar cases from "Eine Seeräubergeschichte," none from "Cola di Rienzi," and one case from "Zur Kritik der preußischen Preßgesetze," accounting for only three in total. Comparing the page numbers of the three manuscripts and H[5c], the former is only slightly more substantial than the latter, as I mentioned already. The former case is 3 for 31. The latter case is 60 for 25. Needless to say, there is a significant divergence.

It would be reasonable to attribute the huge difference to my hypothesis on the possibility of dictation. Engels rarely amends his writings because he completes sentences in his mind first and then writes them down afterwards. However, Marx thinks and writes at the same time. It repeatedly emphasizes, in the case of dictation, the handwritten text reflects the peculiarities of composition of the original author, not of the "physical" writer. Besides, there is also the case of miswriting by physical writers. In general, since the original author constantly changes their speed and tone of speech, it is common for transcribers to require reaffirmation and revision of misheard words caused by rapid utterances and/or a low voice. Although this does not represent all the cases introduced here, it is likely that some of the incorrectly written passages were caused by Engels' mishearing.

Conclusion and our project of online edition of *The German Ideology*

For the reasons stated above, we can be assured that there is little basis for Rjazanov's hypothesis, that H^{5c} "seemed to be written by Engels alone, therefore not by dictation." It is impossible for this hypothesis to explain the examples of such immediate variants, as mentioned in the above sections of this paper, exist in the first place, including the great number of immediate variants.

What about Mayer's hypothesis of "co-authorship"? Provided that the extent of the argument is limited to the previous arrangement between Marx and Engels and the appearance of late variants, it could be unconditionally justified. It is quite unlikely that they started working on *The German Ideology* manuscripts without any advance arrangements, and it is also possible that revisions were made on the basis of their discussions, because in the case of late variants the base text was already written.[16] However, I cannot support the core idea of his hypothesis of "co-authorship." As cited in the preface of this paper, according to Mayer, "Engels wrote more readably, he was quicker and steadier, and therefore constantly ready to commit to paper sections he had conceptualized with Marx jointly." In his opinion, there was discussion between Engels and Marx before Engels began writing. However, it is his conviction that Engels wrote the base text of manuscripts on his own initiative, independently of Marx, that is, without Marx's intervention. I am convinced that this hypothesis of "co-authorship" will face the same problems as those mentioned above, since it will not be able to account for the kind and quantity of variants in the text. In my opinion – even in the case of a previous arrangement between Marx and Engels – the initiative was with Marx, not Engels.

Then, there is another presumption of Engels as initiator, which says, "There are so many immediate variants because the preliminary discussion between Marx and Engels wasn't enough, so that Engels had to ask Marx's opinion constantly while writing the base text."[17]

---

[16] This could be proven by looking at the revisions and corrections to the base text made by Marx and Engels. However, with regard to the case of Engels's lengthy insertion in H^{5a-c}, the possibility of dictation also arises because it could have been composed of many immediate variants, and thus judgment should be based on careful consideration.

[17] I introduced the essence of this paper at international colloquiums held in Tsinghua University (Beijing, in June 2015), Central Compilation and Translation Bureau (Beijing, in June 2015), Tohoku University (Sendai, in August 2016) and Wuhan University (Wuhan, in December 2016). At every colloquium, I have heard this kind of opinions from attendees.

This assumption recognizes only Marx's involvement in the immediate variants produced in the process of preparing the base text, while excluding Marx's influence on the content of these texts. I would like to add a few comments on this presumption.

First, the nature of the immediate variants themselves does not explain the presumption that "the number of immediate variants increased because Engels conferred with Marx." In the case of late variants in which the base text was already completed, it would have been possible for a third party to actively engage in the production and the increase or decrease of late variants. In contrast, in the case of immediate variants, determining factors for their production, increase or decrease depend on the real author of the manuscripts, not on advice from a third party.

When one writes down his thoughts on paper, he may leave "unfinished parts" as they are and make new thoughts. This creates a conflict between the new thought in his mind and the old idea on paper, leading to the production of an immediate variant. The determining factor for the production and number of immediate variants depends on how the real author put his own thoughts onto paper, that is to say, his peculiarities of composition. On one hand, few immediate variants are produced when an author carefully delivers his own words onto paper following reflection. On the other hand, many immediate variants are produced when an author thinks and writes at same time, writing and deleting as he goes. It is apparent that Engels is the former type of writer and Marx the latter; their writing styles contrasted significantly, as mentioned already. In the case of the *Economic and Philosophic Manuscripts of 1844*, there was a case in which a modifier for a noun was eventually deleted after being revised three times[18]. If it was dictated by someone like Marx, with his peculiarities of composition, it would be no surprise that the writer had to revise definite/indefinite articles and reposition nouns, as in the examples listed in Tables 3 and 5. Thus, on the basis of the logic of their peculiarities of composition and the evidence of the text, it is unreasonable in the first place to assume that Engels was the real author of the base text and that Marx was only involved in the immediate variants.

---

[18] See, *MEGA*® I/2, 234, l.31(Text) and 767(Critical Apparatus).

What about the first and second portions of the Feuerbach chapter, namely, H^{5a} and H^{5b}? Tadashi Shibuya first pointed out in the research history of *The German Ideolog*"s authorship problem that the writers of the base text in M25 changed, from Engels to Marx and back to Engels.[19] According to Shibuya, when he made a close investigation of the Feuerbach manuscripts at the International Institute of Social History (IISH, Amsterdam) in 1995, the image of Marx standing at Engels' side came into his head. In consideration of Shibuya's intuition, this paper develops its own argument from a new perspective, addressing the question of why there are so many immediate variants in the Feuerbach manuscripts, in contrast to other contemporary manuscripts written by Engels. M25 is a unique manuscript, as it includes the handwriting of both Marx and Engels in the base text. According to $MEGA^{②}$ I/5, there are 14 cases of immediate variants written by Engels in M25 alone,[20] a figure that is much higher than the average frequency of immediate variants per $MEGA^{②}$ page of Engels' other three manuscripts,[21] suggesting the possibility that Engels' writings were dictated by Marx. I have not yet completed my research on the immediate variants in H^{5a} and H^{5b}, but a glimpse at the preparatory resources at hand suggests that there is not much difference in the frequency of immediate variants between the two manuscripts (H^{5a} and H^{5b}) and H^{5c}. In other words, the implication is that all three manuscripts (H^{5a}, H^{5b} and H^{5c}) were dictated by Marx and written by Engels.[22]

---

[19] See, Shibuya 2006. The history of *The German Ideology* study was profoundly affected when Shibuya presented the issue. See also Carver, 2014a, 110–111. Shibuya pointed out this for the first time in his Japanese translation of *The German Ideology* published in 1998 (Shibuya 1998).

[20] See, $MEGA^{②}$ I/5, 887–888. Additionally, about one page is necessary to reproduce the text of M25 written by Engels on the usual print page of $MEGA^{②}$ format. See, $MEGA^{②}$ I/5, 46–48.

[21] See, section "Many immediate variants inconsistent with other manuscripts by Engels" of this paper.

[22] $MEGA^{②}$ I/5 includes one manuscript written by Engels by himself, namely "Friedrich Engels, [Manuskript über den wahren Sozialismus]"($MEGA^{②}$ I/5, 602–643, this manuscript is called H^{15} in $MEGA^{②}$ I/5 Hereafter referred to as H^{15}). H^{15} was written in the middle of January to April or May 1847 according to $MEGA^{②}$ I/5 (See, $MEGA^{②}$ I/5, 1674–1680). It was written one year after writing the Feuerbach manuscripts. $MEGA^{②}$ I/5 spent 39 pages in the usual print format to reproduce H^{15} and recorded 336 immediate variants in its list of variants. The frequency of immediate variants per $MEGA^{②}$ page of H^{15} therefore is 8.6 ($336 \div 39 = 8.61$). This number is much larger than the number of Engels' three different manuscripts from $MEGA^{②}$ I/3, which I examined in this paper's section "Many immediate variants inconsistent with other manuscripts by Engels", accounting for its 3.4 times ($8.6 \div 2.5 = 3.4$). It is necessary to consider whether this increase of the frequency of immediate variants per $MEGA^{②}$ page from 2.5 ($MEGA^{②}$ I/3,) to 8.6($MEGA^{②}$ I/5) is due to a change in the peculiarities of composition of Engels or a change in recording standard of an immediate variants between both $MEGA^{②}$ volumes. As shown in footnote 13, the number of immediate

On the other hand, as is well known, the Feuerbach chapter of *The German Ideology* manuscripts initially began to be written as a draft of criticism against Bruno Bauer's article "Charakteristik Ludwig Feuerbachs." However, the plan was altered during the writing process, and it became the Feuerbach chapter instead. At the same time, the second chapter of *Saint Bruno* and the third chapter of *Saint Max* had been created. Upon reconstituting the whole of *The German Ideology* manuscripts, Marx not only moved a portion of the Feuerbach chapter, namely a portion of critical arguments against Bauer's article, into the second chapter of *Saint Bruno*, but also moved some arguments written for the third chapter of *Saint Max*, namely two portions corresponding to H^{5b} and H^{5c}, into the first chapter of Feuerbach. Following such editorial adjustments, Marx inserted serial numbers, 1–72, to H^{5a}, H^{5b} and H^{5c}. Given such writing condition and editorial process of H^{5a}, H^{5b} and H^{5c}, we are not able to exclude a possibility that many other portions of the whole manuscripts of *The German Ideology* was dictated by Marx and written by Engels, unless there is some omission in my investigation.

In order to answer the question raised at the beginning of this paper, it is critical to examine the immediate variants in H^{5a} and H^{5b}, which are organized in the list of variants of $MEGA^{②}$ I/5, concretely and in detail. However, it is impossible to verify my hypothesis with $MEGA^{②}$ I/5 alone, such as a homonym mistake, because homonyms are not recorded in both in its list of variants, you cannot recognize them at once. It is necessary to incorporate the deleted texts of immediate variants into base text as is seen in Tables 3–6. The online edition of Feuerbach manuscripts, which I have been working on with my colleagues, will be uploaded within one year with necessary corrections and supplements. This online edition consists of several layers. The most important aspects are found in the following three layers: the first layer includes the base text of the Feuerbach manuscripts as well as the deleted texts of immediate variants marked as

---

variants of H^{5c} is 245 in the *MEJ 2003*, but it changed to 407 in $MEGA^{②}$ I/5, reaching 433 in my research. Therefore, the possibility of the latter cannot be excluded. I am going to obtain images of various manuscripts related to this problem and consider more details in the future. However, what should be noticed here is not this problem but the following fact. That is, even if this increase was due exclusively to a change in the peculiarities of composition of Engels, the frequency of immediate variants of H^{5c} reaches twice as much as that of H^{15} ($17.3 \div 8.6 = 2.0$). Why did this happen? Why are there so many immediate variants found within H^{5c}? This problem is worthy of consideration. In other words, this fact supports a validity of my problem setting in this paper.

seen in Tables 3–6; the second layer consists of the base text without immediate variants; the third layer includes the base text and its late variants marked with several colors, divided further into four categories. Layer 3-1 (L) contains the base text and late variants written by Engels in the left column of the manuscripts. Layer 3-1 (R) contains the late variants written by Engels in the right column of manuscripts. Layer 3-2 (L) contains the base text and late variants written by Marx in the left column of manuscripts. Layer 3-2 (R) contains the late variants written by Marx in the right column of manuscripts. In the first layer, users will be able to examine concretely and in detail the process of Marx's dictation and the writing of Engels. The second layer will show the entire picture of the first draft of the Feuerbach manuscripts. Layers 3-1 to 3-2 (L & R) will help users see the kind of contribution Marx and Engels made towards completing their materialistic conception of history during the period between 1845 and 1846. Since every text from the three layers is attached with a link to the corresponding image of the original manuscripts of IISH, Amsterdam, users are capable of not only freely comparing them with other texts, but also checking the words deciphered by the online project team against corresponding words from the original manuscripts.

Textual variants are very important for research on the formation of texts. Nevertheless, few Marx scholars have shown an interest in the list of variants from *MEGA*②. The reason is quite simple because it is impracticable to grasp meaning of variants only by looking into the list of variants from *Critical Apparatus* of *MEGA*② alone. Its presentation of immediate variants is very simple. An example shown: "89.19l in < der früheren>/" (*MEJ 2003*, 265[23]). But, it alone does not explain why two words "der früheren" belong to immediate variant. However, if we incorporate this immediate variant into base text, as shown in the case of M66 in Table 3, it becomes "Während in der den früheren Perioden". From here we can see the following: an article "der" was deleted and replaced by "den" since a plural form "Perioden" was added after "früheren". Then, it finally becomes clear that the two words initially written as "der früheren" became an immediate variant of "den früheren" from the base text. The editors of the *MEJ 2003* regard the full text (two words) which ends at "früheren" as immediate variants, not just the article, "der", because they consider

---

[23] In *MEGA*② I/5: "111.19l in < der früheren>/" (*MEGA*② I/5 937)

that the article "der", was replaced following the insertion of "Perioden", not "Periode" (singular noun). There are many similar cases to that one. If one puts variants only into the list of variants, there are also numerous incomprehensible cases. This is why the study of variants does not draw much attention. Marx scholars' interest in the research of variants is especially low in Asian countries because it is impossible to translate the list of variants listed only with deletions or replacements of articles into Chinese language, for example, which has no articles in its grammatical system. Therefore, when MEGA was translated in China, variants were excluded from the beginning for grammatical reasons and because of the great number of variants.

However, as shown in Table 3, even if the variant only deletes or replaces articles, one comes to understand from context clues that the deletion or replacement is derived from changing singular nouns into plural nouns or inserting variants into the base text. In other words, users can at least understand the meaning of each variant by using the online edition, because we have incorporated all text variants into the base text in our online edition. I hope that, in addition to $MEGA^{\circledR}$ I/5, our online edition becomes a common platform for Marx-Engels researchers around the world and will be useful for them in verifying my hypothesis.

Acknowledgments

This paper is a condensed version of the Japanese paper of the author with the same title (Omura 2017). This time, the author rearranged the text by condensing some content and changing the order of the arguments, as well as adding some new ideas and fact, especially to $MEGA^{\circledR}$ I/5 and his project of the online edition of *The German Ideology*. The author thanks T. Kurashige for supporting him in the preparation of the translation.

Earlier version of this paper was presented at the international conference "Marx 1818/2018: New developments on Karl Marx's thought and writings" (Lyon, 27–29 September 2017). The author would like to thank the participants for useful comments and two anonymous referees of this journal for their very helpful and constructive comments and suggestions for improving this paper.

Disclosure statement

No potential conflict of interest was reported by the author.

Funding

This work was supported by JSPS KAKENHI Grant Number [16k13159 and 50161659].

References

Carver, Terrell, and Daniel Blank. 2014a. *A Political History of the Editions of Marx and Engels "German Ideology Manuscripts."* New York: Palgrave Macmillan (abbr.: Carver, 2014a).

Carver, Terrell, and Daniel Blank. 2014b. *Marx and Engels' "German Ideology" Manuscripts Presentation and Analysis of the "Feuerbach chapter."* New York: Palgrave Macmillan. (abbr.: Carver edition).

Engels, Friedrich. 1985. *Friedrich Engels Werke Artikel Entwürfe bis August 1844. [Frederick Engels Works Articles Drafts until August 1844.] Marx-Engels-Gesamtausgabe, I. Abteilung, Band 3.* Berlin: Dietz Verlag. (abbr.: MEGA^{②} I/3).

Engels, Friedrich. 1988. *Einleitung. [Einleitung zur Herrn Eugen Dühring's Umwälzung der Wissenschaft.1877.] [Introduction to Mr. Eugen Dühring's Revolution in Science. 1877.] Marx-Engels-Gesamtausgabe, I. Abteilung, Band 27.* 226–241. Berlin: Dietz Verlag.

Engels, Friedrich. 1989. *Karl Marx's Funeral. 1883. Karl Marx Fredrick Engels Collected Works.* Volume 24, 467–468. Moscow: Progress Publishers.

Engels, Friedrich. 2002. *Preface. [Preface to the English edition of "The Manifesto of the Communist Party".1888] Marx-Engels-Gesamtausgabe, I. Abteilung, Band 31.* 117–121. Berlin: Akademie Verlag.

Engels, Friedrich. 2011. *Zur Geschichte des "Bundes der Kommunisten". 1885. [On the History of the Communist League.1885.] Marx-Engels-Gesamtausgabe, I. Abteilung, Band 30.* 89–108. Berlin: Dietz Verlag.

Hiromatsu, Wataru, ed. 1974. Karl Marx/Friedrich Engels: Die deutsche Ideologie. Kritik der neuesten deutschen Philosophie in ihren Reprasentanten, Feuerbach, B. Bauer und Stirner, und des deutschen Sozialismus in seinen verschiedenen Propheten. 1. Bd. 1. Abschnitt. Neuveröffentlichung mit text-kritischen Anmerkungen. [Karl Marx/Frederick Engels: The German Ideology. Criticism of the latest German philosophy in its representatives, Feuerbach, B. Bauer and Stirner, and German socialism in its various prophets. Volume 1, Section 1. New publication with text-critical notes]. Tokyo: Kawadeshobo-Sninsha (abbr.:Hiromatsu-edition).

Marx, Karl. 1982. *Karl Marx Werke·Artikel Entwürfe März 1843 bis August 1844. Marx-Engels-Gesamtausgabe, I. Abteilung, Band 2.* Berlin: Dietz Verlag. (abbr.: MEGA^{②} I/2).

Marx, Karl, and Friedrich Engels. 1932. Die Deutsche Ideologie. Kritik der neuesten deutschen Philosophie in ihren Repräsenten, Feuerbach, B. Bauer und Stirner, und des deutschen Sozialimus in seinen verschiedenen Propheten. 1845–1846. [The German Ideology. Criticism of the latest German philosophy in its representations, Feuerbach, B. Bauer and Stirner, and German socialism in its various prophets. 1845–1846.] Marx-Engels-Gesamtausgabe, I. Abteilung, Band 5. Berlin: Marx-Engels-Verlag G.M.B.H. (abbr.: MEGA① I/5).

Marx, Karl, Friedrich Engels, and Joseph Weydemeyer. 2004. *Die Deutsche Ideologie. Artikel, Druckvorlagen, Entwürfe, Reinschriftenfragmente und Notizen zu I. Feuerbach und II. Sankt Bruno. [The German Ideology. Article, print templates, drafts, fair copies of fragments and notes] Marx-Engels-Jahrbuch 2003.* Berlin: Akademie-Verlag. (abbr.:MEJ 2003).

Marx, Karl, and Friedrich Engels. 2017. *Karl Marx und Friedrich Engels Deutsche Ideologie. Manuskripte und Drucke. [Karl Marx and Frederick Engels German Ideology. Manuscripts and prints.]* Marx-Engels-Gesamtausgabe, I. Abteilung, Band 5. Berlin: De Gruynter Akademie Forschung. (abbr.: MEGA② I/5).

Mayer, Gustav. 1921. "Das Leipziger Konzil von Friedrich Engels und Karl Marx. ["The Leipzig Council of Frederick Engels and Karl Marx."]" *Archiv für Sozialwissenschaft und Sozialpolitik,* Bd. 47:773–808.

Omura, Izumi. 2017. "Re-examining the authorship of the Feuerbach chapter in the German Ideology on the basis of a hypothesis of dictation [Japanese]." Contributions to Marx-Engels-Marxism Research in Japan. No.59: 17–50.

Rjazanov, David. 1926. "Marx und Engels über Feuerbach. Der erste Teil der "Deutschen Ideologie". Einführung des Herausgebers. ["Marx and Engels about Feuerbach. The first part of the "German Ideology". Introduction of the publisher."]" *Marx-Engels-Archiv,* Bd.1: 205–221.

Shibuya, Tadashi. 1998. *The German Ideology by Karl Marx and Frederick Engels: Introduction and Chapter I of Volume I [Japanese translation].* Tokyo: Shin Nihon Publishers.

Shibuya, Tadashi. 2006. "Editorial problems in establishing a new edition of the German Ideology." *In Marx for the 21st Century, With a Special Introduction by Terrell Carver,* edited by Hiroshi Uchida, 193–200. London and New York: Routledge.

Marx, primitive accumulation, and the impact of Sismondi

Nicolas Eyguesier

ABSTRACT

This article re-examines Marx's well-known concept of "primitive accumulation" in relation to Marx's successive attempts to give a historical explanation for the birth of "capitalism". Marx formulated this concept for the first time in *Value, Price, and Profit* (1865), and extrapolated upon it further in the first edition of the first volume of *Capital* (1867). It signified an appreciable alteration to Marx's original historical theory. Indeed, in his writings, preceding the publication of volume 1 of *Capital,* such as *The Communist Manifesto* or *The German Ideology,* Marx had presented a more straightforwardly linear conception of the evolution of human society, consisting of various stages, "capitalism" being the penultimate stage, and "communism", the last. Within this framework, the most advanced nations, such as Great Britain and Germany, were assumed to be those closest to being on the pre-revolutionary cusp of realising socialism. However, from the publication of volume 1 of *Capital* onwards, Marx embraced a less deterministic conception of progress, focussing more than previously on economically backwards countries or societies "at the margins" (Anderson 2010) and envisaging for them possibilities for historical development that did not inevitably entail the sort of industrialisation that Great Britain had experienced. This was particularly true regarding Russia, where volume 1 of *Capital* was welcomed and discussed precisely in light of these questions, as has been underscored by many scholars, notably Shanin, Wada, White, and Stedman Jones.

This article aims at going one step further in examining the question of Marx's ongoing understanding of economic development and modernisation by first comparing the underlying notion of progress implied in Marx's theory of "primitive accumulation" with the development theories of Jean-Charles Léonard Simonde de Sismondi. For Sismondi, the transition to industrial society (characterised by wage labour, mechanisation, rural exodus, etc.) was a diversion from the path of development described by Adam Smith in his 1776 *Wealth of Nations,* wherein commercial society represents the final stage of development for modern societies. Sismondi subscribed to an essentially "romantic" conception of progress, wherein comparison with the past was essential for understanding and evaluating present socioeconomic conditions and cyclical periods of decadence regularly followed periods of progress. In contrast, Marx's conception of progress – notwithstanding whatever scientific dross that Engels and others, like Kautsky, (Stedman Jones 2016, 564) later accorded it after Marx's death – might be called "Utopian", since Marx believed that the future would fulfil the promises of the new era, then developing in Europe in the mid-19th century. Thus, he did not consider industrial society to be a dead end, but rather a tremendous revolutionary opportunity, despite its disastrous social impact on the populations it affected. This article will demonstrate that Marx's position on "primitive accumulation" and the related concept of economic modernisation varied over time, but it will begin by showing how Marx's evolution can be read initially through Marx's mutating assessment of Sismondi and the impact this changing assessment had on his formulation of the concept of "primitive accumulation" in volume 1 of *Capital,* a concept drawn from Sismondi's theory of history.

In his early writings, *The German Ideology* or the *Communist Manifesto,* Marx was clearly critical of Sismondi's vision of economic history. In these writings, he insisted upon the industrial basis of any post-capitalist future communist society as well as a teleological and linear conception of history which could narrate the advent of this desirable future. Later, in *Capital,* Marx advanced another theory of history, less linear, based on the concept of "primitive accumulation", a concept rooted in a historical account he directly borrowed from Sismondi, and one whose initial formulation sparked him to study further the importance of pre-capitalist societies in relation to any imaginable post-capitalist future. In the last decade of his life, the "late Marx" was very interested in Russian debates concerning the interpretation of *Capital* and, more broadly, the question of revolution in economically backward countries, and, subsequently, he was led to reappraise his earlier historical assumptions about progress and modernity. It is a fact that the Russian case stimulated this re-evaluation, bringing the issue of economic development in its relation to capitalism and the means to its supersession into sharp focus and seemingly deeply perplexed the mature Marx in the process. Nevertheless, this article concluded that this last stage in Marx's intellectual development did not fundamentally change Marx's broader assumptions about the logical endpoint of all desirable economic development: his superimposed revolutionary timeline might have been modified, but the goal of his understanding of revolution, an affluent society based on certain desirable scientific and industrial vestiges left over from the capitalist mode of production, remained unaltered throughout his life. In other words, Marx might have drawn closer to Sismondi at the end of his life, but he never converted to anything approximating the supposedly "romantic" position with regards to economic development that Sismondi held.

1. The young Marx and Sismondi on progress

In Marx's early writings, *The German Ideology* (1846) and the *Communist Manifesto* (1848, co-written with F. Engels[1]), Marx put forth a linear theory of historical development in which the economic development of productivity was the principal criterion for measuring the evolution of human societies and there was no real qualitative difference between modern societies and the societies preceding them. To this extent, "capitalism" was a stage of development inscribed within a much larger narrative of human evolution. If principally characterised by the contradiction between the means and forces of production, which was bound to be superseded, it was nevertheless treated by Marx as a necessary preliminary mode of production through which all of humanity had to pass. History was thus a cumulative process charting changes in production, or as Marx put it:

> History is nothing but the succession of individual generations, each of which exploits the improved materials, capital resources, powers of production from all the ones prior to it. (Marx and Engels 1846, 105)

---

[1] The exact relationship between Marx and Engels and their mutual influence on one another from the time of the drafting of the *Manifesto* onwards has been the subject of countless works of scholarship. This article does not directly explore in any detail their possible differences of opinion with regards to primitive accumulation and the question of economic backwardness, even though such differences were important and impacted the particular form taken by the crystallisation of Marx theoretical writings into a seemingly coherent ideological body of doctrine upon Marx's death, courtesy of Engels's robust efforts. On this question, see White (1996) and chapter 11 of Stedman Jones (2016) as well as more generally, on the subject of their possible overarching differences in philosophical orientation, Stedman Jones (2017).

The appearance of "capitalist" society was not a sudden event, but the progressive outcome of the extension of the division of labour, which historically stemmed from gradual developments in the interrelations between city and country in European societies, a process which "commences with the transition from barbarism to civilisation, from tribal life into the state, from the locality to the nation and persists throughout the whole history of civilisation up to the present day" (1846, 213–214).

In this historical context, the birth of the proletariat could be explained by the flight of rural serfs to cities (219) at the same time trade began to grow between cities (233), contributing to "the development of manufacturing" (238), which seriously took off subsequent to the discovery of the Americas by the various European powers (250). Finally, wage relations and forms of revenue dependency fed growing global consumer demand in Europe, which gave birth to the development of large-scale industries. Thus, the extension of commercial exchanges was the cause of world-historical economic transformations of which the capitalist mode of production was the logical and necessary consequence. This argument would be famously reiterated in the *Communist Manifesto*:

> The means of production and trade that formed the basis of bourgeois development were generated in feudal society. At a certain level of development of these means of production and trade, the relations in which feudal society produced and exchanged, the feudal organisation of agriculture and small-scale manufacture, in a word feudal property relations, no longer corresponded to the forces of production already developed. They impeded production instead of advancing it. They became just so many fetters. They had to be sprung open, they were sprung open (1848, 237).

In elaborating a vision of history, which underscored the development of productive forces, the contradictory aspects of these developments and the medieval and burgher origins of the capital mode of production as the fruit of commercial expansion, Marx and Engels famously gave ambiguous praise to the European bourgeoisie, trumpeted for having played the world-historical role of the sorcerer's apprentice responsible for unleashing forces of production it would ultimately be unable to control.

This ambiguity can be found in Marx and Engels's assessment of Sismondi in the *Manifesto*. In their pamphlet, Marx and Engels describe Sismondi as an exemplary representative of "Petty-Bourgeois

Socialism". Indeed, Sismondi is even judged by the duo to be "the head of this school, not only in France but also in England" (Marx and Engels 1848, 247). According to Engels and Marx:

> This school of Socialism dissected with great acuteness the contradictions in the conditions of modern production. It laid bare the hypocritical apologies of economists. It proved, incontrovertibly, the disastrous effects of machinery and division of labour; the concentration of capital and land in a few hands; overproduction and crises; it pointed out the inevitable ruin of the petty bourgeois and peasant, the misery of the proletariat, the anarchy in production, the crying inequalities in the distribution of wealth, the industrial war of extermination between nations, the dissolution of old moral bonds, of the old family relations, of the old nationalities (Marx and Engels 1848, 248).

The authors inadvertently acknowledged here their debt to Sismondi for his description and his understanding of capitalism and its consequences. On the other hand, from a political point of view, Sismondi's "school" is ultimately judged to be both "reactionary and Utopian", because it "aspires either to restoring the old means of production and of exchange and with them the old property relations and the old society, or to cramping the modern means of production and of exchange, within the framework of the old property relations that have been, and were bound to be, exploded by those means". (Marx and Engels 1848, 248).

Thus, in terms of their economic analysis, despite such criticisms, Marx and Engels borrowed critical notions from Sismondi such as the "proletariat[2]" "crisis", "capital", and so on, a point which has been observed by many scholars, such as Andler (1901), M. Leroy (1950), and M. Rubel (1976). On the other hand, Sismondi's "romantic" criticisms of the capitalist phase of economic development ("romantic" in the sense given by Löwy and Sayre (2001)) and Sismondi's scepticism with regards to the supposed benefits to be had from certain scientific and technological developments made him appear to Marx and Engels like someone who was ultimately

---

[2] See, for example, the preface of the second edition of *The Eighteenth Brumaire of Louis Napoleon*: "People forget Sismondi's significant saying: The Roman proletariat lived at the expense of society, while modern society lives at the expenses of the proletariat" (1869, 6). The words of Sismondi are : "Au reste le prolétaire romain ne travaillait pas; car, dans une société qui admet l'esclavage, le travail est déshonorant pour les hommes libres; il vivait presque uniquement aux dépens de la société, des distributions de vivres que faisait la république. On pourrait dire presque que la société moderne vit aux dépens du prolétaire, de la part qu'elle lui retranche sur la récompense de son travail." (1836–1838, 277).

backward-looking and nostalgic for social patterns bound to be displaced. The assessment of Marx and Engels with regards to Sismondi did not differ much from that they gave to those social categories they disparaged such as the petty bourgeoisie and its shopkeepers and artisans they accused of "reactionary for they seek to turn back the tide of modernity". (1848, 235)

Their criticisms were not entirely original, however. Marx and Engels accused Sismondi in terms quite similar to those made by Jean-Baptiste Say (1820, 287), who likewise criticised Sismondi for wanting to "go back" in time to earlier socioeconomic conditions, charges which Sismondi did answer:

> I have been pictured as being, in political economy, the enemy of society's progress, a supporter of barbarous and oppressive institutions. No, I do not desire any part of what has been, but I want something better of what is. I cannot judge what that is, except by comparing it with the past, and I far from want to restore ancient ruins if I show with their help the eternal needs of society (1824, 307).

When Marx accused Sismondi of being reactionary, he implied that the progress of society and the progress of production were largely ones and the same thing, even if in Marx's opinion, progress is dialectically contradictory, as it creates both extreme poverty and alienation as well as the social possibilities for moving beyond global immiseration. For example in the *Theory of Surplus-Value*, Marx writes:

> production for its own sake means nothing but the development of human productive forces, in other words, the *development of the richness of human nature as an end in itself.* To oppose the welfare of the individual to this end, as Sismondi does, is to assert that the development of the species must be arrested in order to safeguard the welfare of the individual. (1861–1863, II: 347–348)

It must be said in the defence of Marx that is true that Sismondi defended, throughout his work, the idea of small ownership, or "dispersed ownership" as he called it (1827, 492). Nevertheless, Marx was unfair in accusing Sismondi of wanting to "restore the old property relations". In fact, in his *New Principles of Political Economy*, Sismondi accepted that the guilds, which he had criticised in his early Smithian work, *De la Richesse commerciale* (1803, 297–306), had disappeared for good, and that only the "defenders of old prejudices and old abuses" (1827, 273), were left still calling for their re-establishment. In his *Études sur l'économie politique* (1837–1838), Sismondi examined in detail the guilds, because they represented for him an example of a social formation which helped to avoid overproduction, albeit in an arbitrary fashion by establishing monopolies over consumers. As he wrote in his *New Principles*, "[the guilds] impeded increases in population, and the swift development of industry" (1827, 463). Ultimately, Sismondi suggested not to "restore" the guilds but to try and recapture their operating principle of legitimacy, which lay in their capacity to sustain and protect the welfare of producers. Sismondi, as it has been frequently noted, did not go into the details about what this "new social form" might look like; he merely analysed the vicissitudes of contemporary economic conditions, openly refusing to offer concrete solutions (1827, 463). Nevertheless, on this specific point, Marx and Engels were insensitive to such nuances.

In fact, the differences between Sismondi and Marx on the larger issue of progress did not stop at the questions of small ownership and guilds insofar as they were derivative of their underlying divergent philosophies of history. Indeed, contrary to his classification today as an economist best known for pioneering a theory of cycles of overproduction and underconsumption, Sismondi was known to his 19th century contemporaries principally for his work as a historian. Indeed, he was famous during his lifetime more as a historian than as an economist – in the words of *The Edinburgh Review*, the "first living historian" (vol. 25, 1815, p. 437). Author of a widely-read and respected *History of the Italian Republics of the Middle-Ages* (1832) as well as a *History of the Fall of Roman Empire* (1834), Sismondi elaborated a theory of progress, whose main thread was the development and spread of the idea of freedom, a kind of ultimate ideal for all human beings, allowing them to reach their highest development from a moral and artistic point of view. Sismondi, along with Benjamin Constant and Germaine de Staël, was a member of the Coppet Circle, most of whose members subscribed to a strong conviction in human perfectibility (Lotterie 1995, 2000). No exception, Sismondi adhered to a "humanist" or "qualitative" vision of progress (Marcuse 1969) according to which the human being was both the driving force and the fundamental unit of measure for all potential progress. This progress did not follow a law that could be scientifically discovered and by means of which the future could be predicted; it was a credo which was at once a belief and a policy. It was quite different from a "quantitative" vision of progress, wherein man's Promethean conquests over nature are the most important criteria. In fact, for Sismondi, those quantitative material achievements were of secondary importance:

> No doubt man can rightly be proud of the influence he exerts over nature and the human results he has compelled nature to accomplish; but neither the power he extracts from the elements, nor the talent with which he exerts it are proof that this has been for the greatest good of society. (1837–1838, 668).

For Sismondi, there can only ever be progress, measured in the accumulation over time of experience (and not of capital, as in the Marxist tradition), as each new generation benefits from the lessons it draws from the past. That explains the importance of history in Sismondi's writings, which, in terms of writings of his writings on political economy, is "the collection of all the facts and experiments which tend to throw light on the theory of public wealth" (1834, I: 1). Nevertheless, Sismondi's conception of history in relation to human perfectibility was strongly influenced by the corresponding idea of decline and decadence, the flipside of progress. This explains why Sismondi devoted so much time to writing about the historical period linking the decline of the Roman Empire and its aftermath to the birth of modern conceptions of freedom in medieval Italy from the political vacuum left by the collapse of Roman imperial institutions (Sonenscher 2018). Likewise, Sismondi openly compared the Roman Empire with modern times:

> It is only by acquiring an accurate conception of the resemblance and the difference between the organisation of the empire and that of modern Europe, that we can venture to foretell whether the calamities by which the former was destroyed, menace us with ruin (1834, I: 12).

In other words, Sismondi's conception of civilizational progress was not automatically linear but was more cyclical, in the sense of being always threatened with decline, reversion, and collapse. Among the causes of the decline of the Roman Empire, Sismondi underscored the death of the middle classes and such excessive concentrations of wealth that Roman society only "consisted of men of enormous wealth and populace" (1834 I: 119). According to Sismondi, as slavery took the place of a free peasantry, the Romans experienced moral decadence, military weakness, and finally imperial collapse. The conclusions that could be drawn from the present situation were not difficult to establish: in Sismondi's opinion, the concentration of wealth inherent to "chrematistics", a term which refers to industrial society, represented a dead-end that contemporaries should seek to avoid at all costs. Indeed, unlike for Marx and Engels, for Sismondi the middle classes composed of small property owners, far from being political conservatives, were the engine driving civilizational progress. When they disappear, society collapses with them:

> It is, in fact, in the middle classes that the domestic virtues – economy, forethought, and the spirit of association –, mainly reside. It is in them that a certain degree of energy is incessantly called into operation, either as a means of rising, or of keeping the position already acquired. It is in them alone that the sentiment of social equality, on which all justice is based, can be kept alive. […]

> The corruption of Rome had begun from the time of the Republic, from the time that the middle class ceased to impress its own peculiar character on the whole nation: this corruption increased in proportion as the intermediate ranks disappeared; it was carried to its highest pitch when the whole empire consisted of men of enormous wealth, and populace (1834, I: 119).

Sismondi's philosophy of history was critically buttressed by two important observations. Firstly, in Sismondi's opinion, the concentration of property had only been completely realised in Britain. Secondly, if Sismondi saw the development of capitalism as a general economic trend in European history, the capitalist transformation of the economy of Continental Europe was nevertheless far from complete. Therefore, although highly probable, industrialisation was not entirely inevitable and the course it would take remained unclear. Some counter-tendencies could even be detected through the study of contemporary European economies. For example, in France, small ownership tremendously increased in the wake of the French Revolution, significantly counterbalancing those vestiges of pre-revolutionary concentrations of landed property. In this respect, France diverged from Britain. On the basis of these historical observations, Sismondi suggested that there were two different paths towards the socioeconomic modernity which could come in the wake of the decline of feudalism and serfdom: either the peasantry could be expropriated from its customary practices and transformed into an urban proletariat (as was the case in Britain), or the land could be more equitably redistributed and either be directly placed into the peasantry's hands as individuated private ownership or be governed by sharecropping contracts, which, in Sismondi's view, would comprise a half-way solution somewhere between serfdom and private ownership, with all of the advantages and disadvantages of both.

The differences between Sismondi and the Marxist tradition become clearer in light of Sismondi's differences with Marx on the specific issue of economic development and European history. What was strictly specific to Britain for Sismondi was true for the entirety of humanity for Marx and his successors. In Marxist thought, pre-capitalist formations are doomed to extinction. This held true not only for communal property, in India, for example but also for small-scale private ownership of land, which strictly speaking, was not synonymous with the capitalist mode of production as Marx and Engels understood it. In fact, to have "capitalism" as an operational mode of production in the Marxist sense, one needs to be able to juxtapose the interests of owners and non-owners, which is much less apparent when the population is mainly composed of small property holders. Thus, there were two historical issues, which Marx was confronted by: how to explain the transition from feudalism to capitalism and how to describe the situation of small-scale production such that it was doomed to be eradicated through industrialisation. Marx would attempt to answer these two questions in the last chapter of volume 1 of *Capital* devoted to "primitive accumulation".

2. Volume 1 of *Capital* and the uses of "primitive accumulation": 1853–1867

The first trace in Marx's work of an argument insisting upon some form of original expropriation as the starting point for capitalist accumulation can be found in *Value, Price and Profit*, a conference given by Marx in 1865 to members of the International Working Man's Association:

> [H]ow does this strange phenomenon arise, that we find on the market a set of buyers, possessed of land, machinery, raw materials, and the means of life, all of them, save land in its crude state, the *products of labour*, and, on the other hand, a set of sellers, who have nothing to sell except their labouring power, their working arms and brains? That the one set buys continually, in order to make a profit and enrich themselves, while the

other set continuously sells, in order to gain their lives? The inquiry into this question would be an inquiry into what the economists call: *The Previous* or *Original Accumulation*, but which ought to be called the *Original Expropriation*. (Marx 1865, 412)

In volume 1 of *Capital*, Marx extended his reflections on this subject, discussing the historical origins of this "original expropriation", and thereby giving the capitalist mode of production both a birthplace and date of birth in Britain between 1500 and 1800. Capitalism's birth certificate was officially given in Part 8 of volume 1, in Chapters 22–33 devoted to the topic of "So-Called Primitive Accumulation". Marx claimed it to be "so-called", because the appropriate word for the "true" story of the origins of the capitalist mode of production should be "forcible expropriation", an extraordinarily violent process wherein the agricultural population is definitively separated from the land it works. For Marx, the historical account typically given by economists of the origins of capitalism in savings is false. Such narrative ascriptions cannot explain the advent of and gradual transition to wage labour in developed economies, a form of remuneration which was qualitatively different from prior forms characteristic of earlier patterns of land tenure. Thus, in the words of E.M. Wood (2017), Marx abandoned in this chapter the "commercialisation model", wherein "capitalism" is characterised by the gradual expansion of international trade, as practised by the bourgeoisie of medieval towns, a characterisation Marx himself extrapolated upon in his earlier writings, notably in his *German Ideology* manuscript, for example. In his new historical modelling, the expropriation of the agricultural population was no longer treated as a specific economic event but rather as a kind of political violence committed by the ruling classes, causing producers to be separated from the means of their production and forcibly transformed into wage labourers. Once capital and labour were face to face as two enemy powers, the capitalist market became sufficiently dynamic and invigorated such that it could radically increase in scope:

The capitalist system presupposes the complete separation of the labourers from all property in the means by which they can realise their labour. As soon as capitalist production is once on its own legs, it not only maintains this separation, but reproduces it on a continually extending scale. The process, therefore, that clears the way for the capitalist system, can be none other than the process which takes away from the labourer the possession of his means of production. (Marx 1872–1875, 632–633[3]).

A long description of the expropriation of the agricultural population follows this quotation, supported by historical sources and examples. The peasantry is, according to Marx, deprived of its access to land, which previously took various forms such as enjoyment of communal lands, small acreages of kitchen gardens adjacent to domestic cottages and other forms of lodging, or access to seigneurial lands in return for fixed fees.

This chapter ends with the description of the "Clearing of the estate" made by the Duchess of Sutherland. Interestingly, the passage on the clearances and the end of the commons in Britain was largely inspired by the fourth essay of Sismondi's *Études sur l'économie politique* (Sismondi 1837–1838: 373–393).

We know, thanks to the *Brussel's notebooks,* that Marx read and copied out partially during his stay in Brussels in 1845 the fourth essay of Sismondi *Études sur les sciences sociales,* as has been revealed through the posthumous publication of these notebooks (Marx 1845, 123–136, and Rubel 1957). Another evidence can be found before the publication of the first and only volume of *Capital* published during his lifetime: in an article which appeared in the *New York Daily Tribune* (1853a), Marx had already drawn in published form from Sismondi's essay.

In this article, Marx singled out the Duchess of Sutherland and her anti-slavery activism for criticism, accusing the Duchess of duplicitous hypocrisy in her protests against the condition of slaves in the Southern United States while expropriating without pity peasants living on her lands who possessed use rights since time immemorial:

> My lady Countess resolved upon a radical reform, and determined upon transforming the whole tract of country into sheep-walks. From 1811 to 1820, these 15000 inhabitants, about 3000 families, were systematically expelled and exterminated. All their villages were demolished and burned downs, and all their fields converted into pasturages. British soldiers were commanded for this execution, and came to blows with the natives. An old

---

[3] I quote from the French edition of *Capital* (1872–1875), because Marx considerably revised the translation, making it almost a second edition of the original German edition and offering diverging opinions on the subject of primitive accumulation (White 1996, 209). It was for this reason that Marx indicated in a note to French readers that "whatever the literary defects of this French edition may be, it possesses a scientific value independent of the original and should be consulted even by readers familiar with German."

woman refusing to quit her hut, was burned in the flames of it. Thus, my lady Countess appropriated to herself *seven hundred and ninety-four thousand acres of land,* which from time immemorial had belonged to the clan. (Marx 1853a, 21).

There is no question that this passage was inspired by Marx's reading of Sismondi, who is even cited as a source in Marx's article. The parallel is even more striking when juxtaposed next to Sismondi's text:

The Gael Nation [...] has been almost completely expelled from its homes by the very same people it regarded as its chiefs [...] the fields it ploughed has been destined to pasturage, and given to foreing chiefs: its houses and villages were destroyed and burnt. We heard that about fifteen thousands peasants had been forced [by the duchess of Sutherland] to flee a country as large as an average French department. [...] It has been asserted that, to force them to withdraw, the man in charge of evacuating the country set fire to their houses; it has been claimed in addition that an old man, some said an old woman, refused to leave her hunt, to brave exile and poverty, but her presence did not stop the fire-raiser, and that the victim has been consumed by the flames. From 1814 to 1820 these fifteen thousands inhabitants, making about three thousand families has been chased away. (Sismondi 1837–1838, 379–382[4]).

Indeed, Marx was clearly pleased with Sismondi's historical example, as he reused it in *Capital*:

This person, well instructed in economy, resolved, on entering upon her government, to effect a radical cure, and to turn the whole country, whose population had already been, by earlier processes of the like kind, reduced to 15,000, into a sheep-walk. From 1814 to 1820 these 15,000 inhabitants, about 3000 families, were destroyed and burnt, all their fields turned into pasturage. British soldiers enforced this eviction and came to blows with the inhabitants. One old woman was burnt to death in the flames of the hut, which she refused to leave. Thus this fine lady appropriated 794,000 acres of land that had from time immemorial belonged to the clan. (Marx 1887, 633[5])

---

[4] La nation des Gaëles [...] a été presque absolument expulsée de ses foyers par ceux mêmes qu'elle regardait comme ses chefs [...] les champs qu'elle labourait ont été destinés au pâturage des troupeaux, et livrés à des chefs étrangers : ses maisons et ses villages ont été rasés par le feu. [...] On apprit qu'environ quinze mille paysans étaient forcés par [la marquise de Stafford, héritière du comté de Sutherland] de sortir d'une contrée grande commme un des départements moyens de la France. [...] On assura que pour les forcer à se retirer, le facteur chargé de faire évacuer le pays mettait le feu à leurs maisons; on prétendit même qu'un vieillard, d'autres disaient une vieille femme, ayant refusé d'abandonner sa cabane, pour aller braver l'exil ou la misère, sa présence n'avait pas arrêté l'incendiaire, et que la victime avait péri dans les flammes. [...] Entre l'année 1811 et l'année 1820, ces quinze mille habitants, formant environ trois mille familles, ont été chassés. (French original version.)

[5] From the french edition of *Capital* (Marx 1872–1875, 647–648): [The duchess of Stafford] avait à peine pris les rênes de l'administration qu'elle résolut d'avoir recours aux grands moyens et de convertir en pâturage tout le comté, dont la population, grâce à des expériences

Thus, the historical question of the evolving expropriation of agricultural populations and its relation to the development of both capitalism and wage labour was not "discovered" by Marx when he was writing volume 1 of *Capital*, but likely goes back to his pre-1848 readings in political economy. Nevertheless, the issue of the historical transition from "pre-capitalist" economies to "capitalist" ones took on a new dimension in the 1860 s, inspiring Marx to return to Sismondi's account. Indeed, a significant change can be noted in Marx's expressed opinions about Sismondi.

In 1853, in a second article published in the *New York Tribune*, whereas Marx describes the expulsion of agricultural population from his ancestral lands as a scandal, he considered that it is would be senseless to try and stop it, like Sismondi had:

> Now I share neither in the opinions of Ricardo, who regards "net-revenue" as the Moloch to whom entire populations must be sacrificed, without even so much a complaint, nor in the opinion of Sismondi, who, in his hypocondriacal philanthropy, would forcibly retain the superannuated methods of agriculture and proscribe science for industry, as Plato expelled pets from his Republic. Society is undergoing a silent revolution, which must be submitted to, and which takes no more notice of the human existences it breaks down than an earthquake regards the house it subverts (1853b: 58–59).

As in the 1848 *Communist Manifesto*, this expropriation is still a requisite step before the ultimate social revolution, understood as the expropriation of expropriators, can ever occur:

> The rural population, the most stationary and conservative element of modern society, disappears while the industrial proletariat, by the very working of modern production, finds itself gathered in mighty centres, around the great productive forces, whose history of creation has hitherto been the martyrology of labourers. Who will prevent them from going a step further, and appropriating these forces, to which they have been appropriated before? Where will be the power of resisting them? Nowhere! Then, it will be of no use to appeal to the "rights of property". The modern changes in the art of production have, according to the Bourgeois Economists themselves, broken down the antiquated system of propriety and its mode of

---

analogues, mais faites sur une plus petite échelle, se trouvait déjà réduite au chiffre de quinze mille. De 1811 à 1820, ces quinze mille individus, formant environ trois mille familles, furent systématiquement expulsés. Leurs villages furent détruits et brûlés, leurs champs convertis en pâturages. Des soldats anglais, commandés pour prêter main-forte, en virent aux prises avec les indigènes. Une vieille femme qui refusait d'abandonner sa hutte périt dans les flammes. C'est ainsi que la noble dame accapara 794 000 acres de terre qui appartenaient au clan de temps immémorial.

appropriation. They have *expropriated* the Scotch clansmen, the Irish collier and tenant, the English yeoman, the hand-loom weaver, numberless handicrafts, whole generations of factory children and women; they will expropriate, in due time, the landlord and cotton-lord (1853b: 59).

As Marx confessed to Engels in a 14 June 1853 letter, he considered himself at the time to be waging a "clandestine" campaign against the editorial line of the *New-York Daily Tribune*, which Marx described as the "Sismondian-philanthropic-socialist anti-industrialism" of "the protectionist i.e. industrial bourgeoisie of America". For similar reasons, Marx had likewise hailed "England's destruction of native industries" in India as "revolutionary". (quoted by Stedman Jones 2016: 582).

In other words, in the 1850 s, Marx ambivalently appreciated the dynamics of capitalism, since the development of economies based on wage labour inadvertently provided the material productive bases for future post-capitalist societies.

In a seeming departure from these assumptions, volume 1 of *Capital* devoted considerable attention to "primitive accumulation" and notably to the "negative aspect" of the dialectic of accumulation, taken for granted in Marx's earlier writings. In this work, Marx underscored the political and unnatural dimension to expropriation which Marx had previously, in 1853, compared to a natural phenomenon, an "earthquake". In this later work, Marx was closer to Sismondi: their explanations of the origins and development of capitalist society were essentially the same. By implication, Marx's shifting historical account of capitalism's origins suggested not only that "primitive accumulation" was not an "earthquake", but that, because of its unnatural origins, it could, to some extent, be avoided.

This did not mean, however, that Marx was willing, like Sismondi, to consider an alternative social form emerging from the end of feudal arrangements and composed of independent small producers. In Chapter 32 of volume 1 of *Capital*, entitled "Historical tendency of capitalist accumulation", Marx clearly discussed this issue. Indeed, he distinguished two different types of private property: one in which labourers owned the means of production; another in which the means of production were the exclusive property of non-labourers (1872–1875, 677). The first one corresponded with Sismondi's property ideal, the second one with capitalism as Marx understood it in terms of the invidious separation of capital from labour. Surprisingly, Marx conceded that there was some obvious desirability to individual ownership in societies characterised by the widespread dissemination of private property:

> The private property of the labourer in his means of production is the foundation of petty industry, whether agricultural, manufacturing or both; petty industry, again, is an essential condition for the development of social production and of the free individuality of the labourer himself. (1872–1875, 677).

But Marx immediately added that this social state was "mediocre", as it excluded "the productive application of the forces of Nature by society, and the free development of the social productive powers" (1872–1875, 677). In this passage, Marx clearly expressed his prejudice in favour of large industry, but he did not compellingly demonstrate that the transition from small-scale to large-scale industry was either inevitable or desirable, much less whether his preferred economic endpoint was practicable. Instead, Marx argued with regards to the "mediocre" mode of production that its dissolution and a replacement was necessary:

> At a certain stage of development, it brings forth the material agencies for its own dissolution. From that moment new forces and new passions spring up in the bosom of society; but the old social organization fetters them and keeps them down. It must be annihilated; it is annihilated. Its annihilation, the transformation of the individualised and scattered means of production into socially concentrated ones, of the pigmy property of the many into the huge property of the few, the expropriation of the great mass of the people from the soil, from the means of subsistence, and from the means of labour, this fearful and painful expropriation of the mass of the people forms the prelude to the history of capital. It comprises a series of forcible methods, of which we have passed in review only those that have been epoch-making as methods of the primitive accumulation of capital. (1872–1875, 678).

Thus, Marx was caught between a teleological post-Hegelian conception of history and his own descriptive difficulties in discussing the metamorphosis of primitive accumulation into something unnatural and obviously worse, in the first instance, for the vast majority of any developing society's population than that which came before it. This passage in *Capital* exemplifies how these two contradictory aspects were at work in Marx's economic thought: capitalism is treated by Marx at once as something inevitable and something whose development was originally an exceptional, unnatural event. Indeed, in this chapter, although he had identified a social form between feudalism and capitalism, he did not want to dwell too much on the transition from feudalism to the "petty mode of production" doomed to its own supersession, and he gave contradictory explanations for the transition from this mode of production to its successor "capitalist" mode of production. His first explanation was that this "mediocre" mode of production "brings forth the material agencies for its own dissolution" in accordance with the commercialisation thesis in which the gradual expansion of private exchanges ends with capitalist society. But Marx's second explanation was that primitive accumulation caused the destruction of individual ownership, signifying, on the contrary, that its disappearance was not inevitable and that without an unnatural socio-political event of some sort or another, it could never have developed on its own. Because "primitive accumulation" was supposed to apply to feudalism alone, not to the "commercialisation model" of the outward expansion of trade, the intermediary "mediocre" mode of production between feudalism and capitalism would seem to raise more flags in Marx's historical account than to clarify matters. Because this "petty" mode of production did not fit neatly into Marx's larger historical account, it was therefore doomed because of its "mediocrity". The boundaries between description and prescription were thus tendentiously blurred in Marx's narrative since it remained unclear why small property arrangements had to face extinction, apart from the fact they either would or should disappear so that capitalism could emerge triumphant in order to usher in a post-capitalist future through the dialectics of class struggle.

Thus, it was not obvious that there existed a path of economic development different from the industrial, capitalist one which characterised the British case. But the possibility that there might be was intriguing to the most eager initial readers of volume 1 of *Capital*: Marx's Russian socialist contemporaries.

3. Marx and the Russians: after 1867

With regards to the question of Russian economic development, Marx wrote that "[o]ne must descend from pure theory to Russian reality" (1881b, 226), and "not to be frightened by the word 'archaïc'" (1881b, 220). Because Marx's historical assumptions were carefully studied and discussed by the Russian Populists, Marx was compelled by his foreign readers to re-examine the question of primitive accumulation from a totally different point of view, one which took into account "pre-capitalist" modes of production and the persistence of the rural Russian commune. Whereas in volume 1 of *Capital* primitive accumulation, as it played itself out in British history, was regarded by Marx as finished, for the Russians, the concept seemed to describe a conceivable future given that the Russia of the 1870 s was still a relatively backward and agricultural country. Because the emancipation of the serfs had occurred only recently in 1861, the period of primitive accumulation described by Marx seemed unfinished to Russian readers of *Capital*, perhaps not yet even underway. To complicate matters further, Russia was not a British colony, so capitalism could not be imported directly from abroad as had been the case for India.

Such foreign interest in *Capital* would force Marx to turn his attention to Russia, however, a country which, until then, he had always denigrated in his journalism for its political backwardness and its geopolitical threat to German interests. In fact, the first translation of *Capital* into Russian was done by Nikolai Danielson and published in March 1872, appearing before even the French and English translations (respectively in 1872–1875 in serial form and in 1887). This Russian translation, published in a time of widespread revolutionary agitation, inspired a sharp interest amongst the Russian progressive intelligentsia for Marx's writings (Walicki 1989; White 1996). Disappointed by the defeat of the Paris Commune and preoccupied with helping the exiled communards trying to find refuge in London, Marx was all too delighted to bask in the attention and turn from Western to Eastern Europe. Russia increasingly monopolised his attention in the 1870 s, driving Marx to read frenetically about Russian and even learn Russian like "it was a question of life or death". After Marx's death, hoping to complete the long-promised and awaited volumes of *Capital*, Engels would find himself, much to his horror, in possession of two cubic metres of annotated Russian books and statistics without an obvious volume 2 in sight. Engels's surprise notwithstanding, it is clear from the manuscripts Marx left unfinished that the "Russian question" had a major impact on the mature Marx's final unpublished writings, influencing even the significant revisions he made to the subsequent 1872–1875 French edition (published serially) of volume 1 of *Capital*. Indeed, in that edition, Marx made important modifications to the original German version, influencing later translations, despite Engels's misgivings. (Stedman Jones 2016, 536 and 581). In doing so he was influenced by the debate than being waged between socialist advocates of industrial modernisation and more "Slavophile" socialist reformers who believed that Russia could achieve socialism through the development of already existing social customs and institutions such as the cooperative associations like the *artel* and the peasant village community, the *obshchina*.[6] The stakes of the debate were well-established when Marx discovered it: despite Russia's relative economic backwardness and the fact that it had never undergone anything closely approximate to the industrial revolution which had happened in Britain, could Russia bypass the British model of economic modernisation altogether and still have a socialist revolution? Marx's response to the question of Russian economic modernisation and its relation to socialist revolution was famously sketched out in a series of 1881 draft letters to Vera Zassulitch unearthed and made public only in 1924 by David Riazanov (Shanin 1983, 127–133). In his attempts to answer the question, Marx argued that the form of primitive accumulation described in *Capital* only applied to Western Europe, where it had found its most complete expression in British history and, consequently, the transformation from primitive accumulation to capitalism need not happen in the exact same way in Russia, since Russia could conceivably bypass the British stage of development and achieve socialism by strengthening the already existing institutions of the *obshchina*:

> The special study I made of [the Russian commune], including a search for original source-material, has convinced me that the commune is the fulcrum for social regeneration of Russia (Marx 1881a, 124).

This affirmation and the general preoccupation of the late Marx with the question of the economic modernisation of Russia have stimulated much speculation on the part of numerous specialists of Marx's thought, particularly amongst those keen on giving a non-dogmatic reading of Marx's thought. Charitable readers have thus

---

[6] The *artel* was a pre-industrial work association, grouping rural craftsmen and seasonal labourers such as construction workers operating outside of their villages. It typically had an elected leader and all net proceeds were shared amongst its members. The term "*artel* relationship" has been used generally to refer to all types of cooperation in production, ownership and landholding within the *obshchina*. (Shanin 1983, 125).

willingly cast Marx as a possibly nuanced theorist of underdevelop-
ment (Shanin 1983) or as a precursor of subaltern studies or even
gender studies (Anderson 2010). It is true that Marx would seem to
have evolved with regards to his assessment of Russia, since the revolution could just as easily happen to the east in the Slavic steppes
amongst the rural mujiks as to the west in the factories of Manchester
amongst the alienated urban proletariat. The uncertainties left by
Marx's unfinished manuscript notes of the 1870s not only would
seem to be at odds with too deterministic a reading of Marx's understanding of economic development. They would also seem to contradict the intellectual legacy elaborated by Marx himself, the "Darwin of
the social sciences" as Engels called him (Stedman Jones 2016:
566–567). After all, Marx explicitly claimed in the preface to the
French edition of *Capital* that is it the "ultimate aim of this work, to
lay bare the economic law of motion of modern society" and that
society "can neither clean by bold leaps, nor remove by legal enact-
ments, the obstacles offered by the successive phases of its normal
development"[7]. Indeed, the Russian material leaves one wondering
what the second and the third volumes of *Capital* would have looked
like had Marx actually written them (and if Engels had not constructed them, after Marx died, out of notes largely written prior to
the publication of volume 1 of *Capital*, signing Marx's name to them
as if he had intended them to work that, in reality, Engels wrote).
Since the third volume was to have focussed on the role of ground
rent, one assumes Marx would have treated at length Russian social
and economic issues in comparative perspective, and not have zeroed
in almost exclusively on examples drawn from British history as Marx
had in volume 1.

Yet Marx's own evolution with regards to his understanding of economic development is obvious in his famous letter drafts to Vera
Zassulitch. In these drafts, Marx now limited himself to discussing
original expropriation and its "historical inevitability" to Western
Europe (Marx 1881a, 100). This marked a major shift when compared
to the earlier claim made in the 1867 preface to the first edition of

---

[7] It should be stressed that this excerpt has been drawn from the introduction of the first
German edition. Here is the original: "Auch wenn eine Gesellschaft dem Naturgesetz ihrer
Bewegung auf die Spur gekommen ist, — und es ist der letzte Endzweck dieses Werks das
ökonomische Bewegungsgesetz der modernen Gesellschaft zu enthüllen — kann sie
naturgemäße Entwicklungsphasen weder überspringen, noch wegdekretiren. Aber sie kann die
Geburtswehen abkürzen und mildem." (MEGA II/5, 13–14).

volume 1 of *Capital*: notably the famous "*De te fabula narratur*" passage addressed to German readers to whom he explained that "the country that is most developed industrially only shows, to the less developed, the image of its own future". Marx's later attenuation and relativisation of his conception of economic development can also be found in a November 1877 letter to Mikhailovsky in which, in the course of comparing Roman proletarians to modern ones, he explained that:

> [E]vents of striking similarity, taking place in different historical contexts, led to totally separate results. By studying each of these developments separately, and then comparing them, one may easily discover the key of this phenomenon. But success will never come with the master-key of a general historico-philosophical theory, whose supreme virtue consists in being supra-historical (Marx 1877, 136)

In his later, mature incarnation, Marx would also admit to the contemporaneousness of diverse social formations, which likewise contradicted his earlier, more sequential conception of the history of economic development:

> Scattered examples survived all vicissitudes of the Middle Ages and have maintained themselves up to the present day — e.g., in my own home region of Trier. (Marx 1881a, 107).

When it came to Russia, Marx conceded that the persistence of the rural commune was not condemned in theory, even if, in practice, it was clearly threatened:

> What threatens the life of the Russian commune is neither a historical inevitability nor a theory; it is state oppression, and exploitation by capitalist intruders whom the state has made powerful at the peasants' expense" (Marx 1881a, 104–105)

Due to such comments, one can plausibly conclude, along with readers like Wada (1983, 60), that Marx "underwent a significant change after he wrote the first German edition of *Capital*", and with Stedman Jones that Marx returned to his first love, romanticism, whereas writings from the early 1840s were resolutely modernist and anti-Romantic in tone (2016, 578). Nevertheless, if one examines the mature Marx's overarching historical vision in light of his earlier differences with regards to a "petty-bourgeois socialist" like Sismondi, the Marx of 1881 still shared many similarities with the Marx of 1848. Marx never considered – except to criticise the idea – the prospects of land being redistributed to the peasantry as an individual property or ex-serfs becoming sharecroppers. In fact, in his draft letters to Vera Zassulitch, he explained that in Western European countries, the birth of capitalism began through capital's expropriation of land which was individually possessed by peasant capitalists and therefore represented a process in which "one form of private property is transformed into another form of private property" (Marx 1881a, 104). In Russia, where individual and communal property were in conflict, communal property persisted, but was directly under attack, notably through taxation. According to Marx, two future scenarios were possible: either the expropriation of land by the capitalist class and the transformation of the peasantry into an urban proletariat or the socialist modernisation of the rural commune through the use of modern "cooperative" methods. Marx never significantly considered the possibility of the rural commune developing through small farming and artisanal labour, however. According to him, "given the present condition of the great majority of Russian peasants, their conversion into small landowners would merely be a prologue to their swift expropriation" (Marx 1881a, 118). Moreover, the type of socialism Marx wanted to see flourish in Russia through the development of the peasant commune was always "industrial" in character:

> [The Russian commune] has maintained itself on a vast, nationwide basis. it is thus placed within a historical context in which the contemporaneity of capitalist production provides it with all the conditions for co-operative labour. It is in a position to incorporate the positive achievements of the capitalist system, without having to pass under its harsh tribute. The physical configuration of the Russian land is eminently suited to machine-assisted agriculture, organised on a large scale and [in the hands] performed by co-operative labour. (Marx 1881a, 113).

Thus, Marx continued to think of socialism as promoting the kind of material abundance furnished by modern science and industry. The cooperative was not run within the factories of the large-scale industry but by the rural commune regularly integrating scientific innovations in production. Marx was unclear as to how the modern cooperative would ever emerge from the archaic, customary traditional institutions of rural Slavs, but he seemed to suggest that British tractors and fertiliser could somehow be unproblematically transplanted to Russia. He thus tried to adapt Russian realities to his conceptual schema rather than modify his conceptual prejudices. Ironically, because many Russian socialists likewise attempted to adapt those same conceptual prejudices to Russian realities, history would prove Marx right, but maybe just not exactly in the sense he intended (Walicki 1989; White 1996). To compound this irony, post-1905 imperial attempts to elim- inate communal village property in Russia and to promote more indi- viduated forms of land tenure would prepare the groundwork (along with the Russian dead of WWI) for the success of the 1917 Revolutions which overthrew forever the imperial regime of the tsars. This might suggest that, ironically enough, before "really existing" socialism's rapid degeneration into a party dictatorship in Russia, the most important and influential historical victory of Marxism as a coherent ideological doctrine was largely facilitated by the Russian peasantry's widespread desire never to leave the stage of "so-called primitive accumulation".

Conclusion

This article has explored the impact Sismondi might have had on Marx as a historian of economic development, notably in the formu- lation of Marx's theory of "primitive accumulation" and its relation to "original expropriation" and the origins of capitalism. A compara- tive exploration of the two writers on these questions suggests that Marx never really resolved his own theories of economic develop- ment. Thus, an author like Sismondi, of whom Marx was categoric- ally dismissive in 1848, seems to have impacted Marx's later reassessment of capitalism's historical origins. However, if Marx's view of history appears to have substantially evolved from 1848 to 1881, this development implied only a partial "return" to Sismondi's observations about economic history since Marx never abandoned his faith in a socialism based on large-scale productive organisation, a conviction sharply at odds with Sismondi's own vision of a better social order.

Acknowledgment

I want to give here warm thanks to the two anonymous reviewers for their inspiring and detailed comments.

Disclosure statement

No potential conflict of interest was reported by the author.

References

Andler, Charles. 1901. *Le Manifeste Communiste de Karl Marx et F. Engels. Introduction historique et commentaire*. Paris: G. Bellais.

Anderson, Kevin D. 2010. *Marx at the Margins*. Chicago: University of Chicago Press.

Leroy, Maxime. 1950. "Simonde de Sismondi, premier analyse de la notion de prolétariat." Chapter 9 in Vol. 2 *of Histoire des Idées Sociales en France*, Paris: Gallimard.

Lotterie, Françoise. 1995. "Le progrès désenchanté: la perfectibilité selon Constant ou le malaise libéral." In *Le groupe de Coppet et le monde moderne: conceptions, images, débats*, edited by Françoise Tilkin, 273–288. Liège: Bibliothèque de la Faculté des lettres et philosophie de Liège.

Lotterie, Françoise. 2000. "L'année 1800. Perfectibilité, progrès et révolution dans *De la Littérature* de Mme de Staël." *Romantisme* 30 (108): 9–12. doi:10.3406/roman.2000.975

Löwy, Michael, and Robert Sayre. 2001. *Romanticism against the Tide of Modernity*. Durham, London: Duke University Press.

Marcuse, Herbert. 1969. "L'idée de progrès à la lumière de la psychanalyse." *L'Homme et la Société* 11 (1): 37–47. doi:10.3406/homso.1969.1175

Marx, Karl. 1845 (1998). "Brüsseler Hefte 1845." P. 115–433 in *Gesamtausgabe (MEGA), Vierte Abteilung, Band 3*. Berlin: Akademie Verlag.

Marx, Karl. 1846 (2014). *Marx and Engel's "German Ideology Manuscripts"*, Translated and edited by Terrell Carver and Daniel Bank. New York: Palgrave Macmillan.

Marx, Karl. 1853a. 1984. "Elections – Financial Clouds – The Duchess of Sutherland and Slavery." P. 16–23 in *Gesamtausgabe (MEGA), Erste Abteilung, band 12*. Berlin: Akademie Verlag.

Marx, Karl. 1853b (1984). "Forced Emigration – Kossuth and Mazzini – The Refugee Question – Election Bribery in England. Mr. Cobden." P. 56–61 in *Gesamtausgabe (MEGA), Erste Abteilung, Band 12*. Berlin: Akademie Verlag.

Marx, Karl. 1861–1863 (1975). *Theories of surplus-value*. 3 vols. Moscow: Progress Publishers.

Marx, Karl. 1865 (1988). "Value, Price and Profit." P. 385–428 in *Gesamtausgabe (MEGA), Zweite Abteilung, Band 4.1*. Berlin: Akademie Verlag.

Marx, Karl. (1869) 1972. "Author preface to the second edition of The Eighteenth Brumaire of Louis Bonaparte." *In The Eighteenth brumaire of Louis Bonaparte*. Moscow: Progress Publishers.

Marx, Karl. 1872–1875 (1989). "*Le Capital*, Paris 1872–1875." *Gesamtausgabe (MEGA), Zweite Abteilung, Band 7*. Berlin: Akademie Verlag.

Marx, Karl. 1877 (1983). "Karl Marx: A letter to the Editorial Board of Otechestvennye Zapiski." P. 134–137 in *Late Marx and the Russian Road*, edited by Theodor Shanin. London: Routledge and Keagan.

Marx, Karl. 1881a (1983). "Karl Marx: Draft of a Reply." P. 99–126 *in Late Marx and the Russian Road*, edited by Theodor Shanin. London: Routledge and Keagan.

Marx, Karl. 1881b (1985). *"Lettres à Vera Zassoulitch (Premier projet, deuxième projet, troisième projet, quatrième projet, et lettre à Vera Ivanovna Zassoulitch), Gesamtausgabe (MEGA), Erste Abteilung, Band 25*. Berlin: Akademie Verlag.

Marx, Karl. 1887 (1990). "Capital. A Critical Analysis of Capitalist Production, London 1887". In *Gesamtausgabe (MEGA), zweite abteilung, band 9*. Berlin: Akademie Verlag.

Marx, Karl, and Friedrich Engels. (2002) 1848. *The Communist Manifesto*, edited by Gareth Stedman Jones. London: Penguin Books.

Rubel, Maximilien (1957) 1974. "Les cahiers de lecture de Karl Marx. I. 1840–1856." Chapter 10 in *Marx Critique du Marxisme*. Paris: Payot.

Rubel, Maximilien 1976. "De Marx à Sismondi ou les emprunts de Marx à la théorie de Sismondi." *Économies et Sociétés*. Hors-Série 21: 39–54.

Say, Jean-Baptiste 1820. *Lettres à Malthus*. Paris: Bossange.

Shanin, Teodor. (ed.). 1983. *Late Marx and the Russian Road: Marx and the Peripheries of Capitalism*. London: Routledge and Keagan.

Sismondi, Jean Charles Léonard 1827 (2015). *Nouveaux principes d'économie politique ou De la Richesse dans ses rapports avec la population*. Vol. 5 of *Œuvres économiques complètes*. Paris: Economica.

Sismondi, Jean Charles Léonard. 1824 (2015). *"Sur la balance des consommations avec les productions."* Chap. 9 in *Écrits d'économie Politique 1816-1842*. Vol. 4 of *Œuvres économiques complètes*. Paris: Economica.

Sismondi, Jean Charles Léonard. 1832. *A History of the Italian Republics, Being a View of the Origin, Progress and Fall of Italian Freedom*. London: Longman, Rees, Orme, Brown, Green and Longman.

Sismondi, Jean Charles Léonard. 1834. *A History of the Fall of the Roman Empire: Comprising a View of the Invasion and Settlement of the Barbarians*. 2 vols. London: Longman.

Sismondi, Jean Charles Léonard. 1837–1838 (2017). *Études sur l'économie politique*. Book 2 & 3 of *Études sur les sciences sociales*. Vol. 6 of *Œuvres économiques complètes*. Paris: Economica.

Sonenscher, Michael. 2018. "Liberty, Autonomy, and Republican Historiography: Civic Humanism in Context." In *Markets, Morals, Politics: Jealousy of Trade and the History of Political Thought*, edited by Béla Kapossy, 161–210. Cambridge, MA and London: Harvard University Press.

Stedman Jones, Gareth. 2016. *Karl Marx: Greatness and Illusion*. London: Allen Lane.

Stedman Jones, Gareth. 2017. "History and Nature in Karl Marx: Marx's Debt to German Idealism." *History Workshop Journal* 83 (1): 98–117. doi:10.1093/hwj/dbx008

Wada, Haruki (1975) 1983. "Marx and Revolutionary Russia." In *P. 40-75 in Late Marx and the Russian Road*, edited by Theodor Shanin. London: Routledge and Keagan.

Walicki, Andrzej 1989. *The Controversy over Capitalism: Studies in the Social Philosophy of the Russian Populists*. Notre Dame: University of Notre Dame Press.

White, James D. 1996. *Karl Marx and the Intellectual Origins of Dialectical Materialism*. London: Palgrave Macmillan.

Wood, Ellen M. 2017. *The Origin of Capitalism: A Longer View*. London: Verso.

Marx's reproduction schemes and multi-sector growth models

Christian Gehrke

ABSTRACT

This paper provides a critical discussion of Marx's analysis of simple reproduction, of reproduction on an extended scale, and of the transition from
simple to extended reproduction. It challenges various interpretations of
Marx's analysis based on steady-state growth models. By referring to Marx's
original manuscripts on the reproduction schemes, the paper shows that
Marx, due to erroneous calculations, *never* arrived at schemes of reproduction
on an extended scale that exhibit steady-state growth. Moreover, it is suggested that Marx identified reproduction on an extended scale with an
expansion path of undisturbed capital accumulation, irrespective of whether
the latter proceeds in a steady or non-steady manner.

1. Introduction

The schemes of simple and extended reproduction in volume 2 of *Capital*
have been appraised by economic theorists as Karl Marx's "finest *analytical*
work" (Samuelson 1982, 46). These schemes were worked out in the mid-
1860s and late 1870s by elaborating on François Quesnay's *Tableau
économique*.[1] Their importance for economic theory relates to the fact that
Marx, in his schemes of simple reproduction, succeeded in disengaging the
schematic representation of the generation, distribution and disposal of the
social surplus provided by his French precursor from its feudal remnants,
and in reformulating it for economic systems with capitalistic production

---

[1]On the relationship between Marx's reproduction schemes and Quesnay's *Tableaux
économiques*, see Tsuru (1942), Samuelson (1982) and Gehrke and Kurz (1995). As Marx
pointed out, however, the physiocratic analysis of simple reproduction was in turn strongly
influenced by Richard Cantillon's *Essai sur la nature du commerce en général* (see MEGA II/11:
34); on the Cantillon-Marx connection, see Ananyin (2014).

relations. However, Marx is extolled mainly by modern economic theorists for having broken entirely new ground with his schemes of extended reproduction, which are regarded as one of the earliest depictions, in the history of economic analysis, of a *balanced* or *steady-state* growth path based on a simple multi-sectoral production model of the Leontief–Sraffa type (Samuelson 1974, 1982). Some scholars have also showered praise on Marx for having provided a highly original analysis of the *transitional dynamics*, because the numerical illustrations of transition paths from simple to extended reproduction that he presented in chapter 21 of volume 2 of *Capital* exhibit particularly strong convergence properties.

> In Marx's economy there prevails a tendency towards balanced growth, which is much stronger than the convergence claimed by neoclassical economists such as Solow, Meade and Uzawa, because any state of unbalanced growth will disappear in Marx's economy in a single year. (Morishima 1973, 120)

With the availability of Marx's original manuscripts in the new MEGA edition[2] it has become possible to see how Engels' version of volume 2 of *Capital* relates to the contents of the original documents, and where his editorial decisions, textual changes, additions or omissions may have changed the meaning, or influenced the interpretations, of Marx's texts. To carry out such a comparative assessment for the entire text of volume 2, and thus for Marx's reproduction analysis as a whole, is however beyond the scope of this paper. In the following, attention will indeed focus rather narrowly on the reproduction schemes and on the problem of the transition from simple to extended reproduction, that is, on chapters 20 and 21 in Part 3 of volume 2 of *Capital*, and on the parts in Marx's original manuscripts relating to the themes discussed in these chapters.

It is known that Marx wrote all in all eight manuscripts for volume 2 of *Capital*,[3] of which only two (i.e., Mss II and VIII) were used by

---

[2]Ms I, composed in 1865, has been published in MEGA II/4.1, and Mss II–VIII have been published in MEGA II/11. Also published are Engels' editorial manuscript ("Redaktionsmanuskript") for volume 2 of *Capital* (MEGA II/12), and the published version of volume 2 of *Capital* (MEGA II/13). All the texts are available online (http://megadigital. bbaw.de).

[3]Eight manuscripts have been identified and numbered by Engels. However, what Engels described as "manuscript III" in his preface to volume 2 (see Marx [1893] 1956, 3; MEGA II/13, 7) was a collection of excerpts, manuscript fragments and other materials belonging to books 2 and 3. Therefore, it is misleading to consider it as a draft for volume 2 (MEGA II/4.3, 423, note 3; II/11, 847, note 15.) It should also be noted that apart from these eight Mss Marx also left several other materials on books 2 and 3.

Engels for composing Part 3 of vol. 2 of his edition.[4] Therefore, the text published by Engels will be compared with the relevant sections of those two manuscripts and, in addition, sections in other manuscripts Marx had written for vol. 2 of *Capital* are identified that should or could have been used by Engels in his edition of chapters 20 and 21 of vol. 2 of *Capital*.

The structure of the paper is the following. In section 2, the conditions for simple and extended reproduction are briefly re-called and alternative readings of Marx's treatment of the problem of the transition from simple to extended reproduction, all based on Engels' edition, are discussed. In section 3, balanced or steady-state growth is shown to be a feature of the capital accumulation paths presented in chapter 21 of Engels' edition of *Capital* only. This feature is *not* to be found in the schematic representations of "Accumulation or reproduction on an extended scale" in Marx's original manuscripts. Section 4 then turns to the discussion of a highly original six-sector model, which Marx had set out in a part of Ms II that was omitted by Engels, and to a specific transition problem that Marx had tried to analyze on the basis of this model. Section 5 of the paper summarizes some material on "The elasticity of reproduction", which Marx had prepared for Part 3 of vol. 2 of *Capital*, where it was meant to precede the "Schematic presentation of accumulation", but which Engels decided not to include in his edition. We then discuss the relevance of this material for the analysis of the transition from simple to extended reproduction. Section 6 contains some concluding remarks.

2. Simple reproduction, extended reproduction and the problem of transition

In the secondary literature on the reproduction schemes, Marx is typically credited with having set out the conditions for simple and extended reproduction, where the latter is identified with a *steady-state* growth path, and with having illustrated the two cases by means of numerical examples that are related to one another. Accordingly, some authors have maintained that Marx could and should have developed his illustration of extended reproduction by directly starting out from the numerical example he had employed for simple reproduction, and by determining explicitly the associated transition path

---

[4]See Engels' "Preface" in Marx ([1893] 1956, 21).

that leads from the former to the latter.[5] Other commentators, however, have denied the feasibility of this: "Had Marx started out with
the Simple Reproduction scheme, there would have been no way to
set the system in motion. ... *The transition to growth remained for
Marx an enigma*" (Hollander 2008, 82–83). In order to discuss these
alternative views on the transition problem, let us first briefly recall
the main properties of the reproduction schemes in chapters 20 and
21 of volume 2 of *Capital*.

2.1. Conditions for "simple reproduction" and for "reproduction on an extended scale"

2.1.1. Simple reproduction

According to Marx, the analysis of the conditions of reproduction and
accumulation of the aggregate social capital must be based on a
decomposition of the economic system that is orientated at the usage
of the different components of the aggregate social product.[6] He
therefore introduced a distinction between two departments:
Department I comprises the production of means of production, that
is, of "commodities having a form in which they must, or at least
may, pass into productive consumption", and department II consists
of industries for the production of articles of consumption, that is,
"commodities having a form in which they pass into the individual
consumption of the capitalist and the working class" (Marx [1893]
1956, 399).[7] The values of the commodities produced in the two
departments (w_i) are given additively by the three components c_i, v_i
and s_i, that is, the value of the constant capital (c_i), variable capital
(v_i) and surplus value (s_i), for $i = 1, 2$.

The reproduction schemes depict the circulation of the components of the social product that must take place between the two
departments, in both physical and value terms, in order to begin a
new cycle of production and consumption on the same (simple
reproduction) or on an extended scale. In the "schematic presentation" of reproduction and accumulation, this is illustrated by

---

[5]See Samuelson (1974, 278) and Turban (1980, 64).

[6]See also Burchardt (1931–2, 122–123).

[7]The disaggregation of department II in chapter 20 into two sub-departments, producing
"necessities of life" and "articles of luxury", respectively, will be ignored here, because in the
present context it is of secondary importance only.

means of various numerical examples, in which generally a given and constant rate of surplus value is assumed, identical for both departments, whereas the organic compositions of capital[8] of the two departments differ from each other in some of the numerical examples. The primary example used for illustrating "simple reproduction" is the following one[9]:

$$I : 4000_c + 1000_v + 1000_s = 6000_w \qquad\qquad I : c_1 + v_1 + s_1 = w_1$$
$$II : 2000_c + 500_v + 500_s = 3000_w \qquad \text{or} \qquad II : c_2 + v_2 + s_2 = w_2$$

Simple reproduction requires that in each period the value of the means of production and of the means of subsistence and articles of consumption produced in the two departments ("supply") is equal to the value of the means of production and consumption annually used up ("demand"),[10] that is,

$$supply = demand$$
$$w_1 = c_1 + v_1 + s_1 = c_1 + c_2$$
$$w_2 = c_2 + v_2 + s_2 = v_1 + v_2 + s_1 + s_2$$

Accordingly, the condition for simple reproduction in the two-department scheme is[11]:

$$c_2 = v_1 + s_1.$$

2.1.2. Extended reproduction

As opposed to simple reproduction, reproduction on an extended scale presupposes that part of the surplus value is regularly converted into additional capital in order to extend the scale of production. Apart from the demand for replacement of the means of production used up in the two departments there thus arises an additional demand for constant capital ($\Delta c_1 + \Delta c_2$) and for means of subsistence for additional labourers in the two departments ($\Delta v_1 + \Delta v_2$), while the capitalists' demand for means of consumption is reduced because part of the surplus value is now used for accumulation purposes. The aggregate supply and demand for means of production and

---

[8]By the "organic composition of capital" we always mean the proportion of constant and variable capital, c/v.

[9]See Marx ([1893] 1956, 401).

[10]See Sweezy (1942, 76–77) and Robinson (1942, 45).

[11]See Marx ([1893] 1956, 406).

consumption therefore amounts to

$$Supply = Demand$$
$$c_1 + v_1 + s_1 = w_1 = c_1 + \Delta c_1 + c_2 + \Delta c_2$$
$$c_2 + v_2 + s_2 = w_2 = v_1 + \Delta v_1 + v_2 + \Delta v_2 + (s_1 - \Delta c_1 - \Delta v_1) + (s_2 - \Delta c_2 - \Delta v_2).$$

Accordingly, the fundamental condition for an undisturbed process of accumulation, or "reproduction on an extended scale", is the equality, in each period, of[12]

$$c_2 + \Delta c_2 = v_1 + s_1 - \Delta c_1.$$

It should be noted that in the analysis of the reproduction schemes it is assumed that at the beginning of the annual cycle of production the variable capital has to be advanced in *money*, whereas the constant capital must already have been acquired in its *use form* by the department in which it is applied in order to start the production cycle. Whereas the means of consumption for the currently employed workers are thus supplied from currently produced output, the elements of the constant capital have to be supplied out of the production of the previous period.[13] With simple reproduction, quantities remain unchanged in each period, so that the distinction is not important, but for the analysis of accumulation and extended reproduction it is highly relevant.

The main numerical example on which commentators have generally based their exposition of Marx's analysis of reproduction on an extended scale, is the one contained in section "1. First Illustration" of chapter 21.[14] At the beginning of this section, the numerical example of simple reproduction is reproduced, under the heading "(A) Scheme of simple reproduction":

$$I : 4000_c + 1000_v + 1000_s = 6000_w$$
$$II : 2000_c + 500_v + 500_s = 3000_w$$

Immediately below this scheme is another one, without further explanation, under the heading "(B) Initial scheme for reproduction on an extended scale":

$$I : 4000_c + 1000_v + 1000_s = 6000_w$$
$$II : 1500_c + 750_v + 750_s = 3000_w$$

---

[12]See Marx ([1893] 1956, 521).

[13]In much of the secondary literature on the reproduction schemes, it is silently assumed that constant and variable capital must be made available at the beginning of the annual production cycle in its use form; see, for instance, the "time-dated framework" of Marx's model of accumulation in Desai (1979, 161).

[14]See Marx ([1893] 1956, 514–517).

Comparing the two schemes (A) and (B), it is easily recognised that in the latter the organic composition of capital in department II has been changed from 4:1 to 2:1. Scheme (B) therefore cannot be supposed to depict the same simple reproduction scheme with "a changed grouping, without which reproduction on an extended scale cannot take place at all" (Marx [1893] 1956, 510). And scheme (B) also cannot be considered as a constellation that has emerged in the course of the transition process from simple to extended reproduction, for instance because department II has experienced problems of insufficient demand for its products.

Next, a very specific hypothesis about the accumulation behaviour of the capitalists in the two departments is introduced. It is assumed that the capitalists in department I first decide to use one-half of the surplus value for capital accumulation in department I and that those in department II then purchase precisely those amounts of the means of production for replacing and enlarging their own capital basis which remain after department I's requirements for reproduction and accumulation purposes have been satisfied. Given these assumptions, the following capital accumulation path results[15]:

$$\text{Initial scheme}: \begin{array}{l} I : 4000_c + 1000_v + 1000_s = 6000_w \\ II : 1500_c + 750_v + 750_s = 3000_w \end{array}$$

$$\text{year 1} \quad \begin{array}{l} I : 4400_c + 1100_v + 1100_s = 6600_w \\ II : 1600_c + 800_v + 800_s = 3200_w \end{array}$$

$$\text{year 2} \quad \begin{array}{l} I : 4840_c + 1210_v + 1210_s = 7260_w \\ II : 1760_c + 880_v + 880_s = 3520_w \end{array}$$

$$\text{year 3} \quad \begin{array}{l} I : 5324_c + 1331_v + 1331_s = 7986_w \\ II : 1936_c + 968_v + 968_s = 3872_w \end{array}$$

$$\text{year 4} \quad \begin{array}{l} I : 5856_c + 1464_v + 1464_s = 8784_w \\ II : 2129_c + 1065_v + 1065_s = 4259_w \end{array}$$

$$\text{year 5} \quad \begin{array}{l} I : 6442_c + 1610_v + 1610_s = 9662_w \\ II : 2342_c + 1172_v + 1172_s = 4686_w \end{array}$$

Readers trained in modern growth theory will easily recognise that after a single period of non-steady growth the economic system is expanding along a *steady-state* accumulation path, with a uniform growth rate of 10%.

2.2. Marx's treatment of the transition problem from simple to extended reproduction

With regard to Marx's treatment of the problem of the transition from simple to extended reproduction, two different interpretative

---

[15]See Marx ([1893] 1956, 514–517).

patterns can be found in the secondary literature. On one hand, it is suggested by several interpreters that this is a problem which Marx had no need to, and indeed did not, address at all, because he regarded simple and extended reproduction merely as two different levels of abstraction in the analysis of the capitalist process of production as a whole. Accordingly, in some of the secondary literature the schemes of simple and extended reproduction are presented independently of each other. To be sure, there are indeed statements in chapters 20 and 21 that could be cited in support of this reading. Thus, in the opening section of chapter 20 we read:

> Simple reproduction, reproduction on the same scale, appears as an abstraction, inasmuch as ... the absence of all accumulation or reproduction on an extended scale is a strange assumption in capitalist conditions ... However, as far as accumulation does take place, simple reproduction is always a part of it, and can therefore be studied by itself, and is an actual factor of accumulation. (Marx [1893] 1956, 398–399)

Moreover, in the first paragraph of chapter 21 it is noted that the analysis of the accumulation of capital discussed in vol. 1 of *Capital* with regard to an *individual capitalist* could be transferred to the annual total reproduction and accumulation of capital in the economic system as a whole only if it is supposed "that production on an extended scale has actually been in process previously. For in order that the money (the surplus value hoarded in money-form) may be converted into elements of productive capital, one must be able to buy these elements on the market as commodities" (Marx [1893] 1956, 494). A further remark, pointing in the same direction, is to be found in the section "Accumulation in Department II", where Marx states: "We had assumed in the analysis of simple reproduction that the entire surplus-value of I and II is spent as revenue. As a matter of fact, however, one portion of the surplus-value is spent as revenue, and the other is converted into capital. Actual accumulation can take place only on this assumption." ([1893] 1956, 507)[16] Clearly, these passages can be read as implying that Marx had no intention of

---

[16]This remark is introduced by Marx in order to formulate an objection to the depiction of the savings-investment nexus based on abstinence theory: "That accumulation should take place at the expense of consumption is, couched in such general terms, an illusion contradicting the nature of capitalist production. For it takes for granted that the aim and compelling motive of capitalist production is consumption, and not the snatching of surplus-value and its capitalization, i.e., accumulation." ([1893] 1956, 507)

studying the transition problem, because the analysis of simple reproduction merely refers to a higher level of abstraction in the analysis of
the same scientific object: the accumulation and reproduction of the
social capital in the capitalistic process as a whole.

There is, however, a second interpretative line, which is found in
contributions by Morishima (1973), Samuelson (1974), Desai (1979),
Turban (1980), Hollander (2008), and others. According to these
authors, chapter 21 of volume 2 of *Capital* contains an attempt,
although an unsuccessful one, at analysing the transition problem.
Thus, according to Turban,

> all of Marx's attempts to solve the problem of the transition from simple
> to extended reproduction failed. He thus only succeeded in providing an
> exposition of the two cases of simple and extended reproduction without
> being able to establish a connection between them. (1980, 64)[17]

For Turban, this is surprising, because it is easy to set out "the
conditions for an adequate solution of the transition problem, in
which the errors committed by Marx are avoided" (1980, 64). The
first condition, recognised also by Marx, is that part of the surplus
value must be saved and invested, that is, must be spent by the
capitalists on purchasing additional means of production instead of
means of consumption. In order for such additional means of production to be supplied, there must first be positive net investment
in department I, which under the prevailing conditions of simple
reproduction can be accomplished only by reducing the capital
replacement in department II. The second condition for an
adequate solution therefore is "that a transfer of means of production and of workers from department II to department I takes
place" (1980, 64). If it is further supposed "that the reduction in
the production of consumers goods corresponds to the reduction in
capitalists' consumption", and assuming in addition that "the change
in the class-specific demand structure for consumption goods causes
no restructuring problems" (1980, 64–65), it becomes possible to
arrive at an undisturbed transition path from simple to extended
reproduction. Overproduction or excess capacity in department II,
presented by Marx as an unavoidable feature of the transition process, can be avoided by simply assuming that the process of restructuring is initiated with a re-allocation of the productive capital

---

[17]Unless otherwise stated, all translations from German sources are mine.

between the two departments. In Marx's numerical example, this could be accomplished along the following lines:

$$
\begin{aligned}
\text{Period } t = 0: \quad & I: 4000_c + 1000_v + 1000_s = 6000 \\
& II: 2000_c + 500_v + 500_s = 3000 \\
\text{Period } t = 1: \quad & I: 4400_c + 1100_v + 1100_s = 6600 \\
& II: 1600_c + 400_v + 400_s = 2400 \\
\text{Period } t = 2: \quad & I: 4840_c + 1210_v + 1210_s = 7260 \\
& II: 1760_c + 440_v + 440_s = 2640
\end{aligned}
$$

At the end of period 0, in which the economic system started out with a capital structure that corresponds to simple reproduction, there is a transfer of capital and workers from department II to department I, so that at the beginning of period 1 the capital in department I is increased by 10%, while that of department II has been reduced by 20%. With the outputs produced in period 1 it would then be possible to increase the capital at the beginning of period 2 in both departments by 10%, so that from now on both sectors could expand in tandem at an accumulation rate of 10%. The transition from a *stationary state* to a *steady-state* growth path could thus be accomplished with only a single period of "not-in-lock-step" growth – which however would still be *undisturbed accumulation* in the sense that in each period the produced outputs are fully absorbed.

Basically the same suggestion for the "correction" of Marx's "transition algorithm" was earlier put forward already by Paul A. Samuelson, together with the remark that "once we permit ourselves unrealistic savings behaviour, why not pick on one of the infinite number of alternative models each with the property of converging in *one* step from simple reproduction" (1974, 278). Samuelson here alludes to another interpretative problem, which concerns the *conceptual* status of Marx's savings (and investment) hypothesis. While Samuelson calls it "unrealistic" and Morishima "unnatural", Desai described it in the following terms: "The capitalists of Department I decide ... for some reason to expand. Quite arbitrarily, Department II then decides to mop up all the excess supply of machine tools" (1979, 154–155)[18] The three authors seem to be agreed that the postulated accumulation behaviour is not a "realistic" depiction of the investment behaviour of producers in competitive markets, who

---

[18]The solution proposed by Turban is a specific variant of Marx's investment hypothesis, according to which department II "mops up" the surplus part (which in this case is *negative*) of the means of production produced in department I, after the capitalists of this department have decided on using a definite part of surplus value (in this case 50%) for accumulation purposes.

clearly would orientate their investment decisions on the sales expectations for their *own* products, rather than on the problems of producers in other industries to find purchasers for *their* products. Furthermore, Marx's assumptions on investment behaviour also entail that surplus value is invested only in the department in which it was generated. Joan Robinson has considered this "a severe assumption to make even about the era before limited liability was introduced, and ... absurd afterwards" (1951, 17). According to Morishima, this assumption "is not only unnatural but conflicts with his reasonings on the formation of the equilibrium rate of profits" (1973, 122). With reference to volume 3 of *Capital*, where Marx analysed the transformation of values into production prices and motivated the tendency towards a uniform rate of profits with free capital mobility among sectors, Morishima dismisses Marx's "peculiar" investment hypothesis employed in volume 2. This argument obviously presupposes that Marx's analyses must be based on the same assumptions throughout the three volumes of capital.[19] Morishima's argument was twisted around by Howard and King, who suggested that Marx, precisely for reasons of internal consistency, in his reproduction schemes could only allow for the internal accumulation of surplus value: If one assumes, as Marx does in volumes 1 and 2 of *Capital*, that commodities exchange at their values, then one must also set aside interdepartmental capital mobility, because the latter implies a uniform rate of profits and prices of production (Howard and King 1985, 183). Whatever we make of this argument, it still leaves unexplained the conceptual status of Marx's peculiar investment hypothesis. In Samuelson's view, Marx's "unrealistic" investment hypothesis clearly shows that his analysis was not meant to be a *positive* analysis. But Samuelson remains agnostic on whether, and in what sense, it could perhaps be seen as a *normative* analysis:

> Marx presumably is not purporting to describe a real-life transition. The algorithm does not take place in the capitalistic marketplace, but rather at Marx's desk in the British Museum. There are an infinite number of alternative unrealistic algorithms that could also be conjured up. (Samuelson 1974, 278)

---

[19]On this premise it could also be argued that it is inconsistent if Marx assumes a constant organic composition of capital in his schemes of extended reproduction, although he elsewhere stated that capital accumulation is generally bound up with changes in this composition.

In Samuelson's reading, the arbitrariness of Marx's treatment calls for using a transition algorithm which starts out from the scheme of simple reproduction. Without making this explicit, Samuelson seems to suppose that Marx's treatment cannot properly be regarded as a *normative* approach, because it lacks clearly defined efficiency criteria. Marx only imposes the criterion of undisturbed accumulation – a criterion, which does not allow the derivation of uniquely determined transition paths. Desai (1979, 172), on the other hand, considered Marx's analysis of the transition to extended reproduction as an anticipation of the Fel'dman-Mahalanobis model, that is, as a forerunner of a planning model.[20]

Why did Marx not develop a transition path that starts out from the scheme of simple reproduction? Samuelson, Morishima, Desai and Turban make out one reason for this in Marx's insufficient grasp of the mathematical properties of the dynamic system that he sought to analyse. Thus, Morishima points out that Marx was unable to solve a system of linear difference equations, and therefore was forced to choose a starting point for his analysis which allowed him to determine in a simple, pedestrian way the transition to a *steady-state* growth path. It can be shown, however, that the "unnatural" investment hypothesis employed by Marx has the remarkable property that the economic system, independently of the initial constellation and of the division of surplus value chosen by the capitalists of department I between accumulation $(\alpha_1 s_1)$ and consumption $(1-\alpha_1 s_1)$, will always reach a steady-state path after a single period of not-in-lockstep growth of the two departments. This is because in his numerical examples Marx assumed that the producers of department I accumulate in each period a certain fraction of their surplus value, $\alpha_1 s_1$, which they employ in the proportions $\left[\frac{c_1}{c_1+v_1}\right]\alpha_1 s_1$ and $\left[\frac{v_1}{c_1+v_1}\right]\alpha_1 s_1$ for additional constant and variable capital, respectively. The producers in department II are then assumed to decide on their reproduction and accumulation requirements in such a way that the remaining means of production are fully absorbed, that is,

$$\alpha_2(t+1)\left[\frac{c_2}{c_2+v_2}\right]s_2(t) = w_1(t)-c_1(t)-\left[\frac{c_1}{c_1+v_1}\right]\alpha_1 s_1(t)-c_2(t).$$

---

[20]The planning models presented by Fel'dman ([1928] 1964) and Mahalanobis (1953) were of course inspired by Marx's ideas on extended reproduction, but there are no hints in Marx's text that he intended such a reading. To put this more formally: For the determination of his capital accumulation paths, Marx omitted to specify optimization criteria and constraints.

As Morishima demonstrates, such an "investment hypothesis" must *always* generate the result that Marx derived for his specific numerical example[21]:

> The accumulation may start from an arbitrary initial point ... in Marx's economy there prevails a tendency towards balanced growth, which is much stronger than the convergence claimed by neoclassical economists such as Solow, Meade and Uzawa, because any state of unbalanced growth will disappear in Marx's economy in a single year.[22] It can easily be shown that such a strange conclusion is not specific to the numerical illustration used by Marx, but is a logical implication of his investment function. (Morishima 1973, 118–120)

According to Morishima, Marx could thus have determined also a transition path that starts out from simple reproduction, but because of his insufficient mathematical skills he failed to see this. A further explanation for Marx's failure was suggested by Samuelson, who pointed out that whereas Marx had elaborated the scheme of simple reproduction already in the 1860s, the scheme of extended reproduction "seems to come from the 1870s[23]; and from the internal evidence of Marx's expositions, one senses that he had not mastered the intricacies of the extended reproduction case in quite the way he had that of simple reproduction" (Samuelson 1974, 271). Because he studied the two cases separately from each other and with a huge time gap, Marx may have lost sight of their connection:

> A gap of years separated Marx's writing on simple and extended reproduction. Perhaps this explains why he did not proceed directly from his original simple reproduction example ... to the new equilibrium configuration when capitalists accumulate part of their incomes to finance golden-age exponential growth of all parts of the system, including the labor supply. (Samuelson 1974, 276)[24]

---

[21]For a proof, see Morishima (1973, 121–122) and Desai (1979, 166–169). Desai also shows that there is no convergence to a *steady-state* growth path, if one assumes that it is the capitalists in sector II who first decide on the rate of accumulation and those of sector I then "mop up" the excess supply (1979, 169).

[22]A comparison of the adjustment speeds of transition paths in models which are based on vastly different adjustment mechanisms is, of course, rather meaningless.

[23]Marx in fact appears to have first worked out the schemes of extended reproduction only in 1880; see note 27 below.

[24]The idea that "undisturbed extended reproduction" is associated with *steady-state* growth in the labour supply is of course not to be found in Marx.

As we shall see below, in Marx's original exposition of the schemes of extended reproduction (in Ms VIII) there is to be found neither a steady-state growth path nor an explicit analysis of the transition from simple to extended reproduction. Therefore, the whole discussion about his alleged failure to come up with a proper solution to the transition problem seems to be misplaced. However, even on the basis of Engels' edition it could be argued that from Marx's point of view there are substantial reasons for not adopting the proposed solution to this problem. First, because in this case in the first period of the accumulation process the means of production (and labour) are simply re-allocated between the two departments.[25] Therefore, the very phenomenon that Marx had declared to be the object of his analysis, namely "accumulation of capital", that is, the transformation of surplus value into *additional* elements of capital, is not present at all. Moreover, such a re-allocation presupposes the existence of non-specific and hence inter-departmentally transferable means of production (and workers). It could be suggested that the following passage in section I of chapter 21 explicitly refers to such non-specific means of production, and that it specifically emphasises their role for the transition from simple to extended reproduction:

> In order that the transition from simple to extended reproduction may take place, production in department I must be in a position to fabricate fewer elements of constant capital for II and so many the more for I. This transition, which does not always take place without difficulties, is facilitated by the fact that some of the products of I can serve as means of production in either department. ([1893] 1956, 500–501)

It must be stressed, therefore, that this passage was phrased, and inserted into Marx's text, by Engels,[26] in order to replace the following statement by Marx:

> Now the products of certain lines of production of I do not enter as means of production into II, but can serve only as means of production in I itself. The product of these branches is decomposable, in terms of its value, into $c + v + m$, like that of any other line. What then becomes of this m *in the condition of simple reproduction*, which does not supply the material for additional constant capital I? This to be investigated under simple reproduction. (MEGA II/11, 797)

---

[25]This shifting of capital (and workers) between the two departments presupposes the existence of non-specific capital (and labour). In modern growth models, this re-allocation mechanism and the corresponding assumption of non-specifity has been employed most prominently by Hicks (1965).

[26]See MEGA II/11, 797 for Marx's original text, MEGA II/13, 461 for the printed version, and MEGA II/12, 458.34–459.2 and MEGA II/12 App, 932 for Engels' insertion.

Obviously, in this passage Marx was discussing neither "the transition from simple to extended reproduction" nor the non-specificity, and hence inter-departmental transferability, of the means of production. On the contrary, his concern was rather with the role of means of production that are *specific* to department I.

Moreover, the proposed solution would be inconsistent with Marx's views of the sequencing of events in the circulation of commodities, capital, and money. In Marx's conceptualisation of the circular flow, the following sequence of transactions is implied: First, department I sells means of production produced in period $t = 0$ in the amount of the variable capital that needs to be replaced plus one-half of its surplus value $(1000 + 500)$ to department II. When department II now purchases additional means of production in the amount of 100, department I can increase its variable capital to 1100 (in money). Department I would then have a constant capital of 4400 (in material form), a variable capital of 1100 (in money), and a consumption fund for capitalists' consumption of 500 (in money). After these transactions department II has means of production in the amount of 1600, a variable capital of 400 (in money) and a "consumption fund" of 1000 units (in consumer goods): "Overproduction" in department II is thus avoided only by assuming that the capitalists of department II reduce their capital by 20% *and simultaneously increase their consumption by 100%*:

Period $t = 0$:	$I : 4000_c + 1000_v + 1000_s = 6000$
	$II : 2000_c + 500_v + 500_s = 3000$
Beginning of period $t = 1 : I : 4400_c + 1100_v + 500\,consumption\,fund = 6000$	
	$II : 1600_c + 400_v + 1000\,consumption\,fund = 3000$
End of period $t = 1$:	$I : 4400_c + 1100_v + 1100_s = 6600$
	$II : 1600_c + 400_v + 400_s = 2400$

This implication of the "transition algorithm" suggested by Samuelson and Turban is not made explicit in their expositions only because they disregard Marx's distinction between the material form and the money form of the variable capital.

3. Marx's discussion of "accumulation or extended reproduction" in Ms VIII

The manuscript material that was to become chapter 21 in Engels' edition formed the final part of Ms VIII, written by Marx in the late 1870s and early 1880. Although he had drafted some material relating to "Accumulation or reproduction on an extended scale" already in his Ms I of 1865, the *schemes of extended reproduction* were only worked out in the course of his work on Ms VIII, and presumably only in 1880 or 1881.[27] At the beginning of the passages from Ms VIII which Engels turned into chapter 21 is a heading, inserted by Marx, which reads: "Anticipated. II) Accumulation or reproduction on an enlarged scale" (MEGA II/11, 790). The editors of the MEGA edition have interpreted this to mean that Marx at this point had meant to insert some further material on issues that belong here, but had decided to postpone this discussion for later treatment when composing his manuscript (and then never came round to fill this gap). Among the themes which were thus not properly covered they mention "the problem of the transition from simple to extended reproduction", which Marx had briefly tackled in Ms I under the heading "The elasticity of reproduction", and "the exposition of the reproduction schemes with various sub-departments", that is, an exposition of simple reproduction based on the six-sector model, which Marx had worked out in a part of Ms II that was omitted by Engels (MEGA II/13 App, 543–544). We shall have a closer look at the material from Ms I on "The elasticity of reproduction", which the MEGA editors consider relevant for the discussion of the transition problem, in section 5 below. The material on the six-sector model from Ms II will be discussed in section 4, where we shall focus attention primarily on Marx's analysis of a specific traverse problem. As we shall see, this traverse problem concerns, however, a transition between two alternative states of simple reproduction, and not a transition from simple to extended reproduction.[28]

Let us return, then, to Marx's exposition of the reproduction schemes in Ms VIII and compare it with the presentation of the material in Engels' edition. We must first note that chapter 21 of

---

[27]See (MEGA II/11 App, 873). An exact dating of individual parts of Ms VIII, on which Marx had worked, on and off, between 1877 and 1881, is not possible. However, the passages in which he set out the schemes of extended reproduction were not written before 1880 (see MEGA II/11 App, 1610–1611). Marx had briefly tackled the problem of accumulation and extended reproduction in his Ms I of 1865 (see MEGA II/4.1, 353–381), but without elaborating any reproduction schemes. In Ms II and in his subsequent attempts at completing the manuscript for vol. 2 of *Capital* the topic was repeatedly postponed for later treatment.

[28]Marx never carried out an analysis of extended reproduction on the basis of his six-sector model in Ms II, although he had intended to do so (see Marx's own table of contents for the "third chapter" of volume 2 of *Capital* in MEGA II/11, p. 4). But he had then broken off his discussion after "(A) Reproduction on a simple scale. (b) Description with the mediating monetary circulation."

volume 2 of *Capital* in Engels' edition is based entirely on the relevant passages in Marx's Ms VIII, with only little additions or omissions by Engels – with one important exception. This concerns Engels' correction of Marx's exposition of the schemes of extended reproduction in Section III of chapter 21, which was introduced by Engels under the heading "Schematic presentation of accumulation" (Marx [1893] 1956, 510–527). The original passage in Ms VIII (MEGA II/11, 810–815), which was presented by Engels under the heading "1. First Illustration", comprises six consecutive schemes over a period of 5 years, based on the same set of assumptions that we listed in section 2 above. But in his calculations for the six consecutive schemes Marx committed several errors, which render the figures of his schemes contradictory with regard to the postulated assumptions. It was Engels who, by correcting Marx's erroneous calculations, arrived at the *balanced* or *steady-state* growth path exposition of extended reproduction. In Marx's original manuscript, the consecutive schemes instead exhibit the following characteristics:[29] (i) the rates of accumulation of the two departments do not align; (ii) the proportions of the two departments change from year to year; (iii) the rate of accumulation in department II changes from year to year. This clearly is not a *balanced* or *steady-state* growth path. The finding that a path of undisturbed accumulation converges, under Marx's set of assumptions, to a *steady-state* accumulation path thus only emerges from Engels' corrected exposition, and cannot be inferred from Marx's original discussion. There certainly is no indication that Marx was aware of this property.

In view of this fact, it seems necessary to reconsider the interpretations suggested by Morishima, Samuelson, Desai, Hollander and others, according to which Marx's schemes of extended reproduction depict not only the conditions for an undisturbed capital expansion path, but also the transition from an arbitrarily chosen initial state of *unbalanced* or *non-steady* growth towards a path of *steady-state* growth. Moreover, it is also necessary to reconsider the issue whether Marx had initially intended to study a transitional path from simple to extended reproduction or, in modern parlance, from a *stationary* equilibrium to a *steady-state* growth path, but then had to give up

---

[29]See (MEGA II/11, 810–815) and (MEGA II/13 App, 545).

this plan because its execution exceeded his analytical powers and mathematical skills.

A comparison of Marx's original manuscript with Engels' edition of chapter 21 leads to the following results.[30] First, Engels generally turned Marx's more tentative wordings and his descriptions of unresolved theoretical problems into more positive statements and a more affirmative exposition. He thus gave the text a much more definitive character than it actually possessed. Secondly, whereas Marx had introduced as section-headings only the numbers "(1)" to "(5)", and for the rest had merely subdivided his text by horizontal lines (often indicating a new beginning after having interrupted his work), Engels inserted a number of section-headings and sub-headings, or connecting introductory phrases, into the text – which, however, do not always correspond to the contents of the respective sections.[31] Third, Marx had sub-divided his text in order to spell out and discuss, under the numberings (1) to (4), various "theoretical difficulties" he was confronted with in the analysis of accumulation (for details, see MEGA II/11 App, 873–874). Accordingly, large parts of Ms VIII were written for self-clarification about theoretical difficulties, rather than with the intention of presenting definitive results. Fourth, in Marx's manuscript there are altogether five different "schemes of accumulation or reproduction on an extended scale". In the first one, also reproduced by Engels (Marx [1893] 1956, 510–514), Marx started out from an initial scheme which is directly derived from the scheme of simple reproduction, with a reduced size of department II:

$$I : 4000c + 1000v + 1000s = 6000$$
$$II : 1500c + 376v + 376s = 2252$$

This suggests that Marx had indeed tried to develop the analysis of extended reproduction by taking the scheme of simple reproduction as his starting point. On the assumption that capitalists in both departments seek to accumulate one-half of their surplus-value, Marx then pointed out problems with the monetary reflux, and broke off his exposition. This was followed by a second set of schemes, which

---

[30]See, on the following, also the editors' "Introduction" in MEGA II/11 App, 873–881. Also relevant for this comparison is the editors' "Introduction" in MEGA II/12 App, 497–523.

[31]See, for instance, Engels' insertion of the introductory sentence: "Let us now take a closer look at the accumulation in department II" ([1893] 1956: 507) in the section "II. Accumulation in department II". In the section under consideration, Marx in fact is *not* discussing accumulation *in* department II, but rather the repercussions *on* department II that result from the attempt of the capitalists in department I to enlarge their capital base.

in Engels' edition were to become the "First Illustration" (with Engels' corrections of Marx's erroneous calculations, discussed above). Marx considered the result unsatisfactory, but *not* because the resulting accumulation path (because of his erroneous calculations) was a non-steady one. He rather was dissatisfied because after the fifth year of reproduction on an extended scale the organic composition of capital was lower than in the initial scheme, "which is in contradiction with the course of capitalistic production" (MEGA II/11, 814). He therefore tried out another initial reproduction scheme with different organic compositions in the two departments, but again committed errors in his calculations and after a few lines again broke off his discussion (see MEGA II/11, 815.8–815.16). In his next attempt, he then changed the rate of surplus value and the organic compositions in the two departments, but because he based his calculations inadvertently on a wrong number for the surplus in department I which remains after one-half of it had been exchanged for means of consumption, he again broke off this discussion, this time already after the first year.[32] And Marx blundered again in some of his calculations also in his next and last example, which Engels presented, with the appropriate corrections, as "2. Second Illustration" (see Marx [1893] 1956, 518–523). Accordingly, Marx *never* arrived at a capital accumulation path along which the two departments are expanding in lock-step.

However, he appears to have considered the accumulation paths depicted in his first and second illustrations as capital expansion paths of *undisturbed accumulation*, and he identified this with *reproduction on an extended scale*.[33] This is confirmed also by Marx's repeated use of the section heading "Accumulation *or* reproduction on an extended scale" ("Die Accumulation *oder* Reproduktion auf erweiterter Stufenleiter"/"Accumulation *od.* Production auf vergrösserter Stufenleiter"; see MEGA II/4.1, 381; MEGA II/11, 790; emphases added). It was Engels who rephrased this as "Accumulation *and* reproduction on an extended scale" and used this as the heading of chapter 21 (Marx [1893] 1956, 493).

---

[32]The editors of the MEGA edition note that if evidence were wanted for showing that in the late 1870s Marx was at times almost incapable of doing serious work, then these documents could be cited (MEGA II/11 App, 878).

[33]Marx in fact did not use the term "undisturbed accumulation". However, in his schematic representation he explicitly referred to the lack of any disturbances in the accumulation process, for instance by introducing his exposition of the accumulation path in his "First Illustration" with the phrase: "If things are to proceed normally [Soll die Sache normal gehn]." ([1893] 1956, 516; MEGA II/11, 812)

4. Marx's six-sector model and his discussion of a specific traverse problem in Ms II

Let us now have a closer look at the parts of Marx's Ms II which Engels decided to omit, in order to find out whether these contain any pertinent material on the transition problem. In the omitted part of Ms II Marx developed a remarkable six-sector model of production (MEGA II/11, 443–522), which he used for studying the conditions of simple reproduction, the monetary reflux, and the transition between two different states of simple reproduction. An excellent description of Marx's six-sector model and a summary account of the research problems Marx sought to address with it can be found in Mori (2009, 2017, 2018) and in the "Introduction (Einführung)" to MEGA II/13.[34]

4.1. Marx's six-sector model

The model exhibits the following structure: The six sectors produce, respectively, (1) means of consumption for workers (sector A3), (2) means of production for A3 and for itself (sector A2), (3) means of production for A2 and for itself (sector A1), (4) means of consumption for capitalists (sector B3), (5) means of production for B3 and for itself (sector B2), (6) means of production for B2 and for itself (sector B1).[35] Multi-sectoral models with a similar structure can be found in Mathur (1965) and Lowe ([1955] 1987, 1976), where the economy is composed of three sectors: heavy equipment, machinery and corn in the former and primary equipment, secondary equipment and consumer goods in the latter. Marx's six-sector model can be seen as a specific variant of these three-sector models, which duplicates the structure of these models by introducing the further analytical division of each of the three sectors into two sub-sectors

---

[34]See MEGA II/13, 540–543 (available online at http://mega.bbaw.de/struktur/abteilung_ii/dateien/mega_II-13_inhalt-einf.pdf).

[35]Note that Marx used in his original manuscript the somewhat awkward notations $II\alpha$, $II\alpha\alpha$, Ia, $II\beta$, $II\beta\beta$, and Ib, which we substitute in this paper – following Mori (2017, 2018) – by A1, A2, A3, B1, B2 and B3, respectively. The same symbols are silently substituted for Marx's notation also in quotations from his manuscripts. Obviously, A3 and B3 make up the sector producing means of consumption (Marx's "department I"), while A1, A2, B1 and B2 together form the sector that produces means of production (Marx's "department II"). In Ms VIII, Marx later reversed the numbering of the two departments (see MEGA II/11 App, 867), and this new numbering was adopted also by Engels in his edition of volume 2 of *Capital*.

Table 1. Marx's six-sector model ($V/S = 1$), Example 1 (See MEGA II/11, 493).

	A1	A2	A3	B1	B2	B3	Workers	Capitalists	Total demand
A1	200	100	0	0	0	0	0	0	300
A2	0	100	200	0	0	0	0	0	300
A3	0	0	0	0	0	0	300	0	300
B1	0	0	0	200	100	0	0	0	300
B2	0	0	0	0	100	200	0	0	300
B3	0	0	0	0	0	0	0	300	300
Wages	50	50	50	50	50	50			300
Surplus value	50	50	50	50	50	50			300
Output	300	300	300	300	300	300	300	300	

producing, directly or indirectly, means of consumption for workers and for capitalists, respectively.[36] As Mori (2009, 2017, 2018) has pointed out, this feature of Marx's six-sector model renders it similar to the four-sector model of Shibata (1939), who divided the economy into four sectors producing, respectively, "workers' consumer goods", "workers' producer goods", "capitalists' consumer goods" and "capitalists' producer goods". A major implication of this feature of Marx's model consists in the fact that the A-sectors are basic and the B-sectors are non-basic, if workers' means of consumption are considered as necessary inputs (Mori 2017).

Marx used the six-sector model in order to derive the conditions of simple reproduction under different assumptions with regard to the rate of surplus value and the organic composition of capital. Based on numerical examples, he carried out some comparative static exercises in order to investigate the properties of his model. He also investigated the monetary reflux, and in particular of the money advanced as wages, on the basis of his six-sector model. The main features of Marx's six-sector model, of the research questions he posed, and of the findings he reached have been discussed by the editors of the MEGA edition (see MEGA II/13 App, 540–543) and, in much greater detail, by Kenji Mori (2009, 2017). In the following, attention will focus on Marx's discussion of a specific traverse problem on the basis of his six-sector model.

---

[36]Marx stressed that this is a purely analytical division and that concrete industries, such as ore mining, would have to be grouped partly in A1 and partly in B1. He also emphasized that the category of "capitalists' means of consumption" comprises not only "luxuries", but also wage goods consumed by servants and capitalists' retainers.

4.2. Marx's discussion of a specific traverse problem in Ms II

As Mori (2017, 12–13) has pointed out, in the part of Ms II that was omitted by Engels Marx also entered briefly into a discussion of a specific traverse problem. The problem he discussed in the passage under consideration (see MEGA II/11, 501–503) concerns the transition from a state of simple reproduction with $V/S = 1$, depicted in Table 1, to a new state of simple reproduction with $V/S = 2$, depicted in Table 2.

The initial state is depicted in Table 1, which can be read in the same manner as a usual input–output table. Each column represents the input components of each sector (in value terms) and each row gives the deliveries of each sector (in value terms). As Marx noted, in an equilibrium of simple reproduction, where the entire surplus value is expended by the capitalists for consumption purposes, the following equations must be satisfied (see also Mori 2017, 10):

$$C_{A3} = (V_{A1} + S_{A1}) + (V_{A2} + S_{A2})$$
$$C_{B3} = (V_{B1} + S_{B1}) + (V_{B2} + S_{B2})$$
$$S_{A1} + S_{A2} + S_{A3} = V_{B1} + V_{B2} + V_{B3}$$

where, C_j, V_j, S_j are respectively constant capital, variable capital and surplus value of sector j ($j = A1, A2, A3, B1, B2, B3$).

Marx first considered the two tables from a comparative static point of view, and noted that in the simple reproduction scheme corresponding to $V/S = 2$ (Table 2) the total social production and the total social capital have remained unaltered, as compared to Table 1.[37] The constant capital also has not changed (in terms of its total amount of value), whereas the variable capital has been increased by 1/3 or $33\frac{1}{3}\%$.[38] In the next paragraph, however, Marx then switched

---

[37]Marx further concluded from this exercise in comparative statics that different relative income distributions (or rates of surplus value) are compatible with the same value of total social production and total social capital: "Here lively view of the fixity of the so-called wage fund. With the same value of the annual social product the wage fund can be 300, 400, 350, 250, etc. It can fall much below the *value of labour power* right up to the absolute minimum, and it can rise above it in innumerable variations. And that it is a *fixed* magnitude is a basic dogma of Political Economy!" (MEGA II/11, 503)

[38]Marx pointed out that the increase of the labour share (and the corresponding decrease of the profit share) implies "not *only a changed distribution of the existing consumption fund or of that part of the annual product of society which enters into their* [i.e. the workers'] *consumption fund.*" This is what is commonly supposed. But it is in fact a changed distribution in the forms of the consumption fund, in the use-forms of which it consists, and a changed allocation of labour power in the different production spheres, and finally also a changed allocation of the constant capital. (MEGA II/11, 501)

Table 2. Marx's six-sector model ($V/S = 2$), Example 2 (See MEGA II/11, 494).

	A1	A2	A3	B1	B2	B3	Workers	Capitalists	Total demand
A1	$266\frac{2}{3}$	$133\frac{1}{3}$	0	0	0	0	0	0	400
A2	0	$133\frac{1}{3}$	$266\frac{2}{3}$	0	0	0	0	0	400
A3	0	0	0	0	0	0	400	0	400
B1	0	0	0	$133\frac{1}{3}$	$66\frac{2}{3}$	0	0	0	200
B2	0	0	0	0	$66\frac{2}{3}$	$133\frac{1}{3}$	0	0	200
B3	0	0	0	0	0	0	0	200	200
Wages	$88\frac{8}{9}$	$88\frac{8}{9}$	$88\frac{8}{9}$	$44\frac{4}{9}$	$44\frac{4}{9}$	$44\frac{4}{9}$			400
Surplus value	$44\frac{4}{9}$	$44\frac{4}{9}$	$44\frac{4}{9}$	$22\frac{2}{9}$	$22\frac{2}{9}$	$22\frac{2}{9}$			200
Output	400	400	400	200	200	200	400	200	

to a different set of assumptions, and thus to a different traverse problem:

> If the same result [i.e. an increase of the variable capital by $1/3$ or $33\frac{1}{3}$ %] were to be brought about through *accumulation of capital*, then with a constant proportion of $V : S$:
>
> Originally the capital produced $= 1500$ £$= C^{1200} + V^{300}$ ——- 300 S.
>
> If V increases from 300 to 400, so also S; and we have:
>
> $300 : 1500 = 400 : x$. $x = \frac{1500 \times 400}{300} = \frac{1500 \times 4}{3} = 500 \times 4 = 2000$.
>
> The capital now would be: $C^{1600} + V^{400} + S^{400}$. Or, the capital increased from 1500 to 2000, that is, by $1/3$ or $33\frac{1}{3}$ %. (MEGA II/11, 501)

Obviously, Marx here poses a different research problem: He now asks how the same increase in the social variable capital (from 300 to 400) could be brought about by accumulation of capital, *supposing the proportion of V:S to remain constant*. The problem then becomes one of studying a transition path from the state of simple reproduction depicted in Table 1 to the one depicted in Table 3. Marx's next remark clearly refers to *this* set of assumptions:

> The growth of capital by $1/3$ is enormous and requires time, quite apart from the fact that it would go along with circumstances and movements which make it very doubtful whether the labour power, represented by V^{400}, is not worse off than the labour power previously, represented by V^{300}. (MEGA II/11, 501)

In the next paragraph, however, Marx then switched back to his previous assumption of an increase in *V/S*, that is, an increase in the labour share (at the expense of the profit share), and noted:

> The mechanism of bourgeois society brings it with it that such changes, like for instance those depicted in [Table 1] and [Table 2] ..., go along with circumstances which paralyze their effects and indeed break those very changes. (MEGA II/11, 501)

What are those "paralysing circumstances" Marx speaks of? And why should the workers be worse off when income distribution is

Table 3. Marx's six-sector model ($V/S = 1$); total capital increased by 1/3.

	A1	A2	A3	B1	B2	B3	Workers	Capitalists	Total demand
A1	$266\frac{2}{3}$	$133\frac{1}{3}$	0	0	0	0	0	0	400
A2	0	$133\frac{1}{3}$	$266\frac{2}{3}$	0	0	0	0	0	400
A3	0	0	0	0	0	0	400	0	400
B1	0	0	0	$266\frac{2}{3}$	$133\frac{1}{3}$	0	0	0	400
B2	0	0	0	0	$133\frac{1}{3}$	$266\frac{2}{3}$	0	0	400
B3	0	0	0	0	0	0	0	400	400
Wages	$66\frac{2}{3}$	$66\frac{2}{3}$	$66\frac{2}{3}$	$66\frac{2}{3}$	$66\frac{2}{3}$	$66\frac{2}{3}$			400
Surplus value	$66\frac{2}{3}$	$66\frac{2}{3}$	$66\frac{2}{3}$	$66\frac{2}{3}$	$66\frac{2}{3}$	$66\frac{2}{3}$			400
Output	400	400	400	400	400	400	400	400	

changed in their favour, that is, in favour of higher wages? Marx's explanation refers to structural imbalances that are bound to arise during the transition from the situation depicted in Table 1 to the one depicted in Table 2:

> If we compare [Tables 1 and 2], this presupposes a *simultaneous* wage increase by 1/3 *in all* lines of production. A large part of the products of [A3] ... consists of foodstuff, which must have been produced (at least in their raw materials) one year earlier. The demand for them would increase considerably. The profits made in [A3] etc. would so far rise as well. In short: capital and labour-power would be drawn from [B3] etc. towards [A3] etc. This change [is] associated with disturbing incidences in [B3] etc. Firstly, a diminished demand for a large part of this production ..., because S is reduced and in the new circumstances there is over-production in [B3] etc. This fall would affect the workers employed in [B3] etc. Their wage would *fall, instead of rise*, insofar as their transfer to [A3] etc. occurs not as quickly as their displacement in [B3] etc. (and this transfer is made more difficult through their subsumption, due to the division of labour, in a specific line of operation). On the other hand, the fall of their wage would check the growing demand for [A3] etc. There is

thus revulsion that would paralyse the change, at least partly. (MEGA II/
11, 501–502)

There is a further element which, according to Marx, tends to
reinforce the "paralysing" effects. The change to a higher labour share
in the social product, he argues, is counteracted also by the adjustment processes which become necessary in the B-industries, through
the fall of the profit share:

> The product of [B3] consists partly of necessary foodstuff etc., which is
> consumed by the retainers of the capitalists, by servants etc., in short: by
> unproductive labourers. A part of them is dismissed with the fall of S by 1/
> 3, … and thrown on the labour market, that is, the labour market for
> [A3] etc. … If one considers that on the one hand the capitalist class can
> for some time just watch the scene, and on the other hand that the
> displacement of productive labourers in [B3] etc. and of unproductive
> labourers that participate in the consumption of the product of [B3] would
> generate a reaction against the process itself, one realizes the difficulty and
> relative impossibility of the change in this way. …

> Not been mentioned yet has been the reaction which a wage increase will
> induce for the application of machinery, that is, for means of further
> labour displacement. (MEGA II/11, 502)

The transition from a lower to a higher labour share would thus
make some members of the workforce worse off, at least temporarily,
and could be curtailed altogether because of the counter-acting effects
which are triggered by it:

> It is these *hindrances* that are *immanent* in the mechanism of capitalistic
> production against all *rapid and general change* of this kind – and if the
> change is only gradual and partial, *the hindrances* which capitalistic
> production instinctively generates against such change *merely accumulate*
> –, which the bourgeois economists regard as so many proofs that the thing
> is generally impossible. (MEGA II/11, 503)

Marx's brief sketch of the problems that are associated with the
transition from a lower to a higher wage share ends here. The
"hindrances" and "paralysing effects" stressed by Marx are clearly
related to his distinction between the industries that produce, directly
and indirectly, workers' means of consumption and those that produce capitalists' means of consumption. These kinds of problems
could not possibly be studied in the three-sectoral models of Lowe
and Mathur, where this distinction is absent. Marx's six-sector model
thus adds an interesting element to their analyses of traverse

processes. On the other hand, the structural adjustment problems stressed by Lowe and Mathur, which concern bottleneck problems in the expansion of primary equipment, are completely ignored by Marx, who made no attempt to address the problem of a traverse from a low (or zero) rate of growth to a higher one. His discussion of the specific traverse problem in Ms II, though interesting in its own right, therefore does not contribute to a better understanding of Marx's ideas on the problem of the transition from simple to extended reproduction.

Before we proceed, it should be noted that Marx critically re-examined the results of the foregoing analysis, as well as of his comparative static exercises, casting serious doubt on their relevance:

> It must be asked whether the results obtained so far are not based on purely abstract and unreal assumptions. It is clear that such an abstract separation between [A3] etc – *production of means of consumption for workers* – and [B3] etc – *production of means of consumption for capitalists* – does not really exist. (MEGA II/11, 503)

The purely analytical division between workers' and capitalists' means of consumption cannot be associated unequivocally with the distinction between "necessaries" and "luxuries":

> The necessary means of subsistence of course make up the most important part of the means of consumption of the labourers. But these also enter to a considerable degree into the consumption of the capitalists. Large part of the foodstuff identical for both. Similarly heating materials. With all the other things, housing, clothing, furniture etc, though of the same genus, nevertheless products of a different kind. On the other hand, many luxury articles also enter into the workers' consumption. (MEGA II/11, 503–504)

Accordingly, shifting means of consumption between the capitalists' and the workers' consumption fund may pose less severe problems than seems to be implied by treating them as products of a strictly different kind. This also holds true, Marx suggested, for the means of production which are used, directly and indirectly, in producing those consumption goods:

> Large part of the constant capital the same, raw materials, machinery, working tools, buildings etc. Where the machine tools are different, buildings, structures and transmission machinery are the same. This shows indeed that the transfer of the constant capital from [A3] to [B3] and *vice versa* is associated with *less difficulties than the transfer of the one-sided labourers (one-sided due to the division of labour).* (MEGA II/11, 504)

In Marx's view, then, means of production are often less specific, and thus more easily transferable between industries, than special-ised workers. Like Lowe and Mathur, Marx thus motivated the idea of the inter-sectoral transferability of constant capital by pointing out that part of the tools, machinery and raw materials that are used in the different sectors are identical. However, it must be stressed that Marx's argument refers to inter-sectoral transferability between the sectors A1 and B1 (and between A2 and B2, or between A3 and B3), whereas Lowe refers to transferability of pri-mary equipment that is used in the production of secondary equip-ment towards producing additional primary equipment, that is, between sectors A2 and A1. In the two department model, it is the latter, rather than the former, which corresponds to transferability between the two departments.

In this part of his manuscript, Marx thus discussed a specific tra-verse problem, but his concern was not with accumulation and extended reproduction but rather with the transition between two states of simple reproduction characterised by different income distributions.

5. Some elements for the analysis of the transition from simple to extended reproduction: Marx's discussion of "elasticity of reproduction" in Ms I

Marx's first draft for volume 2 of *Capital*, Ms I of 1865, contains a discussion of some elements that are relevant for the analysis of the problem of the transition from simple to extended reproduction. This material (MEGA II/4.1, 348–53) was however not used by Engels, in spite of the fact that Marx, at the end of Ms I, had sketched out an outline, according to which the section "The accumulation or repro-duction on an extended scale" was meant to be preceded by a section entitled "The elasticity of reproduction [Die Elasticität der Reproduction]" (MEGA II/4.1, 381). According to the editors of the MEGA (MEGA II/13 App, 543–544) the material discussed below, which in Marx's manuscript has no separate heading, was a first draft of this projected section and it therefore properly belongs (and by implication should have been inserted by Engels) at the beginning of section 3 ("Schematic presentation of accumulation") in chapter 21 of volume 2 of *Capital*.[39]

In the passages under consideration (MEGA II/4.1, 348–353), Marx stressed the elasticity of industrial production that emerges from the possibility of varying the work intensity and the length of the working-day as well as the degree of capacity utilisation of fixed capital items. He in particular pointed out that this elasticity provides a basis for the enlargement of the existing stock of fixed capital, i.e., for *making additions* to the stock of fixed capital *without additional capital* having first to be built up:

> If one considers the predominant and important role which fixed capital (in the form of machinery, ships, etc.) plays in the extractive industries (mining industry, coal industry, fishing, logging, etc.), that is, precisely in those spheres of production that supply the main raw materials (metals, wood) and auxiliary materials (coal, etc.) for the production of *additional* fixed capital, especially also of machinery, it becomes self-evident how much the already achieved level of its development facilitates and supports the production of *additional* fixed capital, i.e. of this part of *accumulation* and reproduction on an extended scale. Quite apart from the fact already mentioned above that the already *existing* fixed capital, in the form of buildings, machinery and means of transport and communication, is capable of functioning as an element in a self-enlarging production process. (MEGA II/4.1, 349)

Marx   further   noted   that   apart   from   the   *elasticity* (*Dehnungsfähigkeit*) of fixed capital, which arises from the possibility of varying its degree of capacity utilisation, it must also be taken into consideration that with the advancement of science and its application the part of the fixed capital stock that needs to be periodically replaced is generally reproduced "in *more productive forms*, so that its simple *reproduction* is associated with a permanent expansion of its productive powers, ... or rather of the productive powers of the labour which it assists". And he emphasised that it is precisely "this *development of the productive power* that is one of the decisive elements for accumulation and reproduction on an extended scale"

---

[39]Some, but by no means all elements of Marx's discussion of "Elasticity of reproduction" in Ms I were in fact later taken up again by him in Ms II, in the section "Money capital considered as part of the aggregate social capital. [Das Geldkapital als Bestandteil des gesellschaftlichen Gesammtkapitals betrachtet.]" (MEGA II/11, 343–347). However, because Engels incorporated these manuscript passages as section "II. The Role of Money-Capital" ([1893] 1956, 358–362) into Chapter 18, "Introduction", of volume 2 its connection to the problem of the transition from simple to extended reproduction was not immediately obvious.

(MEGA II/4.1, 349). The problem of initiating or changing the pace of capital accumulation Marx thus considered to be greatly facilitated by the presence of continuous technical progress. But Marx also stressed that even *without* technical progress, that is, in a *given* state of technical knowledge, "science" typically introduces an additional element of elasticity or flexibility:

> As another *variable* element of production *science* must be mentioned – not only in the sense that it constantly evolves, corrects itself, enlarges itself, etc. This process or this development of science can itself be regarded as a moment of the accumulation process. But the existing amount of technical science at no point in time is distributed equally to all spheres of production, and not *applied* equally to all individual capital advances in every sphere of production. Independently of the process of accumulation and the expansion of the reproduction process the existing fixed capital which must be annually replaced is reproduced, renewed, in *more productive* forms – as is shown e.g. by the merely gradual introduction of improvements … . And of all this there is always a *More or Less*, are the limits quantitatively very elastic. (MEGA II/4.1, 350–351)

After having suggested that also the circulation of commodities entails some further variability for the reproduction process, through the quickening or slowing down of circulation times, Marx then summarised the implications of his deliberations in the following terms:

> For the present purpose, it here suffices to stress that the mechanism of reproduction involves *variability* in the amount of the annual production as one of its principles.[40] This follows from the simple circumstance,
>
> 1. that the time of circulation forms a limit to that part of the capital actually involved in the process of immediate production or reproduction, and that
> 2. that limit itself is not a constant but a variable magnitude, of a given elasticity, so that the limit may constrain in greater or lesser degree.
>
> The *fixed capital*, although its value is a given quantity, is a *variable* quantity, as far as the degree of its actual employment is concerned … ;
>
> the *laboring power*, apart from its constant increase, and although considered as a given and therefore constant quantity, whose value is circumscribed by the value of the variable capital advanced, is a *variable* quantity as to the degree of its actual conservation within a year;

---

[40]My translation ends here; the rest of the text is in English in the original manuscript.

The *technological appliance of science*, apart from its incessant expansion, and only considering its actual degree of development, and so considering it as a given and constant quantity, may in varying degrees be more or less universally applied, within varying limits; and the same holds true with all the *productive powers* of labor, under which the same amount of capital and labor may reproduce commodities; ...

From all these we come to the conclusion, that apart from accumulation, ..., the amount of reproduction, yielded yearly by a given amount of preexisting capital and laboring power, is a variable, and not a constant quantity, and may enlarge or contract. This elasticity or variability forms at the same time a natural basis for accumulation, since there are bases given which will allow of an expansion of reproduction without all the elements of that reproduction being afforded by additional capital and laboring power put in motion. (MEGA II/4.1, 352–353)

Clearly, then, the upshot of Marx's argument set out in these passages is that there exists a high degree of *"elasticity"* (*Dehnungsfähigkeit*) in the industrial production system, and that the constraints imposed on the accumulation process by the currently existing stocks of productive capital and labour power are much less binding than a schematic analysis that operates with given endowments, a given technology, given production coefficients, etc. would make it appear. These ideas have only recently to some extent been incorporated into modern classical theories of growth and technical change in terms of linear production models of the Leontief–Sraffa type which allow for variability in the degree of capacity utilisation.[41]

6. Conclusion

Marx's schemes of simple and extended reproduction represent a considerable advance on the expositions of the reproduction process of the total social capital provided by the French Physiocrats and the English classical political economists. However, while Marx had fully worked out the requirements for simple reproduction, in both physical terms, that is, with reference to use-values, and in value terms, that is, with reference to labour values, already at the beginning of the 1870s, and by then had also studied carefully the monetary reflux in conditions of simple reproduction, he had struggled with the analysis of "accumulation or reproduction on an extended scale" until 1881,

---

[41]See, for instance, Kurz (1986).

but without being able to solve this problem to his own satisfaction. His treatment of the latter problem therefore was in a much more preliminary and incomplete state than that of the former, and its presentation in volume 2 of *Capital* accordingly posed formidable editorial problems for Engels.

With regard to Part 3 of volume 2 of *Capital* Engels' presentation of Marx's unfinished manuscript material appears to have given rise to interpretations that could not possibly have emerged from the original manuscripts. In particular, the reading of the schemes of extended reproduction as a depiction of a *steady-state* growth path could emerge only from Engels' correction of Marx's erroneous calculations of a numerical example in Ms VIII, and could not have been inferred from Marx's own exposition. Marx therefore also could not possibly have associated his extended reproduction schemes with a capital expansion path that converges to a balanced or *steady-state* growth path, after a single period of unbalanced growth. In his understanding it is rather the entire expansion path, including also the first period, which is characterised by "undisturbed accumulation", or "reproduction on an extended scale". Accordingly, a transition from simple to extended reproduction involved, for him, not a traverse from a *stationary equilibrium* to a *steady-state growth path*, but rather a transition from a state of simple reproduction to an accumulation path with undisturbed reproduction of the social capital. In his understanding, this transition could not but be associated with disturbances in the reproduction process, that is, with structural imbalances and (partial) overproduction. The discussion of such disequilibria, however, was not the object of inquiry of the chapter on "Accumulation or reproduction on an extended scale".

Marx had in fact tackled a transition problem in a part of Ms II that Engels chose to omit. However, this discussion concerned the transition from a state of *simple* reproduction, with a given income distribution, to another one with an increased wage share (and a correspondingly reduced profit share), also in *simple* reproduction. As Marx pointed out, this transition also is bound up with the occurrence of structural imbalances. Finally, Marx's discussion of the "elasticity of reproduction" in Ms I, omitted by Engels, shows that from early on he had contemplated a solution to the problems associated with initiating an accumulation process from a state of simple reproduction which relies on variability in the degree of capacity utilisation and other elements related to the elasticity of the production system, rather than on non-specific and thus inter-sectorally transferable capital goods.

Acknowledgements

I would like to thank the participants of the conference "Karl Heinrich Marx 1818–1883" for many useful comments and suggestions. I benefitted in particular from discussions with Kenji Mori and Regina Roth, and also from the comments of two anonymous referees of this journal. The usual caveat applies.

Disclosure statement

No potential conflict of interest was reported by the authors.

References

Ananyin, Oleg. 2014. "'Quorum Pars Magna Fui': On the Cantillon-Marx Connection." *The European Journal of the History of Economic Thought* 21: 950–976.

Burchardt, Fritz. 1931–1932. "Die Schemata des stationären Kreislaufs bei Böhm-Bawerk und Marx." *Weltwirtschaftliches Archiv* 34: 525–564 and 35: 116–176.

Desai, Meghnad. 1979. *Marxian Economics*. Totowa, NJ: Rowman & Littlefield.

Fel'dman, Grigory A. [1928] 1964. "*On the Theory of Growth Rates of National Income.*" In *Foundations of Soviet Strategy for Economic Growth*, edited by N. Spulber, 174–199 and 304–331. Bloomington: Indiana University Press.

Gehrke, Christian, and Heinz D. Kurz. 1995. "Karl Marx on Physiocracy." *The European Journal of the History of Economic Thought* 2 (1): 53–90.

Hicks, John. 1965. *Capital and Growth*. Oxford: Clarendon Press.

Hollander, Samuel. 2008. *The Economics of Karl Marx: Analysis and Application.* Cambridge: Cambridge University Press.

Howard, Michael C., and John E. King. 1985. *The Political Economy of Marx.* New York: New York University Press.

Kurz, Heinz D. 1986. "Normal Positions and Capital Utilization." *Political Economy. Studies in the Surplus Approach* 2: 37–54.

Lowe, Adolph. [1955] 1987. "*Structural Analysis of Real Capital Formation.*" In *Essays in Political Economics: Public Control in a Democratic Society: Adolph Lowe*, edited by Allen Oakley, 60–107. Sussex, England: Wheatsheaf Books. (Originally published in *Capital Formation and Economic Growth*, edited by Moses Abramovitz, 579–632. Princeton, NJ: Princeton University Press.)

Lowe, Adolph. 1976. *The Path of Economic Growth*. Cambridge: Cambridge University Press.

Mahalanobis, Prasanta Chandra. 1953. "Some Observations on the Process of Growth of National Income." *Sankhya* 12 (4): 307–312.

Marx, Karl. [1893] 1956. *Capital. A Critique of Political Economy. Book Two, The Process of Circulation of Capital*, edited by Frederick Engels. London: Lawrence & Wishart.

Mathur, Gautam. 1965. *Planning for Steady Growth*. Oxford: Oxford University Press.

Mori, Kenji. 2009. *Six-Sector Model of Production and Monetary Circuit: Making Sense of Marx's Original Reproduction Schemata*. Tohoku, Japan: Mimeo, Tohoku University.

Mori, Kenji. 2017. "A Non-Basic system in Marx's original Six-Sector Model." Paper presented at the Annual ESHET Conference in Antwerp, Belgium, May 17–20, 2017.

Mori, Kenji. 2018. "New Aspects of Marx's Economic Theory in the MEGA: Marx's Original Six-Sector Model." *The European Journal of the History of Economic Thought, this issue*.

Morishima, Michio. 1973. *Marx's Economics. A Dual Theory of Value and Growth*. Cambridge: Cambridge University Press.

Robinson, Joan. 1942. *An Essay on Marxian Economics*. London: Macmillan.

Robinson, Joan. 1951. "Introduction." In *Rosa Luxemburg: The Accumulation of Capital*, edited by Joan Robinson, 13–28. New York, NY: Modern Reader Paperbacks.

Samuelson, Paul A. 1974. "*Marx as a Mathematical Economist: Steady-State and Exponential Growth Equilibrium.*" In *Trade, Stability, and Macroeconomics: Essays in Honor of Lloyd A. Metzler*, edited by George Horwich and Paul A. Samuelson, 269–307. New York, NY: Academic Press.

Samuelson, Paul A. 1982. "*Quesnay's 'Tableau Economique' as a Theorist Would Formulate it Today.*" In *Classical and Marxian Political Economy. Essays in Honour of Ronald H. Meek*, edited by Ian Bradley and Michael Howard, 45–78. London and Basingstoke: Macmillan.

Shibata, Kei. 1939. "On the General Profit Rate." *Kyoto University Economic Review* 14 (1): 40–66.

Sweezy, Paul M. 1942. *The Theory of Capitalist Development. Principles of Marxian Political Economy*. New York, NY: Monthly Review Press.

Tsuru, Shigeto. 1942. "*On Reproduction Schemes.*" In *The Theory of Capitalist Development. Principles of Marxian Political Economy*, edited by Paul M. Sweezy. New York, NY: Monthly Review Press.

Turban, Manfred. 1980. *Marx'sche Reproduktionsschemata und Wirtschaftstheorie. Die Diskussion ihres analytischen Gehalts in verschiedenen wirtschaftswissenschaftlichen Forschungstraditionen*. Berlin: Duncker & Humblot.

Collected Works of Marx and Engels (MEGA)

Marx-Engels-Gesamtausgabe. 1988. *II. Abteilung, Band 4.1 (Text). Karl Marx. Ökonomische Manuskripte 1863–1867, Teil 1*. Berlin: Akademie Verlag. (cited as MEGA II/4.1)

Marx-Engels-Gesamtausgabe. 2005a. *II. Abteilung, Band 12 (Text). Karl Marx. Das Kapital. Kritik der Politischen Ökonomie. Zweites Buch. Der*

Zirkulationsprozess des Kapitals. Redaktionsmanuskript von Friedrich Engels. Berlin: Akademie Verlag. (cited as MEGA II/12)

Marx-Engels-Gesamtausgabe. 2005b. *II. Abteilung, Band 12 (Apparat). Karl Marx. Das Kapital. Kritik der Politischen Ökonomie. Zweites Buch. Der Zirkulationsprozess des Kapitals. Redaktionsmanuskript von Friedrich Engels.* Berlin: Akademie Verlag. (cited as MEGA II/12 App)

Marx-Engels-Gesamtausgabe. 2008a. *II. Abteilung, Band 11 (Text). Karl Marx. Manuskripte zum zweiten Buch des „Kapitals" 1868 bis 1881.* Berlin: Akademie Verlag. (cited as MEGA II/11)

Marx-Engels-Gesamtausgabe. 2008b. *II. Abteilung, Band 11 (Apparat). Karl Marx. Manuskripte zum zweiten Buch des „Kapitals" 1868 bis 1881.* Berlin: Akademie Verlag. (cited as MEGA II/11 App).

Marx-Engels-Gesamtausgabe. 2008c. *II. Abteilung, Band 13 (Text). Karl Marx. Das Kapital. Kritik der Politischen Ökonomie, Zweiter Band, Hamburg 1885.* Berlin: Akademie Verlag. (cited as MEGA II/13)

Marx-Engels-Gesamtausgabe. 2008d. *II. Abteilung, Band 13 (Apparat). Karl Marx. Das Kapital. Kritik der Politischen Ökonomie, Zweiter Band, Hamburg 1885.* Berlin: Akademie Verlag. (cited as MEGA II/13 App)

Marx-Engels-Gesamtausgabe. 2012. *II. Abteilung, Band 4.3 (Text). Karl Marx. Ökonomische Manuskripte 1863–1868. Teil 3. Manuskripte 1867/68 zum 2. und 3. Buch des „Kapital".* Berlin: Akademie Verlag. (cited as MEGA II/4.3)

New aspects of Marx's economic theory in MEGA: Marx's original six-sector model

Kenji Mori

ABSTRACT
Marx's Reproduction Scheme is widely known as one of the first two-sector economic models in the history of economic theories. However, a close investigation into Marx's original shows that his multi-sectoral analysis contains not (only) two-sector models but six-sector ones, which were totally omitted by Engels in his editing the manuscripts for *Capital*, Volume II. Taking up two interesting theoretical episodes in the ignored six-sector analysis, this paper attempts to make sense of Marx's treatment on the price of production and the dynamic process of traverse between two equilibria.

1. Introduction

It is known that Marx wrote in total eight manuscripts dedicated to Volume II of *Capital*, of which only two manuscripts (Ms. II and Ms. VIII) were used by Engels for the edition of Part 3 of this volume, i.e. the chapters on the so-called "reproduction schemata" (Marx 2005, 529–552, 887–934, 2008a, 8). Although Ms. VIII (written in 1880–1881) was fully utilised, the half of the relevant part of Ms. II (1868–1870), making up 36 manuscript pages, was totally ignored by Engels[1] and was published after 140 years for the first time in MEGA II/11.

In the omitted part of Ms. II, Marx presented a six-sector model of production: (1) means of workers' consumption (sector A3),[2] (2) means of production for A3 (sector A2), (3) means of production for A2 (sector A1), (4) means of capitalists' consumption (sector B3), (5) means of production for B3 (sector B2) and (6) means of production for B2

---

[1] In Ms. II, the text related to Part 3 of Volume II of the edited *Capital* begins on manuscript page 130 (Marx 2008b, 340) and ends on manuscript page 202 (Marx 2008b, 522). The pages 167–202 (Marx 2008b, 443–522) were omitted by Engels.

[2] Note that Marx used in his original somewhat awkward notations $II\alpha$, $II\alpha\alpha$, Ia, $II\beta$, $II\beta\beta$ and Ib, which we substitute in this paper with A1, A2, A3, B1, B2 and B3 respectively.

(sector B1). And simple reproduction was assumed. By means of this multi-sectoral model, he investigated, above all, the following two main issues.[3]

First, Marx tried to find out equilibrium conditions for the quantity system of the six-sector model. Indeed, he succeeded in formulating necessary conditions for the quantity equilibrium in three equations. Furthermore, he carried out some comparative statics in order to examine the shift of equilibrium output, employment etc. by varying a parameter of capital share, i.e. the "rate of surplus value (M/V)".

Marx's investigation of the second issue leads the readers, because of its intensity and persistence, to suppose a large amount of his effort dedicated to it. He illustrated the "law" of monetary reflux using numerical examples in the six-sector model, i.e. he traced each possible route of monetary circuit in which money advanced by capitalists returns to its starting point after realising various components of output of the six-sector economy. Particularly, he concentrated his attention on the reflux of wage paid by capitalists to workers in each sector.

This paper aims mainly to present new results of analytical research in Sections 3 and 4, after characterising Marx's original model in Section 2 based on the earlier version published in Mori (2009, 2018). In particular, Section 2 summarises Marx's treatment of equilibrium conditions and comparative statics as well as inter-sectoral monetary circuit in the six-sector production model. Subsequently, we examine a complementary research question posed by Marx on the price calculation in Section 3 and on the transition process between equilibria in Section 4. Section 5 concludes the paper.

2. Marx's six-sector production model

2.1. Equilibrium conditions

The subject of Part 3 of Volume II of *Capital*, well known as "reproduction schemata", was dealt with in Ms. II as the third "chapter" after the two chapters on "circuit of capital" and "turnover of capital." According to Marx's own table of contents written on the title page of Ms. II, this third chapter was structured as follows (Marx 2008b, 3–4):

---

[3] The first and second issues were presented in Marx's original, respectively, in MEGAII/11 (Marx 2008b, 481–503) and MEGAII/11 (Marx 2008b, 443–481). For the sake of convenience, we changed the original order here.

The real conditions of the processes of circulation and reproduction:

1) Variable capital, constant capital and surplus value from a social point of view
   A) Reproduction on a simple scale
      a) Described without the mediating monetary circulation
      b) Description with the mediating monetary circulation
   B) Reproduction on an extended scale. Accumulation.
      a) Described without monetary circulation
      b) Description with the mediating monetary circulation
2) (no title)

After the description of A) a) and b) based on two-sector reproduction schemata, Marx changed, in a continuation of A) b), to six-sector schemata. This part of Ms. II was neglected by Engels for the edition of *Capital*, Volume II. The section B) a) and the following were never written in Ms. II and to be left to the later Ms. VIII.

As mentioned above, the first issue to investigate in the omitted part of Ms. II consists in the deduction of equilibrium conditions for quantity system of the six-sector production model. This model has following properties:

- The economy consists of six production sectors (A1, A2, A3, B1, B2, B3),[4] household (individual consumption) of workers and that of capitalists. Each sector produces one distinct good (i.e. single production), which is given the same notation as the sector.
- Workers and capitalists consume, respectively, A3 and B3 exclusively.
- Means of production of A3 is A2; that of A2 is both A2 itself and A1; and that of A1 is A1 itself. Similarly, means of production of B3 is B2; that of B2 is both B2 itself and B1; and that of B1 is B1 itself.
- The output value of each sector consists of value of means of production and value added, and value added consists of wage and surplus value.
- The income of workers and capitalists come, respectively, from wage and surplus value exclusively. Both classes do not save.
- Prices are proportional to labour values.

Historically, we can find a similar structure also in multi-sectoral models by Mathur and Lowe, where the economy is composed of three sectors;

---

[4] See Footnote 2.

Table 1. Marx's six-sector model (Example 1).

	A1	A2	A3	B1	B2	B3	Workers	Capitalists	Total demand
A1	200	100	0	0	0	0	0	0	300
A2	0	100	200	0	0	0	0	0	300
A3	0	0	0	0	0	0	300	0	300
B1	0	0	0	200	100	0	0	0	300
B2	0	0	0	0	100	200	0	0	300
B3	0	0	0	0	0	0	0	300	300
Wage	50	50	50	50	50	50			300
Surplus value	50	50	50	50	50	50			300
Output	300	300	300	300	300	300	300	300	

heavy equipment, machinery and corn in Mathur (1965), while primary equipment, secondary equipment and consumer good in Lowe (1976). The most characteristic feature of Marx's model, however, consists in a symmetrical structure between A-sectors and B-sectors, which we can regard respectively as basic and non-basic sectors (in view of augmented input coefficients: see Section 3). More relevant in this respect is Shibata (1939) who divided the economy into four sectors according to "workers' consumers' goods" and "workers' producers' goods" on the one hand, and "capitalists' consumers' goods" and "capitalists' producers' goods" on the other.[5]

For the six-sector model characterised above, Marx devised the following numerical example (Example 1: see Table 1).

One can "read" the table in the same manner as a usual input–output table. Each column from A1 to B3 represents price components of each sector's output; the column of A3, for example, shows that the good A3 of value of 300 is produced by using A2 of 200 and paying wage of 50 and surplus value of 50. Each row from A1 to B3 represents the demand for each good; the row of A2, e.g. shows that the good A2 of value 100 and 200 is sold respectively to the sector producing A2 and A3. The table represents an equilibrium in the sense that for each good the output equals to the real demand. Furthermore, it stands for an equilibrium state of simple reproduction because surplus value is individually consumed by capitalists.

Based on the above example, Marx traced every commodity transaction among production sectors, workers' and capitalists' household to induce general conditions necessary for an equilibrium of supply and demand. He formulated them in the following three formulae[6,7,8]:

---

[5] On the similarity between Marx's and Shibata's construction, see Mori (2007).

[6] Marx (2008b, 483, 493, 495).

[7] Marx (2008b, 483, 488, 490, 494).

[8] Marx (2008b, 488–491, 493, 495).

$$C_{A3} = (V_{A1} + M_{A1}) + (V_{A2} + M_{A2}) \qquad (1)$$
$$C_{B3} = (V_{B1} + M_{B1}) + (V_{B2} + M_{B2}) \qquad (2)$$
$$M_{A1} + M_{A2} + M_{A3} = V_{B1} + V_{B2} + V_{B3} \qquad (3)$$

where C_j, V_j and M_j stand for, respectively, constant capital, variable capital and surplus value of sector j (j = A1, A2, A3, B1, B2, B3). First, constant capital of sector A3 equals the sum of wage and surplus value of both sectors A1 and A2. Second, constant capital of sector B3 equals the sum of wage and surplus value of both sectors B1 and B2. Third, the surplus value of sectors A1, A2 and A3 (we call them together "A-sectors") equals the variable capital of sectors B1, B2 and B3 ("B-sectors"). In both Equations (1) and (2), one can see the well-known condition in the Marxian two-sector model reappear, i.e. that constant capital of consumption-good sector equals the sum of wage and surplus value of means-of-production sector. Furthermore, the third condition anticipates that relationship between subsectors of means of subsistence and luxury which was to be considered in the later Ms. VIII.

2.2. Rate of surplus value and comparative statics

After formulating the equilibrium conditions, Marx carried out some comparative statics in order to examine the shift of equilibrium output, employment, etc. by varying the rate of surplus value (M/V). While the rate of surplus value is unity in all sectors in Example 1, it varies to 1/2 in Example 2[9] (Table 2), 5/7 in Example 3[10] (Table 3) and 7/5 in Example 4[11] (Table 4), where physical input coefficients and the total number of employed workers remain constant.

The conclusion Marx drew from these calculations is that the output, employment and means of production in A-sectors must increase as the rate of surplus value decreases. Theoretical implications of these comparative statics, however, cannot be seen far-reaching because, first, the calculations are nothing more than arithmetic exercises for adapting the equilibrium conditions, and their results are almost self-evident. Second, an assumption of his comparative statics, i.e. that all sectors have a common capital share can sustain its meaning only in case of prices proportional to labour values (i.e. in case of a uniform capital composition across sectors).

Much more interesting about Marx's comparative statics, however, is the fact that he raised some complementary research questions which are

---

[9] Marx (2008b, 481–484, 494).
[10] Marx (2008b, 484-488, 494).
[11] Marx (2008b, 492–494).

Table 2. Marx's six-sector model (Example 2) ($M/V = 1/2$).

	A1	A2	A3	B1	B2	B3	Workers	Capitalists	Total demand
A1	266 $^2/_3$	133 $^1/_3$	0	0	0	0	0	0	400
A2	0	133 $^1/_3$	266 $^2/_3$	0	0	0	0	0	400
A3	0	0	0	0	0	0	400	0	400
B1	0	0	0	133 $^1/_3$	66 $^2/_3$	0	0	0	200
B2	0	0	0	0	66 $^2/_3$	133 $^1/_3$	0	0	200
B3	0	0	0	0	0	0	0	200	200
Wage	88 $^8/_9$	88 $^8/_9$	88 $^8/_9$	44 $^4/_9$	44 $^4/_9$	44 $^4/_9$	0	0	400
Surplus value	44 $^4/_9$	44 $^4/_9$	44 $^4/_9$	22 $^2/_9$	22 $^2/_9$	22 $^2/_9$	0	0	200
Output	400	400	400	200	200	200	400	200	

Table 3. Marx's six-sector model (Example 3) ($M/V = 5/7$).

	A1	A2	A3	B1	B2	B3	Workers	Capitalists	Total demand
A1	233 $^1/_3$	116 $^2/_3$	0	0	0	0	0	0	350
A2	0	116 $^2/_3$	233 $^1/_3$	0	0	0	0	0	350
A3	0	0	0	0	0	0	350	0	350
B1	0	0	0	166 $^2/_3$	83 $^1/_3$	0	0	0	250
B2	0	0	0	0	83 $^1/_3$	166 $^2/_3$	0	0	250
B3	0	0	0	0	0	0	0	250	250
Wage	68 $^1/_{18}$	68 $^1/_{18}$	68 $^1/_{18}$	48 $^{11}/_{18}$	48 $^{11}/_{18}$	48 $^{11}/_{18}$	0	0	350
Surplus value	48 $^{11}/_{18}$	48 $^{11}/_{18}$	48 $^{11}/_{18}$	34 $^{13}/_{18}$	34 $^{13}/_{18}$	34 $^{13}/_{18}$	0	0	250
Output	350	350	350	250	250	250	350	250	

Table 4. Marx's six-sector model (Example 4) ($M/V = 7/5$).

	A1	A2	A3	B1	B2	B3	Workers	Capitalists	Total demand
A1	166 $^2/_3$	83 $^1/_3$	0	0	0	0	0	0	250
A2	0	83 $^1/_3$	166 $^2/_3$	0	0	0	0	0	250
A3	0	0	0	0	0	0	250	0	250
B1	0	0	0	233 $^1/_3$	116 $^2/_3$	0	0	0	350
B2	0	0	0	0	116 $^2/_3$	233 $^1/_3$	0	0	350
B3	0	0	0	0	0	0	0	350	350
Wage	34 $^{13}/_{18}$	34 $^{13}/_{18}$	34 $^{13}/_{18}$	48 $^{11}/_{18}$	48 $^{11}/_{18}$	48 $^{11}/_{18}$	0	0	250
Surplus value	48 $^{11}/_{18}$	48 $^{11}/_{18}$	48 $^{11}/_{18}$	68 $^1/_{18}$	68 $^1/_{18}$	68 $^1/_{18}$	0	0	350
Output	250	250	250	350	350	350	250	350	

anything but trivial and he never posed anywhere else. One of them concerns how to carry out a comparative statics by taking the capital composition (C/V) as a varying parameter instead of the rate of surplus value as before. He asked not only how the quantity equilibrium would change but also what would be a new equilibrium price after varying the capital composition. He was namely well aware that the prices could not remain proportional to labour values when the sectors have different capital compositions. As we examined the detail in Mori (2007) and MEGA II/13 (Marx 2008a, 540–543), this question confronted Marx with the necessity of a different treatment from before.

Another important research question Marx posed complementarily to the comparative statics with regard to varying rates of surplus value was how a dynamic process of transition from one equilibrium to another is possible. Marx was namely confronted with the problem of "traverse" triggered by changing wage rates. In Sections 3 and 4, we will focus on each of both research questions.

2.3. Illustration of the law of monetary reflux

As the second issue in the omitted part of Ms. II, Marx investigated the so-called law of monetary reflux based on the six-sector model of production where the equilibrium conditions are assumed to be satisfied. The method of investigation he applied for this task consists in dividing the commodity transactions of the economy into 12 independent segments called each "partial circulation (teilweise Zirculation)", specifying the route of monetary circulation for each segment and confirming the reflux of money to its starting point. Each segment is considered to be independent in the sense that it has its own starting point of money, and the transactions can be carried out within the segment and without any intersection with another segment.

Marx concluded his investigation on the monetary circuit with the following propositions: First, money advanced by capitalists as wage payments to workers in each sector returns to its starting point.[12] Second, money advanced by capitalists as wage realises, in the course of its reflux, various components of output, i.e. not only the commodity labour power but also variable-capital part, constant-capital part and surplus value of social products.[13] However, finally, some rest ("Überschuß") remains which cannot be realised by circulation of money initially advanced as wage payments. In order to realise the rest, it is necessary for capitalists to advance additional money.[14]

---

[12] "The money of 300£ that is initially advanced in the class I(Ia and Ib), $(II\alpha\alpha + II\alpha)$ and $(II\beta\beta + II\beta)$ as variable capital and then spent by workers as means of purchase, means of circulation of their revenue on necessary means of consumption, has returned everywhere to its starting point in order to begin then with its course anew" (Marx 2008b, 469).

[13] "The same amount of money of 50£ figures here alternately as money form of variable capital $(II\beta)$..., then money form of labours' revenue..., money form of constant capital (Ia)..., money form of constant capital $(II\alpha\alpha)$..., money form of capitalists' revenue $(II\alpha)$..., money form of constant capital (Ib)..., money form of constant capital $(II\beta\beta)$..., and finally returning money form of variable capital $(II\beta)$" (Marx 2008b, 463–464).

[14] "It is therefore the variable money capital that mediates all these transactions. However, there remains as rest (Ueberschuß) a part of surplus value = I(b), $II(\beta\beta + \beta)$ which is not circulated by it, and for whose circulation own amount of money must be advanced" (Marx 2008b, 491). "The sum of value of total circulation is divided into two independent parts of which the one is advanced for circulating variable capital and surplus labour, and the other circulates within constant capital reproduced in their various natural forms. It is a big mistake to think that the amount of money outlaid by consumers (i.e. wage + capitalists' revenue) purchases and circulates the whole product" (Marx 2008b, 481).

These results can be seen to provide us with possibilities to re-evaluate Marx's own contribution especially to the theory of monetary circuit along the line of the so-called "Franco-Italian circuit school". The crucial role which e.g. Graziani (1990, 1998, 2003), Nell (2004) and others ascribed to wage payments in monetary circulation was *de facto* antici-pated by Marx although the bank, one of these authors' three main agents of the economy besides the classes of capitalists and workers, fades into the background in Marx's model. Furthermore, Marx's model of mone-tary circuit has a suitable framework to which the money flow computa-tion of I-O analysis by Leontief and Brody (1993) can be effectively applied (see details in Mori 2009, 2018).

3. Price calculation

3.1. Basics and non-basics in case of augmented inputs

According to Sraffa (1960), if "a commodity enters (no matter whether directly or indirectly) into the production of *all* commodities", it is *basic*, and "those that do not, *non-basic* products" (Sraffa 1960, 8, parenthesis and italics in original). This definition can be in principle adapted to Marx's model although the concept must be extended to "augmented" inputs in that basic products are used directly or indirectly in all sectors as means of production *or* wage good. Non-basic products are used neither directly nor indirectly in at least one sector.

Consider any single production, where each sector produces one dis-tinct good (i.e. there is no joint production). The definition of basic and non-basic products *in the augmented sense* can be formally reformulated as follows (Mori 2011). Let $B \in \mathcal{R}_+^{n \times n}$ denote an augmented input coefficient matrix. If B is indecomposable, all n goods are basic. If B is decomposable, it can be transformed into the following form by suitable simultaneous substitutions of rows and columns.

$$
B = \begin{pmatrix}
B_{11} & B_{12} & \cdots & B_{1n_0} \\
0 & B_{22} & & \vdots \\
\vdots & & \ddots & \vdots \\
0 & \cdots & 0 & B_{n_0 n_0}
\end{pmatrix}
\tag{4}
$$

where $B_{11}, \ldots, B_{n_0 n_0}$ ($n_0 \leq n$) denote each either an indecomposable square matrix or a 1×1 null matrix. Let I_i be the index set of columns (or rows) belonging to B_{ii}, i.e. $I_i := \{j \mid b_{jj} \in B_{ii}\}$. Obviously, all goods in $I_2, \ldots, I_{n_0}$ are non-basic. If B_{11} is a null matrix, there is no basic good.

Otherwise, assume that for each $j = 2, ..., n_0,$ $\begin{pmatrix} B_{1j} \\ \vdots \\ B_{j-1j} \end{pmatrix} \geq \neq 0$ if B_{jj} is inde-

composable, or $\iota \begin{pmatrix} B_{1j} \\ \vdots \\ B_{j-1j} \end{pmatrix} > 0$ ($\iota := (1,...,1)$) if B_{jj} is a null-matrix. If and only

if this assumption is true, any good in I_1 is basic. Note that we use inequality signs for vectors and matrices in this paper in the manner that $X > Y$, $X \geq \neq Y$ and $X \geq Y$ denote that $X - Y$ is positive, semi-positive and non-negative, respectively.

We assume in the following that there are both basic and non-basic goods. As is well known (Bortkiewicz 1907; Charasoff 1910), with respect to the price equation $p = (1 + r)pB$, the rate of profit is determined only among basic goods, and there is a positive price for every good if and only if B_{11} has a strictly larger Frobenius root than B_{ii} for any $i > 1$, i.e. $\lambda_i < \lambda_1$, where λ_j denotes the Frobenius root of B_{jj}.[15]

3.2. Marx's price exercise

Now, in the course of his exercise of the comparative statics with regard to the capital composition, Marx posed himself the following research question. After he admitted that the value composition of capital (C/V) may differ between A-sectors and B-sectors, and also within each of both, he suggested namely: "Let's see in passing how the things turn out to be under the condition of the general rate of profit" (Marx 2008b, 495). He used to set the prices so far equal to labour values because the value composition of capital was the same in all sectors. Now, he asks what happens with production prices representing a general rate of profit if different

---

[15]If there is a group of non-basic goods I_i ($i > 1$) such that the Frobenius root of B_{ii} is not less than that of B_{11}, i.e. $\lambda_i \geq \lambda_1$, then one of the following two alternatives must occur. Either basics' prices are zero while some non-basics' prices are positive with a (possibly) lower rate of profit. Or basics' prices are positive while some prices are negative with a higher rate of profit. The problem was recognised by several authors besides or even before Sraffa (1960, 90–91, Appendix B). Gautam Mathur (1965) treated as a non-basic good a heavy equipment (e.g. dam) in its accumulation process which is being expanded before it can be employed as a means of production for other (machinery) industries in future (Mathur 1965, 115–116). More than 30 years before Sraffa (1960), a mathematician Robert Remak (1929) was well aware of the problem of non-basic system. Adapted to the assumptions and notations in this section, his rather abstract algebraic analysis can be summarised in the following way. First, he assumed an input coefficient matrix whose quantity (column) eigenvector is the aggregation vector ι and the associated Frobenius eigenvalue is unity, i.e. $B\iota = \iota$. Then, for this input matrix B, he proved that there exists a non-negative price eigenvector p such that $p = pB$, and examined how zeros are located in p. Defining I_{n0} as "the highest group (höchste Gruppe)", he concluded that all prices except the highest group must be zero. Obviously, this implies that the prices of all basic goods in I_1 must be zero. This result is true because in Remak's matrix B, we have $1 = \lambda_{n0} > \lambda_j$ for all $j < n_0$.

Table 5. Marx's six-sector model (Example 5) (C/V changed randomly).

	A1	A2	A3	B1	B2	B3	Workers	Capitalists	Total demand
A1	180	120	0	0	0	0	0	0	300
A2	0	100	200	0	0	0	0	0	300
A3	0	0	0	0	0	0	300	0	300
B1	0	0	0	200	125	0	0	0	325
B2	0	0	0	0	75	250	0	0	325
B3	0	0	0	0	0	0	0	300	300
Wage	60	40	50	62.5	62.5	25	0	0	300
Surplus value	60	40	50	62.5	62.5	25	0	0	300
Output	300	300	300	325	325	300	300	300	

value compositions of capital between A-sectors and B-sectors, and within
each of both, are assumed.

Indeed, he changed the value composition of capital (obviously randomly) in both A- and B-sectors and calculated the new equilibrium in
value terms as shown in Table 5.

As mentioned above, since Marx regards not only physical means of
production but also wage goods as inputs based on which the production
price is calculated, we have to use an augmented input coefficient matrix
including wage goods to determine the production price. The augmented
input coefficient matrix implied in his six-sector model can be calculated
from Table 5 in the following way:

$$
B = \{b_{ij}\} := \begin{pmatrix}
\dfrac{3}{5} & \dfrac{2}{5} & 0 & 0 & 0 & 0 \\
0 & \dfrac{1}{3} & \dfrac{2}{3} & 0 & 0 & 0 \\
\dfrac{1}{5} & \dfrac{2}{15} & \dfrac{1}{6} & \dfrac{5}{26} & \dfrac{5}{26} & \dfrac{1}{12} \\
0 & 0 & 0 & \dfrac{8}{13} & \dfrac{5}{13} & 0 \\
0 & 0 & 0 & 0 & \dfrac{3}{13} & \dfrac{5}{6} \\
0 & 0 & 0 & 0 & 0 & 0
\end{pmatrix}
\tag{5}
$$

where b_{ij} denotes the input of good i to produce one unit of good j ($i, j = 1$,
..., 6), goods 1, 2, 3, 4, 5 and 6 stand for A1, A2, A3, B1, B2 and B3,
respectively. As we can easily see from Equations (4) and (5),

$I_1 = \{1, 2, 3\} = \{A1, A2, A3\}$, $B_{11} = \begin{pmatrix} \frac{3}{5} & \frac{2}{5} & 0 \\ 0 & \frac{1}{3} & \frac{2}{3} \\ \frac{1}{5} & \frac{2}{15} & \frac{1}{6} \end{pmatrix}$, and its Frobenius root

   is $\lambda_1 \approx 0.83$

$I_2 = \{4\} = \{B1\}$, $B_{22} = \left(\frac{8}{13}\right)$, and its Frobenius root is $\lambda_2 = 8/13$

$I_3 = \{5\} = \{B2\}$, $B_{33} = \left(\frac{3}{13}\right)$, and its Frobenius root is $\lambda_3 = 3/13$

$I_4 = \{6\} = \{B3\}$ $B_{44} = (0)$, and its Frobenius root is $\lambda_4 = 0$

In Marx's model, A1, A2 and A3 are basic goods because A1 goes into the production of A2, and A2 goes into A3, while A3, i.e. workers' wage good, goes into all six production processes. Therefore, A1, A2 and A3 enter all six production processes, A3 directly while A1 and A2 indirectly. On the other hand, B1, B2 and B3 are all non-basic because they all do not enter A-sectors directly or indirectly. Furthermore, since we have $\lambda_1 > \lambda_j$ for all $j > 1$, the rate of profit is determined within the A-sectors, namely $r = -1 + \frac{1}{\lambda_1} \approx 0.21$, and all goods can have positive production prices, $p = (p_1, p_2, p_3, p_4, p_5, p_6) = (2.39, 1.35, 1, 0.91, 0.91, 1.02)$ by setting A3 to the numeraire, i.e. $p_3 = 1$.

Let us look at Marx's own solution to the price exercise in the six-sector model. When Marx set up his famous formula of the general rate of profit for *Capital*, Volume III in his "main manuscript (Hauptmanu-skript)" of 1864–1865, i.e. more than five years before this six-sector model in Ms. II, the general rate of profit was still calculated by dividing total surplus value (M) by total advanced capital ($C + V$). According to this formula, the surplus value and the capital would each have included those of basic sectors (A-sectors) and non-basic sectors (B-sectors). This would mean in this price exercise $300/1550 \approx 0.19$. However, Marx deviated here obviously from his original formula, and he considered, exactly as our above linear-algebraic price calculation does, only the basic sectors (A-sectors) to determine the general rate of profit. His solution was namely $150/750 = 0.2$.

"… the general rate of profit. Total advanced capital = C600+V150 = 750. Total surplus value = 150. Therefore, M/C = 150/750 = 1/5 = 20%" (Marx 2008b, 495).

This price exercise in the omitted part of Ms. II suggested a different way of calculation of the general rate of profit by ignoring the non-basic sectors although Marx still stuck to his logic of transformation from value to price and did not determine the general rate of profit endogenously within the price equation, but exogenously from the value system. The intentional exclusion of the non-basic B-sectors by Marx from the calculation of the general rate of profit permits, among others, also the interpretation that Marx intuitively regarded the B-sectors such as capitalists' luxuries, etc. as unimportant for the general rate of profit. Immediately after determining the general rate of profit and before calculating each of six prices, however, he interrupted the exercise by saying "This must be investigated later (Dieß später zu untersuchen)" (Marx 2008b, 495). Despite this announcement, unfortunately, he never resumed the exercise nor elaborated on this different approach later in his life.

4. The problem of traverse

As already mentioned, Marx posed a research question concerning a dynamic process of traverse from one equilibrium to another. He assumed that after wage increase by 1/3, the rate of surplus value decreases from the original level of 1 to 1/2. As shown in Table 2, he could calculate without any problem a new equilibrium state, where each of A-sectors must expand its output from 300 to 400 while each B-sector must shrink from 300 to 200. Here, not only the proportion between A-sectors and B-sectors is changed, but this change must be also accompanied by a growth in production and employment in A-sectors. Then, Marx began to consider how to start such a growth process from the stationary state, or how to move from the old equilibrium (300) to the new one (400).

Marx was clear what occurs after such wage increase:

> A large part of products [A3] ... consist of foodstuffs which must be produced (at least in their raw material) beforehand for an annual consumption. The demand for them would increase very much. The profit made in [A3] etc. would rise so far very much. In short, capital and workforce would be drawn from [B3] etc. to [A3] etc. (Marx 2008b, 501–502)[16]

He was, however, well aware that "the mechanism of the bourgeois society brings with it that such changes ... are accompanied by circumstances which *paralyze* their effect and break the changes themselves" (Marx 2008b, 501, italics added). The circumstance Marx meant by the paralysis can be interpreted as follows: Despite the high profit of A3, "[workers'] transfer to [A3] is not so fast as their dismissal under [B3]" so that an ensuing unemployment lowers the wage and annuls in the end the initial effect of wage increase. Due to such paralysis, he concluded with "difficulty and relative impossibility of the change on this way. (Marx 2008b, 502)

Marx, however, did not elaborate in more detail on how such paralysis must occur and why the expected expansion of A-sectors does not take place. A century later, a comparable study on the problem of traverse was

---

[16] Sector indices in square parentheses were changed from the original in order to be consistent with our definition.

resumed by Lowe (1976).[17] There, he identified four phases of the efficient (speediest) course of the expanding traverse (Lowe 1976, 109–114).

(1) Partial liberation of existing capacity
(2) Augmentation of output of primary equipment (which corresponds A1 in Marx's model)
(3) Augmentation of output of secondary equipment (A2)
(4) Augmentation of consumer-good output (A3).

The first phase, in particular, means that we must release means of production from sector A2 and employ them in sector A1 to expand A1 as fast as possible. Lowe regarded this process of "liberation" in the first phase as "paradoxical" in the sense that "in order ultimately to increase the output of consumer goods [A3], such output must, to begin with, be reduced" (Lowe 1976, 110, Square parenthesis added), and he came to the conclusion: The motorial and behavioural conditions in the free market system are "goal-inadequate" and "diverting action in the wrong direction if not blocking it altogether." "[I]ts consequences are not just under- or overbuilding but a total *paralysis* of the adjustment process" (1976, 151, 161, Italics added).

It is true that Lowe treated, unlike Marx, a traverse between *steady growth* equilibria (instead of stationary state equilibria) and a traverse due to a sudden increase of labour supply (instead of a wage increase). Therefore, the situation of the traverse is symmetrically different between both

---

[17] Obviously, there is a difference in the "paralysis" which is directly meant by Marx and Lowe. For Marx, it is the transfer of capital and labour from B-sectors and A-sectors which would be hindered and paralysed while it is the transfer, say, from A/B2 (and A/B3) to A/B1 for Lowe. However, further consideration should be given to what Marx specifically thinks is the hindrance and paralysis in the transfer from B-sectors to A-sectors which is *immanent* in the capitalist production. It cannot be found in the technically given fact that means of production or workers' qualifications are not compatible between A and B due to the division of labour. Such incompatibility would not be immanent only in the capitalist production at all. What is explicitly meant by Marx in the text is rather a characteristic phenomenon that the employment of workers in A-sectors does not increase fast enough, let alone as fast as their release in B-sectors could be absorbed (Marx 2008b, 502). And Marx regards this inertial delay in the growth of employment in A-sectors as "resistance (Widerstandskraft)" which is "immanent in the mechanism of capitalist production" (Marx 2008b, 503). Here is the point where the arguments of Marx and Lowe meet. Although it is focused on A-sectors, Marx pointed out as well as Lowe the difficulty of speedy (efficient) growth of the whole system consisting of consumption goods, secondary equipment and primary equipment. Both considered this difficulty or impossibility as immanent in capitalism (or free market) where they commonly referred to the adverse price incentive. It is true that Marx did not elaborate so much on the specific reason why such a failure of growth in A-sectors must inevitably occur in the capitalist production, as Lowe did in view of the transfer from secondary- to primary-equipment sector. However, as a matter of fact, Marx was well aware that the problem does not lie in the consumption-good sector alone, but it must vertically reach its "root", i.e. the (primary) means-of-production sectors (Marx 2008b, 742–743).

authors: Lowe assumed wage fall and decreasing demand for consumption goods while Marx assumed wage hike and increasing demand for consumption goods. Despite this difference, they reached the same result that the efficient traverse is impossible.

Let us now reconstruct Marx's traverse problem in order to make sense of his "paralysis" by comparison with Lowe's analysis. First, we define the *efficient* traverse as the path of each sector's output which moves the most speedily from the old to the new equilibrium. Formally, the efficient traverse in A-sectors[18] is defined by the solution to the following minimisation problem:

Problem 1.

$$\text{Find } \operatorname{argmin}_{x(t) \geq 0} T!$$

s.t.

$$x(t) \geq \begin{pmatrix} 2/3 & 1/3 & 0 \\ 0 & 1/3 & 2/3 \\ 2/9 & 2/9 & 2/9 \end{pmatrix} (x(t) + \dot{x}(t))$$

$$x(0) \leq \begin{pmatrix} 300 \\ 300 \\ 300 \end{pmatrix}, \quad x(T) \geq \begin{pmatrix} 400 \\ 400 \\ 400 \end{pmatrix}$$

where $x(t) := (x_1(t), x_2(t), x_3(t))'$, and $x_i(t)$ denotes the output of sector i at time t.

Assuming that time is measured continuously, and that there is no storage to be carried over (i.e. the output must be used immediately or disposed for free), the efficient traverse can be determined uniquely (see Appendix) and depicted in Figure 1.

As we can see from Figure 1, the duration of the efficient traverse is about 5.65, and its path can be characterised by the following remarkable features:

(1) Sector A1 starts from a higher point while sectors A2 and A3 must instead start from a lower point than the old level (300).

(2) A1 is the first to reach the new level (400), A2 is the second and A3 the last.

---

[18] The efficient traverse in B-sectors, which subsequently occurs to A-sectors, can be treated in the analogous way, which elaboration we omit in this paper.

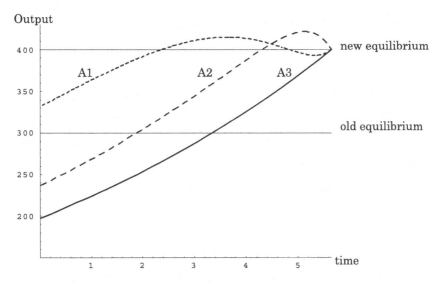

Figure 1. Efficient traverse of A1, A2 and A3.

(3) The growth of A1 and A2 temporarily overshoots the new level to keep sustaining the growth of respectively A2 and A3 to the end.

(4) A3 follows a balanced growth path (with the rate of growth $g = 1/8$) while A1 and A2 are decelerating the growth.

Comparing with Lowe's efficient traverse, we can see that the first feature here corresponds to the first phase of Lowe's traverse, and the second feature represents the order of augmentations of the three sectors characterising the second, third and fourth phases.[19] Note that Lowe's first phase is invisible in the continuous-time model in Figure 1 because the "liberation" takes place there instantly at time 0.

It might be possible to make sense of Marx's "paralysis" by referring to Lowe's "paradox": Sector A3, which must be reduced at first in order to finally expand efficiently to the goal, enjoys instead increasing demand and, therefore, high profit so that it draws capital and workers from other sectors. Obviously, if sector A3 expands, sector A2 as provider of their means of production must expand as well. Then, the liberation of resources from A2 to A1, i.e. the first requirement of the efficient traverse, fails.

---

[19] Lowe admitted that the three phases may not necessarily proceed successively (or "horizontally") but parallel (or "vertically") as shown in Figure 1.

Obviously, such a traverse as is described in this section would not occur in the three-sector model of Engels' edition of *Capital* Volume II, where A1, A2, B1 and B2 are integrated to a single sector, i.e. Sector I, and A3 and B3 are denoted by Sector IIa and IIb, respectively. In the latter model, the efficient transition of equilibrium states after the wage increase would take place instantly because both sectors IIa and IIb are assumed there to use common means of production, so that only a one-time transfer of the common means of production and labour from IIb to IIa would need to be done.

5. Conclusion

In his comparative statics with regard to the capital composition, Marx was confronted with a problem of price calculation including non-basic goods, so that he did not directly apply his formula of profit rate, $r = M/(C + V)$, as before in the manuscripts to *Capital*, Volume III. It is symptomatic of this problem that Marx could not manage to solve the prices and interrupted the exercise.

On the other hand, the research problem on the dynamic process of traverse is a good proof for Marx's awareness that in general the dynamic analysis is a theoretically different question from the comparative statics and a much trickier one because such changes are "paralyzed" by "hindrances that are immanent in the mechanism of capitalistic production" (Marx 2008b, 501–503). And we hope to have been able to show that Marx was *de facto* faced there with the problem Lowe tackled with more than one hundred years later.

These interesting theoretical episodes in his *Capital* manuscript which could have perhaps led readers to question the validity of Marx's price theory in *Capital*, Volume III on the one hand, and to open new perspectives to further develop his multi-sectoral analysis on the other hand, were made invisible in the *Capital* edition after Engels eliminated this part of manuscript in his edition of *Capital*, Volume II. Can Engels' omission of this part of Marx's manuscript be justified? The consideration of this paper would tend to suggest denying the question.

It is true that most of Marx's essential results reappear either in Engels' edition of "reproduction schemata", or they might be no more than trivial arithmetic exercises which would not deserve being published. However, some research questions Marx posed for his own further investigation contain profound theoretical problems although Marx obviously could never give a proper answer to them. If they had appeared in the

Capital edition, it would have been at least clear to the readers that Marx was confronted with critical and significant problems in economic theories. It could be possible that they would have exerted an influence on the course of the posthumous controversies on his economic theories.

Acknowledgments

Earlier versions of this paper were presented at the 21th Annual Conference of the European Society for the History of Economic Thought at University of Antwerp, 18–20 May 2017 and at the conference "Marx 1818/2018. New Developments on Karl Marx's Thought and Writings", Lyon, 27–29 September 2017. I would like to thank the participants for useful comments. I am particularly grateful to two anonymous referees for careful reading and constructive criticism. The usual caveat applies. Mori's research was supported by JSPS KAKENHI Grant Number 16K03572.

Disclosure statement

No potential conflict of interest was reported by the author.

Funding

JSPS KAKENHI [grant number 16K03572].

References

Bortkiewicz, Ladislaus von. 1907. "Wertrechnung und Preisrechnung im Marxschen System. Zweiter und Dritter Artikel. [Value Calculation and Price Calculation in the Marxian System. Second and Third Article.]" *Archiv für Sozialwissenschaft und Sozialpolitik* 25: 1–51, 445–488.

Charasoff, Georg von. 1910. *Das System des Marxismus. Darstellung und Kritk.* [The System of Marxism. Description and Criticism.] Berlin: Hans Bondy.

Graziani, Augusto. 1990. "The Theory of the Monetary Circuit." *Economies et Sociétés, Monnaie et Production* 7: 7–36.

Graziani, Augusto. 1998. "The Marxist Theory of Money." *International Journal of Political Economy* 27 (2): 26–50.

Graziani, Augusto. 2003. *The Monetary Theory of Production.* Cambridge: Cambridge University Press.

Leontief, Wassily, and András Brody. 1993. "Money-Flow Computations." *Economic Systems Research* 5 (3): 225–233.

Lowe, Adolph. 1976. *The Path of Economic Growth.* Cambridge: Cambridge University Press.

Marx, Karl. 2005. *Das Kapital. Kritik der Politischen Ökonomie. Zweites Buch. Redaktionsmanuskript von Friedrich Engels 1884/1885.* [The capital. Critique of the Political Economy. Second book. editors manuscript by Friedrich Engels 1884/1885.] Marx-Engels-Gesamtausgabe, II. Abteilung, Band 12. Berlin: Akademie Verlag. (abbr.: MEGA II/12).

Marx, Karl. 2008a. *Das Kapital. Kritik der Politischen Ökonomie. Zweiter Band. Hamburg 1885.* [Capital. A Critical Analysis of Capitalist Production. Second Volume. Hamburg 1885.] Marx-Engels-Gesamtausgabe, II. Abteilung, Band 13. Berlin: Akademie Verlag. (abbr.: MEGA II/13).

Marx, Karl. 2008b. *Manuskripte zum zweiten Buch des "Kapitals" 1868 bis 1881.* [Manuscripts for the Second Book of "Capital" 1868 to 1881.] Marx-Engels-Gesamtausgabe, II. Abteilung, Band 11. Berlin: Akademie Verlag. (abbr.: MEGA II/11).

Mathur, Gautam. 1965. *Planning for Steady Growth.* Bombay: Oxford University Press.

Mori, Kenji. 2007. "Eine dogmenhistorische Dualität in der Reproduktions- und Preistheorie: Georg von Charasoff und Kei Shibata. [A Duality in the History of Reproduction Theory and Price Theory: Georg von Charasoff and Kei Shibata.]" *Marx-Engels-Jahrbuch* 2006: 118–141.

Mori, Kenji. 2009. "6-Sector Model of Production and Monetary Circuit: Making Sense of Marx's Original Reproduction Schemata [Japanese]." *The Keizai Gaku* [Annual Report of The Economic Society Tohoku University] 70 (3): 81–102.

Mori, Kenji. 2011. "Charasoff and Dmitriev: An Analytical Characterization of Origins of Linear Economics." *International Critical Thought* 1 (1): 76–91.

Mori, Kenji. 2018. "Marx's Original 6-Sector Model of Monetary Circuit." *Executive Committee of K. Marx in the 21st Century Symposium*, Tokyo, September. Accessed 27 February 2018. http://marxinthe21stcentury.jspe.gr.jp/wp-content/uploads/2018/01/mori_full_e.pdf

Nell, Edward J. 2004. "Monetising the Classical Equations: A Theory of Circulation." *Cambridge Journal of Economics* 28: 173–203.

Remak, Robert. 1929. "Kann die Volkswirtschaftslehre eine exakte Wissenschaft werden? [Can the Economics Be an Exact Science?]" *Jahrbücher für Nationalökonomie und Statistik* 131: 703–735.

Shibata, Kei. 1939. "On the General Profit Rate." *Kyoto University Economic Review* 14 (1): 40–66.

Sraffa, Piero. 1960. *Production of Commodities by Means of Commodities. A Prelude to a Critique of Economic Theory.* Cambridge: Cambridge University Press.

Appendix. The solution to Problem 1

The solution of Problem 1 can be found by solving the following differential equations:

$$
\begin{cases}
x_3(t) = x_3(0)e^{t/8} \\[2mm]
\dot{x}_2(t) = 2\left(x_2(t) - \dfrac{9}{8}x_3(t) \right) \\[2mm]
\dot{x}_1(t) = \dfrac{1}{2}(x_1(t) - x_2(t) - \dot{x}_2(t)) \\[2mm]
x_1(0) + \dfrac{1}{2}x_2(0) = 300 \\[2mm]
x_1(T) = x_2(T) = x_3(T) = 400
\end{cases}
$$

The solution can be determined uniquely as follows:

$$x_1(t) \approx -23.71628e^{t/2} + 0.00099e^{2t} + 355.28684e^{t/8}$$
$$x_2(t) \approx -0.00099e^{2t} + 236.85789e^{t/8}$$
$$x_3(t) \approx 197.38158e^{t/8}$$
$$T \approx 5.65061$$

The *Books of Crisis* and Tooke–Newmarch excerpts: a new aspect of Marx's crisis theory in MEGA

Kenji Mori

ABSTRACT
The paper explores a new aspect of the development of the *Books of Crisis*: the fact that Marx's empirical research on the 1857 crisis in these notebooks was undertaken as the direct continuation of his study of Thomas Tooke and William Newmarch's *A History of Prices*. Our investigation will provide clues to better understand the structure and contents of the documents. Particularly, we provide new evidence for why Marx started his research on the 1857 crisis with the French economy, which managed to steer clear of the crisis, rather than with England, which was already acutely affected by it.

1. Introduction[1]

The economic crisis of 1857, the first *worldwide* economic crisis in human history, is known as the historical event that drove the contemporary Marx into strenuous economic research. He collected and systematically classified various economic data from all over the world. They were classified according to countries and topics, and then ordered chronologically. They covered France, Italy, Spain, the United Kingdom, Germany, Austria, the United States, China, India, Egypt and Australia, along with topics pertaining to financial market data (interest rates, share and security prices, bank balance, etc.), commodity market data (prices and sales of agricultural and industrial products, etc.), and bankruptcies, unemployment, short-time working, wages, labour disputes, etc. This voluminous research on the economic crisis of 1857 reached a total of 159 manuscript pages, which would correspond to about

---

[1]The characterisation of the *Books of Crisis* in this chapter is based mostly on my research conducted while editing MEGA IV/14 and writing its Introduction (*Einführung*). For details see MEGA IV/14.

500 print pages, and were known as *Books of Crisis (Krisenhefte)*. The *Books of Crisis* has just been published for the first time in MEGA, Part IV, Volume 14. In parallel with these *Books of Crisis* and based on them, Marx published his research results on phenomena and causes of the crisis in seven articles of *New York Daily Tribune* (*NYDT*).

The paper aims to explore a new aspect in the development of the *Books of Crisis* that was not duly considered in the MEGA edition: the fact that Marx's empirical research on the 1857 crisis in these notebooks was undertaken as the direct continuation of his study of Thomas Tooke and William Newmarch's *A History of Prices*. Our investigation will provide some clues that permit us to better understand the structure and contents of the documents. After characterising the documents and some basic ideas underlying them in Section 2, Section 3 shows how Marx worked on the *Books of Crisis* under the influence of volumes five and six of *A History of Prices*, which had been published shortly before. Section 4 concludes the paper.

2. Basic ideas of the *Books of Crisis*

The *Books of Crisis* consists of three notebooks which cover 191 manuscript pages and contain more than 1500 excerpts from at least twelve newspapers and magazines such as *The Times, The Morning Star, The Standard, The Manchester Guardian* and *The Economist* from 7 November 1857 to 20 February 1858. The first notebook (39 manuscript pages) is entitled "1857 France", the titles of the second and the third notebooks (72 and 80 pages respectively) are "Book of the Crisis of 1857" and "The Book of the Commercial Crisis", respectively. The contents of each notebook are given in Table A1 in Appendix.

As suggested in the introduction of MEGA IV/14 (Marx 2017, 517–522) and Mori (forthcoming), the main motive for making the notebooks was Marx's intellectual need to empirically prove the following hypotheses he had adduced since 1847 concerning the characteristics of a new crisis. First, the next crisis would assume an industrial character unlike the monetary and commercial character in the 1847 crisis, and the monetary crisis would be only the first phase of crisis; it would be followed by a proper industrial crisis.[2] Second,

---

[2]As text evidence, refer to Marx/Engels (1977a, 301–302; 1977b, 448–449, 455–456), Marx (1985b, 347–348; 1986b, 383; 1986c, 390; 1986d, 401–402). The view was shared also by Engels (1990f, 235–236).

the epicentre of the industrial crisis would be found in the three world market industries: the cotton, silk and wool industries.[3] Third, the next crisis would be a "double crisis," i.e., a simultaneous occurrence of *over-production* on the industrial market and *under-production* on the produce market. The extraordinary expansion of production in industry namely tends to cause not only excess supply (over-production) of industrial products but also excess demand (under-production) for raw materials, which causes the price of products to decline, and the price of raw materials to rise. Declining prices and increasing costs put pressure on industrial profit margins.[4] Fourth, the disproportion between fixed capital and circulating capital is assumed to be a cause of crisis.[5] A disproportionally large part of capital tends to be invested to produce for the needs of fixed capital (e.g., machines, factories, railways, ships, etc.), leaving an insufficient amount of capital for the needs of circulating capital (e.g., raw materials, wage goods, etc.). The last two hypotheses, which were of classical (especially Ricardian) origin (Mori 2018a, forthcoming), can be considered to serve as the theoretical backbone directing Marx's empirical research in the *Books of Crisis*. And one of their novel characteristics in view of the usual treatment of Marx's crisis studies would be the fact that Marx's points of view in analysing the 1857 crisis were not (or not yet) dominated by idiosyncratic elements known today as Marxian crisis theory such as under-consumption, the law of falling rate of profit, etc. Instead, they shared essential points with contemporary (and also subsequent) discourses of classical tradition— although Marx may not have been aware of it. Furthermore, we cannot say that this absence of the "class points of view" was due to

---

[3] As text evidence, refer to Marx (1985a, 168; 2001, 23).

[4] As text evidence, refer to Marx (1977b, 456–457; 1986a, 20–21; 1986e, 411; 1986f, 430; 1980, 209; 1992, 189–191, 194–200). This view was also shared by Engels (1981, 235–236; 1987, 6; 1990a, 8–9; 1990b, 194–197; 1990c, 199; 1990d, 205–207; 1990e, 217–218; 2003a, 41–42; 2003b, 67; 2003c, 127; 2003d, 222).

[5] As text evidence, refer to Marx (1986a, 20–21; 1984, 328–329). This view was also shared by Michaelis (1873, 264–265, 326) and Wirth (1890, 310). Although it is unlikely that Marx knew both authors' arguments at the time, it is obvious that Marx's fourth crisis hypothesis has in common with them the focus on the disproportion between circulating capital and fixed capital as a cause of the crisis. And it is exactly the logic of "transformation (or conversion) of circulating capital into fixed capital" that Marx began to theoretically scrutinise after ending the *Books of Crisis* in notebooks VI and VII of *Grundrisse*. It is likely that Marx adopted this logic of transformation (conversion) from James Wilson (1847) since Marx had read Wilson's book and several articles in *The Economist* and excerpted them in detail from 1849 to 1851 in his so-called London Notebooks (Marx 1983, 74, 440–460). See more about it in Mori (2018a, forthcoming).

his theoretical immaturity. As a matter of fact, he never discarded completely his early views, but he held on to them even in the *Capital* manuscripts in 1870s, i.e., his mature years (Mori 2018a).

As demonstrated in detail in Mori (2018a), there are several parallels between Marx's analysis of crisis in the 1850s and Tooke and Newmarch's latest volumes, which both de facto shared the same view of the economic developments leading up to the 1857 crisis as were formulated by Marx as being a "double crisis." *A History of Prices* described—based on the *Reports of the Chief Inspector of Factories and Workshops* by Leonard Horner—details about overinvestment in the boom years 1852 and 1853 that subsequently resulted in increasing raw material costs and decreasing product prices for cotton manufacturers (Tooke and Newmarch 1857, V260, V290, V316, V326–327).

3. The *Books of Crisis* as continuation of *A History of Prices* excerpts

A detailed investigation into Marx's research process in 1857 has revealed that in making the *Books of Crisis* from November, Marx stood under the influence of Thomas Tooke and William Newmarch's *A History of Prices*, volumes five and six, which deal with event from 1848 to 1856 and were published in February 1857. As a matter of fact, what Marx did immediately after (or before) the outbreak of the 1857 crisis in New York, was to read again both volumes of *A History of Prices* carefully and to make thorough excerpts from their description up to 1856.[6] As soon as he completed these excerpts, he undertook a continuation of the excerpt, but now from current newspapers of November 1857. So, began the *Books of Crisis*. In this sense, one may say that both volumes served Marx as models for empirical research.

The *Books of Crisis* were the first data-based empirical research that was systematically conducted by Marx about then current economies. It would be natural to understand that Marx as an autodidact had studied beforehand both of the latest volumes of *A History of Prices* once again, carefully trying to learn how to collect and organise voluminous economic data. It is possible to detect in his *Books of Crisis* signs of this preparatory learning, two of which we will now examine.

---

[6]IISG, Marx-Engels-Nachlasz, Sign. B 83 A, B 89. Special thank goes to Dr. Regina Roth for her kind support in accessing and deciphering the original manuscripts. The usual caveats apply.

The first sign can be traced from the classification of produce markets. As we can see from the contents of "The Book of the Commercial Crisis" (see Table A1), Marx classified the produce market into the following categories, into which he sorted his excerpts.

1) Raw Materials for Textile Fabrics
   α) Cotton
   β) Silk
   γ) Wool
   δ) Hemp and Flax
2) Metals
3) Hides and Leather
4) Mincing Lane
5) Corn Market

We may note that "Mincing Lane" stands for colonial and tropical produce, in which Marx included the following commodities: ashes, cocoa, coffee, drugs and dyes, dyewoods (including logwood), fruit, indigo, molasses, oils, provisions, rice, sago, saltpetre, spices, spirits, sugar, tallow, tar, tea, timber, tobacco, turpentine and wine. Among metals, he counted copper, iron, lead, steel, spelter, tin and tin plates.

To make this classification, he must have consulted the commodity catalogue in *A History of Prices,* which he had just read. In Appendix VII of its volumes V and VI (Tooke and Newmarch 1857, 490–491), the authors (i.e., Newmarch) classified, *besides corn,* the commodities whose prices they were investigating in their book as follows.

I. Colonial and Tropical Produce (food); and Provisions.
    coffee, spices, spirits, sugar, tea, tobacco, provisions
II. Raw Materials of Manufacture.
    ashes, cochineal, cotton wool, flax, hemp, indigo, logwood, oil, saltpetre, silk, tallow, tar, timber, wool
III. Metals.
    copper, iron, lead, tin.

Even allowing for some modifications and interchanges, the similarity between both classifications cannot be denied.

The second evidence of Marx's reference to Tooke and Newmarch in his *Books of Crisis* can be found in the content of "1857 France" as a whole. While all the other parts of Volumes V and VI of *A History of Prices* deal overwhelmingly with British history, Part VI of Volume

VI alone, written by Newmarch, is exclusively devoted to the development of financial policies and institutions in France from 1848 to 1856 (called the "France Part" below). More than 90% of Marx's excerpts[7] from *A History of Prices* concentrate on this part, where he copied (by estimate) more than half of the text almost word-for-word. Closely relevant to the 1857 events is there obviously Newmarch's analysis of the bullion drain from the Bank of France (BOF) in 1855 and 1856, where the bullion reserve at the BOF sank on 9 October 1856 to £6.68 million, the lowest level since 1848. The main points of the analysis can be summarised as follows:

1) The drain and the subsequent rise of the bank rate to 6% was caused by the "New Financial Policy" of the Imperial Government after 1851, which forced upon France excessive expenditure on railways and public works by means of credit (see points 2 to 4 below), expenditures that were disproportionate to its resources of available capital (Tooke and Newmarch 1857, VI 132).

2) The new constitution of the BOF of 3 March 1852 permitted the bank to make advances on railway shares and bonds. In consequence, the BOF decreased its bullion by £18.5 million after the end of 1851, 5.5 million of which was absorbed in the advances on shares and state bonds (*rentes*) (Tooke and Newmarch 1857, VI 66–69).

3) Crédit Mobilier, established in 1852, utilised almost £7 million out of its £7.5 million in assets at the end of 1855 for advances on securities (*rentes*, shares, bonds etc.) (Tooke and Newmarch 1857, VI 123).

4) Besides the BOF and Crédit Mobilier, the Comptoirs Nationaux (Comptoirs d'Escompte or Discount Banks), established 1848, provided not only discounting of bills but also advances on railway shares, shares of public companies and advances on deposits of goods (Tooke and Newmarch 1857, VI 77).

5) The drain was aggravated by the Crimean War, bad harvests and increase of raw silk imports (Tooke and Newmarch 1857, VI 90).

6) "Violent and extraordinary" and "humiliating" governmental measures such as premiums on gold (to prevent gold exports)

---

[7] The rest of excerpt was made from Part VII.

and regulations against melting down and exporting silver were not successful.

7) The drain was only surmounted by gold influx due to a large demand in America and Australia for French manufactures (e.g., silk fabrics) and produce (e.g., wine). In fact, during 1848–1856, the balance of trade in favour of France amounted to nearly £80 million (Tooke and Newmarch 1857, VI 133–134). Without it, a "catastrophe" must have been encountered very early on due to the pressure (Tooke and Newmarch 1857, VI 91).

The very intensive extract of the France Part of *A History of Prices* testifies to Marx's careful study of their analysis about the economic situation in France up to 1856. It is, therefore, quite natural that Marx, immediately after completing the excerpts, undertook their continuation from current newspapers beginning with November 1857, to see how the situation in France could be aggravated again (and hopefully more seriously) by the new crisis that had just occurred in America. As a matter of fact, the resumed excerpt, now entitled "1857 France," was carried out based on the model of the above analysis in the France Part in the sense that such topics were collected that we can follow the development of the things from 1856 to 1857: viz., current conditions of the BOF, Crédit Mobilier, Comptoir d'Escompte, railways, produce markets, foreign trade and manufacturing—as well as governmental policies and a critical assessment of them. Let us summarise Marx's excerpts (Marx 2017, 3–75) and reorganise them in the same numerical order as the above main points of Newmarch's analysis in the France Part (Note: topic 8 was newly added here).

1) After the bank rate rose to 7.5–10% on 11 November 1857, the bullion at the BOF began to increase soon by continued influx of specie, so that the bank rate sank from November 26 step-by-step down to 5% on December 29. From the beginning, the Emperor rejected the proposal of a forced circulation of notes of the BOF. After some further downward trends in November, the *bourse* quotations (including the BOF, Crédit Mobilier and railway companies) soon recovered in December and rose rapidly in January 1858 in all securities and funds. However, the receipts

of railways tended to decline due to their vast prolongations and embranchments so that some companies had to make calls on shares in November and December. The dividends were expected to fall off in shares of railway companies.

2) After negotiations with railway companies, the BOF agreed in December 1857 to advance at once £2 million on deposit of bonds. However, the companies did not need to take advantage of the advance because they had sufficient liquidity to meet their engagements.

3) Crédit Mobilier, Crédit Foncier and Comptoir d'Escompte were said to be negotiating an amalgamation to increase capital and influence.

4) After negotiations with the BOF, Comptoir d'Escompte decided in January 1858 to make advances to Paris merchants on deposit of goods in store.

5) The 1857 harvest was abundant, and corn exports exceeded imports. Therefore, corn prices were so low that the imperial decrees prohibiting export and distillation of corn had to be revoked to sustain its price, and the bakers were obliged to hold one-seventh of their flour reserve in public granaries. Also raw silk's price was held low by falling demand.

6) As the exchange rate of silver to gold (15.5 to 1) was maintained, net exports of silver and net imports of gold continued to grow despite regulations against melting down and exporting silver. In the end, money changers and bullion dealers were not prosecuted.

7) Raw silk and wines remained in high demand. In 1857 (through November), more fabrics (silk, cotton, hemp, flax) and fine wines were exported than in 1856.

8) Nevertheless, manufacturing districts, especially Lyon, were principally affected by the stagnation, where unemployment, short time and stoppages became severe problems. The government took measures to support the manufacturers by a civil list and to provide unemployed workers with food and employment. Besides, a *Mont de Piété* was established for lending money against deposits of silk goods. Failures, however, were limited in number and importance throughout the period in France as a whole.

All in all, Marx's excerpts testify that there were no signs that Newmarch identified in the France Part that would have entailed an acute monetary crisis. Indeed, wine and silk fabric exports increased, and there was no need to import corn. Raw materials (e.g., raw silk) were available at low prices. Despite declining receipts, railway companies needed no special assistance from the BOF. The only sector affected by the 1857 crisis was the textile manufacturing, especially the silk industry in Lyon. Still, a sign of revival was seen there, too, in January 1858. The British media reported at least by 28 November 1857 that France was unaffected by the crisis. *The Economist* published the following report from Paris on that date, which was word-for-word excerpted by Marx.

"French commerce, on the whole, has borne up infinitely better than was to have been expected under the crisis to which the high rate of discount, the general falling off in commercial activity, the return of bills dishonoured from the United States, and, to a certain extent, the numerous failures in England have subjected it. The failures that have taken place have not been considerable in number or important in amount; and there has not been the slightest disposition to have a panic, though circumstances certainly appeared to justify one, and though the French have heretofore been extremely ready to rush into panics on the smallest pretexts. The manner in which they have acted certainly does them credit." (*The Economist*, November 28, 1857, 1319–1320; Marx 2017, 20)

The sentence "there has not been the slightest disposition to have a panic" must have impressed Marx so much that he stressed the phrase by underlining it. This was the development in France in 1857 (and during the beginning of 1858) that Marx studied as a direct continuation of the situation in 1848–1856 described in the France Part of *A History of Prices*.

4. Conclusion

To explain such allegedly unexpected development in the 1857 French economy, Marx reviewed all his excerpts in "1857 France" and came to understand "some results," which he summarised in his letter to Engels on 25 December 1857, and then was published in detail under "The French Crisis" in the NYDT on 12 January 1858. In both the letter and the article, he explained, by using reports from *The Economist* between 7 November and 19 December 1857 (which he excerpted in his notebook), that France did not suffer much during the then present crisis as did England or Germany, that the BOF sustained the prices of railway shares by making advances upon railway securities, and that the prices of French securities were nevertheless expected to fall (Marx 1986e, 413–418; Marx 1990, 229–232). At the same time, Marx dealt in both the letter and article with the so-called French "riddle", viz., why France was not (yet) seriously affected by the 1857 world crisis. In particular, he brought up the argument that France's balance of trade with major trading partners such as the United Kingdom, the United States and also the Hanseatic cities was positive. This argument, however, cannot be considered as original because the article was written mostly through the paraphrasing of newspaper reports excerpted from *The Economist, The Times, The Manchester Guardian, The Daily Telegraph, The Standard* and *The Weekly Dispatch* in his "1857 France" notebook, without specifying the original sources. The French situation must have appeared as a "riddle" to those who shared Newmarch's view that Napoleon III's fiscal policy featuring vast public spending and bailout programs was part of the problem and never of the solution. We know now that Marx endorsed this view.

To the readers (and also editors) of the *Books of Crisis*, the French situation in 1857 must have posed yet another riddle: Why did Marx start his research on the 1857 crisis with the French economy, which managed to keep away from the crisis, and not with England, which had already been so acutely affected to see itself forced to suspend the Bank Charter Act as early as 12 November 1857, i.e., before Marx decided to make the notebooks. Our exposition of a new aspect in the making process of the *Books of Crisis* would suggest that Marx had been intensively studying Tooke and Newmarch's book, and had been firmly convinced of their view of the (allegedly) crisis-prone trend of the 1857 French economy—especially due to the imperial government's fiscal policy.

Acknowledgements

Earlier versions of this paper were presented at the conference "Marx 1818/2018. New Developments on Karl Marx's Thought and Writings", Lyon, 27–29 September 2017. I would like to thank the participants for useful comments. I am particularly grateful to two anonymous referees for careful reading and constructive criticism. The usual caveat applies.

Disclosure statement

No potential conflict of interest was reported by the authors.

Funding

Mori's research was supported by JSPS KAKENHI Grant Number [16K03572].

References

Engels, Friedrich. 1981. "Engels an Marx, 15. Oktober 1851." In *Marx-Engels-Gesamtausgabe*, III. Abteilung, Band 3, Briefwechsel, Januar 1849 bis Dezember 1850. Berlin: Dietz Verlag (abbr.: MEGA III/3).

Engels, Friedrich. 1987. "Engels an Marx, 6. Januar 1852." In *Marx-Engels-Gesamtausgabe*, III. Abteilung, Band 5, Briefwechsel, Januar bis August 1852. Berlin: Dietz Verlag (abbr.: MEGA III/5).

Engels, Friedrich. 1990a. "Engels an Marx, 14. April 1856." In *Marx-Engels-Gesamtausgabe*, III. Abteilung, Band 8, Briefwechsel, April 1856 bis Dezember 1857. Berlin: Dietz Verlag (abbr.: MEGA III/8).

Engels, Friedrich. 1990b. "Engels an Marx, 15. November 1857." In *MEGA III/8*. Berlin: Dietz Verlag.

Engels, Friedrich. 1990c. "Engels an Marx, 16. November 1857." In *MEGA III/8*. Berlin: Dietz Verlag.

Engels, Friedrich. 1990d. "Engels an Marx, 7. Dezember 1857." In *MEGA III/8*. Berlin: Dietz Verlag.

Engels, Friedrich. 1990e. "Engels an Marx, 11. Dezember 1857." In *MEGA III/8*. Berlin: Dietz Verlag.

Engels, Friedrich., 1990f. "Engels, Friedrich. an Marx, 31. Dezember 1857." In *MEGA III/8*. Berlin: Dietz Verlag.

Engels, Friedrich. 2003a. "Engels an Marx, 25. Januar 1858." In *Marx-Engels-Gesamtausgabe*, III. Abteilung, Band 9, Briefwechsel, Januar 1858 bis August 1859. Berlin: Akademie Verlag (abbr.: MEGA III/9).

Engels, Friedrich. 2003b. "Engels an Marx, 18. Februar 1858." In *MEGA III/9*. Berlin: Akademie Verlag.

Engels, Friedrich. 2003c. "Engels an Marx, 9. April 1858." In *MEGA III/9*. Berlin: Akademie Verlag.

Engels, Friedrich. 2003d. "Engels an Marx, 21. Oktober 1858." In *MEGA III/9*. Berlin: Akademie Verlag.

Marx, Karl. 1980. "The State of British Manufactures. March 4, 1859. NYDT, March 24, 1859." In *Collected Works*, vol. 16. Moscow: Progress Publishers (abbr.: MECW 16).

Marx, Karl. 1983. "Londoner Hefte 1852-1853 Hefte I-VI." In *Marx-Engels-Gesamtausgabe*, IV. Abteilung, Band 7. Berlin: Dietz Verlag (abbr. MEGA IV/7).

Marx, Karl. 1984. "Political Movements — Scarcity of Bread in Europe. Sep. 13, 1853, NYDT, Sep. 30, 1853." In *Marx-Engels-Gesamtausgabe*, I. Abteilung, Band 12, Werke, Artikel, Entwürfe, Januar bis Dezember 1853. Berlin: Dietz Verlag (abbr.: MEGA I/12).

Marx, Karl. 1985a. "Der 18. Brumaire des Louis Bonaparte." In *Marx-Engels-Gesamtausgabe*, I. Abteilung, Band 11, Werke, Artikel, Entwürfe, Juli 1851 bis Dezember 1852. Berlin: Dietz Verlag (abbr.: MEGA I/11).

Marx, Karl. 1985b. "Pauperism and Free Trade — The Approaching Commercial Crisis." In *MEGA I/11*. Berlin: Dietz Verlag.

Marx, Karl. 1986a. "The French Crédit Mobilier. Late June, 1856. NYDT, July 11, 1856." In *Collected Works*, vol. 15. Moscow: Progress Publishers (abbr.: MECW 15).

Marx, Karl. 1986b. "The Bank Act of 1844 and the Monetary Crisis in England. Nov. 6, 1857. NYDT, Nov. 21, 1857." In *MECW 15*. Moscow: Progress Publishers.

Marx, Karl. 1986c. "The British Revulsion. Nov. 13, 1857. NYDT, Nov. 30, 1857." In *MECW 15*. Moscow: Progress Publishers.

Marx, Karl. 1986d. "The Trade Crisis in England. Nov. 27, 1857. NYDT, Dec. 15, 1857." In *MECW 15*. Moscow: Progress Publishers.

Marx, Karl. 1986e. "The Crisis in Europe. Dec. 18, 1857. NYDT, Jan. 5, 1858." In *MECW 15*. Moscow: Progress Publishers.

Marx, Karl. 1986f. "British Commerce. Jan. 7, 1858. NYDT, Feb. 3, 1858." In *MECW 15*. Moscow: Progress Publishers.

Marx, Karl. 1990. "Marx an Engels, 25. Dezember 1857." In *MEGA III/8*. Berlin: Dietz Verlag.

Marx, Karl. 1992. "Ökonomische Manuskripte 1863-1867." In Marx-Engels-Gesamtausgabe, II. Abteilung, Band 4, Ökonomische Manuskripte 1863-1867, Teil 2. Berlin: Dietz Verlag (abbr.: MEGA II/4.2).

Marx, Karl. 2001. "Geschäftskrisis – Die Zunahme des englischen Handels und der englischen Industrie in dem Zeitraum von 1849 bis 1853." In *Marx-Engels-Gesamtausgabe*, I. Abteilung, Band 14, Werke, Artikel, Entwürfe, Januar bis Dezember 1855. Berlin: Dietz Verlag (abbr.: MEGA I/14).

Marx, Karl. 2017. "Exzerpte, Zeitungsausschnitte und Notizen zur Weltwirtschaftskrise (Krisenhfte). November 1857 bis Februar 1858." In *Marx-Engels-Gesamtausgabe*, IV. Abteilung, Band 14. Berlin, München, Boston: De Gruyter (abbr. MEGA IV/14).

Marx, Karl, and Friedrich Engels. 1977a. "Neue Rheinische Zeitung. Revue. März/April 1850." In *Marx-Engels-Gesamtausgabe*, I. Abteilung, Band 10, Werke, Artikel, Entwürfe, Juli 1849 bis Juni 1851. Berlin: Dietz Verlag (abbr.: MEGA I/10).

Marx, Karl and Friedrich Engels. 1977b. "Neue Rheinische Zeitung. Revue. Mai bis Oktober 1850." In *MEGA I/10*. Berlin: Dietz Verlag

Michaelis, Otto. 1873. "Handelskrisis von 1857." In Otto Michaelis, *Volkswirthschaftliche Schriften*, vol. 1. Berlin: F.A. Herbig.

Mori, Kenji. 2018a. "Karl Marx's Books of Crisis and the Concept of Double Crisis: A Ricardian Legacy." In *Marx's Capital: An Unfinishable Project?*, edited by van den Linden, Marcel and Gerald Hubmann. Leiden, Boston: Brill.

Mori, Kenji. forthcoming. "Karl Marx's Books of Crisis and the Production Theory of Crisis." In *Studien zur Entwicklung der ökonomischen Theorie XXXII*. Berlin: Duncker & Humblot.

Ricardo, David. 1951. *On the Principles of Political Economy and Taxation, The Works and Correspondence of David Ricardo*, vol. I. Edited by P. Sraffa with the Collaboration of M.H. Dobb. Cambridge: Cambridge University Press.

Tooke, Thomas, and William Newmarch. 1857. *A History of Prices, and of the State of the Circulation, During the Nine Years 1848-1856; Forming the Fifth and Sixth Volumes of the History of Prices from 1792 to the Present Time.* 2 *vols*. London: Longman, Brown, Green, Longmans, & Roberts.

Wilson, James. 1847. *Capital, Currency, and Banking.* London: The Office of the "Economist".

Wirth, Max. 1890. *Geschichte der Handelskrisen.* Frankfurt am Main: J.D. Sauerländer's Verlag.

Appendix

Table A1. Contents of *Books of Crisis*.

France 1857	Book of the Crisis of 1857	Book of the Commercial Crisis
- 1857 France	Failures	I) Money Market
- Crisis	Bank of England	1) Bank of England
- Bank of France	London Money Market	2) Bullion Market
- French Trade	I) General Aspect of the	α) Efflux and Influx of Bullion
- Bank of France	Money Market	β) Price and Movement of
- French Corn trade	II) Bullion Market	Silver
- Ex- and Imports	a) Bullion in the Bank of	γ) Foreign Exchanges
- French Trade	England	3) Loan Market
- Governmental Measures	b) Export and Import of	4) Failures
- Italy	Precious Metals	5) Security Market
- Spain	c) Price of Silver	α) Public Funds
- Bourse Quotations	d) Foreign Exchanges	β) Share Market
- Traffic on the Rhine	Miscellaneous	II) Produce Market
- French Trade	III) Security Market	1) Raw Materials for Textile
- Railways	a) Public Funds	Fabrics
- Northern Europe, etc.	b) Share Market	α) Cotton
- French Bourse	1) Railways	β) Silk
- French State Revenue	2) Joint Stock Banks	γ) Wool
	3) Mining Shares	δ) Hemp and Flax
	IV) Produce Market	2) Metals
	V) Industrial Market	3) Hides and Leather
	VI) Hamburg, Northern	4) Mincing Lane
	Kingdoms, Prussia, Austria	5) Corn Market
	(Germany)	III) Industrial Market
	[Board of Trade Returns]	IV) Labour Market
	IX) United States	V) Miscellaneous
	I) Failures	I) Comparative Statement
	II) Money Market	II) Railway Receipts
	1) Bank of England	Crisis of 1857
	2) London Loan Market	Financial Condition of India
	3) Bullion Market	*Englische Staatseinnahmen*
	a) Efflux and Influx of	1857
	Bullion	Liverpool Ship Trade in
	b) Price of Silver	1857
	c) Foreign Exchanges	China and India, Egypt, etc.
	4) Security Market	United States
	a) Consols	Crisis of 1857
	b) Railway – Joint Stock	[The Supply and
	Bank – Mining Shares	Consumption of Wool]
	III) Produce Market	[The Recent Crisis]
	Raw Materials for	Bank Deposits
	Textile Fabrics	The Recent Crisis
	1) Cotton	Australia et Colonies
	2) Silk	Brazils
	3) Wool	
	4) Hemp and Flax	
	Raw Materials Not for	
	Textile Fabrics	
	a) Metals	
	b) Hides and Leather	
	c) Mincing Lane	
	d) Mark Lane	
	IV) Industrial Market	
	Labour Market	

Marx on rent: new insights from the new MEGA

Susumu Takenaga

ABSTRACT

Marx's theory of rent is usually regarded to be represented in the text of Part VI of Book III of *Capital*, which was originally a chapter in his manuscript written in 1865 on the basis of the manuscript of 1861–1863, into which the theory of rent slipped by accident in the course of its writing. The present article elucidates such particular circumstances relating to the making of Marx's theory of rent composed of two forms, differential and absolute, based on the new MEGA volumes. Special attention is paid to Liebig's agro-chemistry, which considerably influenced Marx's view on modern agriculture.

1. Foreword

The ground rent is one of the three fundamental categories of revenue along with the profit and wages in the modern capitalist economy. As such, it occupied an important place in the economic theory before Marx, who had naturally to pay deserved attention to it and to the theories on it in his economic research and to make efforts to elaborate his own theory of rent in assigning to it an appropriate place in the economic theory conceived as "Critique of political economy." But with the benefit of hindsight, these efforts resulted in his writings of diverse natures: letters, manuscripts, excerpts from other authors, parts in a published book, all of which remain more or less of fragmentary character. Only one among them, Part VI of Book III of *Capital*, can exceptionally be regarded somewhat systematic and this Part VI has been habitually treated as representing "the theory of ground rent of Marx" since it was edited and published by Engels more than a century ago on the basis of Marx's manuscript written in 1865. Between the original manuscript and Engels' published text, there exists a number of non-negligible discordances. Today, thanks to the volumes of the new MEGA, the publication of which is now going on, we can avail ourselves of the literary legacy of Marx in the original. The present article aims at scrutinizing these materials to see how far Marx could go in the elaboration of his own theory of rent. To do so, it will focus on the first several years in the 1860s, the most important phase in his research on rent. It may be useful for this purpose to remount to its prehistory in advance.

For the young Marx who began to study economic theory in 1844 under the influence of Engels, ground rent was from the outset one of the familiar subjects. What was to have a sustained impact on his study of the theory of ground rent till the time, long afterwards, when he conceived his own theory of it, was his study of economic literature with Engels in Manchester during the summer of 1845 (all the excerpts taken by Marx in Manchester are now available in new MEGA volumes 4 and 5 of part IV, published respectively in 1988, 2015, hereafter IV/4, IV/5 for short. In the following, all the MEGA volumes will be indicated in the same way). In relation to the theory of ground rent, particularly important are the excerpts from James Anderson's work, *A calm investigation of the circumstances that have led to the present scarcity of grain in Britain*, London, 1801 (IV/4, 62–65). Some phrases in these relatively short excerpts were to be repeatedly quoted in the manuscript of 1861–1863 and the same points in this work of Anderson were also mentioned, along with his name, in the section on the theory of ground rent of the manuscript for Book III of *Capital* drafted in 1865. We can see that Marx had a long-lasting interest in and high estimation of Anderson from a very early time. Many of these quotations testify to a fundamental opposition to or at least doubt of the basic premises of Ricardo's theory of ground rent. This was before Marx's profound study of the theory of rent contained in Ricardo's *On the Principles of political economy, and taxation*.

One of the main themes of the economic research Marx carried out intensively during his first years in London was centred on landed property, agriculture, and ground rent. The sole outlet for his thinking at that time was his letters addressed to Engels and others. The most important of these is his letter to Engels of 7 January 1851, in which Marx presents the outline of a theory of ground rent he was conceiving while examining critically the theory of Ricardo.

According to Ricardo, "in the advancing state" (Ricardo IV/22–3) of society, the demand for labour and the wages increase with the progress of capital accumulation, which entails a higher demand for food and a rise in food price. This, in turn, makes it possible and necessary to extend cultivation to lands of lower yield, which raises the ground rent as income of the landowner. Such is the scenario depicted by Ricardo, who considers it to be more or less universally valid. It is this one point in Ricardo's theory and the presuppositions supporting it that Marx criticizes in his letter to Engels.

The propositions in Ricardo's theory of rent "are everywhere refuted by history" (III/4, 6). "There is no doubt that, with the advance of civilization, ever poorer types of soil are brought under cultivation. However, equally, there is no doubt that, as a result of the progress of science and industry, these poorer types of soil are relatively good as against those previously regarded as good" (ibid.). The fertility of the land, regarded at a certain time as of an inferior quality, is not invariable, hence the extension of cultivation to such land does not necessarily bring with it a parallel rise in the ground rent and the price of corn. Including the Britain of Ricardo's time, "in all countries, as Petty has already observed, we find that, when the price of corn fell, the country's overall rental rose" (ibid.). Marx affirms that such phenomena apparently contradictory to the theoretical precondition of Ricardo are historically and geographically widely observed and he wonders how to explain this. What is required for this explanation is "to adjust the law of rent to progress in fertility in agriculture generally, this being the only way, firstly, to explain the historical facts and secondly, to eliminate the Malthusian theory of the deterioration, not only of the 'hands', but also of the soil" (ibid.). However, Marx excludes the hypothesis of the diminishing return as a unilateral tendency, considering the progress in agriculture as real enough and unexceptional. "Let us assume that there is a general improvement in agriculture. If this is presupposed, we at the same time assume that science, industry, and population are in a state of growth" (ibid.).

As a conclusion from the above, Marx tries to reconcile Ricardo's theory of rent and the historical facts as follows. This may have been the outline of the theory of rent Marx himself had in mind at that time. "Rent may rise although the price of agricultural produce falls, and yet *Ricardo's law still holds good*" (III/4, 10). This is not to recognize what Ricardo says per se. It means rather that, contrary to Ricardo's assumption, the rent can increase regardless of the price of agricultural products only if the total yield or the differences in fertility (or both of them at the same time) increases, in other words, the rent can increase without any diminishing returns. "The law of rent, as laid down by Ricardo in its simplest form [...], does not presuppose the diminishing fertility of the land, but only −−− and this *despite the general increase in fertility that accompanies the development of society* −−− the *varying* fertility of fields or the varying results obtained by the capital successively employed on the same land" (ibid. emphasis by Marx). The theory of rent Marx was conceiving at that time was constructed, by pursuing, on the one hand, some aspects of Ricardo's theory of rent, but liquidating, on the other hand, the fundamental presuppositions of this same theory. This is the point at which Marx arrived at the beginning of the 1850s regarding ground rent.

2. Marx's research on the (theory of) ground rent in the manuscript of 1861–1863: absolute rent and differential rent

2.1. Industry and agriculture in capitalism, surplus-value and profit

The essential problem consists in contrasting the agriculture and the industry, in shedding light on the particularities distinguishing the former from the latter. Needless to say, agriculture is, just like industry, an indistinguishable branch of capital investment aiming at obtaining profit by employing and exploiting wage labour. This is the fundamental assumption in the theory of rent. Given this shared nature, the question then arises of what the differences and distinctions are between these two branches. As Marx pursues his considerations of various aspects of the differences between agriculture and industry, he approaches the problem of "surplus-profit" which "consolidate(s) itself and accrue(s) to the landlord." He wonders why the surplus-profit arising in a particular branch (agriculture) "accrues to the landlord", because the surplus-profit cannot generally remain in its origin but is socially redistributed to become a general profit and disappears. This is what was to be shown through a series of theoretical processes discussed in the first two chapters in the "main manuscript" of Book III of *Capital*, through which Marx derived the concept of price of production generally deviating from value.

In the section "g Mr. Rodbertus" in the *Theories of surplus value*, Marx already presupposes this concept of "price of production" (II/3.3, p.688). However, in the manuscript of 1861–1863 prior to note-book X including this section "g", he has discussed only the theoret-ical domains concerning value and surplus-value to be treated in Book I of *Capital*, whereas the subjects relating to Book III including the "price of production" are treated only in the first manuscript of Book III entitled "Chapter 3 capital and profit", included in notebook XVI. The whole of the manuscript of 1861–1863 was published for the first time in new MEGA as six books (or fascicles) of volume 3 of Part II (II/3.1–3.6). The notebook XVI was judged by the editorial team in Moscow and East-Berlin to have been written after a tempor-ary interruption of "5 theories of surplus value" in notebook XV, and was published in 1980 as a part of the 5th book (II/3.5). However, as a result of the careful examinations on the original manuscripts of Marx carried out in International Institute of Social History in Amsterdam by Omura and other Japanese researchers, it turned out that "Chapter 3 capital and profit" had been written from December 1861 to January 1862 prior to the main part of "5 theories of surplus-value" and that the number of the notebook (XVI) containing "Chapter 3" and the page numbers therein were allotted ex-post. Then, Marx had already worked out the notion of the price of pro-duction when accidentally tackling Rodbertus' book in mid-1862 to discover the absolute rent.[1]

The last section of the manuscript "Chapter 3 capital and profit" is entitled "7 general law about the fall of the rate of profit with the pro-gress of the capitalist production", which shows that this manuscript covers the theoretical contents of the first three Parts of Book III of *Capital* edited by Engels. In the previous section "6 cost of production", Marx entered probably for the first time into a detailed consideration of a series of issues concerning the transformation of individual profits into the average profit and the resulting

---

[1] The chronological position of the drafting of "Chapter 3" provoked a heated debate on both national and international levels, involving a considerable number of researchers in Japan, East-Germany, and Soviet Union. It continued for a certain time and finally in the mid-1980s, nearly all the contentions of Omura etc. were internationally acknowledged. Thereafter, no major objections to this common agreement have been raised. We will not enter into the details of this debate here, but adhere to the view, which prevailed as a result of the majority consensus. As for the details of the process of this debate and of the grounds of the view newly agreed, see "Chapter 3, Making of the chapter three 'capital and profit' " and "Chapter 4, Formation of the conception of Book III in the manuscript of 1861–1863" in Omura 1998, as well as Müller and Focke 1984, Ohmura [Omura] 1984.

transformation of value into the price of production. He reached the view that the average price of the commodities produced by capitals with different organic compositions varies not around their value but around the price of production generally deviating from the value (though during the time of writing the manuscript of 1861–1863, the price of production was often called "cost price" or in some cases "average price"). As he entered this theoretical domain for the first time, one might imagine that Marx would critically mention the theory of Ricardo "confounding the value and the price of production", but probably because this manuscript was not written as a part of the history of economic theory, but as a first sketch to become a future "Part II" (in Book III of *Capital*), no critical examination of Ricardo's the theory is made here. On the contrary, when Marx approaches the theory of rent in "g Mr. Rodbertus" from a new point of view, different from his own previous view, in this context he severely and repeatedly criticizes Ricardo's theory of value and price as the origin of the serious faults in his theory of rent. This is because he had previously written "Chapter 3 capital and profit".

2.2. Value and price of production, agriculture

Now, in the theoretical context described above, Marx approaches a new concept of rent never imagined before even by himself. To Ricardo's view that "the *average price* of commodities is determined by the labour-time required for their production" (II/3.3, 689) and that "*average price equals value*" (ibid., 690. emphases in original), Marx opposes his point of view as follows:

> But I show that just *because* the value of the commodity is determined by *labour-time*, the average price of the commodities (except in the *unique* case in which the so-called individual *rate of profit* in a particular sphere of production, i.e., the profit determined by the surplus-value yielded in this sphere of production itself, [is] equal to the average rate of profit on total capital) can *never* be equal to their value. (ibid.)

Therefore, "since profit can be less than the intrinsic surplus-value of the commodity, or the quantity of unpaid labour it embodies, profit plus rent needs not be larger than the intrinsic surplus-value of the commodity. Why this occurs in a *particular* sphere of production as opposed to other spheres has of course still to be explained" (ibid. emphasis by Marx). Since for Ricardo, the value of commodities is the price of production, according to the terminology of Marx (cost price plus average profit),[2] he must think that, if the price of a commodity comprises a rent in addition to the average profit, it must be because that commodity is sold at a price above its value. From the point of view of his theory of value, Ricardo, therefore, denies the possibility of a rent arising only in this way. For Marx, however, who has already made clear the distinction between value and price of production, the existence of such a rent can be explained without violating his theory of value, hence it is admissible.

Towards the end of the same lengthy paragraph from which the above quotation is drawn, Marx continues on the subject of rent as follows:

> The commodity which yields rent [is not sold according to its price of production, hence] differs from all these three instances [of ordinary commodities, whose value may be lower than, higher than or equal to the price of production]. Whatever the circumstances, it is sold at a price which will yield *more than average profit—as* determined by the general rate of profit on capital. [...] This instance [in which the rent arises] is thus analogous with case 2 of those [ordinary] commodities whose intrinsic surplus-value is higher than the surplus-value realized in their average price. As with these commodities the profit represents a form of this surplus-value—in this case profit on the capital employed—which has been reduced to the level of the general rate of profit. The *excess intrinsic surplus-value of the commodity over and above* this profit is, *however*, in contrast to [ordinary] commodity 2, also realized in these exceptional commodities, but accrues not to the owner of the capital, but to the owner of the land, the natural agent, the mine, etc. (ibid., 690-1. emphasis by Marx)

This explanation proves that the theory of the price of production was already enrooted in Marx's thinking. The possibility of a new concept of rent absent from Ricardo's theory of rent is thus shown, but the problem is not yet settled. "The commodity which yields rent", these "exceptional commodities" are produced "in a *particular* sphere of production as opposed to other spheres", and their selling prices are not transformed into prices of production. This phenomenon "has of course still to be explained."

---

[2] "Mr. Malthus appears to think that it is a part of my doctrine that the cost and value of a thing should be the same; —it is, if he means by cost, 'cost of production' including profits" (Ricardo, I/47). This passage of Ricardo seems to express conclusively the character of his theory of value in a few very concise and clear words.

Now, Marx showed, on the basis of his theory of the price of production, the existence of a class of commodities among those produced by capital, for which the transformation of value into price of production means virtually a reduction of their price below their value and found here the potential for the rent to emerge. Under what "exceptional" conditions is this reduction in price obstructed, allowing the commodity to be sold at a price beyond the price of production and resulting in the actual emergence of rent? Such was the problem "still to be explained".

> The question is why, […] this particular commodity […] is able to realize a portion of its own surplus-value which forms an excess over and above average profit; so that it is possible for a farmer, who invests capital in this sphere of production, to sell the commodity at prices which yield him the ordinary profit and at the same time enable him to pay the excess in surplus-value realized *over and above* this profit to a third person, the landlord. (ibid., 692. emphasis by Marx)

Here, there seem to be two problems: (1) the emergence of surplus-profit by the obstruction of the transformation of value into the price of production, and (2) the transformation of surplus-profit into rent. Yet, in fact, these two problems mutually presuppose one another and can be reduced to one single and inseparable problem. To the question he raised, Marx answers as follows:

> It is quite simply the *private ownership* of land, mines, water, etc. by certain people, which enables them to snatch, intercept and seize the *excess surplus-value over and above profit* (average profit, the rate of profit determined by the general rate of profit) contained in the commodities of these particular spheres of production, these particular fields of capital investment, and so to prevent it from entering into the general process by which the general rate of profit is formed. (ibid. emphasis by Marx)

It is thus shown that the "landed property" is responsible not only for generating surplus-profit – by obstructing the transformation of the individual rate of profit into the average rate – but also for transforming it into rent. However, the problem reaches further than this. Why can a rate of profit higher than the social average (as the origin of surplus-profit) be obtained in the branch of production where the landed property plays a role (namely agriculture)?

2.3. The composition of Capital in agriculture; Rodbertus' "new theory of rent"

The question just mentioned was the last problem remaining to be solved by Marx in his search for a new theory of rent. The book of Rodbertus (Rodbertus 1851) seems to have given him a certain hint in thinking about it. In his letter to Lassalle of June 16, 1862, Marx frankly recognizes that Rodbertus' book contains a certain merit, in saying that it "does tend in the right direction" (III/12, 133). However, in our view, such an estimation seems to apply only to one point, which we are now going to bring into question.

After a minute examination of Rodbertus' own theory of rent, Marx says in conclusion that "stripped of all this [nonsense], [...] then only the following assertion remains as the real kernel" (ibid.). The "real kernel" Marx talks of here are the following: "agriculture belongs to that class of industries, whose variable capital is greater proportionately to constant capital than in industry, on an average" (II/3.3, 748). This is a paraphrase by Marx, with his own theoretical framework, of what Rodbertus had written: in agriculture, the raw materials such as seeds are self-supplied with value null, so the composition of capital is necessarily low in agriculture, which gives rise to an excess profit proper to the agricultural sector.

The individual rate of profit is higher in agriculture than in industry because the productive forces in agriculture are lower so that the organic composition of the capital invested in agriculture is lower than in industry. The reason for this is that, while in Britain large-scale mechanical industry was widely diffused and developed from the beginning of the nineteenth century, technical innovation in agriculture (the application of natural sciences) did not progress at the same rate, and even in the time of Marx, "manual labour is [was] still relatively dominant in it" (ibid.). Marx seeks the reason for this difference between agriculture and industry in the time lag accompanying the application of production technology based on the different domains of science corresponding to the respective natures of agriculture and industry. A little after the passage quoted above, he says as follows: "Mechanics, the real scientific basis of large-scale industry, had reached a certain degree of perfection during the eighteenth century. The development of chemistry, geology, and physiology, the sciences that *directly* form the specific basis of agriculture rather than of industry, does not take place till the nineteenth century and especially the later decades" (ibid., 762. emphasis by Marx).

Thus, the relative prevalence in the productive forces between agriculture and industry as the foundation of the emergence of surplus-profit to be transformed into rent is dependent on historical conditions, variable with time. It is in observing the general tendency of agriculture up to his time that Marx says that the backwardness of the productive forces in agriculture "appears certain" (ibid., 748). He never considered this situation of agriculture to be due to any necessary reasons. Rather, he thought it possible that the advance in the productive forces in agriculture would become more rapid than in industry with advances in the application of "chemistry, geology, and physiology" to agriculture, developed in the nineteenth century in place of mechanics symbolized by the steam engine. If that happened, the organic composition in the agricultural sector would become relatively high, its surplus-profit would disappear and with it would also disappear the rent. This is precisely the conclusion that Marx drew. No sooner had he shown that a new form of rent Ricardo never conceived of can actually arise on the basis of landed property and of the inferiority of the organic composition of capital, than he sets out the possibility of its disappearance. In spite of this, Marx never excluded this form of rent and seems rather to have continued to stress its theoretical significance.

2.4. Absolute rent and differential rent

As seen above, in creating a new theory of rent while criticizing Ricardo who did not even suppose its existence, Marx simply used the same term "rent" to refer to both the rent in Ricardo's theory and his new conception of rent. However, now that the existence of two kinds of rent of very different nature had become clear, Marx seems to have felt the need to distinguish them by using different names in order to avoid confusion in the discussion. In fact, in returning again to Ricardo immediately after discussing the reason for the existence of surplus-profit in agriculture in his study of Rodbertus' book, he introduces a new term that neither he nor (probably) anyone else had never used before, in saying as follows: "modified in this way, the proposition [of Rodbertus] is correct. It explains the *existence of rent*, whereas Ricardo only explains the *existence of differential rents*"

(II/3.3, 749.emphaisis in original). Here, Marx creates a term he had never used before. The "rent" he mentions at first in saying that "it explains the *existence of rent*" is evidently of a different nature to the rent in Ricardo's theory. In order to distinguish the latter from the former, he says that "Ricardo only explains the *existence of differential rents*". What Marx calls here simply "rent" is actually a new form of rent, the existence of which he has himself just demonstrated theoretically. And in assigning to Ricardo's concept of rent the new term "differential rent", it was also necessary to give a contrasting new term to this new concept of rent of Marx, to distinguish between them.

A little after the above quotation where the term "differential rent" is first introduced, Marx returns to a critical examination of Rodbertus' theory of rent and in criticizing the latter's point that in agriculture the raw materials are used without being reckoned into the calculation of value, Marx explains that rent nevertheless arises from the particularity distinguishing agriculture from industry, as follows:

> It is not the absence of raw materials [...] which raises the value of the agricultural products above the average price [...]. Rather this is due to the higher proportion of variable to constant capital compared with that existing, not in *particular spheres of industrial production*, but *on an average* in industry as a whole. The magnitude of this *general* difference determines the amount and the existence of rent on No. I [the worst land], the absolute, non-differential rent and hence the *smallest* rent. (ibid., 754. emphasis by Marx)

This was the first time that Marx gave the new name "absolute rent"[3] to the non "differential rent". The absolute rent arising equally on the "worst land" not giving rise to differential rent is regarded as a rent arising evenly on every cultivated land. In this way, Marx introduced almost simultaneously – as a pair so to say – the names of the

---

[3] The differential rent is called "differential rent", because it is based on the difference in the productive forces of each of the cultivated lands, determined by their fertility and location. It is not difficult to understand the provenance of this appellation. In contrast, why the absolute rent is called "absolute rent" may require an explanation, but Marx does not give anything like this when beginning to use it. However, the following sentence may give a clue: "if the value of the agricultural produce is higher than its cost-price [price of production], it can pay rent quite irrespectively of differences in land, the poorest land and the poorest mine can pay the same absolute rent as the richest." (II/3.3, 957) We can see from these sentences that the absolute rent is named as such because, in contrast to the differential rent, it arises evenly (absolutely) on the basis of the differences in the conditions of production between agriculture and industry, irrespective of the differences within the agricultural sector.

two forms of rent to be distinguished, but he did not specially define them in introducing them[4] and in the subsequent parts of the manuscript, he uses both of these terms frequently as if they belonged to current vocabulary. Naturally, in the economic works of Ricardo, etc. they are not used (when rent is discussed, it is always simply called "rent". This may have caused no inconvenience since, for these other authors, rent was solely what Marx would call differential rent). These two terms were an entirely new creation of Marx at that moment. Of course, in a very few manuscripts and memoranda he wrote afterward on rent, these terms are used many times as if they belonged to a well-established vocabulary (in Chapter 6 of the "main manuscript" of Book III of *Capital*, these terms are adopted as two main titles).

The twin concepts of absolute and differential rents were created by Marx unnoticed in the mid-nineteenth century and for a long time remained buried in his manuscripts. They became widely known only after a lapse of time of 30 years. Probably, it was from about this time on that these terms came to be widely used as a part of the current economic vocabulary, along with the diffusion of Marxism. At the same time, however, no one seems to have been aware of the background to their creation or even to have known that they existed nowhere before mid-1862. Moreover, they came to be applied even to the theories of rent before Marx, including that of Ricardo, as if it were something self-evident. Today, the expression "Ricardian theory of differential rent" is accepted without resistance. We will also follow the habitual use of these terms. If we have dwelt rather insistently on the circumstances of the birth of these keywords in Marx's theory of rent and of its aftermath, it is in order to reconfirm here that these apparently forgotten circumstances were a quite significant occurrence in Marx's economic research in the manuscript of 1861–1863.

Marx arrived at the concept of absolute rent starting from a critical study of Rodbertus' book. From this point, he was going to wrestle with Ricardo's theory of rent criticized by Rodbertus. The criticism of the absence (rather than negation) of absolute rent in Ricardo's theory had to be carried out by tracing back to his theory of value and price. Marx must have considered the criticism that Ricardo's theory of rent

---

[4] A clear definition of them is given afterwards in a place far from Rodbertus as follows: "*Absolute rent* is the excess of *value* over the *average price* of raw produce. *Differential rent* is the excess of the *market-price* of the produce grown on favoured soils over the *value* of their own produce" (II/3.3, 795. emphasis by Marx).

lacked the absolute rent to be very important because this criticism
was inseparable from the theoretical horizon newly opened by him at
the beginning of the 1860s.

2.5. Anderson, Malthus, Ricardo

Certainly, Marx's critique of Ricardo's theory of rent does not limit
itself to the point seen above. The doubts and criticisms on the
"theory of differential rent of Ricardo" he had harboured since the
very early time when he had become acquainted with Anderson, in
1845, remained as they were. The problems of this kind have nothing
to do with Rodbertus, but as if dragged in by his critique of Ricardo's
theory of rent, Marx was to tackle the problems proper to Ricardo's
theory of rent for the first time since 1851. This theme was addressed
mainly in the part "Notes on the history of the discovery of the so-
called Ricardian law of rent" of "5 theories of surplus value". As this
title suggests, this part studies the prehistory of Ricardo's law (i.e., his
theory of differential rent) and clarifies the relation of Ricardo's theory to this prehistory.

It is James Anderson (1739–1808), who occupies a preponderant
place in this prehistory. Marx describes him as "the source" (II/3.3,
689) of the theory of ground rent and attempts to confirm the relation of the theories of Malthus and Ricardo with that of Anderson. It
is widely recognized that Ricardo's theory of differential rent was not
his original creation. As for the relation between Ricardo and Marx in
the theory of rent, Marx is generally considered to have added his
proper theory of absolute rent to the theory of differential rent inherited from Ricardo, thus constituting the whole of his own theory of
rent, with the reservation that Marx naturally did not accept Ricardo's
theory of differential rent as it was left by Ricardo, but supplemented
it with certain modifications and extensions. Nevertheless, the global
theoretical framework itself is considered to remain from that of
Ricardo. However, there seems to be such a great difference between
their theories that we should question whether they can both be called
with the same name of "theory of differential rent".

Here, I quote a passage in which Marx talks for the first time about
the historical place of Anderson's theory of rent: "Ricardo, it is true
was not the inventor of the theory of rent. West and Malthus had put
it into print before him. The source, however, is *Anderson*" (ibid.). In

other words, the theory of (differential) rent originating from Anderson was inherited by Ricardo via Malthus (not as it originally was, of course, but with various modifications). Indeed, Ricardo recognizes that his theory of rent in *Essay on profits* was under a preponderant influence of that of Malthus, as follows: "in all that I have said concerning the origin and progress of rent, I have briefly repeated and endeavoured to elucidate the principles which Mr. Malthus has so ably laid down, on the same subject, in his 'Inquiry into the Nature and Progress of Rent'" (Ricardo, IV/15 note). Moreover, the framework of the theory of differential rent developed by Ricardo in the first half of this pamphlet is, except for the absence of the connection with the theory of value, the same as the theory of rent in Chapter 2 "On rent" in the first edition of *Principles* published 2 years later.In contrast to Chapter 1 "On value" that was extensively amended every 2 years in the second and third editions of *Principles*, Ricardo made virtually no amendment to Chapter 2 as if there were no debate and criticism of his theory of rent. This may mean that Ricardo's theory of rent maintained until the end of his career, the original form given to it when written (in haste probably, without sufficient preparation) in February 1815.

Then, the question is how to view the relation of succession from Anderson to Malthus and finally to Ricardo. Ricardo may very probably not have known of Anderson and of his theory of rent dispersed in some of his works. Therefore, if Anderson had something to do with Ricardo's theory of rent, we can imagine that it was only via Malthus. The question then focuses on the relationship between Anderson and Malthus. On the relation between these two, Marx says as follows: "Ricardo evidently did not know Anderson since, in the preface to his *Principles of Political Economy*, he treats West and Malthus as the originators [cf. Ricardo, I/5]. [...]. With Mr. Malthus, it is different. A close comparison of his writings shows that he knows and uses Anderson" (II/3.3, 766).

Even if Malthus' theory of rent was heavily influenced by the theory of Anderson, it does not necessarily mean that Anderson's theory was made use of in its original form. In this respect, the verdict of Marx is particularly severe. "As his later polemic about rent with Ricardo shows, Malthus himself did not understand the theory he had adopted from Anderson" (ibid., 689). If Ricardo was "very much indebted" to Malthus in forming his theory of (differential) rent, it would be quite normal that the result should deviate largely from its "source". Indeed, the theory of Anderson as presented by Marx shares only one point in common with the theory of Ricardo that the difference in fertility of the soil is the basis for rent to arise and the amount of rent is determined by this difference. Since this is why a theory of rent is called the differential theory, even with this one sole point in common, it would naturally be possible to speak about the relation of succession from Anderson to Ricardo. However, with regards to how these difference arises, maintains itself (or disappears), and increases (or decreases), Ricardo adopted a position entirely different from that of Anderson. Concretely, in his theory of rent, Ricardo adopted as a matter-of-course presupposition the fixity and invariability of the fertility of the land, the law of diminishing returns and the unilateral extension of cultivation from better to worse land. In getting rid of these presuppositions, Ricardo's theory of rent could hardly be maintained. Marx tries to restore Anderson, the "source" forgotten in Ricardo, through his own reading of the former. This is the central theme for Marx in his research on differential rent in the manuscript of 1861–1863 along with his research on absolute rent beginning with the critique of Rodbertus.

2.6. Anderson and Marx's theory of differential rent

Now, Marx says as follows about how Anderson viewed the fertility of soil:

> He stated expressly that these degrees of relative productivity of *different* types of land, i.e., also the relatively low productivity of the worse types of land compared with the better, had absolutely nothing to do with the *absolute* productivity of agriculture. *On the contrary*, he stressed not only that the absolute productivity of *all* types of land could be constantly improved and must be improved with the progress in population, but he went further and asserted that the *differences* in *productivity* of various types of land can be progressively *reduced*. (II/3.3, 766. emphasis by Marx)

From Anderson's point of view, "in one country, the prices of corn may be high and rent low, while in another country, the price of corn may be low and rent may be high" (ibid., 766–767). Such a situation may be connected to the doubt Marx raised in his letter to Engels of 7 January 1851, where he wrote that the propositions in the theory of rent of Ricardo "are everywhere refuted by history" (III/4, 6). Once the variability of the fertility of land and of the difference in fertility has been recognized, the inverse movements of rent and of the price of corn will cease to be mysterious. If the fertility of the land is variable, the order of fertility of various lands and the differences between them can also vary. The price of corn will move in inverse proportion to the movement of the fertility of lands and the total amount of rent will move in proportion to the differences in their fertility, irrespective of their absolute fertility. Since the price of corn and the total amount of rent are not interlocked, they are independent of each other. The rise in the price of corn necessarily accompanied by the rise in rent, the case supposed by Ricardo, can never be a universal one. "So far as the material is concerned, which Anderson *examined, within the confines of the specific subject he was considering, this was decidedly more extensive than Ricardo's.* [...] in the theory of rent, the reproduction of Anderson's theory, he considered only the economic phenomena relating to the rise in corn prices between 1800 and 1815" (II/3.3, 776. emphasis by Marx).

Marx also emphasizes in other places (cf. ibid., 880) that the historical background for Ricardo's theory of rent was in this way a very narrow and specific situation, only a "status quo in Britain" for him. In widening the range of observation to the entire eighteenth century as Anderson did, a different situation becomes visible. The critical study of Ricardo's theory of differential rent that Marx made in "notes on the history of the discovery of the so-called Ricardian law of rent", based on the works of Anderson, may have been an attempt to definitively settling the doubts he had held from a far earlier time in the 1840s and the 1850s.

Incidentally, in the manuscript of 1861–1863, while Marx makes a multilateral critical study on Ricardo's theory of rent concerning the differential rent arising from the (extensive) extension of cultivation from better to worse lands, he hardly discusses a rent based on the diminishing returns accompanying the (intensive) extension of cultivation with successive capital investment on the same farmlands. He only briefly mentions the latter problem in the following ambiguous words: "a question which is to be later examined in connection with rent: How is it possible for rent to rise in value and in amount, with more intensive cultivation, although the rate of rent falls in relation to the capital advanced? This is obviously only possible because the *amount of capital advanced* rises" (II/3.3, 757. emphasis by Marx). In the manuscript of 1861–1863, these two forms of differential rent are not clearly distinguished with distinct appellations, only the form of rent that was later called "differential rent I" is taken up as the main subject of discussion.

3. Structure of Marx's theory of ground rent and Liebig's agro-chemistry (chapter 6 of the main manuscript of Book III of *Capital*)

3.1. Excerpts from Liebig, new agro-chemistry

While writing the manuscripts of *Capital* at a very high speed, Marx continued to read in the British Museum, taking an enormous amount of excerpts from new resources necessary for writing the manuscripts. "I have been going to the Museum in the day-time and writing at night" (MEW, Bd.31, 178). The notebook including the excerpts he accumulated during the period of writing Chapter 6 on rent in the "main manuscript", is now made available, along with the other original resources of Marx and Engels, on the internet site of the International Institute of Social History (IISG) in Amsterdam (notebook number is B106, the file number including these picture data is Marx*217*). A very voluminous notebook made up of more than 360 pages is assumed to have been filled from August or September 1865 to February 1866, nearly overlapping the period of the writing of the latter half of the "main manuscript" (Sperl 1995). Most of these excerpts are naturally from books with themes like rent, landed property, agriculture, etc. In a number of places in Chapter 6 of the "main manuscript", the excerpts included in this notebook are explicitly and implicitly made use of, so that to study Chapter 6, it is indispensable to refer to this excerpt notebook.[5] On their own, the excerpts from Liebig which comes first occupy a space of more than 100 pages in the notebook, showing how important this book was for Marx. Indeed, he repeatedly mentions Liebig's name and works in Chapter 6.

---

[5] On the contrary, during the period of tackling the theory of rent in the manuscript of 1861–1863 (the notebooks X–XII), Marx did not search for related materials at all while writing the manuscript, probably because then he got unexpectedly involved in the theory of rent. Except for the book of Rodbertus, the literature he referred to then belonged all to the materials he had already read and known before this time. Also in this sense, the writing of manuscript during the latter half of 1865, backed up with the excerpt notes made in parallel, was without precedent in Marx's study on rent.

The 7th edition of Liebig's main work (Liebig 1862) from which Marx drew long excerpts at the end of 1865 had been published 3 years before, following its previous edition published in 1846. This 7th edition was so largely reworked as to become substantially a new book. The most important change in this new edition is the 156-page long "Introduction" newly added at the beginning of the book. In these excerpts, Marx attached importance above all to this "Introduction", and it is Liebig's thought expressed in this part that he mainly mentions in his manuscript on ground rent. The following passage first quoted is from the last section in "Introduction": "Today, we know in the same way that *the soil exhausts itself exactly in proportion to the production of agricultural products* people use for their life." "The labour of farmers obeys the *natural laws*, their task is entirely the same as that of a master of the chemical factory who tries to bring the reactive matters into the best conditions in order to fabricate the desired products without costing manpower" (B106, 29, Liebig 1862, 138. emphasis by Marx). There seems to be expressed the fundamental point of view of Liebig's agro-chemistry that agricultural production is at the same time an exhaustion of land power, that the task of farmer consists in controlling rationally as a purely chemical process, the growth of plants as a kind of vital process in obeying the natural laws acting independently of their will. A little later than this, the following passage is quoted: "just in the case of letting people wastefully lose the products of the material interchange (Stoffwechsel) piled up in towns, any country will certainly become impoverished by the continual export of corn" (B106, 30, Liebig 1862, 141).

The farmland exporting food impoverishes itself because their agricultural products drawn from the land depriving it of its power are consumed by the large urban population far from the farmland and alien to agricultural production, never to be returned back to the land. According to Liebig, the "exhaustion of land" he speaks about in the first quotation progresses in this way. This becomes a noticeable phenomenon in modern agriculture as a commodity production managed capitalistically and targeting remote markets. Liebig calls these cycles between man and nature "material interchange (Stoffwechsel)", the disturbance of which he strongly denounces in the "Introduction". He calls the agriculture that brings about such disturbance "robbery cultivation (Raubbau)" (B106, 45, Liebig 1862, 106). Commercial agriculture under capitalism must become such a "robbery cultivation", because modern agriculture does not obey the "natural laws". These natural laws are: (1) "law of replenishment (Gesetz des Ersatzes)" (B106, 37, Liebig 1862, 151), and (2) "minimum law (Gesetz des Minumums)" (Liebig 1862 (zweiter Theil), 227).

Immediately after taking excerpts from Liebig's main work in the autumn of 1865, Marx refers to this work in several places in Chapter 6 of the "main manuscript", but he only reported to Engels about his global impression of this work in his letter of 13 February 1866. There he says as follows:

> I had to plough through the new agricultural chemistry in Germany, in particular Liebig and Schönbein, which is more important for this matter than all the economists put together, as well as the enormous amount of material that the French have produced since I last dealt with this point. I concluded my theoretical investigation of ground rent 2 years ago. And a great deal had been achieved, especially in the period since then, fully confirming my theory incidentally. (MEW, Bd.31, 178)

The words of general comment on Liebig are almost the same as the eulogy of him ("flashes of light more than the writings of all the modern economists put together") at the beginning of the note 325 in the 1st edition of *Capital* (II/5, 410). We can see from this that Marx then held Liebig in high esteem, just after having carefully read his work. The contents of his study up to that time of which Marx speaks here correspond with those of his excerpt notebook B106. At the end of his letter, probably in reminding himself of his research on the theory of rent in the manuscript of 1861–1863, he says that there appeared many theoretical and empirical studies on this theme from that time to 1865, in reading which he could "confirm my theory". This announcement, made after he had written a new manuscript on the theory of rent, might suggest that there had been no major change in the theory itself.

3.2. Theory of ground rent in *Chapter 6 of the "main manuscript"*

3.2.1. "a. Introduction"

Marx put an "Introduction", absent in the other chapters in the "main manuscript", at the beginning of Chapter 6, to give a general explanation of the "object and method" of his theory of ground rent. He points out the contradictions inherent in the two presuppositions of the appropriation of rent under capitalism: the private property of land and capitalist agriculture managed with the former as its indispensable element. The awareness of these contradictions clearly indicates the influence of Liebig's agro-chemistry that Marx had accepted. Agriculture, managed with the land as private property borrowed by the capitalist for a certain time, aims to sell its products as commodities at as high a price as possible to obtain profits and in pursuing this purpose, it becomes "robbery cultivation" exhausting the land in violation of the "law of replenishment", and will ultimately endanger the procurement of the staple foodstuffs indispensable for the human subsistence. In accordance with this contention of Liebig, Marx criticizes the private ownership of land as follows: "Even a whole society, a nation, or even all simultaneously existing societies taken together, are not the *owners* of the globe. They are only its *possessors*, its *usufructuaries* [fruits users], and, like boni patres familias [good family fathers], they must hand it down to succeeding generations in an improved condition" (ibid., 718. emphasis by Marx). This is precisely the opposite situation to that which arises in capitalist agriculture. With Liebig, Marx criticizes this as follows:

> Large landed property, in reducing the agricultural population to a constantly falling minimum and in confronting it with a constantly growing industrial population crowded together in large cities, creates conditions which cause an irremediable rift [unheilbaren Riß] in the material interchange [Stoffwechsel] prescribed by the natural laws of land. As a result, the power of the soil is squandered, and this prodigality is carried by commerce far beyond the borders of a particular state. (ibid., 752–753)

At the end of this last sentence, Marx adds a note with only one word: *"Liebig"*, probably to transcribe afterward from the excerpt notebook B106 a passage he then had in mind (Cf. B106, 30, 39, Liebig 1862, 141,153 [Einleitung]. Cf. B106, 94, Liebig 1862, 302. Marx emphasizes the last excerpt with a side-line on the left.).

Marx emphasized that the manufacturing only became possible with a certain development in the productive forces of agriculture (II/3.3, 676). The "free hands, as Steuart [Sir James] says" (II/4.2, 727), freed for the first time from the agricultural production in such a historical situation, came to be employed in non-agricultural spheres, which marked the beginning of the development of industry and town separated from the rural agricultural area. The development of town brings about a mass exodus of population from the rural area and at the same time extends the demand for agricultural products (food and raw materials). In such a situation, the agriculture was pressed to increase the supply in spite of the decrease in population, the agricultural products were placed constantly under the pressure of demand and price rise (Cf. ibid., 688). This served as a factor urging the productive forces in agriculture to rise. How far this rise actually went may have become an important factor governing the evolution of agricultural prices (Marx's theory of absolute rent, in which the evolution of productive forces in agriculture relative to the industry is a key factor, should be understood in such a historical context.). In any case, in such situations, an increasingly large part of the products of the land came to be consumed in towns far removed from the land, with none of the nutrients of plants taken away from it being returned to replenish the original land continuing the agricultural production. They were discharged into the rivers and finally to the sea through the water-closet and sewerage system (the development of these devices began in London during the mid-nineteenth century). Following Liebig, Marx calls the development of these processes, irreversible and on a large scale, an "irremediable rift [unheilbaren Riß]" in the "material interchange [Stoffwechsel]" and denounces it. Under capitalism, such a rift does not limit itself to a single country but develops worldwide in the form of the international commerce of primary products like food and raw materials. The theory of Ricardo and the subsequent theories of free trade, encouraging the advanced industrial countries to import primary products from the underdeveloped countries in order to avoid or postpone the fall of the rate of profit of capital in the former countries, were to be regarded from such a point of view.

3.2.2. "c. Absolute rent"

At the beginning of the part on the absolute rent, the problem to be solved is that of the "differential rent on the worst land", raised at the end of the theory of differential rent. Here, Marx starts from the assumption that the worst land does not give rise to differential rent (but what does not arise is only a differential rent but not the rent in general, as in the case of Ricardo.). This point of view seems to be held not only at the starting point of the theory of absolute rent, but also in the theory of differential rent (at least of differential rent I). "The *price of production on the worst soil*, i.e., which yields no rent, is always the one regulating the market-price" (II/4.2, 770. emphasis added). This is Marx's point of view on the differential rent on the worst land.

In his explanation of absolute rent, Marx starts from the situation in which even the landowner of the worst land with no differential rent does not lend his land at no charge but surely levies some money for the use of his land. "And landed property as a limitation continues to exist, even when rent in the form of differential rent disappears, i.e., on soil I [of the worst quality]" (ibid., 693). Even here, the farmer cannot borrow land without paying something to the landowner. However, the farmer can only get the average profit in selling his products on the worst land at the regulating market price, and if he pays some lease money in such a condition, there will be no sense for him to invest on this land. For a rent to arise here, a fund for paying it is necessary and this fund could be ensured only by raising the selling price of agricultural products. This means that, in order to manage agriculture under capitalism on the worst land, the agricultural products produced there must be sold at a price above the cost price + average profit, i.e., the regulating market price. "The general price of agricultural products would, in this case, be significantly modified" (ibid., 691). Landed property plays a decisive role in the rise of prices and the payment of a new rent. If the agricultural products are sold at a price above the regulating market price and if this can serve as a fund for a new rent payable there, they will be sold, irrespective of the classes of soil on which they are produced, at a price above the price of production on the worst land. A new rent will thus arise evenly on every kind of land independently of their qualities. This rent is called absolute rent because it arises equally on every land without any relation to its fertility.

However, if the absolute rent arises, "the differential rent would be the same as before and would be regulated by the same law" (ibid., 692), so it is evident that the theory of differential rent is the theoretical presupposition of the absolute rent. Moreover, as the absolute rent is only evenly superposed on the differential rents, the amounts of differential rents and their relations to each other will not be affected. Marx's explanation of the emergence of absolute rent begins with raising the question of how the rent on the worst soil can be paid, which is liable to give the impression that absolute rent is a phenomenon particular to the worst land. However, Marx never regards absolute rent like this. It is simply the means to explain how it arises.

The factors giving rise to the absolute rent are given by Marx as firstly the force of landed property and then the existence of value superior to the price of production in agriculture. With these two factors put together, a sufficient explanation is given of why the absolute rent becomes the income of landowners, of what is the origin of this income (Cf. ibid., 713). After discussing the latter, Marx stresses that these two factors must necessarily be obtained together. In fact, in Chapter 6 of the "main manuscript" of 1865, the term "absolute rent" is used for the first time in this context (defined, so to say).

> However, the mere existence of an excess in the *value* of agricultural products *over* their price of production would not in *itself* suffice to explain the existence of a *ground-rent* which is independent of differences in fertility of various soil types and in successive investments of capital on the same land — a *rent*, in short, which is to be distinguished in concept from differential rent and which we may, therefore, call *absolute rent* (to distinguish it from the differential rent). Quite a number of manufactured products are characterized by the fact that their *value* is *higher than* their *price of production*, without thereby yielding any excess above the average profit, or a surplus-profit, which could be converted into rent. (ibid., 702–703. emphasis by Marx)

3.2.3. "b. Differential rent", differential rent I

In contrast to the theory of absolute rent, the theory of differential rent "begins with the assumption that agricultural as well as mining products are sold at their *prices of production* like all other commodities". Marx brings into question "how it is possible for ground-rent to develop under these conditions" (II/4.2, 753). The fundamental suppositions and theme of the theory of differential rent are thus given in the first paragraph, making it explicit that the object of the theory is the rent arising in agriculture. However, from the following paragraph, it is the surplus-profit, which can arise in any sector without supposing either landed property or a particular branch of industry that is explained on the basis of the theories of prices of production and market price (value), already developed in the first two chapters of the "main manuscript". Only after that did Marx successively introduce the conditions under which the differential rent arises in agriculture. This way of explanation had never been applied before by Marx, it seems to be his original idea in this manuscript without precedent, including Ricardo. The general framework of the theory of absolute rent had already been conceived in the summer of 1862, but Marx had never positively developed his own theory of differential rent. He seems to have come to the writing of "b. Differential rent" with a strong determination to attempt the first undertaking.

The first sentence of the second paragraph is written as follows: "in order to demonstrate the general character of this form of ground-rent, let us assume that most of the factories of a certain country derive their power from steam-engines, while a smaller number derive it from *natural waterfalls*" (II/4.2, 754). A small number of factory owners who can derive free power from these "natural waterfalls" without driving steam engines can produce the same quantity of a certain kind of commodities with a lower cost than many other factory owners. And, as those who produce the same kind of commodities with steam-engines must all sell them at the above "price of production", a small number of factory owners producing at a lower cost will obtain "surplus-profit" equal to the difference between the costs paid by them and those paid by the others. This can happen because a small number of them enjoy a special advantage from the "natural waterfalls". Here the "waterfalls" are taken at random as an example, it could be any other thing as long as it brings about the same effect.

Every factory owner will naturally endeavor to obtain the extra-profit emerging in this way. And if everyone can succeed in it, this extra-profit will disappear. That is, the surplus-profit subsists precisely because it can only be obtained by some of the capitalists.

> It is by no means within the power of capital to call into existence these *natural conditions* for a greater productivity of labour in the same manner as any capital may transform water into steam. It is found only locally in nature and, not associated with the products which can be produced with labour [...], hence it cannot be established by a definite investment of capital. [...] Those manufacturers who own waterfalls exclude those who do not from using this natural force. (ibid., 758. emphasis by Marx)

For this reason, the surplus-profit can remain in the hands of a small number of factory owners enjoying exclusively a special means of production. Here, Marx says that the waterfalls are in the possession of factory owners themselves who can exploit them at no charge.

The surplus-profit arising in such a situation remains in the hands of the capitalists who first gain it. If these "natural waterfalls" are not owned by the others, it will not pass into the hands of the latter as rent.

Marx only here introduces the relation between a small number of factory owners and the possessors of these "natural waterfalls".

> Now let us assume that the waterfalls, along with the land to which they belong, are held by individuals who are regarded as owners of these portions of the earth, i.e., who are *landowners*. [...] These owners exclude the investment of capital and the exploitation of the waterfalls by capital. They can permit or forbid such utilization. But this condition cannot be created by capital out of itself. [...] Under these circumstances, the surplus-profit is transformed into *ground-rent*, that is, it falls into possession of the owner of a waterfall. (ibid., 759. emphasis by Marx)

Only after these developments is the differential rent defined as follows: "this rent is always a *differential rent*. [...] It invariably arises from the *difference* between the individual *production price* of a capital having command over the natural force that can be monopolized, [...] and the *general production price* of the total capital invested in the sphere of production concerned" (ibid. emphasis by Marx). Since the differential rent arises from the difference in the productive force, which cannot be dissolved by the competition between capitals, it is not the productive force of nature in itself that gives rise to this rent. This must be emphasized as a critique of the erroneous view (also shared by Smith and Malthus) that looks for the origin of rent in the prodigality of nature. "The *natural force* is not the source of surplus-profit, but only its *natural basis*, because [it is a] *natural basis* of an exceptionally heightened productive force of social labour" (ibid., 760).

According to Marx, the capitalist enjoying exclusively the natural conditions giving rise to an exceptional productive force draws a surplus-profit as the fund for paying rent, not in producing a greater quantity of products to sell in taking advantage of this productive force, but in lowering the cost of production and hence his individual price of production. The rent arises not "from the mass" of agricultural products but precisely "from their price" (ibid., 729). In supposing, not a decrease in the productive force like Ricardo, but the case of its increase, Marx deduces the differential rent from the difference in productive force and the ensuing difference in price. The rent arises just because it is exceptional and exclusive, giving rise to the difference.

Up to this point, Marx's reasoning about the differential rent has been developed in supposing that it applies to any branch of production provided that certain conditions are met. It is only after giving the general "definition" of differential rent seen above, that he says as follows: "now that we have described the general concept of differential rent, we shall pass on to its consideration in agriculture proper" (ibid., 761). He thus enters finally into the proper subject of the theory of differential rent, beginning with the differential rent I. At the same time, the example of "waterfalls" which had played a major role is abandoned and instead, different kinds of lands as the fundamental means of production indispensable to agriculture are to play an essential role. This manner of theoretical development is not possible for the theory of absolute rent starting from the contrast between agriculture and industry; from the outset, it had to be a phenomenon specific to agriculture.

First, Marx refers to Ricardo's theory and affirms that he is "quite right" (ibid., 761) in that, according to him, the rent arises from the difference between the conditions of production in agriculture, that it moves upward or downward according to the parallel movement of this difference. This indicates that Ricardo and Marx both adopt the same theory of differential rent originating from Anderson as its "source" (II/3.3, 689), sharing certain common points. However, soon after summarily confirming these points, which Marx recognizes as "right", he emphasizes on the contrary the differences between his theory and that of Ricardo, in saying that "having made these preliminary remarks, I will first present a brief summary of the characteristic features of *my* analysis in contradistinction to that of Ricardo, etc." (II/4.2, 762. emphasis by Marx). This difference concerns how to apprehend the fertility of the land, which plays the decisive role in differential rent I.

To indicate distinctly his difference from Ricardo's theory of rent, Marx says about the fertility of soil as follows, clearly showing the influence of Liebig's agro-chemical theory:

> The *difference in natural fertility* depends on the difference in the *chemical composition of the top soil*, that is, on its different *plant nutrition* content. However, assuming the *chemical composition* and *natural fertility* in this respect to be the *same* for two plots of land, the actual effective fertility

differs depending on whether these elements of plant nutrition are in a *state/form* which may be more or less easily assimilated and immediately utilized for nourishing the crops. Hence, it will depend partly upon *chemical* and partly upon *mechanical* developments in agriculture to what extent the same natural fertility may be made available on the *equally fertile soils. Fertility,* although an objective property of the soil, always implies economically a *relation,* a relation to the existing chemical and mechanical *level of development* in agriculture, and, therefore, *changes* with this level of development. (ibid. emphasis by Marx)

Therefore, with the availability of a technique capable of changing the physical and mechanical conditions of soil so as to make it easier for the crops to assimilate the nutrients contained in it, its fertility will rise. If the tempo and frequency of the development of these processes differ according to the kinds of soil, the relation of fertility between them will also become different. If this really occurs, the ranking of different soils in their fertility also becomes only temporary and relative. Then, the extension of cultivation cannot continue in a certain order or direction. Even if it did go in a certain direction, it would only be in some particular historical or geographical situations. "This shows once again that *historically,* in the sequence of soils taken under cultivation, one may pass over from more fertile to less fertile soils as well as vice versa" (ibid., 763–764).

Founded on this comprehension on the fertility of land endowed with a meaning only for the agriculture actually performed in a certain historical environment, and implicitly criticizing Ricardo's theory of rent, Marx says the following about how the differential rent arises:

Differential rent arises from *differences* in the *natural fertility* of the soil which is *given* for every given stage of agricultural development (leaving aside the question of location); in other words, from the limited area of the best land, and from the circumstance that equal amounts of capital must be invested on *unequal* types of soil, so that an unequal product results from the same amount of capital. (ibid., 770. emphasis by Marx)

Marx agrees with Ricardo in thinking that the differential rent arises under the condition of different fertilities of land, but these fertilities are only given "for every given stage of agricultural development". Marx's theory of differential rent is habitually understood to follow on from Ricardo's theory of rent, but their differences seem far more important.

3.2.4. "b. Differential rent", differential rent II

There are two forms of differential rent ordered from I to II and they are explained in turn, in this order. First, Marx raises problems concerning the differential rent II as follows: "In the last analysis, however, *differential rent* was by its nature merely the result of the different productivity of *equal capitals* invested in land." Therefore, the case in which "*capitals* of different productivity are invested *successively* in the *same* plot of land" (ibid., 778–779. emphasis by Marx) can be called differential rent, in the same way as differential rent I. Here too, Marx confirms that differential rent I does not arise on the worst land. The differential rent is a rent based on "the different productivity of *equal capitals*", in this point the differential rent II is the same as I. The difference is in the form of successive investments of capital.

Since only the difference in productivity is required for the differential rent to arise, it is irrelevant whether this difference is caused by a rise or a fall in productivity. However, in the tradition of the English political economy, the "law of diminishing returns" supposing in such a case a unilateral fall in the productivity was "repeated as a school dogma which had already become a commonplace" (II/5, 413). Marx had held doubts about this supposition since as early as the 1840s. In the consideration on differential rent II, he did not suppose a unilateral fall in the productivity obtained from successive investments of capital on the same land, but he supposed various cases of stationary, rising and falling productivity. Diminishing returns were not excluded but reserved as an object of examination as a possible case.

This stance of Marx in regard to the "law of diminishing returns" made the composition of the theory of differential rent II far more complicated than that of differential rent I, and at the same time made the part of the manuscript dedicated to it quite confused. For this reason, the former grew far longer than the latter, as a result, the theory of differential rent occupied a space considerably larger than that of the absolute rent. In addition, when published by Engels, the theory of differential rent was placed before the theory of absolute rent. The latter was thus overshadowed by the former, which seems to have had a considerable influence on the later reception of Marx's theory of ground rent.

Now, in the case of differential rent I, because each lease contract is concluded for a plot of land of a certain kind and area in supposing a certain amount of capital investment, it may be possible to include in the contract a fixed sum of annual rent calculated on the latest experience of cultivation on that land. The differential rent II is due to an additional surplus-value to be transformed into rent, newly realized by an additional capital investment made in the course of the lease contract concluded as above.[6] We can see from this that differential rent I is the basis of II and that without the former the latter cannot exist and this is also the reason for which the rent called differential rent I is explained first. In the transformation of additional surplus-profit arising in this way into differential rent II, there exist particular difficulties not to be seen in differential rent 1.

> In any case *rent* is fixed when land is leased, and after that the surplus-profit arising from successive investments of capital flows into the pockets of the tenant as long as the *lease* lasts. This is why the tenants have fought for long *leases*, and, on the other hand, due to the greater power of the landlords, an increase in the number of tenancies at will has taken place, i.e., leases which can be cancelled annually. It is therefore evident from the very outset that, even if immaterial for the law of *formation of surplus-profit*, it makes a considerable difference for the *transformation of surplus-profit into ground-rent* whether *equal capitals* are invested *side by side with unequal results*, or whether they are invested *successively on the same land*. The latter method confines this transformation within narrower and more variable limits. (II/4.2, 779–780. emphasis by Marx)

The landowner will attempt to make the tenant farmer pay (if possible the whole of) the surplus-profit the latter raises from his land as rent. For this, the former will continually monitor the behavior of the latter after the conclusion of their contract, to know whether the latter is obtaining a surplus-profit higher than that corresponding to the rent fixed in the contract. On the other hand, the tenant farmer, insofar as he regularly pays the rent after having concluded the lease contract, will consider himself free to increase his profit on the leased land and regard as unjustifiable the surveillance and the additional claim from the landowner.

---

[6] If such an additional investment is already foreseen at the moment of the conclusion of the lease contract, it is substantially not an addition but simply an augmentation of the amount of capital fixed in the contract, hence the rent paid on the basis of such a contract is included in the category of differential rent I. Therefore, differential rent II should necessarily be considered as arising as a result of additional capital investment made ex-post during the period of the contract.

For the landowner placed in such a situation, the opportunity to claim a satisfactory sum of the rent arises when the contract is renewed. Thus, the conflict between landowner and farmer about the period of lease contract continues. However, in any event, the review of the sum of rent at the moment of renewal of the contract is inevitable. If the behavior of tenant farmer increasing the amount of capital investment during the period of the contract becomes general, the sum of rent will be raised every time the contract is renewed. However, this means at the same time that the amount of capital investment foreseen at the moment of agreeing on the contract will gradually rise (Cf. ibid., 786, 812). "In so far as the formation of surplus-profit is determined by the magnitude of operating capital, the *amount of rent* for a certain amount of operating capital is added to the *average rent* of the country and thus provision is made for the new tenant to command sufficient capital to continue cultivation in the same intensive manner.' (ibid., 780. emphasis by Marx) In this way, every time the lease contract is renewed, the additional surplus-profit obtained during the foregoing period to be transformed into differential rent II will become a part of the new differential rent, i.e., differential rent I. As seen above, differential rent II arises on the basis of differential rent I. Here, it becomes clear that the former is of an unstable nature (Cf. ibid., 812–813), constantly returned back or "transformed back" (ibid., 817) to the latter as its foundation.

Under a small subtitle "*Successive capital investment on the worst land A). (Differential rent on the worst land A.)*" (II/4.2, 827), Marx assigns this theme to the last part of his manuscript on the theory of rent. In several points in his manuscript on rent, Marx made clear that he rejected the existence of differential rent on the worst land. However, in actually tackling this problem here, he seems to have arrived at a somewhat different result.

As the productivity of the capital finally invested on the worst land has itself the function of defining the extent to which the capital investment on the other lands can expand, in order for a further additional investment on this worst land to be made, the same change in the market conditions is required, which gave rise to the last investment made (setting the current regulating price of production), i.e., a price rise caused by increasing demand and insufficient supply. In such situations, similar additional investments (which were impossible before the rise in the price of agricultural products) may possibly also occur on the other better lands earlier than on the worst land. "It is assumed in both cases that the increased production is required to meet demand" (ibid., 830). When such an investment is made, differential rent II arises on all the portions of capital invested beforehand on the worst land. This is the "differential rent also on the worst cultivated soil" (title of Chapter 44 in Engels' edition).

In Engels' edition, the theory of absolute rent beginning with the assumption that "differential rent does not arise on the worst soil" immediately follows the theory of differential rent ending with such a result. There is a certain discrepancy in the logical juncture between them. If he could somehow have rewritten the manuscript on rent afterward, Marx would have taken some measures, but he could only leave it as it was. In view of such a serious logical inconsistency remaining at the main turning point in the theory, the manuscript of 1865, despite being Marx's only systematic exposition on rent, is far from its final version. It would be more adequate to regard it as a record of one stage in the long process of his research on the theory of ground rent.

4. Final remarks

In the last section of the present article, we have analyzed Marx's theory of ground rent as it is developed in Chapter 6 of the "main manuscript" for Book III of *Capital*, written at the end of 1865. *Capital*, composed of 3 Books, was conceived by Marx as the very first part in "Critique of political economy", to be followed by "Wage-labour", "Landed property" etc. according to the plan, he had sketched and maintained at least in its outline since the end of 1850s. Hence, he did "not intend to give a detailed exposition of rent till dealing with landed property *ex professo*" (II/3.3, 907), either in the manuscript of 1861–1863 or in the "main manuscript" of 1865. His researches on the ground rent in these manuscripts should, therefore, be understood as its anticipated partial treatment for definite purposes − − − "illustration" of the theory of price of production or "transformation of (surplus-)profit" along with interest − − −. As a matter of fact, Chapter 6 of the "main manuscript" was to be the only draft on the theory of rent Marx left to posterity, with a certain systematic character developing logically the two forms of rent.

These two forms − − − differential rent and absolute rent − − − are integrated and developed in the same chapter of the "main manuscript" respectively as the constituent parts making up a unitary theory, to become known afterwards as "Part VI" of Book III of *Capital*, embodying "Marx's theory of ground rent", in spite of the remaining serious discrepancy seen just above. However, Marx became acquainted with each of these forms of rent and examined them on different occasions at far distant times.

As for differential rent, he came across the works of James Anderson very early, in 1845, before reading Ricardo's original text, and continued the critical study of the latter's theory intermittently for a long time. In the literature, Marx's theory of differential rent tends to be seen as affiliated (though not always directly) to Ricardo, but it seems rather their differences that should be emphasized, and instead of Ricardo, it is Anderson who played a key role in the theory of differential rent of Marx, who always drew explicitly and implicitly on the points Anderson had advanced in his works earlier than Ricardo. Unfortunately, the theory of rent in Anderson's works was not well known before and after Marx (Cf. McCulloch 1845; Anderson 1893). It was rather Marx himself who dug through Anderson's various works to discover his theory of rent scattered through them. These efforts of him are recorded in the manuscript of 1861–1863. In spite of his long commitment, it was rather the theory of differential rent that entailed difficulties for Marx when he tried to develop it positively in Chapter 6 of the "main manuscript".

By contrast, the idea for absolute rent was inspired by accident by Rodbertus' critique of Ricardo's theory of rent. It was equally by accident that the suggestions given by Rodbertus' work led Marx to conceive a new form of rent totally absent in the theory of Ricardo. This was made possible because Marx had elaborated in advance the notion of the price of production based on his theory of value, a few months before he was to tackle accidentally the work of Rodbertus during a very short time from mid-June to the beginning of August 1862. In this context, Marx attached much importance to this unexpected discovery of absolute rent, incidental upon the elaboration of the concept of price of production, and decided to include certain elements of the theory of rent into a chapter in the new book he was just preparing, *Capital*.

Together with Anderson, it is Liebig who played an essential role in Marx's theory of rent in the manuscript of 1865, since his new agro-chemistry became known to Marx just before he set about writing it. Liebig's critical view of modern agriculture under capitalism profoundly influenced Marx's whole theory of rent; he totally accepted it and valued it very highly. However, as his studies on the debate about Liebig's agro-chemistry in Germany after 1862 progressed after the publication of Book I of *Capital* in 1867, this high esteem became qualified: in a note on Liebig, Marx changed his praise from "flashes of light more than the writings of all the modern economists put together" in the first edition, to simply "flashes of light" in the second edition of 1872 (II/6, 477). In any case, Marx continued to take excerpts in reading books on the related natural sciences, aiming at least partly at further elaborating his theory of ground rent, till the last years of his life.

In this way, for Marx, even after 1865, the theory of rent was still to be elaborated, and for this purpose, he wrote some fragments on differential rent during the late 1860s and 1870s. (Cf. II/4.3, 235–243, II/14, 151–152). He continued to take excerpts on landed property and rent from Russian literature. (Cf. II/15, 10) Ultimately, however, all these efforts in his later years did not result in a new manuscript on rent. In such conditions, we can only conjecture what would have been "Marx's theory of rent" from the original materials published or still to be published in new MEGA volumes.

Marx addressed the problems concerning the ground rent for a very long time, during almost the entire period of his economic research. The present article has concentrated on the first half of the 1860s, no doubt the most important period. If it could bring to the fore some points in Marx's unaccomplished theory of rent that have hitherto remained obscure, its objective may be said to have been achieved.

Acknowledgements

The first version of this article was prepared for and presented at the international conference on Marx held in Lyon from the 27th to the 29th September 2017. The author is grateful to the participants of the session on "Ground rent — Falling rate of profit" for their helpful questions and comments. In preparing for the publication in this special issue of EJHET of the abridged version of the original paper, the author could greatly benefit from the helpful comments and suggestions given by the two anonymous referees. If some of the errors and insufficiencies contained in the former versions have been eliminated, it is solely thanks to their help. Evidently, the usual disclaimer applies.

Disclosure statement

No potential conflict of interest was reported by the author.

References

Anderson, James. 1893. "Drei Schriften über Korngesetze und Grundrente mit Einleitung und Anmerkungen von Lujo Brentano." In *Sammlung älterer und neuerer staatswissenschaftlicher Schriften des In- und Auslandes*, edited by Lujo Brentano and Emanuel Leser. No. 4. Leipzig: Duncker & Humbolt.

Liebig, Justus von. 1862. *Die Chemie in Ihrer Anwendung auf Agricultur und Physiologie*. 7te Auflage. Braunschweig: Friedrich Vieweg und Sohn.

Marx, Karl/Friedrich Engels Papers *217*. 2015. Inv. nr. B 106 [B 98], ARCH00860, International Institute of Social History, Amsterdam.

Marx, Karl. (II/3.3). 1978. "Zur Kritik der Politischen Ökonomie (Manuskript 1861–1863), Teil 3." In *Karl Marx Friedrich Engels Gesamtausgabe (MEGA), 2te Abteilung: „Das Capital" und Vorarbeiten*, Band 3.3. Berlin: Dietz.

Marx, Karl (II/4.2). 1992. "Ökonomische Manuskripte 1863–1867, Teil 2". In *Karl Marx Friedrich Engels Gesamtausgabe (MEGA), 2te Abteilung: „Das Kapital" und Vorarbeiten*, Band 4.2. Berlin: Dietz.

Marx, Karl (II/4.3). 2012. "Ökonomische Manuskripte 1863–1868, Teil 3". In *Karl Marx Friedrich Engels Gesamtausgabe (MEGA), 2te Abteilung: „Das Kapital" und Vorarbeiten*, Band 4.3. Berlin: Akademie.

Marx, Karl (II/5). 1983. "Das Kapital. Kritik der Politischen Ökonomie. Erster Band, Hamburg 1867." In *Karl Marx Friedrich Engels Gesamtausgabe (MEGA), 2te Abteilung: „Das Capital" und Vorarbeiten*, Band 5. Berlin: Dietz.

Marx, Karl (II/6). 1987. "Das Kapital. Kritik der Politischen Ökonomie. Erster Band, Hamburg 1872". In *Karl Marx Friedrich Engels Gesamtausgabe (MEGA), 2te Abteilung: „Das Capital" und Vorarbeiten*, Band 6. Berlin: Dietz.

Marx, Karl (II/14). 2003. "Manuskripte und Redaktionelle Texte des „Kapitals"1871 bis 1895". In *Karl Marx Friedrich Engels Gesamtausgabe (MEGA), 2te Abteilung: „Das Capital" und Vorarbeiten*, Band 14. Berlin: Akademie.

Marx, Karl (II/15). 2004. "Das Kapital. Kritik der Politischen Ökonomie. Dritter Band, Hamburg 1894". In *Karl Marx Friedrich Engels Gesamtausgabe (MEGA), 2te Abteilung: „Das Capital" und Vorarbeiten*, Band 15. Berlin: Akademie.

Marx, Karl, and Friedrich Engels. (III/4). 1984. "Briefwechsel, Januar bis Dezember 1851". In *Karl Marx Friedrich Engels Gesamtausgabe (MEGA), 3te Abteilung: Briefwechsel*, Band 4. Berlin: Dietz.

Marx, Karl, and Friedrich Engels. (III/12). 2013. "Briefwechsel, Januar 1862 bis September 1864". In *Karl Marx Friedrich Engels Gesamtausgabe (MEGA), 3te Abteilung: Briefwechsel, Band 12*. Berlin: Akademie.

Marx, Karl, and Friedrich Engels. (MEW, Bd.31). 1965. "Briefwechsel von 1864 bis 1867". In *Karl Marx – Friedrich Engels Werke Band 31*. Berlin: Dietz.

Marx, Karl (IV/4). 1988. "Exzerpte und Notizen, Marginalien, Juli bis August 1845". In *Karl Marx Friedrich Engels Gesamtausgabe (MEGA), 4te Abteilung, Band 4*. Berlin: Dietz.

Marx, Karl (IV/5). 2015. "Exzerpte und Notizen, Juli 1845 bis Dezember 1850". In *Karl Marx Friedrich Engels Gesamtausgabe (MEGA), 4te Abteilung, Band 5*. Oldenburg: De Gruyter.

McCulloch, John Ramsay. 1845. *The Literature of Political Economy: a Classified Catalogue of Select Publications in the Different Department of that Science, with Historical, Critical, and Biographical Notices*. London: Longman.

Müller, Manfred, and Wolfgang Focke. 1984. "Wann Entstand das '3. Capitel: Capital und Profit', das in Marx' Manuskript 'Zur Kritik der politischen Ökonomie' von 1861 bis 1863 enthalten ist?" *Beiträge zur Marx-Engels-Forschung* 16: 175–179.

Ohmura [Omura], Izumi. 1984. "Über die Entstehungsphasen des 'Dritten Capitel. Capital und Profit' und die Miscellanea: Dezember 1862 oder Dezember 1861?" *Beiträge zur Marx-Engels-Forschung* 16: 180–185.

Omura, Izumi. 1998. *Shin MEGA to Shihonron no Seiritsu (in Japanese) [New MEGA and the Making of Capital]*. Tokyo: Hassakusha.

Ricardo, David. (Ricardo, IV), 1951. *An essay on the influence of a low price of corn on the profits of stock etc.*, London 1815. In *The works and correspondence of David Ricardo*, edited by Piero Sraffa with the collaboration of M. H. Dobb, Vol. IV. Cambridge: Cambridge University Press.

Ricardo, David. (Ricardo, I) 1951. *On the principles of political economy and taxation*, London 1817–21. In *The works and correspondence of David Ricardo*, edited by Piero Sraffa with the collaboration of M. H. Dobb, Vol. I. Cambridge: Cambridge University Press.

Rodbertus, Johann Karl. 1851. *Sociale Briefe an von Kirchmann von Rodbertus. Dritter Brief: Widerlegung der Ricardo'schen Lehre von der Grundrente und Begründung einer neuen Rententheorie*. Berlin: Allgemeine Deutsche Verlags-Anstalt.

Sperl, Richard. 1995. *Allgemeiner Prospekt der Bände IV/10 bis IV/32 (Neufassung)*, mimeo.

Is Marx's absolute rent due to a monopoly price?

Saverio M. Fratini ⓘ

ABSTRACT

Absolute rent, in Marx's view, has an upper limit represented by the difference between the value and the price of production of agricultural commodities. The relevance of this limit was questioned by Bortkiewicz because of the difficulties concerning the argument which Marx based it on. The lack of this upper limit prompted some scholars to claim that there is no difference between absolute rent and a rent paid by a monopoly price. Referring to the classical/Marxian theory of monopoly price, we shall argue that it is still possible to distinguish absolute rent from a rent due to a monopoly price.

1. Introduction

In Marx's analysis of ground-rent, agricultural extra-profits are (partially or totally) converted into rent – i.e., appropriated by landlords – due to the class monopoly of private ownership of land.[1] Looking at the mechanism that makes those extra-profits arise, Marx distinguished four

---

[1] In his analysis of ground-rent, Marx claims several times that it has "the monopoly of private owner-ship in land" as its premise. In the capitalist mode of production, every kind of rent – absolute, differen-tial or monopoly – is based on the existence of a class of landowners that is distinct from the class of capitalists and comes into conflict with it, succeeding in intercepting a part of the social surplus-value. In Marx's view, the class monopoly of private ownership of land is therefore a premise for rent just as the class monopoly of the private property of the means of production is the premise for profit. In this sense, the monopoly of soil by the class of landowners is not antithetical to the free competition of products on the market, but rather to the free use of land by capitalists (and workers).

As emphasized by Gehrke (2014), who also refers to Negishi (1985):

the word 'monopoly' should be interpreted here, not in the modern sense that capitalists or landowners act jointly so as to maximize common gains, but in the classical or Marxian sense of an exclusive access to means of production by some specific class. (Gehrke 2014, 125)

According to Piccioni (2014, 63), these different interpretations of the word "monopoly" have their origins in Smith's analysis.

different kinds of rent: extensive differential rent (differential rent I); intensive differential rent (differential rent II); absolute rent; monopoly rent (rent "due to an actual monopoly price").

According to Marx's analysis (that we shall summarise in Section 2), absolute rent is closely related to free competition and the resulting tendency of the rate of profit to reach the same level in every sector of the economy. In particular, if (1) the organic composition of capital in the agricultural sector is lower than the organic composition of capital in the industrial sector and (2) landed property can act as a barrier for the investment of capital in agriculture, then the equality of the rate of profit in the two macro-sectors can be obtained through the transformation of agricultural extra-profit into absolute rent and its appropriation by landlords. In this way, the price of agricultural products does not fall – and can remain equal to the value – notwithstanding the low organic composition of capital in agriculture.

Since Marx's theory of absolute rent is tied to the mechanism of transformation of values into prices, the critiques that affected the Marxian transformation problem, indirectly affected absolute-rent theory as well. In particular, as Marx indicates the difference between value and price of production as the upper limit of absolute rent, once it became clear that the link between values and prices was not of the kind Marx claimed, the existence of a limit was questioned.

Bortkiewicz (1910–11) was the first to develop a critique of Marx's theory of absolute rent along those lines and his position is reported in Section 3. At the cost of a drastic simplification, the point can be summed up as follows: if the class of landlords is able to intercept a part of the social surplus-value by raising a barrier against the investment of capital on land, then there is no reason why the level of absolute rent should be limited by the difference between the value of agricultural products and their price of production.

The same point was taken-up again by Emmanuel (1972) and the lack of the upper limit indicated by Marx for absolute rent prompted a number of scholars to regard it as essentially equivalent to monopoly rent. A brief survey of some different positions about the interpretation of absolute rent as due to a monopoly price will be presented in Section 4.

It is, therefore, necessary to highlight the fundamental features of monopoly price within the classical/Marxian framework. This will be done in Section 5, where we shall consider some common elements of the theories of monopoly price by Smith, Ricardo and Marx. On the basis of this consideration, we shall see that absolute rent cannot be considered as a rent due to a monopoly price, notwithstanding the lack of the limit represented by the labour-value of the products of the soil.

Some conclusions will be drawn in Section 6.

2. Marx's absolute rent

2.1 Absolute rent and the transformation of values into prices

Marx's theory of absolute rent is closely tied to the mechanism of capitalistic competition that tends to level the rate of profit in different sectors and to push it toward the general rate of profit. A detailed analysis of this competitive process is outside the scope of the present paper and therefore we shall simply recall some fundamental elements.

The investment of capital, both in each sector and in the economy as a whole, is made up of two parts: variable capital V (wages paid in advance) and constant capital C (namely the outlay for the means of production: machinery, raw materials, tools, ...). The general rate of profit of the economy, π, results from the ratio between the social amount of surplus-value S and the total amount of capital $V + C$, both expressed in terms of labour-value. Therefore, it depends on the rate of surplus-value S/V and on the average organic composition of capital C/V:

$$\pi = \frac{S}{V + C} = \frac{\frac{S}{V}}{1 + \frac{C}{V}}. \tag{1}$$

Assuming that one unit of labour is paid the same wage in different sectors,[2] the rate of surplus-value will be uniform across sectors. This is due to the fact that both the surplus-value obtained and the variable capital invested are proportional to the employment of (living) labour. Accordingly, if commodities were traded on the basis of their labour-value, then, in the sectors in which the organic composition of capital is lower than average, the rate of profit would be above the general rate π, whereas it would be below π in those sectors with an organic composition

---

[2] As is known, in the classical/Marxian approach, the heterogeneity of the quality of labour can be managed by the structure of wage rates, which is taken as given, in this approach, in order to determine the rate of profit. There is therefore no harm in referring to homogenous labour, cf. in particular, Ricardo (1951, 20–21) and Garegnani (1984, 293, footnote 5).

of capital higher than the average.[3] Therefore, capitalists would move their capital from the latter to the former. Since this movement makes the quantities of commodities brought to market change, it affects their market prices as well. In turn, the change of the relative prices involves a redistribution of the surplus-value from the sectors with a low organic composition of capital toward those with a high organic composition of capital.

This process will come to rest when, in every sector, the prices allow the payment of profits according to the general rate π. Marx calls these prices "prices of production". The price of production is, clearly, below the value for those commodities produced with a low organic composition of capital and is above the value in the opposite case.

Coming back to absolute rent, in Marx's view, it derives from the fact that landed property constitutes an obstacle to the process of capitalistic competition outlined above. In particular, Marx's analysis starts from the assumption that agricultural products are obtained by means of capital with organic composition lower than the one of the capital invested in the industrial sector.[4] Because of this assumption, the agricultural sector initially generates extra-profits and thus attracts more capital as a result. Since further investment of capital in agriculture – with unchanged methods of production – brings about the tilling of new land, it cannot take place without the landowners' permission. Thus, by making the cultivation of new land conditional upon the payment of a certain rent, landowners are able to intercept at least a part of the agricultural extra-profits.

Landed property thus ensures that a share of the agricultural surplus-value will be removed from the mechanism that tends to distribute it

---

[3] Since the capitals invested in the various lines of production are of a different organic composition, and since the different percentages of the variable portions of these total capitals set in motion very different quantities of labor, it follows that these capitals appropriate very different quantities of surplus-labor, or produce very different quantities of surplus-value. Consequently, the rates of profit prevailing in the various lines of production are originally very different. (*Capital III*, 186)

[4] On the low organic composition of capital in agriculture, Marx writes:

If the composition of the capital in agriculture proper is lower than that of the social average capital, then this would be on its face an expression of the fact that in countries with a developed production agriculture has not progressed as far as the industries which work up its products. This fact could be explained, aside from all other economic circumstances which are of paramount importance, from the earlier and more rapid development of mechanical sciences, and especially by their application, compared to the later and partly quite recent development of chemistry, geology and physiology, and particularly their application to agriculture. (*Capital III*, 882)

Table 1. Values and prices of production.

Sector	Constant capital	Variable capital	Surplus-value	Value	Price of prod.
Agriculture	75	25	25	125	120
Industry	85	15	15	115	120

among industries in proportion to the employment of capital. In fact, on the one hand, the low organic composition of capital causes an excess of surplus-value above the ordinary profit – an extra-profit – to arise in agriculture. On the other, the right of property, which gives to landowners the right to withdraw their lands from exploitation, allows them to intercept this excess (or a part of it) in the form of absolute rent.

2.2 An example

In order to enter into the mechanism of determination of the (maximum) amount of absolute rent, let us follow the numerical example provided by Marx (*Capital III*, 886–887),[5] whose data are shown in Table 1.

In Marx's example, of every 100 units of capital (in terms of labour-value) invested in agriculture, 75 are constant capital and 25 are variable capital, while in the industrial sector, 85 are constant capital and 15 variable capital. Assuming that the rate of surplus-value is 100% in both sectors, the value of the agricultural output obtained by 100 of capital is 125 and the value of the industrial one is 115.

In consequence of the different organic composition of capital in the two sectors, with commodities initially traded at their values, the rate of profit on the capital invested in agriculture (25%) will be higher than the rate of profit on industrial capital (15%). In this case, if agriculture was like any other sector, then there would be an increase in the investment of capital in agriculture causing an increase in the output of agricultural products and a fall of their market price. The opposite would happen with reference to the industrial products. This process would stop when the commodities are traded at their prices of production, namely the prices that allow to remunerate capital, in both sectors, by the general rate of

---

[5] A similar numerical example is also given by Marx in the *Theories of Surplus Value* (*Theories II*, 605).

Table 2. Profits, rents and regulating market prices.

Sector	Constant capital	Variable capital	Profit	Rent	Market price
Agriculture	75	25	15	10	125
Industry	85	15	15	0	115

profit: 40/200 = 20%. Therefore, the agricultural products would be sold below, and the industrial products above their value.

However, agriculture is not a sector like any other. The private owner-ship of land represents a barrier against the investment of capital upon uncultivated soil. New land cannot be tilled until the barrier is removed by the payment of rent. In particular, according to Marx's argument, land-owners can intercept as absolute rent up to the entire difference of the surplus-values generated by 100 of capital in the two sectors, namely 25 − 15 = 10. In this way, a part of the agricultural surplus-value is with-drawn from the pool of profits, i.e., from the mechanism that tends to dis-tribute the social surplus-value across sectors in proportion to the investment of capital; therefore, the general rate of profit is lower than the previous case – 30/200 = 15% instead of 20%. The regulating market pri-ces can then remain equal to the values – as shown in Table 2 – while the capital invested in the two sectors receives the same rate of profit, being the entire amount of agricultural extra-profits converted into abso-lute rent.

2.3 The limits of absolute rent

The difference between the value of the agricultural output and its price of production – due to the fact that agricultural organic composition of capi-tal is below the average – represents the theoretical maximum amount of absolute rent. When absolute rent is set within this limit, then (1) it is "a portion of the agricultural surplus-value" (*Capital III*, 887) and (2) it does not prevent the same rate of profit of industrial capital from being realized in agriculture too. Therefore, in Marx's view, if this difference was nil, there would be no room for absolute rent:

> If the average composition of the agricultural capital were the same, or higher than that of social average capital, then absolute rent, in the sense in which we use this term, would disappear; that is, absolute rent which is different from dif-ferential rent as well as from the rent which rests upon an actual monopoly

price. The value of agricultural capital would not stand above its price of production, in that case, and the agricultural capital would not set any more labor
in motion, would not realize any more surplus labor, than the non-agricultural
capital. (*Capital III*, 888)

Once the theory of absolute rent has set the upper limit (and assuming
it is not nil), then its actual level will be determined by the class struggle
between capitalists and landowners and it is therefore further limited by
all those circumstances that can affect the relative strength of the two
sides. In particular, Marx highlights a number of circumstances that may
act in this way and we can try to list some of them.

First, there is the possibility of furthering investments of capital in the
"old leaseholds" (cf. *Capital III*, 873–877). With the aim of fostering the
investment of fixed capital in land (vineyards, plantations, irrigation systems, ...), it is in fact standard practice to let land on a lease for a period
of years with conditions set contractually at the beginning. During the
lease period, the capitalist tenant can invest more capital on the land without altering the conditions of lease agreed at the beginning. Accordingly,
when an increase in the demand for agricultural commodities takes place,
there can be an intensification of the cultivation on the old leaseholds
instead of tilling new land. This possibility – which is, in turn, limited by
the diminishing returns of the further doses of capital on a given surface
of land – can affect the bargaining position of the owners of the last
(worst) soil under cultivation.

A second limit derives from what Marx calls "the general condition of
the market" (*Capital III*, 887), namely the circumstances that can affect
the price level of the products of the soil. In particular, the competition
arising from agricultural commodities of foreign countries can keep the
price of domestic ones low and thus curb the extra-profits upon which the
absolute rent depends.

Finally, there is the competition among landowners, which is, however,
regarded as less important. As is known, in the classical/Marxian
approach to income distribution, competition does not determine the
average or ordinary levels of the distribution variables – since they
strongly depend on social relations – but it simply pushes the actual rates
of wage, rent and profit toward their respective natural rates. In other
words, in this approach, competition starts in the event of a discrepancy
between the actual and natural levels of the distribution rates. Hence, for
Marx, those who maintain that the competition of untilled land can drive

absolute rent toward zero[6] are implicitly assuming that its natural rate is zero. He writes:

> there is always the difference in the cost of clearing for cultivation between the new soil and the last cultivated one. And it depends upon the stand of market prices and of credit whether new land is cleared or not. As soon as this soil actually enters into competition, the market price falls once more to its former level, assuming other conditions to be equal, and the new soil will then produce the same rent as the corresponding soil formerly cultivated as the last. The theory that it does not produce any rent is proved by its champions by assuming what they are precisely called upon to prove, namely that the soil which used to be the last did not pay any rent. (*Capital III*, 895–896)

On this view, the availability of untilled land of the same quality as the last cultivated soil does not bring about an automatic fall in the rate of rent. This fall can only take place if there are capitalists willing to cultivate this land and if its output increases the total supply of agricultural

---

[6] In the case of excess supply of land of the same quality as the worst soil under cultivation, the tendency of absolute rent toward zero can be argued by means of the standard market dynamics. For instance, this is done by Negishi (1989) in the following way (I am indebted to an anonymous reviewer for this quotation):

> the monopoly of landownership does not exclude the possibility that each landowner acts independently. Though Marx made some confusing statements [...], it is clear that he did not have the joint action of all the landowners in mind. For a single landowner, then, there is no reason not to invite additional investment on land when there is absolute rent, i.e., the price of the agricultural product exceeds the price of production. The joint result of such individual actions is, however, the reduction of absolute rent due to an increase in the supply of agricultural products, which continues until the absolute rent disappears. (Negishi 1989, 220)

An even stronger position is taken by Samuelson (1992), who maintains that in the absence of land scarcity there can be no rent (or, perhaps, just a small epsilon).

As an in-depth discussion of this point is beyond the goals of the present paper, we simply propose a possible objection raised by Emmanuel (1972), who writes:

> competition between landowners (like all competition, incidentally) is far from being perfect. [...] a landowner does not usually put his land up to public auction in order to lease it out without delay. He looks around at leisure to find a farmer. He cherishes hopes; the return from each plot has not been defined in centigrams by laboratory analysis and is not posted up on the doors of the Town Hall, but it is estimated subjectively. He regards it as normal to wait a while rather than 'throw away' his plot of land. He becomes stubborn—considerations of self-respect come into the matter—and prefers to lose money rather than seem to have been made a fool of. He is unreasonable. In short, he is a man, and not the infallible electronic machine that marginalists have put in the place of every economic agent. But the mere fact that every landowner is inclined to wait, and does in fact wait a certain time between one farmer and the next, and in no case agrees to go below a certain limit that he regards as equitable, for reasons that have nothing to do with objective economic laws, automatically *sterilizes* part of the supply and causes the market to reach equilibrium at a level higher than that which would have been attained if the economic agents had acted in accordance with marginalist 'rationality.' What was a subjective and irrational attitude in each one's head becomes *ex post* extremely rational and effective conduct, since this is what preserves rents, and above all that rent of the worst plot under cultivation which is an observed fact but which pure political economy has never been able to digest. (Emmanuel 1972, 221, emphasis in the original)

commodities sufficiently to cause a fall in their market prices, thus reducing the surplus profit that allows the payment of absolute rent. Hence, Marx concludes that:

> The competition of the lands among themselves does not, therefore, depend upon the wish of the landlord that they should, but upon the opportunities offered to capital for competition with other capitals upon the new fields. (*Capital III*, 896)

3. The "original law of value" and Bortkiewicz's critique of Marx's rent theory

One of the most important critical analyses of Marx's theory of absolute rent is doubtless provided by Ladislaus von Bortkiewicz in his 1910–1911 essay on Rodbertus' and Marx's theories of rent, and in a further essay of 1919.[7]

Bortkiewicz's analysis starts with an in-depth reconstruction of Marx's argument. In particular, he clearly recognises that Marx, in his discussion of the absolute-rent theory, refers to a situation of developed capitalism in which landed property – modified because of the capitalist mode of production – actually exists and is realised economically through the ground-rent.

According to Bortkiewicz, Marx is right when he says that the issue of the existence of absolute rent cannot be resolved by reference to cases in which its absence is associated with deviations from normal class relations, typical of the capitalist mode of production. One of these outliers is discussed by Marx (*Capital III*, 877–878) and refers to new colonised countries where the availability of land that is not yet private property – and can in fact be appropriated through cultivation – ensures that every farmer is also the owner of the soil he tills. In this case, it is clear that there is no resistance to the investment of capital in agriculture and, therefore, absolute rent cannot ensue. Then, Bortkiewicz writes (1971, 171) that, according to Marx – and in contrast with Rodbertus' standpoint, the presence of this form of rent needs a leasehold system of land tenure.[8]

---

[7] For an extensive discussion on Bortkiewicz's contributions on Ricardo, Rodbertus and Marx, see Gehrke (2014, 109–125).

[8] It is almost unanimously recognised that Marx's absolute rent refers to a situation in which agricultural firms are run by capitalist tenant farmers. Therefore, the thesis advanced by Ghosh (1985, 75) is rather bizarre, in that it suggests considering absolute rent as a "pre-capitalist rent".

Bortkiewicz maintains that, within Marx's theory of absolute rent, the rationale for the removal of a portion of surplus-value from the process that tends to level it in proportion to the investment of capital is the "ineffectiveness" of capitalist competition with respect to landed property.[9] But from this fact, he adds, it does not follow that the amount of absolute rent must be equal to (or at least limited by) the difference between the labour-value of agricultural produce and its price of production (calculated at the industrial rate of profit). The presence of this limit, in Bortkiewicz's reconstruction, requires two further (and different) conditions: (1) the organic composition of agricultural capital must be lower than the industrial one; (2) the "original law of value" must hold. Since we have already discussed the first condition in the previous section, we can focus here on the second.

Albeit admitting that agricultural capital has a lower organic composition than the industrial capital, Bortkiewicz writes that this is not enough to grasp the reason why the labour-value of the agricultural output must be the upper limit for the absolute rent earned by the class of landowners:

> Why should the difference between "value" and "price of production" provide a measure of absolute rent? What does this measure have to do with the reason that, in Marx's view, induces landowners to make their land available for capitalists only upon payment?
>
> [...] it is not possible to understand why the market prices of the products of the soil cannot rise even above their "values", as this increase is due to the fact that landed property has the power to prevent the subordination of agricultural products to the general rules of the capitalistic price formation and to impose deviations from these rules in its own favour. What gives "value", in a Marxian

---

[9] In a well-known passage of the *Theories of Surplus-Value*, Marx imagines that a landowner talks to a capitalist saying:

> Your law will have it that under normal circumstances, capitals of equal size appropriate equal quantities of unpaid labour and you capitalists can force each other into this position by competition among yourselves. Well, I happen to be applying this law to you. You are not to appropriate any more of the unpaid labour of your workers than you could with the same capital in any other sphere of production. But the law has nothing to do with the excess of unpaid labour which you have "produced" over the normal quota. Who is going to prevent me from appropriating this "excess"? Why should I act according to your custom and throw it into the common pot of capital to be shared out among the capitalist class, so that everyone should draw out a part of it in accordance with his share in the aggregate capital? I am not a capitalist. The condition of production which I allow you to utilise is not materialised labour but a natural phenomenon. Can you manufacture land or water or mines or coal pits? Certainly not. The means of compulsion which can be applied to you in order to make you release again a part of the surplus-labour you have managed to get hold of does not exist for me. So out with it! The only thing your brother capitalists can do is to compete against you, not against me. (*Theories II*, 41)

Also, cf. *Capital III*, 896–897.

sense, the capacity to act as a barrier here? Why does the power of landed property reach this precise point? (Bortkiewicz 1971, 172; our translation[10])

The answers to these questions, according to Bortkiewicz, are provided by
Marx in the following important passage (which we shall refer back to in
Section 5.3):

> If landed property gives the power to sell the product *above* its cost-price, at its
> value, why does it not equally well give the power to sell the product *above* its
> value, at an arbitrary monopoly price? On a small island, where there is no for-
> eign trade in corn, the corn, food, like every other product, could unquestion-
> ably be sold at a monopoly price, that is, at a price only limited by the state of
> demand, i.e., of *demand backed by ability to pay*, and according to the price
> level of the product supplied the magnitude and extent of this effective demand
> can vary greatly.
>
> Leaving out account exceptions of this kind – which cannot occur in European
> countries; even in England, a large part of the fertile land is *artificially* with-
> drawn from agriculture and from the market in general, in order to raise the
> value of the other part – landed property can only affect and paralyse the action
> of capitals, their competition, in so far as the competition of capitals modifies
> the determination of the *values of the commodities*. The conversion of values
> into cost-prices is only the consequence and result of the development of capi-
> talist production. Originally, commodities are (on the average) sold at their val-
> ues. Deviation from this is, in agriculture, prevented by landed property
> (*Theories II*, 332–333, emphases in the original).

This passage, in Bortkiewicz's view, reveals that the central point in
Marx's argument about absolute rent is that "originally commodities are
sold at their values". The answer given by Marx is deemed unsatisfactory
by Bortkiewicz since it is based on the idea that a theoretical mechanism,
such as the transformation of labour-values into prices of production, was
also a historical process.

The historical priority of the labour-values with respect to the prices of
production, which Bortkiewicz refers to as the "original law of value", is

---

10 Perché la differenza tra «valore» e «prezzo di produzione» deve fornire una misura della rendita
assoluta? Che cosa ha a che vedere con questa misura il motivo che, secondo l'esposizione di
Marx, induce il proprietario fondiario a mettere il suo terreno a disposizione del capitalista uni-
camente dietro compenso?

[...] non si può capire perché i prezzi di mercato dei prodotti del suolo non possano salire
anche al di là del loro «valore», se questo aumento deve essere condizionato dal fatto che la
proprietà fondiaria ha il potere di opporsi alla subordinazione dei prodotti agricoli alle regole
generali della formazione capitalistica dei prezzi e a imporre deviazioni a proprio favore di
queste regole. Che cos'è che conferisce al «valore», in senso marxiano, la capacità di agire qui
da barriera? Perché il potere della proprietà fondiaria arriva fino a questo preciso punto?

heavily questioned by a number of scholars. He mentions Lexis, Böhm-Bawerk, Sombart and Stolzman, who, although have different (or even opposed) "theoretical tendencies", agree in firmly rejecting the idea that commodities were "originally" traded at prices corresponding to their relative labour-values.

Besides, in his 1919 paper, Bortkiewicz also uses the theoretical criticism of the transformation problem. Contrarily to what Marx believed, there is no link between commodity values and prices of production – in particular, the sum of the values does not necessarily correspond to the sum of the prices for all the commodities. Therefore, even if the labour-values had acted as a limit level in a very early phase, this limit would have no meaning in advanced capitalist systems (cf. Bortkiewicz 1971, 186). The original law of value – even if it were true, but it is not – cannot be used, as Marx does, in order to justify the limit of absolute-rent amount due to the difference between the value and price of production of agricultural products.

Bortkiewicz's conclusion is that:

> Marx was not able to prove in any way that the concept of absolute ground-rent he formulated, understood as an excess of the value above the price of production of the agricultural products, corresponds to something real in the process of price formation. (1971, 173; our translation[11])

Therefore, according to Bortkiewicz (1971, 178), once the limit represented by the difference between the value and price of production is dismissed, Marx's argument on absolute rent becomes theoretically unsound. The conclusion is that, if the class of landowners has the power to interfere with the normal capitalistic process of price formation and earn rent from that, this rent must be deemed due to monopoly pricing.[12]

4. Absolute rent interpreted as a rent paid by monopoly price

The point raised by Bortkiewicz is made even clearer by Emmanuel (1972) by means of a numerical example. In Emmanuel's example, the

---

[11] Marx non ha saputo in alcun modo dimostrare che al concetto di rendita assoluta da lui costruito, nel senso di un'eccedenza del valore sul prezzo di produzione dei prodotti agricoli, corrisponda qualcosa di reale nel processo di formazione del prezzo.

[12] Bortkiewicz remarks pointedly that the problem cannot be easily dismissed saying that in one sector there is a monopoly price and the prices of production prevail for all the other commodities, since the presence of a monopoly situation in one sector affects the process of price formation in the other sectors too (cf. 1971, 184).

production of 200 kilos of agricultural commodities initially requires 100 francs[13] of constant capital and 50 of variable capital. If the rate of surplus-value is 100%, the value of the agricultural output is 100 + 50 + 50 = 200 francs (1 franc the kilo). Assuming 10% is the industrial rate of profit, the value of absolute rent is 35 francs – i.e., the difference between 200 and 150 (1 + 0,1). Now, Emmanuel imagines that productivity doubles and, accordingly, 200 kilos of agricultural commodities are obtained by employing 50 francs of constant capital and 25 of variable capital (and the rate of surplus-value is 100% as before). The value of 200 kilos of output is now 50 + 25 + 25 = 100 (0.50 francs the kilo) and the absolute rent is 17.50 – i.e., 100 − 75 (1 + 0,1). However, Emmanuel wonders:

> But why should the price fall from 1 franc to 0.50? [...] Why should the landlord, who is strong enough to annex the difference between price of production and value, not be strong enough to annex the difference between the new productivity and the old? Why, in the example above, could we not assume that the price would continue to be 1 franc the kilo and the farmer's profit 7.5 francs (10 percent), while the rent rose by 35 francs to 117.50, thus soaking up the entire difference? (Emmanuel 1972, 217–218)

Emmanuel's remark is clear. If, following Marx, the landowner has the power to prevent the fall of the price of the agricultural commodities when this price is greater than the price of production but less than or equal to the value, then the same power should allow the landowner to prevent a fall of the price when it is, for any possible reason, above both the price of production and the value.

Therefore, as already stressed by Bortkiewicz, Marx's arguments about the theoretical upper limit of absolute rent cannot be considered convincing. Summing up, the main problems are three. The first concerns the hypothesis of the organic composition of capital in agriculture lower than average, for which Marx does not give adequate justification. The second derives from the objections to the transformation of values into prices and, in particular, to the idea that commodities were originally traded at their values. The third concerns the power of landed property to intercept also extra-profits that are not due to the difference between the value and price of production of agricultural commodities, and annex them to its rents.

---

[13] As in Marx's analysis, each amount of money corresponds to a certain quantity of embodied labour. There is a commodity (gold) whose monetary price and labour-value determine a parity between the two.

Since – as we shall see in Section 5.3 – this theoretical upper limit, in Marx's analysis, is one of the elements that allow us to distinguish the case of absolute rent from the one of a rent due to a monopoly price, the problems listed above prompted a number of scholars to believe that there is no difference between the two. In particular, they understood absolute rent as due to a situation of monopoly in which the price is not linked to the cost of production but depends on what buyers can afford to pay.

In order to provide an example of the standpoints of those scholars, we can start from Howard and King (1985, 1992). Their dissatisfaction with Marx's original formulation of his theory of absolute rent involves, in particular, its dependence on the hypothesis on the organic composition of capital. They write:

> This ingenious argument has very strange implications, in that absolute rent would disappear altogether if the organic composition in farming were to rise to the social average, even though land remained a scarce, privately owned, non-reproducible resource essential to the production of many commodities. This is not a defensible position. It would be greatly preferable to treat absolute rent as a form of monopoly profit, its magnitude determined by the operation of supply and demand rather than by the theory of value. (Howard and King 1985, 147)

A similar point can be found in Ramirez (2009), who claims that absolute rent would not disappear in the event the organic composition of capital in agriculture was equal to (or even greater than) the average, but it would be a monopoly rent:

> it is incorrect to conclude that absolute rent will disappear altogether once the social productivity of agriculture (reflected in its organic composition) reaches or is equal to that of manufacturing industry because, as long as land is privately owned, landowners will continue to receive a rental payment for the use of the indestructible powers of the soil. The only (major) difference in this case is that absolute rent becomes a form of monopoly rent (surplus profit) whose source is found outside of agriculture and is redistributed to landowners via the price mechanism from more competitive sectors (including wage-goods industries). (Ramirez 2009, 89)[14]

Therefore, Howard and King and Ramirez seem to have more or less the same vision, although their opinions differ on how monopoly price is determined. Ramirez, in particular, refers to "the purchasing power of the buyer" (84) rather than to "the operation of supply and demand", as instead Howard and King do.

---

[14] See also Ramirez (2009, 72–73 and 84).

Moreover, there are scholars that have an intermediate position. They maintain that, in order to avoid its interpretation as a rent arising because of a monopoly price, Marx's absolute rent needs to be either reformulated or set in a different framework. For instance, Tribe (1977, 80) writes that the interpretation of absolute rent as a monopoly rent by some authors follows from Marx's conception of rents as extra-profits intercepted by landowners rather than as part of the costs. Tribe's analysis is criticised by Fine (1979, 273), who maintains that the absolute-rent theory must be considered in a "dynamic context" in which "[i]t is the pace of development of agriculture relative to industry and the movement of capital onto new lands that is of importance". Instead, reporting the opposite standpoint, Fine writes:

> If we restrict our interpretation of Marx's theory of AR to technical considerations alone, then it remains a static theory of surplus value distribution, and the notion of absolute rent as monopoly rent is certain to prevail. (Fine 1979, 260)

Finally, some scholars claim that once the upper limit of absolute rent drops, it also has to change its name in order to emphasise that something relevant changed from Marx's original formulation. Ball, in particular, writes:

> Perhaps the controversy could be resolved by calling AR "absolute rent" when market price is below value, and calling it "monopoly rent II" when market price is forced above value. It would, nevertheless, be mere semantics as the mechanism described by AR has not changed in the slightest. (Ball 1980, 320)

By contrast, Economakis maintains that absolute rent is grounded on a monopoly situation deriving, mainly, from institutional elements. For this reason, he suggests calling it "political rent" (Economakis 2003, 345).

However, differently from the position expressed by many authors who engaged in the study of this part of Marx's analysis, the failure of the upper limit of absolute rent does not imply that it cannot be distinguished with clarity – from a theoretical standpoint – from a rent due to a real monopoly price. This is what we shall try to argue in the next section.

5. Monopoly price and classical theory of value

5.1 Monopoly price in Smith's (and Ricardo's) analysis

As is well known, Adam Smith distinguishes an actual notion of price, namely the "market price", from a theoretical notion that represents the central level toward which the market price "gravitates". This theoretical price is mostly referred to by Smith in the *Wealth of Nations* as the "average or ordinary price". A similar expression is adopted by Marx too: "average market price" or "regulating market price".

Assuming free competition among producers, the ordinary price is the natural price, namely the cost of production determined by wages, profits and rents at their respective natural levels. Once the system of natural prices is introduced, the "effectual demand" for commodities is defined by Smith as the quantities of commodities demanded by those (the "effectual demanders") who are willing to pay the natural prices (1976, vol. II, 73; *WN* I.vii.8).

According to Smith's idea of gravitation, when the quantity of a commodity brought to market is different from its effectual demand, then the market price of this commodity diverges from its natural price. This divergence, in turn, affects the incomes earned in this sector by workers, capitalists and landlords, which differ from those determined by the natural rates. Since workers, capitalists and landlords want to produce where they earn – or expect to earn – the highest rates of remuneration, the discrepancy between natural and market price induces a change of the quantity brought to market. Therefore, the theoretical rest position of this process is a situation in which the quantities of commodities brought to market correspond to their effectual demands and their prices to the natural ones.

However, there are situations in which, for various reasons, it is impossible to fully satisfy the effectual demand and the market is kept in a constant state of scarcity. In particular, Smith refers to those "natural productions" that "require such a singularity of soil and situation, that all the land in a great country, which is fit for producing them, may not be sufficient to supply the effectual demand" (1976, vol. II, 78; *WN* I.vii.24). The ordinary price of these commodities can be much higher than the natural price and the difference between the two is typically appropriated by landlords in the form of rents. As Smith writes:

> Such commodities may continue for whole centuries together to be sold at this high price; and that part of it which resolves itself into the rent of land is in this case the part which is generally paid above its natural rate. The rent of the land which affords such singular and esteemed productions, like the rent of some vineyards in France of a peculiarly happy soil and situation, bears no regular proportion to the rent of other equally fertile and equally well-cultivated land in its neighbourhood. (1976, vol. II, 78; *WN* I.vii.24)

This is clearly the case of a rent due to a monopoly price.

Smith then goes on to discuss the characteristic features of the monopoly price:[15]

> The monopolists, by keeping the market constantly under-stocked, by never fully supplying the effectual demand, sell their commodities much above the natural price, and raise their emoluments [...] greatly above their natural rate.

> The price of monopoly is upon every occasion the highest which can be got. The natural price, or the price of free competition, on the contrary, is the lowest which can be taken, not upon every occasion, indeed, but for any considerable time together. The one is upon every occasion the highest which can be squeezed out of the buyers, or which, it is supposed, they will consent to give. The other is the lowest which the sellers can commonly afford to take, and at the same time continue their business. (1976, vol. II, 78–79; *WN* I.vii.26, 27)

As for Ricardo's view of the monopoly price,[16] it should be emphasised that it seems largely grounded on Smith's one:

> When a commodity is at a monopoly price, it is at the very highest price at which the consumers are willing to purchase it. Commodities are only at a monopoly price, when by no possible device their quantity can be augmented; and when therefore, the competition is wholly on one side— amongst the buyers. The monopoly price of one period may be much lower or higher than the monopoly price of another, because the competition amongst the purchasers must depend on their wealth, and their tastes and caprices. [...] The exchangeable value therefore of a commodity which is at a monopoly price, is no where regulated by the cost of production. (*Works I*, 249–250)

Summing up, there seem to be three fundamental features: (1) the quantity supplied of the commodity in question is constantly insufficient to fully satisfy the effectual demand, the market is "constantly 'under-stocked'" and so "the competition is wholly on one side"; (2) the ordinary price of the commodity is always "much above the natural price"; (3) the level of this monopoly price depends on what "can be squeezed out of

---

[15] A complete analysis of Adam Smith's theory of monopoly is beyond the goal of the present paper. For some interesting insights on it, we can refer the reader to Salvadori and Signorino (2014).

[16] Ricardo does not devote much attention to monopoly price. He mainly considers it in Chapter XVII of his *Principles*, dealing with the effects of taxes on commodity prices.

the buyers"[17] and accordingly is not "regulated by the cost of production."[18]

5.2 Value and monopoly price in Marx

There is no doubt that Marx's notion of monopoly price derives from the one discussed in the previous subsection. In particular, Marx writes:

> When we speak of a monopoly price, we mean in a general way a price which is determined only by the eagerness of the purchasers to buy and by their solvency, independently of the price which is determined by the general price of production and by the value of the products. A vineyard producing wine of very extraordinary quality, a wine which can be produced only in a relatively small quantity, carries a monopoly price. The winegrower would realize a considerable surplus profit from this monopoly price, the excess of which over the value of the product would be wholly determined by the wealth and the fine appetite of the rich wine drinkers. This surplus profit, which flows from a monopoly price, is converted into rent and in this form falls into the hands of the landlord, thanks to his title to this piece of the globe, which is endowed with peculiar properties. (*Capital III*, 900–901)

---

[17] For this reason, when a commodity is sold at a monopoly price, the introduction of a tax on this commodity does not alter its price. As Smith writes:

> When the ordinary price of any particular produce of land is at what may be called a monopoly price, a tax upon it necessarily reduces the rent and profit of the land which grows it. A tax upon the produce of those precious vineyards, of which the wine falls so much short of the effectual demand, that its price is always above the natural proportion to that of the produce of other equally fertile and equally well cultivated land, would necessarily reduce the rent and profit of those vineyards. The price of the wines being already the highest that could be got for the quantity commonly sent to market, it could not be raised higher without diminishing that quantity; and the quantity could not be diminished without still greater loss, because the lands could not be turned to other equally valuable any produce. The whole weight of the tax, therefore, would fall upon the rent and profit; properly upon the rent of the vineyard. (1976, vol. III, 892–893; *WN* V.ii.k.54)

[18] Since land has no production cost, its price – or rather the price of its use – is always above its cost of production. In this sense, rent can therefore be viewed, albeit incorrectly, as a monopoly price, and this is how Smith sees it. As he writes:

> The rent of land, therefore, considered as the price paid for the use of the land, is naturally a monopoly price. It is not at all proportioned to what the landlord may have laid out upon the improvement of the land, or to what he can afford to take; but to what the farmer can afford to give. (1976, vol. II, 161; *WN* I.xi.a5)

The second part of this passage clarifies the point: rent is understood as a monopoly price because it is in no way proportional to what the landowner might have invested in improving its quality. Smith apparently stresses this fact in order to point out that rent is a completely different category of income from capitalist profit, which is instead proportional to the investment made. However, rent is not properly a monopoly price since there is not, in general, any persistent obstacle to meeting the effectual demand. Most of the agricultural products are in fact produced in quantities that meet their effectual demand and, despite that, the lands on which they have been produced yield a rent to their owners.

As emerges from the passage just quoted, Marx's notion of monopoly price presents all the three features listed at the bottom of the previous subsection with reference to Smith's and Ricardo's ideas. Moreover, there is a fourth property of monopoly price according to Marx's analysis. In the case of a commodity traded at a monopoly price, say wine of extraordinary quality, the rent not only annexes a part of the surplus-value obtained in the cultivation of these particular vineyards, but it also absorbs part of the surplus-values of the other sectors. Therefore, according to Marx, the monopoly price is always above both the price of production and the value of the commodity. This is explicitly stated by Marx in the following lines:

> if the equalization of the surplus-value into average profit meets with obstacles in the various spheres of production in the shape of artificial or natural monopolies, particularly of monopoly in land, so that a monopoly price would be possible, which would rise above the price of production and *above the value* of the commodities affected by such a monopoly, still the limits imposed by the value of commodities would not be abolished thereby. The monopoly price of certain commodities would merely transfer a portion of the profit of the other producers of commodities to the commodities with a monopoly price. A local disturbance in the distribution of the surplus-value among the various spheres of production would take place indirectly, but they would leave the boundaries of the surplus-value itself unaltered. (*Capital III*, 1003. Emphasis added)

In a nutshell, since, in Marx's analysis, the total amount of surplus-value of the economy as a whole is fixed and independent of its distribution between profits and rents, if, in the production of the special wine, the sum of profits and rents is greater than the surplus-value extracted from the workers here employed, then the price of this wine must be above its value, so as to attract to this sector part of the surplus-value extracted elsewhere.[19] As in a sector with high organic composition of capital, the price of production must rise above the value in order to allow this sector to

---

[19] That is confirmed in the following passage:

> the sum of average profit plus rent in their normal form can never be larger than the total surplus-value, although it may be smaller. [...] Even monopoly rent [...] must be indirectly always a part of the surplus-value. If it is not a part of the surplus price above the cost of production of the commodity itself, of which it is a constituent part, as in the case of differential rent, or a spare portion of the surplus-value of the commodity itself, of which it is a constituent part, above that portion of its own surplus-value which is measured by the average profit (as in the case of absolute rent), it is at least a part of the surplus-value of other commodities, that is, of commodities which are exchanged for this commodity, which has a monopoly price. (*Capital III*, 969–970)

intercept the surplus-value produced in other sectors; likewise the monopoly price must be above the value. The difference is that the surplus-value absorbed from other sectors –jointly with part of the internal surplus-value – is converted into ordinary profits in the former case and into monopoly rents in the latter.

5.3 Absolute rent vs. (real) monopoly rent

There are many passages in Marx's works where he maintains that absolute rent refers to a situation in which agricultural commodities are traded under competitive conditions and, accordingly, it is not a rent due to a monopoly price. We have already met one of them in Section 3, since it was quoted by Bortkiewicz too. We can add another one here to complete the argument:

> At any rate this *absolute rent*, which arises out of the excess of value over the price of production, is but a portion of the agricultural surplus-value, a conversion of this surplus-value into rent, its appropriation by the landlord; so does the *differential rent* arise out of the conversion of surplus-profit into rent, its appropriation by the landlord, under an average price of production which acts as a regulator. *These two forms of rent are the only normal ones.* Outside of them the rent can rest only upon an actual monopoly price, which is determined neither by the price of production nor by the value of commodities, but by the needs and the solvency of the buyers. (*Capital III*, 887. Emphasis added)

In Marx's view, there are two fundamental differences between absolute rent and the rent paid because of a monopoly price. The first, which emerges rather clearly from the quotation above, has to do with the origin of the surplus-value out of which rent arises. In particular, absolute rent is paid from the difference between the value and price of production of the agricultural output and it is, therefore, a part of the agricultural surplus-value that is converted into rent. By contrast, monopoly rent also absorbs part of the surplus-value of the other productive sectors, as explained at the end of the previous subsection.

The second difference between absolute and monopoly rent is sketched in the quotation given in Section 3, when Marx, referring to the possibility of monopoly prices for common agricultural commodities (corn), writes that that can only take place "on a small island, where there is no foreign trade in corn". In fact, as we have seen in Section 5.1, a commodity can have a monopoly price only if there is a persistent obstacle that prevents the production of a quantity that fully satisfies its effectual demand, as happens, for agricultural products, within an economy characterised by a great scarcity of land and in the absence of foreign trade. Absolute rent refers instead to a completely different case. In fact, the payment of absolute rent is exactly what allows capitalists to remove the barrier raised by landed property. Therefore, once capitalists agree to pay the absolute rent, the barrier is not there any longer and the usual mechanism of capitalist competition will ensure that the increase in the area cultivated coincides exactly with the amount necessary, under normal conditions, to meet the effectual demand.

In a nutshell, while the payment of absolute rent thus ensures that landowners will make an additional amount of land available that will be sufficient to meet the effectual demand, the payment of monopoly rent does not lead to such a result: the obstacle to satisfying the effectual demand persists despite the rent paid.[20]

Now, Bortkiewicz's and Emmanuel's critiques of Marx's idea of the difference between the value and price of production of agricultural commodities as the upper limit for absolute rent clearly affect the first of the two differences with monopoly rent pointed out by Marx. However, the second difference is not touched on by Bortkiewicz's and Emmanuel's arguments and can, therefore, still be used in order to keep absolute rent separated and distinguished from the rent due to a monopoly price.

Finally, once this distinction is made, we can go back to Marx's analysis of the determination of the price of agricultural commodities, both for absolute rent and for monopoly. In particular, in the latter case, as already mentioned, the price does not depend on the rent rate, since it is determined "by the needs and the solvency of the buyers", due to the persistent obstacle to satisfying the effectual demand. Rather the contrary, the monopoly rent (per unit of output) results from the difference between monopoly and production price of this commodity.

---

[20] In the *Theories*, Marx writes:

> Rent arises out of the *monopoly price* of agricultural products, because supply is constantly below the level of demand or demand is constantly *above* the level of supply. (*Theories II*, 523, emphasis in the original)

Instead, absolute rent can be regarded, in Marx's view, as a component of the regulating market price of the product of the soil.[21] In particular, following Marx's analysis, the agricultural products have a regulating market price equal to $P + r$,[22] where P is the price of production and r is the absolute rent (per unit of output) that landowners can earn from their capitalist tenants.

6. Conclusions

In the classical/Marxian approach, income distribution is not a market, but a social phenomenon. Wages, profits and rents are the results of the class struggle and depend, accordingly, on the relative bargaining position of the three classes.[23] As for rent, in particular, the part which derives from the relative strength of the landowners is absolute rent, since both differential rents (I and II) and monopoly rent result from different mechanisms.[24]

However, according to Marx, there must be an upper limit to the agricultural surplus-value that landowners can obtain from capitalists – who, in turn, have extorted it from workers – and he understands it as the difference between the value and the price of production of agricultural commodities. If the rent were above this limit, then the price of the products of the soil would be higher than their value and this is only possible, according to Marx, in the case of a monopoly price.

---

[21] As for the determination of commodity relative prices in cases with absolute rent (understood as a given share of the output of the soil), we can refer the reader to Fratini (2016, 608–610).

[22] As Marx writes:

> In that case [the case of absolute rent] the regulating market price of the total product of all soils existing on the market would not be the price of production, which capital generally makes in all spheres of production, which is a price equal to the cost of production plus the average profit, but it would be the price of production plus the rent, $P + r$, and not merely P. (*Capital III*, 868)

[23] Once the relevance of the class struggle on income distribution is recognised, it follows that the excess supply of a certain input does not imply that its rate of remuneration falls automatically, as instead happens in the Walrasian tâtonnement process. In particular, as is known (cf. Garegnani 1990, 119–121), the presence of involuntary unemployment does not imply an automatic decrease in the wage rate toward its minimum (biological survival) level. Unemployment, if substantial, can only act indirectly on the wage rate by weakening the bargaining position of workers.

In our view, the same can be said of the rate of rent and the possible excess supply of land of the same quality as the worst soil under cultivation.

[24] In both these cases, the price of the product of the soil is determined independently of the rent rate – by the cost of production on the worst land in the first case and "by the needs and the solvency of the buyers" in the second. Accordingly, if extra-profits must be zero in every sector, then differential and monopoly rents are determined by the difference between ordinary price and cost of production of the products of the soil.

Hence, as we have seen in Sections 3 and 4, the theoretical difficulties affecting this upper limit of absolute rent prompted a number of economists to believe that there is no distinction between it and the rent paid by a monopoly price. On the contrary, as we have shown in Section 5, even if the upper limit of absolute rent drops, this does not mean that we are not able to distinguish the case of commodities with a monopoly price from that of commodities whose natural price includes an element of absolute rent. In particular, the difference lies in the persistency of the (natural or artificial) obstacle to the full satisfaction of the effectual demand, which characterises – in the classical approach – a situation of monopoly pricing. Whereas, with absolute rent, once capitalist tenant farmers pay the agreed rent, the barrier to the investment of capital in new lands is removed, and the agricultural output can adjust to the effectual demand by the usual mechanism.

Therefore, concluding, Marx is right when he says that absolute rent – like differential rents – refers to a normal case, in which free competition among producers – modified because of the presence of landed property – involves the "gravitation" of the produced quantities of commodities toward their effectual demand.

Acknowledgments

The author is grateful to Tony Aspromourgos, Ben Fine, Fabio Ravagnani and two anonymous referees for comments and suggestions received. It goes without saying that the usual disclaimer applies.

Disclosure statement

No potential conflict of interest was reported by the author.

ORCID

Saverio M. Fratini 🆔 http://orcid.org/0000-0003-0766-0741

References

Ball, Michael. 1980. "On Marx's Theory of Agricultural Rent: A Reply to Ben Fine." *Economy and Society* 9 (3): 304–326. doi: 10.1080/03085148008538599.
Bortkiewicz, Ladislaus. 1910–11. "Die Rodbertus'sche Grundrententheorie und die Marx'sche Lehre von der absoluten Grundrente." *Archiv für die Geschichte des Sozialismus und der Arbeiterbewegung* 1: 1–40 and 391–434. [Italian translation: "La teoria della rendita fondiaria di Rodbertus e la dottrina di Marx sulla rendita fondiaria assoluta." In *La Teoria Economica di Marx*, edited by L. Meldolesi, 1971, 126–178. Turin: Einaudi.]

Bortkiewicz, Ladislaus. 1919. "Zu den Grundrententheorien von Rodbertus und Marx." *Archiv für die Geschichte des Sozialismus und der Arbeiterbewegung* 8: 248–257. [Italian translation: "Le teorie sulla rendita fondiaria di Rodbertus e Marx." In *La Teoria Economica di Marx*, edited by Luca Meldolesi, 1971, 179–187. Turin: Einaudi.]

Economakis, George E. 2003. "Absolute Rent: Theoretical Remarks on Marx's Analysis." *Science and Society* 67 (3): 339–348.

Emmanuel, Arghiri. 1972. *Unequal Exchange: A Study of the Imperialism of Trade.* New York: Monthly Review Press.

Fine, Ben. 1979. "On Marx's Theory of Agricultural Rent." *Economy and Society* 8 (3): 241–278. doi: 10.1080/03085147900000009.

Fratini, Saverio Maria. 2016. "Rent as a Share of Product and Sraffa's Price Equations." *Cambridge Journal of Economics* 40 (2): 599–613. doi: 10.1093/cje/bev015.

Garegnani, Pierangelo. 1984. "Value and Distribution in the Classical Economists and Marx." *Oxford Economic Papers* 36 (2): 291–325. doi: 10.1093/oxfordjournals.oep.a041640.

Garegnani, Pierangelo. 1990. "Sraffa: Classical Versus Marginalist Analysis." In *Essays on Piero Sraffa. Critical Perspectives on the Revival of Classical Theory*, edited by Krishna Bharadwaj and Bertram Schefold, 112–158. London: Unwin Hyman.

Gehrke, Christian. 2014. "The Reception and Further Elaboration of Ricardo's Theory of Value and Distribution in German-Speaking Countries, 1817–1914." In *The Reception of David Ricardo in Continental Europe and Japan*, edited by Gilbert Faccarello and Masashi Izumo, 76–137. Abingdon: Routledge.

Ghosh, Jayati. 1985. "Differential and Absolute Land Rent." *Journal of Peasant Studies* 13 (1): 67–82. doi: 10.1080/03066158508438283.

Howard, Michael Charles, and John Edward King. 1985. *The Political Economy of Marx.* 2nd ed. Harlow: Longman.

Howard, Michael Charles, and John Edward King. 1992. "Marx, Jones, Rodbertus and the Theory of Absolute Rent." *Journal of the History of Economic Thought* 14 (1): 70–83. doi: 10.1017/S1053837200004405.

Marx, Karl. 1909. *Capital.* Vol. III . Chicago: Charles H. Kerr & Co. In the text quoted as *Capital III.*

Marx, Karl. 1968. *Theories of Surplus Value: Volume IV of Capital.* Part II. Moscow: Progress Publishers. In the text quoted as *Theories II.*

Negishi, Takashi. 1985. *Economic Theories in Non-Walrasian Tradition.* Cambridge: Cambridge University Press.

Negishi, Takashi. 1989. *History of Economic Theory.* Amsterdam: North-Holland/Elsevier.

Piccioni, Marco. 2014. *Production, Value, Distribution and Employment.* Roma: Aracne Editrice.

Ramirez, Miguel D. 2009. "Marx's Theory of Ground Rent: A Critical Assessment." *Contributions to Political Economy* 28 (1): 71–91. doi: 10.1093/cpe/bzp001.

Ricardo, David. 1951. "On the Principles of Political Economy and Taxation." In *The Works and Correspondence of David Ricardo*, edited by P. Sraffa with the collaboration of M. H. Dobb., Vol. I. Cambridge: Cambridge University Press. In the text quoted as *Works I.*

Salvadori, Neri, and Rodolfo Signorino. 2014. "Adam Smith on Monopoly Theory. Making Good a Lacuna." *Scottish Journal of Political Economy* 61 (2): 178–195. doi: 10.1111/sjpe.12040.

Samuelson, Paul Anthony. 1992. "Marx on Rent: A Failure to Transform Correctly." *Journal of the History of Economic Thought* 14 (2): 143–167. doi: 10.1017/S1053837200004971.

Smith, Adam. 1976. "An Inquiry into the Nature and Causes of the Wealth of Nations." In *The Glasgow Edition of the Works and Correspondence of Adam Smith*, edited by R. H. Campbell and A. S. Skinner, Vols. II and III. Oxford: Oxford University Press. In the text quoted as *WN*, book number, chapter number, paragraph number.

Tribe, Keith. 1977. "Economic Property and the Theorisation of Ground Rent." *Economy and Society* 6 (1): 69–88. doi: 10.1080/03085147700000016.

Use values and exchange values in Marx's extended reproduction schemes

Carlo Benetti, Alain Béraud, Edith Klimovsky and Antoine Rebeyrol

ABSTRACT

Marx-Engels' numerical illustrations of the extended reproduction suggest that a two-sector economy reaches a balanced growth path, from the second period onwards. We explain this surprising result and show that for technical reasons, disproportions between sectors can prevent the system from reproducing itself. But, in Marx's reproduction schemes, such a crisis is not only due to purely technical factors and one must wonder what role is played by the relative price in the reproduction of the system. The answer is given by comparing two models having a similar structure but quite different rules for the determination of the relative price. In Marx's model, the price is given by the labour values and thus, it is exogenously fixed. We contrast Marx's analysis with an endogenous price model in which the price depends on the conditions of the accumulation of capital. The Appendices point out the complete accordance of Engels' corrections with Marx's model and Marx's unfruitful quest for a balanced growth path as a tool for the analysis of crises.

1. Introduction

In volume II of *Capital*, Marx analysed the reproduction of a two-sector economy by means of numerical examples in which figures represent monetary flows. His scheme is based on three main hypotheses: accumulation is the only use of the commodities produced by sector I whereas the commodities produced by sector II are accumulated and consumed; the profits are reinvested in the sector in which they were generated, the relative price is exogenous and fixed. Surprisingly, from the second period onwards, the rate of growth is uniform and determined by the rate of accumulation in sector I in the first period. Thus the "extended reproduction scheme" has been commonly interpreted as a balanced growth model in which crises can only occur by modifying some of Marx's assumptions.[1]

On several occasions, Rubel (1968) – in the French Pléiade edition of *Capital* (Marx [1968], Book II, 1735–1737) – points out that the figures in Marx's three examples of the extended reproduction have been corrected by Engels. However, Rubel never mentions either the reasons or the scope of such corrections. The contributions of Mori (2018) and Gehrke (2018) have led us to consult Marx's manuscript.[2] It is merely due to erroneous calculations that no balanced growth path appears. The most important one for our purpose is as follows: while Marx ([1868–1881] 2008, 812) explicitly assumed that the organic composition of capital must remain the same, in his calculations, the organic composition of the additional capital is, in fact, lower than that of the initial capital. Engels did not do anything else than correct such obvious errors, the consequences of which will be examined in Appendix 1. That is why we will study Marx's two-sector model by referring to Engels' text and we name "Marx-Engels' equilibrium" the balanced growth path in the second period.

The construction of a two-sector macroeconomic model is one of Marx's main contributions. M. Morishima (1973, 3), among others, points out its importance: "it is no exaggeration to say that before Kalecki, Frisch and Tinbergen, no economist except Marx had obtained a macro-dynamic model rigorously constructed in a scientific way [...]. Marx's theory of reproduction is very similar to Leontief's input-output analysis [... and ...] contains in itself a way to the von Neumann revolution". The number and the theoretical variety of two-sector models attest to the fertility of the analytical framework developed by Marx.[3]

---

[1] Let us give two significant examples. According to Rosa Luxemburg ([1913] 2003, 335) Marx's result is a consequence of his assumption of a constant technique: the scheme "assumes that the composition of capital is the same in every year, [...i.e., it...] is not affected by accumulation. This procedure would be quite permissible in itself in order to simplify the analysis, but when we come to examine the concrete conditions [...] for reproduction, then at least we must take into account [...] changes in technique, which are bound up with the process of capital accumulation." After a detailed analysis of a Marx's numerical example, Michio Morishima (1973, 120) concludes that "any state of unbalanced growth will disappear in Marx's economy in a single year." That is why he modifies some assumptions of Marx's model. In part 1 and in Appendices 1 and 3, we will show that Marx's results depend on his numerical examples and are not the logical consequence of his model.

[2] Through Mori's article, we have become aware of the existence of a six-sector reproduction scheme in Marx's manuscripts. Its interest does not lessen the importance of studying the two-sector scheme.

[3] At the beginning of the twentieth century, Marx's model was used by the participants in the Marxist debates on the crisis of capitalism (namely, R. Luxemburg, O. Bauer, M.

The theoretical and historical importance of Marx's model justifies a more accurate study of its properties. For the analysis of the reproduction of social capital, Marx underlines the importance of the reproduction of the use values and their interdependence. Yet, to the best of our knowledge, neither Marx nor his successors have developed such an analysis. The use-value system is defined by the technique and the proportion between sectors on which the monetary flows do not provide any direct information. In a previous article (Benetti et al. 2013), we wondered what could be said about the physical reproduction on the only basis of Marx's monetary data. We constructed a matrix of pure numbers having the same eigenvalues as those of the unknown technical matrix and a pure number, which is an index of the unknown physical proportion. These two instruments enabled us to study the physical constraints on reproduction and crises, but they did not provide any insight on the role of the exchange rate in the reproduction of the economy.

This article proposes a complementary approach while adopting Marx's assumptions. We first construct a model of the physical reproduction in which the initial data are the technique and the proportion between the quantities produced in each sector. Then, we explicitly introduce the relative price in the model so that the role of its rigidity in the reproduction of the social capital can be analysed.

The first part of the article studies the reproduction of the use values starting from the balance between resources and uses of each commodity. It amounts to adapting Torrens' analysis (1821, 339–430) to Marx's hypotheses. Torrens was the first one to study, by means of numerical examples, the physical constraints on reproduction when the capitalists accumulate all their production and, as in Marx, the profits are invested within the sectors in which they are generated. Surprisingly enough, Marx did not perceive the importance of Torrens' contribution to the theory of reproduction. We first explain why the economy, from the second period onwards, reaches a

---

Tugan-Baranovsky, K. Kautsky, and R. Hilferding). Later on, the two-sector model is adopted by M. Kalecki, O. Lange, J. M. Keynes, J. Robinson, and by J. Meade and J.R. Hicks in their formalizations of the *General Theory*. At the beginning of the 1960s, the first systematic analyses of the properties of two-sector models are published. Shinkai's model (1960), inspired by J. Robinson, opens this line of research. Immediately after, Uzawa (1961) publishes "a neoclassical version of Shinkai's model" (40, footnote 2). This article and the following (1963) are at the origin of many contributions to the neoclassical theory of the two-sector growth during the 1960s. With regard to Marx's model, the studies of Morishima (1973) and Nikaido (1983 and 1985) are especially important.

balanced growth path. In Marx's analysis, the role of the two sectors is asymmetrical in the sense that the investment in sector II adjusts itself to the accumulation decisions in sector I. The Marxist tradition has emphasized the leading role of the latter and provided historical interpretations. We put forward an analytical interpretation by showing that the leading role of sector I, rooted in the physical properties of commodities, is a necessary condition for the economy to reach, in the second period, a balanced growth path. However, contrary to Morishima's statement (1973, 120), that condition is not sufficient: crises can occur because the technique and the proportion between sectors may be incompatible with the absorption of the available means of production. We determine the critical proportions, which depend on the technique and the rate of accumulation in sector I.

The equations of physical reproduction alone do not represent a capitalist economy. They express the physical constraints to the reproduction regardless of the social institutions and, as such, determine the maximum performance of the economic system.

In the second part, we formalize the capitalist reproduction by integrating the physical equations in a reproduction model in which the price and the profit rates are explicit. The model is built on the basis of Marx's crucial hypothesis of self-financing accumulation in each sector. It determines the conditions for a capitalist two-sector economy achieving the results permitted by its physical data. The model can be solved in two different ways depending on whether the price is endogenous or exogenous. In the first case, the accumulation of capital and the proportion between sectors determine a range within which the price lies, so that the physical reproduction is in no way affected. In the second case, the exogenous price determines the profit rates, thus restricting the possibilities of physical accumulation. By comparing these two interpretations, we bring to light the constraints that the exogenous price imposes on reproduction.

In Appendix 1, we point out that Engels' corrections are in complete accordance with Marx's model. Besides Marx conceived the extended reproduction as a simple reproduction to which net capital accumulation is added. We address that issue in a different manner by studying the transition from the simple to the extended reproduction in Appendix 2. In Appendix 3, we trace Marx's attempts to analyse the extended reproduction and we will show that they all point out an unfruitful quest for a balanced growth path as a tool for the analysis of crises.

This article only deals with the reproduction of use values and values. It leaves out another important aspect of the capitalist reproduction such as the money-circulation.

2. The reproduction of use-values and crises

At the beginning of Chapter 20 on simple reproduction, Marx underlined the main novelty of the analysis of the social capital: "So long as we looked upon the production of value and the value of the product of capital individually, the bodily form of the commodities produced was wholly immaterial for the analysis [...]. This merely formal manner of presentation is no longer adequate in the study of the total social capital and of the value of its products. The reconversion of one portion of the value of the product into capital and the passing of another portion into the individual consumption [...] form a movement [which] is *not only a replacement of value, but also a replacement in material* and is therefore as much bound up with the relative proportions of the value-components of the total social product *as with their use-value, their material shape*" (Marx [1885] 1956, 241 our italics).

In Marx's reproduction schemes – following the tradition initiated by Quesnay's two-sector monetary model – the "system of production and consumption is conceived as a circular process" (Sraffa 1960, 116). The economic relations between sectors are expressed in terms of monetary flows, "the figures may indicate millions of marks, francs or pounds sterling" (Marx [1885] 1956, 243). In order to analyse the reproduction of values and of use values as well, the flows of values are represented as the product of physical quantities and a relative price. After studying the physical system, we bring out first the general conditions for a balanced growth path from the second period onwards; secondly the physical constraints on reproduction and the possibility of crises.

2.1. The physical system

We adopt the following assumptions on the physical system underlying Marx's flows of value. The economy is made up of two sectors: sector I producing the means of production and sector II producing the goods, which are consumed by capitalists and workers. In each sector, there is a unique method[4] with a constant return to scale, which makes use of both types of inputs. The whole capital is circulating. Each unit of labour is replaced by the corresponding wage basket so that labour does not appear explicitly in the system. Only the capitalists save, the workers consume the totality of their wages. At constant real wages, the additional labour required by the extended reproduction is provided by the reserve army and the growth of the population. As a direct consequence of their physical properties, the accumulation is the unique use of the means of production and the consumption goods have a double use, i.e., the accumulation of capital (wage-goods) and the capitalists' consumption.

Let q_i denote the quantity of commodity i available at the beginning of the current period and produced during the previous period, and a_{ij} the amount of commodity j entering into the production of one unit of commodity i. It is assumed that these coefficients are constant and the matrix $A = [a_{ij}]$ is positive and productive (i.e., the Hawkins–Simon conditions are satisfied.) Quantities q_i are in the hands of their producers and must be allocated in both sectors for the production in the current period. We assume that the means of production available at the beginning of the period are fully used. This assumption is removed in subsection 2.3. Let $G_i = 1 + g_i$ be the sectoral factors of accumulation or growth and C the physical capitalist consumption. The balance between resources and uses of each commodity is written:

$$q_1 = a_{11}q_1G_1 + a_{21}q_2G_2$$
$$q_2 = a_{12}q_1G_1 + a_{22}q_2G_2 + C \tag{1}$$

As reproduction does not depend on the quantities produced but only on their proportion, these equations are rewritten as:

$$q = a_{11}qG_1 + a_{21}G_2$$
$$1 = a_{12}qG_1 + a_{22}G_2 + c \tag{2}$$

where $q = q_1/q_2$ and $c = C/q_2$ is the fraction of the production of the consumption goods consumed by the capitalists. Proportion q and matrix A are given. System (2) has one degree of freedom but as the

---

[4] In Marx's terms, "All the various branches of production pertaining to each of these two departments form one single great branch of production, that of the means of production in the one case and that of articles of consumption in the other" (Marx [1885] 1956, 242). There is an "aggregate capitalist" (244) in each sector. The economy behaves as if it were made up of two commodities and two representative capitalists.

physical data can be mutually incompatible, it does not necessarily have an economic solution; c must not be negative and both G_1 and G_2 must be positive, otherwise at least one sector disappears, so the entire economy disappears in the next period.

> We will show that Marx-Engels' equilibrium only exists if 4 necessary conditions are satisfied. The first one is that system (2) of the use-value reproduction has an economic solution. This is obtained if proportion q is less than the highest technical composition a_{11}/a_{12} or a_{21}/a_{22}.

If c is exogenous, both accumulation factors are endogenous and the properties of system (2) are similar to those of the scheme constructed by Torrens (1821, see below Section 2.2). Let D denote the matrix determinant, the solution is $G_1 = \frac{qa_{22} - a_{21}(1-c)}{qD}$ and $G_2 = \frac{a_{11}(1-c) - qa_{12}}{D}$ from which we draw the condition for the existence of an economic solution: $(1-c)\min(k_1, k_2) < q < (1-c)\max(k_1, k_2)$, where $k_1 = a_{11}/a_{12}$ and $k_2 = a_{21}/a_{22}$ denote the technical composition of capital in sector I and in sector II, respectively.[5] For every q out of this range, the economy disappears.

If, as in Marx, c is endogenous (see the next subsection), the capitalist consumption acts as a buffer. Since the capitalists are supposed to be insatiable, the consumption goods cannot be superabundant. In other words, there is no lower bound for q. The second equation of system (2) is rewritten as: $1 \geq a_{12}qG_1 + a_{22}G_2$. Substituting, in this inequality, G_2 and then G_1 as given by the first equation of (2), we see that the solution must satisfy the following inequalities $qDG_1 \geq a_{22}q - a_{21}$ and $DG_2 \leq a_{11} - a_{12}q$. Therefore the condition for the existence of an economic solution is:[6]

$$q < \max(k_1, k_2) \tag{3}$$

This result derives from the assumption on the use of the goods. Unlike the consumption goods, the means of production are only used for accumulation and it is possible that their available quantity cannot be wholly employed.

Marx's model is recursive. One of the factors of accumulation (G_1 or G_2) being given, the first equation determines the other factor and the second equation determines c. Since a single sector cannot absorb all the means of production or all the consumption goods, the

---

[5] If $D > 0$, $k_1 > k_2$: $G_1 > 0 \Rightarrow q > (1-c)k_2$ and $G_2 > 0 \Rightarrow q < (1-c)k_1$. Conversely, if $D < 0$, $k_1 < k_2$: $G_1 > 0 \Rightarrow q < (1-c)k_2$ and $G_2 > 0 \Rightarrow q > (1-c)k_1$.

[6] If $D > 0$, $G_2 > 0 \Rightarrow q < k_1$ but $G_1 > 0 \not\Rightarrow q > k_2$. Conversely, if $D < 0$, $G_1 > 0 \Rightarrow q < k_2$ but $G_2 > 0 \not\Rightarrow q > k_1$

exogenous accumulation factor is bounded: $G_1 < \min(\frac{1}{a_{11}}, \frac{1}{a_{12}q})$ or $G_2 < \min(\frac{q}{a_{21}}, \frac{1}{a_{22}})$.

2.2. The Marx–Engels' equilibrium: the leader and the follower

At what conditions does the solution $G_i > 0$ and $c > 0$ allows us to obtain the Marx–Engels' equilibrium in the second period? One of these three variables must be exogenous. Let us note that an asymmetrical relationship between sectors is the necessary consequence of the choice of one accumulation factor, the other sector having to adapt its own rate of accumulation passively.

> We are going to show that the choice of G_1 as an exogenous variable is a second necessary condition for the existence of Marx-Engels' equilibrium since accumulation is the only use of the means of production. If G_2 or c is the exogenous variable the evolution of the system is unstable.

For a given technique and one exogenous rate of accumulation, the balanced growth path is defined as the proportion such that the rate of growth is uniform:

$$q^*(G) = \frac{a_{21}G}{1 - a_{11}G} \tag{4}$$

That relation is obtained by setting $G_1 = G_2 = G$ in the first equation of system (2). How is that equilibrium achieved? Let $q_i^+ = q_i G_i$ denote the future productions, by definition,

$$q^+ \equiv q\frac{G_1}{G_2} \tag{5}$$

which gives the linear expression $G_2 = \frac{G_1}{q^+}q$. Its substitution in the first equation of system (2) eliminates not only G_2 but q as well and we obtain the following fundamental relation between G_1 and q^+:

$$q^+ = \frac{a_{21}G_1}{1 - a_{11}G_1} \tag{6}$$

This is an astonishing equation. The proportion of future productions only depends on G_1 and not on the initial proportion q. Therefore, q^+ is the equilibrium proportion associated with G_1, as it is shown by comparing with relation (4). We have $q^+(G_1) = q^*(G_1)$. Regardless of the activity level of sector II, hence of q, if equalities (2) hold the knowledge of q_1 and G_1 gives both q_1^+ and $(q_1 - a_{11}q_1^+)$, i.e., the quantity of the means of production which are available for sector II and also the future production in this sector. Thus, the accumulation factor in sector I determine simultaneously q_1^+ and q_2^+, i.e., q^+. For a given G_1, as long as the existing means of production are fully employed, the same proportion q^+ will be obtained from potentially very different values of its initial level. If G_1 remains constant over time, the accumulation factor in sector II will adjust itself from the second period onwards: $G_2^+ = G_1^+$.[7] For all $t \geq 1$, the dynamics are those of a balanced growth (or accumulation) path $q(t) = a_{21}G_1/(1 - a_{11}G_1)$. Hence

$$q^*(G_1) = \frac{a_{21}G_1}{1 - a_{11}G_1} \tag{7}$$

If G_1 changes, a new balanced growth rate results from the adjustment of sector II to the accumulation rate in sector I.

It would have been quite different, if G_2 had been chosen as the exogenous variable in the first equation of system (2). G_2 determines the amount of consumption goods, which is accumulated in sector II. However, this piece of information does not allow us to know the amount of consumption goods available for sector I, which depends on the capitalists' consumption in sector II. If such a difficulty is left out, the amount of consumption goods transferred to sector I is known, but it is by no means enough to calculate the accumulation in sector I, which depends on the capitalists' consumption in this sector.

Let us see now the algebraic expression of this striking contrast to the previous case. The elimination of G_1 between the first equation of system (2) and definition (5) gives the following difference equation:

$$q^+ = \frac{q - a_{21}G_2}{a_{11}G_2} \tag{8}$$

The future proportion is no longer independent of its initial level and a distinctive feature of the physical reproduction in Marx's scheme is lost. The solution of Equation (8) is $q(t) = \bar{q} + (q(0) - \bar{q})(1/a_{11}G_2)^t$, where $\bar{q} = a_{21}G_2/(1 - a_{11}G_2)$. The evolution is now progressive and no longer abrupt. It is unstable under the assumption $G_2 < 1/a_{11}$, which is the condition for a positive stationary solution $\bar{q}$.

In total, by the very nature of the use values in Marx's model, sector I must be the leader and sector II the follower, not the opposite. The adjustment of the accumulation in sector II to the accumulation

---

[7] The demonstration would be the same if, like Marx, we had taken the values without making a distinction between prices and physical quantities of goods.

decisions in sector I is two-fold. Starting from the proportion q, through the first adjustment of G_2, the equilibrium proportion q^* is obtained at the end of the first period. Then, G_2 adjusts once more up to the value of G_1, so that the proportion q^* is reproduced from the second period onwards.

Whatever is exogenously chosen, whether G_1 or G_2, the model is recursive. Such a property disappears if c is taken as exogenous. Such a choice is obviously incompatible with Marx's general approach to the role of accumulation. Moreover, by incorporating in definition (5) the growth rates resulting from the resolution of system (2), we obtain $q^+ = \frac{a_{22}q - a_{21}(1-c)}{a_{11}(1-c) - a_{12}q}$: the future proportion depends on its current level and this is inconsistent with the sharp adjustment to the Marx–Engels' equilibrium. Finally, for $c = 0$, Equations (2) are those of Torrens' unstable dynamic model, which exhibits explosive oscillations around the equilibrium in the case of a negative determinant and monotonic divergence from equilibrium, if the determinant is positive.[8] Such dynamics are independent of the capitalists' consumption if it is given independently of q and of both G_i. They are also the same that Morishima constructed (1973, 125) after correcting Marx's scheme so as to eliminate the asymmetrical relationship between sectors.

2.3. The physical constraints on reproduction

> The crisis is an overproduction of the means of production and not of consumption goods.

If the given proportion q is too low and/or if factor G_1 is too high (but less than $1/a_{11}$), factor G_2 as determined by the first equation of system (2) is positive but may be less than 1. In such a case, a reduction in the size of sector II in the first period allows the economy to reach a balanced growth path in the second period (see Appendix 2). It is a matter of pure and simple adjustment to the Marx–Engels' equilibrium.

However, if the initial proportion q is very high, the adjustment itself may be questioned because the means of production are relatively superabundant and cannot be absorbed or said differently, the

---

[8] The instability can only be avoided if the initial proportion is von Neumann's. In such a case, both accumulation rates are equal and the economy is in equilibrium from the start (see Bidard and Klimovsky 2006, chap. 10).

amount of consumption goods is not sufficient to feed the workers who are required to operate the existing means of production. That failure of reproduction is a crisis caused by a disproportion between sectors. The solution of system (2) implies $c < 0$, i.e., the Marx–Engels' equilibrium does not exist.

Although Marx's analysis of the extended reproduction was centred on equilibrium, Marx did not ignore this kind of crisis, which he mentioned in volume III of *Capital*, Chapter 30 on money-capital and crises: "Let us suppose that the whole of society is composed only of industrial capitalists and wage-workers. Let us furthermore disregard [monetary] price fluctuations […] Let us also disregard the sham transactions and speculations […] Then, a crisis could only be explained as the result of a disproportion of production in various branches of the economy" (Marx [1894] 1996, 347). Apart from the monetary and financial causes of crises, which are the ones he emphasized, by referring to the physical disproportions of activity levels, Marx's analysis is closely related to the classical tradition.

> For a given technique, we are going to determine the third and fourth necessary conditions that the exogenous variables must satisfy: G_1 lies within the range (10) and proportion q is lower than a value which depends on G_1 (see (9)). The maximum value of q is a function of G_1 which is increasing if $D > 0$ and decreasing if $D < 0$.

Let $q_{max}(G_1)$ denote the maximum proportion, which can be reproduced if the capitalists' consumption is nil and the accumulation factor in sector I is G_1. Its algebraic expression is obtained by setting $c = 0$ and by eliminating G_2 between the two equations of system (2):

$$q_{max}(G_1) = \frac{a_{21}}{a_{22} - DG_1} \tag{9}$$

Such a value is positive.[9] Relation (9) is increasing or decreasing according to the sign, positive or negative, of determinant D as it is shown in Figure 1. In the first case, the means of production are more intensively used in sector I ($k_1 > k_2$) and a greater absorption of the means of production is obtained by developing it (i.e., high G_1). Conversely, if D is negative, the same result is obtained by developing sector II (i.e., low G_1).

---

[9] Since $G_1 < 1/a_{11}$, we have $a_{22} - DG_1 > 0$ as it can be verified by replacing D by its expression $a_{11}a_{22} - a_{21}a_{12}$. Note that if $q \leq q_{max}(G_1)$, condition (3) is satisfied: if $D < 0$, we have $q_{max}(G_1) < k_2$ and if $D > 0$, we have $q_{max}(G_1) < k_1$.

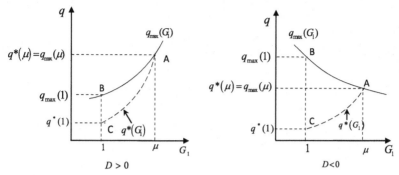

Figure 1. The physical critical proportions.

G_1 must lie within the following range of values:

$$1 \leq G_1 \leq \mu \tag{10}$$

$G_1 < 1$ is discarded, otherwise the economy disappears asymptotic-ally, and the maximum value of G_1 cannot be higher than the von Neumann growth factor (see later). Let μ denote this factor, which is the inverse of the maximum eigenvalue of the input matrix.

On balanced growth paths, the equilibrium proportion is an increasing function of G_1 which is represented by the dotted curve in Figure 1. For $G_1 = 1$, we have $q^*(1) = \frac{a_{21}}{1-a_{11}}$ i.e., the simple reproduc-tion proportion. For $G_1 = \mu$ the equilibrium proportion is von Neumann's.

A crisis occurs if the initial proportion is larger than $q_{max}(G_1)$. For $c = 0$, Equation (2) determine the critical proportions corresponding to the extreme values of G_1 :

- $q_{max}(\mu) = \frac{a_{21}}{a_{22} - \mu D} = \frac{a_{21}\mu}{1-a_{11}\mu}$ is the von Neumann proportion associated with the accumulation structure (μ, μ). This propor-tion is that of the eigenvector $(q_{max}(\mu), 1)$.[10]
- $q_{max}(1) = \frac{a_{21}}{a_{22} - D} = \frac{a_{21}G_2^{max}}{1-a_{11}}$ is the proportion associated with the accumulation structure $(1, G_2^{max})$ where $G_2^{max} = \frac{1-a_{11}}{a_{22}-D}$ is the highest growth factor in sector II, which is the solution of sys-tem (2) for $G_1 = 1$ and $c = 0$.

These proportions are represented on the vertical axis of Figure 1.

---

[10] D is eliminated in the second equality since μ^{-1} is an eigenvalue of A. Therefore, by definition, it verifies the characteristic equation $\mu^{-2} - (a_{11} + a_{22})\mu^{-1} + D = 0$.

A crisis occurs above, and not below, the $q_{max}(G_1)$ graph. For a given G_1 within the range (10), the graph shows the maximum proportion compatible with the productive use of each commodity. The determinant plays a fundamental role. If $D > 0$, the graph determines the minimal value of G_1 to avoid a crisis. If G_1 is too small, the amount of the means of production available for sector II exceeds what this sector can absorb. In this case, the development of sector I should be encouraged. On the other hand, if $D < 0$, the graph determines the maximum value of G_1 to avoid a crisis, in which case, the growth of sector I should be limited in such a way that the accumulation is favoured in sector II. Thus, depending on whether sector I or sector II makes a more intensive use of the means of production, the economic policy recommendations will be radically opposed. If the determinant is zero, as in some of Marx's numerical examples (see Appendix 1), Equation (9) gives q_{max} equal to $a_{11}/a_{12} = a_{21}/a_{22}$ i.e., a constant that does not depend on G_1. The amount of absorbable means of production is independent of the sector in which the accumulation takes place (in Figure (1), we have $q_{max}(1) = q_{max}(\mu)$ and the curve AB is a horizontal line.)

We have seen that inequalities (10) are a necessary condition for the balanced growth at a positive rate from the second period onwards. However, if the initial proportion is larger than q_{max}, the full use of the available means of production may require an accumulation factor in sector I out of range (10). What will the evolution of the system be? Everything depends on the sign of the determinant. If it is negative and the initial proportion is larger than $q_{max}(1)$, factor G_1 must be lower than 1 and low enough so that the available means of production are fully used and $q^+ < q_{max}(1)$. Thus, in the second period, there exists a factor $G_1 \geq 1$ such that a Marx–Engels equilibrium is reached in the third period. On the other hand, if the determinant is positive and the initial proportion is larger than $q_{max}(\mu)$, the means of production can only be absorbed for $G_1 > \mu$. We then have $G_2 < \mu$ and the proportion will increase up to the technical composition in sector I (a_{11}/a_{12}) and inequality (3) will not be met. The available means of production are only absorbed for $G_2 = 0$ and then the entire economy disappears.

3. The reproduction of values and crises

When the previous model is extended to include the relative price, to what extent are the conditions of physical reproduction modified? The notion of profit comes in, which in turn implies two questions on accumulation, namely its financing and the sector in which it takes place. At this stage of the analysis, we introduce the last crucial assumption of Marx's model, i.e., the investment of profits within the sector in which they are generated. Such a hypothesis is often rejected in the later literature (for example, Lange (1961), Morishima (1973), Nikaido (1983 and 1985)). We adopt it not only because it is Marx's, but also because of the many difficulties arising when it is removed.[11]

The exchange rate does not appear explicitly in Marx's scheme, but it can reasonably be assumed that it is determined by the quantities of labour required to produce the commodities we are dealing with. Basically what matters is not the labour theory of value (the calculation of the labour values is useless) but the fact that, in Marx's approach, the price is exogenously fixed in the sense that it does not depend either on the proportion between sectors or on the rate of the accumulation. What are the consequences on the reproduction of social capital? To deal with the problem, we propose a unique model in which both cases, endogenous and exogenous prices, can be treated. We will show that if the relative price is endogenous, Marx's assumption on self-financing sectors does not entail any further constraints on reproduction as compared with the physical model. On the other hand, such constraints arise as a consequence of Marx's exogenous price hypothesis.

Let g_i denote the rates of accumulation, s_i the rates of saving out of the profits, r_i the profit rates, c_i the ratio of the capitalists' consumption to the overall production of consumption goods, and p the relative price of the means of production in terms of consumption goods. The model is written as follows:

---

[11] Such difficulties are related to the information held by agents, to the nature of their expectations, etc.

$$
\begin{aligned}
q &= a_{11}q(1+g_1) + a_{21}(1+g_2) & (i)\\
1 &= a_{12}q(1+g_1) + a_{22}(1+g_2) + c_1 + c_2 & (ii)\\
pq &= (a_{11}p + a_{12})q(1+g_1) + c_1 & (iii)\\
1 &= (a_{21}p + a_{22})(1+g_2) + c_2 & (iv)\\
(1+r_1)&(a_{11}p + a_{12}) = p & (v)\\
(1+r_2)&(a_{21}p + a_{22}) = 1 & (vi)\\
s_1 r_1 &= g_1 & (vii)\\
s_2 r_2 &= g_2 & (viii)
\end{aligned}
\tag{11}
$$

Four conditions are added, the last one being specific of Marx's model, in which the price and the saving rate of the capitalists of sector I are exogenous:

$$
\begin{aligned}
c_1 &\ge 0 & (a)\\
c_2 &\ge 0 & (b)\\
c_1 + c_2 &< 1 & (c)\\
s_1 &\ge 0 & (d)
\end{aligned}
$$

Equations (i)–$(viii)$ formalize the economy at the initial period. (i) and (ii) are the balance between physical resources and uses of each commodity, (iii) and (iv) are the budget constraints, i.e., the balance between resources and uses in each sector. These equations imply that the investment is self-financed and they connect physical equations to price Equations (v) and (vi). Finally, (vii) and $(viii)$ define the rates of saving. Note that s_2 can be negative (see Appendix 2). By combining (i) and (iii) or (ii) and (iv), we obtain the famous exchange equation, i.e., the equality between the value of the means of production bought by sector II and the value of the consumption goods bought by sector I. The sum of the budget constraints (iii) and (iv) gives Walras' law showing that any one of these equations is redundant. Only 7 of the equations are then independent. By taking the physical variables – proportion q and the coefficients a_{ij} – as given, the remaining nine variables are: $g_1, g_2, r_1, r_2, p, s_1, s_2, c_1, c_2$. Thus, the model has two degrees of freedom and therefore, it can be solved in different ways.

We are only interested in the solutions economically meaningful for Marx's theory. The choice of exogenous variables must be consistent with the existence of a balanced growth path in the second period and we showed that one necessary condition is the exogenous decision on accumulation in sector I. The sequence of the solution of physical and value equations is opposite depending on whether the price is assumed as flexible or fixed.

In the following two subsections, we will analyse the reproduction of the economy in both cases, endogenous and exogenous prices.

3.1. Reproduction and crises in the endogenous price model

We will show that the model is recursive: we first solve the physical sub-system (i)–(ii) and then the value sub-system (iii)–$(viii)$.

Let us consider the initial period. Since the price is endogenous, the investments are not constrained by profits and therefore, the accumulation decision in sector I is represented by g_1. We assume that the physical conditions for the reproduction are satisfied: $1 \leq G_1 \leq \mu$ (see inequalities (10)) and $q \leq q_{max}(G_1)$. Equations (i) and (ii) form a sub-system determining respectively g_2 and $(c_1 + c_2) \geq 0$. The reproduction of use-values as a function of g_1 is then determined. Both rates g_i and $(c_1 + c_2)$ are the parameters in the remaining equations. Sub-system (iii)–$(viii)$ is made up of five independent equations and has one degree of freedom. The price is not determined. It must lie within a range defined by a lower bound and an upper bound, which are respectively given by the solution of Equation (v) by setting $r_1 = g_1$ and of Equation (vi) by setting $r_2 = g_2$. Whatever the price, Equations (v) and (vi) give both rates of profit, Equations (vii) and $(viii)$ determine both saving rates and Equation (iii) or (iv) gives the capitalist consumption in each sector. All these variables depend on an undetermined price,[12] but this has no effect on the reproduction of the economy since, in this model, the crisis can only occur if the physical conditions of reproduction are not satisfied. Note that conditions (a) and (b) imply $g_i \leq r_i$, i.e., the physical investments are financed by the corresponding profits. Therefore, this model is compatible with Marx's self-financing assumption.

At the end of the first period, the equilibrium proportion is obtained. If g_1 remains constant in the second period, g_2 changes (see Equation (i)) and the price ceiling also changes. As a consequence of the change in g_2 and (or) in r_2, the rate of saving s_2 is modified in such a way that Equation $(viii)$ is met.

The price range in the first and the second periods is one of the main results of the model. We will study it more carefully in the next two subsections.

---

[12] The indetermination can be eliminated by adding the equality $s_1 = s_2$ which, in this model, is compatible with the asymmetrical relationship between sectors. Furthermore, it has the advantage of entailing a balanced growth path with a uniform rate of profit (see subsection 3.1.2).

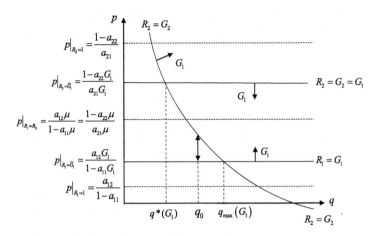

Figure 2. The price range.

3.1.1. The price range in the first period

Since the sectoral accumulation of capital must be self-financed, the accumulation expenses must at least be covered by sectoral receipts. The price lies within a range which changes from the first to the second period.

The relative price must be such that both inequalities $G_i \leq R_i$ (where $R_i = 1 + r_i$) are met. Expressing these limits as a function of the exogenous G_1 and q, we get the following range:

$$\frac{a_{12}G_1}{1 - a_{11}G_1} \leq p \leq \frac{a_{21} - a_{22}q(1 - a_{11}G_1)}{a_{21}q(1 - a_{11}G_1)} \tag{12}$$

The price floor, on the left-hand side of these inequalities, is determined by setting $R_1 = G_1$ in Equation (v) or equivalently, $c_1 = 0$ in Equation (iii). That price is an increasing function of G_1 (it must be higher in order that a higher G_1 can be financed by a higher R_1) and it is independent of the activity level in sector I. When G_1 changes from 1 to μ, the price floor increases from the level at which the rate of profit in sector I is nil, $p_{|R_1 = 1} = \frac{a_{12}}{1-a_{11}}$, to the price of production, $p_{|R_1 = R_2} = \frac{a_{12}\mu}{1-a_{11}\mu}$, as shown in Figure 2.

The price ceiling is calculated by setting $R_2 = G_2$ in Equation (vi) (or $c_2 = 0$ in Equation (iv)) and by using Equation (i) to eliminate G_2. That price is an increasing function of G_1 and a decreasing function of q. For a given q, if sector I accumulates more, factor G_2 decreases (see Equation (i)) and this is compatible with a lower rate of profit in sector II. However, for a given G_1, if q increases, the price ceiling is lower because sector II must accumulate more, so that R_2 must increase and this implies a lower price.

The price floor is a horizontal line and the price ceiling is a hyperbola decreasing from infinity to a negative value of p. To each given G_1, we can associate a $q_{max}(G_1)$ compatible with the reproduction of the economy. If q_0 is the initial proportion, the price must lie within the range represented in Figure 2. That range is reduced to a single point if $q = q_{max}(G_1)$. At the intersection between the prices, ceiling and floor, the rate of growth in each sector is equal to the rate of profit. The capitalists' consumption is nil, and by definition, the proportion is equal to $q_{max}(G_1)$ (see Equation (9)). If the initial proportion exceeds this maximum value, there is no price compatible with the reproduction of the system at the chosen level of G_1.

For $q \leq q_{max}(G_1)$ the price range is not empty. Therefore, if a Marx–Engels equilibrium exists in the physical sub-system, there is at least one endogenous price such that an equilibrium exists in the value model we are studying.

When G_1 increases, both prices, ceiling and floor, move upwards as indicated in Figure 2. The price ceiling increases more or less than the price floor according to the positive or negative sign of the determinant: Equation (9) shows that $q_{max}(G_1)$ is an increasing or decreasing function depending on D being positive or negative.

3.1.2. The price range on the balanced growth path

In the second period, q adjusts to the equilibrium proportion $q^* = \frac{a_{21}G_1}{1 - a_{11}G_1}$ (see Equation (7)). The price floor is unchanged and the price ceiling, now determined by $G_1 \leq R_2$, is independent of the initial proportion. After replacing q by the value of $q^*_{max}(G_1)$ on the right-hand side of inequality (12), we get:

$$\frac{a_{12}G_1}{1 - a_{11}G_1} \leq p \leq \frac{1 - a_{22}G_1}{a_{21}G_1} \tag{13}$$

In the second period, both bounds of the price are horizontal lines. For G_1 varying from 1 to μ, the price ceiling decreases from $\frac{1 - a_{22}}{a_{21}}$, for which $r_2 = 0$, to the production price $\frac{1 - a_{22}\mu}{a_{21}\mu}$. The price floor increases from $\frac{a_{12}}{1 - a_{11}}$, for which $r_1 = 0$, to the price of production. Thus, for $G_1 = \mu$, the price range is reduced to a single point representing the price of production whereas, for $G_1 = 1$, the price range is not empty

since the Hawkins Simon conditions are satisfied: both rates of profit
are non-negative.

If in the first period $G_1 > G_2$, then the proportion q is higher in the
second period and the price ceiling is lower. In such a case, there exist
some prices which satisfy condition (12) in the first period but are
higher than the price ceiling in the second period. If the price is flexible, it can vary from one period to the next so that the investment in
sector II on the balanced path is financed. If the price were not flexible, its minimum ceiling should be imposed from the start.

Finally, a balanced growth path with different rates of profit is a
strange thing, which is common to both the flexible price model and
Marx's fixed price model (see the next subsection). One can wish to
privilege the price of production.[13] In our model, this result is
obtained by adding the equality between sectoral saving rates, as
showed by Equations (*vii*) and (*viii*) (see also footnote 13).

It is instructive to compare our model with the Keynesian tradition,
for instance, Kaldor's model (1955–1956), in which the investment
decision is preeminent and determines the saving by which it is
financed, as in our model. Nevertheless, the mechanisms are quite different. In Kaldor's model, there is no relative price and, the saving
rates being given, the investment rate determines the share of wages
and profits in the national income. The profit share is positively
related to the investment rate and negatively to the rate of saving out
of profits. On the contrary, in our model, the shares of wages and
profits are constant; they do not depend on the rate of growth. The
sectoral saving rates are residual in the sense that they are determined
at the last stage of the solution of the model. They depend on the
price but have no effect on the distribution of income and on the balanced growth path. The choice of a relative price within the price
range determines the rates of profit and therefore, the saving rates
and the distribution of the consumption goods between the capitalists,
but these values do not have the slightest effect on capital accumulation. In Kaldor's sense, a model like ours is Marxist, whereas his is
Kaleckian (when the saving rate of workers is nil, 1955–1956, 96).

---

[13] See, for instance, Morishima's critique of Marx's scheme (1973, 114 and 122). As we have
already seen, in Morishima's formalization, the profits are not necessarily invested in the
sector in which they are generated.

3.2. Reproduction and crises in Marx's exogenous price model

In Marx's schemes the price is exogenous. It determines the rate of profit in each sector and thus the maximum accumulation rates. The model is recursive but now the value relations determine the physical conditions of reproduction.

The relative price does not depend either on the proportion between sectors or on the accumulation of capital. It follows that the accumulation in sector I depends on the price and on the saving rate in sector I, which are assumed as exogenous. Marx's hypothesis implies that the price is not only exogenous but also fixed. If the price changed over time, r_1 (Equation v) and also g_1 (Equation vii) should change and one of the conditions for the Marx–Engels equilibrium in the second period (g_1 constant) would no longer be satisfied.

Proportion q and the technique being given, the two exogenous variables in Marx's model are p and s_1. Equations (v) and (vi) determine r_1 and r_2 as a function of p, Equation (vii) gives g_1 as a function of s_1 and Equation (iii) gives c_1. Equation (i) gives g_2, which may be negative but greater than -1, Equation ($viii$) gives s_2 and finally Equation (iv) gives c_2. Marx's model is recursive. However, contrary to the endogenous price model, in the sequential solution procedure, we first solve the price equations, which allows us to determine the strategic variable g_1.

While r_1 and r_2 in the endogenous price model adjust to the rates of accumulation by means of p, the adjustment mechanism in Marx's model is the opposite: the compatibility of the physical rates g_i with the rates of profit determined by the exogenous price is ensured by the exogenous saving rate s_1 and the adaptation of the endogenous saving rate s_2. The solution $s_2 > 1$ (equivalent to $g_2 > r_2$) expresses a crisis, which only occurs if the self-financing condition is not satisfied in sector II, whereas it is necessarily satisfied in sector I (s_1 is an exogenous variable, not negative and lower than, or equal to 1, by hypothesis.)

We are going to study the consequences of the exogenous and fixed price on the accumulation of the means of production. This analysis enables us to determine the conditions for a crisis in Marx's model. These conditions are then compared with those of the endogenous and flexible price model.

3.2.1. The exogenous and fixed price

Since, in Marx's model, the relative price and the saving rate in sector
I determine the accumulation of capital, the knowledge of their
extreme values enables us to analyse the effects of the exogenous price
on the absorption of the means of production.

(a) The range of the exogenous variables

We are going to show that in Marx's model the exogenous variables, p and
s_1, must lie within a range. The p range only depends on the technique
(see (14)) and the s_1 range depends on both the technique and the price
(see (15)). When the exogenous price is higher than the price of
production sector I cannot accumulate all its profits.

The exogenous price plays a crucial role. By determining both rates of
profit, it imposes a bound to the accumulation of capital in each sector. For the economy not to disappear, none of the profit rates can be
negative. The exogenous price must, therefore, lie within the following
range, defined (as the range of G_1 in the previous model) by the technique:

$$\frac{a_{12}}{1 - a_{11}} \leq p \leq \frac{1 - a_{22}}{a_{21}}. \tag{14}$$

The technical matrix being productive, this range is not empty.
Obviously, Marx's labour values satisfy this condition.

Owing to the self-financing investment hypothesis, the rate of
growth on a balanced path cannot be higher than the lowest rate of
profit. As s_1 is exogenous, we must have $g_1 = s_1 r_1 \leq r_2$.

When the price is lower than the production price, $r_1 < r_2$ and the
rate s_1 can be equal to 1; this is not the case if the price is higher
than the production price, i.e., $r_1 > r_2$. Thus, the s_1 range depends on
the price. We have:

$$0 \leq g_1 \leq \min(r_1, r_2)$$
$$0 \leq s_1 \leq \min\left(1, \frac{r_2}{r_1}\right) \tag{15}$$

Note that, in Marx's model, the maximum accumulation factor
$G_1 = \mu$ can only be reached in the particular case of the exogenous
price equal to the price of production and $s_1 = 1$.

(b) The exogenous price constraint on the absorption of the means of production

Let $q_{max}(s_1, p)$ be the proportion allowing the maximum absorption of the means of production when the relative price is p and the saving rate of sector I is s_1. The maximum value of q supposes a zero capitalist consumption in sector II. For all q beyond it, a crisis occurs because sector II cannot adjust to the accumulation decision in sector I. The maximum proportion is calculated by setting $s_2 = 1$ and by replacing both g_i in Equation *(i)*, by their expression in Equations *(vii)* and *(viii)* of system (11):

$$q_{max}(s_1, p) = \frac{a_{21}(1 + r_2)}{1 - a_{11}(1 + s_1 r_1)} \qquad (16)$$

Proportion $q_{max}(s_1, p)$ is an increasing function of s_1, but the sign of its derivative with regard to p is indeterminate: a rise in p increases r_1 and lowers r_2, with opposite effects on q_{max}.

As we have seen, p and s_1 being given, the exogenous price model determines g_1. Proportion q and g_1 being given, the endogenous price model determines a price range. What is the relationship between the exogenous price and this range?

We will show that in both the first and second period an exogenous price compatible with the reproduction in the fixed price model lies within the endogenous price range.

If we substitute, in Equation (16), $1 + r_2$ by its expression according to Equation *(vi)*, we obtain $p = \frac{a_{21} - a_{22}q_{max}[1 - a_{11}(1 + s_1 r_1)]}{a_{21}q_{max}[1 - a_{11}(1 + s_1 r_1)]}$ i.e., the price ceiling in the endogenous price model (see inequalities (12)) when $q = q_{max}(s_1, p)$.[14] This is a natural result: to calculate $q_{max}(s_1, p)$, we have assumed $s_2 = 1$, which implies $r_2 = g_2$ and this condition defines the price ceiling. Starting from a price satisfying condition (14), we determine both rates of profit and $q_{max}(s_1, p)$. The calculation shows that we obtain a price ceiling equal to the price which we have started with. On the other hand, the price ceiling is a decreasing function of q (see inequalities (12)). For $q < q_{max}$, this ceiling is higher than the exogenous price, which can then be higher than the one associated to q_{max}. As for the price floor, it must be less than the exogenous price because $s_1 \leq 1$. We can conclude that an exogenous price compatible

---

[14] Notice that a change in s_1 has no effect on the price ceiling: according to Equation (16), the product $q_{max}[1 - a_{11}(1 + s_1 r_1)]$ is equal to $a_{21}(1 + r_2)$, which is a constant since it only depends on the fixed price. A change in s_1 is compensated by a change in the same direction of q_{max}.

with the reproduction of the initial proportion in the fixed price model lies within the endogenous price range.

In the second period, the equilibrium proportion is $q^* = \frac{a_{21}(1+s_1 r_1)}{1 - a_{11}(1+s_1 r_1)}$. Since $s_1 r_1 \leq r_2$, this proportion is less than (or equal to) $q_{max}(s_1, p)$, and thus the exogenous price is less than (or equal to) the price ceiling in the second period in the endogenous price model. We have seen that, in the latter model, it may be necessary to lower the price if the proportion increases from one period to the next. This eventuality has no equivalent in Marx's model since the inequality $s_1 r_1 \leq r_2$ in the first period rules out the possibility of a crisis in the second period.

3.2.2. The critical proportions in both models: a comparison

> We will show that the maximal proportion of the means of production which can be absorbed cannot ever be higher in the exogenous price model: $q_{max}(s_1, p) \leq q_{max}(G_1)$.

Proportion $q_{max}(s_1, p)$ should not be confused with $q_{max}(G_1)$ of the endogenous price model. As we have seen, the latter represents the maximum proportion compatible with the reproduction of the use-values, which cannot be exceeded. This proportion is reached when all the profits are accumulated, while $q_{max}(s_1, p)$ supposes the total accumulation of the profits in sector II exclusively. Let us consider a given G_1. In the endogenous price model, it determines $q_{max}(G_1)$ univocally. In the exogenous price model, it is not the case because the same G_1 can be obtained as the product of a plurality of s_1 and r_1 (which depends on p). Thus, there is a plurality of $q_{max}(s_1, p)$ compatible with the same G_1. There is only one price which, for this G_1, gives the equality $q_{max}(s_1, p) = q_{max}(G_1)$, namely the price such that $R_1 = G_1$, which implies $s_1 = 1$.[15] To obtain the same G_1, when the prices are such that $R_1 > G_1$, we must have $s_1 < 1$. The positive consumption of the capitalists of sector I reduces the amount of the consumption goods available to feed the workers and the accumulation of capital is reduced too. Accordingly, $q_{max}(s_1, p) \leq q_{max}(G_1)$. For the same G_1, some initial proportions, which can be reproduced in the endogenous price model, are not reproduced in the exogenous

---

[15] A calculation shows that the difference $q_{max}(G_1) - q_{max}(s_1, p)$ has the same sign, positive or negative, as $R_1 - G_1$.

Table 1. The critical proportions in each model.

		Proportion above which a crisis occurs whatever the rate of growth or the rate of saving in sector I	Proportion below which a crisis never occurs whatever the rate of growth or the rate of saving in sector I
Endogenous Price	$D \geq 0$	$q_{max}(\mu) = \dfrac{a_{21}}{a_{22} - \mu D} = \dfrac{a_{21}\mu}{1 - a_{11}\mu}$	$q_{max}(1) = \dfrac{a_{21}}{a_{22} - D} = \dfrac{a_{21}G_2^{max}}{1 - a_{11}}$
	$D \leq 0$	$q_{max}(1) = \dfrac{a_{21}}{a_{22} - D} = \dfrac{a_{21}G_2^{max}}{1 - a_{11}}$	$q_{max}(\mu) = \dfrac{a_{21}}{a_{22} - \mu D} = \dfrac{a_{21}\mu}{1 - a_{11}\mu}$
Exogenous Price	$p \geq p\big|_{r_1 = r_2}$	$q_{max}\left[\dfrac{r_2}{r_1}, p\right] = \dfrac{a_{21}R_2}{1 - a_{11}R_2}$	$q_{max}(0,p) = \dfrac{a_{21}R_2}{1 - a_{11}}$
	$p \leq p\big|_{r_1 = r_2}$	$q_{max}[1, p] = \dfrac{a_{21}R_2}{1 - a_{11}R_1} = \dfrac{a_{21}}{a_{22} - R_1 D}$	

price model, while any reproducible proportion in the latter model is obviously also reproduced in the former.

The following comparison between the critical proportions in both models brings to light the constraints on the reproduction implied by the level of the exogenous price.

Table 1 is constructed by introducing first the extreme values of G_1 (1 and μ) into the expression of $q_{max}(G_1)$ (see Equation (9)) and second the extreme values of s_1 (0 and r_2/r_1 or 1), into the expression of $q_{max}(s_1, p)$, (see Equation (15)).

> We are going to show that both proportions above which a crisis is inevitable and, with a notable exception, below which a crisis is impossible are higher in the endogenous price model. Furthermore, there exists an extreme case in which an impossible crisis in the endogenous price model is inevitable in Marx's model.

(a) The proportion below which a crisis is impossible

Let us compare the proportions in the second column of Table 1. Two cases must be distinguished according to the sign of the determinant. If $D \geq 0$, we have $q_{max}(1) \geq q_{max}(0, p)$ because $G_2^{max} \geq R_2$. The maximum proportion is the same in both models if $R_2 = G_2^{max}$, which is only obtained for an exogenous price such that $R_1 = 1$. For a higher price, and therefore, a higher R_1, the capitalists' consumption is positive and then the consumption goods available to the sector II workers are reduced and so is the accumulation in this sector.

> There exist some cases in which crises while possible in the endogenous price model are impossible in the exogenous price model.

The case of a negative determinant is interesting in the sense that it gives an unexpected and exceptional result. There exists a price such that $q_{max}(\mu) = q_{max}(0,p) : p = \frac{a_{11}a_{22}-\mu D}{a_{21}(1-a_{11})}$. For any exogenous price below this level, we have $q_{max}(\mu) < q_{max}(0,p)$, because R_2 and G_2 are higher and sector II makes a more intensive use of the means of production. A *fortiori* this inequality is verified for a higher s_1: the amount of the means of production absorbed by sector I is higher while G_2 does not decrease. Therefore, the total absorption of the means of production increases. Thus, the maximum price below which the above inequality is verified increases. A fixed price has a positive effect on reproduction. Why do we observe such a result, which may seem counterintuitive? If the price is endogenous, when G_1 increases, G_2 decreases and this can prevent the system from reproducing itself when $D < 0$. By fixing the price, the capacity of accumulation in sector II is preserved. The increase in s_1 and G_1 makes it possible to increase the reproducible proportion. Accordingly, in such a model, the exogenously fixed price does not necessarily entail a constraint on the accumulation of capital.

(b) The proportion above which a crisis is inevitable

To start with, let us compare the proportions in the first column. If the price is lower than the production price, the critical proportion is $q_{max}(1,p)$. If the determinant is positive, we have $q_{max}(1,p) < q_{max}(\mu)^{16}$ because $R_1 < \mu$. If the determinant is negative, we have $q_{max}(1,p) \leq q_{max}(1)$ because $R_1 \geq 1$. When the price is higher than the price of production, the maximum value of s_1 is equal to r_2/r_1 and $s_1 r_1$ is replaced by r_2. We have $q_{max}(\frac{r_2}{r_1},p) = \frac{a_{21}R_2}{1-a_{11}R_2}$, which appears in Table 1. Thus, q_{max} is a decreasing function of p whatever the sign of the determinant: the accumulation in sector I is bounded by r_2, which decreases when the price increases. We then have:

$$D > 0 \qquad q_{max}\left(\frac{r_2}{r_1},p\right) \leq \frac{a_{21}\mu}{1-a_{11}\mu} = q_{max}(\mu)$$

$$D < 0 \qquad q_{max}\left(\frac{r_2}{r_1},p\right) \leq \frac{a_{21}}{a_{22}-\mu D} < \frac{a_{21}}{a_{22}-D} = q_{max}(1)$$

i.e., the reproducible proportions when the price is exogenous, are equal to, or less than, those when the price is endogenous: the rates of profit, determined by the exogenous price, constrain the sectoral

---

[16] By eliminating p between Equations (v) and (vi) of system (11), one obtains a decreasing relation between the factors of profit: $R_2 = (1-a_{11}R_1)/(a_{22}-DR_1)$. Therefore, R_2 can be eliminated in the expression of $q_{max}(1,p)$ in Table 1.

rates of accumulation and limit the amount of the means of production, which can be absorbed.

There exist some cases in which crises while inevitable in the exogenous price model are impossible in the endogenous price model.

When the exogenous price is higher than the production price, we can establish a stronger proposition: if, in the endogenous price model, the available means of production are fully used whatever G_1, they are not necessarily absorbed when the price is exogenous even if s_1 is maximum. Let us compare $q_{max}(\frac{r_2}{r_1}, p)$ with $q_{max}(\mu)$ and $q_{max}(1)$ in the endogenous price model. If the determinant is negative, since $R_2 < \mu$, we have $q_{max}(\frac{r_2}{r_1}, p) < q_{max}(\mu)$: the maximum proportion that can be reproduced when the price is exogenous is *always* less than the one which is absorbed in the endogenous price model whatever G_1. Let us consider now the case of a positive determinant. There exists a price, equal to $\frac{a_{11}-D}{a_{21}}$,[17] such that $q_{max}(\frac{r_2}{r_1}, p) = q_{max}(1)$. For any price higher than this level, we have $q_{max}(\frac{r_2}{r_1}, p) < q_{max}(1)$: the maximum proportion in the exogenous price model for a maximum rate of saving in sector I, is lower than the maximum proportion in the endogenous price model, whatever G_1.

Thus, for some prices, there are proportions, which are reproduced in the endogenous price model, whatever G_1, and which cannot be reproduced in the exogenous price model, whatever s_1. A crisis, which is impossible at endogenous prices, becomes inevitable at exogenous prices. Why is it so? In the endogenous price model, if the growth rate of sector I decreases, the one in sector II increases. On the contrary, at a fixed price, the growth of sector II does not change because it is constrained by r_2 as determined by p.

In the case favoured by Marx and the Marxist tradition, sector I is deemed as the most capital intensive. The price of production may be considered as the exogenous price most appropriate to the reproduction of the system: first, it is the price allowing to reproduce the maximum proportion when $s_1 = 1$ and secondly, it is the only price compatible with the von Neumann (1938) maximum growth path.[18]

---

[17] Note that the numerator is positive, since $a_{11} - D = a_{11}(1 - a_{22}) + a_{12}a_{21} > 0$.

[18] Note that if $s_1 < 1$, the price of production is not always the price allowing the largest absorption of the means of production. If $D > 0$ and s_1 is large enough, the differential increase $a_{11}qs_1dr_1$ in the amount of the means of production accumulated in sector I as a result from a price increase can exceed the differential decrease $a_{21}dr_2$ of the means of production accumulated in sector II.

Conclusion

Marx's scheme of extended reproduction is a far-reaching macroeconomic model of a two-sector economy in which growth is given an impulse by investing in the sector producing the means of production. For the study of social capital, Marx emphasized the importance of reproducing the "material shape" of commodities. We have shown that such an analysis is based on the physical equations representing the balance, for each commodity, between resources and uses. Our study highlights that the main properties of Marx's scheme derive from its physical specification: a two-sector economy in which one commodity can only be accumulated. Two consequences are drawn of this assumption: first, the leading role of investment in the sector producing the means of production (this asymmetry of investment decisions is a necessary condition for the existence of a balanced growth path from the second period onwards); secondly, the use of one commodity being quantitatively bounded, its overproduction is possible. For a given technique, crises can occur because of an inappropriate accumulation rate in sector I, or because of too high a proportion between sectors. These physical constraints are common to any economy in which accumulation is the only use of one of the commodities, whether capitalist or centralized, monetary or barter, with endogenous or exogenous price.

The integration of physical equations into the value model brings to light that, in Marx's analysis, two assumptions play a key role: on the one hand, the exogenous price and on the other, the investment of profits in the sector in which they are generated. It has been shown that, compared to the physical constraints, the latter hypothesis does not bring about any further constraint if the price is endogenous since it lies within a range such that the exogenous physical investment generates the profits which finance it. On the contrary, by determining the profits, the exogenous price imposes additional constraints on investment. When the self-financing hypothesis is eliminated, the exogenous price in Marx's model does not entail an additional constraint because the investment in a sector can also be financed by the profit generated in the other sector. It follows that some crises in Marx's model could be avoided, if one of these two crucial hypotheses were removed.

A natural extension of this article is the analysis of the dynamics of the crises through which the overproduction of the means of production can be absorbed. It will be the subject of a later study.

Acknowledgements

We wish to express our gratitude to the anonymous referees for their valuable comments and suggestions which enable us to improve our article.

Disclosure statement

No potential conflict of interest was reported by the authors.

Appendix 1

Marx's numerical examples

Marx provided three numerical examples of the extended reproduction. The first one exhibits the same exogenous saving rates and the same organic composition of capital in both sectors. The next two examples are called by Engels "first" and "second illustration." In the first illustration, the most significant one, the organic compositions are different and the accumulation decisions are asymmetric. The second one is similar to the first one except for the uniform organic composition of capital.

(i) Scheme A (Marx, [1885]1956, 307; Manuscript VIII, [1876-1881] 2008, 806)

This scheme is interesting for two reasons: first, all the authors who reject the leading role of sector I more or less rely on it; secondly, it will be seen that the failure of the first example stimulated Marx to adopt the hypothesis about the asymmetrical investment decisions.

Foley (1986, 84–85) uses this example to illustrate his general formulation of the extended reproduction in Marx. He concludes as follows: "If we start with any other proportions [than the 'equilibrium' proportion], it is impossible to meet the conditions of expanded reproduction". In a sense, his assertion is diametrically opposed to Morishima's according to whom, whatever the initial proportion, Marx's economy reaches the balanced growth path in one go.

$$I \quad \underset{c_1}{4\,000} + \underset{v_1}{1000} + \underset{m_1}{1000} = \underset{y_1}{6000}$$
$$II \quad \underset{c_2}{1500} + \underset{v_2}{375} + \underset{m_2}{375} = \underset{y_2}{2250}$$

The organic composition is 4 in both sectors (corresponding to 375 of variable capital in sector II instead of 376 in the text) and the uniform saving rate is 0.5. Since the solution does not depend on the choice of the physical units adopted for measuring the goods, we assume that both monetary prices are equal to 1. The data associated with Marx's example are

$$A = \begin{pmatrix} a_{11} & a_{12} \\ a_{21} & a_{22} \end{pmatrix} = \begin{pmatrix} 2/3 & 1/6 \\ 2/3 & 1/6 \end{pmatrix} \qquad D = 0 \qquad \mu = 1.2 = R_1 = R_2$$

Since the profit rates and the saving rates are uniform, the accumulation rates must also be uniform ($G = 1.1$). The balanced growth path is only possible if the initial proportion is the equilibrium proportion as calculated by Equation (4), $q^* = \frac{a_{21}G}{1-a_{11}G} = 2.75$. Since Marx took q as an exogenous variable ($\frac{6000}{2250} = 2.6667$), his system is overdetermined. It cannot work: a simple calculation shows that 50 is the amount of both the excess demand for the means of production and the excess supply of consumption goods. Marx abandoned the analysis of the first example and moved to the next.

Contrary to what Foley (1986, 84) writes, this is the only example supporting the idea that the economy only works if it starts from the equilibrium proportion. Therefore, Marx's first example is not appropriate for a general analysis of the extended reproduction as shown by the subsequent examples constructed by Marx.

(ii) First Illustration (Marx, [1885] 1956, 310; Manuscript VIII, [1876–1881] 2008, 816))

$$\text{I} \quad \underset{c_1}{4000} + \underset{v_1}{1000} + \underset{m_1}{1000} = \underset{y_1}{6000}$$
$$\text{II} \quad \underset{c_2}{1500} + \underset{v_2}{750} + \underset{m_2}{750} = \underset{y_2}{3000}$$

Hence,

$$A = \begin{pmatrix} 2/3 & 1/6 \\ 1/2 & 1/4 \end{pmatrix} \qquad D = 1/12 \qquad \mu = 1.228 \qquad R_1 = 6/5 \qquad R_2 = 4/3$$

This is the most important illustration, commonly used in the studies on extended reproduction (e.g., Luxemburg, Morishima, etc.). This numerical example clearly shows the asymmetrical relationship between sectors and the existence of the Marx–Engels' equilibrium in the second period. Marx assumed that the capitalists of sector I accumulate one-half of their surplus value, corresponding to $G_1 = 1.1$. Hence, $G_2 = 1.0667$ and, at the end of the first period, the economy reaches its equilibrium proportion equal to 2.0624. In the second period, the uniform rate of growth is equal to 0.1. And so on, in accordance with Engels' edition.

Actually, in Marx's manuscript, the sectoral growth rates are different at all periods. Why? Let us note first that Marx's calculations for the first period confirm that our hypotheses (see Section 2.1) are the same as Marx's and clearly illustrate the asymmetrical relationship between sectors. The saving rate in sector II (equal to 0.2) results from the adjustment of the net investment in this sector (150) so that the available means of production are fully accumulated. The calculations are correct and Marx obtained the equilibrium proportion at the end of the first period (6600/3200). At this stage of the analysis, Marx had all the data to find out the balanced growth path at the next period.

Unfortunately, two pure and simple calculation errors prevent him from seeing that this proportion should remain unchanged. Marx claimed that the organic composition of capital in sector I must remain unchanged, but he calculated the distribution of the accumulated surplus value on the basis of an organic composition equal to 3 instead of 4: "Sub I) ist zu kapitalisiren *550 m*; davon, bleibt frühere Proportion, $412\frac{1}{2}$ *constantes Capital und* $137\frac{1}{2}$ *variables Capital*" (Marx, [1876–1881] 2008, Manuscript VIII, 812).[19] He maintained the erroneous

---

[19] We are very grateful to Michael Gaul for pointing out to us Marx's erroneous calculation.

organic composition in his subsequent calculations. Since the composition of the accumulated capital is less than the composition of the existing capital in sector I, the organic composition will gradually decrease whereas the rate of profit and the rate of accumulation will increase indefinitely. The balanced growth path cannot be reached before "the end of time". This first error is immediately followed by another one. The amount of the means of production which are not accumulated in sector I is 187.5, but Marx made a mistake in copying and writes 137.5. The increase in variable capital in sector II is then 68.5. These two errors explain the fanciful scheme of the second period in the manuscript.

$$\left.\begin{array}{ll} \text{I} & 4812.5_c + 1237.5_v + 1237.5_m = 7287.5 \\ \text{II} & 1787.5_c + 868.75_v + 868.75_m = 3525 \end{array}\right\} = 10812$$

In his edition of volume II of *Capital*, Engels corrected these two errors and under Marx's hypotheses, he found a balanced growth path in the second period and henceforth. The model is Marx's, but it is Engels who drew its logical conclusion. At least on this point, the posterity can only be grateful to him.[20] Therefore, our denomination as "Marx–Engels' equilibrium" is justified.

Let us go back to *Capital*. It is worth pointing out that the initial proportion is very particular because, in Marx's scheme, 2 is the critical proportion $q_{max}(0, p)$. In the case of a positive determinant as in Marx, this proportion excludes any crisis, whatever the rate of accumulation in sector I (satisfying inequalities (10)). For the same $s_1 = 0.5$, if Marx had taken any initial proportion higher than 3.16 (see Equation (9)), a crisis would have occurred in the first period ($c < 0$). It is, therefore, not correct to claim, like Morishima, that in Marx's model, the equilibrium in the second period "is not specific to the numerical illustration used by Marx, but is a logical implication of his investment function" (Morishima 1973, 120). As we have shown, Marx's investment function does not rule out the occurrence of a crisis: the balanced growth depends on the initial proportion between sectors and, for some proportions, on the accumulation decision in sector I.

(iii) Second Illustration (Marx, [1885] 1956, 313 and 316; Manuscript VIII, [1876–1881] 2008, 816 and 821)

$$\begin{array}{ll} \text{I} & \underset{c_1}{5000} + \underset{v_1}{1000} + \underset{m_1}{1000} = \underset{y_1}{7000} \\ \text{II} & \underset{c_2}{1430} + \underset{v_2}{285} + \underset{m_2}{285} = \underset{y_2}{2000} \end{array}$$

Hence,

$$A = \begin{pmatrix} 5/7 & 1/7 \\ 5/7 & 1/7 \end{pmatrix} \qquad D = 0 \qquad \mu = 7/6 = R_1 = R_2$$

---

[20] Obviously, no balanced growth path is found in Marx's manuscript. Nevertheless, Gehrke is not entitled to deduce that "a steady state cannot be inferred from Marx's original discussion" (2017, 16). As we saw the balanced path logically belongs to Marx's model.

Marx is still mistaken in distributing, in sector I, the net accumulation between the constant and the variable capital. The choice of a saving rate equal to 0.5 determines a capital accumulation equal to 500, which Marx divides into 400 and 100. Thus, the capital in sector I is: $5400_c + 1100_v$ (see Marx [1876–1881] 2008, 821). Therefore, the new organic composition of capital lies strictly between 4 and 5. This error is transmitted to the values of sector II. As he did in the previous illustration, Engels corrected it. The distribution of the net accumulation must be 417_c and 83_v (see Marx [1885] 1956, 316) so that the balanced growth path is obtained in the second period after the adjustment of sector II.

Surprisingly, Marx, followed by Engels, rewrote the equation of sector II as follows (Equation II′)

$$\text{II}' \quad \underset{c_2}{1500} + \underset{v_2}{299} + \underset{m_2}{201} = \underset{y_2}{2000}$$

in order to get c_2 equal to what he named the "consumption fund" of sector I. This is wrong because such a fund is actually 1583.3 (i.e., 500 (surplus value) plus 1083.3 (the value of the wage goods to be distributed to the workers in the next period). A noteworthy property of Marx's model is that this error has no consequence on the dynamics and on the Marx–Engels' equilibrium. By starting from the second illustration (Scheme I, II) or from its modified version (Scheme I, II′), we get the same equilibrium system in the next period:

$$\text{I} \quad \underset{c_1}{5416.67} + \underset{v_1}{1083.33} + \underset{m_1}{1083.33} = \underset{y_1}{7583.3}$$
$$\text{II} \quad \underset{c_2}{1583.3} + \underset{v_2}{316.66} + \underset{m_2}{316.66} = \underset{y_2}{2216.6}$$

This system is obtained by only using the sector I equation and factor G_1, which are the same in both schemes ($G_1 = 1.0833$ is the same since R_1 and s_1 are the same). Therefore, the means of production available in sector II are also the same (1583.3). The exchange relationship between sectors is not $v_1 + \frac{1}{2}m_1 = c_2$, but $v_1 G_1 + \frac{1}{2}m_1 = c_2 G_2$ which determines $c_2 G_2$. The accumulation rate in sector II depends on whether one starts from a value of c_2 equal to 1430 or to 1550. After the adjustment of sector II, the equilibrium proportion is the same (3.42) and the balanced growth path is also the same. An increase in the rate of exploitation in sector II makes the capitalists of this sector richer but has no impact on the reproduction of the system.

Appendix 2

The shrinking of sector II and its adjustment

There are some cases in which the adjustment to the balanced growth in the second period implies a reduction in the size of sector II.

Let $q_{min}(G_1)$ be the minimal proportion allowing the simple reproduction of sector II when the accumulation factor in sector I is G_1. This proportion is calculated by comparing the amount of the means of production which has been used in sector II, namely $a_{21}q_2$, with the amount which is not currently used in sector I, namely $q_1 - a_{11}q_1G_1$. Hence,

$$q_{min}(G_1) = \frac{a_{21}}{1 - a_{11}G_1}$$

By definition, sector II shrinks if $q < q_{min}(G_1)$.

Whatever the sign of the determinant, q_{min} is an increasing function of G_1, which varies between 1 and μ (see inequalities (10)).

Two critical proportions are defined:[21]

- $q_{min}(1) = \frac{a_{21}}{1-a_{11}}$ is the simple reproduction proportion below which, whatever G_1, sector II shrinks inevitably.
- $q_{min}(\mu) = \frac{a_{21}}{1-a_{11}\mu}$ is the proportion above which, whatever G_1, sector II never shrinks.

When q is between these two values, sector II shrinks if $G_1 > \frac{q-a_{21}}{a_{11}q}$. Marx was aware of the first critical proportion: he wrote that if $c_2 > v_1 + m_1$, a crisis occurs (Marx [1876–1881] 2008, 823). That is right: we have $v_1 + m_1 = p_1q_1(1-a_{11})$ and $c_2 = a_{21}p_1q_2$, so that $c_2 > v_1 + m_1 \iff q < \frac{a_{21}}{1-a_{11}}$. Marx's inequality means that the initial proportion is less than $q_{min}(1)$. He speaks of an "Überproduction in II", which leads to a "Grossen Krach." Note that such "Krach" is different in nature from what we called "reproduction crisis." Sector II shrinks so that in the next period, the economy is on a balanced growth path at the rate determined by G_1.

A special case of this kind of adjustment is the take-off of an economy starting from the simple reproduction and in which a positive net saving appears in sector I. This case is related to Marx's idea that the extended reproduction should be conceived as the sum of simple reproduction and net accumulation. In our formalization, the traverse from a simple reproduction path towards a balanced growth path is completed in the second period. This is an application of the general property of Marx's model in which the equilibrium proportion is directly determined by the growth rate of sector I in the first period. If, starting from a state of simple reproduction, the capitalists of sector I want to accumulate, sector II must shrink so that the equilibrium proportion of extended reproduction $\frac{a_{21}G_1}{1-a_{11}G_1}$ is reached in the second period (see Equation (4)). This result coincides with the conclusions of Turban's analysis (1980), which we had access to thanks to Gehrke's paper (2018, 9–10).

---

[21] These critical proportions are the same if the price is endogenous. As we have seen, in Marx's model with exogenous price, the maximum value of G_1 is not μ but $\min(R_1, R_2)$.

Appendix 3

Note on the evolution of Marx's position on the extended reproduction

Marx dealt with the "Reproduction and circulation of the aggregate social capital" on three occasions.[22] First, in a manuscript written in 1857–1858 and included in *Grundrisse*. The second text, written in 1868–1870, was published in 2008 in MEGA, under the title *Die realen Bedingungen des Zirkulations und Reproduktionsprozesses*. The third manuscript, written between 1876 and 1881, was published by Engels in volume II of *Capital* under the title *Der Zirkulationsprozeß des Kapitals*. It was also edited in the same volume of MEGA.

In all his writings on reproduction, Marx indicates his interest in the study of crises. In the first manuscript, he deals with a five-sector simple reproduction system and shows that the proportions between different sectors are determined by the technique and the income distribution among profits and wages. He then introduces the accumulation of one-half of the surplus value, the counterpart of which is the reduction of the demand for luxury goods consumed by capitalists, as well as, in Marx's numerical example, the demand for wage-goods due to the decrease in the employment in the luxury goods sector. Marx concludes: "It is clear […] that general overproduction would take place, not because relatively not enough had been produced of the commodities consumed by the workers or of those consumed by the capitalists, but because too much of *both* had been produced – *not too much for consumption*, but too much to retain the *correct relation* between consumption and realization; *too much for realization*" (Marx [1857–1858] 1981, 353).

Marx's proposition stems from his reading of the classical authors. According to them, a crisis results from an abnormally abundant harvest. The problem is not that the food needs are saturated, but that the resources of workers and those that capitalists allocate to their consumption are insufficient to absorb the available consumption goods at their value. The crisis is then transmitted to the other sectors.

In his second manuscript, Marx uses a six-sector model and he studies the effects of changing the organic composition of capital and the rate of surplus value. In the first case, he faces the problem of switching from one simple reproduction equilibrium to another (see Mori 2018).

In his third manuscript, to carry out his study of extended reproduction, Marx radically simplifies the framework of his analysis by abandoning the distinction between luxury goods and wage-goods, so that the industries can be aggregated in a bisector model. He must introduce some new hypotheses, notably of self-financing investment in his first example and of dissymmetry between the two sectors in the second one.

---

[22] We do not examine the major influence of Quesnay's *Tableau économique* on Marx's reflections on reproduction. Marx was literally fascinated by Quesnay's "zig-zag" (see Marx [1861–1863] 1977, 656; [1862–1864] 2013, 398–404).

The numerical examples in Engels' edition of volume II of *Capital* led to the idea that the extended reproduction scheme is a balanced growth model. It is such an idea which attracted Marx's readers' attention, particularly Luxemburg and Morishima. It follows that, according to these authors, a crisis is conceivable only if some of Marx's hypotheses are modified. Luxemburg ([1913] 2003, 337) eliminates the given technique hypothesis and shows that the increasing organic composition of capital results in an overproduction of consumption goods. As for Morishima, he eliminates the self-financing hypothesis and assumes a uniform saving rate. Dynamics are explosive in his model.

Such interpretations are not receivable for two reasons. The first one is based on textual evidence: to study the crisis, Marx explicitly uses his scheme when he considers a "Grossen Krach" (Marx [1876–1881] 2008, 823) caused by an overproduction of consumption goods, as we have seen at the end of Appendix 2. Marx's text is to be found in Engels' edition of *Capital* (Marx [1885] 1956, 317), which was well known by Luxemburg and Morishima. The second reason is a logical one. Morishima wrongly claims that "*any state of unbalanced growth* will disappear in Marx's economy in a single year" (1973, 120, our italics). The existence of Marx–Engels' equilibrium depends on several conditions: physical ones, in particular on the proportion between the two sectors (as shown by Torrens in 1821) and economic ones on price and on the capitalists' saving rate in sector I.

In his numerical examples, Marx did not find a balanced growth path. The question is whether he sought it. His writings show that the answer is positive. The reproduction schemes do not rule out the possibility of crises, on the contrary, they are a theoretical framework which enables us to analyse them. Starting from what he did in the case of simple reproduction, Marx tried to construct a balanced growth model by considering the simplest bisector economy (see "scheme *A*" in Appendix 1). He assumed that both sectors have the same organic composition of capital, the same rate of surplus value and the same capitalists' saving rate, so that the rates of profit and growth are known and uniform, which is exactly what is meant by "balanced growth". As a consequence, the equality of the growth rates must be supported by a unique proportion between the sectoral productions as it can be seen in system (2) where the first equation determines q and the second one determines c. The fatal shortcoming of Marx's example is that such proportion is exogenous. It follows that the model has no solution and, in his comments, Marx did not succeed in finding the cause of this failure. In the second example (see "First Illustration" in Appendix 1), we have an entirely different model. The balanced growth path is now conceived as the outcome of an adjustment of this proportion, which implies different initial rates of growth. The organic compositions of capital and the saving rates are different and the asymmetry between sectors is introduced by considering s_2 as an endogenous variable. That model is quite correct. Marx's right arithmetical calculations enable him to find the equilibrium proportion from the second period onwards. However, his subsequent erroneous calculations prevented him from understanding that what he actually found was the stationary proportion. He vainly continued his numerical calculations for 6 periods.

To sum up, Marx, in his last examples, sought the balanced growth path, conceived as a tool for studying crises. First ("schema A"), he constructed a model with a uniform rate of growth, but he did not realize that such uniformity implied the "good proportion" between sectors. In the second example ("First Illustration") Marx rightly calculated the "good proportion" but arithmetical errors prevented him from obtaining the uniform rate of growth.

References

Bidard, Christian and Edith Klimovsky. 2006. *Capital, Salaire et Crises - Une Approche Classique*. Paris: Dunod. [Spanish translation, México: U.A.M. and Siglo XXI, 2014.]

Carlo, Benetti, Béraud Alain, Klimovsky Edith, and Rebeyrol Antoine. 2013. "Money Values in Marx's Reproduction Model." In *New Contributions to Monetary Analysis: The Foundations of an Alternative Economic Paradigm*, edited by Faruk Ülgen, Matthieu Méaulle, Rémi Stellian, and Ramón Tortajada, 68–90. London: Routledge.

Foley, Duncan K. 1986. *Understanding Capital Marx's Economic Theory*. Cambridge: Harvard University Press.

Gehrke Christian. 2018. "Marx's Reproduction Schemes and Multi-Sector Growth Models." *The European Journal of the History of Economic Thought*, doi: 10.1080/09672567.2018.1475500

Kaldor, Nicholas. 1955–1956. "Alternative Theories of Distribution." *Review of Economic Studies* 23 (2): 83–100. doi:10.2307/2296292

Lange, Oskar. [1961] 1969. *Theories of Reproduction and Accumulation* [English translation]. Oxford: Pergamon Press.

Luxemburg, Rosa. [1913] 2003. *The Accumulation of Capital* [English translation]. London: Routledge and Kegan Paul 1951. Reprint Routledge Classics.

Marx, Karl. [1857–1858] 1981. "Grundrisse der Kritik der Politischen Ökonomie." In *Gesamtausgabe*, (MEGA). Berlin: Dietz Verlag.

Marx Karl. [1861–1863] 1977. "Zur Kritik der Politischen Ökonomie." In *Gesamtausgabe*, (MEGA), Teil 2, Band 3. Berlin: Diez Verlag.

Marx, Karl, and Friedrich Engels. [1862–1864] 2013. "Briefwechsel." In *Gesamtausgabe*, (MEGA), Band 12. Berlin: Akademie Verlag.

Marx, Karl. [1868–1881] 2008. Karl Marx Manuskripte zum zweiten Buch des Kapitals. In *Gesamtausgabe*, (MEGA), Band 11. Berlin: Akademik Verlag.

Marx, Karl. [1885] 1956. *Das Kapital. Buch II: Der Zirkulationsprozess des Kapitals*. Hamburg: Verlag Otto Meissner [English translation, Moscow: Progress Publishers.] https://www.marxists.org.

Marx, Karl. [1894] 1996. *Das Kapital. Buch III: Der Gesammtprocess der kapitalistischen Produktion*. Hamburg: Verlag Otto Meissner [English translation, New York: International Publishers]. https://www.marxists.org.

Marx, Karl. 1968. *OEuvres économie II, French translation*. Paris: Bibliothèque de la Pléiade.

Mori, Kenji. 2018. "New Aspects of Marx's Economic Theory in MEGA: Marx's original Six-Sector Model." *The European Journal of the History of Economic Thought*, doi:10.1080/09672567.2018.1456556

Morishima, Michio. 1973. *Marx's Economics: A Dual Theory of Value and Growth*. Cambridge: Cambridge University Press.

Nikaido, Hukukane. 1983. "Marx on Competition." *Zeitschrift fur Nationalokonomie* 43 (4): 337–363. doi:10.1007/BF01283185

Nikaido, Hukukane. 1985. "Dynamics of Growth and Capital Mobility in Marx's Scheme of Reproduction." *Zeitschrift fur Nationalokonomie* 45 (3): 197–218. doi:10.1007/BF01282561

Rubel, Maximilien. 1968. "Avertissement, Introduction, Notices, Notes, Relevé de Variantes." In *OEuvres Economie II*. Book II: ix-cxxvii. Paris: Bibliothèque de la Pléiade.

Shinkai, Yoichi. 1960. "On Equilibrium Growth of Capital and Labor." *International Economic Review*, 1 (2): 107–111. doi:10.2307/2525290

Sraffa, Piero. 1960. *Production of Commodities by Means of Commodities: Prelude to a Critique of Economic Theory*. Cambridge: Cambridge University Press.

Torrens, Robert. 1821. *An Essay on the Production of Wealth*. London: Longman, Hurst, Rees, Orme and Brown.

Turban, Manfred. 1980. *Marx'sche Reproduktionsschemata und Wirtschaftstheorie. Die Diskussion ihres analytischen Gehalts in verschiedenen wirtschaftswissenschaftlichen Forschungstraditionen*. Berlin: Duncker & Humblot.

Uzawa, Hirofumi. 1961. "On a Two-Sector Model of Economic Growth." *The Review of Economic Studies* 29: 40–47. doi:10.2307/2296180

Uzawa, Hirofumi. 1963. "On a Two-Sector Model of Economic Growth II." *The Review of Economic Studies* 30 (2): 105–118. doi:10.2307/2295808

Von Neumann, John. 1938. "Uber ein Ökonomisches Gleichungssystem und eine Verallgemeinerung des Brouwerschen Fixpunktsatzes." In *Ergebnisse eines mathematischen Seminars*, edited by K. Menger. Leipzig und Wien: Franz Deuticke: 73–83 English translation in *The Review of Economic Studies*, 13, 1 (1945–1946): 1–9. doi:10.2307/2296111

James Steuart and the making of Karl Marx's monetary thought

Rebeca Gomez Betancourt ⓘ and Matari Pierre Manigat ⓘ

ABSTRACT
This paper analyses the influence of James Steuart on Karl Marx's monetary thought. It deals more specifically with Marx's rejection of an automatic mechanism that links variations in the quantity of money to their direct impact on prices. Steuart's pioneering discoveries in economics inaugurate an anti-quantity theory tradition that Marx supported and which fed his own conception of money and credit. Here, we deal with the criticism of the assumptions of the quantity theory of money (QTM), the specifically social character of labour which creates exchange value, the distinction between the functions of money, the difference between income spending and capital advances, and the difference between simple circulation and reflux of money credit.

1. Introduction

In his preface to the fourth German edition of *Capital*, Engels points out that Marx read James Steuart for the first time between 1843 and 1845 in the French translation by Senovert published in five volumes by Didot aîné in Paris in 1789. And indeed, since *Poverty of philosophy* (Marx 1847, 196), Marx's economic works abound with references to Steuart.

By the names of Steuart, Steward and Denham, among others, Marx quoted the author of *An Inquiry into the Principles of Political Economy: Being an Essay on the Science of Domestic Policy in Free Nations* (1767). Steuart occupied a prominent position in the *Grundrisse, Contribution to the critique of political economy*, Book I of *Capital*, and also in the manuscripts of Marx's unfinished later books. And it is also with a chapter on Steuart that Marx begins his *Critical history of economic doctrines*, known as Book IV of *Capital* and published by Karl Kautsky between 1905 and 1910 (now called *Theories of surplus value*).

Marx's references to Steuart cover a variety of domains ranging from the specificity of the modes of production (slavery, serfdom, industry) to the tax foundations of the modern state, including the role of land ownership monopoly in the historical formation of wage labour and the distinction between productive and unproductive labour. In general, Marx finds in Steuart an analysis of the historical processes and mechanisms that led to the separation of direct producers from their objective conditions of production. This separation corresponds to Marx's notion of primitive accumulation (Marx 1905a, 352; Kobayashi 1967; Perelman 1983).

For Marx, Steuart's originality lies in the fact that he "regards things from an historical standpoint." Unlike most of his contemporaries who considered the merchant division of labour, wage labour and the related economic categories as natural data, Steuart avoided the "robinsonades" which obliterated the genesis of the relations of "bourgeois civil society" (Marx 1857a, 17–8). After Steuart, and with the notable exception of some post-Ricardians such as Richard Jones, no English economist will show a "sense of the *historical* differences in modes of production" (Marx 1905b, 320).

Until recently, most studies of Marx's relations with other economists of the eighteenth and nineteenth centuries have shown little interest in the links between Marx and Steuart. In a volume devoted to Steuart and edited by Ramon Tortajada (2002), Henry Denis analyses Marx's judgements on the origin of profit and Steuart's proposal for an ideal standard of money (Denis 1999). McColloch (2011) emphasises the importance of a "theory of history" in Steuart. He also re-evaluates how Marx was influenced by Steuart by reading Hegel, thus extending a hypothesis formulated by Paul Chamley (1963). Yet, none of those studies get at what we believe is crucial: Steuart's influence on Marx's monetary thought and in particular on his criticism of the quantity theory of money (QTM).

Studies of Marx's monetary thought have been structured around the opposition of the author of *Capital* to the QTM. Alfred Pung Hazell, a founding member of the Social Democratic Federation in 1884 and one of the first commentators on Marx's monetary theory, contrasts Marx's ideas with the monetary thought of Mill and Jevons.

Hazell emphasises the interdependence between the theory of money–commodity and the criticism of the QTM (Hazell 1898). Analysing Marx's criticism of the QTM is also the main aim of Hilferding's monetary theory (1909) as well as one of the main goals of Rubin's comments on money (1928, 1929).

Two pioneering studies on the formation of Marx's economic thought, Mandel (1967) and Rosdolsky (1978) trace the parallel evolution of the theories of value and of money from *Poverty of philosophy* to the draft manuscripts of *Capital*. Unifying the two problems, Suzanne de Brunhoff (1967) shows how the anti-quantity theory of Marx is the counterpart to a general theory of money, valuable for any market structure. It is also the problem of the logical and historical genesis of the "general equivalent" that monopolised the attention of scholars when interest was renewed in Marx's monetary thought beginning in the 1970s (see e.g., Brunhoff 1979; Benetti and Cartelier 1980, 1998; Mandel 1981; Aglietta and Orléan 1982; Foley 1983, 2005; Deleplace 1985; Lapavitsas 2003; Reuten 2005; Moseley 2005; Hai Hac 2015).

More recently, an increasing number of studies have proposed clarification on particular aspects of Marx's monetary thought or even tried to project his criticism onto current monetary problems. This is the case, among many examples, of the works gathered in a collective volume edited by Moseley (2005). While some recent studies reconsider the problem of money from a deepening of Marx's analysis of social forms of labour (Baronian 2013), most are essentially based on a rapprochement with Keynesian and post-Keynesian positions (Bellofiore 2005; Itoh 2005; Lapavitsas 2005; Matthews 1996). On the strict ground of the history of monetary thought, perhaps two syntheses – de Boyer (2003) and Arnon (1984, 2010) – broke with an old and tenacious tradition of marginalising or excluding Marx from the history of monetary thought. Only one study reconsiders the monetary theory of Marx from an interdisciplinary perspective, by placing it in the broader context of his philosophical, social, economic and political thought (Nelson 1999, 1).

Among the works cited above, many emphasise the influence of the authors of the *banking school* in the formation of Marx's anti-quantity theory (Mandel 1967; Brunhoff 1979; Rubin 1929). Nevertheless, very few analyse this relationship systematically. One such exception is Arnon (1984, 2010), who reveals the importance of Tooke's influence on Marx's monetary thought.

Our contribution is to emphasise Steuart's role in Marx's criticism of the QTM[1]. This criticism is based on the conception of money and the analysis of its functions, and also on the law of reflux, which Marx understood as a fundamental characteristic of monetary circulation in a capitalist economy. By doing so, we shed light on an important and lesser-known dimension of Marx's critique of political economy: his understanding of the history of monetary thought. According to Marx, two major traditions dominate the history of monetary though. While the first goes back to Hume, the second starts with Steuart. This is crucial for any reconstruction of Marx's monetary view as a result of the critical appraisal of both traditions.

To this end, we take as a starting point Marx's assessment of Steuart's *Theories on surplus-value* as "a rational expression of the Monetary and Mercantile systems" (Section 2). This leads us to consider how the QTM allowed a step forward for economic thought by shifting the study of the exchange value and profit from the sphere of circulation to that of production (Section 3). But, at the same time, this decisive progress is also a step backwards insofar as the QTM obscures the different functions of money, becoming an "abstract opposition" to mercantilism (Section 4). Steuart was Hume's first critic and, as a result, he became the founder of an anti-QTM tradition by developing a "concrete conception of money." According to Marx, Steuart's definition of money allows us to better understand its main functions. Steuart's differentiation of the functions of money is linked to his distinction of the social character of the labour creating value of exchange (Section 5). In doing so, Steuart opens the way for an analysis of the circulation of money in capitalism by connecting income expenditures with capital advances. The distinction between two movements – a "simple" circulation and the "law of reflux" – was Steuart's discovery, long before the nineteenth century's *banking school*. While Money tends to circulate in the circuits of the simple circulation, credit, which Marx defines as a substitute of money as a means of circulation, tends to seize capitalist affairs. Marx emphasises the importance of the law of reflux, but he rejects the confusion of credit with capital (Section 6). All these elements help us to

---

[1]This paper is part of a larger project that soon incorporate Marx's notes on Steuart's French edition of the *Principles* in Marx's personal Library kept in Moscow. For the pages of Steuart's French edition of the *Principles* with Marx's annotations, see the Karl Marx–Friedrich Engels GESAMTAUSGABE (MEGA) *Exzerpte, notizen, marginalien*. Band 32 (1999), 623–624.

understand the ambivalence of Marx criticism of the QTM. This ambivalence, which is the cornerstone of his monetary conception, appears in his critical appraisal of the *currency principle* and *banking school* confrontation, that is the two respective heirs of Hume and Steuart's traditions (Section 7). At the end, we conclude (Section 8).

2. Steuart's "rational expression" of the monetary and mercantile systems

Marx considers the whole capital cycle as a chain of three functional forms: money–capital (M), productive–capital (P) and commodity–capital (C)[2]. These forms produce three different kinds of cycles: M-C → P → C'-M' represents the money–capital cycle, P → C'-M'-C → P' describes the productive–capital cycle, and C-M → P → C' refers to the commodity–capital cycle. These cycles together constitute the entire capital cycle. They also correspond to the three major perspectives that dominate the history of economic thought from mercantilism to the Ricardian School, including the Physiocrats[3].

According to Marx, the problem is that these three points of view result in different interpretations and open the possibility of confusion between capital and the functional forms of capital. From the point of view of the money–capital cycle, capital tends to be confused with money. From the point of view of the productive–capital cycle, capital is confused with objective means of production or with wage goods. Finally, from the perspective of the capital–commodity cycle, capital is confused with commodities. In each of these three cycles, money plays different roles and possesses a different status. Consequently, the point of view one adopts determines the different functions of money and, therefore, the characteristics of money circulation (Marx 1885).

For Marx, the point of view of the money–capital cycle gave rise to "Monetary and Mercantile System" (Marx 1885, 68). In this sense, the mercantilist authors "correctly stated that the vocation of bourgeois society was the making of money, and hence, from the standpoint of simple commodity circulation, the formation of permanent hoards which neither moths nor rust could destroy" (Marx 1859a, 389).

---

[2](M) for money-capital; (C) for the elements of commodity-capital (labour force and means of production); (P) for the process of production or setting in motion of the means of production by the active labour force.

[3]For Marx, modern economic thought (or political economy) begins with Petty and Boisguilbert, and his "classical phase" ends with Ricardo and his first systematic critic, Sismondi.

Paradoxically, the mercantilist emphasis on metallic money as the sole source of wealth and its accumulation as a specific method of enrichment takes place, among other circumstances, under the historical conditions of a weak development of market production, in other words, by the predominance of social forms of labour that do not create exchange value. Besides international trade, "national production was for the most part still carried on within the framework of feudal forms and served as the immediate source of subsistence for the producers themselves" (Marx 1859a, 389). Thus, the mercantilists' tendency to identify money and capital arises precisely because "the sphere of commodity circulation was the strictly bourgeois economic sphere" (Marx 1859a, 390). This confusion of money with capital expresses the commercial capital point of view. Marx insists that this amalgam (between money and capital) does not necessarily result in a confusion between capital and interest-bearing capital although the latter represents, from an historical point of view, an "antediluvian form" of capital "together with its twin brother", commercial capital (Marx 1894, 588).

Marx divides mercantilism into two groups corresponding to two historical moments: the monetary system and the mercantile system[4]. In the latter, "it is no longer the transformation of commodity value into money but the creation of surplus value which is decisive but from the meaningless viewpoint of the circulation sphere and, at the same time, in such manner that this surplus value is represented as surplus money, as the balance of trade surplus" (Marx 1894, 771). As a theoretical expression of merchant and manufacturer interests, the authors of the mercantile system deal with social and political transformations required to cope with the international trade competition between "industrial nations." Therefore, those economists are especially interested in the nature of the State, its regulations and policies. Long before historians of mercantilism as Schmoller (1884) and Heckscher (1931), Marx put into relief the structural and complex articulation between the rise of manufacture capitalism and the emergence of modern State in mercantilist thought:

> Hence the national character of the mercantile system is not merely a phrase on the lips of its spokesmen. Under the pretext of concern solely for the wealth of the nation and the resources of the state, they, in fact,

---

[4]Adam Smith refers to mercantilism as "Commercial or Monetary system" (1776). This is also the case of McCulloch (1824) and others authors later.

pronounce the interests of the capitalist class and the amassing of riches in
general to be the ultimate aim of the state, and thus proclaim bourgeois
society in place of the old divine state. But at the same time they are
consciously aware that the development of the interests of capital and
of the capitalist class, of capitalist production, forms the foundation
of national power and national ascendancy in modern society.
(Marx 1894, 771)

Steuart occupies a special place in the history of the mercantile system. In his *Theories on surplus-value*, Marx attributes to Steuart the
merit of propagating the mercantilist explanation of profit from
exchange operations: only individual profits arise out of an addition
to the value of a commodity (Marx 1905a, 351–2). According to
Marx, Steuart proposes a "scientific form" to the mercantilist argument, distinguishing the "profit upon alienation" from the creation of
new wealth:

> Steuart on the one hand rejects the conception of the Monetary and
> Mercantile systems, according to which the sale of commodities above
> their value, and the profit resulting there from, creates a positive increase
> of wealth. On the other hand he holds to their view that the profit of the
> individual capital is nothing but this excess of the price over the value, the
> profit upon alienation. (Marx 1905a, 352)[5]

In this sense, Steuart is "the rational expression of the Monetary
and Mercantile system" (Marx 1905a, 352). This nuanced judgement
explains the hesitations of commentators who are interested in the
place that Marx grants to Steuart in the history of economic thought.
Heinrich Cunow, one of the first commentators on the *Theories of
surplus value*, rejects the classification of the Scottish author among
the mercantilists (Gaido 2015, 160; Cunow 2017). In contrast, Rubin
and Meek accept Marx's classification of Steuart (Meek, 1967; Rubin
1979, 84–6) as the last mercantilist. For us, Steuart was an author of
transition in the mercantile era who opened the door to a new way of
thinking about the economy.

3. The QTM as a step forward for economic thought

As perhaps the first to think purposefully about capitalism, mercantilists proceeded "from the superficial phenomena of the circulation
process as individualized in the movement of merchants capital, and

---

[5]Despite its importance, we will not discuss Steuart's theory of balance of trade in this paper.

therefore grasped only the appearance of matters. Partly because merchant's capital is the first free state of existence of capital in general" (Marx 1894, 335). Although Marx recognises deep differences among the mercantilists, those doctrinal divergences and nuances do not constitute for him a critical turning point in the history of economic thought. Rather, the abandonment of mercantilist theories is related to the rising influence of industrial capitalists, whose influence and social interests began dominating in the second half of the seventeenth century. This is the concrete and historical basis of the ultimate abandonment of the money–capital cycle point of view and, thus, the catalyst for a decisive turning point in the history of economic thought. For Marx, "the real science of modern economy only begins when the theoretical analysis passes from the process of circulation to the process of production" (Marx 1894, 335).

The definitive decline of mercantilism became effective with the Physiocrats, whom Marx appreciates partly for "going back from merchant's capital, which functions solely in the sphere of circulation, to productive capital, in opposition to the mercantile system" (Marx 1894, 770). Although Marx dates the real science of the economy after the mercantilist age ended, he nevertheless recognised some positive aspects of mercantilism.

Because of the QTM and its "neutralisation" of money[6], the classical economists could develop the capital and profit theories. Marx emphasises this positive aspect of the QTM, what we have called "a step forward" for economic thought[7].

This shift to consider the nature and causes of wealth – from the sphere of circulation to the sphere of production – implies the adoption of the productive–capital cycle and/or the commodity–capital cycle perspective. In both cycles, money appears, fundamentally, as a simple intermediary of commodity exchanges, that is, as a means of circulation.

> It was quite natural that, by contrast with the monetary and mercantile systems, which knew money only as a crystalline product of circulation,

---

[6]The elimination of the different functions of money (replaced only by the means of the exchange function) is the basis of the so-called neutrality of money among classical economists. This is also why the Ricardian and Neo-Ricardian models can be considered systems without money. Note, however, that according to Deleplace (2017), considering Ricardo as a supporter of QTM is a conventional assessment that raises many doubts. For him, Ricardo would not be a supporter of the QTM.

[7]Marx made this point clear in book III of *Capital* (Marx 1894, 770–771).

classical political economy in the first instance should have understood the fluid form of money, that is the form of exchange value which arises and vanishes within the metamorphosis of commodity. Because commodity circulation is looked at exclusively in the form of C-M-C. (Marx 1859a, 391)

Here lies, for Marx, the central point of the monetary theories that consider money as a medium of exchange as their cornerstone. The common elements among the different versions of the QTM are (1) the automatic mechanism that links variations in the quantity of money to their direct impact on prices and (2) the position that money is only a medium of exchange. The immediate consequences are that the QTM hides the monetary character of production and thus obscures the logic of accumulation. But this kind of "neutralisation" of money brought about by the QTM allows the production process to be studied only as a valorisation process in Marx's terms. In any case, money intervenes only as coin, and monetary transactions appear only as an activity subordinated to the circulation of commodities.

By rejecting the mercantilist fetishism of money–capital, the reduction of money to the function of means of circulation opens the way to analyse exchange value and the origins of profit exclusively in the sphere of production. This recognition of the positive implications of the QTM remains a constant for Marx although he will systematically combat all QTM versions from Hume to the *Currency Principle* (including Ricardo's monetary theory), especially in the latter half of the 1850s.

But all of Marx's criticisms of the confusion between money and wealth are simultaneously the negation of a principle highlighted "with a brutal naivety" by mercantilism. By considering money solely as a medium of exchange, the QTM achieved only a unilateral critique of mercantilism, that is, as Marx will say, an "abstract opposition" to the mercantile system, as we will see. Indeed, money no longer appears as a presupposition and as the sole objective of all activity in capitalist economic conditions. With the QTM, both the monetary and capitalist foundations of production disappeared.

Although it is a step forward for research on the nature of capital and the origins of profit, the QTM constitutes also a step back for monetary thought. This is reflected in Marx's criticism of the QTM as the doctrine that stipulates that prices are directly determined by the quantity of money. Marx's approach requires the search for a concrete analysis of money, as inspired by Steuart.

4. The QTM: a step back for monetary thought

Marx very quickly perceived the problematic implications of the identification between means of circulation and money. By conceiving circulation exclusively from the point of view of commodity–capital and productive–capital, money is perceived only as a substitute for barter (the commodity that allows the sale and purchase of other commodities). Marx defines the core as well as the historical genesis of the quantity theory tradition as follows:

> The specific aspect of money as means of circulation is upheld against its specific aspect as money. If the function of means of circulation in serving as coin is isolated, then, as we have seen, it becomes a value token. [...] In accordance with the law relating to the circulation of value tokens, the proposition is then advanced that the prices of commodities depend on the volume of money in circulation, and not that the volume of money in circulation depends on the prices of commodities. This view is more or less clearly outlined by Italian economists of the seventeenth century; it is sometimes accepted, sometimes repudiated by Locke, and firmly set forth in *The Spectator* (in the issue of 19 October 1711) as well as in the works of *Montesquieu* and *Hume* [...] Hume is by far the most important exponent of this theory in the eighteenth century. (Marx 1859a, 391)

Here, Marx's historical exposition of the making of the QTM corresponds completely to that provided by Steuart (1789, 273):

> Who was the first author of this doctrine, I cannot say. I find it in Mr Locke, and in the Spectator for the 19th of October 1711; but they have been beautifully illustrated by Montesquieu; and Mr Hume has extended the theory, and diversified it prettily in his political discourses; which have done much honour to that gentleman, and drawn the approbation of the learned world so much, that there is hardly a nation in Europe which has not the pleasure of reading them in their own language. (Steuart 1767, book II, chapter IV)

Marx reports how the history of the automatic mechanism that links the quantity of money to prices is intimately linked to the great political revolutions that propelled the bourgeoisie to the head of the State in England during the second half of the seventeenth century. Among the predecessors of Hume, Marx mentions especially Locke. In *Grundrisse* and in *Capital* Marx attributes to Locke the paternity of an early version of the QTM (Marx 1859a, 164). But, Marx explains that Locke contradicted his own doctrine by defending opposite views. This financial context and the bourgeoisie class interests explain Locke's ambiguous position in the genesis of the QTM. In other words, this context explains both Locke's positive contributions to the QTM but also his hesitations in the field of monetary theory.

But regardless of these considerations of the different originators of the QTM, the importance of the previous remark lies in the fact that it implies a conceptual distinction between the equation of exchange and the QTM – a distinction which is usually located much later in the history of monetary thought.[8]

If we can say that Marx had something resembling an "equation of exchange," that equation would express the general law of circulation. In his own words, the "quantity of money functioning as the circulating medium is equal to the sum of the prices of the commodities divided by the number of moves made by coins of the same denomination" (Marx 1867, 130). From this point of view, the major problem of the QTM according to Marx is not that it establishes a relation between the mass of transactions, the means of circulation and prices, but rather that it deduces a univocal causal relationship based on money having the sole function of means of circulation. The main problem of the QTM for Marx is the definition of money that it presupposes. Indeed,

> What should have been demonstrated was that the prices of commodities or the value of gold depends on the amount of gold in circulation. The proof consists in postulating what has to be proved: that any quantity of the precious metal serving as money, regardless of its relation to its intrinsic value, must become a medium of circulation, or coin, and then a token of value for the commodities in circulation regardless of the total amount of their value. In other words, this proof rests on disregarding all functions performed by money except its function as a medium of circulation. (Marx 1859a, 404–405)

According to Marx, Hume's theory of money is based on three fundamental propositions: (1) the prices of the commodity are determined by the money supply; (2) the money supply represents all

---

[8]The exchange equation or quantity theory formula $MV = PT$ does not establish a causal relationship between the quantity of money in circulation and the price level. Only under certain assumptions does this equation of exchange become the foundation of the QTM. The amalgam between both will systematically take place at the end of nineteenth and beginning of the twentieth centuries with the works of Irving Fisher (1896 and 1911) and Edwin W. Kemmerer (1903). Fisher attributes the paternity of the algebraic formalization of the equation to Simon Newcomb and Francis Edgeworth (Fisher 1911, 25).

commodities; (3) the increase in the quantity of commodities causes, *ceteris paribus*, a fall in prices or, in other words, an increase in the value of money. Conversely, an increase in the money supply causes an increase in commodity prices or a decrease in the value of money (Marx 1859a, 243 and 393). Note that Steuart also introduces his critical analysis of Hume's QTM by "laying this doctrine in three propositions":

> First, the prices of commodities always proportioned to the plenty of money in the country. So that the augmentation of wealth even fictitious, such as paper, affects the state of prices, in proportion to its quantity. Secondly, the coin and current money in a country is the representation of all the labour and commodities of it. So that in proportion as there is more or less of this representation (money), there goes a greater or less quantity of the thing represented (commodities, etc.) to the same quantity of it. From this it follows that Thirdly, increase commodities, they become cheaper; increase money, they rise in their value. (Steuart 1767, book II chapter IV, 272-3)

For Marx, the three propositions reveal the same error: "the fact that gold and silver are money only as the result of the function they perform in the social process of exchange is thus taken to mean that their specific value and hence the magnitude of their value is due to their social function" (Marx 1859a, 395). By limiting the analysis of the different functions of money to retain only one, the means of circulation, Hume did not develop any concrete analysis of money. This is why Marx considers Hume's monetary theory as an "abstract opposition to the monetary system" (Marx 1859a, 395 and 415). This way of establishing a cause and effect relationship between the money supply and the price of commodities is, for Marx, all the more surprising in that it contradicts Hume's epistemological principle. "Quite contrary to the principles of his own philosophy, [Hume] uncritically turns unilaterally interpreted facts into general propositions" (Marx 1859a, 394). Marx explained Hume's radical position by his extreme opposition to identifying money with wealth in the mercantilist literature (Marx 1867, 133-5).

In contrast, Marx found in Steuart's *Principles* a concrete analysis of the monetary phenomenon. In the same way that Hume is the founding father of a systematic version of the QTM tradition, Steuart inaugurated an anti-quantity theorist tradition (Marx 1859a, 396).

> He [Steuart] is indeed the first to ask whether the amount of money in circulation is determined by the price of commodities or the prices of

commodities determined by the amount of money in circulation. (Marx 1859a, 396)

Steuart rejects Hume's analysis of the relationship between the quantity of money in circulation and the prices of commodities in chapter 28 of his *Principles*, entitled "Circulation considered with regard to the Rise and Fall of the Price of Subsistence and Manufactures." In general, there is "no real or exact proportion between the value of money and that of commodities" (Steuart 1767 book II, 265). In other words, the price of commodities has no fixed proportion with the quantity of precious metals circulating as money. On the contrary, it is the quantity of money which seems to be determined by the price of commodities. For Steuart, the determination of commodity prices depends on "the complex operation of demand and competition," two factors independent of the amount of money in circulation (Steuart 1789). These indications did not escape Marx, and after him Rubin, for whom the Hume–Steuart opposition is the basis of the two great traditions which have marked the monetary theory debates on the relations between the money in circulation and the general level of prices:

> The ideas that Steuart had put forward in contraposition to the quantity theory were extended in the 19th century by Tooke, and then later on by Marx. These two theories – Hume's quantity theory, on the one hand, and Steuart's doctrine, on the other – represent in brilliant fashion the two basic tendencies in the theory of monetary circulation. (Marx 1859a, 415; Rubin 1979)

Steuart's anti-quantity theory position invites us to reconsider the relationship between the quantity of means of circulation and the price of commodities[9]. With this reformulation, the stage is set for the two great discoveries that Marx attributes to Steuart and which constitute the content of the following two sections of this paper: the analysis of the functions of money and the general laws of monetary circulation.

5. The analysis of the functions of money in Steuart and Marx

By claiming that prices are determined by the money supply, quantity-theory supporters such as Hume and Montesquieu assumed that

---

[9]Although Steuart is not the only one, Marx notes that similar ideas can be found in Boiguilbert and Guillaume François Le Trosne in France.

"an aliquot part of the medley of commodities is exchanged for an aliquot part of the heap of precious metal" (Marx 1867, 134). Marx finds an attempt to demonstrate such an "absurd" hypothesis in the writings of Montesquieu:

> That the price of each kind of commodity forms a part of the sums of prices of all commodities in circulation, is a self-evident proposition. But how use values, which are incommensurable with regard to each other, are to be exchanged, *en masse*, for the total sum of gold and silver in a country, is quite incomprehensible. If we start from the notion that all commodities together form one single commodity, of which each is but an aliquote part, we get the following beautiful result; the total commodity = x cwt of gold; commodity A = an aliquote part of the total commodity = the same aliquote part of x cwt of gold. (Marx 1867, 134)

In contrast to Montesquieu, Steuart's merit here, according to Marx, is that he "does not mechanically place commodities on one side and money on the other" (Marx 1859a, 396). For Steuart, "every commodity is in proportion to the sum of money circulating for this commodity" (Steuart 1767, 285). Thus, even under the most favourable conditions for the QTM, there can be no proportionate increase in the general level of prices when the money supply increases, without a distortion of relative prices and also a change in the income structure. This is an argument that we can find often in the history of monetary thought when we examine the criticisms of the QTM[10]. Let us take a closer look at the money functions in the early criticism of the QTM.

We have seen in the previous section how the QTM from the beginning, through the examples of Hume and Montesquieu, holds money to be only a means of circulation. Although he develops his theory in significantly different historical and monetary conditions – that is, in a structurally more developed credit system and temporarily inconvertible bank notes[11] – Ricardo makes the same mistake as Hume and Montesquieu. In Marx's words, "The printing presses in Threadneedle Street played the same role for Ricardo as the American mines played for Hume; and in one passage Ricardo specifically equates these two causes" (Marx 1859a, 29, 400).

But what particularly strikes Marx in the Ricardian theory of money is that "he has nowhere examined [the nature of] money, as

---

[10]Note that this will be also one of Keynes's main anti-QTM arguments in his *Economic Consequences of Mr Churchill* (1925).

[11]During the Napoleonic blockade.

such in the way he has analyzed exchange value, profit, rent, etc."
(Marx 1859a, 29, 401). The heirs of Ricardo and the *currency school*,
represented by Overstone and Torrens, only distinguished themselves
from their mentor by their zeal to apply the QTM to bank money.
The two common denominators of the different versions of the QTM
are the elimination of the different functions of money (replaced with
only the medium of exchange function) and, consequently, the
absence of a concrete analysis of money.

Thus, Marx, reconnecting with a "concrete conception of money"
such as Steuart's, claimed a theory which connects the function of
means of circulation with the other functions of money. Marx begins
by observing how Steuart "deduces [the] various functions [of money]
from different moments in commodity exchange" (Marx 1859a, 396).
Whereas in Hume and the quantity theorists, the circulation function
is the only function that matters, Steuart, on the basis of the different
motives of money demand, distinguishes money as medium of circulation from money as a means of payment:

> The use of money can be reduced to two main purposes: payment of what
> is owed, purchase of what is needed. Both of them together form the
> demand for money in cash … To implement these various payments, a
> certain amount of money is needed. This may increase or decrease
> according to the circumstances, although the quantity of the alienations
> [exchanges] remains the same. In any case, the circulation of a country can
> absorb only a certain quantity of money. (Steuart 1789, Book II)

By distinguishing money from a simple medium of circulation,
Steuart emphasises the role of credit money as well as that of hoarding in the fluctuations of the money supply in circulation:

> The circulation of each country must always be in proportion to the
> industry of the inhabitants who produce the goods which go to the
> market. If, therefore, the currency of a country is less than the proportion
> of the produce of the industry exposed for sale, the industry itself will
> cease, or some invention will be employed, symbolic currency [credit
> money], for example, to provide an equivalent. But if money be found
> above the proportion of industry, it will produce no effect in the price
> increase, and will not enter into circulation; it will be tightened in the
> coffers, and will wait not only for the owners to desire to consume, but
> also for the industrious to satisfy their demand. (Steuart 1767, 288)

Hoarding acts as a regulator of the channels of monetary circulation.
Alongside its function as a means of circulation, money also fulfils a
function of means of payment. Steuart associates this last function to

the development of credit. But this articulation of the different functions of money does not solve the fundamental problem: instead of explaining the circulation of commodities of specific exchange values, QTM supporters circulate use values. The QTM is based on the "absurd" hypothesis that "commodities are without price, and money without value, when they first enter into circulation" (Marx 1867, 134). For Marx, any answer to the question of how money allows for the circulation of commodities presupposes that these commodities already have a price (Marx 1859a, 338, 426). The formulation of the complete answer comes in Marx's writings between the *Grundrisse* and the *Contribution to the critique of political economy* (Mandel 1967, 99; Arnon 2010, 320–1). This was therefore organically linked to the main theme that Marx developed during this period: the specifically social character of labour which creates exchange value.

> Indeed, all the determinations in which money appears – standard of value, means of circulation, and money as such – merely express the different relationship in which individuals take part in overall production or relate to their own production as social production. (Marx 1858, 446)

In this sense, the distinction between concrete labour (source of material wealth) and abstract labour (source of exchange value) was indispensable to deduce the social form in which the commodity expresses its exchange value. This problem, as is well known, determines the genesis of money, what Marx called the "general equivalent" of commodities. This is explained in the *Contribution* and the first section of book I of *Capital*.

In the same way, the present paper highlights the dual specificity of Marx's theory of money–commodity: (a) Money is a commodity like no other; (b) its existence prevents all other commodities from performing the same functions as money itself performs. The first proposition is a criticism directed against Ricardo (Brunhoff, 1967). The second is a criticism against those who think, like John Gray and P. J. Proudhon, that a monetary system can directly reflect social labour and abolish the contradictions of capitalist production (Baronian 2011).

Steuart's writings are crucial for these investigations into the specifically social character of labour which creates exchange value. Steuart develops the whole of his critique of Hume's theory as a framework for an analysis of the division and organisation of social labour necessary for commercial production (Steuart 1767, 267–8; Perelman 1983; Menudo 2014).

Marx emphasises the merits and limits of the categories "real value," "commodity price" and "industry" (Marx 1859a, 297–8; Meek 1967; Dussel 1988, 117–8 et *passim*) for his own discovery of the opposition between "concrete useful labour" and "value-creating labour". What distinguishes Steuart from his predecessors and his successors is "his clear differentiation between specifically social labour which manifests itself in exchange value and concrete labour which yields uses value" (Marx 1859a, 298).

Finally, according to Marx, Steuart defends an erroneous theory based on an "ideal standard of money," a doctrine which arises in the wake of the alteration of gold and silver standards (i.e., their monetary prices) at the end of the seventeenth century. This political practice and his technical problems at that time highlight, for Marx, the difference in meaning between the function of money as a measure of value and that of a standard of prices. Unlike the other aspects of his monetary analysis, Marx points out how Steuart was misled in this case. Here lies the theoretical limit of Steuart's historical exposition of monetary problems according to Marx[12].

The examples put forward by Steuart to demonstrate his theory of an ideal standard of money, instead of complicating the problem or revealing new facets, "disproves its own assertion" (Marx 1859a, 298). Trying to demonstrate a theory of an ideal standard of money was, in the last instance, a way to express that "the labour time is the real standard of money" (Marx 1859a, 320). This was a kind of problematic conclusion that John Gray and the Proudhonians economists also arrived at much later (in the nineteenth century). In short, Steuart "does not understand how the measure of value is transformed into the standard of price" (Marx 1859a, 297; Nelson 1999, 82–3).[13]

---

[12]By making Steuart the founder of the criticism of QTM, Marx does not consider Steuart's approach to be incompatible with his own analysis of money as a developed expression of exchange value. On the contrary, Marx argues that Steuart's "concrete analysis" of money underlines both his historical analysis of the social forms of labour and his difficulties to perceive the specificity of exchange value creating labour. This critical reading of Steuart's monetary criticism contrasts with recent interpretations that make Steuart the founder of a Proto-Keynesian approach, namely purely monetary prices. In this last perspective, there is nothing but money prices, and if we wish to get relative (or real) prices we have to reckon them as ratios of money prices.

[13]We do not develop in this paper Steuart's analysis of the function of money as a store of value for international circulation ("money of the world"). We will discuss this point as well as his theory of balance of trade in another paper.

6. Money advanced, credit and reflux: the iron law of capitalist monetary circulation

According to Marx, to understand the laws that govern monetary circulation in a capitalist economy we must start from the distinction of the two movements of income and capital. In the first case, if we consider money circulation insofar as it deserves final consumption, we observe an expenditure of incomes. In the second case, the circulation of money is considered from the point of view of the advance, that is, the reflux of the value-capital or, to put it another way, the return of (1) the sums which represent wage payments (variable capital for Marx); (2) investments in objective elements of production such as machines, tools and the like needed for production (constant capital) and (3) profits. In this respect, reflux appears as the iron law of monetary circulation, especially as capitalist social relations dominate the entire economy. The circulation of money as capital differs from the circulation of money as a simple means of exchanging commodities. In the first case, money acts as capital and returns to its point of departure; in the second case, the money does not reflux. In the first case, money is *advanced* while in the second it is *spent*.

From a macroeconomic perspective, capitalist circulation always registers three types of transactions according to Marx: (1) income circulation; (2) exchange of capital for income and (3) exchange of capital for capital. This distinction is crucial for Marx's monetary study of "reproduction and circulation of the aggregate," that is, the general form of the accumulation of capital (Marx 1885, 349–57), an analysis which derives from Marx's previous criticism of Adam Smith's theory of capital reproduction (Marx 1905b, 130 and *passim*]). From an exclusively monetary point of view, these transactions make it possible to differentiate currency, or money as a simple means of circulation, from money as a form of capital, insofar as there is reflux. For Marx, the paternity of "the law of reflux" belongs to Sir James Steuart:

> In his investigations into currency, Thomas Tooke underlines that money in its function of capital flows back to its starting point (reflux of money to its point of issue), but in its function simply as currency does not flow back. This distinction [was established] by Sir James Steuart, among others, long before Tooke. (Marx 1868, 39)

In his *Principles,* Steuart says "when a thing is bought, in order to be sold again, the sum employed is called *money advanced*; when it is bought not to be sold, it may be said to be *expended*" (Steuart 1805, 274). Moreover, this distinction between advances and expenditures is also the basis for understanding the necessity for credit development and, more broadly, for a banking system. Steuart defines credit formally as "confidence" in the repayment capacity of a debtor (Steuart 1767 book IV beginning of the chapter I). That is why Steuart distinguishes different forms of credit from different foundations of confidence. In this sense, mercantile or merchants credit,

> is established upon the confidence the lender has, that the borrower, from his integrity and knowledge in trade, may be able to replace the capital advanced, and the interest due during the advance, in terms of the agreement. This is the most precarious of all. (Steuart 1767, book IV part II chapter I on the various form of credit)[14]

From this point of view, the development of credit can only occur with the extension of capitalist production, namely, production for profit, or the generalisation of the use of money as money advanced. Simultaneously, Steuart derives the specific form of circulation of credit instruments from their nature as a substitute for money in his function of means of circulation: they have to "return". This phenomenon becomes much more developed and complex with banks. None of this escaped Marx, who declares that Steuart discovers "the law of circulation based on money credit" (Marx 1859b, 1859a, 397).

As the progress of production for profit objectively consolidates the capacity of economic agents (factory owners, merchants, etc.) to honour their debts, the circulation of capital tends to be increasingly on the basis of credit. Nevertheless, this similarity between the reflux of advance money (as capital) and the reflux of money credit opens the possibility for the confusion of the circulation of credit with the circulation of capital. In the history of monetary thought, this confusion became common since much more developed capitalist conditions led to a much more developed credit and banking system. That is why, according to Marx, this problem is one of the main characteristics of the monetary debates since the nineteenth century and the Bullion report controversy (Marx 1859a, 392 and *passim*). The confusion between credit and capital was commonplace in Tooke and Fullarton.

---

[14]Steuart develops his theory of credit in his *Principles* separately and after solving the problem of money circulation and prices and his critique of Hume. The latter takes place in book II and the former in Book IV. Steuart's theory of credit incorporates a set of financial considerations and thus ranges from interest rates to the role of the state and basic economic forces in determining the interest rate and liquidity of debt securities (See Bentemessek 2012).

While credit is representative of "capital," money in circulation represents "income" (Tooke 1844, 38–9). Marx considers that the development of credit instruments and their reflux constitute an indicator of capital domination of the whole monetary circulation. But he also considers the identification of credit as capital (and vice versa) as an error, claiming instead that there is a clear differentiation between the two.

For Marx, the origin of credit lies solely in the conditions of the exchanges of commodities. From this perspective, credit is just a formal modification of relations between commodity owners due to differences in their respective conditions of production.

> Owing to differences in the period and length of time required for the production of different commodities, one producer comes to the market as a seller before the other can act as a buyer, and if the same commodity owners repeatedly buy and sell one another's product the two aspects of the transaction are separated according to the condition of production of their commodities. This gives rise to relations of creditor and debtor among commodity owners. (Marx 1859a, 375)

That is also the reason why the development of credit constitutes an upheaval in the articulation of two functions of money: means of circulation and means of payment.

> With the development of the credit system there is an extraordinary spread of buying on time. To the extent that the credit system is developed and hence production based on exchange value, the role of money as means of payment will increase, as compared with its role as means of circulation, as agent of purchase and sale. In countries with a developed mode of production, and therefore a developed credit system, money as specy [currency] effectively figures almost exclusively in retail trade and in petty trade between producers and consumers, while in the sphere of large-scale trading transactions it appears as a transient [fugitive] form, a merely notional, imaginary measure of the exchange magnitude of value. Its bodily involvement is confined to the settlement of relatively insignificant balances. (Marx 1858, 432)

Credit accelerates the reflux of money–capital and, more particularly, the part which represents fixed capital of enterprise[15]. This reflux, Marx insists, takes place, and must take place, independently of the use of any kind of credit. This is because, firstly, reflux reflects the movement of money–capital and, secondly, because "all other

---

[15]Fixed capital has the slowest reflux velocity of all capitalist investment.

forms of interest-bearing capital are derivatives of this form and presuppose its existence" (Marx 1894, 390). It is the motives behind the
use of money that determine the mode of circulation. Thus, it is
the motive of the transaction and not its material content – that is,
the particular kind of instrument of credit used – that determines the
necessity (i.e., the "law") for reflux.

Differences in credit instruments or in banking transactions can only
be determined by the particular mode of reflux, or in other words, the
channels through which this reflux takes place. The study of the different forms of this reflux allows distinguishing – little or radically – this
law of reflux from the real doctrine effects (Green 1987; Glasner 1992;
Skaggs 1999; Arnon 2010; de Boyer 2003, 101–2;). Likewise, and more
deeply, the study of the channels of reflux reveals the common denominator of the *banking school* authors (Le Maux 2012). However, to consider the definition and, thus, the description of the channels of reflux
at a purely banking level is to confuse money and capital as well as
Marx's criticism of the *banking school* economists. Hence, the singularity of Marx's monetary position: critic of the *currency school*, close to
the *banking school* but also critical of the latter.

7. The singularity of Marx's anti-quantity theory

Despite its unfinished character and its difficult reconstruction, Marx's
monetary and credit theory clearly deals with a dual challenge. First,
Marx criticises the misunderstanding of the functions of money in the
QTM. The main challenge for him is to define credit and to integrate
it into a general monetary theory. Credit as a substitute for money as
a means of circulation presupposes the development of the function of
money as a means of payment (Marx 1867; Brunhoff 1967;
Likitkijsomboon 2005; Campbell 2005). Second, Marx aims to stop the
tendency of anti-quantity theorists to obliterate the market constraints
of capitalism. This double criticism made Marx's analysis of the difference between the currency school and the banking school original.
The currency and banking's schools are the heirs, according to Marx,
of the two great traditions of thought, since Hume and Steuart. Hume,
Steuart and then the nineteenth century monetary debates gave birth
to important developments of the monetary theory[16].

---

[16]Although Tooke seemed to ignore Steuart's work.

Claiming the scientific authority of Ricardo, *Currency school* partisans applied the quantity theory principle to banknotes and to credit
money in general. Armed with the law of reflux, *banking school*
defenders criticised the alleged influence "of the issue of credit money
(banknotes, etc.) exercises on commodity prices" (Marx 1868, 39). In
other words, money credit does not inflate "the money supply but
substitutes a financial asset by another in the hands of the public"
(Green 1987, 102). This is what Fullarton calls the "impossibility of an
over-issue" because of the law of reflux (Fullarton 1845, 84). Finally,
it is the public demand that determines the quantity of credit instruments. If Marx takes a stand for the *banking school*, then it is because
it discerns the specificity of the circulation of credit instruments
(reflux) and therefore the need for flexible central bank policy, as is
claimed by *banking school* economists (Skaggs 1991; de Boyer 2003,
106–8). For Marx, insofar as the circulation of capital and, thus,
the existence of a system of credit drives the circulation of money,
the Bank charter of 1844 plays the role of accelerator of crises, as
evidenced by the suspension of the Bank charter in 1847 and 1857.

By considering "money in its different moments" and distinguishing it from the simple means of circulation, the *banking school* recon-
nects with a concrete analysis of monetary facts that characterised
Steuart's thought. But Tooke, Fullarton and others are not exempt
from errors. They tend to confuse money and capital, although they,
as Marx nuanced, "are constrained to argue what differentiates them,
and one, and the other (Marx 1859a, 416).

In short, while the *banking school* reflects the characteristics of a
capital circulation, the QTM expresses – in an abstract form – the
market constraints of a capitalist economy. This is the complex
relationship between confidence, which supports credit, and money as
the supreme expression of exchange value:

> In the form of [credit money] the monetary existence of commodity is
> only a social one. It is a *Faith* that brings salvation. Faith in money value
> as the immanent spirit of commodity, faith in the mode of production and
> its predestined order, faith in the individual agents of production as mere
> personifications of self-expanding capital. But the credit system does not
> emancipate itself from the basis of the monetary system any more than
> Protestantism has emancipated itself from the foundations of Catholicism.
> (Marx 1894, 587).

Marx's monetary thought is situated in a tradition inaugurated by
Steuart from several points of view. First, because Marx, like Steuart,

determines the money supply by the sum of the prices of all commodities. Second, because he also distinguishes between bank notes, credit instruments and metallic circulation, and finally because Marx also takes into account the specificity of the circulation of credit to explain the reflux of money. However, Marx's criticism of the QTM stands also in a concrete analysis of the constraints underlying any economy based on the production of commodities.

The social validation of private labour in a society based on mercantile division of labour is an imperative that established what Marx calls the "social metabolism" of contemporary societies. This makes the theory of the "general equivalent" of commodities the "unsurpassable horizon" of any monetary theory.

8. Conclusion

The influence of Ricardo's monetary theory on Marx is relatively well known, as we can see for example in the good use he made of the Ricardian arguments against Proudhon (Marx 1847; Marx 1859b, 393). Nevertheless, the influence of Steuart on Marx's monetary thought remains insufficiently examined.

Steuart positively influences Marx's monetary theory in at least six ways. First, Steuart analyses the origins of the QTM and helps us to understand and criticise Hume and Montesquieu. Second, he develops the different functions of money – as a measure of value, as a means of circulation and payment – and their articulation. Third, Steuart explicitly exposes the specifically social character of labour which creates exchange value although he does not differentiate concrete labour from abstract labour. Fourth, Marx objections to Steuart's theory of the ideal standard of money are the basis of his criticism to Gray, Proudhon and Darimond. Fifth, Steuart distinguishes the money circulation of income expenditure from money used as capital advances. And finally, correlated with the previous one, Steuart defines the specificity of reflux law as the development of credit instruments and the banking system in general, when the money is used for capital advances.

These six elements – which we have exposed analytically for the sake of clarity – are linked and contributed to Marx's criticism of the QTM. For Marx, money functioning as a means of circulation is determined by two main factors: the sum of the prices of commodities in circulation and the velocity of the circulation of money.

Marx develops what he considers as a "general law" of monetary circulation (Marx 1867, 131–2). If velocity of money is constant, "prices are high or low not because there is more or less money in circulation. But there is more or less money in circulation because prices are high or low" (Marx 1859a, 341; Marx 1867, 132).

As the founding father of the anti-quantity theorist tradition, Sir James Steuart, "although his exposition is tarnished by his fantastic notion of the measure of value, by his inconsistent treatment of exchange value in general and by arguments reminiscent of the mercantile system, he discovers the essential aspects of money and the general laws of circulation of money" (Marx 1859a, 396). But Steuart is a childless father. Despite the resumption of the anti-quantity theory with the *banking school* in the 19th century, he will remain largely unknown to this army of heretics of monetary thought, including Tooke. As Marx notes, Tooke "was quite unaware of Steuart's work [as it appears in] his *History of prices from 1839 till 1847*, where he summarizes the history of theories on money" (Tooke, 1848; Marx 1859a, 415). Thus, Marx rescues the anti-quantity theory of Steuart from the dustbin of the history of monetary thought, in the same way Jevons "resuscitated" Richard Cantillon (Rist 1938, 46).

Marx observes how the commentators on and historians of monetary debates in the nineteenth century – with rare exceptions[17] – ignored Steuart's works. "Steuart remained even more of a dead dog than Spinoza appeared to be to Moses Mendelssohn in Lessing's time. Even the most recent historiographer of currency, [James] Maclaren [author of *A sketch of the history of the currency* published in London in 1858] makes Adam Smith the inventor of Steuart's theory, and Ricardo the inventor of Hume's theory" (Marx 1859a, 398). Adam Smith's radical anti-mercantilism and bad faith (*mauvaise foi*) largely explain why Steuart's legacy was forgotten as Marx denounced it in his *Contribution*.[18] Adam Smith himself had announced the fate that he had reserved for Steuart:

> I have the same opinion of Sir James Stewart's book that you have. Without once mentioning it, I flatter myself that any fallacious principle in

---

[17]This is the case of the mathematician Johann Büsch, who "translated Steuart's brilliant English into the Low-German dialect of Hamburg and distorted the original whenever it was possible" (Marx 1859a, 398).

[18]Although Marx will revise his global judgement on Smith's monetary theory between *Contribution* and *Capital* (Marx 1859b, 398-399; Marx 1867, 133).

it will meet with a clear and distinct confutation in mine (Rae 1895, 253–4).

This dismissal of Steuart became almost second nature among the *mandarins* of economic science. Even Keynes and Heckscher seem to ignore Steuart despite the fact that both had good reasons to rediscover the Scottish economist – the first because of his anti-quantity posture and the second as an historian of mercantilism (Ege 1999). The same neglect of Steuart came for later partisans of the theory of the ideal standard of money. "The theory of the [ideal] standard of money was so fully elaborated by sir James Steuart, that his followers – they are not aware of being followers since they do not know him – can find neither a new expression nor a new example" (Marx 1859a, 317).

But beyond this proven pettiness of Smith and others, the silence around Steuart also obeys historical and political reasons no less important. The interests of the rising bourgeoisie were more in keeping with Smith's liberalism than the regulations of Steuart's pre-industrial world. This can explain all the interest in but also the anachronisms that accompanied the "rehabilitation of Steuart" in the post-war, Keynesian intellectual and political context (Sen 1957; Meek 1967). This warning is also valid today on the occasion of the 250th anniversary of the publication of *Principles of Political Economy* by one of the few economists who precisely had a good sense of history.

Acknowledgements

We thank the three anonymous reviewers for their careful reading of our manuscript and their many insightful suggestions. We would also like to thank Paul Dudenhefer for his help in revising and polishing the article and Carole Boulai, Mauricio Coutinho, Carlos Eduardo Suprinyak and Shereen Ilahi for their helpful comments. Last but not least, we want to warmly thank all the participants of the Karl Marx conference organised in Lyon, 27–29 September 2017, specially Claire Silvant, Gilbert Faccarello and Jean Cartelier.

Disclosure statement

No potential conflict of interest was reported by the authors.

ORCID

Rebeca Gomez Betancourt http://orcid.org/0000-0002-5238-6705
Matari Pierre Manigat http://orcid.org/0000-0003-1340-3063

References

Aglietta, Michel, and Orléan André. 1982. *La violence de la monnaie*. Paris: PUF.

Arnon, Arie. 1984. "Marx's Theory of Money. The Formative Years." *History of Political Economy* 16 (4): 555–575. doi:10.1215/00182702-16-4-555.

Arnon, Arie. 2010. *Monetary Theory and Policy from Hume and Smith to Wicksell: Money, Credit, and the Economy*. Cambridge: Cambridge University Press.

Baronian, Laurent. 2011. "La monnaie dans les Grundrisse." *Cahiers d'économie Politique/Papers in Political Economy* 60 (1): 67–86.

Baronian, Laurent. 2013. *Marx and living labour. Routledge Frontiers of Political Economy*. Abingdon: Routledge.

Bellofiore, Riccardo. 2005. "The Monetary Aspects of the Capitalist Process in the Marxian System: An Investigation from the Point of View of the Theory of the Monetary Circuit." In *Marx's Theory of Money: Modern Appraisals*, edited by Fred Moseley, 124–139. Basingstoke: Palgrave Macmillan.

Benetti, Carlo and Cartelier, Jean. 1980. *Marchands, salariat et capitalistes*. Paris: François Maspero.

Benetti, Carlo and Cartelier, Jean. 1998. "Money, Form and Determination of Value." Vol. 1 of *Marxian economics: A reappraisal. Essays on Volume III of Capital*, 157–171. London: Macmillan.

Bentemessek, Nesrine. 2012. "Public Credit and Liquidity in James Steuart's Principles." *European Journal of the History of Economic Thought* 19 (4): 501–528. doi:10.1080/09672567.2010.540337.

Boyer des Roches, Jérôme de. 2003. *La pensée monétaire: histoire et analyse*. Paris: Editions Les Solos.

Brunhoff, Suzanne de. 1967. *La monnaie chez Marx*. Paris: Editions Sociales.

Brunhoff, Suzanne de. 1979. *Les rapports d'argent. Intervention en économie politique 12*. Paris: François Maspero.

Campbell, Martha. 2005. "Marx's Explanation of Money's Functions: Overturning the Quantity Theory." In *Marx's Theory of Money: Modern Appraisals*, edited by Fred Moseley, 143–159. Basingstoke: Palgrave Macmillan.

Chamley, Paul. 1963. *Économie politique et philosophie chez Steuart et Hegel*. Paris: Dalloz.

Cunow, Heinrich. 2017. "Theories of Surplus-Value (1905)." In *Responses to Marx's Capital: From Rudolf Hilferding to Isaak Illich Rubin*, edited by Day, Richard B. and Gaido, Daniel F., 212–245. Vol. 144 of Historical Materialism. Leiden: Brill.

Deleplace, Ghislain. 1985. "Sur quelques difficultés de la théorie de la monnaie marchandise chez Ricardo et Marx." *Economie appliquée* 1: 111–131.

Deleplace, Ghislain. 2017. *Ricardo on Money. A Reappraisal. Routledge Studies in the History of Economics 193*. London: Routledge.

Denis, Henry. 1999. "Marx's Polemics against Steuart." In *The Economics of James Steuart*, edited by Tortajada, Ramon, 76–83. Routledge Studies in the History of Economics 26. London: Routledge.

Dussel, Enrique. 1988. *Hacia un Marx desconocido. Un comentario de los Manuscritos del 61-63*. Mexico: Siglo XXI.

Ege, Ragip. 1999. "The New Interpretation of Steuart by Paul Chamley." In *The Economics of James Steuart*, edited by Tortajada, Ramon, 84–101. Routledge Studies in the History of Economics 26. London: Routledge.

Fisher, Irving. 1896. *"Appreciation and Interest." Publications of the American Economic Association, First Series*, 11 (4): 1–110 [331–442] (Appreciation and Interest, New York: Macmillan. reprinted in The Works of Irving Fisher (Fisher, 1997), Vol. 1).

Fisher, Irving. 1911. *With Brown, Harry Gunnison. The Purchasing Power of Money. Its determination and relation to credit, interest and crises.* New York: Macmillan (Second edit. (1913). Reprinted in Fisher (1997), Vol. 4).

Fisher, Irving. 1997. *The Works of Irving Fisher*, 14 volumes, edited by William J. Barber, assisted by Robert W. Dimand and Kevin Foster; consulting editor James Tobin. London: Pickering and Chatto.

Foley, Duncan K. 1983. "On Marx's Theory of Money". *Social Concept* 1 (1): 5–19.

Foley, Duncan K. 2005. 'Marx's Theory of Money in Historical Perspective'. In *Marx's Theory of Money: Modern Appraisals*, edited by Fred Moseley, 36–49. Basingstoke: Palgrave Macmillan.

Fullarton, John. 1845. *On the Regulation of Currencies*. Second Edition. London: John Murray.

Gaido, Daniel. 2015. "La recepción de las obras económicas de Karl Marx entre 1867–1910". *Izquierdas*, no. 22 (January): 250–267. doi:10.4067/S0718-50492015000100011.

Glasner, David. 1992. "The Real-Bills Doctrine in the Light of the Law of Reflux". *History of Political Economy* 24: 867–894. doi:10.1215/00182702-24-4-867.

Green, Roy. 1987. *'Real Bills Doctrine'. The New Palgrave: A Dictionary of Economics*. London: Palgrave Macmillan.

Hai Hac, Tran. 2015. 'État et capital dans l'exposé du Capital'. In *Nature et forme de l'Etat capitaliste. Analyses marxistes contemporaines*, edited by Artous, Antoine, Solís González, José Luis, Salama, Pierre, and Hai Hac, Tran, 53–92. Mille marxismes. Paris: Editions Syllepse.

Hazell, A. P. 1898. "Two Typical Theories of Money: The Quantity Theory of Money from the Marxist Stand-Point". *Journal of Political Economy* 7 (1): 78–85. doi:10.1086/250557.

Heckscher, Eli. (1931) 1935. *Mercantilism*. London: Allen and Unwin.

Hilferding, Rudolf. (1909) 1981. *Finance Capital. A Study of the Latest Phase of Capitalist Development*, edited by Tom Bottomore. London: Routledge & Kegan Paul.

Itoh, Makoto. 2005. 'The New Interpretation and the Value of Money'. In *Marx's Theory of Money: Modern Appraisals*, edited by Fred Moseley, 177–191. Basingstoke: Palgrave Macmillan.

Kemmerer, Edwin Walter. 1903. *'Money and Credit Instruments in Their Relation to General Prices'. PhD thesis*. New York: Cornell University.

Keynes, John Maynard. 1925. 'The Economic Consequences of Mr. Churchill'. In *Essays in Persuasion*. 244–270. London: Macmillan.

Kobayashi, Noboru. 1967. *James Steuart, Adam Smith and Friedrich List. Economic Series (Nihon Gakujutsu Kaigi. Dai 3-Bu)*. Tokyo: Science

Council of Japan, Division of Economics, Commerce & Business Administration.

Lapavitsas, Costas. 2003. *'Money as "Universal Equivalent" and Its Origin in Commodity Exchange'*. London: SOAS, University of London.

Lapavitsas, Costas. 2005. 'The Universal Equivalent as Monopolist of the Ability to Buy'. In *Marx's Theory of Money: Modern Appraisals*, edited by Fred Moseley, 95–110. Basingstoke: Palgrave Macmillan.

Le Maux, Laurent.. 2012. "The banking school and the law of reflux in general." *History of Political Economy*, 44.4: 595–618. doi:10.1215/00182702-1811352.

Likitkijsomboon, Pichit. 2005. 'Marx's Anti-Quantity Theory of Money: A Critical Evaluation'. In *Marx's Theory of Money: Modern Appraisals*, edited by Fred Moseley, 160–174. Basingstoke: Palgrave Macmillan.

Mandel, Ernest. 1967. *La formation de la pensée économique de Karl Marx: de 1843 jusqu'à la rédaction du 'Capital': étude génétique. Les textes à l'appui.* Paris: François Maspero.

Mandel, Ernest. 1981. 'Introduction'. In *Capital*, edited by Marx, Karl. Vol. III. London: Penguin.

Marx, Karl. (1847) 1976. 'The Poverty of Philosophy'. In *Collected Works*, edited by Karl Marx and Friedrich Engels. Vol. 6: Marx and Engels 1845-48. London: Lawrence & Wishart.

Marx, Karl. (1857a) 1986. 'Introduction to Economic Manuscripts of 1857 58'. In *Collected Works*, edited by Karl Marx and Friedrich Engels. Vol. 28: Marx Economic Works, 1857–1861. London: Lawrence & Wishart.

Marx, Karl. (1857b) 1987. 'Outlines of the Critique of Political Economy'. In *Collected Works*, edited by Karl Marx and Friedrich Engels. Vol.29: Marx Economic Works, 1857–1861. London: Lawrence & Wishart.

Marx, Karl. (1858) 1987. *From the preparatory material for a contribution to critique of political economy.* In *Collected Works*, edited by Karl Marx and Friedrich Engels. Vol. 29: Marx Economic Works, 1857–1861. London: Lawrence & Wishart.

Marx, Karl. (1859a) 1987. *Contribution to critique of political economy.* In *Collected Works*, edited by Karl Marx and Friedrich Engels. Vol. 29: Marx Economic Works, 1857–1861. London: Lawrence & Wishart.

Marx, Karl. (1859b) 1985. Letters to Engels February 25. In *Collected Works*, edited by Karl Marx and Friedrich Engels. Vol 41: Marx Engels 1860–1864 Letters. London: Lawrence & Wishart.

Marx, Karl. (1867) 1996. Capital Book I. In *Collected Works*, edited by Karl Marx and Friedrich Engels. Vol 35: *Capital* Book I. London: Lawrence & Wishart.

Marx, Karl. (1868) 1988. "Letter from Marx to Engels 23 may 1868". In *Collected Works*, edited by Karl Marx and Friedrich Engels. Vol.43: Marx Engels 1864–1868 Letters. London: Lawrence & Wishart.

Marx, Karl. (1885) 1997. Capital Volume II. In *Collected Works*, edited by Karl Marx and Friedrich Engels. Vol. 36: Capital, Volume II. London: Lawrence & Wishart.

Marx, Karl. (1894) 1998. Capital Volume III. In *Collected Works*, edited by Karl Marx and Friedrich Engels. Vol. 37: Capital, Volume III. London: Lawrence & Wishart.

Marx, Karl. (1905a) 1988. Theories of surplus value. In *Collected Works*, edited by Karl Marx and Friedrich Engels. Vol. 30: Marx Economic Works, 1857–1861. London: Lawrence & Wishart.

Marx, Karl. (1905b) 1988. Theories of surplus value. In *Collected works*, edited by Karl Marx and Friedrich Engels. Vol. 31: Marx Economic Works, 1857–1861. London: Lawrence & Wishart.

Matthews, Peter Hans. 1996. 'The Modern Foundations of Marx's Monetary Economics'. *European Journal of the History of Economic Thought* 3 (1): 61–83. doi:10.1080/10427719600000004.

McColloch, William. 2011. 'Marx's Appreciation of James Steuart: A Theory of History and Value'. Working Paper Series. Salt Lake City: University of Utah, Department of Economics.

Meek, Ronald L. 1967. 'The Rehabilitation of Sir James Steuart'. In *Economics and Ideology and Other Essays: Studies in the Development of Economic Thought*. London: Chapman and Hall.

Menudo, José Manuel. 2014. 'Sir James Steuart on the Origins of the Exchange Economy'. WP ECON 14.08. Working Papers Series 3–18. Sevilla: Universidad Pablo de Olavide, Department of Economics.

Moseley, Fred. 2005. *Marx's Theory of Money: Modern Appraisals*. Basingstoke: Palgrave Macmillan.

Nelson, Anitra. 1999. *Marx's Concept of Money. The God of Commodities. Studies in the History of Economics Series 25*. London: Routledge.

Perelman, Michael. 1983. 'Classical Political Economy and Primitive Accumulation: The Case of Smith and Steuart'. *History of Political Economy* 15 (3): 451–494. doi:10.1215/00182702-15-3-451.

Rae, John. 1895. *Life of Adam Smith*. London: Macmillan.

Reuten, Geert. 2005. 'Money as Constituent of Value'. In *Marx's Theory of Money: Modern Appraisals*, edited by Fred Moseley, 78–92. London: Palgrave Macmillan.

Rist, Charles. 1938. *Histoire des doctrines relatives au crédit et la monnaie, depuis John Law jusqu'à nos jours*. Paris: Librairie du recueil Sirey.

Rosdolsky, Roman. 1978. *Génesis y estructura del capital (1968)*. Mexico: Siglo XXI.

Rubin, Isaak Illich. (1928) 1972. *Essays on Marx's Theory of Value*. Detroit: Black and Red.

Rubin, Isaak Illich. (1929) 1979. *A History of Economic Thought*. London: Pluto Press.

Schmoller, Gustav von. (1884) 1902. *The Mercantile System and Its Historical Significance*. London: Macmillan.

Sen, S. R. 1957. *The Economics of Sir James Steuart*. London: G. Bell & Sons for the London School of Economics and Political Science.

Skaggs, Neil. 1991. 'John Fullarton's Law of Reflux and Central Bank Policy'. *History of Political Economy* 23 (3): 457–480. doi:10.1215/00182702-23-3-457.

Skaggs, Neil. 1999. 'Changing Views: Twentieth Century Opinion on the Banking School-Currency School Controversy'. *History of Political Economy* 31 (2): 361–391. doi:10.1215/00182702-31-2-361.

Smith, Adam. (1776) 1981. *An Inquiry into the Nature and Causes of the Wealth of Nations*. Indianapolis: Liberty Fund.

Steuart, James. 1767. *An Inquiry into the Principles of Political Economy, Being an Essay on the Science of Domestic Policy in Free Nations, in Which Are Particular Considered Population, Agriculture, Trade, Industry, Money, Coin, Interest, Circulation, Banks, Exchange, Public Credit and Taxes*. 2 vols. London: A. Millar and T. Cadell.

Steuart, James. 1789. *Recherche des principes de l'économie politique ou essai sur la science de la police intérieure des nations libres*. 5 vols. Paris: Didot l'aîné.

Steuart, James. 1805. *The Works, Political, Metaphisical, and Chronological of the Late Sir James Steuart of Coltness, Bart* (Vol. I), London: T. Cadell and W. Davies.

Tooke, Thomas. 1848. *A History of Prices, and of the State of Circulation from 1839 to 1847 Inclusive*. Vol. 5. London: Longman, Brown, Green and Longmans.

Tooke, Thomas. 1844. *An Inquiry into the Currency Principle*. London: Longman, Brown, Green and Longmans.

Tortajada, Ramon. 2002. *The Economics of James Steuart. Routledge Studies in the History of Economics*. London: Routledge.

Labour values and energy values: some developments on the common substance of value since 1867

Wilfried Parys

ABSTRACT

Marx's *Das Kapital* (1867) singled out labour as the common substance of value in all commodities. Costanza (1980) in *Science* chose energy and propagated energy values (a century after Engels criticised Podolinsky on energy). Mainstream economists quickly questioned Marx's logic. Pareto advocated simultaneous equations, unaware of their use by Mühlpfordt and Dmitriev. Contributions by Charasoff and Potron were also overlooked. Already in 1927, Leontief and Sraffa knew how to replace labour values by other commodity values. Generalising Sraffa's subsystems and using "percentage formulas" for price-value deviations, I discuss some empirical results for labour or energy theories of value.

1. Introduction

In the history of economic thought, various thinkers have been attracted by the problematic idea of a single cause of economic value. Today, such ideas appear mostly in studies on the labour theory of value of Karl Marx. Already in the very first section of *Das Kapital*, in 1867, Marx uses the following argument: the fact that two commodities, for example, one quarter of corn and x cwt. of iron, are exchanged against each other in the market, implies that "there exists in equal quantities something common to both". Marx then continues:

> The two things must therefore be equal to a third, which in itself is neither the one nor the other. Each of them, so far as it is exchange-value, must therefore be reducible to this third ... If we then leave out of consideration the use-value of commodities, they have only one common property left, that of being products of labour (Marx [1867] 1954, 45).

Then Marx explains the values of commodities by a special common substance, the quantity of abstract labour embodied in them.[1] Marx's theory of value was criticised from several angles. Several well-known mainstream economists (for example, Philip Henry Wicksteed, Eugen von Böhm-Bawerk, Knut Wicksell, and Vilfredo Pareto) quickly pointed out that labour was not the only common substance in commodities. Another problem was Marx's suboptimal mathematics. In Marx's system, the same commodities can appear on the side of the inputs and on the side of the outputs. Today, it is well-known that many analytical problems in such circular systems can be solved by means of simultaneous equations of the input-output type. Here the most original contributions were not made by leading economists mentioned above, but by rather unknown outsiders (Wolfgang Mühlpfordt, Vladimir Dmitriev, Georg Charasoff, Maurice Potron), whose pioneering works were neglected for decades. In December 1927, both Piero Sraffa and Wassily Leontief, independently of each other, argued that the reduction of all commodities to labour values was not a unique process; from a formal point of view, it was possible to compute not only labour values but also wheat values, coal values, etc. Although both Sraffa and Leontief were well-known economic scholars already at a young age, their above insights of 1927 remained rather unnoticed for several decades.

Not every bibliometric search on value theory will lead to the above-mentioned economists or to 21st century top-economists. Suppose a complete outsider consults the bibliometric specialists of the library of a top university. These specialists claim to know objective criteria to assess the scholarly prestige of the thousands of journals in their library: the impact factor. A certain journal in the library seems to be really scientific beyond doubt. It wears the clear and simple name *Science*, its 2016 impact factor was more than 37. This prestigious journal contains several papers by non-economists on the theory of value, advocating the use of the concept of *energy value*, where a commodity's energy value corresponds to the quantity of direct and indirect energy necessary to produce that commodity. The most conspicuous study of this type in *Science* is the often cited article *Embodied Energy and Economic Valuation,* by Robert Costanza (1980), claiming that both theory and empiry suggest a close connection between relative prices and energy

---

[1] For more background information, see Faccarello, Gehrke and Kurz (2016). Related material is also found in several essays in Bellofiore (1998).

values. The works of Costanza and some other influential non-economists are usually discussed outside the networks of orthodox or Marxian economics, but the empirical and the theoretical studies on energy values and labour values show several remarkable cases of analogous arguments and imperfections, both trying to support the use of a single substance of economic value.

My paper considers both theoretical and empirical aspects of such discussions on labour values and energy values.[2] I also use a numerical example of a simple three commodity economy and illustrate the computation of both labour values and energy values in two ways: via a system of simultaneous input-output equations, or via subsystems (vertically integrated systems that produce only one net output). The two computation methods are well-known from the rich literature on labour values. However, my example is useful here, because comparing energy values and labour values forces me to a generalisation of the notion of a subsystem: in order to define this notion unambiguously, I need to specify not only the net output of the subsystem but also its net input. If the only net input of the subsystem is energy, I use the expression "energy subsystem". This concept is needed to establish a percentage formula on the deviation between prices and energy values, analogous to my formula for labour values. By generalising Sraffa's notion of subsystems, it is possible to explain why supporters of labour values and energy values both present "good" empirical results for their favourite theory. Both groups should be more aware of the non-uniqueness of their exaggerated claims and then be more humble when trying to defend their one-sided theories and their empiry.

2. Wicksteed, Böhm-Bawerk, Wicksell, and Pareto on the common substance

Already in the 19th century, many important mainstream economists questioned Marx's arguments about the common substance. Wicksteed (1884) claimed that the common something in all exchangeable things is not abstract labour, but abstract utility. Wicksell ([1893] 1954, 44) mentioned that other common substances could exist, for instance, a certain area of land, a certain quantity of power (coal), etc. Wicksell

---

[2] In this way, I try to counteract too much fragmentation; see also the general remarks by Trautwein (2017).

never propagated the idea of a land theory of value or a coal (energy) theory of value. It is well-known that he ultimately emphasised the role of marginal utilities in his Marx critique.[3]

Marx had suggested that all types of skilled and unskilled labour could be reduced to the same sort of average or abstract labour and that the latter was the common substance of value in all commodities. Böhm-Bawerk tried to ridicule Marx's argument:

> With the very same reasoning one could affirm and argue the proposition that the quantity of material contained in commodities constitutes the principle and measure of exchange value – that commodities exchange in proportion to the *quantity of material incorporated in them*. Ten pounds of material in one kind of commodity exchange against ten pounds of material in another kind of commodity. If the natural objection were raised that this statement was obviously false because ten pounds of gold do not exchange against ten pounds of iron but against 40,000 pounds, or against a still greater number of pounds of coal, we may reply after the manner of Marx that it is the amount of *common average material* that affects the formation of value, that acts as unit of measurement. Skillfully wrought costly material of special quality *counts* only as compound or rather multiplied common material, so that a small quantity of material fashioned with skill is equal to a larger quantity of common material (Böhm-Bawerk [1896] 1949, 85).

Pareto also pointed out the arbitrariness of claims about the common substance, for example, in his book *Les systèmes socialistes* (Pareto [1902] 1965, vol. 2, 343n). Elsewhere in the same book (287–293), he suggested that the classical economists and Marx should have used simultaneous equations, to handle the interdependent nature of their systems. Pareto and his contemporaries were not aware that the relevant equations for Marx's analysis had been formulated already in 1893 in Königsberg, in a doctoral dissertation that would fall into oblivion till the end of the 20th century.

3. Mühlpfordt formulates input-output price equations

In his 1893 dissertation in Königsberg, Wolfgang Mühlpfordt (1872–1928) reviewed both some objective theories of value (classical or Marxian) and the subjective value theory of the Austrians. Mühlpfordt (1893, 25–26) formulated the same input-output price

---

[3] More detailed quotations for this and for some other sections can be found in a much longer, earlier version of my paper (Parys 2018).

equations that were presented by Sraffa (1960, 6), for a system of production of n commodities by means of the same n commodities, where the wage goods for the workers enter the system on the same footing as the other inputs. Two years later, Mühlpfordt's (1895) article on Marx again showed how such simultaneous equations were able to determine the average rate of profit in Marx's system. As far as I know, Mühlpfordt was the first Marx critic who used modern input-output coefficients with two subscripts (the a_{ij} coefficients, where a_{ij} = physical quantity of commodity j used to produce a unit of commodity i, where i and j vary from 1 to n).

At the very end of his article, Mühlpfordt (1895, 99) saw "kein unüberbrückbarer Widerspruch" (no irreconcilable contradiction) between the classical and the Austrian school. He was neither a mathematician nor a Marxist, but surely a pioneer of Marxian mathematical economics. He spent his career outside the networks of the specialists of value theory; after 1895, he never published on value theory again (he wrote a few articles on other topics, for example, on accountancy and on actual political problems).

He was deeply disappointed by the lack of recognition that plagued him from the very beginning. His doctoral dissertation deserved better than the insulting jokes in March 1894 in *Die Neue Zeit*, where a hypercritical reviewer failed to understand the dissertation's strong points and started his sarcastic review as follows:

> Judging from the present treatise, it seems not to be very difficult for the faithful to become a doctor in Königsberg by means of an economic work. What the author has to say about price and income contains absolutely nothing new. (Anonymous 1894)

It took a century before Mühlpfordt's brilliant originality was discovered by Howard and King (1987) and then generated further comments; see, for example, the bibliographical references given by Quaas (1994).

4. Dmitriev formulates the modern labour value equations

Completely unaware of Mühlpfordt's results, another remarkable case of early input-output analysis was presented by Vladimir Dmitriev (1868–1913), in the first pages of his Russian essay of 1898, reprinted in his 1904 book. The editor of the English translation, Domenico Mario Nuti (1974, 30), mentions that in the West he knew only one original copy of Dmitriev's Russian book, in the rich library of Piero

Sraffa. According to the recent catalogue by Giancarlo de Vivo (2014, xxxix, 138), Sraffa acquired a copy of Dmitriev's 1904 book only in the 1960s. Apparently, it is not widely known that Leontief too owned the Russian text in the 1960s. There exists no catalogue of Leontief's library, but in a letter of 20 October 1969 to William Jaffé, Leontief writes:

> Under separate cover I am mailing to you – registered mail – a photostat copy of Dmitrieff's book. I have received it a year ago from Russia, and, most likely it is the only copy in this country. So, please return it to me as soon as possible by registered mail (Leontief Papers, HUG 4517.6, General Correspondence 1969-70, G-O, Box 11, folder J).

Dmitriev ([1904] 1974) used modern simultaneous equations of the input-output type to show explicitly how to compute the labour values, but as soon as he studied the price system, he employed the less general method of finite dated labour series. Modern discussions of Marx's value theory construct two systems of simultaneous equations: one system for labour values and one system for prices and the rate of profit. Here, Dmitriev and Mühlpfordt each performed 50% of the task: Dmitriev formulated the modern system of labour value equations, but not the related system of prices, whereas Mühlpfordt had explicitly shown us the latter, but not the former.

Dmitriev tried to offer an organic synthesis of the labour theory of value and the theory of marginal utility. Moreover, in some later writings he strongly leaned towards the marginal productivity theory (Schütte 2003, 186–275). Both his mathematical approach and his non-Marxian standpoints decreased the official recognition of Dmitriev to nearly zero in Stalin's Soviet Union.

5. Bortkiewicz does not use the general Mühlpfordt and Dmitriev equations

Ladislaus von Bortkiewicz (1868–1931) knew both the mainstream and the Marxist literature unusually well. It is surprising that even Bortkiewicz overlooked the Mühlpfordt (1895) article on Marx in the *Jahrbücher für Nationalökonomie und Statistik*, then one of the leading economic journals. On the other hand, Bortkiewicz knew Dmitriev's originality and praised it explicitly in his influential Marx critique (Bortkiewicz 1907, 34). Later, he even took care of the entry on Dmitriev in the authoritative *Encyclopaedia of the Social Sciences*

(Bortkiewicz 1931). In spite of this, Bortkiewicz never used the system of simultaneous input-output equations that was used by Dmitriev for the determination of labour values. Bortkiewicz (1907, 34) rather laconically mentions about Dmitriev: "Ich habe seine Darstellung nur etwas vereinfacht" (I have only simplified his presentation a bit). That "simplification" deleted Dmitriev's brilliant simultaneous input-output equations.

Later, Bortkiewicz also underestimated Wassily Leontief's potential, when in 1928 he wrote a rather critical report on Leontief's doctoral dissertation (Leontief 1991a; Bjerkholt 2016, 32–40). Leontief's other supervisor in Berlin was Werner Sombart, but he lacked the mathematical sophistication necessary to understand Leontief's (and Bortkiewicz's) ideas on value theory. Ironically, Sombart (1905) did not forget to include the article by Mühlpfordt (1895) in his long chronological bibliography of works on Marx. However, the 300 items in Sombart's bibliography were not annotated, and the name Mühlpfordt generated no interest among his contemporaries.

6. Charasoff reduces everything to a basket of Urkapital (in the limit)

Unlike Marx, Georg Charasoff (1877–1931) did not reduce everything to a *single* substance, but to a specially designed *composite* commodity, a basket of so-called *Urkapital*.

After obtaining a doctoral degree in mathematics in Heidelberg in 1902, Charasoff planned a trilogy on the economic theories of value. First, he presented a short book on Marx (Charasoff 1909), based upon lectures he had organised in the preceding three years. A review by Gustav Eckstein (1909) was as negative as possible: "If one wanted to note all the nonsense which is in this book, one would have to transcribe it". Most other reviewers were more polite, but all showed little enthusiasm. The following year Charasoff (1910) published a much stronger and longer work, his *Das System des Marxismus*. For various reasons, this book too was neglected by most specialists. Charasoff held no university position, lived a rather Bohemian life as an independent scholar, had a less than ideal book publisher (who went out of business in 1913) Moreover, Charasoff sometimes behaved in a shocking nonacademic way in everyday life (for more biographical details, see Gehrke 2015).

One of the many original insights in Charasoff (1910) is his clever treatment of the circular nature of production. In his analysis, we find the same commodities on the side of the inputs and on the side of the outputs. Charasoff (1910, 290) suggests that Marx argues in a circle when he first takes the labour values of the inputs as given and then determines the labour values of the outputs. In a system of production of commodities by means of commodities, we need to determine the values of all commodities via a system of simultaneous equations. Charasoff (1910, 290–291) then supports Pareto's claim that most economists do not seem to know how to construct or to handle a system of simultaneous price equations due to a lack of mathematical expertise. Those who look for a simple unique cause of economic value do not understand the nature of a general equilibrium system.

Charasoff invented the device of *Urkapital* ("original capital"), a specially designed basket of different commodities.[4] Charasoff shows that in the limit all commodities can be reduced to this special Urkapital, as follows. Suppose we consider two arbitrary commodities X and Y. Their input baskets (Charasoff's "capitals of the first order") will correspond to X' and Y'. In general these two baskets have different proportions. To produce X' and Y', we need input baskets X'' and Y'' ("capitals of the second order"), again with two different proportions in general. If we go back k rounds we find the "capitals of the k-th order" $X^{(k)}$ and $Y^{(k)}$. The further we go in this series (the higher k), the more the baskets $X^{(k)}$ and $Y^{(k)}$ seem to become proportional to each other.[5] "In the limit" the baskets become exactly proportional to each other, being different quantities of the same composite commodity, namely baskets of Urkapital.

If in the limit X needs three times more Urkapital than Y, then the price of X will be three times higher than that of Y (Charasoff 1910, Chapters 9 and 10). In this sense, Charasoff considers Urkapital as the common substance in the commodities X and Y that "explains" their relative prices. Strictly speaking, within the usual assumptions of the model (given inputs and outputs, single

---

[4] From a mathematical point of view, a basket of Urkapital corresponds to an eigenvector of the augmented input matrix: see Egidi and Gilibert (1984) or Parys (2014). Compare with Sraffa's (1960) standard composite commodity, which corresponds to an eigenvector of the non-augmented input matrix (by the latter, I mean the original input matrix, not including consumption by workers).

[5] Charasoff presents an example with three commodities, where the proportions of the Urkapital basket become already visible after four rounds. See the figures in the original tables from Charasoff (1910, 114) or their representation in matrices (Parys 2014, 998).

product industries, homogeneous labour, circulating capital only, a given basket of wage goods for the workers, etc.), Charasoff was the only one whose search for a common substance of value was logically correct. However, remember that his common substance of Urkapital was not an individual commodity, but a basket of commodities, and that Charasoff's construction of it involved the nontrivial computation of a mathematical limit.

Some rather unimportant remarks by Charasoff on Marx were discussed or quoted by Nikolai Bukharin (1927, 56, 127, 179, 184, 188), in *The Economic Theory of the Leisure Class*. Sraffa's copy of the 1927 English edition of Bukharin's book contains many annotations. In his unpublished papers (D3/12/3:54), Sraffa makes some positive comments on Bukharin's book. Hence, Sraffa seems to have read Bukharin's book thoroughly. Sraffa surely must have noticed the name Charasoff, especially on pages 127 and 179, where Sraffa places a line in the margin close to or near a Bukharin quote of Charasoff. For example, on page 179, Bukharin provides the full bibliographical reference of Charasoff's (1910) book, and then continues:

> Charasoff's assertion that even certain Marxian studies contain a subjective interpretation of the Marxian theory, is entirely correct; but this is not the place to discuss this question (Bukharin 1927, 179)

Sraffa put a straight line in the margin of this passage. Charasoff's (1910) book introduced some original devices that were related to some later Sraffian tools (Sraffa's standard commodity, the distinction between basics and non-basics, determination of labour values by dated labour series and subsystems, for example). However, Bukharin mentioned only a few less important remarks of Charasoff and did not draw attention to any of Charasoff's really innovating devices. There is no trace of Charasoff's book in the catalogue of Sraffa's library (de Vivo 2014). Charasoff finally started getting some recognition only in the 1980s, when Egidi and Gilibert (1984) drew special attention to many of Charasoff's original results.

7. Potron's unintended contribution to a solution of some Marxian problems

Most studies on Marx (including Mühlpfordt, Dmitriev, Bortkiewicz, Charasoff) concentrate on systems with homogeneous labour. Of course, it is well known that Marx himself spent several

paragraphs on the problem of reducing heterogeneous types of labour
to a sort of standard labour, i.e., on the reduction of skilled labour to
multiple simple labour. One of the most creative technical contributions in this context was implicit in the works of the French Jesuit
mathematician Maurice Potron (1872–1942), although Potron never
read Marx and surely did not like his ideology. Without studying the
relevant economic literature, Potron wrote on economics in the periods 1911–1914 and 1935–1942. His economic papers contained pioneering anticipations of input-output economics, but they were
published in journals for mathematicians or for Roman Catholic intellectuals, hence outside the networks of economics.[6] For more than
half a century, economists neglected his work, until Émeric Lendjel
(2000) finally drew attention to Potron's novel mathematical economics. A few years later, Kenji Mori (2008) explicitly emphasised that
Potron's work *de facto* included remarkable analytical results on the
relation between surplus values and profits in Marxian systems with
heterogeneous labour.

8. Simultaneous equations are necessary

Potron's wealthy parents (and their family) intellectually and finan-
cially supported Catholic social action, and in this context Potron
became interested in the study of just prices and just wages. Potron
emphasised that wages and prices could not be studied separately in
isolation. To judge whether a wage was just or not, one had to know
the prices of the commodities consumed by the workers. To judge
whether the price of a commodity was just or not, one had to know
its cost of production, thus the prices of the physical inputs and especially the wage. Just wages and just prices were interdependent. To
handle this interdependence, Potron developed an original system of
simultaneous input-output equations and inequalities.

   Just like Potron, Charasoff held a doctoral degree in mathematics
and understood the power of simultaneous equations. Unlike Potron,
Charasoff knew mainstream economics, including Pareto's work and
his insistence on the necessity of using simultaneous equations. In
circular models where A, B, C, etc., depend on A, B, C, etc., it was
useless to look for one "single cause" explaining A, B, C, etc.

---

[6] For many details on Potron's life and work, and a recent annotated Potron bibliography,
I refer to Bidard, Erreygers, and Parys (2009), and Parys (2016a).

Although Sraffa's (1960) book never refers to Pareto, Sraffa's unpublished papers clearly show how he took notice of Pareto's remarks (Kurz and Salvadori, 2010, 198, 212).

9. Sraffa on reducing everything to labour, or to wheat, or to something else

It is probably not widely known that in 1929 Maurice Dobb and Piero Sraffa planned an English translation of Marx's *Theorien über den Mehrwert* and asked Karl Kautsky's permission to use his German edition as a starting point (Parys 2013, 44). In 1930, Sraffa abandoned the idea of the Marx translation project, in order to concentrate on the academically more prestigious Ricardo edition. Dobb never translated Marx's *Theorien über den Mehrwert* but helped Sraffa to edit Ricardo. Unlike other Cambridge economic colleagues in the 1930s, both Dobb and Sraffa retained a strong interest in Marx's economics. Sraffa's unpublished notes of the 1940s often contain more Marxian terminology than Sraffa's (1960) book. For example, the latter mentioned "proportions of labour to means of production", the former often argued in terms of "organic composition of capital". A striking feature of his unpublished papers is that Sraffa, already in the 1920s, wrote down very sceptical remarks about Marx's labour values (see Sraffa D3/12/9:89):[7]

> It is a purely mystical conception that attributes to human labour a special gift of determining value.

A small card in the archives (Sraffa D3/12/10:71) has the following text:

> Method of "substitution" in equations: corresponds exactly to "historical" method of showing that all values are "due" to labour, or to wheat or to any other thing that enters in the production of every one of them.

Here Sraffa is referring to methods for solving simultaneous equations. From a purely formal point of view, we can define not one, but several common factors. We can reduce all commodities to embodied labour (labour values), but we might as well reduce everything to embodied wheat or embodied energy, for example (see further on

---

[7] Also quoted by Kurz and Salvadori (2001, p. 168).

energy values). Kurz (2015, 224) emphasises that the above insight from Sraffa's papers dates from as early as December 1927.[8]

10. Leontief on reducing everything to A or to K

In exactly the same month of December 1927, independently of Sraffa's research in Cambridge, the 22-year-old Leontief submitted the text of his doctoral dissertation in Berlin.[9] Due to bureaucratic problems (Bjerkholt 2016, 32–40), Leontief obtained his degree only at the end of 1928. The last algebraic formulas at the end of the dissertation (Leontief 1928, 621–622; 1991b, 210–211) are relevant for the problem of reducing everything to one common substance. With some goodwill, we can see here the same insight as in Sraffa's unpublished files. Leontief's example was rather primitive because it presented a no-surplus system. In such a special case, the A-value of A is simply one. Leontief should have worked out a better example; it would have been more meaningful if he had computed the A-value of K, or the K-value of A. Or he should have considered a system with a surplus. Then the A-value of A or the K-value of K will be smaller than one, which is typical of economies that are able to produce a surplus.[10]

In the late 1920s, Leontief resp. Sraffa mentioned the different reductions to a single input only in an old German text resp. unpublished personal papers. These insights remained rather unnoticed for decades. One of the first published numerical examples in English of computing commodity values was provided in the book *Proportions, Prices, and Planning* by András Bródy (1970, 85–86), for a no-surplus system; in this special case, the labour values were proportional to other commodity values.

11. A simple corn-energy-labour economy

To simplify my exposition, I use the following numerical example of an economic system where a unit of corn (also denoted below by

---

[8] In a section on "tertium comparationes" Kurz and Salvadori (2010, 202–203) discussed embodied electricity in relation to some Sraffa notes of early 1928.

[9] On the limited interaction between Leontief and Sraffa during their long careers, see Parys (2016b).

[10] See Gintis and Bowles (1981). A few years ago, *Metroeconomica* published several sophisticated articles on such commodity values, in more general frameworks than the simple systems of the pioneers. See the bibliographical references provided by Fujimoto and Opocher (2010a, 2010b).

1 corn) means one kilo of corn, a unit of energy (1 energy) means one kilo of coal, and a unit of labour (1 labour) means one hour of labour time. It is an example of ex post accounting: at the end of the year, after it is known which quantities of inputs and outputs have been used and produced (including knowledge of the workers' consumption and the labour hours they performed), an accountant expresses all quantities per kilo of corn, per kilo of coal and per hour of labour. I make the traditional simplifying assumption that all inputs are completely used up (no fixed capital):

$$0.4 \text{ corn} + 0.5 \text{ energy} + 0.05 \text{ labour} \rightarrow 1 \text{ corn}$$

$$0.1 \text{ corn} + 0.4 \text{ energy} + 0.25 \text{ labour} \rightarrow 1 \text{ energy}$$

$$0.2 \text{ corn} + 0.5 \text{ energy} + 0.15 \text{ labour} \rightarrow 1 \text{ labour}$$

These data can be compatible with various economic theories. An orthodox Marxist could interpret the last row above as the outcome of tumultuous struggles about the length of the working day, such that in the past year every individual worker ultimately performed 10 hours of labour per day and everyday consumed 2 kilos of corn, burned 5 kilos of coal for heating at home, and needed 1.5 hours of labour services at home.[11]

11.1. Labour values and labour subsystems[12]

The coefficients of the first two rows allow us to compute λ_c and λ_e, the labour values of a unit of corn and energy: $\lambda_c = 0.5$ and $\lambda_e = 0.5$. A working day (10 hours) involves the consumption of 2 corn, 5 coal, and 1.5 labour, hence $2\lambda_c + 5\lambda_e + 1.5 = 1 + 2.5 + 1.5 = 5$ hours of necessary labour. Hence, every working day consists of 5 hours of necessary labour and 5 hours of surplus labour. Marx's rate of surplus value is 100% here.

The same labour values can also be computed via subsystems (see also Sraffa 1960, 89). In case of corn, I can construct *the labour subsystem of corn*, a sort of vertically integrated system for the production

---

[11] In my example, all input coefficients are positive. If one prefers the more traditional assumption of zero units of labour input in the consumption basket of the workers, the methods for determining labour values and other values remain the same.

[12] The computation of the labour values via equations or via subsystems is "textbook material". A much longer, earlier draft of my paper (Parys 2018) presents more details on these computations for my numerical example.

of corn, with 0.5 units of labour as the only net input and with 1 unit of corn as the only net output. We can project the net input into the net output and claim that the 0.5 units of labour are now embodied (incorporated, crystallised, congealed) in 1 unit of corn. This is just an alternative method to compute the labour value of corn, $\lambda_c = 0.5$.

I draw special attention to the following: I use the expression "*labour* subsystem" here instead of the shorter "subsystem". In the traditional Sraffian literature it is taken for granted that labour is the net input of the subsystem, but in the present article I will need a more general approach and terminology. In general, suppose IN is an arbitrary basic input, and consider any other commodity OUT. Then we can construct a subsystem with commodity IN as the only net input and with one unit of commodity OUT as the only net output. Such an IN-subsystem of OUT will show how much IN is embodied in OUT, or in other words, it shows the IN-value of OUT. When discussing energy values, IN will be energy.

11.2. Energy values

If I use the ideas of Costanza's (1980) energy values in the high-status journal *Science,* applied to my simple corn-energy-labour example above, I consider not labour, but energy as the ultimate substance of value, and I give the energy input a special status, separated from the two other inputs (corn and labour). I then treat corn and labour, the non-energy sectors, as the two endogenous sectors, and therefore choose the following layout:

$$0.4 \text{ corn } + \ 0.05 \text{ labour } + 0.5 \text{ energy} \rightarrow \ 1 \text{ corn}$$

$$0.2 \text{ corn } + \ 0.15 \text{ labour } + 0.5 \text{ energy} \rightarrow \ 1 \text{ labour}$$

Both corn and labour require a direct input of 0.5 units of energy. However, it would be wrong to conclude that their energy values are the same. To the 0.5 units of direct energy input, we have to add the indirect energy input, i.e., the energy values of the corn and labour inputs. Hence, the energy values for corn and labour, denoted ε_c and ε_ℓ, are computed via simultaneous equations:

$$0.4\,\varepsilon_c + 0.05\,\varepsilon_\ell + 0.5 = \varepsilon_c$$
$$0.2\,\varepsilon_c + 0.15\,\varepsilon_\ell + 0.5 = \varepsilon_\ell$$

My example gives $\varepsilon_c = 0.9$ and $\varepsilon_\ell = 0.8$.

In my example, the production of 1 unit of energy (coal) required 0.1 corn, 0.25 labour, and 0.4 energy itself, hence a total energy value of 0.1 ε_c + 0.25 ε_ℓ + 0.4 = 0.09 + 0.2 + 0.4 = 0.69. Hence in the production of 1 unit of energy, we use up an energy value = 0.69 and thus we create 1-0.69 = 0.31 surplus energy value here. Just like supporters of labour values have found a positive rate of surplus *labour* value in my example, the energy accountants now find a positive rate of surplus *energy* value (0.31/0.69 = 0.45 or 45%). In my example, it takes less than a kilo of direct and indirect coal to produce 1 kilo of coal. Such a condition is also mentioned in Sraffa's unpublished drafts of 22 September 1944: "If condition 'one ton of coal requires dir. ± indir. less than 1 ton of coal' is satisfied …" (Sraffa Papers D3/12/39:41).

11.3. Energy subsystems

I define *the energy subsystem of corn* as a sort of vertically integrated system for the production of corn, with energy as the only net input and with corn as the only net output.

Consider again the system with the exogenous energy of the preceding Section 11.2. Multiply the quantities consumed in the corn process by 1.7 and those consumed by labour by 0.1. This gives:

$$0.68 \text{ corn} + 0.085 \text{ labour} + 0.85 \text{ energy} \rightarrow 1.7 \text{ corn}$$

$$0.02 \text{ corn} + 0.015 \text{ labour} + 0.05 \text{ energy} \rightarrow 0.1 \text{ labour}$$

Both on the left and the right we find a total of 0.1 labour.

The only net input = 0.85 + 0.05 = 0.9 energy.
The only net output is 1.7 − 0.68 − 0.02 = 1 corn.

I can project the net input into the net output and claim that the 0.9 units of energy (here 0.9 kilos of coal) have been embodied into 1 unit of corn. This is an alternative method to compute ε_c = 0.9, the energy value of corn. I called the above system *the energy subsystem of corn*. In a similar way, I can construct *the energy subsystem of labour*. The latter will generate the energy value of labour.

12. Leontief's early empirical examples of labour values and subsystems

In the 1920s, the young Leontief in Russia read a very large amount of texts from classical economists and Marx, but Leontief never emphasised the importance of labour values for his own economics. In the last decades of his long career, Leontief was rather often interviewed. In an interview in French, edited by Bernard Rosier, Leontief discussed the theory of value of the classical economists and Marx; here Leontief expressed his scepticism as follows:

> Je pense toujours que c'est un peu métaphysique. C'est pourquoi j'ai toujours des difficultés avec les marxistes. Quelle est la valeur, qu'est-ce que la plus-value? Vous pouvez interpréter les choses de la manière que vous voulez. Cependant on peut calculer le quotient de travail quand on a un tableau, mais aussi celui de l'acier, ou maintenant celui de l'énergie. Tout cela est identique *du point de vue du calcul* (Leontief, in Rosier 1986, 89)

Here Leontief clearly points to possible computations of labour values or steel values or energy values, and at the same time he does not believe that such single input theories provide a useful theory of value. Ironically, Leontief (1944), in his paper *Output, Employment, Consumption, and Investment*, was perhaps the first who (implicitly) computed real-world labour values by means of input-output methods. His paper wanted to solve questions such as "How many new jobs will be created by the consumers' demand for an additional one million of passenger cars?" (Leontief 1944, 290). His Table IV (312) contains "the direct and the total employment coefficients" for different industries, i.e., thousands of persons per one million dollars worth of final demand. The total employment coefficients correspond to ratios of labour values to prices, Leontief's table was thus tailor-made for empirical studies on the deviation between prices and labour values, but Leontief was not interested in this question, and supporters of labour values for many years missed the opportunity to look at such input-output data.

In the fifties, Leontief (1953) presented his classic results on the labour intensity of American imports versus exports and concluded that the exports were more labour intensive than the imports. This "unexpected result", the Leontief Paradox, captured wide attention and generated numerous debates among specialists and standard paragraphs in many textbooks on international economics. Some tables of Leontief (1953) implicitly contained comprehensive empirical examples of subsystems. For example, his important Table 1 presents a vertically integrated system for the production of automobiles: its only net output consists of automobiles, it is a detailed description of a subsystem of automobiles, and its total direct labour requirement implicitly reveals the labour value of automobiles. Table 2 of Leontief (1953) offers a summary of the figures for all other subsystems, and thus implicitly the labour values of all other commodities.

13. Deviations of prices from labour values and energy values

The real world prices of the input-output tables differ from the "prices of production" analysed in many theoretical studies on Marx. The latter prices assume a uniform rate of profit r in all sectors. In addition, suppose now that such prices and labour values are expressed in comparable units: take an arbitrarily chosen commodity h and choose units for labour values and prices so that:

$$\lambda_h = p_h = 1$$

Then, for an arbitrary commodity j, Parys (1982, 1210) established the following "percentage formula":

$$\frac{p_j}{\lambda_j} = 1 + r\left(k_j - k_h\right)$$

where r is the uniform rate of profit, k_j is the capital-labour ratio of the labour subsystem of commodity j, and k_h is the capital-labour ratio of the labour subsystem of the numeraire commodity h. To obtain this simple formula, it is necessary to measure capital in prices, not in labour values, and to consider the capital-labour ratio of a sub-system, not that of an individual industry.[13]

Subsystems contain various individual industries and therefore the capital-labour ratios of subsystems are often less different than those of individual industries. Moreover, the expression $(k_j - k_h)$ is multi-plied by r, usually a small number (rates of profit are usually much lower than 100%, thus r is much lower than 1). This is one of the rea-sons why the percentage deviation indicated by $r\left(k_j - k_h\right)$ can be

---

[13] See the numerical example in Parys (1982, 1211). It shows that Marx's approach in terms of the organic compositions of individual industries and measurement in terms of labour values, can sometimes be strongly misleading. Sraffa, already in the 1940s, suggested that the ranking of the organic compositions of capital of two subsystems could be the reverse of that of the two original industries (Sraffa Papers, D3/12/36/60).

rather small in some empirical studies, especially when the numéraire h is close to a sort of average commodity.

Moreover, the empirical exercises employ input-output tables, which contain only a few dozens of heavily aggregated industries, and they usually aggregate outputs and inputs by simply using prices, including the reduction of heterogeneous labour and heterogeneous energy to homogeneous labour and energy.[14] A perfectly disaggregated study for a modern Western economy surely needs to consider more than a dozen *million* different commodities. Remember the planning problems of the old Soviet Union, where consumers enjoyed less variety than in the West:

> In the USSR at this time there are *12 million identifiably different products* (disaggregated down to specific types of ball-bearings, designs of cloth, size of brown shoes, and so on) (Nove 1983, 33–34).

Aggregation of millions of commodities into a few dozens cancels out many extreme differences and reduces the reported deviations of prices from labour values or energy values.

I can also present a formula for the deviation of prices from energy values, if I consider now special cases where the uniform rate of profit r also rules in the price equation for labour.[15] If I then choose units for prices and energy values so that $\varepsilon_h = p_h = 1$, some word processing generates a similar expression for the deviation between prices and energy values:

$$\frac{p_j}{\varepsilon_j} = 1 + r\,(E_j - E_h)$$

---

[14] There is a large literature on the Marxian problem of the reduction of heterogeneous labour to homogeneous labour, for example, using simultaneous equations that take into account the direct and indirect labour time necessary to produce skilled labour-power. A similar problem exists for heterogeneous energy. In my simple numerical example above, one unit of energy simply corresponds to one kilo of coal. In more complicated cases, various types of energy inputs are used. There are many energy papers on the reduction of heterogeneous energy inputs to one homogeneous unit; see Parys (2018) for more details on Costanza's (1980) use of the BTU, the British Thermal Unit, the amount of heat needed to increase the temperature of one pound of water by one degree Fahrenheit. Note that many empirical studies on labour values or energy values choose the unsophisticated method of aggregating heterogeneous labour or heterogeneous energy by means of the corresponding dollar costs.

[15] Denote the price of a unit of labour by p_ℓ, denote the price of the corresponding consumption basket by p_b, and then define the symbol r_ℓ such that $p_b\,(1 + r_\ell) = p_\ell$. The rate r_ℓ can be equal to r, the uniform rate of profit in all the other price equations, in the following two special cases. First, when a pure slave system rules, where slave labourers are "produced" at the profit rate r just like any other product. Second, consider a capitalist system where workers are "free", earn a wage, and have a positive savings rate s. Then, by definition, $s = (p_\ell - p_b)/p_\ell$ and thus, $s = r_\ell/(1 + r_\ell)$. The rate r_ℓ then equals the uniform rate of profit r, if the savings rate $s = r/(1 + r)$. For example, if $r = 0.10$, then $r = r_\ell$ if the savings rate $s = 1/11$.

where the symbol E_j refers to the energy subsystem of commodity j and it denotes the ratio between non-energy inputs (aggregated at prices) and the energy input in this subsystem; similarly, E_h refers to the energy subsystem of the numeraire commodity h. Again, this formula might be useful to explain relatively small deviations in highly aggregated empirical studies on energy values.

14. Costanza's energy values

The *Science* article by Costanza (1980) employs input-output analysis, but never uses such subsystems or percentage formulas. In the first page of his paper, Costanza (1980, 1219) invoked the prestige of a Nobel laureate, not in economics, but in chemistry, namely Frederick Soddy (1877–1956), who tried to unite physical and social sciences into one framework, emphasising the unique role of energy:

> If we have available energy, we may maintain life and produce every material requisite necessary. That is why the flow of energy should be the primary concern of economics (Soddy 1933, 56).

Soddy's switch from chemistry to economics was not well-received by mainstream economists.[16] Some energy studies supported the energy theory of value with the same enthusiasm that many Marxists used in their defense of the labour theory of value. At a rather late stage, the energy values supporters turned their eyes to input-output methods, and publication in *Science* generated a lot of prestige and funding. After the ambitious article by Costanza (1980), some later input-output computations also tried to support the energy theory.[17]

Costanza (1980) employed American input-output tables, for an ambitious empirical exercise on the relation between prices and energy values. He presented the results of various econometric regressions. Their very high determination coefficient R^2 was employed by Costanza to suggest a strong relation between prices and energy

---

[16] There is a surprisingly large group of non-economists who produced heterodox economic theories based upon a special role for energy. See Berndt (1985), Martinez-Alier (1987), and Mirowski (1988) for some historical details on the economic ideas of such adventurous outsiders.

[17] See a compilation of many of his essays in Costanza (1997); in the introduction (xviii), he complained that his results "have been more or less completely ignored by both conventional economists and environmentalists". However, Nicholas Georgescu-Roegen wanted to attack the fundamentals of Costanza's approach, but *Science* rejected his criticism; see the long letter of 20 May 1991, from Georgescu-Roegen to James Berry, published by Bonaiuti (2011, 236–240); see also Georgescu-Roegen (1986).

values, and thus a strong case for the energy theory of value. Ironically, in the same period, Wolff (1979) in the *American Economic Review* had reported equally high determination coefficients, when regressing prices on labour values, using similar American input-output tables. Wolff (1979, 335) suggested that "this indicates that empirically relative prices were close to relative labour values for the U.S. economy". Most authors of *Science* do not read intensely the *American Economic Review*, and vice versa.

It is risky to emphasise the importance of high values of R^2. Consider my following example of three goods, with prices $p_1 = 102$, $p_2 = 106$, $p_3 = 112$, and energy values $\varepsilon_1 = 1$, $\varepsilon_2 = 3$, $\varepsilon_3 = 6$. Here, a perfect linear relation holds ($p = 100 + 2\ \varepsilon$), an econometric regression will yield $R^2 = 1$. Do we meet a 100% perfect energy theory of value in this case? No! On the one hand, relative prices are 106/102, 112/102, 112/106, thus all close to 1. On the other hand, the corresponding relative energy values are extremely different: 3/1, 6/1, 6/3. Statistical studies on deviations between prices and values are sometimes careless.[18]

15. Problems of imperfect communication

Usually energeticists and Marxists belonged to two separated intellectual networks, with different conferences, different journals, etc. Of course, a minority of scholars studied both Marxian and energy accounting approaches. In point of fact, Marx himself tried to read widely in the natural sciences. In the final years of Marx's life, he and Engels paid some attention to novel ideas on the relation between energy and labour, presented by the Ukrainian socialist Sergei Podolinsky (1850–1891).

After publishing a Russian version of his thoughts, Podolinsky tried to spread his ideas in the West. He sent a letter to Marx on 30 March 1880, including a draft of a paper (in French) "to which your work *Das Kapital* has given me the first stimulus".[19] He received a reply

---

[18] For a comprehensive discussion of many measures of deviation between prices and labour values, see the recent books by Mariolis and Tsoulfidis (2016), and by Shaikh (2016, Chapter 9). Both books contain many bibliographical references about recent empirical studies on the labour theory of value. They do not discuss the literature on energy values, but implicitly they pay attention to many subtle problems of empirical measurement that are overlooked in the energy literature.

[19] Marx-Engels Papers D 3701–3702 (D VI 240–241): letters from Podolinsky, Archives of the International Institute of Social History, Amsterdam.

from Marx, but this is not extant. A somewhat longer Italian text appeared the next year in *La Plebe* (Podolinsky 1881), and a slightly different German version two years later in *Die Neue Zeit* (Podolinsky 1883). At that moment, Marx had just passed away and Podolinsky had stopped his creative activities due to an incurable mental breakdown. In recent years, Podolinsky's work received increasing attention in studies on ecology and Marxism, and this led to English translations of the above Italian and German articles.

The existence of different versions might be slightly confusing. For example, the Italian version refers to Marx, but not to Quesnay; the German version mentions Quesnay, but not Marx. Engels read the Italian version, which contains the following passage on the opening page:

> According to the theory of production formulated by Marx and accepted by socialists, human labour, expressed in the language of physics, accumulates in its products a greater quantity of energy than that which was expended in the production of the labour power of the workers. Why and how is this accumulation brought about? (Podolinsky 1881)[20]

Many modern readers might be tempted to answer Podolinsky's question by means of simultaneous equations, but Podolinsky himself concentrated on the general distribution of energy in the universe, the role of energy on the earth, the special properties of human labour, etc., without offering equations or well-rounded conclusions. In December 1882, Engels wrote two letters to Marx about Podolinsky's ideas. Engels did not believe that a sort of energy accounting could be a useful addition or improvement of Marx's work:

> The energy value, according to the production costs, of a hammer, a screw, a sewing needle, is an impossible quantity. In my opinion, it is completely impossible to express economic relations in physical magnitudes. (Engels to Marx, letter of 19 December 1882)[21]

Since Podolinsky presented no new analytical method for value theory, it is easy to understand Engels's scepticism. The extensive study by Martinez-Alier (1987) and other 20th century writings might have suggested that Marx and Engels handled Podolinsky's work rather

---

[20] Foster and Burkett (2017, 243–287) reproduce the complete English translations of Podolinsky's Italian and German articles, plus some editorial notes.

[21] Der Energiewert, den Produktionskosten nach, eines Hammers, einer Schraube, einer Nähnadel ist eine unmögliche Größe. Ökonomische Verhältnisse in physikalischen Maßen ausdrücken zu wollen, ist meiner Ansicht nach rein unmöglich (Marx and Engels 1973, 134).

hastily, but some more recent literature challenged this interpretation. Foster and Burkett (2017, Chapter 2) mentioned that there exist around 1800 words long extracts from Podolinsky's texts in Marx's notebooks and that such yet unpublished material will be included in a future volume IV/27 of the Marx–Engels Gesamtausgabe (MEGA).[22]

The majority of contemporary economists raise eyebrows when confronted with strong results claimed by adherents of labour values or energy values. Sometimes it is clear that these adherents believe that their approach possesses a simple "definitional" obviousness. Compare, for example, Hunt and Costanza. Hunt defended Marx's labour theory of value in the *Cambridge Journal of Economics*:

> The natural environment must be transformed if it is to support human life. Production is this transformation. And production has only one universally necessary social or human ingredient: labour. [...] The sun is as essential to human productive activity as is the crust of the earth. But no one speaks of the sun being a factor of production on the same footing as labour (Hunt 1983, 337–338).

Hunt was surely not familiar with the Costanza article on energy values in *Science* a few years earlier. Here Costanza attaches great relevance to the obvious fact that in the universe the sun and its energy can exist without human beings, but not vice versa:

> The question might be asked whether the same thing we have done with energy could not be done with any of the other currently defined primary factors and thus support capital, labor, or government service theories of value. The answer is that on paper this could be done. We must look to physical reality to determine which factors are net inputs and which are internal transactions. No one would seriously suggest that labor creates sunlight (Costanza 1980, 1224).

Often, the studies on labour values and energy values neglect each other and also neglect the criticism from more sophisticated economists. Many empirical studies on labour values concede that the labour theory has logical deficiencies, but is a good empirical approximation. Ironically, this approach does not defend Marx, who claimed that labour values were absolutely necessary to explain prices and the

---

[22] I refer to Foster and Burkett (2017) for more details. They spend a very large part of their book on Podolinsky, and they also present interesting details on how Marx and Engels studied the new results in the natural sciences: on the one hand, Marx and Engels read widely about such topics, and on the other hand, they strongly rejected trials to construct a theory of value based upon energy. In the first chapter of *Das Kapital* (and some other places) Marx mentions that human labour involves an expenditure of human brains, muscles, nerves, hands, etc., but his theory of value is based upon labour time, not upon units of energy.

rate of profit, but it supports Stigler's Ricardo. Stigler (1958) coined the expression "Ricardo's 93% labour theory": he claims that Ricardo did not hold an analytical labour theory of value, but an empirical one: labour values often give a good approximation in practice.

I suppose that especially the supporters of energy values do not realise that the critique by Steedman (1977) and others with respect to labour values also holds for energy values. Both labour values and energy values are ex post accounting magnitudes. In the real world, an extremely complex mechanism, involving actions of numerous decision-makers (consumers, producers, politicians, etc.), all operating under many complicated influences and constraints, leads to a certain combination of inputs and a certain gross output. Ex post and making some simplified assumptions, accountants can then compute labour values or energy values afterwards. These values are derived quantities; they are not theoretically necessary for explaining prices or profit rates.

16. Conclusion

In the history of economic thought, several scholars propagated the problematic idea of a single cause of value. My article concentrated on some developments after 1867, when Marx, in the opening pages of *Das Kapital*, singled out labour as the ultimate determinant of value, the common substance in all commodities, the source of the surplus, etc.

Mainstream economists like Wicksteed, Böhm-Bawerk, Wicksell, and Pareto casted doubts on Marx's arguments. Pareto also questioned the amateurish logic of many non-mathematical economists and recommended the use of simultaneous equations for a professional treatment of interdependent systems. Today, such simultaneous equations are the standard tool for determining labour values and discussing their relation with prices. In the 1890s and later, Pareto, Bortkiewicz, and many others overlooked the pioneering price equations of Mühlpfordt (1895), despite their publication in the *Jahrbücher für Nationalökonomie und Statistik*, which was internationally regarded as one of the top journals of economics in that period. Unaware of Mühlpfordt, Dmitriev formulated the complementary input-output equations for labour values. Bortkiewicz read Dmitriev's Russian essay, and "simplified it a bit", thereby missing the opportunity to use Dmitriev's pioneering input-output coefficients. In 1928, Bortkiewicz also underestimated the potential of his doctoral student Leontief, who received a Nobel Prize in 1973 for his input-output analysis. Working outside the intellectual networks of all the above economists, and therefore neglected by them, Charasoff (1910) reduced all commodities "in the limit" to a special composite commodity (Urkapital), and anticipated several analytical tools used in Sraffa's (1960) book. Sraffa intensively studied Bukharin's book on economic theory, which contained several references to Charasoff, but Bukharin concentrated on rather superficial Charasoff references and did not draw attention (and probably did not understand) the original devices created by Charasoff. Sraffa's impressive library does not contain a copy of Charasoff.

Both Leontief and Sraffa constructed the fundamentals of their theories on their own. In 1927, at an early stage of their career, unaware of each other, both realised that the reduction of all commodities to labour values was not a unique process. From a formal point of view, it was possible to compute wheat values, coal values, etc. Leontief never published this result in English, until his German dissertation was partially translated in 1991. Sraffa's remarks on this problem remained hidden in his unpublished papers until after his death. In the 1940s, Leontief's statistical computations on direct and total employment coefficients yielded important information for debates on the deviation of prices from labour values, but it took rather long before Marx scholars took notice of such empirical input-output material. Moreover, it took nearly a century before it was detected that the Roman Catholic economic model of Potron had implicitly and unintentionally solved some Marxian problems about the relation between surplus values and profits in a system with heterogeneous labour.

The energy crisis of the early 1970s generated an increasing interest in energy problems and led some influential non-economists to advocate an energy theory of value. This culminated in the prestigious article on energy values that Costanza (1980) ultimately published in *Science*, claiming that input-output computations revealed a close connection between relative prices and energy values.

I presented a generalisation of Sraffian subsystems for energy values and a formula for the percentage deviation of prices from energy values (formally similar to my formula for labour values) and I discussed why both adherents of labour values and energy values often claimed "good" empirical support for their favourite theory of value. The histories of labour values and energy values present unusual combinations of originality, amateurism, and several cases of imperfect communication, though Marx and Engels themselves paid critical attention to the papers on energy by Podolinsky. However, Podolinsky did not anticipate modern input-output methods for computing energy values.

Mainstream economists of the 21st century will regret that both adherents of labour values and energy values often miss the opportunity to study more sophisticated modern approaches to value theory. Moreover, many studies on energy values and labour values underestimate the similarity of each other's arguments. Not only the formal input-output analysis often looks analogous, but even the methodological arguments can look rather similar, for example, when both currents of thought, often unaware of each other, claim that their favourite input (labour resp. energy) obviously is the unique ultimate input. Finally, note that both currents of thought also discuss much wider issues than the pure theory of value, for example, when presenting broad historical studies. In this context, Marx and Engels (1848) made the well-known statement that the history of all hitherto existing societies is the history of class struggles. Here, Marx and Engels seem to be rather modest, limiting themselves to human societies on the Earth, whereas the scope of some energy specialists is infinitely much wider, as they emphasise the dominating role of energy for the history of all human and nonhuman systems in the Universe.[23]

Acknowledgements

I wish to thank three anonymous referees, whose comments improved the article. I am grateful to Lord Eatwell (literary executor of the Sraffa Papers), Jonathan Smith and his colleagues (Sraffa Papers, Wren Library, Trinity College, Cambridge, U.K.), the staff of the Harvard University Archives (Leontief Papers, Cambridge, Massachusetts, U.S.A.), and the International Institute of Social History (Amsterdam). I owe special thanks to Heinz Kurz.

---

[23] See the statement by Cleveland (2009, xv) on energy: "its central role in human affairs dates to the time of the first humans, its role in shaping the physical and biological nature of the Earth dates to the planet's birth, and the story of Big Bang itself is told in terms of energy and matter."

Disclosure statement

No potential conflict of interest was reported by the author.

References

Anonymous. 1894. "Review of Mühlpfordt (1893)". *Die Neue Zeit* 12 (26): 826–827.

Bellofiore, Riccardo, ed. 1998. *Marxian Economics: A Reappraisal.* 2 vols. Basingstoke: Macmillan.

Berndt, Ernst. 1985. "From Technocracy to Net Energy Analysis: Engineers, Economists, and Recurring Energy Theories of Value." In *Progress in Natural Resource Economics*, edited by Anthony Scott, 357–367. Oxford: Clarendon Press.

Bidard, Christian, Guido Erreygers, and Wilfried Parys. 2009. "Our Daily Bread: Maurice Potron, from Catholicism to Mathematical Economics." *European Journal of the History of Economic Thought* 16 (1): 123–154. doi:10.1080/09672560802707456

Bjerkholt, Olav. 2016. *Wassily Leontief and the Discovery of the Input-Output Approach.* University of Oslo: Department of Economics. Memorandum 18/2016.

Böhm-Bawerk, Eugen von. [1896] 1949. *Karl Marx and the Close of His System.* New York: Kelley.

Bonaiuti, Mauro, ed. 2011. *From Bioeconomics to Degrowth: Georgescu-Roegen's "New Economics" in Eight Essays.* London: Routledge.

Bortkiewicz, Ladislaus von. 1907. "Wertrechnung und Preisrechnung im Marxschen System. Zweiter Artikel." *Archiv für Sozialwissenschaft und Sozialpolitik* 25 (1): 10–51.

Bortkiewicz, Ladislaus von. 1931. "Dmitriev, Vladimir Karpovich." In *Encyclopaedia of the Social Sciences*, Vol. 5, edited by Edwin R.A. Seligman and Alvin Johnson, 185–186. New York: Macmillan.

Bródy, András. 1970. *Proportions, Prices and Planning.* Amsterdam: North-Holland.

Bukharin, Nikolai. 1927. *The Economic Theory of the Leisure Class.* London: Martin Lawrence.

Charasoff, Georg. 1909. *Karl Marx über die menschliche und kapitalistische Wirtschaft. Eine neue Darstellung seiner Lehre.* Berlin: Hans Bondy.

Charasoff, Georg, 1910. *Das System des Marxismus. Darstellung und Kritik.* Berlin: Hans Bondy.

Cleveland, Cutler J. 2009. "Foreword." In Fred Cottrell. *Energy and Society.* Revised Edition, xv–xvii. Bloomington: Author House.

Costanza, Robert. 1980. "Embodied Energy and Economic Valuation." *Science* 210 (4475): 1219–1224. doi:10.1126/science.210.4475.1219

Costanza, Robert. 1997. *Frontiers in Ecological Economics.* Cheltenham: Edward Elgar.

De Vivo, Giancarlo. 2014. *Catalogue of the Library of Piero Sraffa*. Milan: Fondazione Raffaele Mattioli; Turin: Fondazione Luigi Einaudi.

Dmitriev, Vladimir Karpovich. [1904] 1974. *Economic Essays on Value, Competition and Utility*. Cambridge: Cambridge University Press.

Eckstein, Gustav. 1909. "Zur Marxschen Wertlehre." *Vorwärts. Berliner Volksblatt*, Second Supplement, February 21.

Egidi, Massimo, and Giorgio Gilibert. 1984. "La teoria oggettiva dei prezzi." *Economia Politica* 1 (1): 43–61. [English translation: "The Objective Theory of Prices." *Political Economy. Studies in the Surplus Approach*, 1989, 5 (1): 59–74.]

Faccarello, Gilbert, Christian Gehrke, and Heinz D. Kurz. 2016. "Karl Heinrich Marx (1818–1883)." In *Handbook on the History of Economic Analysis. Volume 1. Great Economists since Petty and Boisguilbert*, edited by Gilbert Faccarello and Heinz D. Kurz, 211–233. Cheltenham: Edward Elgar.

Foster, John Bellamy, and Paul Burkett. 2017. *Marx and the Earth*. Chicago: Haymarket.

Fujimoto, Takao, and Arrigo Opocher. 2010a. "Commodity Content in a General Input-Output Model." *Metroeconomica* 61 (3): 442–453.

Fujimoto, Takao, and Arrigo Opocher. 2010b. "Commodity Content in a General Input-Output Model: a Reply to Bellino, Yoshihara, and Veneziani." *Metroeconomica* 61 (4): 754–758. doi:10.1111/j.1467-999X.2010.04109.x

Gehrke, Christian. 2015. "Georg von Charasoff: A Neglected Contributor to the Classical-Marxian Tradition." *History of Economics Review* 62 (1): 1–37. doi: 10.1080/18386318.2015.11681279

Georgescu-Roegen, Nicholas. 1986. "The Entropy Law and the Economic Process in Retrospect." *Eastern Economic Journal* 12 (1), 3–25.

Gintis, Herbert, and Samuel Bowles. 1981. "Structure and Practice in the Labor Theory of Value." *Review of Radical Political Economics* 12 (4): 1–26. doi: 10.1177/048661348101200401

Howard, Michael Charles, and John Edward King. 1987. "Dr Mühlpfort, Professor von Bortkiewicz and the Transformation Problem." *Cambridge Journal of Economics* 11 (3): 265–268. doi:10.1093/oxfordjournals.cje.a035030

Hunt, Emery Kay 1983. "Joan Robinson and the Labour Theory of Value." *Cambridge Journal of Economics* 7 (3/4): 331–342. doi:10.1093/cje/7.3-4.331

Kurz, Heinz D. 2015. "Sraffa's Equations 'Unveiled'? A Comment on Gilibert." In *Revisiting Classical Economics: Studies in Long-Period Analysis*, edited by Heinz D. Kurz and Neri Salvadori, 193–225. London: Routledge.

Kurz, Heinz D., and Neri Salvadori. 2001. "Sraffa and von Neumann." *Review of Political Economy* 13 (2): 161–180. doi:10.1080/09538250120036628

Kurz, Heinz D., and Neri Salvadori. 2010. "Sraffa and the Labour Theory of Value. A Few Observations." In *Economic Theory and Economic Thought: Essays in Honour of Ian Steedman*, edited by John Vint, J. Stanley Metcalfe, Heinz D. Kurz, Neri Salvadori and Paul A. Samuelson, 189–215. London: Routledge.

Lendjel, Émeric. 2000. "Une contribution méconnue dans l'histoire de la pensée économique: le modèle de l'Abbé M. Potron (1935)." *Cahiers d'Économie Politique* 36: 145–151. doi:10.3406/cep.2000.1280

Leontief, Wassily. 1928. "Die Wirtschaft als Kreislauf." *Archiv für Sozialwissenschaft und Sozialpolitik* 60 (3): 577–623. Partial English translation in Leontief (1991b).

Leontief, Wassily. 1944. "Output, Employment, Consumption and Investment." *Quarterly Journal of Economics* 58 (2): 290–314. doi:10.2307/1883321

Leontief, Wassily. 1953. "Domestic Production and Foreign Trade: the American Capital Position Re-Examined." *Proceedings of the American Philosophical Society* 97 (4): 332–349.

Leontief, Wassily. 1991a. "An Introductory Note by Professor Leontief." *Structural Change and Economic Dynamics* 2 (1): 179.

Leontief, Wassily. 1991b. "The Economy as a Circular Flow." *Structural Change and Economic Dynamics* 2 (1): 181–212. Partial translation of Leontief (1928). doi:10.1016/0954-349X(91)90012-H

Mariolis, Theodore, and Lefteris Tsoulfidis. 2016. *Modern Classical Economics and Reality*. Tokyo: Springer.

Martinez-Alier, Juan. 1987. *Ecological Economics*. Oxford: Blackwell.

Marx, Karl. 1867. *Das Kapital. Erster Band*. Hamburg: Otto Meissner. [I quoted from the English translation: Marx, Karl. 1954. *Capital, Volume 1*. Moscow: Progress.]

Marx, Karl, and Friedrich Engels. 1848. *Manifest der Kommunistischen Partei*. London: Burghard.

Marx, Karl, and Friedrich Engels. 1973. *Werke. Band 35*. Berlin: Dietz.

Mirowski, Philip. 1988. "Energy and Energetics in Economic Theory: A Review Essay." *Journal of Economic Issues* 22 (3): 811–830. doi:10.1080/00213624.1988.11504810

Mori, Kenji. 2008. "Maurice Potron's Linear Economic Model: A *De Facto* Proof of 'Fundamental Marxian Theorem'." *Metroeconomica* 59 (3): 511–529. doi:10.1111/j.1467-999X.2008.00315.x

Mühlpfordt, Wolfgang. 1893. *Preis und Einkommen in der privatkapitalistischen Gesellschaft*. Königsberg: Hartungsche Buchdruckerei.

Mühlpfordt, Wolfgang. 1895. "Karl Marx und die Durchschnittsprofitrate." *Jahrbücher für Nationalökonomie und Statistik* 65 (1): 92–99.

Nove, Alec. 1983. *The Economics of Feasible Socialism*. London: Allen and Unwin.

Nuti, Domenico Mario. 1974. "Introduction." In Dmitriev (1974, 7–32).

Pareto, Vilfredo. [1902] 1965. *Les systèmes socialistes*. Genève: Droz.

Parys, Wilfried. 1982. "The Deviation of Prices from Labor Values." *American Economic Review* 72 (5): 1208–1212.

Parys, Wilfried. 2013. "All But One: How Pioneers of Linear Economics Overlooked Perron-Frobenius Mathematics." Research Paper 2013-030, University of Antwerp. Online via RePEc (EconPapers) at https://repository.uantwerpen.be/docman/irua/69ba06/112841.pdf

Parys, Wilfried. 2014. "Why Didn't Charasoff and Remak Use Perron-Frobenius Mathematics?" *European Journal of the History of Economic Thought* 21 (6): 991–1014. doi:10.1080/09672567.2014.951672

Parys, Wilfried. 2016a. "Annotated Potron Bibliography." *Cahiers d'Économie Politique* 71: 151–179. doi:10.3917/cep.071.0151

Parys, Wilfried. 2016b. "The Interaction Between Leontief and Sraffa: No Meeting, No Citation, No Attention?" *European Journal of the History of Economic Thought* 23 (6): 971–1000. doi:10.1080/09672567.2016.1201958

Parys, Wilfried. 2018. "Labour Values and Energy Values." Research Paper 2018-006, University of Antwerp. Online via RePEc (EconPapers) at https://repository.uantwerpen.be/docman/irua/9bc2b3/150541.pdf

Podolinsky, Sergei. 1881. "Il socialismo e l'unità delle forze fisiche." *La Plebe* 14 (3): 13–16; 14 (4): 5–15.

Podolinsky, Sergei. 1883. "Menschliche Arbeit und Einheit der Kraft." *Die Neue Zeit* 1 (9): 413–424; 1 (10): 449–457.

Quaas, Friedrun. 1994. "Wolfgang Mühlpfordt and the Transformation Problem: Some Remarks on Articles by Howard and King and Gilibert." *Cambridge Journal of Economics* 18 (3): 323–326. doi:10.1093/oxfordjournals.cje.a035277

Rosier, Bernard, ed. 1986. *Wassily Leontief. Textes et itinéraire.* Paris: La Découverte.

Schütte, Frank. 2003. "Die ökonomischen Studien V.K. Dmitrievs." Doctoral Dissertation, Technical University of Chemnitz.

Shaikh, Anwar. 2016. *Capitalism: Competition, Conflict, Crises.* Oxford: Oxford University Press.

Soddy, Frederick. 1933. *Wealth, Virtual Wealth and Debt.* 2nd ed. London: Allen and Unwin.

Sombart, Werner. 1905. "Ein Beitrag zur Bibliographie des Marxismus." *Archiv für Sozialwissenschaft und Sozialpolitik* 20 (2): 413–430.

Sraffa, Piero. 1960. *Production of Commodities by Means of Commodities: Prelude to a Critique of Economic Theory.* Cambridge: Cambridge University Press.

Steedman, Ian. 1977. *Marx after Sraffa.* London: NLB.

Stigler, George Joseph. 1958. "Ricardo and the 93% Labor Theory of Value." *American Economic Review* 48 (3): 357–368.

Trautwein, Hans-Michael. 2017. "The Last Generalists." *European Journal of the History of Economic Thought* 24 (6): 1134–1166. doi:10.1080/09672567.2017.1378694

Wicksell, Knut. [1893] 1954. *Value, Capital and Rent.* London: Allen and Unwin.

Wicksteed, Philip Henry. 1884. "Das Kapital. A Criticism." *To-Day* 2 (4): 388–409.

Wolff, Edward Nathan. 1979. "The Rate of Surplus Value, the Organic Composition, and the General Rate of Profit in the U.S. Economy, 1947–67." *American Economic Review* 69 (3): 329–341.

The employment contract with externalised costs: the avatars of Marxian exploitation

Rodolphe Dos Santos Ferreira and Ragip Ege

ABSTRACT
The paper pursues two aims. The first is to argue that the foundation of Marx's theory of capitalist exploitation is to be found, not in the labour theory of value, but rather in the contract of employment, the legal frame of the capital-labour relation. The second is to suggest that the partial externalisation of the reproduction cost of labour power has been an important source of relative surplus value, along with the productivity increase, emphasised by Marx, in the industries supplying wage goods.

1. Introduction

Neoclassical economic theory views the employment relationship as a transaction between a supplier and a demander of labour services. In this context, exploitation can only mean an excess of the marginal productivity of labour over its remuneration. This approach mistakenly considers the employment relationship as a *contract for services* (the *locatio conductio operis* of Roman law), wherein a person (the *conductor operis*) undertakes to perform a particular service, committing to produce a certain specified result. Marxian theory of capitalist exploitation is on the contrary based on the *contract of employment* (the *locatio conductio operarum*), by which a person consents to render certain services (*operae*) as directed and controlled by an employer in return for an agreed upon remuneration (*merces*).

Through the latter contract the employer hires the worker's labour power for a specified working time. Working time adds value to the value of intermediate consumption plus that of wage goods. The ratio of this added value (surplus labour time) to the value of wage goods (necessary labour time) measures the degree of exploitation. This way of conceptualising exploitation has suggested to both adepts and opponents of Marxian theory an intimate dependence of the concept of exploitation on the so-called labour theory of value, which takes working time, ultimately the unique limited resource in Marx's argument, as the sole source of value. However, a rejection of the labour theory of value does by no means imply a rejection of the concept of exploitation, which is compatible with any coherent general equilibrium theorising of prices.

That the status of the concept of exploitation is divorced from the status of the labour theory of value has already been consistently argued by analytical Marxism (Cohen 1979; Roemer 1981, 1982), without necessarily convincing conventional Marxists, for whom only referring to the labour incorporated in the wage goods can one establish a difference between what the worker gives and what he receives (Napoleoni 1991). Paradoxically, the two approaches end up in a similar position: while rejecting the labour theory of value as a necessary ingredient to define the concept of exploitation, Roemer nonetheless accepts to begin with to define it as "the unequal exchange of live, direct labor for labor embodied in goods" (1986, 63).[1] Eventually, he redefines exploitation, still in terms of "distributive injustice", as applying to a person who "does not have access to his fair share [...] of the alienable productive assets of society" (1986, 82). This redefinition is admittedly related to a precondition of Marxian capitalist exploitation: the proletarian, not having access to capital, is doomed to sell his sole alienable productive asset, namely labour power. Two objections are however in order. First, justice is not at stake, at least in Marx's conceptualisation. *Unequal exchange* applies to a contract for services that would violate the Aristotelian principle of justice: "in the interchange of services Justice in the form of Reciprocity is the bond that maintains the association [...]; if proportionate equality between the products be first established, and then reciprocation takes place, the requirement indicated will have been achieved, but if this is not done, the bargain is not equal and intercourse will not continue" (Aristotle [c. 335 BC] 1934, 281:   V.v.6–8). Marx makes a partial comment on a closely related passage of Aristotle in the *Capital*

---

[1]Veneziani and Yoshihara (2017) also analyse the concept of exploitation as an *unequal exchange of labour,* without attributing it to Marx.

(Marx [1867] 1887, 40–41), but he never refers to the principle of justice. This neglect makes sense: Marxian exploitation is a positive, rather than a normative, concept. Furthermore — this is our second objection — in the contract of employment, the worker exchanges his labour power against a wage covering its reproduction cost: the transaction concerns equal values. To quote Marx, "the exchange between the worker and the capitalist is a simple exchange; each obtains an equivalent; the one obtains money, the other a commodity whose price is exactly equal to the money paid for it; what the capitalist obtains from this simple exchange is a use value: disposition over alien labour" (Marx [1857] 1973, 281–282). Exploitation does not concern *exchange*; it starts only after it has taken place, within the *production* process.

The rate of exploitation may increase through the lengthening of working time (creating absolute surplus value) or through the shortening of necessary labour time, a systemic outcome due either to productivity increases in industries producing, directly or indirectly, wage goods or to a contraction of the basket of wage goods (both creating relative surplus value).[2] Assuming that labour power is paid for at its own value, Marx concentrates on productivity increases as the source of relative surplus value. However, a reduction of the cost of labour power does not necessarily entail a decrease of the workers' standard of living, if that reduction stems from cost externalisation, labour reproduction costs being in part taken over by the government or other institutions. The welfare state, born in Germany with Bismarck's Health Insurance Act of 1883, in the year of Marx's death, has certainly been an important source of such cost externalisation. The recent evolution of labour market relations, exhibiting in particular diverse types of flexible employment contracts, which culminate in the zero-hour contract and in the so-called self-employment, is another effective way of externalising costs.

In the following, we first recall in *Section 2*, the formal argument showing that the Marxian concept of capitalist exploitation does not depend substantially upon the labour theory of value, the role of which is mainly expositional and rhetoric. We then argue in *Section 3* that the Marxian concept of capitalist exploitation is by contrast intimately linked to the nature of the contract of employment, through the

---

[2]The distinction between *absolute* and *relative* surplus value corresponds to the distinction between what Marx calls the *formal* and the *real* subsumption of labour under capital. The former modifies only the form of the relation between the labourer and his exploiter, without changing the production process, the latter requires on the contrary such a change, operating at an intersectoral (hence systemic) level. See Marx ([1861–63] 2010, 93–117).

distinction between labour and labour power that it supposes. We further suggest in *Section 4* that a significant source of relative surplus value, disregarded by Marx, has been the partial externalisation of the reproduction cost of labour power. We conclude in *Section 5*.

2. Capitalist exploitation and the labour theory of value

We resort to the simplest way of formalising the labour theory of value, by assuming homogeneous labour, constant returns to scale and the absence of joint production in the capitalist sector.[3] Denoting by v the line matrix of unit values, by A the Leontief square matrix of unit intermediate consumptions, and by l the positive line matrix of unit labour inputs (in working hours), the matrix of added values is $v - vA = l$ when added value is entirely imputed to labour,[4] in conformity with the Marxian labour concept of value. Unit values can then be straightforwardly determined as $v = l(I - A)^{-1}$.

If we now denote by T the duration in hours of the working day and by ω the column matrix of the worker's necessities per day, $v\omega$ is the value of this basket and, since value is conceptualised as labour time, $v\omega$ is also the *necessary labour time*. The difference $T - v\omega$ is then the surplus value created by worker-day and can also be viewed as the *surplus labour time*. Finally, the ratio $(T - v\omega)/v\omega$ is the rate of surplus value or the *rate of exploitation*. As well known, the rate of exploitation can be increased through a higher T (*absolute* surplus value) or through a lower $v\omega$ (*relative* surplus value), itself obtained by higher productivity decreasing v (the phenomenon emphasised by Marx) or by a lower wage basket ω.

This presentation might suggest that the labour theory of value is an essential ingredient of the theory of capitalist exploitation. It is not. Marxian value is just a convenient aggregator, which has the essential property of stemming entirely from production conditions, here described by the two matrices A and l. The use of arbitrary prices would indeed create the suspicion that exploitation emerges in the *sphere of circulation*, as the consequence of "unequal exchange",

---

[3]A more general analysis, extending to joint production, can be found for instance in Morishima and Catephores (1978, ch. 2) or, covering in addition the case of decreasing returns, in Roemer (1981, ch. 2).

[4]Notice that we are here taking the value of workers' consumption as being a component of value added, whereas it might alternatively be treated on the same footing as intermediate consumption, by augmenting the Leontief matrix A.

whereas Marx insists on inserting exploitation in the *sphere of production*. Moreover, the Marxian concept of value has the additional advantage of being simply defined, without resorting to algebra, as the total labour time that must be expended, directly and indirectly, to produce a given commodity. This is less the case of equilibrium prices, Marxian *prices of production*, supposedly to be derived by *transformation* of labour values.[5]

Let us come back to the Leontief matrix A. This matrix exhibits a technological property that is necessary for the existence of exploitation, namely productiveness. In other words, the technology allows to generate a *net product*, as first conceptualised (and termed "neat proceed") by Petty (1662, ch. 4, §§13–15)[6] and later on used by Quesnay (1766). If we denote by x and y the column matrices of gross and net products, respectively, the technology is productive if there exists a positive x such that $y = x - Ax > 0$ or, equivalently, in value terms, if there exists a positive price line vector p entailing positive value added: $p - pA > 0$. Positive value added entirely imputed to labour, as postulated by Marx's labour concept of value, that is $v - vA = l$ is just a particular case where $p = v$. We now know from the Perron–Frobenius theorem (proved more than twenty years after Marx's death) that the very property of productiveness of the Leontief matrix allowing a consistent determination of labour values $v = l(I - A)^{-1}$, since the inverse $(I - A)^{-1}$ is then well defined and positive, also ensures that there exists a positive eigenvector p^* such that $p^* - p^*A = Rp^*A$, where $1 + R > 1$ is the reciprocal of the dominant eigenvalue of A. The vector p^* is the vector of prices of production if capital is reduced to circulating capital, completely used up in each period, and if wages are not advanced. This vector appears as an aggregator completely and uniformly imputing value added at rate R to capital p^*A, rather than to labour l.

Does this full imputation of value added to capital destroy the Marxian concept of capitalist exploitation? It does not. Consider the production of any commodity, possibly composite, taking as its unit the net product $\hat{y}$ that can be obtained with one hour of direct and indirect labour ($v\hat{y} = 1$). In the system of production of this commodity,

---

[5]Notice that Marx uses a labour *concept* of value (as an aggregator and as the supposed foundation of equilibrium prices), without in fact defending a labour *theory* of value, since his equilibrium prices diverge systematically from labour values.

[6]Quoted and commented by Marx ([1861–63] 2010, 171–175).

the worker creates per day $Tp^*\hat{y}$ units of (redefined) value. If in addition $\hat{y}$ is chosen as the numeraire, we have by construction $p^*\hat{y} = 1 = v\hat{y}$, so that the working day can still be decomposed into necessary labour time $p^*\omega$ and surplus labour time $T - p^*\omega$, although $p^*\omega$ differs in general from $v\omega$, implying that the redefined rate of exploitation $(T - p^*\omega)/p^*\omega$ will not coincide with the Marxian one, a discrepancy that does however not threaten the concept itself.[7] Indeed, like labour values, prices of production stem entirely from production conditions. Like labour values, they are well defined only if the technology is productive. And like labour values, they entail existence of exploitation only if the value of the worker's necessities, be it $p^*\omega$ or $v\omega$, is smaller than the value he can create in a working day, namely T.[8]

The Sraffian construct (Sraffa 1960) generalises these two extreme aggregators, while keeping the same required properties for a consistent concept of exploitation. Sraffian prices $p(w)$ are extended prices of production such that value added computed at these prices decomposes into wages at rate w and profit obtained by applying to capital a uniform rate r:

$$p(w)(I - A) = wl + rp(w)A.$$

Sraffa's numeraire, the *standard commodity*, is the net product $\hat{y}$ generated by a system of production using one unit of labour and where the gross product is an eigenvector x^* of the Leontief matrix (associated with the dominant eigenvalue $1/(1 + R)$): $\hat{y} = x^* - Ax^* = RAx^*$. We thus obtain (after post multiplication by x^* of the two sides of the preceding equation):

$$p(w)\underbrace{\overbrace{(I - A)x^*}^{\hat{y}}}_{1} = wl\underbrace{\overbrace{x^*}^{(I-A)^{-1}\hat{y}}}_{v\hat{y}=1} + r\underbrace{p(w)\overbrace{Ax^*}^{(1/R)\hat{y}}}_{1/R}.$$

---

[7] An alternative choice of numeraire would be labour power, or rather the disposal of labour power during one day, in the line of Smith's "labour commanded" measure of value. If the wage w is equal to the (redefined) value of labour power $p^*\omega$, this choice of numeraire leads to $(1/w)p^*\omega = 1$, hence to the expression of the rate of exploitation as $T(1/w)p^*\hat{y} - 1$.

[8] After having shown that, under joint production, positive profits are compatible with negative surplus value, depriving this magnitude of its intended significance, Steedman (1977, ch. 11) suggests to abandon all reference to Marxian values and to concentrate on observable magnitudes. This is not our position. Negative surplus value is the consequence of persisting to use a system of equations, in a context where one should instead resort to inequalities, allowing for some slack in the production of by-products (see Morishima and Catephores, 1978, s. 2.2). Thus, while dispensable, the reference to Marxian values when characterizing exploitation is not doomed to be a source of confusion.

Hence, $r = (1 - w)R$, so that a share w of value added is imputed to labour and the complementary share $1 - w$ to capital, at rate R. The corresponding rate of exploitation is simply $(T - p(w)\omega)/p(w)\omega$, defined independently of the labour theory of value, which corresponds to the extreme imputation to labour of the whole value added ($w = 1$). Let us emphasise that even the other extreme imputation, to capital, of the whole value added ($w = 0$), leading to prices of production strictly ($p^* = p(0)$), does not suppress exploitation, as we have already seen. So, the core of the concept of capitalist exploitation is not essentially linked to the labour theory of value and must be grounded on another foundation, the employment contract.

3. Capitalist exploitation and the employment contract

Under slavery, workers are placed on the same footing as farm animals or machines. Working time is not contractually defined and the slaves' necessaries have the same status of intermediate consumption as fuel or feed. Under capitalism, workers are free but their labour power is leased for some *limited* time, a lease which is remunerated by a wage covering the workers' necessaries. Notice that the wage is not paid for the work done but for the disposal of the capacity to work (*Arbeitsvermögen*), not for the act but for the potency, so that the wage is not the price of labour but the remuneration of labour power. This distinction is already sketched in Marx's *Wage labour and capital* [1849][9] but is in fact implied by the very nature of the employment relationship as a leasing contract under Roman law, at a time in which this contract coexisted with slave property: the worker who hires out his services should receive full time wage, even when working less for any reason independent of his will (*Qui operas suas locavit, totius temporis mercedem accipere debet, si per eum non stetit, quo minus operas praestet*, Paulus, *Digest*, 19.2.38). Marx recalls in the *Grundrisse* this principle ruling the contract of employment: "If the capitalist were to content himself with merely the capacity of disposing, without actually making the worker work, for example, in order to have his labour as a reserve, or to deprive his competitor of this capacity of disposing [...], then the exchange has taken place in full"

---

[9]"The day labourer [...] receives in place of his productive power [*Produktivkraft*], the effect of which he has bargained away to the farmer, five silver groschen, which he exchanges for means of subsistence" (Marx [1849] 2010, 214).

(Marx [1857] 1973, 282). And in his *Philosophie des Rechts*, Hegel explicitly refers to the contract of employment (*locatio operae*) as "alienation of my productive capacity or my services so far, that is, as these are alienable, the alienation being restricted in time or in some other way" (Hegel [1820] 1896, 86), and comments: "Single products of my particular physical and mental skill and of my power to act I can alienate to someone else and I can give him the use of my abilities for a restricted period, because, on the strength of this restriction, my abilities acquire an external relation to the totality and universality of my being. By alienating the whole of my time, as crystallised in my work, and everything I produced, I would be making into another's property the substance of my being, my universal activity and actuality, my personality" (Hegel [1820] 1896, 73–74; quoted by Marx [1867] 1887, 123, n.3).

Exploitation is present in both modes of production, slavery and capitalism, since the working time is divided into necessary labour time, required to reproduce the worker's capacity to work, and surplus labour time, performed for the benefit of the master or of the capitalist. However, exploitation, which is so to say self-revealing under slavery, becomes disguised under capitalism. This contrast is emphasised in Marx's *Capital*: "The wage-form [...] extinguishes every trace of the division of the working-day into necessary labour and surplus-labour, into paid and unpaid labour. All labour appears as paid labour. [...] In slave-labour, even that part of the working-day in which the slave is only replacing the value of his own means of existence, in which, therefore, in fact, he works for himself alone, appears as labour for his master. All the slave's labour appears as unpaid labour" (Marx [1867] 1887, 381).

Marxian exploitation is by contrast absent in the context of the contract for services, a relation pertaining to the sphere of circulation: "For example, when the peasant takes a wandering tailor, of the kind that existed in times past, into his house, and gives him the material to make clothes with. Or if I give money to a doctor to patch up my health. What is important in these cases is the service which both do for one another. *Do ut facias* here appears on quite the same level as *facio ut des*, or *do ut des*. The man who takes the cloth I supplied to him and makes me an article of clothing out of it gives me a use value. But instead of giving it directly in objective form, he gives it in the form of activity" (Marx [1857] 1973, 465).

Of course, whether the price for the service fits some criterion of justice is a relevant question that was tackled by Aristotle, as already mentioned. However, the possibility of an unjust price, or of unequal exchange, is a rather different question, which does not involve exploitation in Marxian sense.

There is also a just price (or rather a just wage) issue in the context of the contract of employment, an issue that has been implicitly addressed by Nash (1950) in his bargaining solution, which must satisfy the symmetry axiom, reminiscent of the Aristotelian principle of justice: equals must be treated equally. The modern theory of the labour market has made an extended use of the so-called "generalised" Nash bargaining solution, where different weights are attributed to the partners, so as to take differences of bargaining power into account, but at the same type dissolving any reference to the principle of justice.

Marx essentially considers the wage to be at its floor, the cost of reproduction of labour power, even if this cost is historically determined and may reflect quite different living standards in different periods and societies. Even if the capitalist is not the owner of the worker himself, and does not have to directly ensure his reproduction, which is left to the worker, the cost of reproducing labour power is supposed to be internalised, as far as it must be covered by the wage paid to the worker. This internalisation is patent when the wage is partly paid in kind, in the context of nineteenth century industrial paternalism, providing to the workers welfare services such as cultural and sports activities, housing, education, medical services and so on.

4. Capitalist exploitation and cost externalisation

By taking over a significant part of the cost of reproduction of labour power, concerning health insurance (1883), accident insurance (1884) and old-age pension (1889), the welfare state, theorised by the *Kathedersozialisten* and implemented as "State Socialism" (*Staatssozialismus*) by Bismarck, initiated a partial cost externalisation. This externalisation should be understood as relative to the individual firm but also to the whole capitalist sector of the economy, since the social expenditure taken over by the government is financed by taxes which are more or less disconnected from the wage base, impending partly on noncapitalist sectors. It appears as one source of relative surplus value by erasing part of the basket of workers' necessities, without necessarily reducing the workers' standard of living. The importance of the welfare state has greatly increased during most of the last century, pursuing the course of cost externalisation in the fields of education, housing, transportation or social insurance, for instance.

Another important source of externalisation results from the increased labour market flexibility targeted by the political authorities. As already emphasised, one of the distinctive traits of the contract of employment is the obligation for the employer to pay a full time wage, even when unfavourable technical or market conditions impose a temporary activity drop. When flexibility is achieved by allowing workers' remuneration to be adjusted to part-time work or by relaxing employment protection, the risk normally impending on the employer is partly transferred to the employee. Under extreme forms of employment precariousness, culminating in the zero-hour contract, reproduction of the labour power ceases to be ensured by the capital-ist sector. Workers are seen as self-employed – even as capital owners, in uberised industries – hence as completely responsible for their own reproduction. Signs of this evolution were already observed by Marx:

> "If the hour's wage is fixed so that the capitalist does not bind himself to pay a day's or a week's wage, but only to pay wages for the hours during which he chooses to employ the labourer, he can employ him for a shorter time than that which is originally the basis of the calculation of the hour-wage, or the unit-measure of the price of labour. Since this unit is determined by the ratio *daily value of labour-power/working day of a given number of hours* it, of course, loses all meaning as soon as the working day ceases to contain a definite number of hours. The connection between the paid and the unpaid labour is destroyed. The capitalist can now wring from the labour a certain quantity of surplus labour without allowing him the labourtime necessary for his own subsistence. He can annihilate all regularity of employment, and according to his own convenience, caprice, and the interest of the moment, make the most enormous overwork alternate with relative or absolute cessation of work" (Marx [1867] 1887, 385).

One might be tempted to view such evolution as the progressive vanishing of the contract of employment in favour of the contract for services, and consequently as the announced death of the capital-labour relationship and eventually as the end of Marxian capitalist exploitation. One of the characteristics defining the employment con-tract is however resilient: the so-called self-employed are economically dependent on an employer, under whose control they work, so that they should be viewed as employees and not misclassified as independent contractors, according to the U.S. Department of Labor Administrator's Interpretation (15 July 2015).[10] This guidance, issued under the Obama administration, has admittedly been withdrawn, without a replacement guidance, by the Trump administration (7 June 2017), but such a reversal will not necessarily entail dramatic changes in courts' positions, often consistent with the guidance of the former administration. Marxian capitalist exploitation is not yet dead.

5. Conclusion

Marxian exploitation occurs in the sphere of production and stems from the excess of working time over the time necessary for reproducing the capacity to work. It does not refer to any criterion of justice which would apply to the sharing of this surplus and allow to characterize an "unequal exchange". Marxian exploitation results from the capacity of the master, the lord or the capitalist to appropriate the product of surplus labour time.

Capitalist exploitation in particular is founded on the employment contract, which puts labour power, the labourer's capacity to work, at the capitalist's disposal and under his control, for some time exceeding the necessary. We have argued that the distinction between labour and labour power, translating into economic concepts the legal characteristics of the employment contract, is crucial, not the way the necessary labour time, and hence, the rate of exploitation is evaluated. The labour concept of value, imputing to labour the whole value added, magnifies exploitation but, contrary to a widespread belief, is not essential for its existence.

When describing the creation of relative surplus value, Marx emphasised productivity increases in wage goods production. We have instead stressed the important process of wage cost externalisation ascribable to the development of the welfare state on the one hand and to the flexibilisation of the employment contract on the other.

---

[10]Several tests of economic dependence are listed by the Administrator: the integration of the work performed to the employer's business, the inexistence of an opportunity for profit or loss, the disproportion between the worker's and the employer's investments, the engagement on a permanent or indefinite basis (typically as at-will employment), the control being exercised over the worker. The natural implication of this battery of tests is that "most workers are employees."

Acknowledgements

The authors wish to thank Harald Hagemann, Julian Wells and two anonymous referees for useful comments and suggestions.

Disclosure statement

No potential conflict of interest was reported by the authors.

References

Aristotle [c. 335 BC] 1934. *The Nichomachean Ethics*. Translated by H. Rackham. 2nd edition. London: William Heinemann.

Cohen, Gerald A. 1979. "The Labor Theory of Value and the Concept of Exploitation." *Philosophy & Public Affairs* 8: 338–360. http://www.jstor.org/stable/2265068

Hegel, Georg W. F. [1820] 1896. *Philosophy of Right*. Translated by S. W. Dyde. London: G. Bell.

Marx, Karl [1849] 2010. "Wage Labour and Capital." In *Marx & Engels Collected Works (Volume 9: Marx and Engels 1849)*, 197–228. London: Lawrence & Wishart. https://archive.org/details/MarxEngelsCollectedWorks Volume10MKarlMarx

Marx, Karl [1857] 1973. *Grundrisse [der Kritik der Politischen Ökonomie]: Foundations of the Critique of Political Economy (Rough Draft)*. Translated by M. Nicolaus. Harmondsworth: Penguin Books.

Marx, Karl [1861-63] 2010. "A Contribution to the Critique of Political Economy" In *Marx & Engels Collected Works (Volume 34: Marx 1861-64)*. Translated by B. Fowkes, 5–336. London: Lawrence & Wishart. https://archive.org/details/MarxEngelsCollectedWorksVolume10MKarlMarx

Marx, Karl [1867] 1887. *Capital, A Critique of Political Economy. Book One: The Process of Production of Capital*. Translated by S. Moore and E. Aveling. https://www.marxists.org/archive/marx/works/download/pdf/Capital-Volume-I.pdf

Morishima, Michio, and George Catephores. 1978. *Value, Exploitation and Growth*. London: McGraw-Hill.

Napoleoni, Claudio. 1991. "Value and exploitation: Marx's economic theory and beyond." In *Marx and Modern Economic Analysis*, edited by Giovanni Caravale. Adershot: Edward Elgar.

Nash, John. 1950. "The Bargaining Problem." *Econometrica* 18: 155–162. http://www.jstor.org/stable/1907266

Petty, William. 1662. *A Treatise of Taxes and Contributions*. London: N. Brooke.

Quesnay, François. 1766. "Analyse de la formule arithmétique du Tableau Economique de la distribution des dépenses annuelles d'une nation agricole." *Journal d'agriculture, du commerce et des finances* V (3): 11–41. https://gallica.bnf.fr/ark:/12148/bpt6k1114600/f36.image.r=Analyse

Roemer, John E. 1981. *Analytical Foundations of Marxian Economic Theory.* Cambridge: Cambridge University Press.

Roemer, John E. 1982. *A General Theory of Exploitation and Class.* Cambridge, MA. Harvard University Press.

Roemer, John E. 1986. *Value, Exploitation and Class.* Chur: Harwood Academic Publishers.

Sraffa, Piero. 1960. *Production of Commodities by Means of Commodities: Prelude to a Critique of Economic Theory.* Cambridge: University Press.

Steedman, Ian. 1977. *Marx after Sraffa.* London: NLB.

U.S. Department of Labor, Wage and Hour Division, *Administrator's Interpretation No. 2015-1,* July 15, 2015. Issued by Administrator David Weil. https://www.blr.com/html_email/AI2015-1.pdf

Veneziani, Roberto, and Naoki Yoshihara. 2017. "The Theory of Exploitation as the Unequal Exchange of Labour." University of Massachusetts, Amherst, Department of Economics WP 2017-04. https://scholarworks.umass.edu/econ_workingpaper/220

Marx and Kalecki on aggregate instability and class struggle

Michaël Assous and Antonin Pottier

ABSTRACT
Michal Kalecki developed his original model of the business cycle in the early 1930s. Several versions referred as versions I, II and III have been developed until the late 1960s from which Kalecki draw three central propositions on instability and class struggle: (1) the capitalist system "cannot break the impasse of fluctuations around a static position" unless it is shocked by "semi-exogenous factors", (2) the dynamics of the profit rate and investment – as in version I and II – may be disconnected from "class struggle" and (3) when class struggle impacts the dynamics of the economy – as in version III – this is happening in a context in which expected profitability of new investment projects is negatively related to the profit share. In this article, we want to show that each of these three proposals represents key differences with Marx.

1. Introduction

Kalecki credited Marx for having clearly disentangled the problems of the origin of profit from the conditions of its realization. The former applies to the sphere of production in connection with the exploitation of workers. The second concerns the sphere of circulation and the issue of effective demand.[1] While Kalecki showed a low level of interest for the first problem,[2] he praised Marx for having forcefully brought up the second problem. Focused on that latter

---

[1] As he put it: "That Marx was deeply conscious of the impact of effective demand upon the dynamics of the capitalist system follows clearly from this passage of the third volume of the *Capital*: 'The conditions of direct exploitation and those of the realization of surplus-value are not identical. They are separated not only by time and space but logically as well. The former are limited merely by the productive capacity of the society, the latter by the proportions of various branches of production and by consumer power of the society.'"(Kalecki 1968b, 73–74)

[2] Kalecki considered Marx's labor theory on which he based his theory of exploitation mostly "metaphysical". See Sebastiani (1989, 22).

[3] See Steindl (1981).

issue, the objective of this article is to bring new elements of comparison between Marx and Kalecki on aggregate instability and class struggle.

Kalecki (1933a, 1939) initially developed a model couched in terms of a dynamic equation he wanted to be simple enough to be solved analytically and yet rich enough to capture salient aspects of the world. Two modifications referred to below as version II (Kalecki 1943, 1954, 1962) and III (Kalecki 1968a)[3] were undertaken on the basis of which Kalecki put forward three central propositions: (1) the capitalist system is bound to fluctuate around a static equilibrium unless it is shocked by "semi-exogenous factors", (2) the dynamics of profitability and investment – as in version I and II – may be disconnected from class struggle and (3) when class struggle impacts the dynamics of the economy – as in version III – this is happening in a context in which profitability is negatively related to the profit share.

These propositions represent three significant departures from Marx. First, the idea that deviations from long-run paths may end up in cycles around a static position does not fit with Marx's vision of capitalism whose reproduction and even more development was far from certain. Second, if among "semi-exogenous factors" innovations are considered by Kalecki to be essential for the growth of the capitalist system, they are, according to Marx, the ultimate cause of the collapse of the system. Third, if Kalecki finally introduced an effect of class struggle on cyclical growth, he, unlike Marx and later Goodwin (1967), resorted to a negative relationship between profitability of marginal plants and the profit share.

We discuss in Section 2 key aspects of Kalecki's view of instability by presenting Kalecki's early model and its subsequent modifications on the basis of which a first comparison with Marx on aggregate instability is done. Section 3 extends the comparison – but now only in reference to Goodwin's model – by paying attention to the impact of class struggle in Kalecki's model. The rationale is that (1) Goodwin's model had a critical impact on macroeconomics and (2) it allows a closer comparison with Kalecki, due to a shared methodology of mathematical modelling. A summary of the paper's main findings is given in the conclusion.

---

[3] See Steindl (1981).

2. Two different visions of economic development

2.1. Kalecki's model and its modifications

With the aim to show that the capitalist system is not a "harmonious" regime the purpose of which is the satisfaction of the needs of its citizens, but an "antagonistic regime" prone to repetitive crises, Kalecki came up with a new conception of instability in the early 1930s that one can be summarised as follows: economies are unstable and bound to stagnate in absence of any external perturbations.

Following Marx, Kalecki considers an economy with two classes: a class of people possessing all means of production – the capitalists; and a class of people possessing nothing but their labour force – workers. Because capitalists, unlike workers, are not constrained on their current income, Kalecki argues that as long as the economy operates below capacity, "capitalists as a class gain exactly as much as they invest or consume" (Kalecki 1933a, 79). In a way, capitalists "are masters of their fate" (ibid, 79–80). However, if "capitalists do many things as a class they certainly do not invest as a class" (Kalecki 1968b, 78). So, without any control over past and present decisions taken by others, they have no way to regulate the flow of profits occurring to them and to prevent the profit rate to fluctuate. The trade cycle is due to these fluctuations and is the form taken by this coordination failure on which Kalecki based a series of paradox.[4]

Along that line, Kalecki pointed out that cycles are "automatic". So, whenever a recession occurs, there are always mechanisms that will pull the economy out of it. In the context of the mid-1930s, he went further and argued that the Great Depression was no more than one phase of the trade cycle that would, at least in theoretical terms, end up in an upswing (Kalecki 1933b). Obviously, "anti-slump intervention" may significantly impact the pattern of the business cycle. Such interventions, however, were assumed to "barely scratch the surface of the capitalist system" (Kalecki 1964, 238) whose structure, with

---

[4] This statement neatly summarizes one of these paradoxes: "Investment considered as capitalists' spending is the source of prosperity, and every increase of it improves business and stimulates a further rise of spending for investment. But at the same time investment is an addition to the capital equipment and right from birth it competes with the older generation of this equipment. The tragedy of investment is that it calls forth the crisis because it is useful. I do not wonder that many people consider this theory paradoxical. But it is not the theory which is paradoxical but its subject —the capitalist economy." (Kalecki 1939, 148). See Lipinski (1977) and Besomi (2006) for a discussion of these paradoxes.

only a few exception, was assumed to remain largely unchanged all along the adjustment process.

Towards the end of the 1930s, Kalecki, hence, reached the idea that the world was cycling around a static position. To move forward meant addressing two issues: (1) to be able to explain why cycles do not die away and (2) to clarify the conditions likely to explain growth. Drawing upon a property of his original model so far left implicit, Kalecki eventually finalized his conception of instability.[5] Dynamic analysis indeed reveals that his original model displays two solutions: cycles around a static position or sustained growth. Because these two solutions are mutually exclusive, picking the cyclical solution necessarily means assuming that growth, if any, is generated by external shocks.

Kalecki was convinced that for realistic values of the parameters of his model, there was hardly a satisfactory substitute for cycles. Therefore, he was led to the conclusion that the source of long-term growth should be found in factors somewhat external to the mechanism generating the cycle, namely forces superimposed to the basic mechanism and which could not be explained by current economic events. This source he saw in innovations. He considered this a semi-exogenous factor because innovations could not, in his view, be made dependent on the current economic situation or on purely economic factors having taken place in the recent past. His point was that the stream of inventions has an impact on investment similar to a continuous increase in profits while each new invention, like any rise in profits, makes certain projects *ceteris paribus* more attractive. Thus, a stream of inventions may cause investment over and above the level which would otherwise obtain.

Kalecki, especially, considered that an important factor contributing to a positive long-run trend is the link between the profitable investment opportunities opened up by invention and the size of the capital stock. Investment flowing from the application of a given flow of new ideas will "be proportionate to the volume of capital equipment" (Kalecki 1943). This represents the "semi-exogenous" aspect of investment associated with innovation as well as the sense in which long-run growth is semi-exogenous.

---

[5] See Assous et al. (2017) for a discussion of that property in Kalecki's version I of his model (Kalecki 1933a, 1939).

Discussing Harrod and growth theories of the early 1960s, Kalecki felt the need to underline the implication of that aspect of his approach.

> Harrod observes rightly that his theory exhibits the basic 'antinomy' of the system; he thinks that 'antinomy' leads to fluctuations around the trend line. I believe that the antinomy of the capitalist economy is in fact more far reaching: the system cannot break the impasse of fluctuations around a static position unless economic growth is generated by the impact of semi-exogenous factors such as the effect of innovations upon investment. It is only in such a case that cyclical fluctuations do occur around the ascending trend line. (Kalecki 1962, 134)

Along that line, Kalecki could eventually kill two birds with one stone: producing an explanation of (1) why cycles do not die away and (2) why they are occurring along an ascending trend line.[6] This certainly accounts for the fact that from the 1950s Kalecki stuck to a linear approach although he had resorted earlier to non-linearities. Indeed, non-linearities *per se* had proven to be insufficient for yielding at the same time endogenous cycles and exponential growth. Like Kaldor (1940), he could only prove the existence of endogenous fluctuations around a static position.

In the end, Kalecki perceived a cost associated with the way in which he had incorporated innovations and technical change into his model. This cost was a relative neglect of the connection between the trend and the cycle. For the most part, these are separate aspects, at least in the formal parts of the argument. It is thus with the aim to fix that problem that he eventually developed a new version of his model. The innovative aspect of that work was to explore how cycles and growth could be connected via technical progress.

> I myself approached this problem in my *Theory of Economic Dynamics* [1954] and my 'Observations on the Theory of Growth' [1962] in a manner which now I do not consider entirely satisfactory: I started from developing a theory of the 'pure business cycle' in a stationary economy, and at a later stage I modified the respective equations to get the trend into the picture. By this separation of short-period and long-run influences I missed certain repercussions of technical progress which affect the dynamic process as a whole. I shall now try to avoid splitting my argument into these two stages as much as applying the approach of moving equilibrium to the problem of growth. (1968a, 263)

---

[6] See Gomulka, Ostaszewski, and Davies (1990) for a stability analysis of Kalecki's (1962) paper.

This last argument deserves some elaboration. As for previous versions (I and II), the analysis of the impact of effective demand upon profits and national income determination is considered to involve no "particularly intricate questions". As long as workers spend all their wages, the following relation holds between capitalists' consumption, accumulation and profits:

$$P_t = C_t + I_t,$$

where P_t is profits, C_t capitalists' consumption and I_t gross accumulation, i.e., the reproduction and expansion of fixed capital and the increase in inventories, at time t. Capitalists' consumption consists of an amount $A(t)$ slowly changing over time and a part proportionate to profits, i.e., $C_t = \lambda\, P_t + A(t)$, where λ is capitalists' marginal propensity to consume.[7]

Substituting capitalists' consumption into the profit equation allows Kalecki to obtain the profits corresponding to any "short-period equilibrium": that is, the equilibrium level of profit for a given level of investment and capital stock:

$$P_t = \frac{I_t + A(t)}{1 - \lambda}.$$

To determine the level of output Y_t by the level I_t and $A(t)$, Kalecki assumes a certain relationship – discussed in the next section – between profits and output. When the profit share, q is constant, he gets:

$$Y_t = \frac{P_t}{q}.$$

A key aspect of the analysis is the "determinants of investment decisions" (Kalecki 1968b, 78). A feature common to Kalecki's models is to have a time lag – let us say a year – between investment decision orders D_t and the actual output of investment goods I_t – in the form of new capacity ready to produce I_t, we have $D_t = I_{t+1}$. The innovative aspect of version III is the assumption that in the presence of unused productive capacities, new investments capture only a part of the current change in profit $n\Delta P_t$ (where coefficient n is assumed to be small). Then, Kalecki introduces the influence of technical progress and argued that depending on its importance, the profits yielded by

---

[7] See Trigg (2001) for a discussion of the connection between Kalecki's theory of profit and Marx's schemes of reproduction.

old equipment will fall in the year in line with productivity gains in favor of new firms. After transformation, he eventually shows that profits of working old equipment decline by a fraction δ per unit of time where δ is the higher the greater is the rate of increase in productivity resulting from technical progress, and the lower the profit share q. So, any level of investment "capturing" any given profit rate π will depend on two main determinants: "the increment in total profits and the transfer of profits from old to new equipment" (1968a, 267). Besides these two determinants, Kalecki adds:

> In the year considered new inventions come within the compass of the entrepreneurs. Thus they expect to do better out of their investment than those whose investment materialized in the year considered. In fact, this will not prove true for the investing entrepreneurs as a body: if the increase in productivity is not accelerated the investment materializing in the next year will not be more profitable on the average than that in the present one. Nevertheless, those entrepreneurs who are first to avail themselves of the technical novelties will do better than the average. To account for this additional stimulus to investment which is a direct outcome of innovations we shall add to the right side of the formula for investment decisions a slowly changing magnitude depending $[B(t)]$ – similarly to the stable part of capitalists' consumption – on past economic, social and technological developments. (Kalecki 1968a, 269)

After some transformations, one then gets a dynamic equation of investment in the following form:

$$I_{t+1} = aI_t + b(I_t - I_{t-1}) + F(t) \tag{1}$$

with $F(t)$ assumed to be a "slowly changing function of time" and coefficient a and b assumed to account for the impact of technical progress and class struggle through its impact on the profit share q.

The difference between two possible trajectories of the economy is a solution of the homogeneous system $I_{t+1} = aI_t + b(I_t - I_{t-1})$, so that any trajectory is the sum of a particular solution plus a solution of the homogeneous system $I_{t+1} = aI_t + b(I_t - I_{t-1}) + F_t$. If the solutions of the homogeneous system are cyclical and if we have a steadily growing particular solution, it means that the economy will exhibit trajectories with both growth and cycles. But, in the absence of any information on the properties of a particular solution, it is not possible to determine the trajectory of the economy based on the solutions of the homogeneous system alone. For instance, if the solutions of the homogeneous system are tending to zero, it does not mean that the trajectory of the economy will not be cyclical. It only means that all trajectories of the economy will finally be identical, that differences in initial conditions fade away.

According to Kalecki, with $F(t)$ being slowly changing functions, there is a particular solution of (1) that grows slowly and steadily. Once the existence of a steady growth path is taken for granted, the study of the homogeneous system makes it possible to move from a particular solution to all possible trajectories of the economy. Solutions of the homogneous system are of the form $I_t = \lambda_1 \beta_1^t + \lambda_2 \beta_2^t$ where β are roots of the equation $X^2 - (a+b)X + b = 0$. It may be noted that the product of roots is $b > 0$, which means that the roots will always be of the same sign. The form of the solutions depends on the discriminant of the equation and of the module of the roots. For example, if the discriminant is negative and the module of the roots are both below 1, the generic solution of the homogeneous system is a dampened cycle around the x-axis. In this case, the generic trajectory will be a dampened cycle around the growing trend: the difference between two trajectories will oscillate and shrink towards 0. As an opposite example, consider a positive discriminant with one of the roots above 1. The generic solution of the homogeneous system is a sum of exponential, one of which is explosive. In this case, the generic trajectory would be an increasing path, but the difference between two trajectories will exacerbate over time.

To discuss the possible trajectories of the economy submitted to dynamics (1), we have introduced a particular solution of (1) and solutions of the homogeneous system. The reader could have associated the particular solution with the trend and solutions of the homogeneous system with cycles. This would, however, obscure a key point emphasized by Kalecki in the quotation above. The separation between trend and cycles does not exist in the model itself. All particular solutions are perfectly non-distinguishable from the point of view of the model. It is only the analyst that picks out a particular solution, labels it the "trend", and examines solutions as difference from this trend. In Kalecki's 1968 version, any solution can be seen as a trend: all solutions are symmetric and not a single one is privileged by the theory. The trend is only in the eye of the analyst, a convenient concept to describe the possible trajectories of the economy.

It is important to notice that the trend is not built in the functioning of the economy because Equation (1) that forms the basis of the dynamics has not been derived from a distinction between a trend and an out-of-the-trend solution. The theory does not presuppose the existence of the trend to investigate investment decisions in the long run. This is the reason why Kalecki (1968b, 78) found that his new version although of a "pioneer nature" was a move in the right direction. The approach can be contrasted with the 1962 version that Kalecki no longer found satisfactory. In the 1962 version, the dynamics is based on the existence of a trend. The equation that determines investment (Equation 1) has a pure business cycle component and a trend one. This breaks symmetry between solutions from the start: the trend concept is within the economy and is necessary to formulate the determinants of investment.[8] Getting rid of this two-stage approach was, as we recall above, a great achievement for Kalecki.

In this model where the trend is not built in, we can ask whether growth is endogenous or exogenous, that hobby horse of the growth economist. Where does the growth of a particular solution come from? It does not arise from pure economic forces, that is from the dynamics of investment but it develops from the slowly increasing function $F(t)$. If $F(t)$ is constant, the economy is no longer growing. So, the growth relies on this increasing semi-exogenous factor $F(t)$. Fully endogenizing this factor would prove a dead end: the investment equation will be of the same sort, but with $F(t)=0$, and we will be back to the dichotomy between cycles and growth. It is certainly for that reason that Kalecki eventually concluded his paper by the idea that going further does not mean to endogenise the elements $A(t)$ and $B(t)$ but rather to provide a new analysis of the dynamics of the coefficient a and b.

> To my mind future inquiry into the problems of growth should be directed not towards doing without such semi-autonomous magnitudes as $A(t)$ and $B(t)$ but rather towards treating also the coefficients used in our equations (m, n, δ, q) as slowly changing variables rooted in past development of the system. (1968a, 276)

With these considerations in mind, one can get now new insights on how far Kalecki moved away from Marx.

---

[8] In mathematical terms, solutions of the 1962 version form a vector space, with the trend as the origin, whereas in the 1968 version, solutions forms an affine space. One can always set an origin to the affine space, but this origin is conventional.

2.2. Aggregate instability: Marx and Kalecki

Kalecki praised Marx for having been "deeply conscious of the impact of effective demand upon the dynamics of the capitalist system" (Kalecki 1968b, 73). He was, however, far from convinced by his theory of investment, which, in his mind, left no scope for highlighting the economic adjustments at work. His point – based on Marx's schemes of reproduction – was that Marx had, in fact, no theory of investment and was "absolutely in the dark concerning what [would] actually happen" (ibid, 79) in case of disequilibrium.[9]

To understand Kalecki's critic, it may be useful to shortly recall how Marx addressed growth issues with the help of his schemes of reproduction. Marx considered an economic system consisting of two sectors, with sector I producing capital goods and sector II producing consumption goods. For each sector, total value produced is divided into value of capital goods used up, value of wage goods purchased by workers who spend their entire wage bill on them and surplus value. The rate of surplus value is assumed to be the same and given in the two sectors.

In simple reproduction, supply of capital goods is equal to demand of capital goods from sectors I and II while supply of consumer goods is equal to demand of consumer goods by workers and capitalists from both sectors. Because the whole surplus is entirely consumed, there is no growth and the economy reproduces identically.

In extended reproduction, with the aim to rule out disequilibria that might appear, Marx assumes that in any period and for any level of investment decided by capitalists of sector I, capitalists of sector II are willing to invest until the whole supply of capital goods is sold. From then on, as long as surplus value is completely spent, he can show that demand of consumer goods by capitalists is automatically determined and the economy settles down on a balanced growth path by the next period.[10]

Kalecki praised Rosa Luxemburg for her "skepticism as to the possibility of long-run expanded reproduction" and her refusal to take for granted "self-propelled growth of capitalist economy" (1968b,

---

[9] According to Kalecki (1939, 45), Marx failed to develop a theory of the inducement to invest and to explore the impact of investment upon total profits.

[10] According to Morishima, "The unnatural adjustment of the rate of accumulation by capitalists of departement II to the exogenously determined rate of accumulation in departement I was by Marx merely as a *deux ex machina*". (1973, 125)

79).[11] Like Luxemburg, Kalecki refused to resort to Marx's specific investment analysis. Unlike her, however, he did not think that any deviation from "the initial unstable path" could eventually – in the absence of "external markets"[12] – lead the economy to break down. Instead, he argued, in line with the property of his model discussed above, that "once [the economic system] has deviated downwards from the path of expanded reproduction, it may in fact find itself in a position of long-run simple reproduction" (Kalecki 1968b, 78) while if the economy is growing at all, this is primarily because of technical progress.

It is very unlikely that Kalecki ignored Marx's prediction elsewhere in his work of a capitalist economy liable to crisis as a result of increasing contradictions and antagonisms. Furthermore, Kalecki was, without doubt, aware of the specific nature of Marx's hypotheses – at least through the reading of Luxemburg's works – for which extended reproduction was possible. From this point of view, one can conclude that both Marx and Kalecki had in common to be concerned with showing that the capitalist system was unstable. However, by ruling out the possibility of economic collapse and pointing out to the possibility of cycles around a static position, Kalecki, unlike Marx, limited the scope of such instability.

Again, Kalecki knew Marx's cyclical-growth analysis rooted in class antagonism and technical progress. But, here again, important differences exist between the two.

Marx argues that class antagonism and technical progress, prompted by competition, will sustain endogenous growth. In particular, as accumulation accelerates during the boom phase, he pointed out that the bargaining power of workers would increase and profits would be threatened. So, accumulation would slow down and the economy would eventually enter a recessionary phase, which, by reducing the bargaining power of workers, would lay the

---

[11] Sebastiani (1989, 23) recalls that Luxemburg regreted that Marx had developed a "wholly arbitrary picture" of the working of the economy while "there is no rule in this accumulation and in this consumption [on the part of the capitalists of section II], both being only justified with the requirements of accumulation in section I". Recent works based on the MEGA have however revealed that Marx never concluded - on the basis of his schemes of reproduction – that the economy could reproduce itself and still less that the economy could grow steadily. This mostly resulted from Engels editing work.

[12] As Kalecki points out, "by 'external markets' she understood those outside the world capitalist system consisting not only of underdeveloped countries but also of the non-capitalist sectors of developed capitalists economies, for instance, peasant agriculture as well as governement purchases." (1968b, 79)

ground for a new recovery. On top of this cyclical mechanism, capitalists would have the opportunity to maintain their profitability by switching to more productive capital-intensive technologies and hence sustain growth. The problem is that the breakneck quest for productivity gains arising out of competition would lead to the widespread replacing of "circulating capital" by fixed capital and thus to the rise in the organic composition of capital and the fall in the profit rate. By, hence, seeking to restore their profitability, capitalists would end up undermining the foundations of the very regime of capitalist development and thus set the stage for its replacement.

The idea that technical progress could lead the system to grow cyclically is common to Kalecki and Marx, even though Kalecki draws no conclusion on the very long term tendency of capitalism. The dividing line between Marx and Kalecki is that technical progress is endogenous and has a destructive side in Marx[13] while in Kalecki, growth can only come from exogenous technological shocks. In addition, Kalecki sees no obstacle to long-term growth as long as technical progress occurs. Besides these two important differences, a third one related to class struggle needs finally to be highlighted.

3. Key differences on class struggle

Kalecki's theory of distribution posits that the "degree of monopoly" of the economy determines the functional distribution of income. Ignoring initially the effect of trade union's strength, Kalecki showed that as long as the "degree of monopoly" remains unchanged, any change in money wages resulting from class struggle will be followed by a proportional change in prices and no change in employment: if workers manage to get a higher wages, the firms will simply react by raising prices and keeping their real wages constant. This, of course, is subject to the qualification discussed by Kalecki in the 1930s that the rate of interest would not change following the rise in price, which tacitly amounts to assume that the supply of money is elastic. Otherwise, the higher demand for money would increase the rate of interest, which adversely would affect investment and consequently the employment level.

---

[13] We want to thank the referee for helping us to clarify that point.

In his last paper entitled "Class Struggle and the Distribution of National Income", Kalecki slightly changes his view and makes the argument that class struggle may be a major determinant of the degree of monopoly. Alongside the degree of industrial concentration and the nature of the strategic interactions among firms, his point was that "class struggle as reflected in union bargaining power" may affect the size of the markup and ultimately income distributive shares.[14] The mechanism was the following: If markup and profit share are high, trade unions can increase their wage demands, which tends to increase the money wage and hence costs. It follows that high-profit margins cannot be maintained without creating a tendency towards rising prices. Fearful of losing their competitive position, firms may accept a reduction in their profit margins. Thus, the power of the trade unions effectively imposes a limit on profit share fluctuations.

> High mark-ups in existence will encourage strong trade unions to bargain for higher wages as they know that firms can afford to pay them. If their demands are met but ... [the markup] is not changed, prices will also increase. This will also lead to a new round of demands for higher wages and the process would go on with prices levels constantly rising. But certainly an industry will not like such a process making its products more and more expansive and thus less competitive with products of other industries. To sum up, the power of the trade unions restrains the markup. (Kalecki 1971, 5–6)[15]

Kalecki constantly argued that an increase in the bargaining position of workers would, by redistributing income from profit to wage earners, increase aggregate demand (given a higher propensity to consume out of wage income) and hence the level of output and employment in the economy. Though, as concerns its impact of the dynamics, his position significantly changed between versions I and II and version III.

---

[14] Resorting initially to Lerner's analysis, he concluded that the profit share was depending on the "degree of monopoly of the economy". In the case of monopolistic competition in which the monopolist firm sets its price given a constant marginal cost, he admitted that the degree of monopoly was given by $1/\varepsilon$, where ε is the elasticity of demand while the markup set by firms was equal to $1/(\varepsilon-1)$. Kalecki later mentioned the process of concentration in industry and the development of sales promotion through advertising and selling agents as major factors determining the markup elasticity of demand. See Rugitsky (2013) for a detailed analysis of the concept of class struggle in Kalecki's writings.

[15] Besides unions, Kalecki easily recognized that there may exist "other forms of class struggle" likely to affect the distribution of national income "in a more direct way" as in the case of price controls which can maintain workers purchasing power or the subsidizing of prices of wages goods financed by a direct taxation of profits.

Versions I and II have in common to disconnect the dynamics of the economy from changes in income distributive shares that could result from class struggle. In both versions indeed any change in the profit share let investment and thus the trajectory of the economy unchanged. Class struggle is neutral in terms of its effect on the cycle. This is because there is a strong complementarity between income distribution and income determination, which finds expression in the idea that even though the profit share might vary during the business cycle, its changes will have no impact on the profit rate. The profit level, in accordance with the view that capitalists earn what they spend, remains uniquely determined by investment decisions taken in the recent past.

Suppose for instance that there is a rise in the profit share, as long as capitalist spending stays constant, the total amount of profits does not change. But, while profits remain unyielding, real wages and real national product decrease because of the fall in workers' consumption, with a consequent fall in output, which adjusts just so much that the higher percentage share of profits in aggregate output results in an unchanged absolute amount of profits. Hence, we find the striking Kaleckian proposition that changing profit shares cannot impinge on the course of the cycle. Certainly, such evolution affects the amplitude of aggregate output changes over the cycle, but it simply has no effect on the profit rate and thus the dynamics of investment. Even though class struggle would come with changing profit share, we see that it will have no impact on the dynamics of the economy.[16]

Version III (1968a) makes a decisive break with versions I and II. For the first time, one can see that income distributive parameter and thus class struggle can have a direct impact on the dynamics of the economy. As we have just seen, in versions I and II, income distributive parameter does not enter the equation for the evolution of investment, were it investment within the cycle or trend investment. On the contrary, in version III, the profit share enters the equation with the parameter a of the reduced form of equation (see Section 2). This is because in version III, the transfer of profits from old to new firms is directly related to the profit share q. So, as soon as a rise in the bargaining power of workers reduces the profit share, the profit rate of new investments increase and the dynamics is

---

[16] See Assous et al. (2017) for a discussion of that property in Kalecki's original model (Kalecki 1933a, 1939).

impacted. The model, hence, highlights the existence of a negative relationship between the profit share and the profit rate of new investments. So, the profit rate of old equipment falls while the profit rate of new equipment increases. But, because accumulation is depending on the profit rate of new investments and not on the overall profit rate, it can be deduced that accumulation is positively related to wage share.

Concerning cycles and growth, the influence of the profit share is of two sorts. A change in the profit share will change parameter a and will thus modify the future course of the economy. In the most frequent cases, such a change will not alter the form of the dynamics. This means that the possible economic trajectories will still have the same form as before. Mathematically speaking, a change in profit rate and so in parameter a will not change the solution type of the homogeneous system. If the system before the change was characterized as the particular solution plus a solution of the homogeneous system that is, let's say, cyclical, the system after the change in profit rate will still be the particular solution plus a cyclical solution of the homogeneous system.

In some less frequent cases, however, the change in profit rate would have a more dramatic effect, which alters the form of the solution. Such a change affects the parameter a, so that it changes the types of the solution of the homogeneous system.

If we start from an economy where the discriminant of the homogeneous system is negative and parameter b is below 1, this economy will exhibit cycles as the difference between two different initial conditions oscillates. A change in parameter a only affects the discriminant and not the product of the roots of the homogeneous system. Starting from the case stated, it is possible, for a particular combination of a and b, that a change in parameter a makes the discriminant positive (such a situation is relatively easy to design). After the change, solutions of the homogeneous system are relaxation towards zero. Cycles between two pathways with different initial conditions are thus no longer possible: all solutions relax towards the same long run trajectory. A change in the profit rate would in this example suppress the cycles.

Whether one considers version I and II or version III, one can see that Kalecki departs from Marx on the understanding of the impact of class struggle. We can make a more detailed comparison if we rely on macroeconomic interpretation of Marx by Goodwin (1967). In Goodwin's model, greater workers' strength "carries the seed of its own destruction". Indeed, it reduces the profit share, which is, up to a factor, the profit rate, as Goodwin, contrary to Kalecki, assumes a full utilization of capital. Because Goodwin resorts to the classical saving hypothesis, where all profits are invested, that reduction of the profit share reduces investment and hence growth of capital stock, with decreases in labour demand and employment and consequently leads to the formation of a reserve army of labour. So, class struggle turns, after a wage spike, in favour of capitalists. Wage share declines and the profit rate recovers and increases, leading to a boom of investment. By engendering a too vigorous expansion of employment, the improved profitability does not last forever: workers' bargaining power is eventually strengthened so that the cycle then repeats itself. As Goodwin concludes: "this is, I believe, essentially what Marx meant by the contradiction of capitalism and its transitory resolution in booms and slumps" (Goodwin 1967, 58). With its non-linear model, Goodwin shows how cycle sustains itself around an increasing trend generated by technological progress and population growth.

The contrast with Kalecki is marked. First, class struggle and wage bargaining are essential in Goodwin's model to sustain the cycles. In booms, intensifying class struggle is due to the fact scarce labour compress the profit share, whereas in bust, unemployment pressures wages down- wards, increasing profit share and sows the seeds for the recovery. In Kalecki's versions I and II, the degree of labour strength in the struggle over wages has no effect at all on the profit rate and investment and thus on the trajectory of the economy!

Second, in Goodwin's model, a change in the profit rate is positively related to a change in the profit share, whereas any change in the profit share that could possibly happen will let the profit rate unchanged in Kalecki's version I and II.

The contrast is even stronger if one refers to version III based on a negative relationship between the marginal rate of profit and the profit share. This is because in that version, a rise in the profit share (of all capitalists) comes with a fall in the marginal rate of profit. So, while Goodwin's model – in which the profit rate does not vary among firms – is based on the idea that a rise in the profit share stimulates the profit rate, accumulation and growth, in Kalecki's version III a rise in the profit share depresses the marginal rate of profit and slows down accumulation and growth.

Third, an important difference between Kalecki and Goodwin is about the role played by class struggle on growth. In Goodwin's model, growth is generated by population growth and exogenous technical progress while change in income distribution has no impact on the growth rate of the economy. It only explains cyclical fluctuation around an exogenously determined trend. In Kalecki's version III, things are different. Because the trend and the cycles are no more separable, change in income distribution impact, so to speak, both the cyclical and trend component of growth.

4. Conclusion

The article has paid attention to Kalecki's model and its later modifications, particularly the 1968 version. The analysis has led us to identify three notable differences between Kalecki and Marx. First, in all Kalecki's versions, the economy is supposed to fluctuate around a static position in the absence of any increasing semi-exogenous factors. So, as soon as one admits that Marx offers an argument to indicate that the balanced growth rate is unstable except under very specific assumptions, one can see that Kalecki drastically reduced the scope of economic instability. The economy is fluctuating but risk of collapse is eliminated. Second, an examination of Kalecki last version allowed highlighting the role played by technical progress. Unlike Marx, Kalecki concludes that change in productivity has a positive effect on growth and does not undermine the economic development. Finally, the analysis has help pointing out key differences between Marx and Kalecki on the role played by class struggle on the dynamics. It was in particular possible to show that while class struggle is central in Marx works for establishing a positive link between the profit share and the profit rate, this is not the case in Kalecki's works who either disconnected the profit rate dynamics for the profit share dynamics as in version I and II or assumed a negative link as in version III whose effects are considerably different from those found in Goodwin's (1967) model.

Acknowledgements

The authors gratefully acknowledge the motivating and helpful suggestions they received from the two anonymous referees and the participants at the conference

New developments on Karl Marx's thought and writings, Lyon, 27–29 September 2017.

Disclosure statement

No potential conflict of interest was reported by the authors.

References

Assous, Michaël, Amitava Dutt, Paul Fourchard, and Antonin Pottier. 2017. "(In)-stability in Kalecki's Early Macroeconomics." *Journal of the History of Economic Thought* 39 (1): 69–87. doi:10.1017/S1053837216001097.

Besomi, Daniele. 2006. "Formal Modelling vs. Insight in Kalecki's Theory of the Business Cycle." *Research in the History of Economic Thought and Methodology: A Research Annual* 24: 1–48. doi:10.1016/S0743-4154(06)24001-X.

Goodwin, Richard. M. 1967. "A Growth Cycle." In *Socialism, Capitalism and Economic Growth. Essays Presented to Maurice Dobb*, edited by C. H. Feinstein, 54–58. Cambridge: Cambridge University Press.

Gomulka, Stanislaw, Adam Ostaszewski, and Roy O. Davies. 1990. "The Innovation Rate and Kalecki's Theory of Trend, Unemployment and the Business Cycle." *Economica* 57 (228): 525–540. doi:10.2307/2554717.

Kaldor, Nicholas. 1940. "A Model of the Trade Cycle." *The Economic Journal* 50, (197): 78–92 doi:10.2307/2225740.

Kalecki, Michal. 1933a. "Essay on Business Cycle Theory." In *1990. Collected Works of Michal Kalecki*, edited by Michal Kalecki, Vol. 1, 65–108. Oxford: Clarendon Press.

Kalecki, Michal. 1933b. "The Present Phase of the World Crisis." In *1996. Collected Works of Michal Kalecki*, edited by Michal Kalecki, Vol. 6, 183–187. Oxford: Clarendon Press.

Kalecki, Michal. 1939. *Essays in the Theory of Economic Fluctuations*. London: Allen & Unwin.

Kalecki, Michal. 1943. "Studies in Economic Dynamics." In *1991. Collected Works of Michal Kalecki*, edited by Michal Kalecki, Vol. 2. Oxford: Clarendon Press.

Kalecki, Michal. 1954. "Theory of Economic Dynamics." In *1991. Collected Works of Michal Kalecki*, edited by Michal Kalecki, Vol. 2. Oxford: Clarendon Press.

Kalecki, Michal. 1962. "Observation on the Theory of Growth." *Economic Journal* 72: 134–153. doi:10.2307/2228620.

Kalecki, Michal. 1964. "Econometric Model and Historical Materialism." In *On Political Economy and Econometrics. Essays in Honour of Oskar Lange*, edited by Oskar Lange, 233–238. Warsaw: PWN.

Kalecki, Michal. 1967. "The Problem of Effective Demand with Tugan-Baranovsky and Rosa Luxemburg." In *1991. Collected Works of Michal Kalecki*, edited by Michal Kalecki, Vol.2, 451–458. Oxford: Clarendon Press.

Kalecki, Michal. 1968a. "Trend and the Business Cycle Reconsidered." *The Economic Journal* 78 (310): 263–276. doi:10.2307/2229463.

Kalecki, Michal. 1968b. "The Marxian Equations of Reproduction and Modern Economics." *Social Science Information* 7 (6): 73–79. doi:10.1177/053901846800700609.

Kalecki, Michal. 1971. "Class Struggle and the Distribution of National Income." *Kyklos* 24 (1): 1–9. doi:10.1111/j.1467-6435.1971.tb00148.x.

Kalecki, Michal. 1990. "Collected Works of Michal Kalecki." *Capitalism, Business Cycles and Full Employment*, edited by Jerzy Osiatynski, Vol. 1. Oxford: Clarendon Press.

Kalecki, Michal. 1991. "Collected Works of Michal Kalecki." *Capitalism: Economic Dynamics*, edited by Jerzy Osiatynski, Vol. 2. Oxford: Clarendon Press.

Kalecki, Michal. 1996. "Collected Works of Michal Kalecki." *Studies in Applied Economics, 1927–41*, edited by Jerzy Osiatynski, Vol. 6. Oxford: Clarendon Press.

Lipinski, Edward. 1977. "Michal Kalecki." *Oxford Bulletin of Economics and Statistics* 39 (1): 69–77.

Morishima, Michio. 1973. *Marx's Economics, A Dual Theory of Value and Growth*. Cambridge: Cambridge University Press.

Rugitsky, Fernando, M. 2013. "Degree of Monopoly and Class Struggle: Political Aspects of Kalecki's Pricing and Distribution Theory." *Review of Keynesian Economics* 1 (4): 447–464. doi:10.4337/roke.2013.04.06.

Sebastiani, Mario. 1989. "Kalecki and Marx on effective demand." *Atlantic Economic Journal* 17 (4): 22–28. doi:10.1007/BF02309967.

Steindl, Josef. 1981. "Some Comments on the Three Versions of Kalecki's Theory of the Trade Cycle." In *Studies in Economic Theory and Practice. Essays in Honour of Edward Lipinski*, edited by J. Los, 1990. Amsterdam: North-Holland. Reprinted in Josef Steindl, *Economic Papers, 1941–88*. New York: St. Martin's Press, 139–148.

Trigg, Andrew. 2001. *Surplus Value and the Kalecki Principle in Marx's Reproduction Schema. Open Discussion Papers in Economics*, Vol. 40. Milton Keynes, UK: The Open University.

Searching for New Jerusalems: P.H. Wicksteed's "Jevonian" critique of Marx's *Capital*

Michael V. White

ABSTRACT

In 1884, P.H. Wicksteed published a critique of the first volume of Marx's *Capital*, the first detailed analytical encounter in English between Marx's value theory and the new discourse of "marginalism". In revisiting that episode, this article has three principal objectives. The first is to show how Wicksteed developed his understanding of political economy, as he moved from initially following Henry George's *Progress and Poverty*. The second is to examine why Wicksteed's defence of George necessitated criticizing the Marxist Social Democratic Federation. The third is to show that Wicksteed's criticisms of Marx were simply incorrect.

[Marx's] spider-web scholasticism has been swept away, and his theory of 'surplus value' sent to the limbo of 'keys to all the mythologies'. (Philip Wicksteed 1890).[1]

I have never kept careful records of my life and have next to no documents. (Philip Wicksteed 1921).[2]

The socialist journal *To-Day* was relaunched in January 1884 with Henry Hyndman, founder of the Social Democratic Federation (SDF), as the proprietor.[3] If Friedrich Engels and, until his death, Karl Marx had previously been unimpressed with Hyndman, Engels' disdain was evident in September:

> Under Hyndman's direction *To-Day* gets worse and worse. To make it more interesting they accept anything and everything. The editor has written to me saying that the October issue will contain a critique of

---

[1] Wicksteed 1890, 530. The reference is to the provisional title of Casaubon's unfinished book in George Eliot's *Middlemarch*. Greg Moore has reminded me that this was a particularly dismissive reference as Casaubon was not simply wasting his time on a useless and never-to-be completed research project. He was also doing so in a selfish and arrogant manner.

[2] P.H. Wicksteed to J.M. Connell, 18 October 1921 (Dr. Williams' Library MS 24.103).

[3] The Democratic Federation was formed in 1881 and became the Social Democratic Federation in 1884. It will be referred to here as the SDF.

Capital !!, and invites me to reply – which I refused with thanks. Thus a socialist organ has turned into an organ in which the pros and cons of socialism are discussed by every Tom, Dick and Harry.[4]

The article was a critique of the first volume of *Capital* by the Unitarian minister, Philip Henry Wicksteed.[5] It was the first detailed analytical encounter in English between Marx's value theory and the new economic discourse of "marginalism", as Wicksteed explicitly based his analysis on W. Stanley Jevons' *Theory of Political Economy* (*TPE*). The general conclusion reached by subsequent commentators was that Wicksteed had scored a clear victory in the ensuing debate during the following years. This was in large part because of the clarity of Wicksteed's analysis compared with the analytical weakness of his critics.[6] Some Marxists were also impressed. At the onset of the Cold War, Paul Sweezy commented that Wicksteed's critique "is one of the earliest and also one of the best from the point of view of the subjective theory" (Sweezy 1949, 244n) while Eric Hobsbawm acknowledged that "[f]ew critiques of Marx have been more effective" than Wicksteed's, which was "written with sympathy and courtesy" (Hobsbawm 1957, 37).

Drawing in part on a newly available archive,[7] this article has three principal objectives. The first is to provide a detailed context for the production of Wicksteed's article, showing how he utilized the network centred on the Cambridge economist H.S. Foxwell in moving from an initial theoretical position embracing Henry George's *Progress and Poverty* (1879) to Jevons' marginalism (Section 1). The second is to broaden that context by showing how, again drawing on the Foxwell network, Wicksteed's defence of George necessitated criticizing, and hence differentiating his approach from, that of the SDF (Section 2). The third objective is to reexamine the specific arguments in the *To-Day* article. The principal focus here is not whether

---

[4] Friedrich Engels to Eduard Bernstein, 13–15 September 1884 (in Marx and Engels 2010, 192). The editors of To-Day were Ernest Bax (1854–1926) and James Leigh Joynes (1853–93). It seems likely that Bax had solicited Engels' contribution.

[5] Wicksteed 1884f. Wicksteed used the German and French editions as there was no English translation at the time.

[6] See previous accounts of this episode in Howey (1960, ch.13); McBriar (1966, 29–35); De Vivo (1987); Steedman (1989); Flatau (2004).

[7] Specifically, the H.S. Foxwell Digital Collection, Kwansei Gakuin University Library, now available online: http://library2.kwansei.ac.jp/e-lib/keizaishokan/foxwell/index.html. Items from this remarkable archive will be cited here by the author, date, KGU and item number. For the history of the Foxwell archive, see Freeman (2006); "Foxwell's Papers", *Economists' Papers. Preserving Economic Memory* website: http://www.economistspapers.org.uk/?p=1034.

Wicksteed accurately represented Marx's position. Instead, the analysis is concerned with the coherence of Wicksteed's representation of Jevons' analysis that, he argued, was superior to Marx in terms of its generality and analytical coherence. It is concluded that, in misreading Jevons, Wicksteed's arguments were clearly incorrect (Section 3). The reception of Wicksteed's critique and its significance for his subsequent work in economics is also considered (Section 4).

1. The Kepler of political economy

Working in England and Ireland as the correspondent for the *Irish World*, Henry George was arrested in Ireland, along with the Eton master James Joynes, in August 1882.[8] The arrests were made on the ground that George was a "suspicious person" under the Protection of Persons and Property Act (1881), also known as the "Coercion Act" (Salt 1897). On his return to London in September, George delivered a well-attended and successful lecture calling for the nationalization of land, without compensation for landlords, to overcome the problems of poverty and low wages.[9] It was Bernard Shaw's attendance at that lecture that led him, for a time at least, to become a "Georgian" (Jones 1988, 474–5). In late October, Philip Wicksteed went to Aberdeen for a meeting of the British and Foreign Unitarian Association, where another delegate was the Georgian and Christian socialist, Alexander Webster. Earlier in the year Wicksteed and Webster had been among thirteen signatories to a letter published in the Unitarian magazine *The Inquirer*, protesting against the "recourse to an old and discredited system of coercion" in Ireland. The signatories hoped that "henceforth the troubles which unjust laws or uses may occasion among the Irish peasantry may be met by thorough and speedy reforms, and by firm administration of the ordinary laws of the land."[10] Given the reference to "thorough and speedy reforms", it is unsurprising that Webster presented Wicksteed with a copy of George's *Progress and Poverty* in Aberdeen. Wicksteed subsequently agreed that reading the *Progress* on the train back to London "set my

---

[8] As noted above, Joynes was subsequently an editor of *To-Day*.

[9] "The Nationalization of the Land", *The Times*, 6 September 1882, 5.

[10] "Coercion in Ireland", *Inquirer*, 6 May 1882, 292. For Wicksteed at the Aberdeen meeting, *Inquirer*, 18 October 1882, 704. On Webster (1840–1918), "The Rev. Alexander Webster", *Inquirer*, 24 August 1918, 273–74; Aberdeenprotest 2017.

brain on fire" (Wicksteed 1918), a reaction that was evident in a letter
he wrote to George on 26 October:

> I have been for years an occasional student of Political Economy and long
> ago I became profoundly convinced that some great fallacy or fallacies lay
> at the root of the science, especially in its utter inability to explain not
> only the cause but the nature of commercial depressions. I lost no
> opportunity of speaking to friends who were well versed in the science but
> could get no kind of satisfaction. [Your book] has given me the light I
> vainly sought for myself ... [and] has made for me 'a new heaven & a
> new earth' (Dorfman 1949, 147–48).[11]

If George found a ready audience in Ireland, his enthusiastic reception in London followed the 1878/9 recession and subsequent years of
indifferent trade. That was not the only reason for a widely perceived
crisis by the early 1880s, characterized by "the collapse or decay of
staple industries, the expansion of casual and sweated trades,
increasing overcrowding, poor health, hard winters, prolonged
unemployment, and chronic poverty". With the "chronic shortage of
working-class housing in the inner industrial perimeter" and rapidly
rising rents in London, the fear "amongst politicians, press and
church dignitaries" was that the members of the "respectable" working
class were being "forced to cohabit with the casual poor and the crim-
inal classes in insanitary areas". The danger of moral infection was
compounded by the enthusiasm for George and the SDF, "seen as dis-
turbing symptoms of a change in the popular temper". While
George's rent theory "provided an arresting and convincing explanation of housing conditions in London" (Stedman Jones 2013, 222,
218, 243, 281, 284), the success of *Progress and Poverty* was due not
only to the rent theory, but also, as Wicksteed indicated, to George
using that theory to explain depressions as primarily the result of
speculation in land (George 1883, Book V, Ch. 1).

If Wicksteed was in something of a fervour about *Progress and
Poverty*, he was also worried by his lack of a detailed knowledge of
political economy. On the same day that he wrote to George,
Wicksteed sent a letter to Herbert Foxwell, the Cambridge economist
who was also professor of political economy at University College

---

[11] *Revelation* 21: "Then I saw 'a new heaven and a new earth', for the first heaven and the first
earth had passed away, and there was no longer any sea. I saw the Holy City, the new
Jerusalem, coming down out of heaven from God, prepared as a bride beautifully dressed for
her husband."

London.[12] Noting that he had just finished reading George's *Progress*, Wicksteed asked Foxwell if he could provide the "title of any defence – if such there be – of the old formula division labour/dividend capital/product wages & the old divisions of capital and the functions of capital".[13] Although only Wicksteed's side of the correspondence remains, Foxwell evidently provided an extensive reply, suggesting in part that Wicksteed read Emile Laveleye's critique of George (Laveleye 1882) and the *Economics of Industry* by Alfred and Mary Paley Marshall (Marshall and Marshall 1879). In response, although he was unconvinced by Laveleye and had yet to read the Marshalls, Wicksteed urged on Foxwell

> the propriety – or rather I should say the necessity – of some economist of established position to undertake a detailed and systematic review of George's system .... I cannot but think that I must represent hundreds if not thousands of hitherto desultory students of Political Economy who have been prevented from undertaking more serious ... studies by a feeling that the science is chaotic and contradictory, with some fallacy at its root vitiating its conclusions and to whom George's work looks like the work of the Kepler of Political Economy. If the economics of the book are unsound I cannot imagine a more truly significant work or one that lies upon economists as a more imperative duty than to expose the fallacies.[14]

Following a suggestion by Foxwell, Wicksteed then arranged for the Oxford academic Arnold Toynbee to deliver two lectures on George in January the next year.[15] Having undertaken further reading, Wicksteed told Foxwell that he was "surprised how far [J.S.] Mill's dictatorship has been already rejected by recent economists" and asked Foxwell whether he "thought well of Shadwell's and Hearn's books which I am often referred to".[16] Given his high opinion of Jevons, it would be surprising if Foxwell had not previously mentioned *TPE* and Wicksteed purchased a copy of the second edition (1879) in late 1882 (Robbins 1933, vi). Although he made no mention of Jevons in his letter to Foxwell, Wicksteed's reference to "Mill's dictatorship" could well have reflected his reading of Jevons' attack on

---

[12] Wicksteed had graduated from UCL and the affiliated (Unitarian) Manchester New College.

[13] Wicksteed to Foxwell, 26 October 1882 (KGU 7-589).

[14] Wicksteed to Foxwell, 8 November 1882 (KGU 6-599).

[15] It is no exaggeration to say that Foxwell regarded Toynbee as 'saint-like' (Winch 2009, 250–57; see also Foxwell 1887c, 93–4). Toynbee had previously lectured on George at Oxford. That material was incorporated in his posthumous publication, *Lectures on the Industrial Revolution* (1884).

[16] Wicksteed to Foxwell, 28 November 1882 (KGU 8-599).

the "noxious influence of authority" in *TPE*, where Jevons also praised John Lancelot Shadwell and William Hearn for their general explanations of wages.[17]

The wages question was a key feature of Wicksteed's first article on George for the *Inquirer* in which he publicised Toynbee's forthcoming London lectures. He repeated his previous point, made to Foxwell, that George's work "has been published for several years. It has been read by the economists" and yet "*it is unanswered*".[18] Political Economy was criticised for "her" failure to satisfactorily explain "*where the industrial sore really is* that drains the strength of the labouring masses, while the fortunate few grow ever richer and richer". Rejecting suggestions that the prevalence of "gaunt and hungry want" was inevitable or the "fault" of the poor,[19] Wicksteed criticised Political Economy for failing to satisfactorily explain "long periods of 'depression'" marked by "naked and starving" families. He also attacked any explanation of wages in terms of population pressing against the means of subsistence. In general, when population increased, wealth actually increased in "*a greater ratio*" while "in Ireland the gradual expatriation of a nation is being executed, and with decreasing population poverty is lightened by no shade" (Wicksteed 1882). Wicksteed's focus on depressions and the explanation of wages in terms of capital and population were the same issues that George discussed in the first chapter of *Progress and Poverty*.

While the *Inquirer* had previously published sympathetic reviews of the *Progress* and A.R. Wallace's *Land Nationalization*, there was a virulent reader response to the Georgians, particularly regarding Ireland. The initial target was Harold Rylett, minister at Monmeath, Georgian, friend of Joseph Arch and a former student of Jevons'.[20] Having previously supported the letter by Wicksteed and other

---

[17] In the second edition of *TPE*, Jevons praised T.E. Cliffe Leslie, Shadwell's *System of Political Economy* (1877) and Hearn's *Plutology* (1864) for the "general idea that wages are the share of the produce which the laws of supply and demand enable the labourer to secure" (Jevons 1879, xlix-l). Using the same wording as Jevons when citing the relevant page of *TPE*, the Marshalls added the name of F. A. Walker and referred to William Thornton's *On Labour* (Marshall and Marshall 1879, 205n). Wicksteed's reference to Mill's dictatorship could not have come from the Marshalls – although it could have been fed by Foxwell – and it is unlikely that Wicksteed was enthused by their discussion of land ownership where they wrote: "If a vote could be taken from all Economists throughout the world, it would probably be given in favour of the system under which the land is owned by its cultivator" (63).

[18] All emphases in quotations appear in the original material.

[19] "Which one of us has not felt as though the shadow of a curse fell across the purity and comfort of his home when he is told that it is the outcome of a 'struggle for existence' in which he is the winner, and the pauper and harlot the losers?" (Wicksteed 1882).

[20] For Rylett (1851–1936), see White (1994b); "Harold Rylett", *Land and Liberty*, No.158, September 1936, 138.

ministers on coercion (see above), Rylett became a particular target as a member of the proscribed Irish Land League. In the number after Wicksteed's article on George was published, the *Inquirer* reported a speech by Rylett following the execution of three men in December 1882 for the Maamtrasna murders, which Rylett depicted as a result of the "evils of Irish landlordism". The editor commented that, while Rylett was sometimes capable of "injudicious utterances", the *Inquirer* "heartily sympathise[d]" with the speech.[21] The responses were incandescent. One correspondent, "J.P.", attacked the *Inquirer* for approving "the violent and disgraceful language of Mr. Rylett". But that was not the only recent crime of the journal as Wicksteed's article had also used "language far too sensational", such as his reference to "starving families", which, in reality, only applied to "exceptional" cases. Wicksteed's language was "sadly misleading and mischievous, tending to set class against class, and to encourage discontent and disloyalty." It was well-known that the problem in Ireland was partly that rents withheld under the Land League campaign were spent on alcohol and also used "to swell the immense sums at the command of the Land Leaguers for their infamous uses." Contra Wicksteed, the basic problem in Ireland had nothing to do with landlords but with "over-population" which should be allowed to carry out its God-given work: "The pressure of population upon production is … a most beneficient ordination, pervading as it does all nature, and has long been a settled truth, now, however, taking a new name, 'The survival of the fittest'."[22]

While Wicksteed had supporters in the subsequent *Inquirer* correspondence regarding George during 1883–4, much of it, like the J.P. letter, was basically abusive, relying on crude versions of a wage fund or a "population principle" that Wicksteed swatted away as superceded irrelevancies. At the same time, however, he had to deal with, and had a quite different response to, the economists who were hostile to George. One example was F.Y. Edgeworth who wrote to Foxwell in January 1883, noting that he could only attend the second of Toynbee's lectures and that he agreed with a "slashing review" of George that had appeared in the *Pall Mall Gazette* some months before.[23] In February, Edgeworth delivered a public lecture on "Land and Rent" at

---

[21] "The Maamtrasna Massacre", *Inquirer*, 13 January 1883, 29–30.

[22] J.P. "Progress and Poverty", *Inquirer*, 27 January 1883, 57.

[23] F.Y. Edgeworth to Foxwell, 3 January 1883 (KGU 22-259).

Hampstead, where he characterised rent as an "unearned increment" and announced his agreement with John Stuart Mill that "the state should for the future appropriate such unearned increment". That did not mean the state "should appropriate existing rents" although "this did not apply to those schemes of nationalization which accepted the principle of compensation". Limits could also be set by taxation to the amount of property acquired by bequests. In a swipe at George, however, he also criticized a "simple formula, such as 'Interest falls with wages, and rent devours them both'" while protesting

> against the employment of such exaggerations to excite odium against landlords and justify a policy of confiscation. He ... submitted that the stability of society would best be secured by respecting the rights of property which had already come into existence, and endeavouring to check the growth of inequality in the future.

Foxwell was later to describe Edgeworth's lecture as directed at "some of the more simple-minded bourgeois of Hampstead" who were impressed by George.[24] He was also, and typically, more vehemently critical than Edgeworth, characterising George in a public lecture at Cambridge as "a *Physiocrat gone mad*", who shared "an ethics of savagery" with Hyndman and the SDF: "Mr George would have us commence this program of a wholesale act of robbery, while Mr Hyndman regards class hatred as its only possible motive force. What is such teaching as this but an ethics of savagery?"[25] Nevertheless, Foxwell remained friends with Wicksteed, apparently managing to restrain himself in any further discussion about George. Indeed, in early March 1883, Wicksteed told Foxwell that "many" of those who attended Toynbee's lectures "insist on having the discussion promised" and he had thus arranged a hall for that purpose. Toynbee was by now seriously ill, so Wicksteed would open the discussion, Alfred Milner (see below) had promised to attend, Shadwell "promised to speak" and Wicksteed asked Foxwell if he would do the same.[26]

---

[24] Edgeworth's lecture was reported in "Town Club – Land and Rent", *Hampstead and Highgate Express*, 17 February 1883. Copy in Foxwell, "Notes on Deaths of Economists and Press Obituaries', n.d. (KGU 577-1). In an accompanying note, Foxwell wrote that, at the time, "*Progress and Poverty* had begun to disturb the minds of some of the more simple-minded bourgeois of Hampstead, who were impressed by George's constant invocation of the Deity & the moral law to justify his proposed confiscations. But this was a stale trick".

[25] Foxwell's lecture was reported in "Study of Social Questions", *Cambridge Review*, 13 February 1884, V (114), 183. The quotation above is taken from his "MS notes on Henry George, land, property in land", n.d. (KGU 530-1), which seem to be part of his notes for the lecture.

[26] Wicksteed to Foxwell, 9 March 1883 (KGU 55-259).

Toynbee died the same day and the meeting was cancelled, but Wicksteed's request confirms his interest in hearing and responding to the arguments of Georgian critics, provided that he regarded them as serious economic commentators. If Foxwell was in that camp, the same can be assumed about Shadwell, who was a foundation member of the Property and Defence League.

In his *Inquirer* article promoting Toynbee's lectures, Wicksteed foreshadowed that, if George's arguments remained "victorious", "we shall hope to lay before our readers in a series of communications the main lines of his argument" (Wicksteed 1882). He subsequently published six major pieces in the *Inquirer* during 1883 and early 1884, the first three of which were a response to Toynbee's lectures, published posthumously in early 1883.[27] There was no indication in any of the articles that Wicksteed's fundamental faith in George's remedy of land nationalisation had been shaken. Nevertheless, the articles also indicate how Wicksteed utilized recent work in political economy to reinforce, amend and make a significant analytical departure from George's analysis. This was most evident in Wicksteed's response to Toynbee's critique of George's argument that the rates of wages and interest could fall while rents rose.[28] Responding to a Toynbee parable by reworking Chapters II and III from Book IV of the *Progress*, Wicksteed revealed an aptitude for abstract argument that was far superior to Toynbee's in positing a "model" of a colony with a core region, surrounded by a periphery of free land. Considering a series of long-period positions

---

[27] Wicksteed 1883a–c. Working from a shorthand writer's notes, Alfred Milner (who joined the staff of the *Pall Mall Gazette* in 1881, staying until 1885) edited Toynbee's lectures for publication (Toynbee 1883). Due to his ill health, Toynbee was unable to edit the notes before his death and Milner asked Foxwell to check the proofs. Foxwell declined, suggesting Alfred Marshall instead, although Milner thought that was not feasible (Alfred Milner to Foxwell, 8 February 1883 (KGU 53-259); 10 February 1883 (KGU 57-259)). On the lectures, see Kadish (1986, 213–16), who notes (216) that Milner censored a number of Toynbee's statements on Ireland and abolishing the House of Lords because they were politically embarrassing. The text of the published lectures was appended to the first printing of Toynbee's *Industrial Revolution* in May 1884, although it was omitted from all subsequent reprints and editions. This was because, Kadish also suggests, the edited lectures were still too radical for Milner as they could be read as supporting Irish Home rule and a more general anti-imperialist position.

[28] In the relevant chapters of the *Progress* (Book IV, chs II-III), George tended to switch without warning between referring to 'wages' as a real rate and as a share of output. When Toynbee (1883, 14–15) accused George of inconsistency on this and other matters, Wicksteed acknowledged the inconsistency in "one or two unfortunate passages" of the "two very important chapters", but argued that it was not a fundamental problem. Toynbee's critique was "a perfectly fair polemic against *Mr. George*, but it does not affect *his system*" (Wicksteed 1883b, 276). In any case, "it is, of course, no argument against the tenable theories of a writer to say that he has in several places advanced untenable theories on the same subject" (Wicksteed 1883c, 292).

where labour was the only variable input, the core was characterized by a rising "average product of labour" with increasing returns due to an expanding division of labour. The minimum and average wage was determined by the product of labour (corn) in the free belt. In the first stage of the model, pressure of population would lead to further cultivation of the belt with a constant real wage although the average rising product of labour in the core meant that rent absorbed a larger share of total output (Wicksteed 1883b, 276). The second stage allowed for a rising value of land in the core and hence the emergence of a speculative belt between the core and periphery. This entailed that land would be held idle due to "anticipated *value*", a waste of resources that was also a feature of the core.[29] Labourers would now either have to pay rent in the belt or move further out to free land. In the latter case, even assuming constant returns to land, the real wage rate would fall as, with a given exchange rate for corn set in the core, the farmers in the periphery would have to pay for the "time, labour, and expense of transport ... [as well as] the privations ... [of] many things [which] cannot be transported to the farm at all" (Wicksteed 1883c, 292). A Georgian analysis could thus argue that the rates of wages and interest (although the latter was not explained in the model) would fall at the expense of rent, even without diminishing returns to land, a result in which land speculation played a pivotal role.

Wicksteed argued that the model showed "what really takes place"[30] and a modification to one assumption could also explain how "the deepest and most hopeless poverty" was due to rents. Even Toynbee acknowledged, Wicksteed noted, that this occurred in Ireland, Dorset and London. It was largely because, in many cases, it was "impossible" to migrate to (peripheral) land overseas so that "what is to keep the wages of the lowest stratum of workmen above that starvation line euphemistically described in the books of political economy as 'the standard of comfort'. The remuneration of labour and a corresponding remuneration of capital, is all that the landowners need allow" (Wicksteed 1883c, 292; cf. Toynbee 1883, 32–5). While Wicksteed did not discuss wage rates above the "standard of comfort", the

---

[29] Mines, shops and building sites would be deliberately kept idle "because the landlord asks too high a rent" (Wicksteed 1883c, 292). Wicksteed cited Toynbee (1883, 37) in support of that point.

[30] When Toynbee argued that empirical evidence showed wage rates had not fallen in the US, Wicksteed amended the argument to say that speculation had a "tendency" to lower wages that would "otherwise" have been higher (Wicksteed 1883c, 292).

implication here was that any such rates in the core were a residual of rent and the result of possible bargaining. Hence, the explanation of the aggregate wage share in the core was, within limits, indeterminate.

The analysis illustrates three aspects of Wicksteed's developing understanding of political economy. It first indicates how he read recent work in part to find arguments that could be regarded as consistent with a Georgian position. The reliance on increasing returns in manufacturing and constant returns in agriculture, for example, could find support in Shadwell's analysis, as could the argument that the minimum or average wage was determined by the return on marginal land.[31] The second aspect concerns the indeterminate wage share in the core sector which appeared to be a residual (see above). While that was an amendment to George's analysis (cf. George 1883, 120–21), it was consistent with Jevons' argument in the final chapter of *TPE* and with the work of F.A. Walker, whose *Wages Question* (1876) Wicksteed had read by May 1883 (Wicksteed 1883b, 276). When Wicksteed subsequently reviewed Henry Sidgwick's *Principles of Political Economy* (1883), Walker's *Political Economy* (1883) and Jevons's *Methods of Social Reform* (1883) in early 1884, he praised Sidgwick's critique of the wage-fund theory while noting that the "general public has recently been familiarised [with the argument] by Mr. Henry George, and, as no reference is made to him or his work by Mr. Sidgwick, we are authorised in supposing that the latter regards the new theory of the relation of capital and wages as the natural outcome and completion of economic thought, quite independent of its statement by Mr. George" (Wicksteed 1884e, 399). He was, however, generally, although not completely, far more enthusiastic about Walker, whom he had previously described as "the most eminent ... of living Economists" (Wicksteed 1884d, 115). Wicksteed now praised Walker for making profits (as compared with interest) analogous with rent, so that "the workman, in reality, makes what terms he can with landlord, capitalist, and employer, and then keeps what is left of the product for himself; whereas in appearance it is the employer who makes what terms he can with landlord, capitalist and workman, and keeps what is left of the product for himself" (Wicksteed 1884e, 401).

The third aspect of Wicksteed's analysis indicated a significant departure from the *Progress*. Toynbee had criticized George for his

---

[31] Shadwell (1877, 134–6; 1880, 23–4, 54–5). For Shadwell, see Steedman (2000).

lack of a satisfactory explanation of relative prices, arguing that had led to a misunderstanding of Ricardo's rent theory (Toynbee 1883, 15). Noting the criticism that George had left "out of sight the mechanism of exchange", Wicksteed initially claimed that George had not "neglected" it, "although he does not enter in technical details on the subject" (Wicksteed 1883b, 276). Nevertheless, it is evident that Wicksteed regarded this as a substantive problem because when he assumed a given set of relative prices to explain a long-period position in his model, he gave this justification:

> In any given condition of the community there is a certain exchange value of corn (fixed by what Jevons might call the equation of final utilities), such that when corn rests at this value there is no greater or less advantage in applying labour and capital to the production of corn than in applying it to the production of other commodities (Wicksteed 1883c, 292).

That statement referred to a long-period equilibrium position as set out in Chapter V of TPE and was significant on two grounds. The first, as suggested above, is that it indicates Wicksteed recognised a critical deficiency with George's analysis in explaining a long-period equilibrium position and that he was now following Jevons in that regard. That point is reinforced by the second, which is that, although, as will be explained below, it was a peculiar reading of TPE, it was to provide the fulcrum for his critique of Marx in the following year. Evidently, Wicksteed had decided on that reading of Jevons by May 1883. The effect of TPE in that context is also suggested by Wicksteed beginning to experiment with a notation to characterize the real wage rate on the periphery where he discounted the farmers' revenue by a "fraction" l, which was the "local coefficient" (Wicksteed 1883c, 292).

While the serious study of TPE, which would subsequently take Wicksteed far into the intricacies of Jevons' analysis, was now in train, it is important to note that, by early 1884, Wicksteed gave no indication that he saw anything fundamentally inconsistent between a Georgian proposal for land nationalisation and a marginalism that treated ground rent as a surplus and wages as a residual. To this extent at least, marginalism could be made consistent with the basics of a Georgian position. If Wicksteed ignored Jevons' dismissal of Progress and Poverty,[32] he could refer to Leon Walras, "who shares

---

[32] For Jevons' dismissal of George in letters to Harold Rylett, see White (1994b). Although part of a relevant letter was printed in the Letters and Journal (Jevons 1886, 444), Wicksteed made no mention of it in his review of that text (Wicksteed 1886).

with Jevons the honour of the successful application of the exact methods of mathematics to the illustration and elucidation of economics, as published in an elaborate essay to defend his favourite thesis (inherited from his father) of land nationalization" (Wicksteed 1884d, 116).[33] Indeed, Wicksteed apparently felt that the mainstream tide was turning in the Georgians' favour because although there might be some

> differences between Mr. George and the English economists ... I believe that many English economists rejoice ... in the vividness and force which Mr. George has brought home to us the supreme importance of the study of economic problems, and the directness with which he has shown their bearing upon our actual lives. (*Inquirer* 1884)

While that statement might have reflected some (temporary) waning of overt hostility on Foxwell's part,[34] two months later Alfred Marshall was to show that there was little rejoicing at Oxford University when he attacked George at a rowdy public meeting.[35] If that was disappointing, a more dangerous opponent was at hand.

2. The stockbroker and the Marxist(s)

There was a further departure from George worth noting in Wicksteed's later *Inquirer* articles when he responded to a critic who demanded to know how he could justify George's policy of land nationalisation which would fall "*without compensation*" on current landowners.[36] Wicksteed argued that the policy should be based on the taxation of land, supplemented by an income tax, so that the incidence would not fall only on landowners. Those who should pay were the

> governing classes ... roughly coincident with the propertied and income-receiving classes, except, perhaps, the humblest stratum ... [The] loss would affect the whole capitalist class immediately, in so far as it holds

---

[33] Wicksteed might have been referring to Walras (1881). Foxwell had asked Walras for a copy of that pamphlet after it was reviewed in the *Journal of the Statistical Society* (Jaffe 1965, vol. 1, 524–5).

[34] From Foxwell's diary: On dining with Wicksteed at the Beetons', "Interesting discussion on George" (16 April 1883); "Dined with Henry George at [Sydney] Olivier's rooms. V. pleasant party" (8 April 1884) (KGU 15^1/$_2$).

[35] On Marshall at Oxford, see Stigler 1969, 217–26. There had been another rowdy meeting the previous week at Cambridge ("Mr. Henry George", *Cambridge Review*, 12 March 1884, V (118), 255–6).

[36] Juvenis. "Mr. Wicksteed and Mr. George", *Inquirer*, 19 January 1884, 37. Wicksteed's response to the use of the Juvenis pseudonym provides a striking example of how well he could employ the rhetorical device of an iron fist in a velvet glove (Wicksteed 1884b).

land for transportation, manufacturing, mining or other purposes, as in the case of railways and other industrial joint-stock companies; and contingently, in so far as it has advanced money on the security of land, as in the case of insurance companies, banks and other financial associations.

Wicksteed noted that this policy had been suggested to him by a

friend whose professional occupations lead him to look at all of these questions from the floor of the Exchange as well as from the bench of the lecture-room, and who assures me that his knowledge of practical finance tends to remove than to magnify the difficulties of the problem of nationalizing the land. (Wicksteed 1884c, 100, 101)

Wicksteed's collaborator was almost certainly the stockbroker Henry Raimie Beeton (1851–1934), another friend and correspondent of Foxwell's. Beeton had first met Foxwell in 1879, was his collaborator in the bimetallism agitation of the 1890s and maintained a voluminous correspondence with him until his death.[37] A Wicksteed "family legend" had it that Wicksteed and Beeton first met in March 1884 at a meeting of the Hampstead Liberal Club attended by several members of the "Economic Circle". Having both expressed "emphatic approval" of Henry George and finding common cause, they "'fell into each other's arms'" (Herford 1931, 207). The origin of the Circle (which, at the time, Wicksteed and Beeton referred to as the Economic Society) has been traced to a study group formed in 1883 at Manchester New College to examine *Progress and Poverty*. Wicksteed's biographer reported that he led the discussion "from the first", requiring the group "to equip themselves" with Jevons' mathematical analysis.[38] The Circle itself initially met at the home of Hodgson Pratt in early 1884.[39] After Beeton joined the group, meetings were transferred to his home at Hampstead in October. The Circle, which met for roughly the next five years, is well known to historians of economics as its membership included, at various times, Wicksteed, Edgeworth, Foxwell, Henry Cunynghame (sometimes mistaken for William Cunningham in this context), Bernard Shaw, Sidney Webb and, occasionally, Alfred

---

[37] Little detail has been published about Beeton's activities in economics. See, for example, the obituary by Bonar (1934).

[38] At some points in the 1880s, Wicksteed took lessons in the differential calculus from John Bridge, mathematics tutor at UCL, although the dates of this are not clear (Herford 1931, 200n).

[39] Pratt (1824–1907), a pacifist credited with founding the International Arbitration and Peace Association in 1880, met Walras at Lausanne in 1871 and, in April 1874, following a request from Walras, sent him the names of 17 British economists who might be interested in his work (Jaffe, 1965, vol. 1, 361n, 383–85). The list "excluded Marshall and mislocated Fawcett in Oxford" (Whitaker and Kymn 1993, 55).

Marshall (Herford 1931, 205–11; Howey 1960, ch.13). Wicksteed's *Alphabet of Economic Science* (1888) was dedicated to Beeton and his wife, Elizabeth, for their "genial hospitality" at Hampstead where the book's contents had been first "set forth".

The family legend of Wicksteed first meeting Beeton in March 1884 provides a tidy timeline for a depiction of their relationship that turns on the Circle and its history. It is, however, incorrect and obscures a further aspect of their collaboration. Beeton first contacted Wicksteed in January 1883 regarding tickets for the Toynbee lectures. By April, Foxwell recorded that he had had dinner with Wicksteed at the Beetons' where there was an "interesting discussion on George".[40] Apart from the enthusiastic promotion of their Georgian project, Wicksteed and Beeton were united with Foxwell in opposing the analysis and activities of Hyndman and the SDF.

Foxwell had initially contacted Hyndman in late 1882 asking about the policies of the SDF. The correspondence did not begin well (Foxwell declaring that he was not a democrat) and, with Hyndman responding in combative mode, it quickly deteriorated. Foxwell then developed something of an obsession with denouncing Marx, Hyndman and his works in lectures and letters. At the time, political positions were more fluid than subsequently, with the SDF supporting George. Hyndman and George were on friendly terms and Hyndman told George that it had been initially suggested that Toynbee's London lectures be sponsored by the SDF, a proposal he rejected because "I disapprove of attacking allies and Toynbee calls himself a Radical Socialist" (Barker 1955, 390; Kadish 1986, 203). If Hyndman was in an ecumenical mood, the Foxwell circle was oblivious to it. In early January 1883, Toynbee wrote to Foxwell that "I agree with you entirely about his [Hyndman's] attempt to sow dissent between classes. It is wicked". He had, however, written to Hyndman saying he had been informed that an attempt would be made to disrupt the lectures and had asked Hyndman to "use what influence he has" to prevent it.[41] After Toynbee's death when he informed Foxwell that

---

[40] Foxwell diary, 16 April 1883 (KGU $15^1/_2$). Wicksteed referred to another dinner at the Beetons' in January 1884 (Wicksteed to Foxwell, 8 January 1884 (KGU 18-123)).

[41] Toynbee to Foxwell, 5 January 1883 (KGU 63 – 259). There is further evidence that Hyndman was sympathetic to Toynbee's George lectures. Hyndman subsequently told Bernard Shaw that, with regard to Toynbee's statistics on rent, "I went over them ... with him before he lectured" (Letter from Hyndman to Shaw, 12 July 1889, British Library, G.B. Shaw Papers, Series 1, vol. XXXI, Add MS 50538).

the plan for the public meeting to allow responses to the lectures had been cancelled (see above), Wicksteed also announced that he had had not completely abandoned the idea for the future. Hyndman, however, was a problem. Wicksteed claimed that Hyndman "is on rather cold terms with the Georgians" and that, while not one of those pressing for the public discussion of the Toynbee lectures, he would "take advantage" of it. What "I do know [of him] is consistent with your estimation of him and I have certainly no desire to help him!"[42]

Beeton drew closer to Wicksteed from the beginning of 1884. In January, he told Foxwell that he had listened to George lecture at St James Hall. While impressed, he was particularly taken with Wicksteed, who "made a very fine speech emphasizing the differences between land reformers & the Democratic Federation". He would send Foxwell a copy of Wicksteed's speech that "was far and away the best thing of the evening outside the lecture itself".[43] Given that the charge of sowing class conflict had previously been levelled at Wicksteed, one purpose of his writing in this period was to differentiate a Georgian approach from that of the SDF or "Socialists", for which the reader could readily substitute followers of Marx. As Wicksteed put it, he wanted to make very clear the "radical opposition" between a Georgian analysis "and the doctrines of communism" (Wicksteed 1884d, 116). Since the Georgian analysis held that land was the only source of a persistent economic surplus, Wicksteed rejected any "socialist" suggestion that a structural surplus could derive from the exploitation of labour. Responding to Toynbee's argument that employers were largely to blame for low wages and the adverse distribution of wealth (Toynbee 1883, 40–43), for example, Wicksteed claimed that only "the most pronounced socialists" would agree that the employers were the source of the problem. That argument was a diversion because as

> the system of credit is perfected, competition amongst employers of labour will become more and more perfect, and it is difficult to see how the 'earnings of supervision and direction,' or, in other words, the remuneration of employers, can be permanently maintained at an exorbitant rate … [If at present profits were] largely increased by the

---

[42] Wicksteed to Foxwell, 12 March 1883 (KGU 54-299).
[43] Beeton to Foxwell, 14 January 1884 (KGU 20-123); 21 February 1884 (KGU 16-123).

monopolizing power of great capitals the progressive perfecting of the credit system must tend to reduce them by making it comparatively easy for outsiders who possess business talent to cut them down by free competition (Wicksteed 1883b, 275).

By early 1884, Wicksteed also registered his opposition to the policies of the SDF in a review of Jevons' *Methods of Social Reform*. Focussing on Jevons' chapters on the organisation of industries by the state, Wicksteed commented that,

> although the State-socialism of the late Karl Marx and his followers contemplates a 'State' such as we have not yet seen, its advocates cannot afford to ignore Jevons' weighty words on the subject of state management, and they ought to attach the more weight to them inasmuch they come from an enemy of the laissez faire system hardly less pronounced than themselves (Wicksteed 1884e, 402).

Beeton's collaboration with Wicksteed on the taxation proposals sketched in the *Inquirer* indicates that they were as one in promoting a radical liberal program of land reform that was to be clearly differentiated from the Marxists in the SDF. Their friendship would have been further strengthened because, while they both remained friends and correspondents with Foxwell, in general, the Cambridge economist remained hostile to George, regarding land nationalisation as a slippery slope to Marx and Hyndman. Indeed, Beeton had to beat a hasty retreat after he had gently mocked Foxwell for that argument and received an angry response.[44] By 1887, Foxwell had found a pseudo-sociological explanation for the supporters of George and Marx, which echoed his comments on Edgeworth's 1883 Hampstead lecture (see above):

> It is ... among the middle classes that socialistic theories are most discussed. Mr. H. George's land proposals and the recently translated *Capital* of Karl Marx both found sympathizers in this social stratum. They were well calculated to appeal to the somewhat *dilettante* enthusiasm of those who were educated enough to realize and to be revolted by the painful condition of the poor, but not patient or hardheaded enough to find out the real causes of this misery, nor sufficiently trained to perceive the utter hollowness of the quack remedies so rhetorically and effectively put forward (Foxwell 1887c, 99).

Despite his well-known hostility to Marx, Foxwell does not seem to have played any direct role in the production of Wicksteed's *To-Day*

---

[44] Beeton to Foxwell, 23 February 1884 (KGU 17-123).

Figure 1. Henry Raimie and Elizabeth Beeton, c. 1891.

critique. He spent the summer of 1884 in the USA and, on his return, it was Beeton who sent him a copy and to whom Foxwell responded, criticizing Wicksteed's conflation of the "standard of comfort and starvation point" when referring to wages (see below).[45] Evidently, Foxwell

---

[45] Beeton to Foxwell, 20 October 1884 (KGU 15-123); 30 October 1884 (KGU 14-123). Nor was Foxwell an active member of the Economic Circle in October 1884. Beeton referred to "A few friends who meet at my house every other Tuesday to discuss Economic questions … Wicksteed & Edgeworth having held on the last occasion that Jevons & Walras teaching on the Theory of Exchange is true & Ricardo & Mill false [George] Armitage Smith (I don't know whether you know him) is going to reconcile the two, as I understand it" (KGU 14-123).

Figure 2. Beeton family with chauffer, c.1902.

had not seen the article before its publication. It was subsequently claimed that Wicksteed's article followed his being challenged when studying in a "fellowship" of "Marxist" Fabians, "to write an article … confuting Marx". Wicksteed emphatically denied that was the case. The article was not "written in answer to a challenge but was sent by me *proprio motu* and accepted by the editorial staff".[46] The "editorial staff" may have been a reference to one of the editors,

---

[46] The 'challenge' claim was made by Robert Rattray (1918). For Wicksteed's rejection, Wicksteed (1918). Despite this, Rattray, who had met Wicksteed "a number of times", repeated the claim in 1946 (Rattray 1946), which helped to create a false trail regarding Wicksteed's submission of the *To-Day* article. At the same time that the Economic Circle shifted to Hampstead, the anarcho-socialist Charlotte Wilson organized a 'Karl Marx Club', also in Hampstead, to read Volume I of *Capital*. Over the next four years, the discussion group subsequently became the 'Proudhon Club' and then the 'Hampstead Historic Society'. At least in the early stages, members of the group included Edgeworth, Sidney Webb, Shaw, Annie Besant, Sydney Olivier, Graham Wallas and H.H. Asquith (!) (Hinely 2012, 13). Shaw also listed Belfort Bax as an early participant (Shaw 1889, 129). Noting Wolfe's claim (1975, 178–9, 206) that Wicksteed had also attended what Webb patronizingly referred to as "Mrs Wilson's economic tea party", and that the group was dominated by Fabians, Ian Steedman cited Rattray to suggest that it was in that group that the 'challenge' had been issued to Wicksteed (Steedman 1989, 118–19; see also Stigler 1986, 291). Apart from the point that Wicksteed explicitly denied Rattray's claim, there is, so far as I am aware, no evidence that Wicksteed ever attended meetings of the Karl Marx Club.

J.L. Joynes (see above), who had collaborated with Wicksteed (and others) in founding the Land Reform Union to promote land nationalisation (Steedman 1989, 121). At the same time, Wicksteed's response might give the impression that the article was constructed in a political vacuum and entirely without reference to anyone bar himself ("*proprio motu*"). However, quite apart from Wicksteed's previous public criticism, someone else was particularly interested in a critique of the SDF. At the close of 1883, Beeton had written to Foxwell. *To-Day* had just been relaunched and Beeton enclosed a copy of an article from the journal on diminishing returns (Kinnear 1884), asking for Foxwell's assessment.[47] Beeton was not reading the magazine out of idle interest or because he was in any way sympathetic. As he told Foxwell: "I should like to see someone of first rate rank and admittedly free from the so-called "bourgeois" bias (whatever that might mean) show up that squirt Hyndman. Do you know a man who could bring his mind to do it?" [48] A few months later he had found his man.

3. Homage to Jevons?

In the *To-day* article, Wicksteed used two main arguments to criticise Marx's analysis of the economic surplus. The first was that Marx had no satisfactory theory of relative prices based on labour, whereas the second was that his explanation for the value of "labour-force" was analytically incoherent.[49] Hence, there could be no satisfactory explanation for surplus value. Each component of the critique will be considered in turn.

3.1. Explaining relative prices

The relative price argument itself had two separable albeit connected elements. The first was that the exchange value of all commodities, in any time period, was determined by their final degrees of utility. Even

---

[47] Although the date for that issue of *To-Day* was January 1884, it was evidently available the previous month.

[48] Beeton to Foxwell, 31 December 1883 (KGU 33-7). For an example of Beeton's unremitting hostility to Hyndman and the SDF, see his letter, "Political Economy and Socialism", *The Times*, 7 October 1885, 4.

[49] Wicksteed translated Marx as referring to 'labour-force' rather than to 'labour-power', for which he subsequently blamed Bax, the editor of *To-Day* (Flatau 2004, 81). I use Wicksteed's terminology for the most part here.

in the case of reproducible commodities in a long-period, where commodities exchanged according to the labour contained in them, it was the final degrees of utility that determined the exchange ratio and, accordingly, how much labour was used in their production.[50] The second element was to argue that Marx's commodity domain was seriously limited, as he could not explain the prices of irreproducible and other commodities in terms of labour embodied. The marginal utility theory could, however, explain such prices. Before discussing each argument in turn, it will be helpful to briefly consider the basis for Wicksteed's framework.

When he referred in *To-Day* to the difficulty with explaining the relations between utility, labour and exchange value, Wicksteed declared that:

> It is the complete and definitive solution of the problem ... which will immortalize the name of Stanley Jevons, and all that I have attempted ... in this article is to bring the potent instrument of investigation which he has placed in our hands to bear upon the problems under discussion. (Wicksteed 1884f, 399)

When he also wrote of being "under his [i.e. Jevons'] guidance" in that regard, Wicksteed was referring to Chapters IV and V of *TPE*.

---

[50] Wicksteed claimed that "the great logician has ... fallen into formal (if not ... substantial) error" (Wicksteed 1884f, 398) in excluding value in use from the determination of value in exchange. According to Wicksteed, Marx argued that the exchange value of commodities was to be explained only as the *"products of labor"*, having been "stripped of all physical attributes, *i.e.* of everything which gives them value in use". However, Marx then added the "important statement that *the labour does not count unless it is useful*". This "surrenders the whole of the previous analysis" for, if only useful labour was relevant, the commodities cannot have been "stripped" of the "abstract utility, conferred on them by abstractly useful work". Hence, it was not the case that the exchange value of commodities could be explained in terms of "abstract human labour" alone (Wicksteed 1884f, 395, 396). In the pages to which Wicksteed referred, Marx was discussing the long-period exchange value of reproducible commodities, a point that Wicksteed acknowledged (Wicksteed 1884f, 397). Marx argued that, as there was no common unit for designating use values, units of abstract labour were all that remained to explain exchange value. It was clear from this account that while value in use could not determine value in exchange, it was a precondition for it (Marx 1990, 126–31). (That was also, of course, the position of Ricardo). While it might be argued that Marx's discussion of value in use, especially in Volume 3 of *Capital*, is not without problems (Steedman 1989, 134–40), the analysis in Volume 1 was not illogical as Wicksteed claimed. Indeed, having made his claim about Marx at some length and then arguing that "value in exchange is rigidly determined by value in use", Wicksteed made essentially the same distinction as Marx between a precondition and a determinant of exchange value within the terms of his own argument: "labour is ... one of the sources ... alike of value in use ... and value in exchange ... but in no case is it a *constituent* element of the latter any more than of the former ... Labour ... *confers* upon suitable substances both ... value in use ... [and] value in exchange ... but it is not an element of either" (Wicksteed 1884f, 404, 398). Wicksteed was apparently unable to extend to Marx the rather generous reading method that he had previously accorded to Henry George (see above).

Chapter IV considered a market period where trading took place
from a parametric stock of commodities. The following chapter discussed a long-period outcome, where production levels changed with
labour as the variable input, working with a stock of raw materials.
Using Jevons' notation as far as possible, the long-period equilibrium
condition, discussed in some detail in the second edition (Jevons
1879, 205–9), was

$$\phi x/\psi y = dy/dx = y/x = p_1/p_2 = \omega_2/\omega_1 = c_1/c_2$$

where, with two commodities X and Y, $\phi x/\psi y$ is the final degree of
utility ratio for them, dy/dx is the marginal exchange ratio, y/x is the
market exchange ratio and p_1 (p_2) is the price of X (Y) measured in
gold. The equilibrium condition to the left of the price ratio corresponds to that for trading in a market period. The following chapter
added ω_1 and ω_2 for the marginal labour product ratio and c_1/c_2 for
the cost of production ratio of X and Y, respectively. Cost of production was equal to the inverse of the marginal labour product ratio
multiplied by a given wage rate.[51] The marginal labour productivity
ratio, which Jevons termed the "degree of productiveness", was initially assumed constant, giving a "uniform rate of production" that
was characteristic of the manufacturing sector using "machine labour"
(Jevons 1879, 192).[52]

The equilibrium condition helps in explaining the first component
of Wicksteed's critique. He argued that "value in exchange is rigidly
determined by value in use" in both a market and a long period. It
was the "abstract utility of the last available unit of any commodity
[that] determines the ratio of exchange of the whole of it" (Wicksteed
1884f, 404, 400). Making no mention of the increasing returns
assumption used in his Georgian "model" (see above) and following
Jevons in assuming constant returns but ignoring his references to
cost of production, Wicksteed illustrated the long-period case by positing a labour-saving technical change for some commodities. Labour
would transfer to the production of those commodities as an

---

[51] I have added the term for cost of production as the definition was not clearly explained and
no symbol was given in *TPE*. The argument entails, however, that there is a given wage rate,
presumably measured in gold, which is the same in both industries. Cost of production can
thus be represented, for X and Y respectively, as $c_1 = (1/\omega_1)w$; $c_2 = (1/\omega_2)w$, where w is the
given wage rate.

[52] For detailed discussion of the long-period equilibrium condition, including Jevons'
assumption of constant labour productivity and his odd treatment of cost of production, see
White (1994a, 2004, 2005). Cf. Black (1970, 25) and Steedman (1989, 123, 126) who assert
that Jevons only discussed diminishing returns.

increased output could be obtained for the same input. (There is no capital in the analysis). With an increased supply, the relative value of the commodities would fall, *"not because they contain less labour,* but because the recent increments have been *less useful,* and by the "law of indifference" the utility of the last increment determines the value of the whole" (405).[53] At equilibrium, where the ratio of labour units equalled the exchange ratio driven by the utility ratio, it was the latter which explained why labourers were "willing" to supply that amount of labour. Even the most favourable case for Marx, where the exchange ratio reflected the (marginal) labour embodied in reproducible commodities, was only a coincidence:

> [The] 'law of variation of utility' fully accounts for all the phenomena of supply and demand and for the coincidence, in the case of articles that can be indefinitely multiplied, between the relative amounts of labour they contain and their relative values. (406)[54]

This claim that the utility ratio drove the exchange rate in a long period misrepresented Jevons' analysis. Even if the cost of production in *TPE* is put to one side, so that only the marginal labour product ratio is referred to, in the case of constant returns, the productivity ratio would act as an attractor for the system and the utility ratio would adjust to it. Jevons acknowledged this with his remark that "the ratio of exchange of commodities will conform in the long run to the *ratio of productiveness,* which is the reciprocal of the ratio of the costs of production" (Jevons 1879, 202). He also made clear that, in the case of diminishing returns and hence increasing costs in the raw material sector, the "ratio of exchange governs the production as much as the production governs the ratio of exchange" (204). Both the ratio of productiveness (or the cost of production) ratios and final degree of utility ratio governed the price since if, for example, the exchange ratio changed, the amount demanded would change and so would the level of production. Even in that case, the cost of production ratio also governed the price. If Wicksteed's claim that, in a long period, the final degree of utility ratio alone governed the price was simply incorrect, he was not following Jevons but rather resurrecting

---

[53] The law of indifference was Jevons' term for the assumption that all commodities exchanged at the same ratio in any market 'at any moment'. It required highly restrictive conditions (White 2001), none of which was mentioned, let alone considered, by Wicksteed.

[54] Wicksteed added that labour "can indefinitely modify the number of ... things, and by so doing can modify their (final) utility, and so affect their values" (Wicksteed 1884f, 407).

the value analysis of Archbishop Richard Whately (Whately 1832, 152–53; 1853, 32–3).[55]

The second component of Wicksteed's critique was that, unlike marginalism, Marx's analysis was of limited use because of its restricted commodity domain. It could not explain the prices of a number of commodities, particularly irreproducibles: "specimens of old china, pictures by the deceased masters, and to a greater or lesser degree the yield of all natural or artificial monopolies. The value of these things changes because their utility changes" (Wicksteed 1884f, 407).

If the question of the pricing of "natural or artificial monopolies", for which Wicksteed provided no explanation and for which there is no warrant in *TPE*, is put to one side, it is possible that Wicksteed's remarks about irreproducibles drew on a polemical passage by Jevons at the close of Chapter IV when, criticizing the argument that labour was "the *cause of value*" which would entail that "value will be proportional to labour", he claimed that Ricardo "disposes of such an opinion" when he acknowledged that the value of some commodities "is determined by their scarcity alone". These included "rare statues and pictures, scarce books and coins, wines of a particular quality which can be made only from grapes grown on a particular soil". Irreproducible commodities played a crucial role in understanding that it was the existence of "many things, such as rare ancient books, coins, antiquities, etc., which have high values, and which are absolutely incapable of production now, [that] disperses the notion that value depends on labour" (Jevons 1879, 176–77).

While Wicksteed may well have drawn on that passage, his claim about irreproducibles was mistaken as the Jevonian framework could not explain the price of irreproducible commodities. The problem with irreproducibles was that they were simultaneously indivisible and heterogeneous because unique. While Wicksteed acknowledged that the Jevonian theory turned on "infinitesimal increment(s)" (Wicksteed 1884f, 404), he nowhere explained its significance for understanding divisibility. Nor, although he referred to the assumption of commodity homogeneity (399), did he explain its significance. Yet, it was Jevons

---

[55] It is possible that Wicksteed's reading of *TPE* drew on Jevons' notorious 'catena' near the close of Chapter IV: "*Cost of production determines supply. Supply determines final degree of utility. Final degree of utility determines value*" (Jevons 1879, 179). Even if that was the case, it depended on ignoring Jevons' clear statements about the determination of long-period values in the following chapter.

who, in discussing indivisibility, turned to the "much more difficult problem" of exchange, between two transactors, of an indivisible commodity for a divisible one, such as money:

> In all such cases our equations must fail to exist, because we cannot contemplate the existence of an increment or decrement to an indivisible article ... A bargain of this kind is exceedingly common; indeed it occurs in the case of every house, mansion, estate, factory, ship, or other complete whole ... The theory seems to give a very unsatisfactory answer, for the problem proves to be, within certain limits, indeterminate (Jevons 1879, 131–33).

As the result would depend on bargaining, the

> transaction must be settled on other than strictly economical grounds ... [such as the] disposition and force of character of the parties, their comparative persistency, their adroitness and experience in business, or it may be feelings of justice or kindliness ... These are motives more or less extraneous to a theory of Economics ... It may be that indeterminate bargains of this kind are best arranged by an arbitrator or third party. (134–35)

These examples involved elements of both indivisibility and heterogeneity although the point was particularly clear in the case of irreproducibles. The examples Jevons cited to criticize a labour theory in *TPE* thus could not be explained by his own theory although he was more explicit about that point in his unfinished *Principles of Economics* (1905).[56] Jevons was not alone in that regard as other theorists were (and continued to be) hampered by similar continuity problems, which turned, in part, on the impossibility of constructing a marginalist utility or demand function for a unique and hence heterogeneous commodity (White 1999). At the same time, Wicksteed made no mention of how Jevons had limited the domain of the science of political economy by distinguishing between activities in terms of their ethical characterization, so that bargaining, for example, was precluded.[57] Wicksteed was subsequently to erase any trace of his Jevonian heritage in that regard when his *Common Sense of Political Economy* (1910) made almost any action an "economic" one.

---

[56] For a more detailed discussion of this problem for Jevons, see White (2001).
[57] For an explanation of how Jevons limited the domain in *TPE*, see White (1994a).

The value of "labour-force"

Wicksteed claimed that Marx had followed "the old school of economics" in arguing that the wages of "manual labour normally tend
... to a point at which they barely suffice to support existence and
allow of reproduction". That "starvation" wage could only be altered
by "collective [action] on the part of the working-classes" which was
assumed impossible. Wicksteed took that assumption as given, noting
that he would not "stay to examine" it, thereby giving the impression
that he disagreed with it (Wicksteed 1884f, 389), although he had
used precisely that assumption in his Georgian analysis of the year
before. He was thus concerned with Marx's argument that the (long-
period) value of labour-force "is fixed by the amount of labour needed
to produce it". However, on Wicksteed's preceding analysis, value
only sometimes coincided with the amount of "labour contained" and
that coincidence depended on labour being "freely directed" to move
between the production of different commodities until equilibrium
was reached. That, however, was not possible for labour-force because,
as the worker was powerless

> to direct labour at his will, then there is no reason whatever to suppose
> that the value [of labour-force] will stand in any relation to the amount of
> labour which it contains, for its value is determined by its utility at the
> margin of supply, and by hypothesis it is out of the power of labour to
> raise or lower that margin (Wicksteed 1884f, 408).

The only type of economy where Marx's result could occur was in
a "slave-breeding" one, which meant that, in all other economies,
"there is no economic law the action of which will bring the value of
labour-force, and the value of other commodities, into the ratio of the
amount of labour respectively embodied in them" (408–9). The value
of labour-force was indeterminate in Marx's system and so his claims
about surplus value had no secure theoretical basis.

Three points can be made about this analysis. First, the conclusion echoed Shadwell's claim that the long-period wage analysis of
David Ricardo and Thorold Rogers was "applicable to the rate of
renumeration which is given to slaves" and could not explain "the
ordinary rate of wages received by free labourers" (Shadwell 1877,
141). Second, to derive his specific argument that Marx had made a
logical blunder, Wicksteed assumed that the value of labour-force
should be explained, like that of any other commodity, in marginalist terms. That simply dismissed, without any acknowledgement, the

non-marginalist terms of Marx's analysis, thereby erasing the complexity and analytical lineage of his discussion. It also erased Marx's clear statement that, whereas the (exchange) value of labour power in a long period was explained in terms of labour embodied, the bundle of commodities that made up a minimum "subsistence" were historically conditioned. By contrast with "other commodities, the determination of the value of labour-power contains a historical and moral element" (Marx 1990, 275). The general point about "a historical and moral element" was, of course, hardly new, as Marx's own references indicate. But, Wicksteed's critique conflated the explanation for the value of labour-power with the explanation of the commodity bundle whose value had to be determined. The argument was thus constructed wholly within the terms of Wicksteed's marginalist framework, erroneously attributing an important assumption to *Capital*.

Third, the context of the claim about the value of labour-force can help clarify the one specific matter for which Wicksteed praised Marx's analysis. He closed the article by noting that, in the "latter portion" of Volume I, Marx had made "contributions of extreme importance to the solution of the great problem, though I cannot see that they stand in any logical connection with the abstract reasoning of his early chapters" (Wicksteed 1884f, 408). Although the reference here was not particularly clear, Wicksteed had earlier referred to the analysis of unemployment and the industrial reserve army of labour in Chapter 25, where Marx

> shows that the alternative expansions and contractions of the several branches of industry, aggravated by the disturbances caused by the introduction of labour-saving machinery and so forth, tend constantly to throw upon the market a number of unemployed labourers, who will offer their 'labour-force' to the purchaser at prices barely adequate to support existence. (Wicksteed 1884f, 390)

Although Wicksteed suggested that this matter "seems worthy of the most earnest attention", he did not "dwell on it further" because it was concerned with fluctuations around, and not with the actual explanation of, the (long-period) value of labour-force. It is, however, somewhat ironic that it was Marx who had drawn Wicksteed back to mention one of the two topics underpinning his initial support for George but which had received virtually no attention from him in

print after December 1882.[58] And while he declared that the analysis
of unemployment was "worthy of the most earnest attention", it was
not, so far as I am aware, a matter to which he was to return.

4. Aftermath

Although Wicksteed's analysis was by no means immune from criticism, there was, initially at least, no published defence of Marx.
Wicksteed and his supporters were, however, impatient for a response
with the *Inquirer* providing an early (and shameless) example:

> *To-Day* under its new management maintains its interest ... [R]eaders of
> the *Inquirer* will probably be chiefly attracted by Mr. P.H. Wicksteed's
> criticism of Karl Marx, for the sake of which alone the magazine is well
> worth buying this month. Whether we agree with it or not it is a model of
> fair and appreciative criticism, and his anxiety to anticipate criticism to his
> own theory is worthy of Darwin.[59]

Foxwell adopted another tack. Although he had played no direct
role in the production of Wicksteed's article, he was highly impressed.
After receiving and commenting on his copy, he had dinner at the
Beetons' where Wicksteed and value theory dominated the conversation.[60] Foxwell then used the club network to contact Engels. Shortly
after dining at the Beetons, he arranged to have dinner at his club,
the Savile, with Marx's collaborator. The conduits here were E.R.
Lankaster, who had attended Marx's funeral, and H.B. Donkin who,
as the family doctor, went to the Marx house on a number of occasions with Lankaster in the last years of Marx's life. Although Foxwell
recorded a "long & interesting chat" at the dinner,[61] it is not known
whether Wicksteed's article was mentioned. As noted above, however,
Engels had dismissed the possibility of a reply and it is not known
whether he actually ever read the article. It can, however, be surmised
that the arcana of Wicksteed's analysis was not part of the

---

[58] Wicksteed did note that Toynbee had not mentioned George's theory of commercial crises.
However, because crises were, on George's account, "only an acute form of a disease which is
chronic in progressive industrial societies we need not so much lament this omission"
(Wicksteed 1883c, 292).
[59] "Reviews", *Inquirer*, 15 October, 682. The previous week, Wicksteed had also written to Leon
Walras enclosing a copy of the critique, which Walras praised in response (Jaffe 1965, vol. 2,
12, 14).
[60] "Dined at Beeton's. 7.0. Discussion on Theory of Value – Wicksteed etc." Foxwell diary, 11
November 1884 (KGU 15$^1/_2$).
[61] Foxwell diary, 2 December 1884 (KGU 15$^1/_2$).

conversation, especially as Engels was accompanied by Donkin and Lankaster.[62]

Although Engels had attributed the publication of Wicksteed's critique to Hyndman's "direction" of *To-Day* (see above), Hyndman apparently had less control over the contents of the magazine. A note in *Justice*, the "organ" of the SDF edited by Hyndman, mockingly referred to "the generosity of Socialist editors" in publishing Wicksteed, commenting that "the late Stanley Jevons is a queer champion indeed for the Rev. P.H. Wicksteed to set up against such a thinker as Karl Marx." A further note on the following month's issue of *To-Day* praised the contents but asked: "Why is not Mr. Wicksteed's weak article answered?"[63] According to Bernard Shaw's subsequent amusing, if at times misleading, account, Hyndman had refused to respond to Wicksteed (Shaw 1889, 128). Shaw then decided he would write a reply, although, as he also later acknowledged, it was unsuccessful.[64] He was, then, presumably more than somewhat miffed when his contribution was criticized in *Justice* on the basis that he had mistakenly attempted to focus on the analytical coherence of Wicksteed's argument:

> We are not satisfied with Mr. Shaw's answer to Mr. Wicksteed; it seems to us that Mr. Jevons' metaphysical vagaries filtered through Mr. Wicksteed should have been met with a plain statement of the economic theory worked out by Marx. Surely this is *necessary* if a naturally clever man like Mr. Wicksteed can thus miss the whole point of Marx's exposition.[65]

This was a clear indication that Hyndman would simply refuse to engage with Wicksteed's critique. At most he would set out "a plain statement" summarising Marx's position. Otherwise, he did not respond or ran interference on Marx's critics. An example of the latter occurred in 1887 when the *Pall Mall Gazette* published an anonymous and often vitriolic review by Foxwell of the English translation of the first volume of *Capital*, which claimed that Marx's value theory had

---

[62] Donkin told Foxwell that, while he was "ignorant of the subject of his work", he had seen "a good deal" of Marx in the last years of his life. He also had a "great regard" for Engels "as I think anyone does who knows him. Marx too was one of the most delightful men in private life that I have ever known." Donkin to Foxwell, 14 November 1884 (KGU 15-61).

[63] "To-Day", *Justice*, 4 October 1884, 5; "Tell-Tale Straws", *Justice*, 1 November 1884, 5. Although the comments were unsigned, they were presumably written by Hyndman.

[64] Shaw (1885). It might be noted that, while he did not make much of it, Shaw identified a continuity problem in Wicksteed's account which, as Howey (1960, 123) noted, Wicksteed ignored in his response (Wicksteed 1885).

[65] "The Socialist Magazine", *Justice*, 3 January 1885, 2.

been *"réfuté sans réplique* by the Rev. P.H. Wicksteed, with unneces-
sary patience" (Foxwell 1887a).[66] When Shaw, who had by then been
converted to Wicksteed's position via his attendance at the meetings
of the Economic Circle, protested that "modern Socialism is not based
on Marx's value theory", Hyndman mocked him, in part by recalling
his response to Wicksteed in *To-Day*.[67] Hyndman was, however, willing to give space to the Jevonians in *Justice*. Wicksteed's *Alphabet* was
published in late 1888 where he again criticized the "delusion" of a
labour theory of value, extending the argument he had first made 4
years before.[68] The next year, *Justice* published a long letter by the
Fabian Walter De Mattos, citing the *Alphabet* to demonstrate that the
"Jevonian – Wicksteed" critique of Marx was correct.[69] This produced
a prolonged correspondence, including a letter from Shaw attacking
Hyndman, which, for the most part, simply restated the positions of
the two sides. Contemporaneously, *To-Day*, now edited by the Fabian
Hubert Bland, published what was ostensibly a review of the *Alphabet*
by Graham Wallas with responses by Hyndman and Shaw. While
Hyndman simply restated a Marxist position on value, Shaw used
much of his space to attack Hyndman, particularly his failure to
respond directly to Wicksteed (Wallas 1889; Hyndman 1889; Shaw
1889). It has often been noted that the Marxist responses to
Wicksteed were of a poor quality. It would be more accurate to say
that, for the most part, Hyndman and others (for example, Bax 1895)
simply failed to engage with Wicksteed's critique.

By 1895, however, Hyndman had belatedly decided he could attack
the analytical coherence of Jevons' value analysis. To do so, however,
he relied to a significant extent on the critique of Jevons' *TPE* in
Alfred Marshall's *Principles of Economics* (Hyndman 1895a, 1895b). In
the *Economics of Industry*, the Marshalls, without naming Jevons, had

---

[66] Foxwell did acknowledge, however, that the "most truly original and valuable parts of Marx's
work are those in which he describes the economic evolution of society. His ... vivid
perception and portrayal of the immense social significance of industrial development will be
long studied for the sake of the strong stimulus it gives to the economic imagination; a
stimulus greatly needed in this country" (Foxwell 1887b, 5). A subsequent remark by
Wicksteed suggests that he broadly agreed with Foxwell on that point (Wicksteed 1890, 530),
although he had appeared to be dismissive of Marx's more general historical analysis in 1884
(see the peculiar remark in Wicksteed 1884f, 391n).

[67] See letters by Shaw and Hyndman in the 1887 *Pall Mall Gazette*: 7 May, 3; 11 May, 11; 12
May, 11; 16 May, 2. In his May 12 letter, Shaw claimed that his reply to Wicksteed was
written "from the Ricardian or Cairnesian point of view". For discussion of Shaw's conversion
and attendance at the Economic Circle, see the references in note 5 above.

[68] Wicksteed 1888, 116–22; see Flatau 2004, 82–88.

[69] W.S. De Mattos, "Value", *Justice*, 8 June 1889, 3.

criticised the argument that "utility alone ... [is] the basis of Value", albeit (and confusingly) in the context of discussing a long-period equilibrium position ('Normal Value'). Although it was acknowledged that "the price of every commodity must be the measure of its Final Utility", Jevons' argument would hold only with a perfectly inelastic supply. Moreover, it was not "true [in general] that final utility determines value" since the latter depended on "the relation between the circumstances of supply and those of demand" (Marshall and Marshall 1879, 145, 148). Marshall developed that critique in the *Principles*, directly criticizing Jevons' "catena" in *TPE*. According to Marshall, Jevons had privileged the role of demand and thus failed to explain the roles of supply price, demand price and the amount produced in "mutually determining one another (subject to certain conditions) ... The 'cost of production principle' and the 'final utility' principle are undoubtedly component parts of the all-ruling law of supply and demand; and [each] may be compared with one blade of the scissors" (Marshall 1961, 817–20).[70]

Given that Hyndman had previously rejected analysing the coherence of the Jevons–Wicksteed discussion of value, it took some chutzpah for him to then cite Marshall's critique. It should be noted, however, that a number of the Fabians had already indicated they agreed with Marshall's position. One of the earliest signs of this appeared, somewhat ironically, in *Commonweal*, the journal of the Socialist League that had split from the SDF in late 1884. In November 1888, *Commonweal* published a note commemorating the drowning of Jevons four years before. Signed "S.W.", the note referred to Jevons "discovering, and compelling the economic world to accept, what is now universally regarded as the true theory of value". (Here, William Morris added an irritated editorial note that this was only the case for "the Jevonian wing of the 'orthodox' economists"). However, S.W. proceeded to argue that Jevons'

> principle that normal value is the ratio between the relative 'final' utilities of the commodities ... has now definitely succeeded the crude form of its rival, the Smith-Ricardo-Marx 'labour cost' theory. The two theories are, however, seen to harmonise, upon a proper recognition of the 'law of diminishing return,' and normal value may therefore now be stated

---

[70] This was the basis of the claim, often repeated since, that Jevons had privileged demand to counter Ricardo's privileging of supply. Although the validity of Marshall's criticism will not be pursued here, in my opinion, although Jevons' account was not without fault, Marshall's account caricatured the analysis in *TPE*.

indifferently as a ratio either between final (marginal) utilities, or between the respective costs of production of the most costly item of the contemporary supply of a commodity, according as the psychical or the industrial point of view is more apposite.[71]

If that account was confusing, the use of "normal value" suggests the language of the *Economics of Industry*. When the Fabian Graham Wallas reviewed Wicksteed's *Alphabet* in *To-Day* a few months later (see above), he argued that Jevons' and hence Wicksteed's account was one-sided because they

> paid too much attention to variations in the "utility" of commodities, *i.e.*, in the conditions of demand, and too little to the difficulty of producing them, *i.e.*, the conditions of supply. To explain the ratio of exchange by considering either demand alone or supply alone is to explain the position of the tongue of a balance by referring only to the weight placed in one of the two scales (Wallas 1889, 85).[72]

If some of the Fabians were echoing Marshall by the late 1880s,[73] his critique of Jevons in the *Principles* was subsequently widely accepted. At the turn of the century, Foxwell railed against that reading of Jevons as part of his argument that the emphasis on cost on production in Ricardo had led to Marx:

> It is conceivable that production might cease, & economic activity be confined to exchange of existing resources. Take the case of a siege, e.g. The phenomenon of value would still remain & still be of central and fundamental importance. There could be no question of the factor of cost of production as a determinant of value, but Jevons' principle of marginal utility would be as operative as ever. And this assumption ... is only an extension of what is today the fact in regard to an important class of commodities, occupying the attention of whole trades, e.g. the picture trade, old booktrade, curio trade, old furniture trade &c &c. Moreover, for short periods it is the case of almost all commodities.

---

[71] S.W. "Death of W. Stanley Jevons", *Commonweal*, 4 (135), 8 November 1888, 251. Could S.W. have been Sidney Webb?

[72] On this basis, Wallas argued that Marx and Wicksteed/Jevons could be reconciled: "Each grants ... the truth of the other's propositions, but attaches more importance to his own" (Wallas 1885, 83).

[73] Historians have noted that the 'Jevonian-Wicksteedian' influence on the Fabians has been exaggerated (see references in note 5 above). The exaggeration was due in no small part to Shaw who continued to retail his version of the Wicksteedian victory over Marx on value and his own conversion well into the next century. In a report of a discussion with Shaw, however, G.V. Portus recorded that when he objected that Jevons and Marx were both wrong because value "could not be derived from supply alone [Marx] nor from demand alone [Jevons]", Shaw could not provide a satisfactory rebuttal (Portus 1927).

The mischief caused by the undue emphasis laid upon cost of production since Ricardo appears to me greater every day I live ... The fact is that the 'exceptional cases' of Marshall & Ricardo are of enormous importance in practice, and his [i.e, Marshall's] typical case of strict mutual determination much more rarely reached than he assumes ... It is the great merit of Jevons that his principle of Marginal Utility requires none of these arbitrary restrictions of its application, but is ... as universal in its application as the phenomenon of value which it is put forward to explain.[74]

Given Foxwell's previous criticism that Wicksteed's *Alphabet* had failed to deal satisfactorily with the problem of continuity,[75] that later statement of fealty to Jevons was remarkably blind to the inability of a marginalist framework to deal with the prices of irreproducible commodities. Nevertheless, for the majority of the emerging economics profession, Jevons had been crucified on the Marshallian supply and demand cross. Since Wicksteed had taken the Jevonian position on value to its limit, that might, in part, help explain why the *To-Day* critique seems to have been generally ignored by that profession. One other factor, however, was at work in that regard. The *Economic Journal*, for example, generally regarded Marx on value as an uninteresting topic, so far as articles were concerned (Steedman 2004, 45). Edgeworth, the first editor of the *Journal*, indicated why that was the case: "We have much sympathy with those who hold that the theories of Marx are beneath the notice of a scientific writer" (Edgeworth 1921, 71). The *Journal* did, however, print a review of the third volume of *Capital* in which there was no mention of Wicksteed (Butlin 1895). And while high praise was bestowed on Eugen Bohm-Bawerk's critique, in *Karl Marx and the Close of his System*, of what became known as the "transformation problem" (Butlin 1898), mention of Wicksteed was again notable only for its absence. This suggests that Bohm-Bawerk's analysis was regarded as superior to and having

---

[74] H.S Foxwell to J.N. Keynes, 24 January 1901 (J.N. Keynes papers, 1/49, Marshall Library, University of Cambridge). Foxwell used almost identical language in his lectures. See the undated lecture notes, "Notes on the Theory of Value, Supply and Demand" (KGU 572-1, sheets 29 and 36).

[75] Foxwell was generally effusive about the *Alphabet* and had recommended that it be published by Macmillan. However, he did argue that "Mr. Wicksteed does not seem adequately to recognise the extent to which habit, custom, inertia, and social institutions give rise to discontinuity, even in large communities; nor does he deal satisfactorily with the determination of value in the cases, such as that of the labour bargain, where discontinuity must be assumed" (Foxwell 1889, 301; cf. Wicksteed 1888, 128). Foxwell also thought that Wicksteed had gone "too far" in claiming that exchange value was "never" a function of cost of production.

superseded that of Wicksteed, which was consequently ignored or forgotten. In the early 1930s, Lionel Robbins attempted to remedy that situation when he reprinted the critique in his edition of Wicksteed's *Common Sense*, lauding it as the "first scientific criticism of Marx's theory". Having "mastered the essential material", Wicksteed had shown that the labour theory of value was "false" and could only explain some "special instances of a more comprehensive theory" (Robbins 1933, vii, viii). By the early 1960s, however, Wicksteed had joined the list of unread classics in economics. In a presidential address to the American Economic Association, Paul Samuelson declared, that Marx had failed to "clear up the contradiction between 'price' and 'value' in later volumes [of *Capital*] … On this topic the good-humoured and fair criticisms of Wicksteed and Bohm-Bawerk have never been successfully rebutted" (Samuelson 1962, 13). As Wicksteed was not concerned with a contradiction between price and value, Samuelson had apparently not bothered to read the *To-Day* article. It was not until after the subsequent revival of interest in Marx that Wicksteed's analysis received its first careful and detailed examination (Steedman 1989).

Wicksteed's reading of Jevons on value, hinted at in his defence of Henry George and set out in his critique of Marx, could be characterised as the theoretical linchpin for his subsequent conceptualisation of cost as opportunity cost and for the supply curve as a "reversed" demand curve (cf. Steedman 1999, xxii–ii; Spencer 2003). However, while he made few published references to the *To-Day* article after replying to Shaw in 1885, he did contribute a comment on Bax's defence of Marx (see above), which was delivered to the National Liberal Club in 1895. In a cryptic outline of his 1884 analysis, Wicksteed noted that, in summarising his "vindication" of the "Jevonian Theory of Value", he had also "made out an irresistible case for land nationalization as distinct from the nationalization of the "instruments of production" generally" (Wicksteed 1895, 40), thereby signalling the original political context of his article. Drawing on his marginalist framework a few years later, he delivered his own paper to the Liberal Club, explaining why land nationalization could and should be supported from the position of economic "individualism" (Wicksteed 1901).[76]

---

[76] It has been claimed, in a reference to the 1880s, that "Wicksteed's … radical leanings … diminished subsequently" (Stigler 1986, 291). While it not clear what, precisely, 'radical

Wicksteed once amused himself by claiming that "I am sometimes supposed to be a Socialist by my friends who are not Socialists, and I am generally not considered one by my friends who are" (Wicksteed 1908, 761). Unless a land nationaliser of the Wicksteed (or Beeton) stripe is to be unproblematically designated a socialist, it is difficult to classify Wicksteed in that way.[77] Indeed, as noted above, he provided a justification for land nationalisation from the perspective of an "economic individualist". It would be more accurate to characterize him, at least until 1914, as a member of a radical faction in the Liberal Party, promoting land reform by taxation, supporting Home Rule, opposing the opium trade and the Boer War. It was from this position that he identified *TPE* as providing a more secure theoretical framework from which he could support land nationalization in a Liberal reform program where "socialists" were the principal critical target. Those political concerns were also evident in the next phase of his work. Following the publication of the Marx critique, Wicksteed began a series of lectures at the Economic Circle on the theory of interest. While he was dissatisfied with Jevons' explanation, one of the strengths of *TPE* was that it "laid the foundations of the true theory of interest, thereby at once confuting the logic and the methods and justifying the aspirations of Mr. Ruskin and the Socialists" (Wicksteed 1886, 646).

Conclusions

Wicksteed's path to his critique of Marx traversed a series of networks. He was already familiar with the Scottish radical Unitarians when one of their number induced him to read *Progress and Poverty*. Presumably via his association with (the Unitarian) Manchester New College and UCL, he then contacted H.S. Foxwell and, subsequently, members of his circle. As he began to read more widely in political

---

leanings' means, if the reference was to land nationalization, it is clearly incorrect (cf. Wicksteed 1918).

[77] Although Wicksteed characterized himself as a sympathiser with the 'social ideals' of socialism (Wicksteed 1908, 761), there was little sign of that in his review of William Morris' utopian *News from Nowhere*: "many readers may be partly convinced by it that life would be more endurable without misery, without smoke, without competition, without drudgery, without enterprise, without pedantry, without conventions. Can we reach such a state by Trafalgar Square meetings, and could we preserve it without stern self-discipline? Morris seems almost inclined to say, yes, to both these questions. 'O sancta simplicitus!' we cry" (Wicksteed 1891, 133).

economy, Wicksteed's initial belief that Henry George may have been the Kepler of the discourse was tempered by the realization that not all political economists could be reduced to a crude caricature of J.S. Mill. In particular, components of recent "new" approaches to the subject could be made consistent with George's analysis, while others could be used to buttress it by meeting objections to *Progress and Poverty*. If Jevons' *TPE* was performing the latter role as early as May 1883, that text also offered a much broader and different theoretical perspective, albeit one that could be yoked to a Georgian program of land reform. Wicksteed was able to work through those arguments in part by the generous space offered to his articles in the Unitarian *Inquirer* and by drawing on the encouragement and sometime collaboration of Henry Beeton, another member of the Foxwell network. Their defence of the liberal Georgian program also necessitated criticizing "the socialists", specifically the Marxism of Hyndman and the SDF. Jevons' utilitarian framework, helpful in the defence of George, could thus be turned into an attack on a labour theory of value.

Wicksteed claimed that, unlike the theory in *Capital*, Jevons' marginalist theory of value "is equally applicable to things that can, and cannot, be multiplied by labour ... is equally applicable to market and normal values ... and fits all the complicated phenomena of our commercial society like a glove" (Wicksteed 1884f, 407). This claim depended on a striking misreading of *TPE* for Wicksteed's key claims regarding the role of utility in a value analysis and the generality of the marginalist program.[78] It is important to stress that the conclusion reached here about the *To-Day* article does not rest simply on the misreading of Jevons. It is rather that, because of that misreading, Wicksteed's two principal arguments about value theory were demonstrably incorrect. His critique of the explanation of the value of labour-power then presented Marx's argument only in the terms of a marginalist theory, relying on a key assumption that was inconsistent with Marx. The result was that, regardless of whatever verdict might

---

[78] It was also not the case that Jevons' "'law of the variation of utility' fully accounts for all the phenomena of supply and demand" (Wicksteed 1884f, 406). While Jevons argued that 'law' was the principal explanatory factor, other factors were necessary to account for the 'laws of supply and demand'. Indeed, it was for this reason that Jevons never drew supply and demand curves (White 1989). See also, in this regard, the discussion of Jevons' analysis of labour supply in Spencer (2004).

be held about the analytical adequacy of the first volume of *Capital*, it remained untouched by Wicksteed's critique.

Acknowledgements

I am indebted to staff at Dr Williams' Library; John Holliday for information and materials regarding H.R. Beeton; and Takutoshi Inoue for copies of material from the H.S. Foxwell Digital Collection, Kwansei Gakuin University Library, before it went online. For comments and suggestions, thanks to Ben Fine, Peter Groenewegen, Prue Kerr, John King, Greg Moore and anonymous referees at this *Journal*. The usual caveat applies on responsibility for the final product.

References

Aberdeenprotest. 2017. "Rev. Alexander Webster, Unitarian Minister and Socialist (1840–1918)." *Aberdeenprotest Blog*, 29 January. https://aberdeenprot-est.wordpress.com/2017/01/29/rev-alexander-webster-unitarian-minister-and-socialist-1840-1918/

Barker, Charles Abro. 1955. *Henry George*. New York: Oxford University Press.

Bax, E. Belfort. 1895. "I. – E. Balfort Bax." In Levy 1895, 5–16.

Black, R. D. Collison. 1970. "Introduction." In *Theory of Political Economy*, by W. Stanley Jevons. Harmondsworth: Pelican.

Bonar, James. 1934. "Obituary. Henry Raimie Beeton." *Journal of the Royal Statistical Society* 97 (4): 693–4.

Butlin, F. 1895. "Untitled Review of Das Kapital, Vol. *III*. by Karl Marx." *Economic Journal* 5 (18): 249–51. doi:10.2307/2955771

Butlin, F. 1898. "Untitled Review of *Karl Marx and the Close of His System* by E. Bohm-Bawerk." *Economic Journal* 8 (31): 375–8.

De Vivo, Giancarlo. 1987. "Marx, Jevons, and Early Fabian Socialism." *Political Economy. Studies in the Surplus Approach* 3 (1): 37–61.

Dorfman, Joseph. 1949. *The Economic Mind in American Civilization, Volume Three 1865–1918*. New York: Viking.

Edgeworth, F. Y. 1921. "Untitled Review of *The Revival of Marxism* J.S. Nicholson; *Karl Marx* by A. Loria." *Economic Journal* 31 (121): 71–3. doi: 10.2307/2223292

Flatau, Paul. 2004. "Jevons's One Great Disciple: Wicksteed and the Jevonian Revolution in the Second Generation." *History of Economics Review* 40: 69–107. doi:10.1080/18386318.2004.11681191

Foxwell, Herbert S. 1887a. "The Textbook of Modern Socialism (First Notice)." *Pall Mall Gazette* 6 May: 5.

Foxwell, Herbert S. 1887b. "The Textbook of Modern Socialism (Second Notice)." *Pall Mall Gazette* 13 May: 4–5.

Foxwell, Herbert S. 1887c. "The Economic Movement in England." *Quarterly Journal of Economics* 2 (1): 84–103.

Foxwell, Herbert S. 1889. "Mr. Wicksteed's 'Alphabet of Economic Science'." *Inquirer* 11 May: 300–1.

Freeman, R. D. 2006. "The R. D. Freeman Collection of Foxwell's Papers — Its Rescue." *Journal of the History of Economic Thought* 28 (4): 489–95.

George, Henry. 1883. *Progress and Poverty. An Inquiry into the Cause of Industrial Depressions, and of Increase of Want with Increase of Wealth – The Remedy.* London: Kegan, Paul, Trench.

Hinely, Susan. 2012. "Charlotte Wilson, the 'Woman Question', and the Meanings of Anarchist Socialism in Late Victorian Radicalism." *International Review of Social History* 57(1): 3–36. doi:10.1017/S0020859011000757

Hobsbawm, E. J. 1957. "Dr. Marx and the Victorian Critics." *New Reasoner* 1: 29–38.

Herford, C. H. 1931. *Philip Henry Wicksteed. His Life and Work.* London: Dent.

Howey, Richard S. 1960. *The Rise of the Marginal Utility School 1870–1889.* Lawrence: University of Kansas Press.

Hyndman, H. M. 1889. "Marx's Theory of Value." *To-Day* 11 (65), April: 94–104.

Hyndman, H. M. 1895a. "VII. H.M. Hyndman." In Levy 1895: 41–6.

Hyndman, H. M. 1895b. "The Final Futility of Final Utility." *Transactions of the National Liberal Club Political Economy Circle* II: 119–33.

Inquirer. 1884. "The Rev. Philip H. Wicksteed and Mr. Henry George." *Inquirer* 12 January: 23.

Jaffe, William, ed. 1965. *Correspondence of Leon Walras and Related Papers.* 2 vols. Amsterdam: North Holland.

Jevons, Harriet A., ed. 1886. *Letters & Journal of W. Stanley Jevons.* London: Macmillan.

Jevons, W. Stanley. 1879. *The Theory of Political Economy.* 2nd ed. London: Macmillan.

Jevons, W. Stanley. 1905. *The Principles of Economics. A Fragment of a Treatise on the Industrial Mechanism of Society and Other Papers*, edited by Henry Higgs. London: Macmillan.

Jones, Peter d'A. 1988. "Henry George and British Socialism." *American Journal of Economics and Sociology* 47 (4): 473–91. doi:10.1111/j.1536-7150.1988.tb02078.x

Kadish, Alon. 1986. *Apostle Arnold. The Life and Death of Arnold Toynbee 1852–1883.* Durham: Duke University Press.

Kinnear, J. Boyd. 1884. "Doctrine of Diminishing Returns from Land." *To-Day* January: 58–71.

Laveleye, Emile de. 1882. "Progress and Poverty. A Criticism." *Contemporary Review* 42, July–December: 786–806.

Levy, J. H., ed. 1895. *A Symposium on Value.* London: King.

Marshall, Alfred and Mary Paley Marshall. 1879. *The Economics of Industry.* London: Macmillan.

Marshall, Alfred. 1961. *Principles of Economics.* Variorum edition. Edited by C. W. Guillebaud. 2 vols. London: Macmillan.

Marx, Karl. 1990. *Capital. A Critique of Political Economy*. vol. I. London: Penguin.

Marx, Karl and Frederick Engels. 2010. *Collected Works*. vol. 47. London: Lawrence and Wishart.

McBriar, A. M. 1966. *Fabian Socialism and English Politics 1884–1918*. Cambridge: Cambridge University Press.

Portus, G. V. 1927. "Bernard Shaw at Home." *Sydney Morning Herald* 14 November: 10.

Rattray, Robert. F. 1918. "The Late Rev. Alexander Webster." *Inquirer* 31 August: 279.

Rattray, Robert. F. 1946. "I Met – 7. Philip Wicksteed." *Inquirer* 9 March: 66–7.

Robbins, Lionel. 1933. "Introduction." In *Phillip H. Wicksteed, The Common Sense of Political Economy and Selected Papers and Reviews on Economic Theory*, edited by Lionel Robbins, vol. I. London: Routledge and Kegan Paul.

Salt, Henry S. 1897. "James Leigh Joynes: Some Reminiscences." Social Democrat no. 8, August. http://www.henrysalt.co.uk/bibliography/essays/james-leigh-joynes-some-reminiscences

Samuelson, Paul A. 1962. "Economists and the History of Ideas." *American Economic Review* 52 (1): 1–18.

Shadwell, John Lancelot. 1877. *A System of Political Economy*. London: Trubner.

Shadwell, John Lancelot. 1880. *Political Economy for the People*. London: Trubner.

Shaw, G. B. 1885. "The Jevonian Critique of Marx." *To-Day* III, January: 22–6.

Shaw, G. B. 1889. "Bluffing the Value Theory." *To-Day* 11 (66), May: 128–35.

Stedman Jones, Gareth. 2013. *Outcast London. A Study in the Relationship between Classes in Victorian Society*. London: Verso.

Spencer, David A. 2003. "The Labor-Less Labor Supply Model in the Era before Philip Wicksteed." *Journal of the History of Economic Thought* 25 (4): 505–13. doi:10.1080/1042771032000147533

Spencer, David A. 2004. "From Pain Cost to Opportunity Cost: The Eclipse of the Quality of Work as a Factor in Economic Theory." *History of Political Economy* 36 (2): 387–400. doi:10.1215/00182702-36-2-387

Steedman, Ian. 1989. "P.H. Wicksteed's Jevonian Critique of Marx." Ch. 7 in *From Exploitation to Altruism*, 117–44. Cambridge: Polity.

Steedman, Ian. 1999. "Introduction." In *Collected Works of Philip Henry Wicksteed*, edited by Ian Steedman, vol. 1. Bristol: Thoemmes.

Steedman, Ian. 2000. "John Emilius Lancelot Shadwell on Value and Wages." In *Contributions to the History of Economic Thought*, edited by Antoin Murphy and Renee Prendergast, 169–200. London: Routledge.

Steedman, Ian. 2004. "British Economists and Philosophers on Marx's Value Theory, 1920–1925." *Journal of the History of Economic Thought* 26 (1): 45–68. doi:10.1080/1042771042000187862

Stigler, George J. 1969. "Alfred Marshall's Lectures on Progress and Poverty." *Journal of Law and Economics* 12 (1): 181–226. doi:10.1086/466665

Stigler, George J. 1986. "Bernard Shaw, Sidney Webb and the Theory of Fabian Socialism." In *The Essence of Stigler*, edited by Kurt R. Leube and Thomas Gale Moore, 290–302. Stanford: Hoover Institution.

Sweezy, Paul M. 1949. "Fabian Political Economy."*Journal of Political Economy* 57 (3): 242–8. doi:10.1086/256809

Toynbee, Arnold. 1883. *Progress and Poverty. A Criticism of Mr. Henry George*, edited by Alfred Milner. London: Kegan Paul Trench.

Wallas, Graham. 1889. "An Economic Eirenicon." *To-Day* 11 (64), March: 80–6.

Walras, Leon. 1881. "Théorie Mathématique du Prix des Terres et de leur Rachat par l'État." *Bulletin de la Societe Vaudoise des Sciences Naturelles* 17 (85) June: 189–284.

Whately, Richard. 1832. *Introductory Lectures on Political Economy, Delivered in the Easter term, MDCCCXXXI.* 2nd ed. London: Fellowes.

Whately, Richard. 1853. *Easy Lessons on Money Matters for Young People.* 13th ed. London: Parker.

Whitaker, J.K and K.O. Kymn. 1993. "Did Walras Communicate with Marshall in 1873?" In *Leon Walras. Critical Assessments*, edited by John Cunningham Wood, vol. 3, 54–58. Routledge: London.

White, Michael V. 1989. "Why are there no Supply and Demand Curves in Jevons?" *History of Political Economy* 21 (3): 425–56. doi:10.1215/00182702-21-3-425

White, Michael V. 1994a. "Bridging the Natural and the Social: Science and Character in Jevons's Political Economy." *Economic Inquiry* 32 (3): 429–44. doi:10.1111/j.1465-7295.1994.tb01341.x

White, Michael V. 1994b. "A Five Per Cent Racist? Rejoinder to Professor Hutchison." *History of Economics Review* (21) Winter: 71–86. doi:10.1080/10370196.1994.11733151

White, Michael V. 1999. "Obscure Objects of Desire? Nineteenth-Century British Economists and the Price(s) of Rare Art." In *Economic Engagements with Art*, edited by Neil de Marchi and Crauford Goodwin, 57–84. Durham: Duke University Press.

White, Michael V. 2001. "Indeterminacy in Exchange: Disinterring Jevons' Trading Bodies." *The Manchester School* 69 (2): 208–26. doi:10.1111/1467-9957.00243

White, Michael V. 2004. "In the Lobby of the Energy Hotel: W.S. Jevons' Formulation of the Post-Classical Economic Problem." *History of Political Economy* 36 (2): 227–71. doi:10.1215/00182702-36-2-227

White, Michael V. 2005. "Strange Brew: The Antinomies of Distribution in W.S. Jevons' *Theory of Political Economy*." *European Journal of the History of Economic Thought* 12 (4): 583–608. doi:10.1080/09672560500370227

Wicksteed, Philip H. 1882. "Progress and Poverty." *Inquirer* 30 December: 839–40.

Wicksteed, Philip H. 1883a. "Mr. Toynbee's Lectures on Progress and Poverty [First Notice]." *Inquirer* 21 April: 243–4.

Wicksteed, Philip H. 1883b. "Mr. Toynbee's Lectures on Progress and Poverty [Second Notice]." *Inquirer* 5 May: 275–6.

Wicksteed, Philip H. 1883c. "Mr. Toynbee's Lectures on Progress and Poverty [Concluding Notice]." *Inquirer* 12 May: 291–3.

Wicksteed, Philip H. 1884a. "The Rev. P.H. Wicksteed and Mr. Henry George." *Inquirer* 12 January: 23.

Wicksteed, Philip H. 1884b. "Mr. Wicksteed and Mr. George." *Inquirer* 2 February: 68–9.

Wicksteed, Philip H. 1884c. "The Nationalisation of Land." *Inquirer* 16 February: 100–1.

Wicksteed, Philip H. 1884d. "The Nationalisation of Land." *Inquirer* 23 February: 115–16.

Wicksteed, Philip H. 1884e. "Some Recent Books on Political Economy." *Modern Review* April: 398–402.

Wicksteed, Philip H. 1884f. "Das Kapital. A Criticism." *To-Day* 2 (4), October: 388–409.

Wicksteed, Philip H. 1885. "The Jevonian Criticism of Marx: A Rejoinder." *To-Day* 3, April: 177–9.

Wicksteed, Philip H. 1886. "Reviews." *Inquirer* 2 October: 645–6.

Wicksteed, Philip H. 1888. *The Alphabet of Economic Science. Part 1. Elements of the Theory of Value or Worth.* London: Macmillan.

Wicksteed, Philip H. 1890. "Fabian Essays in Socialism." *Inquirer* 16 August: 530–31.

Wicksteed, Philip H. 1891. "Untitled Review of *News From Nowhere; or, an Epoch of Rest*, by William Morris." *International Journal of Ethics* 2 (1): 132–3. doi:10.1086/intejethi.2.1.2375819

Wicksteed, Philip H. 1895. "VI. – Phillip H. Wicksteed." In Levy 1895: 38–40.

Wicksteed, Philip H. 1901. "Land Nationalization." *Transactions, National Political Economy Club.* London: Pewtress: 214–38.

Wicksteed, Philip H. 1908. "Social Ideals and Economic Doctrines of Socialism." *Inquirer* 28 November: 761–3.

Wicksteed, Philip H. 1918. "Dr. Wicksteed and Henry George." *Inquirer* 21 September: 304.

Winch, Donald. 2009. *Wealth and Life. Essays on the Intellectual History of Political Economy in Britain, 1848-1914.* New York: Cambridge University Press.

The reception of Marx in France: *La Revue Socialiste* (1885–1914)

Michel Bellet

ABSTRACT
The aim of the present article is to provide context to reading, interpreting and using Marx from 1885 to 1914 in *La Revue Socialiste*, the main journal of socialist movements in France. The article first states some quantitative elements on the absolute and relative importance of the references to Marx and the words "Marxism" and "Marxist" in the journal. The central editorial line of the review – to restore a French descent to socialism and to try to found a socialism not exclusively "Marxist" – is then analysed. This line is maintained over time, with variations, in different national and international contexts. Finally, three key economic themes defining the relation to Marx in the journal are presented. Based on this quantitative and qualitative analysis, a brief conclusion stresses some of the most specific aspects of the socialist reception of Marx in France before WWI.

1. Introduction

In 1885, the creation of *La Revue Socialiste* (henceforth referred to as *LRS*) by Benoît Malon (Rebérioux 1987; Vincent 1992; Girin 2011; Vuilleumier 2011; Jousse 2017, chap. 5 and 9) was based on a commitment of openness with respect to the different branches of socialism. Especially after the sobering experience of the Paris Commune of 1871, and the outbreak of the Socialist movement, Malon wanted to offer "a collection open to all socialists of knowledge and good will" (in *LRS*, I(1), 1). In what was then, over a long period (1885–1914), the main journal of socialist movements in France[1] and one of the most significant journals in Europe, Karl Marx was by far

---

[1] *La Revue Socialiste* published its last issue on June 15, 1914, having been unable to cope with difficulties of distribution. On July 31, Jean Jaurès, contributor to the review since June 1892, was assassinated. On 3 August, Germany declared war on France. The review was relaunched only in 1925 by Jean Longuet, under the name of *Nouvelle revue socialiste*. Over the period 1885–1914, *La Revue Socialiste* was then the main journal linked to French socialism, with *Le Mouvement socialiste*, created in 1899 by Hubert Lagardelle, in an orientation often marked by revolutionary trade unionism and Georges Sorel's influence. This journal also ceased to appear in 1914.

the most important reference. Therefore, a careful analysis of the *Revue Socialiste* is a useful way to define the real influence of Marx on French socialist thought before 1914.

This analysis reflects the division between socialist organisations (1879–1905), but also the constitution of a unified party in 1905, the SFIO (Section Française de l'Internationale Ouvrière) influenced by the Second International (1889–1916) and its German section; a climate of specific relationship with mutualist and cooperative organisations; the Boulanger and Dreyfus crises; and finally some nationalist and imperialism tensions. Within this context, *LRS* was preoccupied with the promotion and redevelopment of the French sources of socialism, especially modern socialism ("collectivism"), against German socialism and its Marxist framework, or its Guesdist political equivalent (Jules Guesde, Gabriel Deville, Paul Lafargue). All the successive directors of this journal (Malon, Georges Renard, Gustave Rouanet, Eugène Fournière, Albert Thomas) served that line, with different critical views on Marx.

Our study is organised as follows. In Section 2, we provide some quantitative elements on the references to Marx and the words "Marxism" and "Marxist", during the 29 years and the 2158 articles of the life of the journal. In Section 3, we examine the central line of the review in its connexion to Marx: to elaborate a French definition of "socialism". This central issue, however, leaves open interpretive paths that are not strictly identical according to the successive directors of the journal, and according to some prominent people (Jean Jaurès, Charles Andler and Georges Sorel) – the real place given to "revisionism" in *LRS* has to be linked to this line. In Section 4, we deal with the three key economic themes defining the relation to Marx: economic materialism; historical evolution and the so-called Marxist fatalism; and finally the necessary complementarity between moral and economic concepts. Section 5 concludes stressing the desire to go beyond a "Marxism of the first book" or "the era of the first volume" of *Capital* and to consider Marx as already limited by the developments of "reality".

2. Marx as a reference: a quantitative overview[2]

Marx's name appears on p. 4 of the introduction to the first issue of the journal in 1885, and the references to Marx are by far the most

---

[2] The data are derived from processing carried out by the author from digitised texts accessible through Gallica.

Table 1. Most referenced authors in *LRS* (1885–1914).

	Page number	Percent/total pages of selected names (7945)	Percent/total pages of LRS (43833)
Marx	**2034**	**25.5**	**4.64**
De Paepe	1002	12.7	2.28
Proudhon	833	10.6	1.9
Fourier	587	7.4	1.33
Engels	551	7	1.25
Lassalle	463	5.8	1.05
Saint-Simonians	428	5.4	0.97
Bernstein	340	4.3	0.77
Blanc	286	3.6	0.65
Babeuf	221	2.8	0.50
Pecqueur	211	2.6	0.48
Blanqui	211	2.6	0.48
Bakounine [Bakunin]	195	2.4	0.44
Cabet	194	2.4	0.43
George	179	2.3	0.4
Leroux	124	1.5	0.28
Vidal	86	1.1	0.19
Total		100%	17.96%

numerous among the 13 most referenced authors in *LRS* over the entire period 1885–1914 (Table 1).[3]

If other criteria are introduced, this position is further enhanced. Thus, if we take into account the criteria of the dedicated[4] articles, we see that Marx, with 18 articles, is in the first row ahead of Caesar De Paepe (13 articles), Pierre-Joseph Proudhon and Constantin Pecqueur (9 each). Then come Ferdinand Lassalle (7 articles), Étienne Cabet and Émile de Laveleye (6 each), Gracchus Babeuf, Henry George, Piotr Lavroff, Michaïl Bakunin and Nikolai Tchernychewski (5 each), Friedrich Engels, George Bernard Shaw, Henri Saint-Simon with the Saint-Simonians (4 each), Georgi Plekhanov and Auguste Blanqui (3 each) and finally Pierre Leroux and Charles Fourier (2 each).

The strong presence of De Paepe in *LRS* is linked to Malon's defence of the so-called collectivist orientation. That of Proudhon is linked to the desire to represent another type of French socialism, associated at the time with revolutionary trade unionism and Sorel. *LRS* trade-offs between tendencies in opposition in the international and national socialist congresses sometimes presented as an opposition between "collectivists" and "mutualists", also play a role. The

---

[3] The other figures of socialism present in *LRS* but weakly represented are: Jean-Hippolyte de Colins, Dom Léger Marie Deschamp, Piotr Lavroff, Jean Meslier, Georgi Plekhanoff, Karl Rodbertus, George Bernard Shaw, and Nikolai Tchernychewski.

[4] "Dedicated" article means: article specially dedicated to the author and article presenting a text (usually unpublished) of the author. It is the presence of the name in the title that has been chosen as the criterion.

presence of Lassalle (who died in 1864), to whom Malon was particularly attached, although linked to the German context, is mainly due to the desire to refer to German socialism that was an alternative to that of Marx. The other names refer to the will to construct a French historiography of socialism (Pecqueur, Cabet, Babeuf, Saint-Simonians, Blanqui, Leroux, Fourier). However, this central orientation does not call into question the central place of Marx, nor the diversity of representations in *LRS*: English Fabian socialism (Shaw), American socialism (George), Belgian socialism (de Laveleye, often assimilated to the 'socialists of the chair'), Russian socialism (Tchernychevski and Lavroff), German non Marxian socialism (Lassalle).[5]

As regards the strictly dedicated articles (see Table 2), there are 18 papers and a note; but if Marx's name dominates the journal, it is also through questions about "Marxism" and "neo-Marxism" (Table 3).[6] As a benchmark, we provide an overall indication of the tone of these *LRS* articles concerning Marx: "positive" means support for Marx's theses (including different interpretations), "negative" means calling into question, "positive/negative" means critical support (Malon or Jaurès' position), and "indifferent" means no position.

In a second step, we expand the count by taking into account the presence of the term "Marxism" in the titles (15 articles and 2 notes, Table 3).

In evolution, according to three criteria (pages, citations, articles), the presence in the *LRS* of the name of Marx is indisputable (Figure 1). It is fairly regular, except for a peak in 1899, 1900 and 1901 (partially linked to the debate on revisionism) and through 1911 and 1912 (partially because of a new context: *La Revue Socialiste* became *La Revue Socialiste, Syndicaliste et Coopérative*, after the merger with the *Revue Syndicaliste*, with Thomas as editor-in-chief).

Data taking into account the terms "Marxism" and "Marxist" follow the same trend over the period (Figure 2). However, these references remain considerably more limited than those referring to the name "Marx" itself: citations are less than half as numerous

---

[5] In the minority representations concerning dedicated articles, we find: Collins (Jean-Hippolyte de Colins), Wilhelm Liebknecht, Svetozar Markovic, Carlo Pisacane and Wilhelm Weitling.

[6] If we counted the terms "modern" or "contemporary" socialism, "collectivism", "socialist systems", "historical materialism", "economic materialism" etc., the number would be higher (see below). For a view of the time, in *LRS*, of the use of the term "Marxism", see Paul Buquet, alias Pierre Boz (1897b).

Table 2. List of papers dedicated to Marx in *LRS* (1885–1914).

Author	Title	Date	Dimension of reception
Halpérine, Elie (1858–1936)	Karl Marx	1885 (tribute for the 2nd anniversary of Marx's death)	Positive
Malon, Benoît (1841–1893)	Karl Marx et Proudhon	1887	Positive
Rouanet, Gustave (1855–1827)	Le matérialisme économique de Marx et le socialisme français	1887 (series of 5 articles)	Positive/Negative
Lafargue, Paul (1842–1911)	La théorie de la valeur et de la plus-value de Marx et les économistes bourgeois	1892	Positive
Boz, Pierre, alias of Paul Buquet (1852–?)	Le matérialisme historique d'après Marx et ses disciples	1897	Positive/Negative
	La Correspondance de Karl Marx et ce qu'on appelle « Marxisme » (*Die Neue Zeit*)		Positive/Negative
Vandervelde, Émile (1866–1938)	A propos du *Manifeste du Parti communiste*	1898 March.	Negative
Slepzoff, N. (1836–1906[a])	Analyse du Troisième Livre du *Capital* de Marx	1998 (2 articles)	Indifferent
	Analyse du Deuxième Volume du *Capital* de Marx	1899	Indifferent
Rappoport, Charles (1865–1941)	Idées et faits socialistes. Le matérialisme de Marx et l'idéalisme de Kant	1900	Positive/Negative
Cornelissen, Christiaan (1864–1942)	La Dialectique hégélienne dans l'œuvre de Marx	1900	Negative
Marx, Karl (1818–1883)	Les Théories de Marx sur la rente foncière *Introduction à une Critique de l'Économie Politique. Document inédit*	1901 1903 (ed. Karl Kautsky, translation by Edgar Milhaud)	Indifferent
Bernstein, Eduard (1850–1932)	Une œuvre posthume de Marx. *Les théories sur la plus-value*	1905	Negative

[a]The author's real name would be Slepzoff Aleksandr Aleksandrovich. We thank F. Alisson for this information on an author often cited for his articles on Marx, but strangely unknown.

Table 3. List of papers dedicated to "Marxism".

Authors	Articles	Date	Dimension of reception
Fournière, Etienne (1857–1914)	Benoît Malon et le marxisme	1893	Positive/Negative
Renard, Georges (1847–1930)	Socialisme intégral et marxisme	1896	Negative
Boz, Pierre, alias of Paul Buquet (1852–?)	Les bases philosophiques et sociologiques du marxisme, Th.-G. Mazaryk	1899	Positive/Negative
L. M.	Une révision des doctrines marxistes (A propos du livre de Bernstein)	1900	Positive
Kellès-Krauz, Casimir de (Kazimierz Kelles-Krauz (1872–1905)	L'inventeur de la « crise du Marxisme »	1900	Positive
	Comtisme et Marxisme	1901	
Vandervelde, Émile (186–1938)	L'idéalisme marxiste	1904	Negative
Bourgin, Georges (1879–1958)	Materialismo storico ed economia marxista	1908 April (a note on B. Croce)	Positive/Negative
Walter-Jourde, J. (?)	Le néo-marxisme	1908–1909 (series of 4 articles)	Positive/Negative
Staudinger, Franz (1849–1921)	L'Organisation des Consommateurs et la Théorie marxiste	1912 Feb (transl. by C. Mutschler)	Positive/Negative
Andler, Charles (1866–1933)	Fréderic Engels. Fragment d'une étude sur la décomposition du marxisme	1913–1914 (series of 4 articles)	Positive/Negative

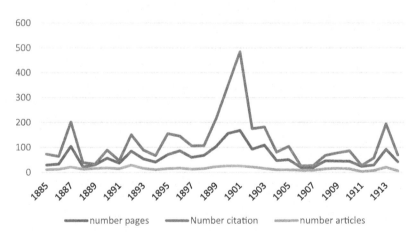

Figure 1. "Marx" in *LRS* (1885–1914).
*1914: only one semester of publication.
Number of pages: pages in which Marx's name appears (articles and usual headings).
Number of citations: number of mentions of Marx's name in *LRS* (articles and usual headings).
Number of articles: number of articles in which the name of Marx appears (excluding usual headings).

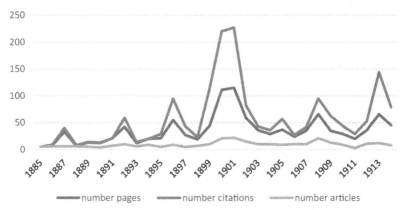

Figure 2.   References to "Marxism" or "Marxist" in *LRS* (1885–1914).

(1747 vs. 3587), and the number of pages and articles involved in *LRS* is also significantly lower (respectively 1082 vs. 1864, and 284 vs. 452).

Marx's importance can also be identified by taking the total number of *LRS* articles over the period, per year, referring either to Marx or to "Marxism" or "Marxist". It shows that it does, of course, focus on the targeted articles, but also that a very large number of other articles, on various subjects (religion, justice and law, literature, modern art, etc.) are also permeated (again notably more by "Marx" than by "Marxism" and "Marxist").

Marx, during the period, is thus indisputably the first reference: more than 25% of the citations of the "masters" of socialism, more than 20% of the 2158 articles published during the period, 13% of total articles with indirect permeation through the presence of the terms "Marxism" and "Marxist", and 33 dedicated articles – here in a broader sense – and a report.

3. Benoît Malon and the interpretation of Marx: a new historiography of socialism

The mass of references to Marx in *LRS* is organised around a dominant orientation: the will to restore the sources and the contribution of French socialism to international socialism, to counter the weight of a German socialism strongly influential in the Second International – with a Sozial-demokratische Partei Deutschlands (SPD) created in 1890 and soon powerful – and under Marxist influence. This editorial line should not be understood as opposition to Marx, but often as his integration into an older and broader heritage. Three elements support this line. The first concerns a heavy task of restitution, and sometimes re-invention, of the history of socialist thought. The second concerns the modern definition of socialism as "collectivism", and the third concerns the flexibility of implementation of this line, which allowed the management of the journal despite political and intellectual tensions between currents of socialism.

3.1. Malon, LRS and Marx's role in a history of world socialist thought

Malon and his successors were very actively involved in the constitution of a history of socialism that put in perspective the role of Marx, German socialism and its party (SPD), as well as that of those who claimed to be "Marxist"[7] within the LRS. To this end, the journal's management published a series of articles dedicated to past authors: these were then integrated into the French contribution to socialism, or more strictly, in the French roots of international socialism. Saint-Simon,[8] the Saint-Simonians (Saint-Amand Bazard, Hippolyte Carnot), Fourier, Leroux, Pecqueur, François Vidal, Blanqui, Proudhon (with more caution), and even Babeuf, Jean Meslier and Dom Léger Marie Deschamps, were thus subject to this re-reading. As Malon said, "the socialist home is elsewhere" (1887a, 314) and it had to be refocused on France: the thought (and actions) of Marx were an additional contribution in a wider project, whose continuity had to be restored. His contribution was, therefore, not denied but integrated into two ways.

---

[7] That is the Parti Ouvrier, with Jules Guesde, from 1882 to 1902, then, from 1902 to 1905, the Parti Socialiste de France (after merging with the Blanquists). In the party reunified in 1905 under pressure from the Second International (SFIO, with Jaurès as effective leader), this Marxism was often presented as the emanation of this International, with the powerful role of its German section (see the reaction of Fournière, 1905).

[8] This is the great era of official integration of Saint-Simonianism into a history claimed to be socialist. This will is particularly clear in Jaurès (1903). "Yes, I know that Marx has rendered this incomparable service to the proletarians, but I also know that in the thought of the proletarians of France, and in the thought of the proletarians of the world on whom our country's history has had decisive repercussions, I know that the name of Marx would be the most recent one, but he would not be the only one, if our history had not been broken, and it is because it seems necessary to me that the proletarians of France should regain consciousness of their past, of their entire past … that I now call on them to think quickly about the thought and the work of the great initiator that was Saint-Simon" (1903, 131).

First of all, Marx gave great importance to "economic determinism" in socialist conceptions. For most interpretations, this means that, of all the strictly social factors in the development of humanity, the economic factor is most important and determines all the others: it is the basis on which they erect the superstructure, it is the content of which they are the form. This "economic materialism" refers basically to a labour theory of value, which Malon considered to be "penetrating" (1887a, 315). Certainly, for Malon, the economic determination was not alone and there was a simultaneous evolution of various factors. "There is no opposition, but extension of one by the other, or rather complement" (1887a, 316). These expressions of economic determinism are obviously not random, and are linked to an exegesis of volume I of *Capital* and a few texts available or selected, most often through interpretations of the Marxists (Guesde, Lafargue, Deville essentially) and their political representation (the Parti Ouvrier).

The second contribution of Marx recognised by Malon concerns the philosophy of history. It was a question of confronting the idea that French theoretical socialism lacked philosophical principles, contrary to German socialism. Malon, in fact, admitted a French weakness in the demonstration of a law of evolution which would show that socialism is a historical category, a stage in the course of history, whereas this conception, together with the socialisation of productive forces, differentiates modern socialism from "utopian" socialism. If many precursors to this law of evolution can be found including Saint-Simon, Fourier and Robert Owen, it must be admitted that "the great glory of Marx and Engels will be to have given modern collectivism its scientific method, uncovered the great secret of social evolution, and so to speak brought it into the philosophy of history" (1887a, 241). Malon then contrasted the rich period of French socialism (especially with Pecqueur) with the period after 1850, which did not grasp the philosophy of history and the laws of development of the social process:

> The new French socialists did not understand [them] any more (even less perhaps) than their predecessors, the great utopians. It was a serious fault, a weakness for nascent collectivism ... Socialism in France, rich with so much glory, so many ideas, and so many works, had, after 1851, only survivors; while Germany produced Marx, Lassalle, Karl Grün. (1887a, 242)

To this reconsideration of the French heritage of socialism and Marx's role, Malon and *LRS* put in perspective the definition of the modern stage of international socialism as "collectivism". This definition actually referred to a much broader filiation. Marx, who was supposed to support this orientation, should certainly be included in this framework, but the French socialists (and in particular Pecqueur) were the initial formulators of "collectivism" – that is, in economic terms, the gradual socialisation of productive capital (land and labour instruments) used by associations controlled by the State: the central bank, the railways, the mines and canals; the substitution of associated labour for wage labour, in industrial, then commercial, and then agricultural labour; and finally the free use of his remuneration by the worker. For the Malonists, this theory has been neglected until Louis Blanc in 1846, Jean-Hippolyte de Colins in 1850 and especially 1868, but de Paepe[9] succeeded in popularising it with its new name of collectivism at the congresses of the International (1868–1869–1874). The modern stage of international socialism had, therefore, a French source.

In his six articles on "French collectivists" (1886–1887a), Malon uses Pecqueur's contribution[10] to put the role of Marx in perspective but also to push back the claims of the Proudhonians. Unlike the so-called utopian communism, it was a question of limiting socialisation to productive forces alone (and not to current goods and income which are associated with labour), with a recognised role in the intervention of the State – the conquest of the State was part of a necessary strategy. This also questioned mutualism and a legacy of Proudhon, which, according to Malon (1887b), negatively marked the socialist movement in the 1860s. From this point of view, the proximity to Marx was required. But the French roots of this modern socialism are still claimed.

As we can see, this interpretation of Marx's role and writings is highly dependent on the balance of power between the different socialist tendencies. Thus this particular status, together with the semantic uncertainties associated with the term socialisation and

---

[9] In his first article in *LRS* on the "silhouette of a collectivist society" (1888: 386), De Paepe himself invokes the role of Pecqueur and indicates that collectivism "is basically a sort of transaction between communism and individualism. It does not say that everything must be jointly owned, but only that some objects should belong to the great national community represented by the State, while others could belong to more circumscribed communities, such as the Commune and the professional group, and still others could remain private, individual property".

[10] Andler's famous commentary on Marx's *Manifesto* (1901) also underlines Pecqueur's very strong influence on Marx. In this attempt, Malon advances rather that Marx is an extensive reproduction of Pecqueur.

the precise relations with the economic role of the State, would be the subject of constant discussions over the lifetime of *LRS*, in connection with the re-reading of the texts of Pecqueur, but also, and above all, in relation to the possibility for the Malonians to play, according to varying periods and alliances, between socialist factions: in the face of the Guesdists, Pecqueur is often invoked to limit socialisation to the instruments of production and defend indirect state intervention, as a simple regulator and promoter. On the contrary, in the face of the Mutualists, Pecqueur is invoked to defend marked centralisation. This dual interpretation was for a long time that of the journal, for example for Renard, the successor of Malon as editor. Collectivism is then presented as a synthetic socialism: man is individual and social, and must, therefore, emancipate himself from the authority of the State in political and intellectual matters, hence socialism is "decentralising and libertarian in politics"; and, on the other hand, the State "regulate the production and distribution of wealth (not consumption)"; hence, socialism is "collectivist in economic matters" (Renard 1894, 514).

3.2. Malon'successors and Marx: inflections around a centre

In this reinsertion of Marx into a much broader lineage, the interpretation of Malon's successors to the leadership of *LRS*, from 1894 onwards, became more critical. Renard, in his 4 articles on "Le socialisme actuel en France" (1887–88), attempted a typology of the doctrines of socialism from different groups: he classified Marx and his followers among the modern socialist statists and considered that "socialist theorists have been more strongly influenced by German thinking for ten years", even if "French socialism was not completely Germanised" (1887, 3rd paper, 595). The importance attached to "economic facts" was still credited to Marx (1887, 585), but, overall, Renard made little reference to Marx, with the exception of his 1896 article on Marxism and Malon's so-called "integral socialism". The reading of Marx by Renard, which remained fairly rapid, therefore proposed, still in Malon's lineage, absorption of all economic and moral dimensions of socialism into a broader conception.

In the same way, Renard's successor as editor of the *LRS*, Rouanet (1898–1905), maintained the approach of reintegrating Marx into a wider field, based on the rediscovery of French socialist traditions. In his five articles (1887) on "Le matérialisme de Marx et le socialisme français" he wrote: "Marx's thought... is essentially anti-French" (1887, 307): this meant that Marx belonged to a philosophical tradition linked to the German Historical School of Law (especially Friedrich Carl von Savigny), opposing fact and law. This school was formed in reaction to the philosophy of the French Revolution, which, in connection with the Greek and Roman heritage, was based on an idea of law. Hegel drew up a synthesis of the two philosophies, but which subjected law to the evolution of the Idea and its successive achievements: the law becomes an integral part of the fact. Marx's philosophical thought is only the transcription of the Hegelian frame-work, replacing the evolution of the Idea by the succession of "forms of work". There is, therefore, a "purely German descent of Marx" (1887, 400)[11]. Compared to Malon, who admitted certain weaknesses of the French authors regarding the philosophy of history, Rouanet's project is to show the power of French philosophy and the role of the French Revolution as a phase not only of national but also of human development. All in all, for Rouanet, there are two Marxes: Marx the economist, whose proposals are correct even if they are sometimes radical; and Marx the philosopher and doctrinaire, who is, in fact, breaking with the tradition of socialism. Following in Malon's foot-steps, Rouanet praised, for example, an essay to rehabilitate the so-called utopian socialism, which he defended as "idealistic socialism". Against Marx's contempt for utopians, he defended, in particular, the socialism of 1848, which "had developed to the highest degree this moral side, appropriate to the philosophical state of the period" (1887, 531). In this lengthy presentation of more than 120 pages, which was taken up later in a book, there are only two specific references to Marx (the *Communist Manifesto* and volume I of *Capital*) and numerous references to Deville, Lafargue and Guesde. Rouanet finally proposed to get rid of the unsuitable part of Marx (a philosophy based on a material fatalism and the power of force) and to preserve the rest (the new emphasis on economic factors), in a development that takes up the Malonian framework of "integral socialism" or "scientific relativism in socialism": socialism, like modern sociology,

---

[11] In this reconstitution, Rouanet nevertheless feels the need to add a note indicating that Marx drew on French philosophy: but it is the simplistic materialism of Claude-Adrien Helvétius or Julien Offray de La Mettrie. By writing that the "Marxists were even more anti-French than Marx", Rouanet provoked heated argument with Deville.

must combine an evolutionary determinism with economic content and the recognition of the role of an "ideal".

The line of the last two editors of *LRS* is more distant from Marx's thought. For Fournière (editor from 1898 to 1914, but in partial retirement from 1910), there was indeed a diversion by Marx from socialist history. The rupture is on the question of individualism and contract. In his series of eight articles on "Les systèmes socialistes (de Saint-Simon à Proudhon)" (1903),[12] Fournière, in turn, reconstructed a historiography of socialist thought. The Utopians (e.g., Saint-Simon, Fourier) are not pre-figurations of the Hegelian dialectic, as Marx and Engels maintain, but they descended from French philosophy. Even economic determinism is present in Saint-Simon, Pecqueur, and Proudhon's writings: Marx simply expands it considerably. Socialism, because of this inspiration linked to French philosophy, is fundamentally individualist and contractualist. It is individualist because the French philosophy that inspires it is utilitarian sensationism, derived from Claude-Adrien Helvétius and Jean-Jacques Rousseau. For Fournière, this philosophy leads to a morality based on utility. But this morality is social because man is not alone: it is, therefore, necessary to seek the means to reconcile individual interest and social interest, in a socialised morality and social individualism. That means is the contract. Rousseau's social contract merely legitimises a state power through the supposed contractualisation of individuals with society and the total alienation of each partner. But Proudhon, according to Fournière, has opened a new path with the contract in a federative system. The contract, for Fournière, is not the origin of society, but it is at its end, in societies nearing completion. The objective contract exists in the spontaneous or voluntary association of independent individuals, who, by association, become free (1903, 1908). But Marx and Marxist socialism break with this heritage. They absorb the individual into the general community, "under a compact mass of individuals, not individual but undivided" (1908, 144):

> It was from the individual that Fourier and Proudhon began, and it was with him that they ended up. Saint-Simon himself did not deviate from the great individualist trend, against which only the democratic communists from Babeuf and Buonarotti ruled. ... What Marx added to the concepts

---

[12] The series was published in 1904. The direct references to Marx concern *Misère de la philosophie*, *Le Manifeste* (translated by Andler) and volume I of *Capital*, as well as Engels' preface to volume II.

of Fourier and Proudhon, both permeated by an economic determinism that he absorbed in his historical materialism, was therefore not a rectification of what they had been wrong and absolute, but a total erasure of the path imperfectly traced by them, and a deviation from the road up to that point followed by French socialism. (1908, 146)

Moreover, Marx and Marxist socialism make the state an end, not a means; the conquest of the state would then make everything possible. They are opposed to the contractualism of association, in which the State is not the master of individuals, but only an instrument of balance between the various groups. A system of federated associations ("sociocracy"), different from the Marxist "Social Republic" and different from the Democratic Republic initiated by the 1789 Revolution, would represent the modern socialist path.

The last director of *LRS*, Thomas, at Fournière's death (January 1914), but a general editor since 1910, still spoke of "practicing the most absolute eclecticism in the journal" ("We maintain the line", 1914, 5, 6). Moreover, during this period, we can see an expansion of references to economists (Antoine-Augustin Cournot, Léon Walras, Gaëtan Pirou and Vilfredo Pareto) in particular. In Thomas's texts, we also find the continuation of the reconstitution of a non-Marxist legacy of socialism (5 articles on Babeuf in 1904 and 1905, as a basis for what was supposed to become a book on Pecqueur). In short, Thomas was the first director of the *LRS* who, in the review, did not explain his relation to Marx. There is, therefore, for the first time, a sort of personal crowding out effect, even if references to Marx did not decrease – in 1913 and the first half of 1914, extensive articles were published: by Edmond Laskine, Andler, Otto Effertz in 1913; Andler, L.-A. Tcheskis (on Plekhanov), Ludovic Meister (on Max Adler) in 1914.

3.3. Variations around or outside a line: Jaurès, Andler and Sorel

The variability of the implementation of the Malonian perspective and its opening to various currents are also perceptible in the articles of a few prominent and well-known political and/or intellectual men: Jaurès, Andler and Sorel.

We have already mentioned Jaurès's active participation in reconstituting a historiography of French socialism. But, it is important to revisit the earlier publication in three articles (1892) in *LRS* of his complementary thesis on "Les origines du socialisme allemand", written in Latin and translated by Adrien Veber (4 chapters, including a final chapter on collectivism in Fichte, Hegel, Marx and Lassalle). Jaurès explains his reading of the origins of German socialism from Martin Luther to Lassalle and Marx from the following perspective: first of all, events flow from ideas, and history from philosophy; second, German socialism is profoundly linked to a philosophical thread based on a "certain dialectic which changes the forms of things and the relations of men" (1892, 643), on a human freedom based on a universal order of things (and not on a false individual freedom), with the claim of equality between men; finally, even behind the conversion of this dialectic to materialism (particularly in Marx), "in the deep folds of socialism survives the German breath of idealism" (1892, 644). Without going into the details of Jaurès' reasoning, we can clearly see that this line has a very close connection with the *LRS* relationship with Marx: Jaurès is indeed on the Malon line, but from a different perspective, since German socialism, in its philosophical origin, contains a patent or latent idealism. The proposed combination of German socialism and French socialism, in the name of a dialectic of history, of things and of the world, will ultimately be the victory of humanity itself: "dialectical socialism is thus in harmony with moral socialism, German socialism with French socialism ... " (1892, 167). In our view, this risky philosophical apparatus is based on some references to Marx. Concerning the social question and equality, Jaurès' reading of Luther is based on the passages of Marx's *Capital* on money and usury when the latter quotes this author (1892, 657)[13]. Likewise, according to Jaurès, Marx transposes the Hegelian dialectic into economics: relying on the famous introduction to the 1873 second German edition of *Capital*, Jaurès points out what Marx owes to Hegelian philosophy, but, for him, it is a positive filiation, whereas for other *LRS* authors it is this filiation that poses a problem. In the other articles published in *LRS*, Jaurès follows the line of complementarity between Marx and the French heritage of socialism, but with limited references to this author.

The presence of Andler in *LRS* remains minor and late (seven articles, from 1910 onwards) but represents an important and different orientation. This Germanist was known since 1901 for having participated in his own way in the evaluation of the originality

---

[13] The reference is not indicated by Jaurès, but it is Chapter III, but also Chapters VII, XI and XXIV, of volume I of *Capital*.

of Marx and Engels in the long historical introduction and commentary of his translation of the *Communist Manifesto*, which was generally used in *LRS*. This documented text stressed the heavy borrowings of Marx and Engels from French authors (Babeuf, the Saint-Simonians like Bazard, Pecqueur, etc.); but, it also underlined Marx's own contributions (awareness of the working class as a class, role of practice, materialism based on the role of tools, but without fatalism, exclusion from dogmatism). However, Andler's position was clearly changing. In his attempt to define a "socialist civilisation" in *LRS* (1910), he immediately opposed the German *Weltanschauung* (conception of the universe) to the French *Kulturanschauung* (theory of the destiny of culture), linked to the philosophers of the 18th century. Through the notion of civilisation, the question was to provide a moral foundation for socialism: socialism comes through moral experience, a "new mentality", a "total inner regeneration" (1910, 199), which was despised by the Marxist "socialism of the stomach" (below) and negative protest. In a reading with strong Nietzschean accents, where everything, production work and political forms, should be a work of social art, Andler nevertheless retained an ambivalent attitude towards Marx. He was not strictly within *LRS*'s dominant line on this point as on others: while the state is not a delegate of the capitalist class, it is true that capitalist forces try to make it its instrument. But if the state becomes democratic, under pressure from socialism, social laws favourable to workers would be edicted. Andler' series of four articles (1913–1914b) on Engels and the "decomposition of Marxism" was initially intended to form the basis of a work that had not yet been completed.[14] His publication was encouraged by a bitter controversy with Jaurès concerning German social democracy, by a certain isolation within the SFIO and also by his willingness to respond to the accusations of his "old hate for Marxism" (1913–1914b, 386n).

He, first of all, notes the diversity of Marxisms:

> We will actually see that there has never been a single Marxism. There were as many nuances of Marxism as there were interpreters. In the great community of Marxist convictions, the agreement was constantly imagined and crossed by unconscious heresies. (1913–1914b, 386)

---

[14] As Sorel would also repeat, for Andler the term "decomposition" also means "transformations of Marxism", with research into elements that can help to cope with the present, new, conditions of society.

He defended the thesis of a doctrine that Marx had deliberately left unfinished, and of a reconstruction and modification by the disciples (originally German). Engels, because of his particular relationship with Marx, was the first to change the doctrine, presenting it as a complete system, not only economically but also philosophically. After a reading of Engels' *Anti-Dühring* and its confrontation with recent ethnographic works, Andler returned to Marx's works by showing how the obscurities left by Marx (especially the relationship between productive forces and the mode of production, or the metaphor of "determination-in-the-last-instance" and the superstructure) are dealt with by Engels in an over-simplified way. Marx was more ambiguous. And above all, Andler argued that Engels' historical reading of the birth and evolution of the German state emphasised the role of commercial profit: in this way, Engels further underscored the weakness of *Capital* with regard to surplus-value and profit. Commercial capitalism would basically be at the origin of a surplus, prior to any exploitation of the labour force. By relying on Effertz (1913–1914b), Andler drew the consequences from his reading, as we will see below in the debate on the labour theory of value. However, if Andler was important in *LRS*, it is also because he pushed the debate on the French sources of socialism to an unexpected but latent end. Indeed, the question of the relationship with the German Social Democrats[15] gradually came to dominate his reasoning, with the questioning of a "Pan-Germanism" of German socialism. The terms of his texts triggered the controversy with Jaurès. In three articles on imperialism in German Socialism (1913–1914a), Andler questioned, not "classical Marxism and its current offspring", but a new revisionism, a "neo-Lassallian and imperialist revisionism" (1913–1914a, 448) – that would come from Bruno Hildebrand, but would be supported by Eduard Bernstein, Rudolf Hilferding, and even August Bebel: this revisionism would be based on the assumption that the convulsions created by a war would shake up industrial nations and promote socialism. This "bloody romanticism" (1913–1914a, 459) would mask a German nationalism preparing a war against France. As we can see, even with a cultured intellectual, the debate on Marx is not in fact independent of nationalist considerations running through socialism itself.

---

[15] There would also be a heated argument with Mehring about the *Manifesto* in *Le Mouvement social* in 1902.

The last important figure is Sorel. A Polytechnic engineer, and engineer from the École des Ponts et Chaussées, Sorel was an author of Proudhonian inspiration and was often portrayed as the philosopher of Revolutionary Trade Unionism (SR). Initially linked to the other socialist journal (*Le Mouvement socialiste*) in which he presented his theses on violence, Sorel, even before the break with this journal, intervened in *LRS* from 1900 (eleven articles). His interventions represent both the open-minded policy of *LRS* and a calculated trade-off between the tendencies of the socialist movement within the journal. Compared to the central line of the review, he refused to participate in the reconstruction of a French lineage of socialism in the face of Marx and more generally German influence. For him, the relevant cut was chronological and took place in 1848: before that date, approaches were dominated by feelings, in the sense of a call to kindness, enthusiasm, sympathy, even religion, accompanied by a claim to rights. With the philosophers of the 18th century, but also with Fourier, with the Saint-Simonians, and even more with Pecqueur, who believed that nature has provided everything it takes to be happy, "we can follow the same concept of an economy based on enthusiasm until 1848: the highest expectations were based on what was called the spirit of association" (1902a, 303).

According to Sorel, Proudhon and Marx are at odds with this concept. Rigorous socialism is based on the role of the division of labour and trade as a truly collective force, as Marx thought. Concrete knowledge of production mechanisms and technology in human labour (1902a, 299) is essential. In his first two articles, which focus on a critique of Anton Menger's legal doctrine of the right to the integral product of labour, he even argued that the rules of law also depend more and more on the progress of the productive forces, as some of Marx's texts proposed; but this does not exclude in any way Marx's recognition of the role that "the moral feeling of the mass" can play in retributive justice (1900, 412). The imperative of material progress incorporates moral change.

Moreover, for Sorel, Marxism has made it clear that socialism "is less a philosophy than a change that is taking place in all institutions" (1902a, 295). It is, therefore, not necessary to adopt a general doctrine, nor to be surprised that "neither Marx, nor Engels, nor any Marxist, has given a regular and complete didactic exposition of the system" (1902a, 297). This is due to the difficulty of highlighting regularities in economic facts, to the ongoing economic transformations, but also to the importance of action, which does not need to have "perfect scientific coordination" (1902a, 297). Abstract and uniform laws are not a scientific guarantee, and we must stop reading Marx from this so-called necessity. Many of Sorel's writings in *LRS* (particularly 1902b) stress the relevance of Marx's historical and analytical remarks, on industrial unions and the role of State in capitalism, the role of violence or force, usury, mergers, investments abroad, the role of commercial capital, and the employment contract as a sale and not as an association (including on the basis of volume III of *Capital*). Even if Marx does not succeed in making it possible to grasp all the transformations of capitalism, sometimes makes mistakes and is out of step with the reality of the twentieth century, he has identified an essential principle, namely that the theory of capital must not be freed from the practical struggle, and must "follow it step by step" (1902a, 539). In *LRS*, Sorel thus makes a measured and relative defence of Marx against the Marxists who want to turn his thinking into an absolute and ultimately utopian doctrine (like Engels); he questions the content of the texts, often relying on Benedetto Croce's work and on part of what he considers to be Bernstein's emancipation: "Everyone recognises that Marxism is in decadence today" (1902a, 519). The unity of the Sorelian analysis, sometimes delicate, is also made, as we will see more clearly below concerning the labour theory of value, on the necessary role of myths, capable of mobilising in a symbolic way a people, a party or a class beyond the logical imperatives. These myths – for example, the general strike by revolutionary trade unionists – are indispensable for action, even if they are not implemented. Consequently, Sorel appeared to be more interested in Marx's thinking as a social myth based on the opposition between bourgeoisie and proletariat than in the scientific nature of his intellectual construction.

3.4. The role of the revisionist debate

The debate over revisionism was an opportunity to strengthen the implementation of the *LRS* core line. While Fournière (1900) did not hesitate to identify revisionism with Malon's approach the line of *LRS* is more moderate. First of all, it should be pointed out that the so-called revisionist debate, opened between 1896 and 1898 in *Die Neue Zeit*, entered the *LRS* from 1898: Émile Vandervelde, in his critical article on Marx's *Manifesto*, resumed the debate on the Marxist law of the concentration and centralisation of capital, launched by Bernstein; in October followed Hendrikus Van Kol (alias Rienzi)'s article, which invoked the need for perpetual revisions in socialist theories, identifying some important themes and references (Bernstein, Karl Kautsky, Vandervelde, Jaurès). In 1899, the debate gained momentum with the article by Edgar Milhaud (January) who reported on the Socialist Congress in Stuttgart, followed in February by Einaudi's text on profit, based on the 1899 book by Antonio Graziadei (and which evoked more broadly the discussions in Germany, Italy and Great Britain with the Fabians), by Arturo Labriola's article in June, by a report on Tomas-Garrigue Mazaryk's book (1899) by "P. B." (Pierre Boz) in August, in November by Bernstein's own article – which was the preface to the French edition of his 1899 book – and finally by a very serious presentation of the "Bernstein, Kautsky and Bebel discussion" in an article by Dr Summachos (Charles Rappoport's alias). It can, therefore, be said that *LRS* had been in the debate since its inception, sometimes anticipating the publication in French of certain works (Bernstein's and Antonio Graziadei's in particular). Then, in 1900, there were three direct texts (by Kautsky, Bernstein and "L. M."), an account of the French version of Bernstein's texts by Fournière, a report by Olivier Prawdine (1900) on the German debates, an article by Casimir De Kellès-Krauz on the "crisis of Marxism" (and the intervention of other protagonists in this movement, beyond Mazaryk and Croce) and finally two directly linked articles by Rappoport. In 1901, Rappoport continued with two articles (1901b, 1901c) still linked to the debate, but with a specific and detached reading and a report on freedom of criticism at the Lubeck Congress (1901d). In the same year, Prawdine published two texts on the German debates: a review of Rosa Luxemburg's interventions on French socialism (1901a), and a review of new elements on the debate between Bernstein and Kautsky (1901b). The years 1902–1904 were much less lively (with the exception of Vandevelde 1904). But as early as 1905, Bernstein made a critical assessment of the interest in publishing Marx's *Theorien über den Mehrwert*, edited by Kautsky – there were also two critical studies of Maurice Halbwachs on

Bernstein. Two articles by Bernstein himself appeared in 1909 (on trade unionism and the revision of the social-democratic programme). In 1910–1911, Eugenio Rignano's two articles returned to the Marxist theory of value from the point of view of equity. Thus, in *LRS*, the references to Bernstein continued despite the decision of the German party of 1903 to officially condemn Bernstein's theses, which was often analysed as "the failure of revisionism" and its disappearance (by Jousse 2007 for example). There was still ample reference to Marx and Bernstein's "revisionist" readings in 1913 (Laskine on the historical materialism and interpretation of Rodolfo Mondolfo; Andler on Engels (1913–1914b), and, in 1914, articles on Plekhanoff by L.-A. Tchetsis). There was also, in the last issue of *LRS*, a paper by Meister (1914) on Adler.

Apart from its significant quantitative importance, the debate, the debate is certainly at the service of the Malonian line and is partly filtered out by this objective: the opening of a broader discussion on Marx's interpretation relativized the weight of this author within the German component of socialism and supported the attempt at a not exclusively Marxist socialism, or of an eclecticism sometimes claimed. But at the same time, it remained open and contradictory because it was also marked by the respect of a certain pluralism. The idea of an overlay between an orthodox/revisionist line and a Marxist/reformist current is not defensible: at this time, the fracture lines were diverse and evolutionary. The open debate on revisionism must, therefore, be seen in a broader context: *LRS* testified to this and made a significant contribution.[16]

4. Three central points of disagreement in economics

Three decisive points informed the various interpretations of Marx and Marxism in *LRS*. They related to questions about the development of socialism after Marx (a Marxist or non-Marxist socialism) and they were not independent of the power relations between French and international socialist currents. The first concerned variations on Marx's "economic materialism", with two themes: the labour theory of value and the question of cooperatives. The second concerned the laws of evolution of the economic system and the debate on Marx's

---

[16] Other French socialist journals have of course contributed to this (*Le Mouvement Socialiste, La Revue Blanche, le Devenir Social*).

catastrophism – and, as a consequence, capitalist concentration and the question of agriculture. The last point involved the role of morality in its relation to economic determinism and historical evolution.

4.1. "Economic materialism"

The expression "economic materialism" has in fact been associated with Lafargue's course of social economy (1884). This "Guesdist" link inaugurated in *LRS* a series of variations in criticism and defence, based on a selection (sometimes a translation) and an interpretation of Marx's texts (*Misère de la philosophie*, the *Manifesto*, *Capital* and the 1859 *Critique of Political Economy*). What was at stake was both the importance of the "economic factors", sometimes themselves reduced to "technique" or "tooling", and their relation to other factors (political, moral, etc.) in historical causality. At the same time, the economy was presented as the material and even materialistic basis of society.[17] The Guesdists gave a very strict and mechanical interpretation of this economic determination – expressed for example by the phrase "socialism of the stomach" (*socialisme du ventre*), an expression used by Guesde in a debate. Beyond the caricatures of Marx's own positions, and beyond the evolution of Marx himself, it is ultimately the question of the significance of historical materialism (Engels' term) and the role of economic relations[18] that is posed.

The general Malonian line of *LRS* is as follows: there is a positive achievement brought by Marx concerning the role of the economy, but excessive weight has been given to economic factors; therefore, other factors must be reintroduced. In this perspective, *LRS* published several texts challenging both the mechanical interpretation of Guesdists and revisionists (for example, the thesis of the elimination of materialism in Marxism put forward by Mazaryk 1899). It was Vandervelde (1904) who stressed, using several texts (including volume III of *Capital* or the *Theses on Feuerbach*), that Marx did not defend an economic exclusivism, but an economic preponderance, and did not underestimate the importance of ideological factors

---

[17] It should be noted that Marx's 1857 "Introduction", translated by Milhaud and published by *LRS* (1903) is not exploited in the debates on so-called economic materialism.

[18] This phrase "rapports économiques" is very rarely used in debates. Together with Vandervelde (1904) and Laskine (1913), Meister (1914), who reports on Max Adler's work on Marx, is one of the few to point out that Marx does not speak of an economic "matter" but of an economic relationship, and that the chapter on "commodity fetishism" in *Capital* is sufficient to question a certain interpretation of historical or "economic" materialism.

(1904, 169). According to these authors, one can find an idealistic Marxism, but never explicit because of the necessities of the political struggle against its opponents. Rappoport (1901c) finally argued that the most interesting, solid and useful point raised by Bernstein is this:

> Without rejecting Marx's considerable body of work as a whole, we will be obliged more and more to cut off the weak parts of it, especially its economic and materialistic exclusivism ... And contrary to what has been written quite often, it is Marx's method, even more so than doctrine, that will have to suffer from this criticism ... an exclusive and unilateral method by definition that makes any integral conception of society impossible. (1901c, 534)

Socialism must, therefore, cease to be exclusively Marxist, without falling, as Bernstein sometimes did, into scepticism about socialism (1901b). Other, more numerous *LRS* articles defended combination, synthesis or eclecticism. This is the case, for example, for Kelles-Krauz (1900, 1901), who gave an overview of the "initiators of the Marxism crisis" (Mazaryk, Antonio Labriola and Croce, but also Nicolas Kareieff) concerning economic materialism in order to refuse to purge Marxism of materialism, as Mazaryk argued, and defend a way of synthesis, giving each of the factors its place. This relativism certainly referred to the recognition that several readings are possible: but, like other authors in *LRS*, Kelles-Krauz admitted that the present historical phase temporarily encouraged a materialistic point of view based on work and its material conditions as the basis of class struggle. If a general interpretative monism was not desirable for the future, it was advisable for the present, and Marxism represented this monistic social philosophy. Léon Winiarski (1895) pointed out that the hypothesis of "economic materialism" in the hierarchy of social factors "is very useful in systematising the facts" but that a serious analysis does not allow the material factor to be placed above other factors (1895, 390, 394). On the one hand, measuring the degree of material development is not easy. On the other hand, it was impossible in sociology to define strictly where the influence of various social factors begins and ends. Many other texts pointed to the diversity of definitions of historical materialism within Marx's writings and are in favour of a reconciliation between what they call materialism and idealism (in the sense of ideal motivations of individuals or groups playing a role in the material structure), while questioning the validity of this reconciliation (e.g., Boz 1897b, 1899). Any monistic position is, in fact, metaphysical, but the terms of an overtaking are not very clear. The broad and serious exposition of Plekhanoff's ideas on historical materialism, in reaction to revisionism and revolutionary trade unionism, carried out by Tcheskis (three articles, 1914) clearly points to an exaggerated "objectivism" in some Marx's own formulas (sometimes followed by Plekhanoff), but at the same time the recognition of the phenomena of consciousness. Tcheskis linked these two tendencies around a path of synthesis that would be a philosophy of action, fundamentally pragmatic and linked to economic and social evolution, taking into account the new facts that emerged after Marx.

Laskine's three articles (1913) on the interpretation of historical materialism, based on Mondolfo's 1912 text on Engels, are also high-quality texts, which are still worth reading today.[19] They are not strictly in line with the review, while seriously emancipating themselves from strict orthodoxy. It is for Laskine to "defend the hardcore of Marxism against Marxism itself" (1913, 405), taking into account the debates stemming from German revisionism (Bernstein in particular, sometimes critically) but also Giovanni Gentile or Sorel.

> Whether Marx and Engels are to a large extent responsible for the persistent error ascribing to them an entirely different doctrine, cannot be seriously contested ... the economy can only be represented as the sole springboard of history through confusions of words and reductions denounced by Marx himself and by Engels as inadmissible. (1913, 6–7)

Laskine shows that there is no dualism in Marx between action and economic determinism and therefore no economic monism; there is no "refusal on the part of Marx to grant any manifestation of human activity either its own existence, autonomous development or, above all, the dignity of causality" (1913, 13). "The State is not the product of purely economic cause, especially it is not the passive product of it" (1913, 26–27). Force (violence) is also economic. Economics is the matter whose law is the form, writes Laskine by invoking the texts of Marx and Engels on the legislation of factories. This question of the status of the law in Marx's "economic materialism" also leads to the attempt to develop a legal socialism, which, according to Jean Neybour (1907)

---

[19] Laskine was the translator of Engels' *Herrn Eugen Dührings Umwälzung der Wissenschaft*, (*Anti-Dühring*), under the title *Philosophie, économie politique, socialisme (Contre Eugène Dühring)*, 1911, Paris: Giard & Brière.

would represent a real ground for reconciling materialism and idealism, the legal phase being presented as the third phase of development of socialism, after a materialistic phase based on the economy, and an idealistic phase based on the role of moral ideas (1907, 336). André Mater (1903 especially) attempted to synthesise the contributions of certain jurists (Emmanuel Levy, Maurice Hauriou, partly Anton Menger, partly Sorel 1900), presenting law as a science of facts, based mainly on jurisprudence. Legal socialism is revolutionary. The link to Marx was claimed, based on the *Critique of Political Economy*, and certain passages from *Capital* and the *Manifesto*: "I even believe that legal socialism could be presented as an application of this Marxist method, which, based on historical materialism, consists in determining the meaning of future changes on the basis of the meaning of present changes, and then, not by decrees abolishing the phases of natural development, but shortening the period of gestation and softening the evils of their childbirth" (1903, 13 – part of the sentence is actually taken from Marx himself). Legal socialism can also help to transform the police state into a managerial state, as socialism demands.

It is, therefore, clear that *LRS* did not represent the classical defenders of so-called economic materialism. The review gave way to a more subtle debate: beyond certain tactical aspects and differences between authors, there is a desire for creation, intellectual and practical innovation beyond Marx, but also in support of Marx. More precisely, two specific economic points were discussed in this perspective: the question of the theory of value[20] and the creation and management of cooperatives.

Let us deal first with what is said of the theory of value in *LRS*. Its defence is a first perspective. This was initially carried out in response to opponents not linked to socialism, even if it is visibly addressed to the various socialist currents. Lafargue (1892) sought to complement the 1884 polemic with the "bourgeois or official economists", Paul Leroy-Beaulieu and Maurice Block,[21] by showing that the labour

---

[20] Let us recall the sentence of Jaurès (1892, 25): "The theory of value is, so to speak, the cornerstone of socialism". It is likely that Jaurès actually drew this sentence from Marx's *Misère de la philosophie* (1847), who himself quoted Proudhon: ""[Venal] value is the cornerstone of the economic edifice" (I, 90). The "constituted" value is the cornerstone of the system of economic contradictions" (1847, I, 2).

[21] These 1884 articles are well known: an article by Lafargue in response to Leroy-Baulieu's work on collectivism, a response from Block, then a reply from Lafargue, followed by Block's last observations, then an article by Achille Loria. It should be noted that other, probably stronger opponents, Philip Wicksteed, Vilfredo Pareto or Eugen von Böhm-Bawerk, are not mentioned.

theory of value finds its foundations in many economists: in Adam Smith and David Ricardo, but also in Jean-Baptiste Say. Labour is the source of value, capital does not create value and therefore the added value can only be linked to labour. Questioning the labour theory of value means questioning the theory of surplus value, the reality of exploitation and all of socialism. The doctrine, with its foundation linked to human labour power, forms an indivisible whole, but its source lies in a large part in bourgeois economics: Marx only drew the strict consequences from it (see also Ely Halpérine 1885). As we have seen, Malon (1886–1887a, 315–320) and Jaurès (1892) supported the labour theory of value in a very general way. In short, it can be said that explicitly or implicitly, until 1898, the Guesdist interpretation of labour value is accepted in *LRS*. After the publication of volume III of *Capital*, the rather painstaking summary of volumes II and III of *Capital* published as early as 1898–1899 in *LRS* by Aleksandr Slepzoff remains on this line: Slepzoff argued that Marx had solved all contradictions victoriously, especially on the question of price and value in their reciprocal relations (1899, 210). The only exception was Auguste Chirac (1892), who rejected any possibility of finding a fixed principle of value, an intrinsic value or an absolute measure of it. Value depends only on social conventions for the same community. We can, therefore, only use the theory as an "anti-capitalist theory, a means of fighting against the seizures of capital: but in my opinion, Marx never wanted to make it a formula for setting up a socialist system" (1892, 662–63).

The irruption of the revisionist debate changed the situation. Since then, the dominant position in the journal was the questioning of the labour theory of value. When it was actually carried out, the reading of volumes II and III of *Capital* was in fact interpreted not as a solution but as an increase in the confusion on this question and the relationship between value and price. It was Van Kol (alias Rienzi) who, in 1898, for the first time with a reference to Bernstein, launched a more general questioning including the theory of value (1898, 418). Criticism can, therefore, be read according to the following interpretations.

Quite composite views support the elimination of the theory because it simply would not be necessary. For Fournière (1903, 280–81), who used Bernstein's argument, the law of value is only an ideological key to opening the doors of communism, a pure critical instrument, and socialism must "cheerfully grieve over the theory of value" and pose the real problem, namely the increased importance of the value of the individual in society (1908, 518; see also Boz 1899, who drew on Mazaryk 1899). On this interpretation, however, we also find the Sorelians linked to revolutionary socialism (Sorel, Arturo Labriola, Edouard Berth) and politically distant from Fournière: for instance Labriola (1899), while tearing apart the scientific value of Bernstein's theses in economics, indicated that it is appropriate to abandon Marx's law of value. Sorel criticised the reductionism of skilled to simple labour (a true "calorimetry", according to him), arguing that this type of labour comparison is impossible except to take into account the prices paid for wages and the price of goods (1902a, 395–97), just like Marx did. While stressing Marx's hesitations, and building on some of Albert Schaeffle's, Croce's and Pareto's works, he ultimately argued that Marx did not really seek to demonstrate economically the determination of value through labour employed in production. According to him, Marx put forward this theory as a symbolic call, in a particular situation at the beginning of the 19th century, a situation that was further examined in a sort of normal state that excluded evolutions. The article by Luigi Einaudi (1899), published rather surprisingly by *LRS*, skillfully presented 1899 Graziadei's theses (Graziadei 1899), but ultimately to push them further and bring down the whole of Marx's theses. For Graziadei, according to Einaudi, Marx's value theory was contradictory to the facts (role of monopolies, case of goods that are difficult to reproduce, the role of technical capital that goes on expanding). If the premise is wrong, however, it should be possible to separate the theory of profit from value analysis: profit no longer consists in surplus-labour but in surplus-product. If profits consist in surplus-product, there is nothing to prevent wages from increasing if at the same time the products of working hours that are devoted to the capitalist's advantage are increased (1899, 167). The theory of exploitation remains valid but is not based on the theory of value. On the basis of this presentation, Einaudi argued that there would be no conflict of interests between the capitalists and the working class. Marx had overlooked the human basis of economic phenomena: the relationship between the two classes depends on moral and intellectual conditions and a peaceful struggle between them is possible, as the English orientation of socialism would show (1899, 175). The point of view expressed by the philosopher-sociologist and jurist Halbwachs (1905b) is noteworthy because it amounts to validating an abandonment of the law of value, for broader methodological and sociological reasons. This author poses Marx, his revisionist critics and even the entire profession of economists with a fundamental problem of methodology. Inspired by François Simiand, Lucien Levy-Brühl and Émile Durkheim,[22] Halbwachs argued that the so-called theory of value is an abstraction of a normative type among economists, which responds to extralogical reasons, and in fact to practical rules (in the case of Marx a practical principle of remuneration favourable to the producer proletariat, or a principle of "fair" remuneration for all factors of production in the case of other theories of value). The theory of value is not a theory in the true sense of the word because it does not methodically submit to experimental data and direct findings of actual facts. Its subtle analysis is only the support of a preconceived idea. It wrongly rejects what it considers a flat and sterile empiricism – even Walras is referred to here for his theory of value. This viewpoint is well represented in LRS, either implicitly or explicitly, and reflects the desire to deal more directly with new social realities.

Other theses, very strongly represented in LRS from the revisionist debate, defend a combination of Marx's labour value and other approaches (in particular the so-called utility theory associated with Stanley Jevons, Eugen von Böhm-Bawerk and Walras: see for example Renard 1897–1898, or Christiaan Cornelissen 1901c, 1902). These theses remain compatible with the overall line of LRS: compatible with Malon's motto of eclecticism, compatible also with certain socialist measures (land collectivism for example) or with a more distant perspective of socialism.

Another analysis can also be found in the Effertz (1913), Landry (1906) and Andler (1913–1914b) group.[23] Adolphe Landry presented the new "ponophysiocratic" socialist system of Effertz in LRS (1906), a system emphasising the symmetrical role of labour and nature in the economy and based on a critique of the so-called "ponocratic" system

---

[22] The links between LRS and the theses of the journal l'Année sociologique concerning political economy are quite clear, and go far beyond the collaboration and direct presence of Simiand in the journal (for example, a collective article on agriculture in 1907 under the direction of Renard). The influence of Belgian sociology, through the role of Guillaume de Greef, is also important in LRS.

[23] Andler prefaced Landry's book on economic antagonisms, a preface reproduced in the 1906 Journal de métaphysique et de morale, under the same title as Landry's article on Effertz. Despite differences, this trio of authors refer to each other in LRS.

of Marx, solely concerned with the exploitation of labour. By purporting to organise society on the basis of the principle that goods cost labour and nothing but labour, Marx eliminated the role of other factors, land in particular. An equation is established between labour and land for the determination of value, resulting from the direction that men give to their demand, the importance they give to the products of labour and products of the land. Socialism must, therefore, choose a land-labour equation, because there is no indefinite increase in production, contrary to what Marx suggested. Landry, drawing on Effertz, suggested a more general shift to utility as the sole source of value (1906, 263). Andler (1913–1914b), moreover, argued that Marx defended the labour value only to offer hope and consolation for the workers and that a broader theory is needed. Socialist civilization should not be consoling, but constructive.

A final orientation was the pure and simple abandonment of the theory of labour value and its replacement by the theory of utility, but uncritical of this theory, contrary to Cornelissen's position: the five Walras texts in *LRS* (from 1896 to 1909) are representative of this orientation – it may however still appear to be a kind of synthesis, insofar as some consequences are compatible with a type of collectivism.[24] In particular, as it is well-known, Walras defended individual property but not that of land. On this basis, as well as that of questioning monopolies, Walras had no reluctance to call himself a collectivist and defend a "synthetic socialism (or synthetism)" (1896, 35).[25]

Co-operative organisation is the second issue linked to the debate on Marx's economic materialism in *LRS*. This question is related to the question of the labour theory of value, although it also refers to the classic question of the transformative or non-transformative role of cooperatives (see the inaugural address of Marx at the AIT, the letters of February 1865 to Engels and Johann Baptist von Schweitzer

---

[24] We must remember that it was *LRS* who published Charles Péguy's famous article in February 1897: "Un économiste socialiste: M. Léon Walras" and that this article was immediately followed by Jules Magny's article: "Un autre économiste socialiste: H.-M. Hyndman" (Hyndman is often presented as a dogmatic Marxist in England). It is difficult to better represent the strategy of *LRS*. It was Renard, former director of *LRS*, who gave the eulogy at Walras' graveside in 1910.

[25] The question of the various sources of socialism (and thus not exclusively Marxist) is also raised in Laskine (1912a) about Cournot. Based on the review of Cournot's 1877 *Revue sommaire des doctrines économiques*, Laskine argues that Cournot's analysis would be compatible with a "practical and moderate socialism, a legal, reformist or Fabian socialism" (1912a, 73).

and, in our period, the relationship between the cooperative movement, the trade union movement and the socialist forces). Charles
Gide's first article in LRS on "L'avenir de la coopération" recalled that
the victory of the collectivist or Marxist doctrine at the 1879 congress
had consecrated the break between a cooperative movement and a
collectivist or Marxist movement at the international and national
levels (1888, 589–91). In France, the attempt to merge the Union
Cooperative (Gide) and the Confederation of Socialist consumer
co-operatives experienced various vicissitudes from 1907 to 1912. This
different strategic and practical approach was accompanied by theoretical debates. The criticism of Marx's theory of value often led to the
hypothesis that surplus-value (and therefore exploitation) is realised
in exchange, and thus in the relations between producers and consumers. It is, therefore, not only production that must be socialised
but above all exchange and consumption, through consumer cooperatives. While a long-standing debate concerned production cooperatives, supported by Marx,[26] consumer cooperatives were condemned,
particularly by the Marxist school (Guesde, Lafargue in particular), or
set aside (Kautsky, Vandervelde), as Fournière (1908) pointed out in
his synthesis of the evolution of the socialist doctrine on cooperation.
Fournière defended a position integrating the role of consumer cooperatives and the union of the co-operative movement. LRS in italisque,
among the many texts on the cooperative movement, published also a
text by Fritz Staudinger, presented as the "well-known theorist of
cooperation in Germany" (1912, 151), claiming to complete "what is
still, in the Marx doctrine, truly fruitful" (1912, 156), by fully integrating consumers into economic relations.

Andler (1913–1914b) supported this viewpoint, which gave new
credit to the cooperative movement, and which was also reinforced by
developments questioning Marx's insufficient analysis of the role of
theft, robbery, and commercial capitalism monopolies in the primitive
accumulation, prior to the exploitation of the labour force. Sorel
(1901) also took up his Proudhonian theses on the decisive
importance of the socialisation of exchange or circulation to defend
consumer cooperatives and municipal services of warehouses and
retail trade.

---

[26] Sorel (1902) reports openly on this issue, from Marx's early texts to remarks on
Gotha's program.

4.2. History and laws of evolution: fatalism and catastrophism in Marx

In *LRS*, the second point of economic debate on Marx concerns the notion of historical law, the questioning of what would be Marx's fatalism or even an economic catastrophism. Here, it is the interpretation of Chapter XXXII of volume I of *Capital* ("The historical trend of capitalist accumulation") that is mainly at stake. This materialist fatalism would imply the continuous increase in the relative power of the proletariat, with the proletarisation of all sectors of activity, and, at the same time, the reduction in the number of members of the capitalist class and the disappearance of the middle class. What is also at stake is the law of increasing impoverishment of the proletariat, attributed to Marx.[27] Finally, what is discussed is the supposedly automatic and necessary transition towards overcoming capitalism, based on its internal economic evolution. *LRS* opened a significant debate on Marx's fatalism – which this time clearly intersects with the revisionist debate and the interpretative conflicts between Bernstein, Kautsky and Bebel – and echoes a large number of disputes through the analysis of economic data. As regards proletarisation, the data would thus be contrary: the social pyramid widens at its base, instead of shrinking, with the role of the middle classes of small, medium and large employees replacing the self-employed people. In fact, the class of capitalists would constantly expand, with it its global wealth and power. A problem of homogeneity would arise on both sides of the capitalist class and the working class (Rignano 1910–1911, who took up part of Bernstein's theses). Summachos [Rappoport] (1899) defended Bernstein on the statistical data on the evolution of capitalist society: it seemed indisputable to him that the proletariat is only a minority and that the rural population and other urban components will not be expropriated. This raised new strategic questions for socialism (alliances around the proletariat). As for the law of increasing impoverishment, "it is false" (Fournière, 1903; Cornelissen 1904 in particular), and, once again, Marx's use of the Hegelian method of the negation of the negation, that claims to demonstrate a victory for the proletariat because the economic evolution of capitalism, is said to be erroneous. Marx, in this perspective, was the

---

[27] There was often an assimilation between this interpretation and Lassalle's iron law of wages. However, in *LRS*, this assimilation disappeared at the end of the 1890s.

economist of the first phase of great capitalism (transition to the factory) but did not report on subsequent developments.

Nevertheless, some texts contested that economic fatalism could be attributed to Marx. For Rappoport, for example (1901a), a distinction must be made between the law of tendency and the law of evolution. The latter, which acts continuously, cannot be deduced from the former (which may be transitory); then Chapter XXXII would have to be interpreted using only the law of tendency.[28] Laskine (1913) believed that on this issue too, Marxism may be distorted by certain formulas used by Marx and Engels and that an attempt should be made "to protect the core of Marxism against Marxism itself" (Laskine 1913, 405). Thus, based on numerous texts, he indicated that catastrophism is fundamentally outside the spirit of Marx; it is the category of praxis, central to Marx, which, according to Laskine, prohibits both catastrophic (Labriola's criticism of Marx) and voluntaristic (Bernstein's criticism of Babouvism and Blanquism against Marx) interpretations. There are no absolute and necessary historical laws in Marx, as long as one grasps the role of consciousness that allows mass action and modification of pre-existing objective conditions.

In order to understand the precise content of the debate in *LRS*, it is also important to refer to two issues: concentration and agriculture. Most of the references to concentration imply that Marx is responsible for a law of increasing concentration of capital and diminishing number of capitalists, as indicated in Chapter XXXII of volume I of *Capital*. While most of the general texts accepted this reading (trend towards private concentration paving the way for public or social expropriation), the revisionist debate opened up questions more clearly. Cornelissen (1901a, 196) makes Marx's presentation a pure effect of the adoption of the Hegelian method; moreover, in addition to the possible discussions of an absolute or relative measure of the phenomenon of concentration, it highlights the contradiction between the thesis of volume I on this point and Chapter XIII of volume III. In order to validate an increase in the absolute mass of profit and a fall in its rate, Marx (1894, 325) argues that "the growing

---

[28] Volume III of *Capital*, with Chapter XIV on "Counteracting Influences", is never taken into account in *LRS* to understand the notions of law ("immanent laws", "natural law", "general law") and tendency ("historical tendency", "inherent tendency", "natural tendency", "tendency in contradiction with its other tendency", "constant tendency"). Even Cornelissen (1901a: 192–196), who examines precisely the chapter XIII of volume III, and notes a contradiction with some passages from volume I, does not make the link with the next chapter.

concentration of capital (accompanied at the same time, though in lesser degree, by a growing number of capitalists) is, therefore, both one of its material conditions and one of the results that it itself produces" (see Cornelissen 1901a, 192). This contradicts what is advanced in volume I, and shows, according to Cornelissen, that everything is possible in an infinite game of Hegelian dialectics. For Walter-Jourde (1908–1909, 484–85), it is useless to discuss whether Bernstein or Marx is right on this point, because, even if one can see an increase in the number of capitalists in France rather than a reduction, this increase occurs under the domination of the biggest and therefore the analysis of Marx is already realised. In order to overcome many uncertainties about notions (concentration, centralisation of capital, monopolisation, socialisation) sometimes used in the same paragraph by Marx, a real effort of rigour and measurement is made in the texts of Hubert Bourgin (1910) and Halbwachs (1905b). For Bourgin, "until now, the scientific theory of the phenomenon has not yet been stated" (Bourgin 1910, 487). Marx rightly understood concentration as an indicator of socialisation. However, in order to progress after the criticisms of Vandervelde (1898) and Bernstein (1899), a distinction must be made between the logical value of the concept of concentration (which is still confused) and its positive value, in terms of precise statistical data: Bourgin's conclusion indicates that since the middle of the 19th century (since the *Manifesto*), industrial concentration has clearly manifested itself – increase in the average size of industrial establishments, in the maximum size of these establishments and in the relative number of the largest establishments; decrease in the number of the smallest establishments; concentration of the working population in the largest establishments. Halbwachs' work (1905b), which also reacted to Bernstein's text, pointed out that the theory of concentration in Marx, contrary to value theory, is neither an ideology nor a practical ideal, and can, therefore, be studied as such, by detaching it from Marxism. The facts support Marx, "if not in agriculture, at least in industry" (1905b, 532). This raises the methodological problem of grouping different facts into the same set and therefore into a potential law (1905b, 533).

The case of agriculture precisely raised a lot of debate in *LRS*, insofar as the Marxist theory of concentration (in *Capital* I, chapter XXV, but also chapter XV on machinery and large industry, as well as in the *Manifesto*) appeared to be less verified there, and the status of small peasant property in an agrarian socialism had been hesitant. Élie Soubeyran (1908, 361) stated at the outset that "the small peasant property that Marx's economic materialism had condemned to vanish entirely in the name of the fatalities of a special and often treacherous science" had remained. Georges Desbons (1912) used French data from 1852 to 1908 to prove that peasant property was fragmented, and that "Marx's thesis must be rejected – at least in France" (1912, 440). However, using data over a longer period of time, he came up with a more complex but also much more general conclusion: capitalists do not possess the means of agricultural production as directly and to the same extent as the means of industrial production, but the essence of Marx's thesis is validated, because "they are nonetheless the main beneficiaries of agricultural activity ... and ... consequently, they enrich themselves to the detriment of the rural class" (1912, 451), especially because of the rural exodus and the domestic system associated with small property. Sorel (1901) argued that any general formula for concentration must be rejected and that in agriculture "the advantage of a production system does not obviously depend on the extent of an area or the size of the capital invested" (1901, 423). Finally, the collective text by Renard, Aimé Berthod, Landry, Paul Mantoux and Simiand (1907) recalled that the Ricardian theory of land rent, which indicates, in their opinion, that an element of agricultural product does not come from labour, is the basis of agrarian socialism. The monopoly of the landowner must, therefore, be abolished, as indicated by many economists (Marx, but also Herbert Spencer, Walras and John Stuart Mill). While the question of ownership seems to be clear, the question of the type of exploitation (small or large) is not – but the ambiguity of the term "collectivism" seems to indicate exploitation by the community, particularly in Marx, with a preference given to large enterprises. Using a number of French and foreign works, the authors argue that the division of labour cannot be applied to the same degree of precision and perfection in agriculture, that machines can be used unevenly according to relief, and that the development of land productivity depends less on advances in mechanics than on chemistry. Clearly, in agriculture, large exploitations do not have the same superiority as in industry. The authors, therefore, defend small-scale exploitation, accompanied by association in commercial matters as a means of organisation, "as Saint-Simon, Fourier and Pierre Leroux proclaimed" (1907, 240).

4.3. Marx, morality and economics

The third and final point of discussion revisits the question of morality. It is closely linked to the two preceding points, since, according to some interpretations, the definition of economic materialism, associated with economic fatalism in Marx (and even more so in orthodox Marxism), would leave little room for the role of morality and of the ideal in socialist motivations. One decisive feature of *LRS*, and undoubtedly of French types of socialism, is the recognition of moral factors. This moral claim presents three quite different aspects.

The first is the Malonian "integral socialism", which is the most represented in *LRS*. It is a matter of completing "the steel realism of the master", Marx (Malon, 1890, 149). French thought gave socialism its sentimental and idealistic reading; German thought, with Marx, gave it its historical and critical armor: "it only remains to combine the two forces, sentimental and scientific, to make the contemporary thrust irresistible" (1890, 137). More specifically, it is a question of recognising the role of the ideal, and the innovative effectiveness of moral forces. Moral regeneration and social transformation go hand in hand; feeling is the motor of human acts. Jaurès, Rouanet and Fournière upheld this line, although the composite character of this montage is sometimes underlined: in Malon's view, the coherence of Marx's historical materialism with Alfred Fouillée's theory of "forceful ideas" is not obvious; as well as the enigmatic mix made by Walter-Jourde (1908–1909) between energeticism and organicism, Marx and Charles Darwin, in order to recognize the strength of the ideal in a "Neo-Marxism".[29]

The second aspect, clearly marked by the revisionist debate, is that of a connection between Marx and Immanuel Kant. The starting point is the search for Marx's philosophical foundations, but it quickly leads, in *LRS*, to a contradiction between Marx's economic materialism and the recognition of the ideal, or more strictly a universal moral imperative.[30] While the manuscripts of the young Marx are almost

---

[29] The moral law is then a law of biology. The term "neo-Marxism" is very rare, with the exception of Walter-Jourde. It can be found once in Laskine (1913, 408).

[30] The issue of the support for Captain Dreyfus sometimes appears in the background of *LRS* debates, even if, apart from Guesde's position of withdrawal, divisions on this issue cross the various currents. See especially Berth (1901) and support for Dreyfus marking the entry of the proletariat into its phase of "living ethics" (Sorel), autonomous, universal, as Marx advocated (as opposed to a national and calculating socialism).

totally unknown, this interpretation, following Mazaryk (1899), tends
to indicate that the originally German Hegelian Marx would have
become a positivist economist under Franco-English influence and
that this evolution made it impossible for him to understand the role
of morality. There would be an amoralism of Marx: morality is only
historical (it only condemns what history has already condemned),
there is a historical function of evil, and morality is dependent on a
class, disguising class interests. However, contrary to Werner
Sombart's opinion, which is sometimes mentioned, a reconciliation
would be possible, with a return to Kant within Marxism. The
Kantian imperative of never employing a human being as a technical
means, an imperative ignored by capitalism, would be related to
Marx's desire to replace the reign of necessity by the reign of freedom,
or the alliance between "Denkenden und Leidenden" (a phrase from
the 1844 *Deutsch–Französische Jahrbücher*). Socialism would, in fact,
be the socio-economic realisation of the moral law: it would not be a
pure economic interpretation, but an ethical necessity linking economics and morality. Authors such as Rudolf Stammler, Karl
Vorländer, Ludwig Woltmann or Mazaryk, all referred to in the
articles of *LRS* (but there are no reference to Hermann Cohen and
the school of Marburg), and in forms which are not always identical,[31] wanted to renew Marxism, substituting for economic and external material causality a moral inner purpose. Lafargue's answer to this
debate is a classic response of Marxist Guesdism, the report of which
can be found in the polemic with Rappoport (1900b): any attempt at
reconciliation, or even correspondence between Kant and Marx, translates into an intolerable intrusion of idealism into materialism and
Kant is denounced as sophistic. In *LRS*, two texts express an interesting
willingness to displace the classical debate between materialism and
idealism. For Laskine (1910), for example, there is indeed a sense of
justice in Marx, and this author implied, rather than depreciated, the
influence of moral factors in history. The Republic of free men, the
development of each person's faculties (Marx's formulas), are obviously not foreign to Marxism; and class struggle is not morally indifferent either. For Laskine, however, there has never been perfect
coherence in scientific socialism and morality in Marx. And this is for
a fundamental reason: Marx did not seek a morality, but a science of

---

[31] Adler, mentioned once in a summary of Meister 1914, was still apart from the Neo-Kantians.

mores, in a sociological sense[32] – there are only moral facts and a science of these facts. Marxism is, therefore, opposed to traditional theoretical morals, just like modern sociology.

The return to Kant in a part of the revisionist debate is then explained: it is only a potentiality and a vengeance of morality suffocated by a science of morals; Marx sometimes gave in because he was torn between militant revolt and scientific method. Rappoport (1900a, especially about Woltmann) clearly refused to accept Kant's installation with Marx: "the alliance ... doesn't make sense. Kant has nothing to do with Marxism" (1900a, 168). It is not necessary to seek, as the Neo-Kantian Marxists wanted, an objective reality that would be animated by a metaphysical principle, an ideal, a goal. Any objective conception of the human ideal must be rejected (1900a, 173–4): objective reality provides us with objective conditions, means of combat, but the ideal, the goal comes from us alone, and the ideal is not an extension of objective reality. Rappoport's interpretation thus presupposes a form of irreducible and evolving autonomy of ideas based on objective conditions. In *LRS*, therefore, we find the opening of a debate on an underlying normativity in Marx's thinking, in honourable philosophical and sociological forms, with a real internationalised culture for some of the editors.

The third aspect of the moral claim is Nietzschean. It is found, with differences, in the Sorelians (Sorel, Berth) and Andler. It is a question of finding an acknowledgement of the role of the value transmutation that is important in Marx, in the face of a moral degeneration linked to capitalism or more precisely to its current exhaustion. To Sorel, this necessary transmutation, with a genuine morality of producers and consumers, beyond the recognised material well-being, must allow a new genealogy of the morality of free men without masters (present or future). The Marxist emancipation of the working class, linked to Marx's attachment to his labour theory of the value, is, therefore, worth a promise, but a valid promise only if it leads to a victory of true values, allowed by violence and the general strike. Andler, in his articles on socialist civilisation (1910), was not always very clear on these true values, but he clarified them in his later work on Friedrich Nietzsche. He used terms often common to those of Sorel and with the same inspiration (regeneration, absolute

---

[32] It should be noted that the title of Laskine's article is based in part on Levy-Brühl, *Morale et science des moeurs* (1903).

transformation of all things, power and vigour).[33] The bourgeoisie is a class in decadence because its organisational instinct has weakened, while others express this instinct, with the force of attraction of the new ideal.

5. Some concluding remarks

This study of almost 30 years of *LRS*' life has allowed us to identify several characteristics of Marx's reception in France. First of all, it has shown that Marx's direct place was important quantitatively, and much more important than references to the terms "Marxism" or "Marxist": he was the most frequently mentioned author in *LRS*.

We have shown that this role could not be examined independently of the power relations between socialist currents in the Second International, in divided socialist organisations in France, and then in the SFIO currents from 1905 onwards. The interpretations of Marx are filtered by this context. Other elements are also involved: trade union movements, cooperative movements, various crises at the national or international level. For example, the weight of the national and even nationalistic dimension in the Marx discussions of the period is all too often underestimated: the questioning of the "nationalisation of French socialism" in the face of German historicism, with, in the background, the strength of the victors of the War of 1870, plays a role: Chirac[34] (from 1887) and Fournière (1905, 664) probably gave the clearest texts in this respect. German hegemony is a strong theme (Chirac, Rouanet, Fournière, and later Andler on Pan-Germanism). In the debate concerning the penetration of Marxism in France, this line of reading remains unfortunately hidden (Prochasson 1989 excepted). Starting from French philosophy as a vector of socialism, some authors ended up associating the weight of Marx and Marxism with an anti-France and Pan-Germanist position – however,

---

[33] See the assessments at first fairly close to the two authors on the modern development of American capitalism: in Sorel, the American financiers are "the new conquistadores" (1902a: 311), in spite of a trivialization of the standardized product; in Andler (1910, 205): "the modern American production workshops translate the social feeling, with vigorous men working exactly and willingly ... in a good form of agreed discipline". See also the amazing articles of *LRS* on Taylorism in the company, generally affected by very positive values.

[34] Chirac is the fifth largest producer of articles in *LRS* with 31 articles over the period (behind Fournière (124), Malon (110) Rouanet (76) and Renard (38) and ahead of Jaurès (29), Rappoport (16) and Thomas (15).

Jaurès, Rappoport, Laskine (at least until 1916) and many others were not involved in this nationalistic attitude.

Nevertheless, *LRS* ensured a real debate on Marx, and it was often a valuable debate in a pluralistic framework. The "Marxism of the first volume" took an important but not fatal blow. The supporters of this very often limited reading of Marx are poorly represented in *LRS*: Guesde was absent and Deville wrote only one article although Lafargue wrote another five. Their place, compared to the first aborted version of *LRS* (1880) and to the journals of the previous period (especially the three series of Jules Guesde's *L'Egalité* (1879–1883), was very limited, even if the Guesdist shadow was felt indirectly (see Rappoport, 1900b). The number of contributors to an interpretation of Marx had grown and the quality had also increased. There was a widening of references to Marx's work and an internationalisation of the debate and cultural transfers. The dominance in *LRS* is indeed that of an enlarged socialism beyond Marx. There was at the same time an enlargement in the reference texts of Marx and the interpretations of them. The contingent of Germanists was more important than is usually indicated, and the hypothesis of a French confinement is erroneous. Of course, these references depended on the availability, at the time, of Marx's writings, and on the edition of the manuscript, especially by Engels.

Some currents are certainly missing, or almost absent, in this opening: first of all the German historical schools (except Cornelissen who reported on Sombart in 1903), even though the first edition of *Sozialismus und soziale Bewegung*, the Sombart conferences, were published in French in 1898, and two books by Gustav von Schmoller were translated into French (Schmoller 1902, 1905). Likewise, the emergence of Austro-Marxism is hardly envisioned, apart from a text by Meister (1914).[35]

This openness of *LRS* is undoubtedly less marked with regard to the discipline of economics: authors were more concerned with sociology or economic sociology.[36] The analysis of Marx's texts remained weak in economics. The role of the circles of the École

---

[35] In 1904, Adler founded the *Marx-Studien* with Hilferding, published in Vienna until 1923. In 1910–1911, with the Russian Marxist historian David Riazanov and Otto Bauer, Adof Braun and Karl Renner, he participated in the project for the complete publication of Karl Marx's texts.

[36] One can refer to the contents of the *Annals of the International Institute of Sociology* (1902) with its 300 pages of analysis on historical or economic materialism.

Normale Supérieure (Renard, Thomas, Andler, Bourgin, Buquet, Halbwachs) or the École Polytechnique (Sorel) were insufficient, and that of the autodidacts (Malon, Fournière) as well. Moreover, the contributors were often literary or philosophical writers: the economists were very few in number (Chirac, Laveleye, Hector Denis, Effertz in a certain way, Landry, and Milhaud). Halbwachs and Simiand[37] had trained as economists, but they were more interested in economic sociology. The discussions over volumes II and III of *Capital* remained limited. Only one reference to Ladislaus von Bortkiewicz's work can be found in *LRS*, in a review written by Laskine (1912b) on the German journal *Archiv für die Geschichte des Sozialismus und der Arbeiterbewegung*, with no real impact on the whole debate. Hilferding appeared because of his *Finanzkapital* (1910), but his 1904 text on "Böhm-Bawerks Marx-Kritik" is never referred to. By contrast, the contributions from the "outside world" are much more striking, especially with regard to the theory of value. On this theme, the French-speaking authors (especially Walras) argued for a non-Marxist socialism, and they had difficulties in finding good quality debaters. The regular economic columns of *LRS* were long held by the journalist, politician and director Rouanet himself; it was not until 1905 that the economist Milhaud kept the "Bulletin économique" of the journal. The difficulties also stemmed from the fact that the journal was not primarily a scholarly journal – unlike for example *L'Année sociologique*, founded in 1896 by Durkheim.

Finally, the effective opening up of knowledge and debates on Marx's texts during the period and the constitution of various "Marxisms" were to be severely weakened by the contradictions of the Second International and Social Democratic or Socialist Parties. The vote on military credits, the support for war (Guesde included) despite the initial anti-war posturing of the socialist representatives, the rallying to the cause of the *Union sacrée* and the terrible consequences of the First World War would break the international intellectual dynamic on Marxism. With rare exceptions, the new Bolshevik situation and a new orthodoxy, this time "Marxist-Leninist", would crush for a time the diversity of Marx's reception and interpretations in France as elsewhere.

---

[37] Both collaborated on the newspaper l'*Humanité*. Simiand intervened only once in *LRS*, in a collective article (Renard et alii, 1907).

Acknowledgements

I gratefully thank Gilbert Faccarello, Heinz D. Kurz, and two anonymous referees for their helpful remarks and suggestion.

Disclosure statement

No potential conflict of interest was reported by the author.

References

Andler, Charles. 1901. *Traduction historique et commentaire du Manifeste communiste de K. Marx et F. Engels.* Paris: SNLE Bibliothèque socialiste G. Bellais.

Andler, Charles. 1910. "La civilisation socialiste." *La Revue Socialiste* 309: 197–212; 310: 289–305.

Andler, Charles. 1913–1914a. "Ce qu'il y a d'impérialisme dans le socialisme allemand d'aujourd'hui." *La Revue Socialiste* 347: 446–465; 349 54–76; 350: 147–168.

Andler, Charles. 1913–1914b. "Fréderic Engels. Fragment d'une étude sur la décomposition du marxisme." *La Revue Socialiste* 348: 385–397 and 481–501; 349: 54–75; 350: 147–168.

Annales de l'institut international de Sociologie. 1902. *Le matérialisme historique ou économique, par Casimir de Kelles-Krauz, J. Novicow, A. Loria, Maxime Kovalewsky, R. de la grasserie, Ad. Coste, N. Abrikossof, F. Toennies, G. De Greef, Lester Ward, Ch. Limousin, A. Groppali, F. Puglia, E. De Roberty, René Worms, Alfred Fouillée, G. Tarde,* edited by Eduardo Sanz Y Escartin, and Léon Winiarski. Vol.VIII of the Travaux des années 1900 & 1901. Paris: Giard & Brière.

Bernstein, Eduard. 1899. "Réponse à mes Critiques Socialistes." *La Revue Socialiste* 179: 527–540.

Bernstein, Eduard. 1900. "Réponse à Kautsky (Observations personnelles)." *La Revue Socialiste* 183: 293–304.

Bernstein, Eduard. 1900, *Socialisme théorique et socialdémocratie pratique. Translation of Die Voraussetzungen des Socialismus,* 1899 by Alexandre Cohen. Paris: Stock.

Bernstein, Eduard. 1905. "Une œuvre posthume de Marx. Les théories sur la plus-value." *La Revue Socialiste* 242: 137–149.

Berth, Édouard. 1901. "De l'utopie à la science." *La Revue Socialiste* 196: 398–420.

Bourgin, Georges. 1908. "Materialismo storico ed economia marxista (B. Croce) – Sulle organizzazioni operaie (R. Musto)." *La Revue Socialiste* 280: 378–379.

Bourgin, Hubert. 1910. "Le socialisme et la concentration industrielle." *La Revue Socialiste* 306: 486–501; 307: 52–62; 308: 155–163; 309: 271–284.

Boz, Pierre. 1897a. "Le matérialisme historique d'après Marx et ses disciples." *La Revue Socialiste* 149: 595–602.

Boz, Pierre, 1897b. "Revue de la Presse Étrangère. La Correspondance de Karl Marx et ce qu'on appelle « Marxisme » (Die Neue Zeit)." *La Revue Socialiste* 154: 461–465.

Boz, Pierre. 1899. "Revue des livres. "Les bases philosophiques et sociologiques du marxisme, études sur les questions sociales", par Th. G. Mazaryk, professeur à l'Université de Prague." *La Revue Socialiste* 176: 250–252.

Chirac, Auguste. 1887. "Analyse socialiste." *La Revue Socialiste* 31: 1–25.

Chirac, Auguste. 1892. "Théorie de la Valeur." *La Revue Socialiste* 96: 659–675.

Cornelissen, Christiaan. 1901a. "La Dialectique hégélienne dans l'œuvre de Marx." *La Revue Socialiste* 194: 185–200.

Cornelissen, Christiaan. 1901b. "Les Théories de Marx sur la rente foncière." *La Revue Socialiste* 198: 690–715.

Cornelissen, Christiaan. 1901c. "Critique de la théorie moderne de la valeur." *La Revue Socialiste* 203: 185–200.

Cornelissen, Christiaan. 1902. "La valeur pré-capitaliste." *La Revue Socialiste* 206: 161–176.

Cornelissen, Christiaan. 1903. "Revue des livres: Werner Sombart, Der moderne kapitalismus." *La Revue Socialiste* 222: 758–762.

Cornelissen, Christiaan. 1904. "Des modes d'organisation technique de la production." *La Revue Socialiste* 236: 151–173.

De Paepe, César. 1888. "Silhouette d'une société collectiviste." *La Revue Socialiste* 43: 383–391.

Desbons, Georges. 1912. "Capitalisme et agriculture." *La Revue Socialiste* 329: 433–451.

Effertz, Otto. 1913. "L'étatisme des Entreprises et des Propriétés. Maximes d'application pratique du Socialisme et du Communisme." *La Revue Socialiste* 347: 349–371; 45–73; 311–333; 521–536.

Einaudi, Luigi. 1899. "Une nouvelle théorie du profit et de la production capitaliste." *La Revue Socialiste* 170: 163–175.

Fournière, Eugène. 1893. "Benoît Malon et le marxisme." *La Revue Socialiste* 107: 541–543.

Fournière, Eugène.1900. "Revue des livres. Socialisme théorique et socialdémocratie pratique, par Edouard Bernstein." *La Revue Socialiste* 182: 228–234.

Fournière, Eugène. 1903, "Les systèmes socialistes (de Saint-Simon à Proudhon)." *La Revue Socialiste* 218: 129–152; 219: 257–287; 219: 385–414; 221: 663–690; 224: 150–179; 226: 395–423; 227: 513–546.

Fournière, Eugène. 1905 "La Crise Révolutionnaire du Socialisme Français." *La Revue Socialiste* 107: 660–680; 247: 49–66.

Fournière, Eugène. 1908. "Le socialisme et l'association." *La Revue Socialiste* 288: 517–534.

Gâcon, Gérard, Latta Claude, Lorcin Jean, and Bourdier René-Michel. 2011. *Benoît Malon & La Revue socialiste. Une pensée en débat.* Lyon: Jacques André éditeur.

Gide, Charles. 1888. "L'avenir de la coopération." *La Revue Socialiste* 42: 574–597.

Girin, Charles-Henri. 2011, "La Revue Socialiste, à l'ombre de Benoît Malon." In *Benoît Malon & La Revue socialiste. Une pensée en débat*, edited by Gâcon Gérard, Latta Claude, Lorcin Jean, and Bourdier René-Marie, 185–193. Lyon: Jacques André éditeur.

Graziadei, Antonio. 1899. *La produzione capitalista*. Torino: F. Bocca.

Halbwachs, Maurice. 1905a. "La psychologie de l'ouvrier moderne. Étude critique." *La Revue Socialiste* 241: 46–57.

Halbwachs Maurice. 1905b. "La Science et l'Action sociale d'après Bernstein. Étude critique." *La Revue Socialiste* 245: 523–535.

Halpérine, Ely. 1885. "Karl Marx." *La Revue Socialiste* 3: 238–246.

Jaurès, Jean. 1892. "Les origines du socialisme allemand." *La Revue Socialiste* 90: 641–659; 91: 11–30; 92: 151–167.

Jaurès, Jean. 1903. "La Doctrine Saint-Simonienne et le Socialisme." *La Revue Socialiste* 224: 129–149.

Jousse, Emmanuel. 2007. *Réviser le marxisme? D'Édouard Bernstein à Albert Thomas (1896–1914)*. Paris: L'Harmattan.

Jousse, Emmanuel. 2017. *Les hommes révoltés. Les origines du réformisme en. France*, Paris: Fayard.

Kautsky, Karl. 1900. "Réponse à Bernstein." *La Revue Socialiste* 181: 26–39.

Kellès-Krauz, Casimir. 1900. "L'inventeur de la « crise du Marxisme »." *La Revue Socialiste*, 192: 695–707.

Kellès-Krauz, Casimir. 1901. "Comtisme et Marxisme." *La Revue Socialiste* 197: 589–605.

L. M. 1900. "Une révision des doctrines marxistes (A propos du livre de Bernstein)." *La Revue Socialiste* 184: 405–418.

Labriola, Arturo. 1899. "Bernstein et le socialisme." *La Revue Socialiste* 174: 663–679.

Lafargue, Paul. 1884. *Le matérialisme économique de Karl Marx*. Paris: Oriol.

Lafargue, Paul. 1892. "La théorie de la valeur et de la plus-value de Marx et les économistes bourgeois." *La Revue Socialiste* 93: 288–295.

Landry, Adolphe. 1906. "Un système nouveau de socialisme scientifique." *La Revue Socialiste* 261: 257–267.

Laskine, Edmond. 1910. "Socialisme, morale et science des mœurs." *La Revue Socialiste* 310: 333–350.

Laskine, Edmond. 1912a. "Cournot et le socialisme." *La Revue Socialiste* 325: 51–73.

Laskine, Edmond. 1912b. "Mouvement des idées. Une revue d'histoire du socialisme." *La Revue Socialiste* 332: 163–175.

Laskine, Edmond. 1913. "Le matérialisme historique et son nouvel interprète." *La Revue Socialiste* 337: 404–437; 338: 5–30, 115–125.

Malon, Benoît. 1886–1887a. "Le développement du collectivisme en France." *La Revue Socialiste* 23: 90–101; "Le programme de 1880. Suite des Collectivistes français." 25: 39–58; "Les Collectivistes français (suite). Pièces justificatives du 4ème chapitre." 26: 107–132; "Les collectivistes français (suite). Les précurseurs théoriques du parti ouvrier." 27: 221–243; "Les collectivistes français (suite). Les précurseurs théoriques du parti ouvrier." 28: 306–327; "Les collectivistes français. Les précurseurs théoriques du Parti Ouvrier français. Ferdinand Lassalle." 31: 57–68.

Malon, Benoît. 1887b. "Karl Marx et Proudhon." *La Revue Socialiste* 25: 15–22.

Malon, Benoît. 1890. "Les précurseurs du socialisme moderne." "Principes et tendances du socialisme contemporain." *La Revue Socialiste* 61: 22–51; 62: 137–166.

Marx, K. (1894), *Das Kapital. Kritik der politischen Ökonomie. Dritter Band. Der Gesamtprozess der kapitalistischen Produktion*, edited by F. Engels, Hamburg: Meissner. English trans. by D. Fernbach, *Capital*, vol. 3. London: Penguin Books and New Left Review, 1981.

Mater, André. 1904. "Le socialisme juridique." *La Revue Socialiste* 235: 1–27.

Mazaryk, Tomas-Garrigue. 1899. *Die philosophischen und sociologischen Grundlagen des Marxismus*. Vienna: Carl Konegen.

Meister, Ludovic. 1914. "Max Adler et le matérialisme historique." *La Revue Socialiste* 354: 509–518.

Milhaud, Edgar. 1899. "Le Congrès socialiste de Stuttgart." *La Revue Socialiste* 169: 1–34.

Milhaud, Edgar. 1903. "Introduction à une Critique de l'Économie politique (Document inédit par K. Marx)." *La Revue socialiste* 222: 691–720. (published by Kautsky K., translation by Milhaud E.)

Mondolfo, Rodolfo. 1912. *Il materialismo storico in Federico Engels*. Genova: Formiggini.

Neybour, Jean. 1907. "Droit et socialisme." *La Revue Socialiste* 268: 336–344.

Prawdine, Olivier. 1900. "Revue des revues. Orthodoxes et critiques." *La Revue Socialiste* 192: 713–722.

Prawdine, Olivier. 1901a. "Revue des revues. Questions diverses." *La Revue Socialiste* 195: 343–352.

Prawdine, Olivier. 1901b. "Revue des revues. Deux méthodes." *La Revue Socialiste* 200: 213–220.

Prochasson, Christophe. 1989. "Sur la réception du marxisme en France: le cas Andler (1890–1920)." *Revue de synthèse*, 1: 85–108.

Rappoport, Charles [alias Dr. Summachos]. 1899. "Idées et faits socialistes. La Discussion Bernstein, Kautsky et Bebel." *La Revue Socialiste* 179: 591–602.

Rappoport, Charles. 1900a. "Idées et faits socialistes. Le Matérialisme de Marx et l'Idéalisme de Kant." *La Revue Socialiste* 182: 160–175.

Rappoport, Charles. 1900b. "Idées et faits socialistes. Kant était-il « un sophiste bourgeois »? (réponse à Paul Lafargue)." *La Revue Socialiste* 183: 349–361.

Rappoport, Charles. 1901a. "Qu'est qu'une loi de l'histoire?" *La Revue socialiste* 193: 90–106.

Rappoport, Charles. 1901b. "Y-a-t-il un socialisme scientifique?" *La Revue socialiste* 200: 195–212.

Rappoport, Charles. 1901c. "Les « problèmes » de Bernstein." *La Revue Socialiste* 203: 513–536.

Rappoport, Charles. 1901d. "La liberté de critique au congrès de Lubeck." *La Revue Socialiste* 203: 575–584.

Rebérioux, Madeleine. 1987. "La Revue socialiste." *Cahiers Georges Sorel*, 5: 15–38.

Renard, Georges. 1887–1888. "Le socialisme actuel en France." *La Revue socialiste*, 1887, 33: 225–248; 35: 456–480; 36: 583–600; 37: 21–39.

Renard, Georges. 1894. "Notre programme." *La Revue socialiste* 112: 513–519.

Renard, Georges. 1896. "Socialisme intégral et Marxisme." *La Revue socialiste* 137: 560–576.

Renard, Georges, Berthod Aimé, Landry Adolphe, Mantoux Paul, and Simiand François. 1907. "Le socialisme et l'agriculture. Ce qu'on a fait. Ce qu'on peut faire." *La Revue Socialiste* 267: 229–240.

Rignano, Eugenio. 1910–1911. "Le socialisme." *La Revue Socialiste* 310: 306–320; 313: 30–43.

Rouanet, Gustave. 1887. "Le matérialisme de Marx et le socialisme français." *La Revue Socialiste* 29: 395–422; 30: 579–602; 31:76–86; 33: 278–294; 35: 507–531.

Schmoller, Gustav von. 1902. *Politique sociale et économie politique (Questions fondamentales)*. Paris: Giard et Brière.

Schmoller, Gustav von. 1905. *Principes d'économie politique*, translated by G. Platon, and I. Pollack, 5 tomes. Paris: Giard et Brière.

Slepzoff, N. Aleksandr. 1898. "Analyse du Troisième Livre du Capital de Marx." *La Revue Socialiste* 158: 195–210.

Slepzoff, N. Aleksandr. 1899. "Analyse du deuxième volume du Capital de Marx." *La Revue socialiste* 180: 641–662.

Sombart, Werner. 1898. *Le socialisme et le mouvement social au XIXème siècle*. Paris: Giard et Brière.

Sorel, Georges. 1900. "Les aspects juridiques du socialisme." *La Revue Socialiste* 190: 385–415; 191: 558–586.

Sorel, Georges. 1901. "Économie et agriculture." *La Revue Socialiste* 195: 289–301; 196: 421–441.

Sorel, Georges. 1902a. "Idées socialistes et faits économiques au XIXème siècle." *La Revue Socialiste* 207: 294–318; 208: 385–410; 209: 519–544.

Sorel, Georges. 1902b. "Les syndicats industriels et leur signification." *La Revue Socialiste* 211: 41–65.

Soubeyran, Élie. 1908. "La propriété et la question du sol." *La Revue Socialiste* 281: 405–428.

Staudinger, Fritz. 1912. "L'Organisation des Consommateurs et la Théorie marxiste." *La Revue socialiste* 326: 151–181 (translated by Mutschler).

Tcheskis, L.-A. 1914. "Les idées philosophiques et sociales de G. Plekhanoff. Son interprétation du matérialisme historique. Etude critique." *La Revue Socialiste* 351: 248–262; 353: 414–439; 354: 527–547.

Thomas, Albert. 1914. "Eugène Fournière est mort. "Nous maintenons la ligne"." *La Revue socialiste* 349: 5–9.

Vandervelde, Émile. 1898. "A propos du Manifeste du Parti communiste." *La Revue Socialiste* 159: 327–343.

Vandervelde, Émile. 1904. "L'idéalisme marxiste." *La Revue Socialiste* 230: 162–176.

Van Kol, Hendrikus [alias Rienzi]. 1898. "Arrière les dogmes!" *La Revue Socialiste* 166: 418–425.

Vincent, Steve K. 1992. *Between Marxism and Anarchism: Benoît Malon and French Reformist Socialism.* Berkeley-Los Angeles-Oxford: University of California Press.

Vuilleumier, Marc. 2011. "Aux origines de *La Revue socialiste* (1877–1882)." In *Benoît Malon & La Revue Socialiste. Une pensée en débat*, edited by Gérard Gâcon, Claude Latta, Jean Lorcin, and René-Marie Bourdier, 23–95. Lyon: Jacques André éditeur,

Walras, Léon. 1896. "Théorie de la propriété. Suite et fin." *La Revue Socialiste* 139: 23–35.

Walter-Jourde, J. 1908–1909. "Le Néo-Marxisme." *La Revue Socialiste* 288: 481–500; 290: 150–164; 292: 326–342; 294: 529–543; 299: 998–1012.

Winiarski, Léon. 1895. "Le Matérialisme économique et la Psychologie sociale." *La Revue Socialiste* 130: 388–410; 131: 998–1012.

Index

abbreviated forms of commonly-used nouns 153–4
absolute rent (AR) 10, 271–4, 282–9, 292–3, 297–311, 316–19; an example of 301–2; interpreted as a rent paid by monopoly pricing 308–11; limits of 302–5, 309–11, 319; and transformation of values into prices 299–301
abstract labour 10, 53, 129–33, 373, 380, 389–91
Adoratsky, Vladimir Viktorovich 4
advances and expenditures of money 375–6
agricultural improvement 103
agro-chemistry 279, 281, 287, 294
alienation 7–8, 46–62, 67–71; critique of economic categories 49–56; in exchange and in production 56–9; *internal* and *external* critiques of 53–6; of labour 67; terminology of 67–8
Alison, Archibald 103
Althusser, Louis 46, 55
analytical developments 10–11
analytical Marxism 6
Anderson, James 263, 274–7, 287, 293–4
Andler, Charles 173, 491, 503–6, 517–19, 526
Andrews, David 7
Angaut, Jean-Christophe 50
animals, nature of 84
Aristotle 57, 84–7, 121, 129, 418–19, 425
Arnon, Arie 360
Arthur, Christopher J. 81
"artistic whole" 119–20
Assous, Michaël 11
autodidacts 528–9

Backhaus, Georg 5
balanced growth 322–6, 329–30, 334, 340, 348, 439, 446

Ball, Michael 311
Bank of France (BOF) 253–6
banking school economists 360, 378–81
barter 367
base text, authorship of 146–8, 161–5
basic and *non-basic* products 236–9
Bauer, Bruno 18, 22, 30, 35–41, 49, 164
Bauer, Edgar 7, 15–22, 25, 28, 31–4, 40–3
beauty as a social concept 84
Bebel, August 506, 509, 520
Bellet, Michel 11
Benetti, Carlo 10
Béraud, Alain 10
Berlin Young Hegelians (*die Freien*) 15, 20–4, 28–43; *see also* Young Hegelian movement
Bernstein, Eduard 78, 506–16, 522
Berth, Édouard 526
Bismarck, Otto von 425
Blanc, Louis 499
Blaug, Mark 92
Block, Maurice 514
Böhm-Bawerk, Eugen von 308, 389, 391, 410, 517, 529
Books of Crisis 248–52, 257, 261
Bortkiewicz, Ladislaus von 297–8, 305–8, 316–17, 393–4, 410–11, 529
bourgeois mode of production 67, 80
bourgeois society 52, 56, 61, 70, 363–4, 527
Bourgin, Hubert 522
Boyer des Roches, Jerôme 360
Boz, Pierre (P.B.) 509
Breckman, Warren 5
British Museum 278
Brody, András 236, 399
Brunhoff, Suzanne de 360
Brussels notebooks 180
Buhl, Ludwig 18
Bukharin, Nikolai 396, 411
business cycle 432, 434, 438

Cantillon, Richard 381
capital: as alienation 64–7; as an "alien power" 62–4; forms of 362–3; organic composition of 300–2, 306, 309–10, 315, 398, 441
Capital (Das Kapital) 1–10, 46–7, 55, 62–7, 71, 75, 82, 86, 92–110, 113, 119–23, 126, 128, 169–70, 178–89, 195–8, 202–5, 210–11, 221, 225, 229, 231, 239, 244–5, 251, 262–7, 273, 278, 280, 292, 316, 322, 332, 358–60, 367, 373, 388, 407, 410, 418–19, 424, 491, 498, 504–8, 514–15, 520–1, 529
capitalism 66–8, 169–73, 177–9, 182–6, 190–1, 423, 432, 441, 516, 520–2; origins of 179, 183, 190–1
capitalist mode of production 124–5, 136–41, 171–2, 178–80, 185, 305
Carver, Terrell 48, 55, 148
catastrophism 510–11, 520–1
censorship 19–20, 24, 27, 32
Charasoff, Georg 388–9, 394–7, 411
Chinese language 166
Chirac, Auguste 515, 527
"chrematistics" 177
Christianity 36–7
circular flows of commodities 209
circulation of money 235–6, 361, 368–72, 375–80; iron law of 375
class struggle 412, 430–1, 441–6, 449, 525
clearances, Scottish 180–1
Cohen, Gerald 6, 81
Cohen, Hermann 525
Colins, Jean-Hippolyte de 499
collectivism 491–2, 497–500
Colletti, Lucio 5, 8
commodity fetishism 74–83, 87–9; standard interpretation of 75–9; understood as an error 76–7, 80
commodity production, system of 79–84, 89
"common third" 10
communes and communal property 190–1
communism 169–70
The Communist Manifesto 103, 172, 505, 514
comparative statics 233–7, 244
Comptoirs Nationaux 253
concentration: industrial 522; of capital 521–2
Condorcet, Marquis de 89
Constant, Benjamin 175
contracts for services 417, 424, 426
contracts of employment 417, 419, 423–7

co-operative organisations 518
Coppet Circle 175
Cornelissen, Christiaan 518, 521, 528
Costanza, Robert 388–90, 401, 406–11
credit 361, 372–3, 376–8; definition of 376; origin of 377
Crédit Mobilier 253, 255
crisis theory 249–57, 348
Croce, Benedetto 508
Cunow, Heinrich 364
currency principle 362, 366
currency school 372, 378–9
cyclical behaviour 362, 365, 431–4

Danielson, Nikolai 186
"the Darwin of the social sciences" 188
Darwinism 3
Debord, Guy 47
de Brosses, Charles 78
decadence 176
definite and indefinite articles, replacement and deletion of 157–60
deforestation 105
Delphic Oracle 80
de Paepe, César 492, 499
Desai, Meghnad 203–6, 211
Desbons, Georges 523
de Vivo, Giancarlo 393
de Vriese, Herbert 7
dialectical materialism 3
differential rent 271–8, 282–93, 298; two forms of 289
diminishing returns 102–4, 264–5, 277, 289, 303
division of labour 78, 85, 172, 380, 507
Dmitriev, Vladimir 388, 392–4, 410–11
Dobb, Maurice 398
Dos Santos Ferreira, Rodolphe 11
Drummond, Victor 110
Dühring, Eugen 95, 101, 109
Durkheim, Émile 517, 529

Eckstein, Gustav 394
Economakis, George E. 311
Economic and Philosophical Manuscripts (EPM) 46–56, 62, 69–70, 95, 122, 152, 162
economic materialism 511–14
The Economist 104, 256
The Edinburgh Review 175
Effertz, Otto 517–18
L'Egalité (journal) 528
Ege, Ragip 11
Egidi, Massimo 396
Einaudi, Luigi 509, 516

elasticity: of industrial production 222, 224; of reproduction 210, 225
Elster, Jon 6, 81
Emmanuel, Arghiri 298, 308, 317
endogenous prices 322, 335–44, 348
energy theory of value 406–7
Engels, Friedrich 1–3, 92–113, 119–28, 134–5, 138, 144–6, 149, 153–4, 160–5, 170–7, 196, 211–14, 221–2, 225, 388, 408, 506; as editor and literary executor to Karl Marx 127–8; time spent on a wide range of pursuits 128; Works: "Cola di Rienzi" 152, 158, 160; *Condition of the Working Class in England* 101; *Entäußerung* and *Entfremdung* 49–51; *Herrn Eugen Dührings Umwälzung der Wissenschaft* 109; *Outlines of a Critique of Political Economy* 103
"entelechy" 87
equilibrium conditions 230–3
Es leben feste Grundsätzel (novella) 15–33, 41, 43; portrayal of Karl in 16–18, 23–33, 41
exchange: money as a medium of 372; propensity for 85; social process of 369
exchange rates 335
exchange value 57–62, 65, 68–9, 79, 87, 366, 373–80, 388
exogenous prices 322, 325, 335–6, 341–8
exploitation 418–27, 430, 517–18, 523; concept of 418–19; and cost externalisation 425–7; and the employment contract 423–5; rate of 420, 423
expropriation 179–82, 190–1
extended reproduction 195–201, 209–13, 224–5
externalisation of costs 425–7
Eyguesier, Nicolas 9

Faccarello, Gilbert (co-editor) 129–30
faith in money 379
fatalism 520–1
fertilisers 103
fertility of land 264–5, 276–9, 287–8
"fetishism", use of the word 7, 78–82, 88–9; *see also* commodity fetishism
feudalism 61, 172, 177–8, 183, 185, 363
Feuerbach, Ludwig 3, 8–9, 36, 49–50, 53–6, 66, 70, 164
Feuerbach manuscripts 144–66; inconsistent intermediate variants 149–54, 157–8; online edition of 164–6; possibility of dictation 144–8, 153–61, 164–5

Fine, Ben 76–7, 311
First World War 529
Foley, Duncan 76–7
foreign trade, absence of 316–17
Fourier, Charles 498, 502–3, 507, 523
Fournière, Eugène 502, 508, 515–16, 519, 527
Fraas, Carl 105
France 177, 252–7, 490–1, 498, 504, 510, 519, 522–3, 527
"Franco-Italian circuit school" 236
Fränkel, Albert 33–4
Frankfurt School 6
Fratini, Saverio Maria 10
freedom, conceptions of 175–6
Fromm, Erich 47–8
Fullarton, John 376, 379

Gehrke, Christian 9, 129, 323
Geikie, James 110
Gentile, Giovanni 513
George, Henry 11
Germany 419, 500–1, 504–6, 510, 524, 527–8
Gide, Charles 519
Gilibert, Giorgio 396
Goldendakh, David Borisovich 4; *see also* Rjazanov, David
Gomez Betancourt, Rebecca 10
Goodwin, Richard M. 431, 444–6
Gospel narratives 37
Gray, John 373–4, 380
Graziadei, Antonio 509
Graziani, Augusto 236
Great Depression 432
growth theories 434
Grün, Karl 498
Grundrisse, the 5, 7, 46–56, 62, 68–70, 95, 122, 358, 367, 423
Guesde, Jules 511, 515, 528–9
guilds 175

Halbwachs, Maurice 509–10, 516–17, 522
handwriting analysis 146–8
Harrod, Roy 434
Harrod-neutral technical change 139
Hawkins-Simon conditions 339–40
Hazell, Alfred Pung 360
Heckscher, Eli 363, 382
Hegel, G.W.F. (and Hegelianism) 2–5, 37, 39, 49–50, 53, 424, 501, 504, 521–2
Heinrich, Michael 6–7
Helvétius, Claude-Adrien 502
Herwegh, Georg 21, 42–3
Hess, Moses 5, 49–50, 55–6, 70

Hildebrand, Bruno 506
Hilferding, Rudolf 360, 506, 529
Hiromatsu, Wataru 148
historical materialism 3, 144, 503, 512–14
history, theories and philosophies of
 170–1, 175
hoarding 372
Hoff, Jan 6
Hollander, Samuel 198, 203, 211
homonym mistakes 164
homophones 154–7, 164
Horner, Leonard 251
Howard, Michael Charles 74, 78, 205,
 310, 392
human nature 51
human society, evolution of 169
Hume, David 361–2, 366–74, 378–81
Hunt, Emery Kay 409
hyperlinks 99–100

ideal standard of money 382
idealism 512
income distribution 318
India 178, 183, 186
industrialisation 169–70, 177–8
innovation 433–5
instability, economic 430–3
intermediate variants 149–54, 157–65;
 restoration of 159–60
International Institute of Social
 History 278
International Working Men's
 Association 100
Internationale Marx–Engels Stiftung
 (IMES) 4
intrinsic value of a commodity 81
"invisible hand" metaphor 135–6

Jaffé, William 393
Jaurès, Jean 491, 493, 503–6
Jesus Christ as a historical person 37
Jevons, Stanley 11, 381, 517
Johnston, James 103
Jousse, Emmanuel 510

Kaldor, Nicholas 340, 434, 441
Kalecki, Michal 11, 323, 430–9, 442–6
Kant, Immanuel 525–6
Kautsky, Karl 3, 170, 359, 398, 509, 520
Kellès-Krauz, Casimir 509, 512
Keynes, John Maynard 1, 340, 360, 381
King, John Edward 74, 78, 205, 310, 392
Klimovsky, Edith 10
Krisenhefte 9
Kurz, Heinz D. (co-editor) 8, 129, 399

labour: different meanings of 133–4;
 productive and unproductive 107; social
 character of 363, 373, 380; as the soul of
 production 51
labour, labour capacity and labour power
 63–7, 87, 423, 427
labour contracts 11; see also contracts of
 employment
labour market flexibility 426
labour theory of value 122, 388, 393, 410,
 417–20, 423, 498, 508, 510, 514–15, 526
Labriola, Arturo 509, 516
Lafargue, Paul 511, 514, 525, 528
landed property 269, 271, 281–4, 294, 298,
 300, 305–9, 317, 319
Landry, Adolphe 517–18
Laskine, Edmond 510, 513, 521, 525, 529
"law of motion" 121, 123
"law of value" 129
lease periods 303
legal socialism 513–14
Lendjel, Émeric 397
Lenin, V.I. 3, 123
Leontief, Wassily 236, 388–9, 393–4, 399,
 403–4, 411
Leontief matrix 420–2
Leontief Paradox 403
Leontief–Sraffa models 224
Leopold, David 5
Leroux, Pierre 523
Leroy, M. 173
Leroy-Beaulieu, Paul 514
Levy-Brühl, Lucien 517
Lewis, Haskel 81
Liebig, Justus von 10, 102–5, 137–40, 262,
 278–82, 287, 294
living labour 65–6, 69, 125, 137
Locke, John 129, 367–8
Lowe, Adolph 9, 219–221, 231–2, 241–3
Löwy, Michael 173
Lubeck Congress (1901) 509
Lukács, Georg 50
Luther, Martin 504
Luxembourg, Rosa 439–40, 509
Lyon 255–6

Maclaren, James 381
McLellan, David 47–8
Malon, Benoît 11, 490–3, 496–504, 508–11
Malthus, Thomas 264, 274–5, 286
Mandel, Ernest 360
Manigat, Matari Pierre 10
Marburg 525
Marcuse, Herbert 47
marginal utility theory 81, 391, 393

Martinez-Alier, Juan 408–9
Marx, Karl: character traits 28–30; complex and wide-ranging thought of 4; deteriorating health of 127; early years 5–8, 24–31, 41–2, 46–7, 263; as a historian 191; need for a comprehensive edition of the works of 3–4; quest for social recognition and intellectual influence 31–2; reception of the works of 11–12; reinterpretation of 5; secondary literature on 122; way of working 8; Works: *Theorien über den Mehrwert* 509; *Value, Price and Profit* 169, 178–9; *Wage labour and capital* 423; *see also Capital*
Marx-Engels equilibrium 323, 328–34, 341
Marx–Engels Gesamtausgabe (MEGA and MEGA²) 4–9, 12, 21, 35, 92–101, 113–14, 119–23, 126–8, 134–40, 149, 152, 164, 166, 196, 210, 249, 262–3, 266, 294, 409; connections between the parts of 101; full-text retrieval from 98; historical-critical text in 98; modes of presentation of 99; order of texts in 96; status of editorial work 94–9
Marx-Engels Werke (MEW) 4–5
Mater, André 514
materialism *see also* economic materialism; historical materialism
materialistic conception of history 144, 165
Mathur, Gautam 220–1, 231–2
Mayer, Gustav 8, 148, 153, 161
Mazaryk, Tomas-Garrigue 509–12, 525
Meade, James 196, 207
"mediocre" mode of production 185
Meek, Ronald L. 364
MEGAdigital 83, 97–113
Meister, Ludovic 510
Mendelssohn, Moses 381
Menger, Anton 507
mercantilism 361–6, 369, 380–2
Meyen, Eduard 22
middle classes 177
Milhaud, Edgar 509, 529
Mill, John Stuart 52, 55, 523
Mondolfo, Rodolfo 510, 513
monetary theory 360–2, 365–70, 375, 378, 380
money 76–7, 69, 87, 111; definition of 368, 361; demand for 372; functions of 361–2, 369–74, 377–80; and social relations 56–9; supply of 368–9, 372, 379–80
monism 513
monopoly pricing 297–9, 303, 308–19; and classical theory of value 311–18; and value in Marx 314–16

Montesquieu, Baron de 367, 370–1, 380
morality and moral sentiments 85, 524–6
Mori, Kenji 9, 214, 216, 230, 234, 323, 397
Morishima, Michio 196, 203–7, 211, 323, 325, 331
Morris, Jacob 81
Moseley, Fred 360
Le Mouvement socialiste (journal) 507
Mühlpfordt, Wolfgang 388, 391–3, 410

Napoleon III 257
Nash, John 425
natural price 84, 312–13
Negri, Antonio 70
Nelson, Anitra 360
Neue Rheinische Zeitung 99
New York Daily Tribune (*NYDT*) 124, 180–3, 249, 256
Newmarch, William 9, 248–57
Neybour, Jean 513–14
Nietzsche, Friedrich 526
Nuti, Domenico Mario 392

objectification 51–2
Omura, Izumi 8–9, 266
overpopulation 102
overproduction of the means of production 348
Owen, Robert 498

Pareto, Vilfredo 388–91, 395–8, 410
Parys, Wilfried 10
payment, money as a means of 372–3
peasantry 180, 190–1, 522–3
Pecqueur, Constantin 11, 498–502, 507
Perron-Frobenius theorem 421
Petty, William 421
philosophical aspects of Marxism 3, 5
Physiocrats 107, 109, 224, 365
Plato 182
Plekhanov, Georgi 3, 510, 513
Podolinsky, Sergei 388, 407–9, 412
political economy 106, 135, 292
"ponocratic" system 517–18
Potron, Maurice 388–9, 397, 411
Pottier, Antonin 11
Prawdine, Olivier 509
praxis 3
price determination 366–71
primitive accumulation 169–70, 179, 183–6, 191, 359
"principledness" 15–16, 32–4, 42
private property 51, 54, 63, 178, 183–4, 190, 281, 310

product markets, classification of 252
production price 238, 268–9, 282–6, 293, 297–301, 306–9, 317, 422–3
productiveness 421
productivity 68–9, 139, 171, 289, 446; of the soil 103
profit rate 111–13, 119, 121, 125, 130–40, 237, 239, 269–71, 298–9, 302–3, 404, 441–6
progress, different conceptions of 170, 174–6
proletariat, the 172
Proudhon, Pierre Joseph 30, 53, 67–8, 373–4, 380, 492, 499, 502–3, 507
"pure critique" model 38–41

Quaas, Friedrun 392
quantity theory of money (QTM) 358–73, 378–80
Quesnay, François 106–9, 195, 326, 408, 421

radicalization 38
Ramirez, Miguel D. 310
Rappoport, Charles 509, 512, 521, 525–6
Rebeyrol, Antoine 10
reflux, monetary 230, 235–6, 361, 375, 378–80
Reichelt, Helmut 5
Renard, Georges 500
Renault, Emmanuel 5
rent, theory of 262–80, 283–4, 287–8, 291–4, 297, 312–13; Marx's research on 265–78; see also absolute rent; differential rent
reproduction, extended 322–5, 348, 354–6, 439
revisionism 508–10
La Revue Socialiste (LRS) 11, 490–528; papers dedicated to Marx/Marxism in 494–5
Rheinische Zeitung 19, 21–2, 24, 28, 34, 40–3
Ricardo, David 1, 10, 84, 104, 124–6, 130, 133, 136–40, 182, 263–8, 271–7, 282, 286–8, 293, 298, 313, 315, 366, 371–3, 379–81, 398, 410, 515, 523
ridicule as a philosophical strategy 39–40
Rienzi see Van Kol, Hendrikus
Rignano, Eugenio 510, 520
Rjazanov, David 4, 8, 96, 148, 161, 187
"robbery cultivation" 281
Rodbertus, Johann Karl 266–7, 270–4, 293, 305
Roemer, John 6, 418

Rojahn, Jürgen 5
Roman Empire 176–7
"romantic" conceptions 170–3
Rosdolsky, Roman 360
Rosier, Bernard 403
Roth, Regina 8, 127
Rouanet, Gustave 500–1
Rousseau, Jean-Jacques 502
Rubel, Maximilien 173, 323
Rubin, Isaak Illich 5, 8, 77, 81, 129, 360, 364, 370
Ruge, Arnold 20–2, 30–1, 34–5, 40–2
Russia 169–70, 185–91

Saad-Filho, Alfredo 76–7
Sachs, Joe 84, 87
Saint-Simon, Comte de 497–8, 502, 507, 523
Saitō, Kōhei 102, 105, 138
Samuelson, Paul A. 195, 203–6, 211
Savigny, Friedrich Carl von 501
Say, Jean-Baptiste 174, 515
Sayre, Robert 173
scarcity, value depending on 81
Schmalz, Theodor 107
Schmoller, Gustav von 363, 528
Science (journal) 389, 401
Section Française de l'Internationale Ouvrière (SFIO) 491, 527
self-moving value 86, 89
"semi-exogenous factors", shocks from 431–4
Shanin, Teodor 169
Shibata, Kei 232
Shibuya, Tadashi 163
Simiand, François 517
Sismondi, Jean-Charles Léonard 9, 169–83, 189, 191
six-sector production models 214–19, 229–36
slavery 423–4
Slepzoff, Aleksandr 515
Smith, Adam 1, 51, 84–9, 107–8, 124, 129, 132–6, 286, 298, 311–12, 375, 381–2, 515; Works: The Theory of Moral Sentiments 85; The Wealth of Nations 78, 85–8, 169–70, 312
social capital 324, 326, 348, 355
social contract 502
social validity 80
socialisation 59–62, 70–1
socialism 141, 173, 187–91, 490–3, 496–507, 510, 512–14, 518, 523–8; phases of 513–14
Soddy, Frederick 406

Sofortvarianten 146
Sombart, Werner 308, 394, 525, 528
Sorel, Georges 491–2, 503, 507–8, 513, 516, 519, 523, 526
Soubeyran, Élie 523
Spätvarianten 147
specialisation by producers 60
species, propagation of 85
The Spectator 367
Spencer, Herbert 523
Sperber, Jonathan 6–7
Spinoza, Baruch 381
Sraffa, Piero 6, 132, 236, 326, 388–93, 396–9, 402, 411, 422
Staël, Germaine de 175
Stammler, Rudolf 525
Staudinger, Fritz 519
steady-state growth path 196–7, 201, 206, 211, 225
Stedman Jones, Gareth 6–7, 169, 189
Steedman, Ian 410
Steuart, Sir James 10, 281, 358–64, 367–82
Stigler, George Joseph 409–10
Stoffwechshell 281–2
Strauss, David Friedrich 36–7
Der Streit der Kritik 40
surplus value 52, 67, 87, 130, 133, 137, 139, 174, 199, 202, 233–5, 239, 266–9, 290, 299–301, 306, 311, 315–18, 361–4, 419–20, 425–6, 515, 519
Sutherland, Duchess of 180–1

Tableau économique 106–9, 195
Takenaga, Susumu 9
Tchetsis, L.-A. 510, 513
technical progress 125–6, 133, 136–9, 223–4
textual variants 165–6
Thomas, Albert 493, 503
timber growth 105
Tomberg, Friedrich 47–8
Tooke, Thomas 9, 248–51, 258, 360, 370, 375–6, 379, 381
Torrens, Robert 324, 372
trade unions, power of 442
transition from simple to extended reproduction 196–8, 201–9
traverse from one equilibrium to another 240–4

Tribe, Keith 311
Der Triumph des Glaubens 35–6
Turban, Manfred 203, 206

undisturbed accumulation 204, 213, 225
United States 124–5, 140
Urkapital 394–6, 411
use-values 58, 64, 82, 324, 326, 374, 419
Utopianism 170, 173, 501–2
Uzawa, Hirofumi 196, 207

value theory 130, 275, 389–94, 403, 411–12, 514–19, 522; classical 78; *see also* energy theory of value; labour theory of value
Van Kol, Hendrikus 509, 515
Vandervelde, Émile 509, 511, 522
velocity of circulation of money 380–1
von Neumann, John 323, 333, 347
Vorländer, Karl 525

Wada, Haruki 169, 189
wages, nature of 423–5
"Während in den früheren Perioden" 165
Walras, Léon 336, 517, 523, 529
Walter-Jourde, J. 522
waterfalls, power from 285–7
Watts, John 101
Weitling, Wilhelm 30, 123
welfare state provision 419, 425–7
Westphalen, Jenny 24–5
Westphalen, Ludwig von 24–5
White, James D. 169
White, Michael 11
Wicksell, Knut 389–91, 410
Wicksteed, Philip Henry 11, 389–90, 410
Winiarski, Léon 512
Wittmann, David 49
Wolff, Edward Nathan 407
Woltmann, Ludwig 525–6
Wood, E.M. 179
writing styles of Marx and Engels 162

Young Hegelian movement 48–50, 56; *see also* Berlin Young Hegelians

Zassulitch, Vera 95, 187–8, 190
zero-hours contracts 426
Zoubir, Zacharias 7

Printed in the United States
by Baker & Taylor Publisher Services